ADMINISTRATIVE LAW
IN THE POLITICAL SYSTEM

ADMINISTRATIVE LAW IN THE POLITICAL SYSTEM

Abridged Third Edition

KENNETH F. WARREN

Professor of Political Science and Public Policy
St. Louis University

PRENTICE HALL
Upper Saddle River, New Jersey 07458

Congress Cataloging-in-Publication Data

WARREN, KENNETH F.
    Administrative law in the political system / Kenneth F. Warren.—
Abridged 3rd. ed.
      p.   cm.
   Includes index.
   ISBN 0–13–339987–7 (pbk.)
    1. Administrative law—United States.   2. Delegated legislation—
United States.   3. Administrative agencies—United States.
I. Title.
KF5402.W37   1997
342.73'06—dc20
[347.3026]   96-28614
                                     CIP

Editorial director: Charlyce Jones Owen
Editor-in-chief: Nancy Roberts
Acquisitions editor: Michael Bickerstaff
Assistant editor: Jennie Katsaros
Project manager: Merrill Peterson
Prepress and manufacturing buyer: Bob Anderson
Electronic art manager: Michele Giusti

This book was set in 10/12 Times by NK Graphics
and was printed and bound by Courier Companies, Inc.
The cover was printed by Phoenix Color Corp.

 ©1989, 1976 by Prentice-Hall, Inc.
Englewood Cliffs, New Jersey 07632

Printed in the United States of America

10   9   8   7   6   5   4

ISBN 0-13-339987-7

Prentice-Hall International (UK) Limited, *London*
Prentice-Hall of Australia Pty. Limited, *Sydney*
Prentice-Hall of Canada, Inc., *Toronto*
Prentice-Hall Hispanoamericana, S. A., *Mexico*
Prentice-Hall of India Private Limited, *New Delhi*
Prentice-Hall of Japan, Inc., *Tokyo*
Prentice-Hall Asia Pte. Ltd., *Singapore*
Editora Prentice-Hall do Brasil, Ltda., *Rio de Janeiro*

To my cute and loving wife, Annette

and

To all those who struggle to achieve

procedural due process

CONTENTS

CHAPTER FOUR

PROTECTING ADMINISTRATORS FROM UNDUE INTERFERENCE AND HARASSMENT   **149**

CHAPTER FIVE

RULE-MAKING: AGENCIES AS LEGISLATIVE BODIES   **182**

CHAPTER SIX

ORDER-MAKING: AGENCIES AS JUDICIAL BODIES   218

CHAPTER NINE

SUING THE GOVERNMENT AND ITS ADMINISTRATORS   365

CHAPTER TEN

AN ADMINISTRATIVE LAW CHALLENGE: BALANCING SOCIETAL
AND INDIVIDUAL RIGHTS   408

APPENDIX

TABLE OF CASES

PREFACE

The third and abridged edition of *Administrative Law in the Political System* represents an attempt to satisfy a need in the public administration field for a comprehensive, yet streamlined, administrative law text written by a social scientist especially for social science students. The general purpose of the book is to convey to students the role of administrative law in the American political system, but, more specifically, its role in shaping, guiding, and restricting the actions of administrative agencies to make regulatory practices more in line with due process standards. The book is unique in that all traditional administrative law topics covered (for example, rule-making, adjudication, tort law) are written, as much as possible, in nontechnical language, with an emphasis on points of particular interest to social science students. Special attention is given to the impact politics has on efforts by administrators to comply with administrative law dictates. Systems theory is employed in this abridged edition in a limited way to stress that agency regulators must respond not only to the "demands" placed upon them by administrative law, but also to the conflicting socioeconomic and political pressures stemming from their total environment.

An enormous effort has been made to make this abridged third edition as up-to-date as possible. Emphasis has been placed on current trends in administrative law, recent court decisions, happenings during the Clinton administration, and especially the impact the era of "re-inventing government" and neo-conservatism has had on the development of administrative law.

In sum, this abridged edition should be appreciated by social science students, particularly in the area of public administration, because it (1) provides comprehensive, yet streamlined coverage of administrative law written especially for social science students; (2) does not assume prior legal training or command of technical legal vocabulary; (3) draws upon both the legal and social science literature to help provide insights into the nature of administrative law; (4) plays down the case approach, commonly employed in law school contexts, in favor of a more direct descriptive and analytical approach, which makes the relatively difficult subject matter of administrative law considerably easier to understand; (5) employs systems analysis, a popular analytical framework familiar to most relatively advanced social science students, to place administrative law in the perspective of the American political system; (6) relates administrative law to topics of particular concern to social science students (for example, the politics of drafting and implementing regulatory policies); and (7) is current, thus placing administrative law developments in the perspective of the 1990s.

Obviously, many people provided assistance as I struggled to finish this book. I wish to thank them for their unselfish and valuable services. First, I want to acknowledge the students in both my undergraduate and graduate administrative law classes, who, over the years, have made valuable constructive criticisms. For the first, second, and third editions of the book, valuable research assistance was provided by many loyal and dedicated people. I have already thanked them by name in my previous editions. For this abridged third edition, I want to thank the following people for their technical assistance, scholarly insights, and just plain emotional support and encouragement: Cindy Hartson, Sue Moore, Reeder Thompson, Joe Miller, Homer Teng, Amber Miller, Terry Wells, Dave Hagedorn, Murphy Sullivan, Ron Medley, Clarissa Valdivia, Leo Garvin, Paul Brown, Tom Connelly, Phyllis Forchee, Joe Simeone, George Wendel, Jay Shafritz, David Rosenbloom, Bernard Schwartz, and especially my wife, Annette, for her loving support and profound insights.

Kenneth F. Warren
St. Louis, Missouri

ADMINISTRATIVE LAW
IN THE POLITICAL SYSTEM

CHAPTER ONE

ADMINISTRATIVE LAW: AN INTRODUCTION

OBJECTIVES OF THIS BOOK

The first edition of this book, published in 1982, was written to fill a conspicuous void in the literature of political science, public administration, public policy, and public affairs. Up to that time no comprehensive administrative law textbook had been written by a social scientist for social science students. Fortunately, since that time a few other social scientists have written administrative law textbooks specifically geared for social science students, thus helping to fill that conspicuous void.[1]

Before these recent administrative law publications by social scientists, virtually all comprehensive administrative law textbooks had been written by law professors (for example, Kenneth C. Davis, Walter Gellhorn and Clark Byse, Bernard Schwartz, and Louis Gaffe and Nathaniel Nathanson) who were indeed scholarly legal writers, yet who seldom treated in any depth the relevant public policy issues quite obviously implied by administrative law questions. This is not to suggest that these writers did not on occasion entertain important policy issues. Obviously, some of them did. Davis's *Discretionary Justice* and Gellhorn's *When Americans Complain* are two excellent examples of specialized works in which the authors transcended mere technical discussion of administrative law doctrines and searched for solutions to related and obstinate public policy problems.[2] Consequently, these particular books have been widely used and applauded by social scientists.

Even a cursory inspection of these pre-1982 administrative law texts shows that they were intended primarily for students in law school. The prose reflects the technical legal language of the authors. These authors are not attempting primarily to motivate their readers to think about vital public policy questions in our society;

rather, they are chiefly concerned with trying to teach students how to win administrative law cases. Why, for instance, do so many of their problem-oriented discussions end with the traditional legal casework rhetoric: What judgment or what decision? While public administration students are somewhat interested in the "what judgment" controversies, they are more concerned with administrative law issues pertaining to important public policy questions. For example, what regulatory procedures are employed by the Nuclear Regulatory Commission (NRC), the Federal Aviation Administration (FAA), and the National Aeronautics and Space Administration (NASA) when those agencies make rules and conduct hearings? And how do these regulatory procedures affect each agency's ability to function to prevent, for example, another Three Mile Island accident, or another fatal plane crash, or another tragic shuttle disaster.

In sum, the focuses of the lawyer and the public administrator in regard to administrative law are quite different, and an appropriate book for students in public administration should mirror this reality and emphasize pertinent subject matter. Touching on this difference in perspective, Peter Woll asserted: "Therefore, lawyers become advocates for the government as well as for private interests. Their formal training, however, fits them better for acting as advocates of private rights than of the public interest, at least of a public interest defined separately from the rights and needs of private parties. *Administrative lawyers are formally trained in how to prevent government from acting arbitrarily against private interests, rather than in how to make a government action more effective in the public interest*" (italics mine).[3]

The basic twofold goal of this book is to provide students oriented to public administration with a comprehensive coverage of administrative law fundamentals while simultaneously linking administrative law issues to relevant, topical public policy questions. For example, in discussions of the order-making power of agencies, a special effort is made to place order-making procedures and decisions in the context of rather well-publicized and relevant current events. This is done with the hope of making the somewhat difficult and tedious administrative law doctrines and principles applicable to the real world of public administration.

Another central objective is to promote among public administration students a greater appreciation of the genuine legal obstacles which must be recognized and confronted in the handling of administrative problems. Traditionally, social scientists have not given much more than a flirtatious glance at the technical legal aspects associated with public administration. On the other hand, law schools have been content to produce graduates with a relatively solid understanding of legal doctrines, but only a flimsy grasp of the connection between technical legal doctrines and the normative operational needs of democratic government and society. While the social scientist is typically educated to reflect in a relatively abstract manner upon the problems of simultaneously achieving justice for both the individual and society, the law student is trained chiefly as a legal technician whose purpose is to use the law to argue for the singular interests of a client.[4]

Thus, social scientists tend to place administrative law in the perspective of the entire political system. This allows them to examine administrative law from the standpoint of its role in the larger political system. This is obviously the chief strength of the social science, sometimes called the liberal arts, approach. However, social scientists naturally tend to express this bias in their thinking, since they have been conditioned to respect and reject certain values. As far back as the days of Confucius and Plato, students have been taught to respect the knowledge of the generalists over that of the expert. It is this sort of bias which has unfortunately allowed those learning public administration to stress abstract theory and de-emphasize technical knowledge. Yet before the public administrator can play ball to win in our system, he or she should learn some of the finer points of the public administration game. It is hoped that this book on administrative law will help public administration students learn and apply technical administrative law factors that must be understood and employed if the students are going to be competent future participants in the serious business of administering in the public interest.

ORGANIZATION OF THIS BOOK

The book is organized to make administrative law applicable to public policy concerns. (1) Administrative law is defined and described from the perspective of the American political system. The legal and political roles governmental agencies play in the American political system vis-a-vis the Congress, the courts, the White House, the bureaucracy, the regulated industries, other interest groups, and the American public are presented, along with public policy-making implications. This systems approach should be both helpful and encouraging to social science students because many have already been exposed to and feel comfortable with this useful approach. (2) Throughout the text public policy examples and illustrations are employed to provide added insights on how administrative law applies to making and implementing public policies. (3) Comprehensive summaries are added to reiterate the major points conveyed in each chapter, especially regarding the administrative law-public policy relationship.

Although there are many ways in which the chapters and chapter sections in an administrative law book could be organized, the order selected appears to be as logical as any for the stated objectives. Chapter 1 conveys the chief goals and basic approach. Systems theory and analysis are described and the rationale for selecting this particular approach is given. Students are then introduced to the fundamental character of administrative law, its scope and distinctiveness, and to its growing importance in American legal and political life.

In Chapter 2 the focus is on the growth of administrative power and its impact on American political life. The delegation doctrine is examined early in the chapter since the great size, power, and pervasiveness of bureaucracy today stem largely from the questionable delegation of quasi-legislative and quasi-judicial powers to administrative agencies by Congress. To illustrate the practical effects of administrative power, concrete examples, which convey the tremendous impact administrative decisions may have on virtually all participants in the system, are given. For example, the FAA's decision to ground the DC-10s and NASA's decision to postpone future shuttle missions are particularly enlightening. Because the growth of administrative power has challenged the traditional tripartite model of democratic government, traditional democratic standards are evaluated in light of the demands placed upon modern government. Logically, the chapter concludes (short of its presentation of cases, questions, and comments) with a treatment of the controversial subject of regulation versus deregulation. An attempt here is made to evaluate both the pros and cons of governmental regulation.

Chapter 3 focuses upon the relationship between Congress and the administrative agencies with an emphasis on attempts by Congress to keep administrators responsible. Special attention is devoted to key congressional acts designed to regulate administrative procedures. Because of its critical importance to understanding prescribed administrative action, considerable space is given to the Administrative Procedure Act (APA) and its key amendments—among them, the Freedom of Information Act, the Sunshine Act, and the Privacy Act.

To ensure responsible administrative actions, administrators must be protected from unethical and illegal influence peddling from outsiders. Chapter 4 examines the various internal and external pressures placed upon administrators and their likely corruptive impact. Conflict of interest legislation, loyalty oaths, constitutional prohibitions, and the United States president's appointment and removal powers are discussed in the context of administrative law and public interest theory.

Chapter 5 deals with rule making, a basic administrative law topic. Rule making is defined and justified in this chapter. APA requirements governing formal and informal rule-making procedures are presented and assessed, especially in terms of the act's various loopholes. Particular emphasis is placed on analyzing the democratic character of rule-making procedures and how certain procedural steps tend to shape public policy outputs.

Administrators not only have the power to make "laws" (rules), but they also have the power to judge the appropriateness of their rules when holding hearings and issuing orders. Order making, a quasi-judicial function, is covered in Chapter 6. At the beginning of the chapter, order-making activities are defined and distinguished from rule-making functions. Most of the chapter is concerned with the elements considered to be part of the fair hearing process, with extensive description and analysis of the differences between administrative hearings and court trials.

Chapter 7 confronts one of the most perplexing questions in administrative law: How much administrative discretion is too much? Although both formal and informal administrative activities are examined in the chapter, most of it focuses on the use and misuse of discretion. Because discretionary actions seem to conflict with the principle of the rule of law, it is vital to stress the critical importance of this issue. Kenneth C. Davis believes this matter to be the most pressing administrative law issue today.[5] Because democratic government is threatened by abuses of discretionary power, different ideas for structuring and controlling administrative discretion are evaluated.

Chapter 8 focuses on the role played by the courts in evaluating the appropriateness of agency actions. Initially, the role of judicial review in the administrative process is presented. Next, discussions center around the reviewability and nonreviewability of agency activities. This chapter makes clear that the courts do not normally want to meddle in agency affairs. Consequently, the courts have made use of several doctrines which allow them to stay clear. Court orders and their effectiveness in forcing public officials to execute sanctioned public policies (for example, school integration) are evaluated. The chapter concludes with an assessment of the overall effectiveness of judicial review on administrative action.

Chapter 9 considers some of the most intriguing administrative law questions, those that always seem to arouse intense interest among students: Can the government and/or its officers be sued and under what conditions? What political and legal distinctions are made between *governmental* and *official* immunity? What justifications can be given to the existence of the sovereign immunity doctrine? How immune is the president of the United States from tort liability suits?

In the final chapter, administrative law is placed in the perspective of social contract theory, which emphasizes questions pertaining to the rights and obligations of individuals versus the rights and obligations of society. Because administrative law focuses largely upon the makings of administrative due process, administrative law becomes caught in the middle of the perplexing and ageless political dilemma involving efforts by a constitutional government to strike an equitable balance between societal and individual rights when formulating and administering public policies. In this context administrative due process controversies are considered, especially in terms of procedural steps taken by governmental agencies when conducting administrative searches and seizures. Administrative searches and seizures have taken on a heightened interest in the 1990s because of a variety of federal forfeiture statutes that allow real estate and personal property to be seized, sometimes even from innocent third parties, when the property is thought to be connected to certain illegal activities.[6]

THIS BOOK'S APPROACH: SYSTEMS THEORY

To study anything in the absence of a sound theoretical framework is both difficult and foolish because a well-constructed theoretical framework provides a conceptual tool which can be used to focus on particular situations (for example, agency decision making) and to help interpret specific events (for example, Federal Trade Commission (FTC) orders). Social science researchers have used theoretical frameworks, or models, to help them systematically pinpoint, order, and conceptualize what they intend to study. To state it simply, models are useful because they allow one to see at a glance what variables and relationships are being considered and examined. Thus, models help to simplify, accelerate, and refine the discovery and learning process. The study of administrative law is in crucial need of theoretical approaches, approaches which can relate administrative law to real administrative behavior. For example, Erwin G. Krasnow, Lawrence D. Longley, and Herbert A. Terry acknowledged the need for rigorous, systematic approaches to the study of regulatory behavior (the focus of administrative law) in their book on broadcast regulation. They

**'Don't You Know Crime Doesn't Pay —
Unless You've Got The Law On Your Side?'**

Source: Reprinted with permission of Tom Englehardt and the *St. Louis Post-Dispatch,* May 2, 1991.

commented: "It is remarkable that so little effort has been devoted to the systematic understanding of broad-scale regulatory systems such as those affecting broadcasting. That is not to say that people have not attempted to understand broadcasting regulation. It is to point out that they have tended to shy away from attempts to explain it in analytic systems terms."[7] In this book there is an honest attempt to go beyond the formal-legal approach by developing a conceptual framework (systems model) which is quite useful in analyzing administrative law in the context of actual agency actions. A next step would be to begin the empirical testing of worthwhile hypotheses implied by the various independent-dependent relationships in the model (for example, the influence of a certain interest group over the policy decisions, as seen in the rules and orders, of a particular regulatory agency).[8]

The systems approach is popular in the social sciences for good reason. Systems theory probably provides the learner with the simplest, yet most revealing analytical framework or model on how participants (frequently called actors) relate functionally to one another. The *system* is defined by researchers or writers to suit their research or descriptive needs. The system may be conceptualized on the micro or macro level: one might focus research on the environment of a small-town police chief or on a nation in an international setting.

Systems analysis has the advantage of often simplifying very complex interrelationships among actors in a system. *Actors* may be perceived as individuals (a judge), agencies (Environmental Protection Agency), interest groups (American Medical Association), and so on. They tend to influence the behavior of the focal political actor. Despite the relative simplicity of a systems model, such a heuristic model (a heuristic model is, simply, a conceptual helping device) is excellent for specifying relationships between participants, as well as indicating possible hypotheses to be tested.

The systems model's conceptual strength lies in its basic isomorphic character, that is, in its ability to reflect real-world behavior in a model. For our purposes, we can use the system framework as an analytical tool, to place the administrative system into perspective with its environment. In particular, we can demonstrate quite well the complex role administrative agencies play in the American political system.

It should be emphasized that systems analysis is excellent for stressing the functional relationships between participants in a system. Systems theory is best suited for those who want to study not static but active and continuous behavior among systemic actors. In our case we can employ systems analysis to focus on administrative law issues in the context of real administrative agencies as they interact with their environment, which includes at least the White House, the Congress, the courts, the regulated industries, other governmental agencies, the media, and the general public.

Systems theory helps to explain how agencies struggle to survive in an always potentially hostile environment while carrying out their statutory mission of making, adjudicating, and executing public policies. Systems theory accepts and assumes one basic truth: as the English philosopher Thomas Hobbes conceived it some four hundred years ago, the first instinct of any actor (our example is an administrative agency) is to survive. This maxim cannot be overemphasized. Systems analysis would have no analytical starting point without it. For centuries political theorists and sociologists have acknowledged that this fundamental instinct exists in all individuals and organizations. Self-preservation is something, then, that all administrative agencies seek, and it is impossible to understand their role in the political system without recognizing this reality.[9]

David Easton, who developed the systems model for political scientists, stresses that survival, or *system persistence,* is actually linked to whether the focal actor or actors (again, the example is an administrative agency) can continue to authoritatively allocate values, in this case, policy decisions or outputs. It is important to understand what Easton means by the "authoritative allocation of values." Easton believes that if an agency has real power in its environment, it must have the ability to force its policies (values) on others. This is really a description of power, and one must have power to survive.[10] Thus, if the FAA, for example, made policy decisions, yet not authoritatively, the FAA would presumably perish, since the allocated policies would carry no significant weight and thus would not be obeyed.

The major structural and functional features of the systems model are sketched in Figure 1.1. Basically, the conceptual design illustrates continuous reactions that must take place in a focal actor's environment if the focal actor is to survive as an authoritative force in the system. The focal actor must react properly to environmental *feedback,* which is expressed in terms of *demands* and *supports.* In systems theory, *reacting properly* to environmental stimuli (inputs) essentially means acting in a way that is consistent with furthering the actor's chances of survival. Appropriate reaction may not necessarily consist of maximizing supports since it is not always necessary for the focal actor to have maximum support to survive. However, proper reaction does consist of action which must be committed to avoid *demand overload.* Demand overload can be conceptualized simply as a red alert situation in which the focal actor must respond immediately and appropriately to reduce the dangerous demands or, if the response is inadequate, face devastation. For example former president Richard Nixon noted in his resignation speech that he was resigning because he had lost a sufficient basis of support. Nixon's description of why he felt he had to resign closely captures the essence of systems theory. Indeed, in light of the demands placed upon him by the Watergate affair, Nixon failed to respond adequately to this demand overload situation. This failure still further eroded the environmental supports he needed to survive. Finally, Nixon had no alternative but to resign because he had lost the environmental supports which were absolutely essential to sustain his survival as president. In specific systems terms, he had to step down because he could no longer

FIGURE 1.1   *A General Systems Model*

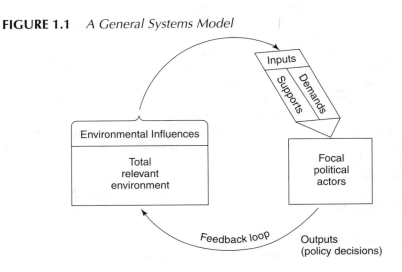

authoritatively allocate values (make respected public policy decisions) in the absence of sufficient and sustaining environmental supports for his leadership.

The merit of systems theory to the study of administrative law cannot be overemphasized. Administrative law involves essentially the study of the legally sanctioned procedural activities of administrative agencies as they interact with their environment. But administrative law cannot be fully appreciated and understood if it is studied only in the context of formal organizational theory—that is, in the context of how administrative organizations ought to perform in the system. Systems theory makes possible the examination of formal administrative law prescriptions in the context of actual behavior in real organizations. Every organization has what is referred to as a *natural system,* which consists of basic survival goals which often depart quite radically from the formal system's prescribed goals (for example, regulating plane safety). A major reason people often cannot comprehend why a certain decision was made is because they try to understand the decision from an unrealistically limited perspective. They tend to exclude factors which are not rational in terms of the organization's formal objectives, yet nevertheless contribute rationally to the organization's ability to cope successfully with its environment.[11] Thus, administrative procedure cannot be studied realistically from the narrow perspective of what administrative law would dictate. It must instead be viewed from the perspective of the total demands placed on administrative agencies by a complex and active environment.

Simply put, agency administrators cannot respond only to what administrative law demands, because public administrators must respond to other environmental demands as well. After reading an administrative law case, a student in class will often ask me why the administrator so blatantly violated the law. My typical response is that the administrator was probably aware of what administrative law required, yet chose to yield to what he or she perceived as a greater pressure. Students must never ignore or underestimate the role politics can play in agency decision making.

Figure 1.2 expands Figure 1.1, applying the systems model directly to the special focus in this book—the involved interactions and interdependence between administrators within public agencies and their unique environments. The model in Figure 1.2 should still be considered a general framework because it is more useful for illustrating the systems picture for a typical administrative agency than for achieving an understanding of the specific interactions within the system for a particular agency. However, Figure 1.3, which depicts the unique environment of the Federal Communications Commission (FCC), is presented to show how the general systems model can be easily adapted so that the focus can be shifted readily from the general administrative system to a specific agency.

Figures 1.2 and 1.3 convey quickly and vividly that administrative decision making must be viewed within the context of an agency's environment. Actually, two environments should be considered—the outer and the inner. Both environments tend to influence administrators as they formulate agency decisions. Whether making internal procedural rules or major public policy statements, all prudent agency decision makers must acknowledge and respond to common outer environmental inputs

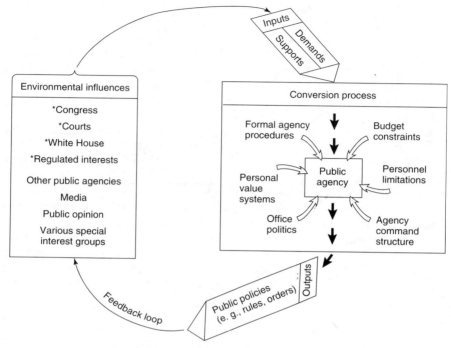

FIGURE 1.2   *The Administrative System*

Note: Asterisks denote significant influence.

(demands and supports). In the typical agency's environment, these inputs would include such major political actors as: (1) the Congress; (2) the courts; (3) the White House; (4) the regulated; (5) other governmental agencies; (6) the media; and (7) the public. Each of these powerful forces in the environment presents a potential threat to the survival, continued success, or at least good health of any public agency. Therefore, their messages (inputs) cannot be taken too lightly or ignored. Successful agency administrators have learned to make decisions which are at least minimally acceptable to their environments. In this vein, then, it should be apparent by now that administrative law dictates constitute only one environmental demand that administrators should consider when reaching decisions. Thus, an administrative decision which complies with what legal formalism may require, but is otherwise environmentally unacceptable, should probably be regarded as a poor or impractical decision—a decision which will be unlikely to be effective when implemented.

Although not indicated in Figure 1.1, the inner environments of agency officials shown in Figures 1.2 and 1.3 also play a crucial role in shaping agency decisions. Ira Sharkansky, who has led the way in the effort to apply systems analysis to the public administration field, refers to these inner environmental factors as *with inputs* because they represent inputs into the decision-making process which occur

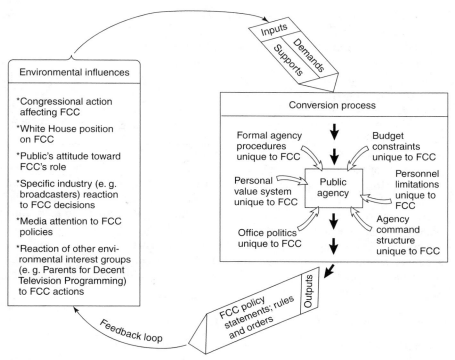

FIGURE 1.3   *FCC's Administrative Environment*

Note: Asterisks denote significant influence.

"within" the agency itself during the "conversion process."[12] During the conversion process the demands and supports from the environment are transformed (converted) into outputs. These outputs represent decisions which reflect agency responses to the inputs from the outer environment and from the inner environment (with inputs) as well. That is, administrators cannot ignore realistically the inputs stemming from inside the agency itself. Internal agency stimuli typically consist of such influential forces as internal agency rules and regulations, office politics, the chain-of-command network, budgetary constraints, staff competencies, employee morale and attitudes, and the like.

It should be emphasized that the heuristic models shown are simply conceptual tools for helping an analyst to envision in a more accurate and sophisticated manner administrative agencies as they interact in a complex systems network. Any environmental force, even some forces not represented in the models, could play a key role in swaying agency decisions—for example, a major international incident. However, it makes sense to draw parameters around the causal variables to include only those factors which the relevant social science and administrative law literature suggest would be most likely to describe agency interactions under normal systemic circumstances.[13]

It should also be noted that legal influences are not given separate, categorical status in the models. This might appear odd for a book which focuses primarily on questions pertaining to the legal relationship between administrative agencies and their environments. But there is a logical reason. Administrative agencies have only implicit constitutional status at best. While the legislative, executive, and judicial branches each have clear constitutional sanctioning as specified in Articles 1, 2, and 3, respectively, of the U.S. Constitution, no article exists which provides for what is perceived commonly as the fourth branch of government—the federal bureaucracy. Consequently, the legal demands and supports which tend to influence agency actions are represented in the other environmental forces indicated in the models. Of course, most of the legal parameters which tend to restrict agency behavior are imposed rather formally on agencies by Congress and the courts at the federal level. On the state level the legislatures and the courts would restrict state agencies in a similar manner. However, the way public agencies read and actually respond to the formal legal dictates depends largely on the important signals (feedback) from other actors in an agency's environment. For instance, public opinion and media may be quite influential on a more informal level in determining agency attitudes toward how the legal mandates from the more formal institutional authorities should actually be interpreted and applied in our society.

ADMINISTRATIVE AGENCIES PLAY THE LEAD ROLES

To obtain a realistic and insightful understanding of administrative law in the United States, it is necessary to develop an appreciation for how the American administrative system actually functions. Accordingly, a few crucial elementary questions should be addressed. Specifically, it would be helpful to know such pertinent information on public agencies as these: (1) Who are our public administrators? (2) Where do they work? (3) What do they do? (4) How do they do it? (5) What overall role do they play in our political system?

Who Are Our Public Administrators?

In many respects public administrators, at least collectively, constitute the most powerful class of workers in the United States. According to the Bureau of Labor Statistics, by 1996 those working in what are regarded as traditional governmental agencies accounted for just under 19 million, a sizable percentage of our entire civilian work force of almost 133 million. Public administrators, especially those near the top of their respective agencies, are in reality responsible for making major policy decisions and spending most of our tax dollars, despite the fact that very few public administrators are elected. Only the president and the vice president are elected on the national level, although many more administrators are elected at the state and local levels (for example, governors, mayors, attorneys general, treasurers, auditors, sheriffs). Still, compared to the many millions of civil servants in the U.S. public bureaucracy, only a very tiny fraction are, in the final analysis, elected. Because many of these nonelected public administrators possess vast policy-making powers, many people believe that these administrators pose a potential threat to traditional democratic governmental processes in this country.

It is very difficult to generalize about the character of public servants since their functions and backgrounds are so varied. Nearly all public servants have their occupational counterparts in private enterprise. While this was certainly not true during the nineteenth century, expanded governmental activities during the twentieth century have compelled government to employ those from all career areas, ranging from such professionals as doctors, lawyers, scientists, and professors, who normally handle highly sophisticated tasks, to those needed to perform clerical and janitorial functions that may require limited talents and very little prior training. Those public servants at low employee classification levels have normally not been perceived as public administrators; yet many of them, such as administrative assistants, clerks, and policemen, in fact exercise significant discretionary powers and should rightfully be viewed as part of the administrative corps, especially since they must follow certain administrative procedures as prescribed in statutes and court decisions.

Looking at job classifications and job descriptions today, one would find it challenging to discover a measurable difference between public and private bureaucracy. Only the goals that they seek appear to be strikingly different. Generally speaking, public administrators seek to promote the public welfare by providing needed goods and services, but not necessarily or usually at a profit. Unlike private businesses, which seek to maximize profits, governmental agencies are frequently obligated because of an environmental demand to provide vital goods and services at a loss. Those administrators in the business world who criticize their public counterparts for being inefficient in handling programs often fail to realize that public administrators must administer many programs that businesses dropped because they could not operate them at a profit; the inner-city transportation services of most municipalities serve as an example here.

In sum, administrators in the private and public sectors are more similar in job functions than might be expected. In many cases they have even had the same basic college preparation, although some may have placed more emphasis on one area of expertise than another. This is becoming more true because of the recent and continuing popularity of master of business administration (MBA) and master of public administration (MPA) programs, which often are quite similar in program content, although the former is geared more toward private than public management. Commonly, because of the interdisciplinary nature of these degree programs, some even leading to joint MBA-MPA degrees, students are required to complete the same core courses (for example, organizational theory and behavior, micro and macro economics) in order to satisfy the degree requirements. MBA and MPA students, those most likely to be our future leaders in private and public administration, also may focus on the same advanced areas; public finance, accounting, administrative law, labor-management relations and management information systems are common examples. Of course, many who emerge as administrators in private and public enterprise are engineers, scientists, or those who have had little to no formal administrative training.

Private and public organizations also face common problems as they struggle to survive when interacting with their environments. There are many examples of managerial successes and failures in both sectors. Critics may find examples of poorly administered public programs (the General Accounting Office, called the GAO, finds several every year), but the managerial blunders which led both Lockheed and Chrysler to inevitable bankruptcy, had it not been for life-sustaining governmental loans, and more recently the collapse of hundreds of banks and savings and loan institutions, do not speak well for administrative efficiency in the private sector either. Thus we can put to rest the old, yet unsubstantiated generalization that private businesses are run more efficiently than public organizations. In short, for at least the reasons noted, it is important not to put unrealistic stress on the differences between private and public administrators, because of the common bonds they share in regard to administrative structure, operations, personnel, and efforts to achieve functional efficiency.

Like people within the American business community, those employed by public agencies come from all segments of society. However, evidence indicates that public agencies are actually more representative of the American people (i.e., by reflecting a better cross section of the diverse socioeconomic classes in America) than business organizations, as well as the legislative, executive, or judicial branches on the national level. Despite fair employment practices legislation that should have forced notable American businesses to open their doors to all persons, social scientists find that public agencies are still more open to women and minorities than private enterprise.[14] Statistics show that women and minorities stand a better chance of being hired and promoted into responsible positions in public agencies, especially federal agencies, than private enterprise. But as Frederick C. Mosher notes, white males are still found in greater numbers in public bureaucracy and in the better positions. "There can be no doubt that there are wide statistical disparities in the employment of white males as compared with females and with blacks, Hispanics, and other minorities."[15] Regarding women alone, Mary E. Guy concludes: "We know that women are making advances into management posts. But there is a long way to go before women will hold management positions proportional to their representation in the work force. . . ."[16]

Where Do Our Public Administrators Work?

Our public administrators work in a great variety of administrative agencies. Public agencies vary in size, location, complexity of functions, and goals. Most public administrators, as common sense would dictate, are probably in agencies which reflect their particular skills, especially since the agencies have been created to handle a specific area of concern in society, such as housing, transportation, energy, or health. Thus, one would expect to find administrators with training and experience in housing matters in the U.S. Department of Housing and Urban Development (HUD), while one would expect to find a disproportionate number of energy experts working in the U.S. Department of Energy (DOE).

Especially important to the focus of this book, public agencies also vary according to their prescribed statutory status in the administrative system. An agency's defined legal status plays a major role in determining the extent of political power the agency can probably wield as it interacts with other political actors in its environment. Essentially, there are three basic types of public agencies, although their legal distinctions are commonly blurred: (1) independent regulatory agencies; (2) quasi-independent regulatory agencies; and (3) executive (cabinet) departments. After a consideration of these three agency types comes a brief discussion of other forms of public agencies in the public administrative network where quasi-public administrators (those administrators who may be in technically private organizations, yet work for government in some capacity) are commonly found.

Independent Regulatory Commissions   Although interest group theorists present credible arguments for the position that no true independent governmental agencies exist, there are nevertheless in the U.S. administrative system public agencies commonly known as independent regulatory commissions or boards. These commissions perform powerful regulatory functions in American society; yet they exist outside the executive departments and beyond the jurisdiction of the president. Congress has given commissioners in these agencies great quasi-legislative and quasi-judicial powers. They are supposed to employ these powers to create rules and orders deemed necessary to regulate specific industries. They have also been granted limited powers to determine whether the regulated have complied with the rules and orders and to punish violators, usually through fines, revocation of licenses, failure to renew permits, and so on. Because the actions (rules, orders, and penalties) of these commissioners may result in the loss of, say, the right to operate a business, those caught in the regulatory embrace of independent regulatory commissions frequently perceive their power to be awesome. The first independent regulatory commission, the Interstate Commerce Commission, was established in 1887, about one hundred years after the founding of our republic. Other such agencies were created later, including the Federal Trade Commission (FTC), Federal Power Commission (FPC), Securities and Exchange Commission (SEC), Federal Communications Commission (FCC), National Labor Relations Board (NLRB), Federal Reserve Board (the Fed), Federal Maritime Commission, and Consumer Product Safety Commission.[17]

Actually, these independent regulatory agencies were created in response to the feedback from the environment, which placed imposing demands on Congress to create bodies of administrative experts able to deal with the varied and complex problems which plagued modern technological society. As the decades passed, it became obvious that Congress no longer had the time, patience, or special talents to regulate all of the vital activities necessary to preserve social order and prosperity in American society. Nor did the courts have the capability to settle all of the disputes between parties and agencies which emerged inevitably as a natural consequence of public policy implementation efforts.

To prevent politics from interfering with the legislative and judicial judgments of these administrative experts, certain structural and procedural precautionary measures were taken by Congress in the creation of these agencies to help protect them from outside contaminative and disruptive political pressures. All independent regulatory commissions are multiheaded and usually consist of five to seven members, although there are exceptions to the general rule. All independent regulatory commissioners are appointed by the president with the consent of the Senate, but they cannot be removed except for *cause* (malfeasance, misfeasance, or nonfeasance). To help insulate commissioners from inappropriate White House meddling into their business affairs, the courts have ruled against presidents who have tried, without proper cause, to remove such commissioners. Political reasons are inadequate grounds for removal.

To further add to their structural independence, the president must appoint these commissioners to fixed terms, and these fixed terms are staggered to prevent any single president from appointing too many people to the commissions. One further check—the rule that no more than the simple majority of a commission may consist of members of the same political party—has kept presidents from stacking independent commissions with appointments in their favor. The role partisan politics can play in commission decision making is thus minimized.

But such independence from viable political controls has caused many critics to refer to this independent regulatory commission system as the headless fourth branch of government, and critics feel that such structure makes centralized administrative planning and coordination of policy virtually impossible.[18] Systems theory would suggest that, although the independent commissions are not immune from external environmental pressures, external influences could, nevertheless, be minimized by their particular structural arrangement. Independent regulatory commissions are never so independent, as the systems model implicitly conveys, that they are not subject to budgetary controls placed upon them by the president and Congress, by public disclosures of their performance, by verbal reprimands by governmental and civic leaders, by investigations by Congress, and by other systemic demands to which they must respond. For example, because of the wide publicity given to General Accounting Office reports (GAO is the investigatory arm of Congress), critical GAO reports can be quite damaging to the image of any independent regulatory commission, thus tending to destroy any illusion independent regulatory commissioners may have of their actual independence from environmental forces.

Quasi-Independent Regulatory Agencies   Many writers who focus attention on administrative structure make no distinction between independent and quasi-independent regulatory agencies, especially since no distinction is made formally in the *United States Government Manual.* However, a practical distinction, important for students of administrative law, does exist. The first independent regulatory commission, the Interstate Commerce Commission (ICC), which was established in 1887, best exemplified the purest independent regulatory agency. The ICC (terminated on December 31, 1995) was structurally independent, not even attached structurally to the Department of Commerce, and it was also rather well protected from outside interference by statute. But not all so-called independent regulatory agencies and commissions are so structurally or statutorily independent; thus their independent status is somewhat compromised. For example, the Federal Aviation Agency (FAA) was created as an independent regulatory commission to promote the airline industry and regulate air safety. Yet a number of experts believe that the FAA's regulatory independence is compromised somewhat because it is housed in the Department of Transportation and is therefore under that department's sphere of influence. Other agencies, such as the Environmental Protection Agency (EPA) and the Food and Drug Administration (FDA), were created as independent agencies with vast adjudicative powers, as is typical for the model independent regulatory commission. However, the EPA and FDA, like several other agencies, find that their regulatory independence is more imagined than real since Congress saw fit to place them within the executive branch: their leaders are not protected by statute from removal by the president. Nevertheless, the courts have slammed the door shut on presidents who have tried to meddle with administrative officials who perform quasi-judicial functions in such agencies, regardless of whether they are specifically protected by statute from presidential intrusion (*Wiener* v. *United States,* 357 U.S. 349; 1958).

Executive Departments   According to some public administration scholars, it is frequently very difficult to separate a quasi-independent regulatory agency's operational status from that of a regular executive department's, although executive departments are generally regarded as more prestigious, possibly because they have "Cabinet" status. However, presidential supervision over executive departments tends to make them considerably less independent than either independent regulatory commissions or quasi-independent regulatory commissions.[19]

Essentially, Cabinet departments (such executive departments as the Department of Defense, Department of Transportation, Department of Health and Human Services, and the Department of Energy) have been created as administrative agencies to assist the president in refining and implementing those public policies enacted by Congress. In contrast, independent regulatory and quasi-independent regulatory agencies play a more traditional regulatory role, thereby relying more heavily upon the standard regulatory tools of rule making and order making. Since administrative law students have focused primarily on procedural due process procedures in agency rule making and order making, generally less attention has been given to Cabinet departments than to those agencies which are more regulatory than administrative in function and purpose. Nonetheless, administrative law pervades all governmental agencies, even those agencies or offices, such as police departments and the White House, once considered beyond the proper scope of administrative law.[20]

Other Public Agencies   In addition to working in independent regulatory agencies and executive departments at the federal or state levels, public administrators are also found in other governmental offices, government-supported corporations, and private agencies and corporations working under government contract.

Other governmental offices can range from relatively well-known and important ones, such as the Small Business Administration and the National Science Foundation, to obscure and relatively inconsequential ones (for example, the American Battle Monuments Commission and the Renegotiation Board). These agencies, commissions, and boards were created as a response to special and narrow demands placed on government; and they normally function with very limited staffs and budgets, especially as compared to such giant government agencies as the U.S. Department of Defense (DOD).

The Federal Crop Insurance Corporation, the Federal National Mortgage Association, the Tennessee Valley Authority, the Smithsonian Institution, the U.S. Postal Service, and the National Railroad Passenger Corporation (Amtrak) provide examples of federal government corporations that are totally or partially owned by government and yet sell goods and services (mail delivery, electric power, bank deposit insurance, transportation service) much like private businesses. Government corporations also exist at the state level, where they are frequently called *authorities*. These authorities must often operate turnpikes, harbors, and airports.

Before 1945 government corporations possessed a great deal of independence and flexibility and functioned practically like any business. However, increasing concern during the 1930s about the unaccountable democratic character of such corporations as the Tennessee Valley Authority (TVA) led to the 1945 passage of the Government Corporation Control Act. Essentially, this act gives government corporations policy direction and fiscal control. Specifically, the act subjects these agencies to the usual congressional investigations and budgetary checks, such as audits, and to civil service statutes. For administrative purposes, some of these corporations are attached loosely to major departments, and their governing boards are staffed by persons appointed by the president.

The government corporations that provide goods and services at both the federal and state levels frequently cannot break even at the relatively low rate they charge (rates which private businesses, incidentally, would regard as too low to make a healthy profit). But because the goods and services provided are considered by the government to be vital to the promotion of the public welfare, they are usually supported in part by governmental subsidies. The challenge, in regard to government corporations, is to find the correct balance between granting these corporations the flexibility necessary for quick and wise business decisions in a rapidly changing environment and maintaining safeguards essential to preserving their democratically responsible character.

Such institutions as Gallaudet College, Howard University, and the American Printing House for the Blind are regarded as federally aided corporations. They function as private institutions, their boards of directors and personnel free from governmental intervention. However, because they are funded by tax dollars, they must be considered quasi-public agencies which must comply with numerous procedural due process restrictions required of the more traditional governmental agencies. Thus, they are legitimately within the jurisdiction of administrative law, although admittedly on the fringe.

It is difficult today to judge just which organizations are beyond the scope of administrative law. The role of government expands as increasing demands are placed upon government; with it grows government pervasiveness. It appears that there are few, if any, sizable organizations left in America today which do not have to comply with required governmental procedures of some kind; equal opportunity employment requirements are frequently cited examples. Actually, some scholars argue that most of us today work for government, at least indirectly. Should those of us who work for private corporations, universities, and the like consider ourselves quasi-governmental employees? Maybe not, but the fact is that Harvard University, IBM, McDonnell Douglas, General Motors, and other such organizations must enter into certain quid pro quo agreements with government as a condition for receiving governmental contracts, grants, loans, and subsidies. Ideally, the arrangements are mutually beneficial. While the government obtains such necessary supplementary goods and services as airplanes, scientific information, transportation service, and trained future leaders, the private organizations benefit financially, and in many cases receive the added benefit of prestige. Nevertheless, the bottom line is that in order to do business with government, these private enterprises must play by government's rules, many of which entail following elaborate procedures related to fair employment practices, work safety, use of human subjects in research, and so on. Completing compliance and various data forms to demonstrate that proper procedures are in fact being followed normally occupies a great deal of time, so much time that some administrators have seriously questioned whether playing ball with government is really worth it.

The purpose of this discussion has been to familiarize the reader with the various types of public or quasi-public administrative agencies which fall within the legitimate purview of administrative law. For the most part, however, this book will be concerned with administrators in this immense administrative system who work in the independent regulatory agencies, quasi-independent regulatory agencies, and cabinet departments. In our political system these administrators interact most with each other and the other branches of government. They also attract by far the most attention from interest groups in the administrative system's environment because these public administrators are responsible for making important policy decisions of major consequence for those affected.

What Do Our Public Administrators Do?

It is clear that if one broadly classifies as public administrators all civil servants who function as administrators (or employ administrative discretion) at least part of the time, public administrators perform a vast array of job tasks in providing goods and services for the public. Even so, and despite the apparent similarities in employee character and structural bureaucratic features between private and public employment, for various reasons the American people do not feel that governmental employees, including public administrators, do very much. A Gallup Poll showed that 67 percent of those surveyed thought that public employees work less than those in private enterprise.[21] The pollsters also found, though these views are certainly debatable, that the public believes that civil servants not only have easier times on the job, but that they also do so for more pay (the opinion of 64 percent) and better fringe benefits (the opinion of 77 percent).[22] Consequently, George Gallup concluded that the "federal government civilian employees—the well-known 'Washington bureaucracy'—has a giant public relations problem."[23] Despite these perceptions by the public, however, it is virtually impossible, because of the mass of intervening variables, to compare productivity accurately between "sister" industries, let alone between the public and private sector. But it is worth noting, in fairness to our public employees, that Robert Townsend, a business efficiency expert and former president of Avis Rent-a-Car, claimed in his books *Up the Organization* and *Further Up the Organization* that people in business are lazy, working at only 50 percent of their capacity, and tend to check their brains at their company's gate.[24]

Governmental administrators in general are paid to regulate. Virtually all of their job tasks relate to reaching regulatory goals assigned to them by Congress and expected of them by the general public. Despite the Gallup finding that Americans believe government is too big (67 percent of those polled held that "government employs too many people"),[25] U.S. citizens keep on asking for more to be done—and spent—in the areas of defense, education, health care, and crime prevention.[26]

Regulatory activities are designed, ideally, to aid in the promotion of the general welfare or public interest—concepts which have always eluded precise definition. Nevertheless, Congress has created virtually every department, agency, commission, board, and so on, and assigned their administrators the task of performing their regulatory mandate in a manner not inconsistent with the public interest. As the systems model demonstrates, increasing demands have caused the regulatory governmental umbrella to expand rapidly to the point where public administrators today are regulating practically all functions believed linked to the maintenance of social health and stability; energy, environment, transportation, commerce, and consumerism are some of the major examples. The English philosopher John Locke's notion of limited government was incorporated into the U.S. Constitution, but it seems to have vanished from practice long ago, replaced by the idea of the welfare state.

Essentially, public administrators regulate in order to protect American society against market defects and failures. Public administrators are concerned especially with preventing people from being exploited by private interests. In every society there are those who do not mind tyrannizing and abusing others while they seek what James Madison believed every free country should permit and nurture—the right of all parties to pursue their selfish interests as long as they do not seriously jeopardize the same rights of others. Stephen G. Breyer and Richard B. Stewart believe that public administrators in their regulatory role particularly aim at: (1) controlling monopoly power; (2) preventing windfall profits; (3) correcting spillover costs; (4) promoting the release of essential public or consumer information; (5) eliminating excessive, destructive, and unhealthy competition in some areas; (6) alleviating and distributing scarce resources, especially in times of crisis; and (7) other areas where the political leaders believe public administrators need to act in a parental capacity (for example, occupational and personal safety and collective bargaining).[27]

The question asked in the title of this section—"What do our public administrators do?"—has been answered here only in very general terms (they regulate vital socioeconomic activities). The question can best be answered by examining the specific procedures public administrators employ while trying to obtain specific agency goals.

How Do Our Public Administrators Regulate?

Our public administrators employ a variety of methods to regulate, but most regulatory approaches can be classified into four general modes. The choice of basic regulatory methods selected by administrators, or originally by Congress, depends largely on the type of activity being regulated (for example, supply of electrical power) and the specific sort of regulatory problem which needs to be addressed (for example, monopolistic or near monopolistic dominance of a market).

The four commonly used regulatory practices are: (1) licensing and granting permissions; (2) rate-setting and price controls; (3) establishing and enforcing public interest standards; and (4) punishing. Naturally, most regulatory agencies use these procedures eclectically, but public administrators tend to emphasize only those regulatory techniques which are best suited for the type of industry that they are entrusted with regulating. Thus, for example, because the Federal Communications Act of 1934 created the FCC to control interstate and foreign communications (the Communications Satellite Act of 1962 has expanded the FCC's responsibilities), mostly connected to radio, television, telephone, and telegraph communications, the FCC commissioners have relied primarily upon the licensing method to control the communications industry. Ideally, the commissioners grant and renew licenses only to those applicants who demonstrate that they can provide, or have in the past provided, communication services in the public interest. Since the FCC cannot regulate rates that, say, television and radio stations charge their sponsors, the licensing approach is about the only viable method FCC commissioners can employ to regulate the quality of programs aired.

The idea that public administrators should be delegated the responsibility for regulating economic activities in society and that they should be given the necessary regulatory tools to do their jobs effectively is hardly a new one. Governments throughout history have always regulated economic activities to some extent. For example, in ancient Egypt the economic activities of the complex canal system were regulated by the governing authorities, while during the Roman Empire the state's administrators were entrusted with regulating diverse economic activities. In 1887 in the United States the Interstate Commerce Commission, the first independent regulatory commission, was established for the general purpose of regulating interstate commerce, but particularly the railroads, although even more specifically the apparent rip-off short haul rates charged to some farmers. These rates were criticized widely at that time by public interest groups and civic leaders as contrary to the best interest of American society. To grant public administrators the authority to establish fair rates in various industries has since become a very common practice aimed at promoting the public good.

Agency administrators have always had the regulatory authority to try to control socioeconomic activities through the practice of simply establishing compulsory standards and voluntary guidelines believed to be in the public interest. Through legislative mandates Congress has given public agencies the power to be flexible in their particular regulatory spheres in setting standards through rules and orders to protect and promote the public interest.

Finally, public administrators have always been able to regulate through threatening or actually using the punitive measures which they have been given by Congress. Congress has allowed administrators to enforce their regulatory policies by permitting them, for example, to impose fines on violators or to suspend or revoke licenses permanently. The penalties may be quite stiff if serious violations have occurred. For example, in 1986 the Securities and Exchange Commission revoked the license of Ivan F. Boesky and imposed a record fine of $100 million on him for his illegal insider stock-trading transactions.[28]

THE NATURE OF ADMINISTRATIVE LAW

Perspectives on Administrative Law

Since the study of administrative law involves the probing of many challenging concepts, it is ironic that one of the most difficult concepts to understand definitively is administrative law itself. One reason for the conceptual vagueness of administrative law stems from the fact that the administrative law field is really in its infancy and is desperately trying to cut the cord from the more traditional law areas (constitutional law, contract law, criminal law) from which it emerged. Although it appears that most legal scholars today recognize administrative law as a fast-growing, independent legal field,[29] some still refuse to perceive administrative law as separate from other legal fields, thus stirring mud in its definitional waters. For instance, Nathaniel Nathanson once wrote in an *Administrative Law Review* article: "But I often tell my students that administrative law is nothing but a mixture of constitutional law and statutory construction, seasoned, I hope, with liberal sprinklings of common sense or sophisticated in the ways of government."[30] However, although written over twenty years ago, this glib perception of administrative law not only does a disservice to its development as a separate field, but it is also a patently false and unfair view. In fact, not only do all developed legal areas overlap somewhat (can we separate completely criminal law from constitutional law?), but administrative law itself is also a much richer and more unusual blend of various other legal fields than Nathanson acknowledges.

The term *administrative law* is like many other conceptual words, such as *love, power, justice,* and *democracy.* It is a lot easier to describe these concepts than to define them. Definitions have been attempted, but they always seem to lack something. Also, because the definitions are frequently so different, they sometimes only confuse the reader. For example, administrative law is defined in *Daniel Oran's Dictionary of the Law* as "1. Laws about the duties and proper running of an administrative agency that are handed to agencies by legislatures and courts. 2. Rules and regulations set out by administrative agencies." In the old standby, Black's *Law Dictionary,* administrative law is defined as: "Body of law created by administrative agencies to implement their powers and duties in the form of rules, regulations, orders, and decisions." Stephen G. Breyer and Richard B. Stewart define administrative law as "consisting of those legal rules and principles that define the authority and structure of administrative agencies, specify the procedural formalities that agencies employ, determine the validity of particular administrative decisions, and define the role of reviewing courts and other organs of government in their relation to administrative agencies." Possibly the dean of administrative law in twentieth-century America, Kenneth Culp Davis, defines it as "the law concerning the powers and procedures of administrative agencies, including especially the law governing judicial review of administrative action."[31]

Together, these definitions provide some clues as to what administrative law entails. But in truth these definitions seem to raise more questions than they answer because each definition employs words, phrases, and concepts—public law, sovereign power, administrative agencies, rules and regulations, judicial review, and so forth—which are also vague in meaning. The real role played by administrative law in our governmental system is only implied. Thus, because of acute definitional problems, it seems wiser to try to describe administrative law and its related concepts in the context of administrative law history and its modern role vis-a-vis administrative agencies, the legislatures, the courts, the White House, and outside parties.

Broadly speaking, administrative law deals with (1) the ways in which power is transferred from legislative bodies to administrative agencies; (2) how administrative agencies use power; and (3) how the actions taken by administrative agencies are reviewed by the courts. More specifically, administrative law is concerned with the legal developments which have so dramatically increased the powers and scope of the administrative branch. The law-making (technically, quasi-legislative or rule-making) and judicial (technically, quasi-judicial or order-making) powers, which have been delegated to administrators by the legislative branch at both the national and state levels, have created an extremely powerful administrative branch, thus changing the meaning we have traditionally attributed to the separation of powers doctrine. As a result, students of administrative law have been particularly concerned over the significance of this change in the balance of power within our traditional tripartite governmental structure, especially since such alterations necessitate new interpretations of what we mean by "rule of law," "liberty," and "democracy." Consequently, administrative law scholars in recent decades have devoted much attention to evaluating the impact of the growth of administrative power on democratic society. Considerable time has been spent on seeking new and effective measures for controlling and checking the activities of administrative officials so that the public interest can be better protected. Since the 1930s the courts have been very active in reviewing agency actions and watching out for administrative abuses. Agency hearing examiners (administrative law judges) and court judges have given special attention to situations in which the discretionary power of administrative officials seemed to come dangerously close to violating procedural due process rights as guaranteed by the Constitution, by statutes, and by the agency's own prescribed rules of fair conduct.

SCOPE OF ADMINISTRATIVE LAW

Although the scope of administrative law is impossible to determine, especially at this time in its youthful development, it is apparent that administrative law is broadly concerned with the role and power relationships of administrative agencies in society or, simply, the ways in which administrative agencies use their power in implementing public policies. One can expect, then, almost all critical issues in administrative law to center ultimately on questions of power politics, which are vitally important to the character of any democratic political system. Sallyanne Payton, acknowledging that administrative law is inherently a political subject concerned primarily with procedure, puts it this way: "Procedures are power; they may assist or hinder the agencies in accomplishing their missions, may force agencies to redefine their missions or their constituencies, may provide visibility into decision-making processes and thus facilitate political accountability, and so on. . . . Preferences for one type of decision maker or process over another are at the base of political preferences. . . ."[32] More generally, Marshall Breger notes that ". . . administrative law today deals with central issues in our political landscape. The enlarged curriculum (sic) can only spark the interest of its practitioners and scholars."[33]

The following is a relatively long list of vital administrative law questions reflecting power considerations which should provide more insights into the scope and nature of administrative law: (1) How much power should be delegated to administrative agencies? (2) How much administrative discretion is too much? (3) Does the doctrine of sovereign immunity extend too much power to governmental agencies? (4) What constitutes "arbitrary and capricious" agency decisions? (5) What are the components of a "fair hearing"? (6) How can administrative officials be allowed to administer needed public policies without infringing on the rights of individuals? (7) How does an extreme interpretation of "executive privilege" square with "rule of law," "popular sovereignty," "limited government," "separation of powers," and other notions of popular government? (8) How much "official immunity" should be extended to governmental administrators? (9) Under what circumstances should the "burden of proof" be allowed to be placed on persons coming before administrative agencies? (10) How free can a country remain if administrative agencies are permitted to make laws, administer them, and decide on the appropriateness and fairness of their own laws? (11) Are administrative agencies becoming too oppressive and threatening to our freedom? (12) Is procedural due process less important than substantive law? (13) How can administrative abuses be effectively checked? (14) What internal and external safeguards can be developed to keep public administrators in line? (15) What role should the courts play in the review of agency decisions? (16) How can legislative bodies better control agency activities to guarantee that "legislative intent" is carried out responsibly in the administrative process? (17) What should be done to control the "regulators"?

One of the best methods for gaining a quick understanding of the scope of administrative law is to scan some of the major basic textbooks on the subject.[34] Even a cursory examination of administrative law books shows that certain topics are treated by virtually all writers, but others receive little or no coverage. This can be explained easily by making a distinction between administrative law purists and nonpurists.

The purists think in an ideal mode, taking a very narrow perception of what should be regarded as legitimate areas of administrative law. They believe that administrative law should be confined essentially to the study of the independent regulatory agencies or commissions (for example, the Interstate Commerce Commission, the Federal Trade Commission, the Nuclear Regulatory Commission). This attitude is rooted in the argument that only these agencies have traditionally exercised quasi-legislative (rule-making) and quasi-judicial (order-making) powers, while other administrative agencies (for example, the Office of the President, executive departments, and police departments) do not normally possess such powers. Since administrative law focuses primarily on rule-making and order-making procedures, the purists have basically concluded that only agencies which exercise such authority should be given significant attention. In short, the purists have concentrated primarily on the formal aspects of agency operations as they relate to administrative law. Specifically, they have focused mostly on the statutory authority of agencies, rule-making and order-making processes, and judicial review of the "formal" actions of the independent regulatory commissions.

Unlike the purists, the nonpurists have taken a much broader view of what administrative law should entail. To the nonpurist, there is no valid reason for not studying administrative agencies of virtually all descriptions, even if these agencies perform only "purely" administrative functions. For example, to Davis, a nonpurist, police departments fall within the legitimate scope of administrative law analysis even though the police possess no formal quasi-legislative or quasi-judicial powers. However, police, as well as other purely executive officers, exercise administrative discretion when making decisions that affect the community. Because informal discretionary acts may have profound consequences for individuals and groups, Davis recommends that considerable attention be devoted to improving the quality of discretionary justice in America, especially since such informal decision making makes up more than 90 percent of all agency actions. Once more, such informal agency discretionary action often falls outside the jurisdiction of the Administrative Procedure Act and the reviewing courts.

The purists and nonpurists have also disagreed over whether certain executive officials, particularly the president and state governors, should be included in administrative law analysis. This controversy stems from the fact that the president and state governors do not derive their powers from legislative statutes, as do administrators in all regulatory agencies. The president of the United States draws power from Article 2 of the U.S. Constitution, while state governors, as well as other administrators in some states, derive their authority from their respective state constitutions.

Consistent with the separation of powers doctrine, this does insulate these executives from the congressional controls which other administrators must endure. And since administrative law has focused traditionally on the relationship between legislators and administrative agencies under legislative supervision, the purists have questioned whether administrators with separate constitutional status are within the legitimate scope of administrative law or whether they should be left to the constitutional law scholars. However, the crucial point is not whether these executives are considered within the power subject area of administrative law but rather that students recognize the difference between these two types of administrators in the administrative system.

The purists would also maintain that elected and nonelected public administrators are not the same and that administrative law covers the latter but not the former. Once again, if the purists consider the focus of administrative law to be congressionally created regulatory commissions whose quasi-legislative and quasi-judicial officials are appointed, not elected, then applications of administrative law would hardly seem appropriate for elected officials. This is an important distinction to consider when reflecting upon the fairness of administrative actions by elected and nonelected officials: the behavior of elected officials can be checked directly by the voters, but the actions of nonelected public administrators cannot.

Additionally, the purists hold that administrative law is not concerned with substantive public policies (that is, the actual policy content of the orders and rules) but only with the procedural steps leading to orders and rules. However, it is absurd to try to pretend that procedural due process can be separated from substantive due process. To do so would be like suggesting that good wine has nothing to do with the steps taken in producing and maintaining its fine quality. Chapter 5 will show that the content of rules is very much affected by the procedures adopted by agency administrators. Obviously, for example, agency officials in the rule-making process can shape the final public policies produced by using their broad discretionary powers to determine in practice not only who participates, but also what weight is given to the inputs of the different participants.

In reality, the study of administrative law, despite the purists, is like the study of almost anything else. That is, everything sensibly pertaining to the subject is open for inclusion as part of the legitimate subject sphere. Robert Lorch put it this way: "One may wonder where administrative law ends and other kinds of law begin. Where, for example, does the law of civil rights leave off and administrative law begin? The answer to that cannot be supplied any more than an answer to the question where blue ends and purple begins. Administrative law is not a thing of clear boundaries, nor is any other branch of the law, for they are all *neighborhoods* in the world of law which fade into one another block by block."[35] In 1990 the administrative law section of the American Bar Association held a workshop on what should be covered in an administrative law course. The participating fifty or so administrative law professors concluded that virtually any relevant topic could be covered given how interdisciplinary administrative law has become, now legitimately including such fields as psychology, economics, organizational theory, public policy, and political science. About the only limiting factor was available time.[36]

This book takes a nonpurist approach so that a conceptually broad and sophisticated comprehension of the role of administrative law in our political system can be presented. It seems unwise to exclude certain subject matter from administrative law study simply because it fails to pass the administrative law purity test. Besides, many informal aspects that affect administrative law may not interest traditional law students; yet they may intrigue public administration and public policy students.

The Distinctiveness of Administrative Law

What makes the administrative law field distinct from other areas of law? After what has already been said about the eclectic nature of administrative law, it would now be absurd to argue that administrative law is a purebred species. It is obviously a mongrel. But even a mutt has a distinct personality.[37] And it should be reiterated that administrative law is a mixture of various legal areas, just as other law fields are. (See Figure 1.2 for an illustration of this practical concept.) For some reason, however, possibly their youthful innocence, administrative law scholars are simply less secure and, therefore, less pretentious.

What makes administrative law unique is its special focus. However, probably every field of study, whether in law, the social sciences, or another area, is distinguished by its particular emphasis. Despite disagreements regarding the proper scope of administrative law, virtually all administrative law scholars focus on the makings of fair

FIGURE 1.4   *The Eclectic Nature of Administrative Law*

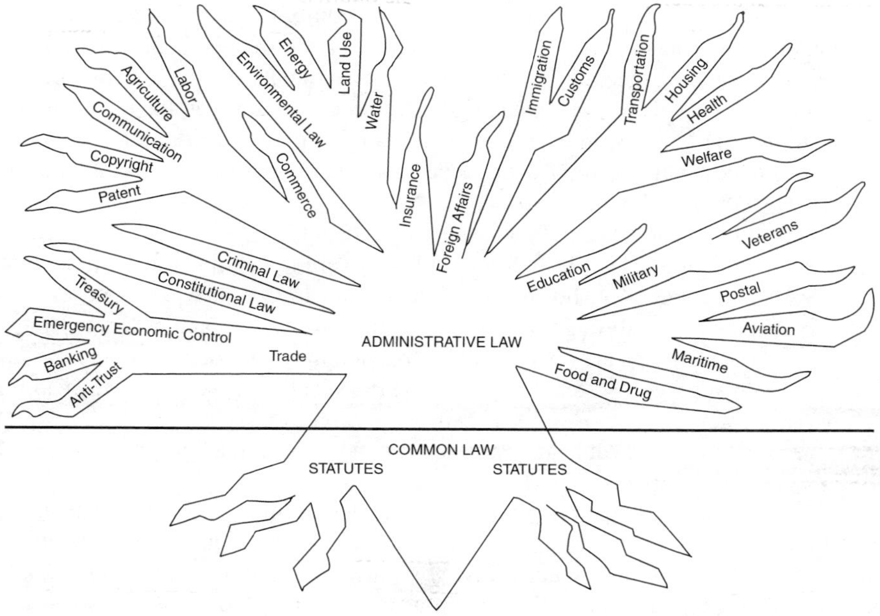

procedure in administrative agencies. Thus, administrative law is made distinct by its attention to the procedural activities of all public administrators. Whether analysis is on agency rule making, order making, official immunity, or judicial review of agency actions, administrative procedural due process considerations provide the chief focal points. Even after acknowledging the vague character of administrative law, Lorch maintained that "the central business district of administrative law is fair administrative procedure."[38]

Because of administrative law's emphasis on procedural due process, as contrasted to substantive due process, its interest in the U.S. Constitution is confined mostly to sections in the Constitution or state constitutions that pertain directly or indirectly to procedural due process considerations. Therefore, in the federal Constitution, administrative law issues frequently touch upon the Fourth, Fifth, and Fourteenth Amendments. While the Fifth and Fourteenth Amendments specifically call for due process of law to be executed when governmental actions are taken, other amendments and sections of the Constitution have been interpreted by the courts to imply such a call. For example, the Fourth Amendment says nothing about due process specifically. But the Amendment prohibits unreasonable searches and seizures, thus forcing police and other administrators to follow due process procedures when carrying out searches.

Administrative law is unique, compared to other legal fields, in the sense that probably more than 90 percent of administrative law is derived from common law.[39] Common law is that body of law which accumulates over the years as the result of judicial decisions. It is judge-made law. In the case of administrative law, judges over the decades have, on an incremental or case-by-case basis, given practical meaning to due process requirements in administrative procedure. In fact, although the Constitution mentions due process, due process is never, even weakly, defined in it. Legislative enactments, especially in such major enactments as the Administrative Procedure Act, have given some meaning to due process. However, the most authoritative and lasting insights on what due process or fair procedure should entail have come from major policy-setting court decisions, such as *Morgan* v. *United States,* 304 U.S. 1 (1938); *Goldberg* v. *Kelly,* 397 U.S. 254 (1970); *Connecticut* v. *Doehr,* 111 S.Ct. 2105 (1991), and *McCarthy* v. *Madigan,* 112 S.Ct. 1081 (1992). Such cases have formed the giant reservoir of common law governing administrative procedure today. Practically speaking, however, public administrators provide the everyday meaning of due process through their interpretations of statutes and court decisions. Statutes and court rulings are never so definitive that they are not open to interpretations by administrators. Consequently, unless their specific actions are overruled by the courts, administrators can employ their broad discretionary powers to determine the meaning of procedural due process in the context of the public programs that they are responsible for implementing.

The fact that administrative law today is rooted only weakly in substantive, or statutory, law also helps to give administrative law its unique character and, to some, its relative lack of respectability. Administrative law's heavily judge-made common law backing not only makes administrative law very difficult to understand

and follow, since major changes can occur in the law with each court decision, but it may also detract from its democratic soundness. That is, democratic theory holds that laws should ideally be made by elected representatives of the people. Democratic theory has never placed judges at the heart of democracy. Thus, one may ask: "How democratic is a body of laws if under 10 percent of them were made by legislators?"

The answer is self-evident, and it poses a serious threat to democratic life in the United States. Many readers may regard this contention as mere alarmist academic rhetoric. But to those a warning should be issued. Theory is not impractical. Theory has very practical applications. Those who continue to insist that theory and practice mix like oil and water are distorting reality. The truth is that the wisdom in democratic theory has been increasingly compromised in America for the sake of expediency. In its present form administrative law clashes too sharply with the sound principles embraced in democratic theory. Administrative law is a unique body of law which stresses procedural due process. In practice, procedural due process may mean much more to the preservation of democratic life than substantive law. Davis was absolutely correct when he noted that any knowledgeable person of law would acknowledge this reality.[40] For example, legal experts and political scientists long recognized that the Soviet Constitution was substantively more democratic than the U.S. Constitution. But what good is a democratic constitution if it is not upheld by fair procedures which in fact give constitutions their real meaning for the citizenry? In the words of Justice Robert H. Jackson: "Procedural fairness and regularity are of the indispensable essence of liberty. Severe substantive laws can be endured if they are fairly and impartially applied. Indeed, if put to the choice, one might well prefer to live under Soviet substantive law applied in good faith by our common-law procedures than under our substantive law enforced by Soviet procedural practices" (*Shaughnessy* v. *United States ex rel. Mezei,* 346 U.S. 206, 224;1953). And this perspective endures. Recently in *Riverbend Farms* v. *Madigan,* 958 F.2nd 1479, 1482 (9th Cir. 1992), the court exclaimed: "Procedure, not substance, is what most distinguishes our (system) from others."

The breakdown of the traditional tripartite model of democracy in America has resulted in a preponderance of what might be called undemocratic power in the administrative branch with the courts trying desperately, yet futilely, to keep these new, mighty administrative agencies democratically accountable.[41] In many respects administrative law is distinct because it plays a critically important and powerful role in our society; yet its significance to the preservation of our democratic way of life has not been fully appreciated. If it were, there would be a more serious effort to develop and structure administrative law so that administrative procedures could reach higher levels of efficiency and fairness. The untidy and frequently unfair procedures followed by many of our administrative agencies in implementing public policies at all governmental levels attest clearly to our need to strengthen the procedural and substantive character of administrative law. And it should not be overlooked that citizens judge public policies not as they are written but as they take on life when implemented by administrators.

ADMINISTRATIVE LAW'S INCREASING RELEVANCE

There is no need to spend much time noting the growing importance of administrative law in modern America. The critical nature of administrative law should be already apparent to any casual observer of governmental developments in American society, especially those advanced enough to be reading this administrative law text. Nevertheless, let me emphasize some of the factors which have made administrative law one of the more vital subjects today.

Although the development of the American administrative system is elaborated on in Chapter 2, it is worth acknowledging here that the great expansion of public administration in the United States, starting with the presidency of Franklin Delano Roosevelt, has been enormous. This reality is the single most important reason for administrative law's rapid growth and heightened status. Since the beginning of the Great Depression, Americans have been increasingly willing to allow government to respond to and resolve a great variety of societal problems that had previously been handled outside government. This attitude has encouraged the widespread use of administrative agencies to regulate in what is considered to be the public interest.[42] Increased regulation of socioeconomic life by government has resulted in a massive number of new statutes and an especially vast quantity of agency rules and orders.

As an academic and practical field, administrative law has become more popular and relevant as the impact of public administration on American lives has become more profound. Davis claims that administrative law has passed through three stages of development and is presently, and simultaneously, entering a fourth and fifth stage.[43] Generally, as public administration activity has increased in vitality and depth in the American political system, interest in administrative law has been transformed from a more theoretical interest to serious concern for resolving the practical problems that have plagued administrative law. For example, during the first stage, Davis notes that focus was on the constitutional foundations of administrative law. A chief theoretical concern was where constitutional law ended and administrative law began. During this lengthy stage, which lasted from the beginning of the republic to about the 1920s, special emphasis was placed on issues pertaining to the separation of powers and delegation doctrines. Stage two, running throughout the 1920s and 1930s, was dominated by judicial review of agency actions as the courts tried to determine the constitutionality of certain new agency practices. For the courts, the central focal question was essentially this: what role does the Constitution permit the emerging administrative state to play in our political system? Toward the end of the 1930s, at the height of agency proliferation, increased attention began to focus on formal administrative procedures, especially order making and rule making. During this third stage, concern for fair formal administrative procedures led, in 1946, to the passage of the Administrative Procedure Act (60 Stat. 237), a major act aimed at regulating administrative behavior in virtually all federal agencies. Since the 1960s a good deal of attention has been devoted to informal agency conduct, which makes up more than 90 percent of all agency actions. Special focus in this fourth stage has been on increasing the fairness, efficiency, and effectiveness of informal agency decision-making processes. Emphasis has been placed on balancing the needs of society against the requirements of sound administrative practices. Stage five is characterized by a new concern for the technical and democratic complexities of the rule-making process, especially since regulatory agencies in recent years have relied heavily on the rule-making procedure to promulgate a host of new governmental regulations. The scope of these new regulations has broadened considerably during the past decade or so.[44]

According to comments by Ernest Gellhorn presented to members of the American Bar Association in the "Presidential Showcase Program," we have now passed the fifth stage and have entered still another stage. Gellhorn contends that in what Davis calls the fifth stage (Gellhorn's second modern stage), the mood was set that virtually guaranteed swift movement to another stage. During this fifth stage governmental regulation reached its most intense and pervasive level, yet the integrity of the administrative process was doubted and challenged, especially the seemingly arrogant role played by powerful agency experts. Administrative policies were often perceived as cost ineffective, lacking any sensible regulatory wisdom. Consequently, a new representational approach to administrative law and regulatory government developed, characterized by significant public participation in agency decision making. Throughout the late 1960s and well into the 1970s, Congress passed legislation and the courts reached decisions that promoted broad interest-group participation in the administrative process. The courts even liberalized standing law, making it easier for interest groups to challenge agency actions in the courts. When the courts heard administrative law cases, they employed the "hard look" rationale, scrutinizing not just administrative procedures, but also the quality of expertise employed by agency administrators.[45]

The sixth stage, or Gellhorn's third modern stage, emerged then as a reaction to the apparent runaway regulatory character of modern regulatory government. Starting around the time of President Jimmy Carter's administration, reformers began to question the reasonableness and even legitimacy of so much governmental regulation.[46] Contending generally that regulatory government had become too domineering and cost-ineffective, these reformers pushed for governmental deregulation and other measures to reduce the size and force of what they considered constitutionally illegitimate public administration. The deregulation movement began during President Carter's administration but picked up pace during the relatively conservative presidential administrations of Reagan and Bush, led by a Supreme Court dominated by Reagan and Bush appointees. Ironically, this era of serious popular skepticism and cynicism toward governmental regulation has stretched into the Clinton years, causing the courts to return to fundamental administrative/constitutional law issues concerning delegation, separation of powers, and legitimacy so commonly debated before the 1930s [e.g., *INS* v. *Chadha,* 462 U.S. 919, 1983; *Bowsher* v. *Synar,* U.S., 1986; *Morrison* v. *Olson,* 108 S.Ct. 2597 (1988); *Skinner* v. *Mid-America Pipeline Co.,* 109 S.Ct. 1726 (1989); *Touby* v. *United States,* 111 S.Ct. 1752 (1991); and *Metropolitan Washington Airports Authority* v. *Citizens for the Abatement of Aircraft Noise,* 111 S.Ct. 2298 (1991)].

THE REGULATORY ARM FALLS ON GROVE CITY COLLEGE

In modern America virtually nothing seems to be immune from the far-reaching grasp of governmental regulators. Much to the dismay of laissez-faire conservatives, governmental intrusion in the private sector has become so widespread that the word *private* has been losing its practical meaning, so much so that now it is becoming more popular—because it is really more accurate—to refer to many private organizations as quasi-public organizations. Quasi-public organizations can be described as organizations or companies under private ownership whose behavior is controlled rather rigorously by governmental regulations. Some examples are auto manufacturers, universities, restaurants, and advertising firms.

The controversy between Grove City College, a small private college in western Pennsylvania, and the U.S. Department of Education illustrates the continuing efforts of government to establish a sphere of influence in what were once considered private policy matters.[47] To put the story in a nutshell, a Department of Education (DOE) decision ordered Grove City College (G.C.C.) to acknowledge compliance with a DOE regulation prohibiting sex discrimination. Asserting its independence, G.C.C. refused to sign the DOE compliance forms in principle, arguing that it had never received a dime from federal funds. DOE, however, took the position that G.C.C. received funds indirectly through student loans which, of course, students used to pay tuition. DOE admitted that it had no evidence that G.C.C. was guilty of sex discrimination. In this case, the sex discrimination issue is completely beside the point. The real question being tested by G.C.C. is whether there is such a thing as a private college or university in modern America. Even the relatively conservative Burger Court reluctantly answered that it is unlikely, because colleges and universities have to comply with Section 9011a of Title IX (20 U.S.C., Section 1681, a). Expanding the role of governmental regulation just a bit more, the Court held that G.C.C. was the recipient of federal financial assistance, although indirectly through a student loan program (Basic Educational Opportunity Grants), and therefore must comply with the statutory provision prohibiting sex discrimination in any of its educational programs linked to this aid (*Grove City College* v. *Bell,* 465 U.S. 555, 575; 1984). In concurring, Chief Justice Burger and Justices Powell and O'Connor noted that they had no choice under law but to concur, even though in their view "the case is an unedifying example of overzealousness on the part of the Federal Government. . . . It was and is the policy of this small college to remain wholly independent of government assistance, recognizing—as this case will illustrate—that with the acceptance of such assistance one surrenders a certain measure of the freedom that Americans have always cherished" (at 576–77).

Although the Grove City College case is linked specifically to the U.S. government's policies in higher education, the case obviously has widespread implications. In the G.C.C. dispute, DOE administrators used government-sponsored student loans, a somewhat indirect source of revenue for G.C.C., to justify their demand for compliance with DOE standards. This justification led one scholar, after reviewing the *Grove City* decision, to conclude that *"Grove City's* expansive definition of federal financial assistance is, in effect, another step toward limiting the autonomy of private entities through further federal government encroachments."[48] More recently a New York court, citing *Grove City College,* held that ". . . since Colgate is unwilling to make a change, it is the duty of this court to order change." So it ordered Colgate ". . . to grant varsity status to the women's ice hockey program starting with the 1993/94 school year, . . ." [*Cook* v. *Colgate University,* 802 F.Supp. 737,751 (N.D.N.Y. 1992)].

Has history not shown that federal and state agencies have employed similar techniques and rationales to enforce their will? Will not the influence of governmental bureaucracy continue to increase in the private sector as public administrators adopt an even more prevalent parental attitude in their attempts to protect and promote the public health and safety in more and more areas of American life? Has not administrative law been thrust to the forefront by the enthusiastic encroachment of governmental regulators on the wilting private sector? In light of these developments, would it not be wise to understand administrative law?

Some of the questions may indicate a conservative bias on the part of this author, but the questions are meant only to reflect reality. In fact, the rapid expansion of the administrative system may be perceived as part of a noble effort by government to provide Americans with a higher quality of life through increased and better regulation. And, in truth, despite some administrative problems, a strong case could be made by liberal thinkers that expanded governmental regulation has indeed improved the quality of life for the average American citizen since welfare state ideas and policies began to be accepted and rapidly implemented after the New Deal. For example, governmental regulation has helped to improve working conditions, made transportation safer, curbed the marketing of dangerous consumer products, and so on. In any event, it is true that as public agencies become more involved in the areas of transportation, housing, energy, environment, communications, health, safety, education, welfare, human rights, and the like, administrative law issues will become more prevalent. Specifically, administrative law will play a greater role in helping to resolve the increasing number of disputes between the regulated and the regulators. In so doing, administrative law will have the very difficult task of fairly balancing the need for efficient and effective governmental administration with the interests and rights of the regulated.

SUMMARY

In this administrative law textbook the noncasebook approach is employed, making it ideally suited for students in the social sciences. Its basic purpose is to familiarize students in political science, public administration, public affairs, public policy, and the like with the role played by administrative law in the American political system. To fulfill this central goal, the book devotes considerable space to the examination of the major principles and issues in administrative law. This book has been written primarily for social science students; therefore, every attempt is made to apply administrative law to public policy implementation problems in the context of the realities confronted by public administrators in political life. To help clarify the role of administrative law in the political system, a systems approach, quite familiar to most social science students, is employed, on a somewhat limited basis.

Only recently has the importance of administrative law been recognized by public administration scholars. However, administrative law is now perceived as so crucial to understanding the functions of administrative agencies that administrative law has become one of the hottest, if not *the* hottest, field in the public administration discipline. Modern regulatory government has become so complex and pervasive that it has strained the relationship between the regulators and the regulated. Heated disputes between these two natural rivals have increased in recent decades as the regulatory arm of government has grown stronger. Recently many Americans, clinging to the freedoms that they have left, have even challenged the very legitimacy of the administrative state. To ease the tension between the regulators and the regulated, administrative law has been developing rapidly. Legislators, and especially judges, have been trying to develop an administrative law system in which administrative procedures are effective and efficient and still embrace the principles of due process under law. The developmental pace of administrative law has been so rapid that the state of administrative law is uncertain, unstable, and, thus, quite difficult to understand. Quoting Bernard Schwartz, administrative law in recent years has been in a ". . . continual state of flux" and we are witnessing ". . . a virtual administrative law explosion."[49]

NOTES

1. Donald D. Barry and Howard R. Whitcomb, *The Legal Foundations of Public Administration,* 2nd ed. (St. Paul: West Publishing Company, 1987); Lief H. Carter, *Administrative Law and Politics: Cases and Comments,* 2nd ed. (Little, Brown and Company, 1983); Phillip J. Cooper, *Public Law and Public Administration,* 2nd ed. (Englewood Cliffs, N.J.: Prentice Hall, 1988); and Florence Heffron with Neil McFeeley, *The Administrative Regulatory Process* (New York: Longman, 1983).
2. Kenneth C. Davis, *Discretionary Justice: A Preliminary Inquiry* (Westport, Conn.: Greenwood Press, 1980); and Walter C. Gellhorn, *When Americans Complain: Governmental Grievance Procedures* (Cambridge, Mass.: Harvard University Press, 1966).
3. Peter Woll, *American Bureaucracy,* 2nd ed. (New York: W. W. Norton, 1977), 77.
4. For fascinating viewpoints on how administrative law should be taught, see Richard J. Pierce, Jr., "How Much Should an Administrative Law Course Accomplish?: A Response to Schotland's Five Easy Pieces," *Administrative Law Review,* 43 (Winter 1991), 123–133; and Sidney A. Shapiro, "Reflections on Teaching Administrative Law: Time For a Sequel," *Administrative Law Review,* 43 (Summer 1991), 501–509.
5. Kenneth C. Davis and Richard J. Pierce, Jr., *Administrative Law Treatise,* 3rd ed. (Boston: Little, Brown, 1994), vol. 111, chap. 17.
6. Today there exist over one hundred federal forfeiture laws applying to many illegal activities. See Laura J. Kerrigan, Project Editor, "Project: The Decriminalization of Administrative Law Penalties," *Administrative Law Review,* 45 (Fall 1993), 388–389, 412–413.

7. Edwin G. Krasnow, Lawrence D. Longley, and Herbert A. Terry, *The Politics of Broadcast Regulation,* 3rd ed. (New York: St. Martin's Press, 1982), 133.

8. Acknowledging the need for empirical studies in the area of administrative law, the editors of the *Administrative Law Review* decided to begin the 1980s with two volumes devoted to empirical research efforts. See "Symposium on Empirical Research in Administrative Law, Parts 1 and 2," *Administrative Law Review,* 31, 32 (Fall 1979, Winter 1980). More empirical studies in administrative law, although not an impressive amount, have been published in professional journals since 1980.

9. For an excellent book devoted solely to explaining the survival instincts of governmental agencies see Herbert Kaufman, *Are Government Organizations Immortal?* (Washington, D. C.: Brookings Institution, 1976).

10. David Easton, *A Framework for Political Analysis,* 2nd ed. (Chicago: University of Chicago Press, 1979).

11. Judith R. Gordon, *A Diagnostic Approach to Organizational Behavior* (Boston: Allyn and Bacon, 1993), 21–23.

12. Ira Sharkansky, *Public Administration: Policy-Making in Government Agencies,* 4th ed. (Chicago: Rand McNally, 1978), 10–11.

13. Thomas R. Dye, *Understanding Public Policy,* 7th ed. (Englewood Cliffs, N.J.: Prentice Hall, 1992), 42–44.

14. Cole Blease Graham, Jr., "Equal Employment Opportunity and Affirmative Action," in Steven W. Hays and Richard C. Kearney (eds.), *Public Personnel Administration: Problems and Prospects,* 2nd ed. (Englewood Cliffs, N.J.: Prentice Hall, 1990), chap. 13; Mary E. Guy, "Three Steps Forward, Two Steps Backward: The Status of Women's Integration into Public Management," *Public Administration Review,* 53 (July/August 1993), 285–291; and Angela M. Bullard and Deil S. Wright, "Circumventing the Glass Ceiling: Women Executives in American State Governments," *Public Administration Review,* 53 (May/June 1993), 189–202.

15. Frederick C. Mosher, *Democracy and the Public Service,* 2nd ed. (New York: Oxford University Press, 1982), 223.

16. Guy, "Three Steps Forward, Two Steps Backward: The Status of Women's Integration into Public Management," 290.

17. As of July 1, 1993, sixty-two agencies were listed as "Independent Establishments and Government Corporations," although not all are truly established independent regulatory agencies. See *The United States Government Manual,* 1993–1994 (Washington, D.C.: Government Printing Office, 1993), 539–774.

18. See, for example, Susan Bartlett Foote, "Independent Agencies Under Attack: A Skeptical View of the Importance of the Debate," *Duke Law Journal* (1988), 223–237.

19. James P. Pfiffner, *The Modern Presidency* (New York: St. Martin's Press, 1994), chap. 5.

20. Kenneth C. Davis, *Police Discretion* (St. Paul, Minn.: West Publishing Company, 1975).

21. *The Gallup Opinion Index,* Report No. 146 (Princeton, N.J.: Gallup Poll, 1977), 23.

22. *The Gallup Opinion Index,* Report No. 146, pp. 22, 24. According to the *Statistical Abstract of the United States, 1987,* 107th ed. (Washington D.C.: Government Printing Office, 1986), 400, governmental employees in 1985 did average slightly greater pay when compared to "all domestic industries," a factor of $22,186 to $20,991. However, if one excludes just one of the eleven categories listed ("agriculture, forestry, fisheries"), which significantly reduces the average because of its $11,320 annual wage and salary figure, civil servants fall below the average income level, $22,186 to $24,728.

23. *The Gallup Opinion Index,* Report No. 146, p. 20.
24. Robert C. Townsend, *Up the Organization* (New York: Fawcett, 1978), chap. 1; and Robert C. Townsend, *Further Up the Organization* (New York: Alfred A. Knopf, 1984).
25. *The Gallup Opinion Index,* Report No. 146, p. 20.
26. "Wishing for More for Less," *Time,* October 23, 1978, 29.
27. Stephen G. Breyer and Richard B. Stewart, *Administrative Law and Regulatory Policy,* 2nd ed. (Boston: Little, Brown, 1985), 14–20. For comprehensive treatment of the regulatory function see Robert E. Litan and William D. Nordhaus, *Reforming Federal Regulation* (New Haven, Conn.: Yale University Press, 1983); and Kenneth J. Meyer, *Regulation: Politics, Bureaucracy, and Economics* (New York: St. Martin's Press, 1985).
28. "SEC Imposes Record Fine," *St. Louis Post-Dispatch,* November 15, 1986, 1 and 6A.
29. Bernard Schwartz noted recently that "During recent years we have been in the midst of a virtual administrative law explosion." "Recent Administrative Law Issues and Trends," *Administrative Law Journal,* 3 (1990), 543. Responding directly to Schwartz's observation, Marshall Breger agreed in "Comments on Bernard Schwartz's Essay," *Administrative Law Journal,* 5 (1991), 347.
30. Nathaniel L. Nathanson, "Proposals for Administrative Appellate Court," *Administrative Law Review, 25* (Winter 1973), 89.
31. Henry Campbell Black, *Black's Law Dictionary,* 5th ed. (St. Paul, Minn.: West Publishing Company, 1979), 22; Stephen G. Breyer and Richard B. Stewart, *Administrative Law and Regulatory Policy,* 2nd ed. (Boston: Little, Brown and Company, 1985), 12; Davis, *Administrative Law Treatise,* 1:1; Daniel Oran, *Oran's Dictionary of the Law* (St. Paul: West Publishing Company, 1983), 15.
32. Sallyanne Payton, "Administrative Law: What Is It, and What Is It Doing in Our Law School?" *Law Quadrangle Notes* (Fall 1983): 30.
33. Breger, "Comments on Bernard Schwartz's Essay," 349–350.
34. For example, see Barry and Whitcomb, *Foundations of Public Administration;* Breyer and Stewart, *Administrative Law and Regulatory Policy;* Carter, *Administrative Law and Politics;* Cooper, *Public Law and Public Administration;* Kenneth C. Davis, *Administrative Law* (St. Paul: West Publishing Company, 1977); Walter Gellhorn and Clark Byse, *Administrative Law* (Mineola, N.Y.: Foundation Press, 1984); Heffron with McFeeley, *Administrative Regulatory Process;* Glen O. Robinson, Ernest Gellhorn, and Harold H. Bruff, *The Administrative Process,* 2nd ed. (St. Paul: West Publishing Company, 1986); and Bernard Schwartz, *Administrative Law,* 2nd ed. (Boston: Little, Brown and Company, 1984).
35. Robert S. Lorch, *Democratic Process and Administrative Law,* 2nd ed. (Detroit: Wayne State University Press, 1980), 60–61.
36. For reflections on this workshop, see Roy A. Schotland, "How Much Truth Is Too Much Truth for Judicial Review? and other Easy Pieces After An AALS Workshop On Teaching Administrative Law," *Administrative Law Review,* 43 (Winter 91), 113–121; and Richard J. Pierce, Jr., "How Much Should an Administrative Law Course Accomplish?: A Response to Schotland's Five *Easy Pieces," Administrative Law Review,* 43 (Winter 91), 123–126.
37. Barry and Whitcomb, *The Legal Foundations of Public Administration,* 7.
38. Lorch, *Democratic Process and Administrative Law,* 61.

39. Davis, *Administrative Law Treatise, 1:* 140. Davis claims that not only is 90 percent of administrative law judge-made, but also that even the remaining 10 percent of statutory law chiefly codifies judge-made common law.

40. Kenneth C. Davis, *Administrative Law and Government,* 2nd ed. (St. Paul: West Publishing Company, 1975), 157.

41. For what I still believe is the most absorbing analysis of the alleged collapse of the tripartite American governmental structure see Eugene P. Dvorin and Robert H. Simmons, *From Amoral to Humane Bureaucracy* (San Francisco: Canfield Press, 1972), especially chap. 4. Also see R. Ship Melnick, "Administrative Law and Bureaucratic Reality," *Administrative Law Review,* 44 (Spring 1992), 245–254.

42. Kenneth F. Warren, "We Have Debated Ad Nauseam the Legitimacy of the Administrative State—But Why?," *Public Administrative Review,* 53 (May/June 93), 249–254.

43. Davis, *Administrative Law Treatise,* 1:14–15.

44. Ibid. Davis's comments on the five stages provided only the core for this summary.

45. Ernest Gellhorn, "Opening Remarks: Administrative Law in Transition," *Administrative Law Review,* 38 (Spring 1986): 107–114.

46. Ibid. Also, see Aaron Wildavsky, "Ubiquitous Anomie: Public Service in an Era of Ideological Dissensus," *Public Administration Review,* 48 (July/August 1988); Brian J. Cook, "The Representative Function of Bureaucracy: Public Administration in Constitutive Perspective," *Administration and Society,* 23 (February 1992); and Michael W. Spicer and Larry D. Terry, "Legitimacy, History, and Logic: Public Administration and the Constitution," *Public Administration Review,* 53 (May/June 1993).

47. The dispute was originally between Grove City College and the Department of Health, Education and Welfare. When HEW was reorganized into two agencies, the Department of Education handled the dispute.

48. Beverly Brandt Tiesenga, "Title IX and the Outer Limits of the Spending Powers: *Grove City College* v. *Bell, Chicago-Kent Law Review,* 61 (1985), 729–30.

49. Schwartz, "Recent Administrative Law Issues and Trends," 543.

CHAPTER TWO

THE GROWTH OF ADMINISTRATIVE POWER AND ITS IMPACT ON THE AMERICAN SYSTEM

GROWTH OF THE ADMINISTRATIVE SYSTEM

There is an old saying that a picture is worth a thousand words. In attempting to convey the dramatic growth of the administrative system since the early years of this republic, a glance at a couple of pictures would certainly be helpful. Imagine looking at a picture of a typical busy street in the United States during the early 1800s, and compare it with a typical busy urban street today. What striking differences would be expected, reflecting changes in American living patterns which have promoted major and necessary alterations in American institutions and government? A careful scrutiny of the early nineteenth-century street scene would show, for example, fewer people; unpaved streets; shorter and simpler building structures; no large department stores; no televisions, VCRs, dishwashers, refrigerators, electronic games, and the like on display in store windows; fewer entertainment spots; no motorized transportation; no endless rows of street signs and lights; no planes or helicopters flying overhead; no electronic noises; no telephone poles or lines; no indications of elaborate sewer, plumbing, heating, or electrical systems; no street monitors. And there would be other missing items, things which are symptomatic of the complexities in modern American life.

Selected indicators, which have been extracted from various tables in the *Historical Abstract of the United States* and the *Statistical Abstract of the United States,* convey vividly America's rapid growth in various socioeconomic areas.[1] For example, in 1790 the total population of the United States was less than 4 million, not even the size of one major metropolitan area today. Now, in 1996, our population runs around 260 million, about 65 times the 1790 figure. The growth in federal civilian employment has been even more spectacular, going from only 4,837 federal employ-

TABLE 2.1   Growth in Federal, State, and Local Civilian Employment

Year	Number of Federal Employees	Number of State and Local Employees
1816	4,837	Not Available
1831	11,491	Not Available
1851	26,274	Not Available
1871	51,020	Not Available
1891	157,442	Not Available
1911	395,905	Not Available
1921	561,142	Not Available
1931	609,746	2,704,000
1941	1,437,682	3,372,000
1951	2,482,666	4,287,000
1961	2,435,808	6,616,000
1971	2,862,926	8,806,000
1981	2,865,000	13,103,000
1995	2,821,000	16,457,000

Sources: Historical Abstract of the United States, Colonial Times to 1970 (Washington, D.C.: U.S. Government Printing Office, 1975), pt. 1, Series D, Specs. 139, 140, 141; and *Statistical Abstract of the United States, 1995,* 115th ed. (Washington, D.C.: U.S. Government Printing Office, 1995), 326 and 351.

ees in 1816 to 2,821,000 by 1995 or 583 times the 1816 number, with state and local governmental employment increasing still more dramatically (see Table 2.1). Of course, urban growth statistics reflect the overall increase in population. For instance, in 1820 New York City's population was 123,700; today it is more than 7 million. Dramatic increases also occurred in population in many other American cities, especially in Boston and Philadelphia.

Agency Proliferation: The Administrations of George Washington and Bill Clinton

President George Washington headed the first national administration, which was tiny and very limited in its powers and scope of activities. At this time in our history there was enthusiastic support for the free market system and the theory of limited government. Without doubt, governmental administration then epitomized the laissez-faire slogan: "For forms of government let fools contest; What'er is *least* administer'd is best."[2] In Washington's administration only the basic governmental functions were performed. Only three executive departments existed. Washington's cabinet consisted of John Jay, secretary of state (succeeded by Thomas Jefferson in 1790); Alexander Hamilton, secretary of the treasury; and Henry Knox, secretary of war. Also part of Washington's cabinet, but not heads of departments, were Edmund Randolph, attorney general (not until 1870 was the Department of Justice established) and Samuel Osgood (succeeded by Timothy Pickering in 1791), postmaster general (not established as a department until 1872).[3]

No "independent" regulatory agencies existed for about the first century of the republic because, to most citizens, just the thought of a governmental regulatory agency was repulsive. As noted in the last chapter, a vocal minority today still perceive any form of governmental regulation as repugnant. Nevertheless, enough public sentiment against free market abuses emerged toward the late 1800s that the people turned to government for help. Government responded initially by creating the Interstate Commerce Commission in 1887, but this independent regulatory agency was only the first of many more to come in the twentieth century.

While virtually no governmental bureaucracy existed during the simpler times of Washington's presidency, in sharp contrast today's administrative apparatus is gigantic, pervasive, and powerful, reflecting the complex problems and challenges of a greatly transformed American society in the new age of space exploration. President Clinton's administration includes fourteen huge cabinet-level departments or agencies, a large White House staff, and a host of so-called independent agencies to help in administrative and regulatory functions (see Figure 2.1).

Figure 2.2 traces the growth in the number of federal agencies from 1789 to 1996. What is not shown, however, is that our public agencies have not only increased in number but, more importantly, they have increased in size as well. Actually, the growth of the administrative system can be attributed more to increases in agency size than increases in the number of agencies.

Why Have Agencies Increased in Size and Number?

Exponential Agency Growth Requires Birth Control   Herbert Kaufman studied the life cycle of organizations for a period between 1923 and 1973 to respond to the question, *Are Government Organizations Immortal?,* which became the title of his book.[4] Kaufman demonstrated the clear tendency for bureaucracy to expand in an exponential manner. Kaufman contends that once organizations are born, they tend to resist death by taking on traits of immortality. In reflecting on the growth patterns which have led to today's giant administrative system, Kaufman commented that such growth tendencies bear "some challenging implications for policy-makers and managers of governmental machinery."[5] No doubt this is true, but what specifically seems to have nurtured the hearty development of the administrative system? Why has it occurred?

Kaufman cites seven reasons, all linked to an agency's bid to survive. In the first place, he points out that agencies endure after birth because they are given legal sanctioning, which provides them with formal powers. This formal authority, usually embedded in several statutes, is difficult to take away. Second, each agency has guardians in Congress, especially among powerful congressional leaders who head key congressional committees. Kaufman notes that although specific legislators may come and go, agencies retain their security by befriending congressional committees on the whole (that is, members and their staffs) so that they will survive when their particular legislative friends leave. Third, incremental budgetary procedures favor extended agency life after birth. Kaufman argues that congress persons tend to become prisoners of their own creations. That is, once Congress approves an annual

THE GOVERNMENT OF THE UNITED STATES

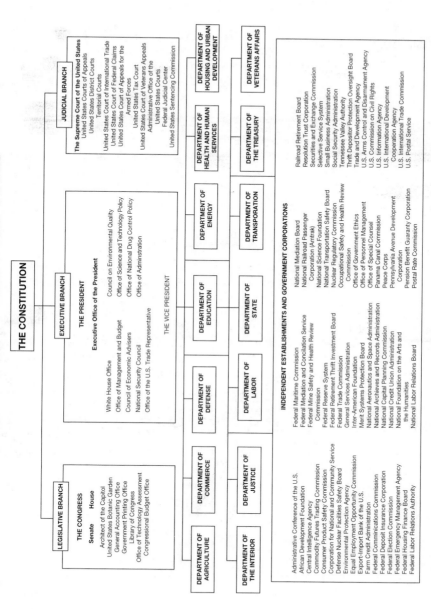

FIGURE 2.1 *The Government of the United States*

Source: United States Government Manual (Washington, D.C.: U.S. Government Printing Office, 1995–96), 22

41

budget for an agency, the next year's budget is practically impossible to cut completely or shave: "Total elimination of funds for an agency or even massive slashes approaching total elimination are unknown, for all practical purposes."[6] Actually, agency budgets tend to increase automatically and incrementally from year to year because of "the sheer momentum of the budgetary process."[7] Kaufman also contends that agencies benefit from the lack of time legislators have to scrutinize the validity of submitted agency programs and budgets, thus making it exceedingly difficult for Congress to defend any agency cuts in the face of agency protests.

Fourth, agency expertise, protected by statutes and court decisions, provides agencies with relative independence and strength to resist hostile political attacks by intruders. Fifth, agency employees tend to fight hard to preserve the life of their agencies, and thus their jobs. Not only do agency leaders fight out of loyalty to protect their agency's future, but, Kaufman maintains, they fight to protect their professional reputations and their future employability. Sixth, as emphasized in Chapter 1, agency administrators learn to form strong ties with their clientele. Because many agencies were created to serve a specific clientele (for example, veterans), it would be expected that those an agency serves would likely be the agency's most ardent supporters. And to reiterate another major point from the last chapter, regulated industries also stand to benefit from a symbiotic relationship with regulatory agencies. Last, Kaufman holds that professional and trade associations also function to protect those agencies which tend to be supportive of their occupational interests. "When all seven of the foregoing factors are taken together," he concludes, "the contention that government agencies are virtually immortal seems incontestable."[8]

FIGURE 2.2   *Cumulative Totals of Agencies That Survived to 1996*

Source: Adapted from Herbert Kaufman, *Are Government Organizations Immortal?* (Washington, D.C.: Copyright © 1976 by the Brookings Institution, p. 62). Data since 1973 drawn from the *U.S. Government Manual* (Washington, D.C.: U.S. Government Printing Office, 1995–1996).

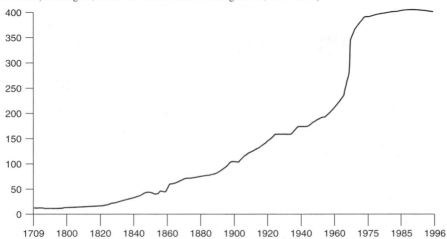

Although Kaufman acknowledges the existence of certain hazardous forces in the administrative system's environment that may serve to curb agency proliferation (competition, leadership and policy changes, alienation of key supporters, completed missions), agency expansionism appears assured because certain systemic characteristics allow many agencies to be born but few to die. Kaufman found that agency fatalities were so rare that it would probably be wise for the government to investigate different agency birth control methods. Otherwise, assuming the normal growth rate of five new agencies a year, this country can expect to have another 266 federal agencies by 2023, whether they are needed or not.[9] Reflecting back on Kaufman's research, Glen O. Robinson notes that it is risky to predict future growth trends, but Kaufman appears to be right. Bureaucratic growth, Robinson acknowledges, has continued through Republican and Democratic administrations, despite political rhetoric and apparently honest efforts to stop it. Robinson comments that "[T]here seems to be a kind of political racket at work that permits change in one direction only."[10]

'... AND HERE, WE'LL CUT A SLOT IN THE DOOR TO MAKE IT EASIER FOR CITIZENS TO PAY THEIR TAXES'

Source: Reprinted with permission of Tom Engelhardt and the *St. Louis Post-Dispatch,* September 8, 1993.

Growth Induced by Distrust and Expertise   According to William L. Morrow, the expansion of the administrative system has emerged from a basic distrust for the ability of existing agencies to perform new functions fairly: "Distrusting existing organizations and seeking to provide new spark and thrust to new policies, interest groups, politicians, and public officials have usually preferred creating *new* organizations to the prospect of adding new policy responsibilities to existing ones."[11] The call for increased specialization has also helped to spur the creation of new agencies. John Kenneth Galbraith argues that a new elite forming a technostructure has emerged in modern, industrialized countries of the world. The *technostructure* consists of technical and managerial experts found in industry as well as in public agencies. According to Galbraith, this new technostructure, whether in industry or governmental agencies, places a high priority on productivity because increased production tends to increase and strengthen the technostructure itself.[12] Recognition of the technostructure's experts' knowledge by the other governmental branches has allowed bureaucracy to expand with little resistance.

The political climate must also be conducive to stimulating waves of bureaucratic growth, according to James Q. Wilson. He contends that there were four periods in our history when the political climate favored the rapid growth of regulatory agencies. To Wilson, conditions favoring the creation of agencies have to be just right because agency proliferation is generally resiste   asserted that each wave "was characterized by progressive or liberal presiden   ee (Cleveland, T. R. Roosevelt, Wilson, F. D. Roosevelt, Johnson); one   of national crisis (the 1930s); three were periods when the Preside   rdinary majorities of his own party in both houses of Congress (19   940, and 1964–1968); and only the first preceded the emergen   ass media of communication. These facts are important beca   culty of passing any genuinely regulatory legislation. . . . with   circumstances—a crisis, a scandal, extraordinary majorities, an es   President, the support of the media—the normal barriers to legislat   may prove insuperable."[13] These periods are sketched in Table 2.2. I have added to Table 2.2 a fifth stage, the "deregulation stage," which took place mostly during the Reagan and Bush years, reflecting the sentiment that bureaucracy is "too fat" and even illegitimate (discussed in Chapter 1). This movement may have slowed the growth pace, but it flatly failed to prevent bureaucracy from expanding, especially in the area of defense and entitlement programs. Deregulation also failed because it led to financial insecurity in some industries (for example, the airline industry), public inconvenience (for example, problems for air and bus commuters, especially on "unpopular" routes), price gouging (for example, cable TV rate hikes), and even some outrageous and well-publicized scandals (for example, the savings and loan debacle.)[14] As a result of some deregulation failures, some reregulation has occurred, possibly taking us into a sixth stage of a combination of reregulation/deregulation.

Attitudinal Changes Have Aided Growth   Insights on the apparent causes of increased governmental regulation seem endless, but one can say with certainty that the

TABLE 2.2   James Q. Wilson's Four Periods of Bureaucratic Growth

Period	Focus	Key Acts Passed
1887–90	Control monopolies and rates	Interstate Commerce Act Sherman Act
1906–15	Regulate product quality	Pure Food and Drug Act Meat Inspection Act Federal Trade Commission Clayton Act
1930–40	Extend regulation to cover various socioeconomic areas, especially new technologies	Food, Drug, and Cosmetic Public Utility Holding Company Act National Labor Relations Act Securities and Exchange Act Natural Gas Act
1960–79	Expand regulation to make America a cleaner, healthier, safer, and fairer place to live and work	Economic Opportunity Act Civil Rights Acts of 1960, 1964, and 1968 National Environmental Policy Act Clean Air Act Occupational Safety and Health Act
1978–93	Deregulation movement as a reaction to bureaucratic overexpansion	Paperwork Reduction Act Air Deregulation Act Radio and TV Deregulation Banking Deregulation

Source: This table is based on James Q. Wilson's "The Rise of the Bureaucratic State," *Policy Making,* edited by Francis E. Rourke, 4th ed. (Boston: Little, Brown, 1986), pp. 125–148, but table categories and descriptions were created and supplemented by this author.

public administration system grew rapidly from the late 1800s to the present because, simply, (1) the American people called upon government for help, and (2) U.S. government officials were very eager to provide this help. Of course, systems analysis theorists would expect this demand-response pattern to emerge, since acknowledging public demands would be considered the appropriate response of democratically responsible public servants, especially if they wanted to remain in office. Edwin W. Tucker has done an admirable job in summarizing the attitudinal changes which, in roughly the past century, have led the American public and politicians to sanction and encourage increased governmental regulation, as well as administrative law. Although Tucker's dozen reasons overlap somewhat, he makes the clear point that the regulatory process grew because: (1) the public began to change its mind and to perceive government as a viable instrument for solving many social problems; (2) public officials were willing to accept the responsibility for resolving social problems; (3) public attitudes gradually changed from a feeling of fear toward government to a more positive and euphoric attitude about the potential of public administration to cause positive social change; (4) the public began to question the conventional wisdom that government is best which governs least, arguing now that under certain conditions governmental intervention is necessary; (5) Americans started to abandon the dogmatic belief that the private sector would and could take the necessary corrective measures to alleviate problems in society; (6) public opinion began to turn against the prevailing idea that public administration can only have a negative impact on society; (7) the public adopted a more humane, welfare state concept and an accompanying rejection of the attitude that what's good for GM is necessarily good for society; (8) the public increasingly believed that certain state-of-nature liberties should be sacrificed so that social order, an important social condition, can be achieved; (9) Americans began to adopt an increasingly egalitarian philosophy that emphasized the virtues of equality over values that promoted the interests of a favored few; (10) the people felt disenchantment with property-based theory, which tends to emphasize individual property rights over social and human rights; (11) there was an increasing realization that population growth, shifts, and related issues are important matters for social planners to consider; and (12) the American people became more willing to challenge the status quo on all socioeconomic fronts in an effort to search for and establish an increasingly equitable social system.[15]

Court-Inspired Administrative Growth   Decisions of American legislators and presidents over the decades, in their efforts to serve constituent demands, helped to shape today's large public service system. However, judicial decisions have also played a major role in expanding the size, scope, and power of the government's administrative network.[16] A few examples of this type of court decision would include *Munn* v. *Illinois,* in 1876. In this case, the U.S. Supreme Court upheld the constitutional and statutory authority of the Granger laws, thus enabling Illinois administrative agencies to regulate railroads. This case was significant because it allowed public agencies to regulate private property, so long as it was in the public interest to do so. Chief Justice Waite justified governmental regulation by arguing that "property does become clothed with a public interest when used in a manner to make it of public consequence, and affect the community at large" (94 U.S. 113, 126; 1876).

Obviously, because it is difficult to know which regulation is in the public interest, this decision helped to open the door to all sorts of regulatory measures regarded by various agencies to be in the public interest. But the Mann decision left an important question unanswered: Can a state regulate activities of industries which are not only engaged in *intrastate* commerce, but *interstate* commerce as well? Shortly afterwards, in *Peik* v. *Chicago and Northwestern Railway Co.,* the Court answered yes, thus expanding even further state regulatory power and paving the way for the regulatory movement at the national level. The Court reasoned that "until Congress acts in reference to the relations of this company to interstate commerce, it is certainly within the power of Wisconsin to regulate its fares, etc. so far as they are of domestic concern. With the people of Wisconsin this company has domestic relations. Incidentally, these may reach beyond the State" (94 U.S. 164, 178; 1877). Although the railroads and other industries attempted to thwart governmental efforts to regulate their businesses, eventually the courts supported critics who argued that the public interest would suffer if government failed to regulate socioeconomic activities to some extent. In reviewing the growth of regulation in the United States, Stephen G. Breyer and Richard B. Stewart concluded that "the decisions of federal and state courts reviewing the actions of these early regulatory agencies laid the foundations of modern administrative law."[17]

Despite some court support for governmental regulation before the New Deal, significant judicial sanctioning for administrative regulations did not come until the impact of the Great Depression on society became so crippling as to create a critical need for governmental intervention in the economy. Breyer and Stewart point out that at first the federal courts sided with the critics of the New Deal's regulatory programs, but "in a relatively short time, the Supreme Court (and with it, much of the lower federal judiciary) swung from almost undisguised hostility toward the new programs of administration to conspicuous deference. The availability of judicial review of administrative action was curtailed, and particular agency decisions were frequently sustained with judicial obeisance to the mysteries of administrative expertise."[18] Evidence of this can be seen in the following Court decisions: *NLRB* v. *Jones and Laughlin Steel Corp.,* 301 U.S. 1 (1937); *Steward Machine Co.* v. *Davis,* 301 U.S. 548 (1937); *Switchmen's Union* v. *National Mediation Board,* 320 U.S 297 (1943); and *NLRB* v. *Hearst Publications, Inc.,* 322 U.S. 111 (1944). The Court's increasing willingness to bow to agency expertise, as we shall see, has played a major role in the development of agency dominance today.

The strength and pervasiveness of the administrative system were developed in other rather typical court rulings. Recognition of the legitimacy and power of the administrative process was given by Justice Robert Jackson in *FTC* v. *Ruberoid Co.,* when he wrote: "The rise of administrative bodies probably had been the most significant legal trend of the last century and perhaps more values today are affected by their decisions than those of all the courts, review of administrative decisions apart" (343 U.S. 470, 487; 1952). In *U.S.* v. *Caltex,* 344 U.S. 149 (1952), Chief Justice Fred Vinson strengthened the power of administrative action during times of emergency. Specifically, Justice Vinson fortified the government's police power by giving administrative agencies total immunity from suits filed under the just compensation clause of the Fifth Amendment challenging the legitimacy of certain administrative actions taken while responding to an emergency, such as the destruction of property. Vinson noted in his opinion that "the common law had long recognized that in times of imminent peril—such as when fire threatened a whole community—the sovereign could, with immunity, destroy the property of a few that the property of many and the lives of many more could be saved" (at 154). In *Heart of Atlantic Motel, Inc.* v. *U.S.,* (379 U.S. 241; 1964), Justice Tom Clark significantly broadened the scope of federal administrative authority under the commerce clause. Essentially, Clark held that federal agencies can regulate any activity which is related directly or indirectly to commerce, so long as Congress has sanctioned such regulatory activity. Justice Clark "argued that Congress could have pursued other methods to eliminate the obstructions it found in interstate commerce caused by racial discrimination. But this is a matter of policy that rests entirely with the Congress not with the courts. How obstructions in commerce may be removed—what means are to be employed—is within the sound and exclusive discretion of Congress" (at 261–62). This decision has enabled federal agencies to use the threat of the commerce clause to regulate within states virtually any business activity having possible interstate impact. Drug traffic, prostitution, gambling, deceptive sales practices, professional sports, and racial discrimination in businesses are a few examples.

A variety of court decisions in more recent years have added still further to the growing strength of both national and state administrative agencies. In *Vermont Yankee Nuclear Power Corp.* v. *Natural Resources Defense Council,* 435 U.S. 519 (1978), the U.S. Supreme Court was not impressed with the public interest intervenor's argument that the courts should make administrative agencies employ stricter rule-making procedures when dealing with complicated scientific matters that could lead to the promulgation of potentially dangerous rules or public policies. The Court held that agency officials have the discretion to follow only rule-making procedures required specifically by the Administrative Procedure Act or other pertinent statutes. The Court stressed that to require more elaborate procedures "almost compels the agency to conduct all rule-making proceedings with the full panoply of procedural devices normally associated only with adjudicatory hearings" (at 525). In brief, the Court said Congress would have to limit the discretionary power of agency administrators when drafting rules because the courts have no business in this area. Six years later in *Chevron, U.S.A.* v. *Natural Resources Defense Council,* 104 S.Ct. 2778 (1984), the Supreme Court reiterated its position by stating in essence that courts should defer to agency expertise or discretion as long as agency discretion is based on a "permissible" application of what a law permits. In the words of the Court, "a court may not substitute its own construction of a statutory provision for a reasonable interpretation made by the administrator of an agency" (at 2782).

According to Michael Herz, the *Chevron* decision ". . . has become perhaps the central case of modern administrative law."[19] It was cited by over 2,000 federal courts by 1992, only eight years after *Chevron,* and has caused much heated debate.[20] In "Deference Running Riot: Separating Interpretation and Lawmaking Under *Chevron,*" Herz contends that *Chevron* goes too far, permitting administrators to exercise too much power without subjecting the exercise of such power to judicial review. To Herz, application of the *Chevron* doctrine, which permits broad and possibly irresponsible deference to public administrators, tends to make public agencies too powerful, illegitimate, and unaccountable.[21]

Legal scholars argue that nothing has contributed more to the growth of administrative power than decisions such as *Chevron* because the *Chevron* doctrine sanctions broad deference to administrative expertise by the courts, thus severely limiting what administrative action or decisions will be subjected to judicial review. Once more, *Chevron* also endorses broad, vague, and frequently irresponsible delegations of legislative power by Congress to public agencies, tending to strengthen even more the "independent" power of administrators, causing an increasing number of citizens to question the very legitimacy of the power they hold.[22]

But making matters worse, critics charge that too many state and federal courts have been too quick to embrace and even expand *Chevron.* In 1991 the U.S. Supreme Court itself expanded the *Chevron* doctrine in *Rust* v. *Sullivan,* 111 S.Ct. 1759, holding that the *Chevron* doctrine requires deference to the agency's interpretation of a statute, not just a *reasonable* agency interpretation, as originally held in *Chevron,* but an interpretation that is merely *plausible.* Critics, already bothered that *Chevron* had caused courts to retreat from their obligation to review agency action, became more disturbed by *Rust.* One leading scholarly critic, Bernard Schwartz, exclaimed: "Now *Rust* transforms the reasonableness requirement to one of plausibility—a test met by an interpretation that has only an appearance or show of truth—i.e., it is only superficially fair or reasonable. In this respect, *Rust* makes for a dilution in scope of review even beyond that made by *Chevron* itself."[23] Originally applied only to rulemaking, *Chevron* now applies to all agency interpretations of statutes, including adjudicatory decisions. In short, *Chevron,* as applied by the courts, has greatly expanded the power of the administrative state.

There is an irony to this development. During the New Deal FDR and his liberal supporters fought fiercely the conservative courts, eventually getting them to defer more to agency expertise and discretion. Of course, this deference allowed for the growth of the administrative state and the emergence of awesome administrative power. However, by the mid-1960s political observers, especially liberal critics led by such public interest groups as Common Cause, Union of Concerned Scientists, and consumer advocate Ralph Nader, became disillusioned and distrustful of "unfettered" administrative actions and began to urge the courts to reassert their power of judicial review and use it to check abuses of administrative power. Generally, for the next dozen years or so, the courts did respond, overruling various agency actions that seemed to undermine the public interest, especially when related to safety, civil rights, and environmental hazards. The courts seemed determined to make public administrators more democratically accountable. But by the mid-1980s, under the influence of a more conservative public and Reagan administration politics, state and federal courts, led by the U.S. Supreme Court, started once again to defer to agency expertise and discretion, with *Chevron* dramatically and emphatically "kicking off" the movement. Courts were responding to outcries, mostly from conservatives, that the courts had been violating the separation of powers doctrine by meddling too much in the administrative process and making too many public policy decisions that should be made by legislators and public administrators. Clinton administration politics, including especially his judicial appointments, will undoubtedly cause the reversal of this trend.

On the whole, court decisions in various legal areas related to public administration (for example, hearing rights, rulemaking, torts, delegation, judicial review of agency actions, administrative searches and seizures) have had the impact of increasing the power and scope of administrative action. These specific legal areas will be the focus of later discussions. In a real sense, the courts have had little practical choice but to sanction the development of the administrative state because the growth of American society has unquestionably demanded a greater role to be played by our public administrators at all levels of government.

A Concluding Macro View   Obviously, numerous factors have caused the expansion of the administrative system; yet mere bureaucratic inertia has probably been the most crucial factor. Rapid bureaucratic expansion has not been confined only to the public sector. Red tape, the unfortunate symbol of modern bureaucracy, has engulfed private enterprise as well. Nor has swift bureaucratic growth been limited to the American system. Henry Jacoby, in *The Bureaucratization of the World,* like Max Weber before him, makes it quite clear that bureaucratization is a natural process which eventually invades the private and public institutions of all nations.[24] It may be simply a case of Britain, Germany, the Soviet Union, and the United States today and Uganda, Iran, and Guatemala tomorrow.

Despite much well-publicized public opinion against bureaucratic growth, Americans have turned continually to government for helpful services, thus stimulating the growth of the public administration system. It also seems true that modern bureaucracy, as conceptualized by Max Weber (that is, a structure in which administration is meritorious and separated from flagrant political manipulation by non-experts), can survive only in a fairly wealthy country with a relatively stable socioeconomic, legal political order. Certainly, administrative law cannot be expected to mature in a volatile environment. Thus, despite some of the administrative system's shortcomings, (for example, too many and confusing procedures, abuses of administrative discretion, unfair hearings), public agencies overall have increased the quality of American life.

A SIGNIFICANT HISTORICAL DEVELOPMENT: THE DELEGATION OF POWER TO ADMINISTRATIVE AGENCIES

The American colonists fought against what they considered an abuse of power by British governors in the American colonies. As a result, the founding fathers made sure after the Revolutionary War that the powers granted to the executive branch were limited and controllable. This pattern was also established in the states. In some cases, state governors were not even given enough power to govern properly, a fact of political life which still plagues some governors today. But despite the fact that most state governors and even city mayors are still relatively weak, most governmental administrators today enjoy tremendous power—power that would almost certainly make our constitutional writers gasp with alarm. What has happened between then and now? Should Americans fear the trend toward more and more powerful administrators who cannot be checked through the ballot box?

The demand for public services caused government to increase, especially since President Franklin D. Roosevelt was elected and given a mandate by the people to employ administrative machinery to end the suffering caused by the Great Depression. As government expanded its operations and agency tasks became more specialized, legislators lost the ability and enthusiasm to scrutinize administrative activities as closely as they had done when governmental bureaucracy was smaller and simpler. To allow the president to lead and the government's bureaucracy to administer public programs expeditiously, U.S. congress persons increasingly began to delegate and subdelegate their legislative powers to agency heads and their subordinates. But could legislative power be so delegated? Did this transfer of power from one branch to another violate the separation-of-powers doctrine, which seemed to be such a vital part of the U.S. Constitution?

Glen O. Robinson asserts that delegating legislative power to administrators has always presented a problem to liberal constitutionalists because concepts of trusteeship, rooted in English Common Law and Lockean theory, strictly prohibits the entrusted lawmaking power from being delegated away to undemocratically accountable administrators. Robinson notes that such ". . . is a simple notion that requires no elaborate legal or political theory to defend, at least in principle. If the legislature is truly a trustee, any general transfer of entrusted power would seem a plain evasion of responsibility. The irresponsibility is heightened by the transfer of powers to a politically unresponsible bureaucracy."[25] Of course, delegation is also restricted in theory by the separation-of-powers doctrine, which the founding fathers regarded as fundamental to the U.S. Constitution.

A literalist look at the Constitution seems to indicate that the constitutional framers did not intend for the legislative branch to weaken itself by giving away its policy-making powers. The framers clearly made the legislative branch the strongest of the three branches, at least rhetorically. Article 1, Section 1 of the U.S. Constitution states clearly that "all legislative powers herein granted shall be vested in a Congress of the United States, which shall consist of a Senate and House of Representatives." Section 8 of the same article also makes clear that "the Congress shall have power . . . to make all laws which shall be necessary and proper for carrying into execution" all the enumerated powers listed in the section.

Article 1, Section 8, specifically grants to Congress the powers to "collect taxes," "borrow money," "regulate commerce," "coin money," "establish Police offices and post roads," "declare war," "raise and support armies," "provide and maintain a navy," and so on. Could these specific powers be legally delegated to an administrative branch, thus encouraging the growth of vast bureaucratic power? Why did the constitutional framers spell out what powers the Congress should have if they did not really care who, for example, regulated commerce or maintained a navy? These questions are tough ones to answer comfortably, especially since what was said in the Constitution and what was practiced by the constitutional framers clashed so sharply in the early years of the Republic, when many who developed the Constitution served as congressmen. Despite what was written in the Constitution, as soon as the framers became congressmen, they enacted legislation which had the effect of giving away some of their legislative powers. For example, they authorized the president to regulate the provision of military pensions and establish pay scales for injured or disabled soldiers as he saw fit.

Before *Curtiss-Wright:* Court Ambivalence toward Delegation

Ironically, especially in light of the rocky history of the delegation doctrine until well into the twentieth century, the first real challenge to the legitimacy of Congress to delegate legislative powers to administrators was overruled. In *The Cargo of the Brig Aurora, Burnside, claimant* v. *United States,* 11 U.S. (7 Cranch) 382 (1813), it was charged that the president should not be able, even under statutory authority, to determine when the Non-Intercourse Act of 1809 should come into force because this task is legislative in nature and not purely executive in function. Justice William Johnson held, however, that it would be improper for such discretion not to be granted to a president: "We can see no reason, why the legislature should not exercise its discretion in reviewing the act . . . either expressedly or conditionally, as their judgment should direct." In an extremely perceptive decision that even today sounds contemporary, Chief Justice John Marshall gave more support to the delegation doctrine in 1825, although his insightful decision was later overruled but then restored to some extent during the 1930s. In reflecting on the ability of Congress to handle *all* legislative tasks itself, Marshall commented: "It will not be contended that Congress can delegate to the courts, or to any other tribunal, powers which are strictly and exclusively legislative. But Congress may certainly delegate to others, powers which the legislature may rightfully exercise itself, the line has not been exactly drawn which separate those important subjects, which must be entirely regulated by the legislature itself, from those of less interest, in which a general provision may be made, and power given to those who are to act under such general provisions to fill up the details" (*Wayman* v. *Southward,* 23 U.S. (10 Wheat) 1, 15–16). When Marshall talked about distinguishing between "important subjects" and those which amount to only "provisions to fill up the details," he put his finger on the basic delegation doctrine controversy which is still argued heatedly among some scholars today.[26] That is, what constitutes significant legislative activity by administrators? What types of legislative functions by administrators seem truly minor or quasi legislative in character? This is an important distinction, especially for those persons who are interested in preserving the democratic operating procedures in government, because different answers to the question make meaningful differences in how our system approaches the making of public policies.

The key to settling the dispute really centers around what the framers meant by "law" and what they felt constituted the "law-making" function. In 1852 a judicial attempt was made to distinguish between laws which should only be made by legislators, and those "laws" (actually rules) which could be made by administrators. The position was taken that only legislators have the authority to make basic laws or determine what laws Americans should live under. It was argued that the power to decide on what "shall be" our laws should not be delegated: "The true distinction is between the delegation of power to make the law, which necessarily involves a discretion as to what it shall be, and conferring authority to discretion as to its execution to be exercised under and in pursuance of the law" (*Cincinnati, W. & Z.P. Co.* v. *Commissioner,* 1 Ohio St. 77, 88).

The *Cincinnati* case had the effect of helping to develop a nondelegation doctrine because it was held that legislators should not be allowed to permit those outside the legislative branch to engage in meaningful rule making that might infringe, even slightly, upon their policy-making powers. The opinion that significant legislative power should not be delegated was developed further in *Field* v. *Clark,* 143 U.S. 649 (1892), and *United States* v. *Shreveport Grain and Elevator Co.,* 287 U.S. 77 (1932). In these two cases the principle of nondelegation was upheld, although specific limited delegations were allowed. In *Field* the Court permitted the president to alter import duties at his discretion, yet acknowledged: "That Congress cannot delegate legislative power to the President is a principle universally recognized as vital to the integrity and maintenance of the system of government ordained by the Constitution" (at 1692). In *Shreveport Grain and Elevator,* a relatively recent case in terms of the long court history of delegation disputes, the Court paid lip service to the virtues of nondelegation, yet allowed "reasonable variations" so that the specific delegation could be upheld: "That the legislative power of Congress cannot be delegated is, of course, clear" (at 85). But Kenneth C. Davis argues that such court decisions have befuddled the status of delegation before the courts: "It is statements of this kind that have caused much of the difficulty in law development. Congress persisted in delegating, and the Court perceived that delegational was often necessary if the tasks of government were to be performed."[27] Nevertheless, there exists a long list of cases, even since 1930, in which the courts have allowed the specific delegation and yet opposed delegation in principle.

However, for practical reasons, and the courts admitted this by their actions, the nondelegation doctrine could not survive in a climate which demands that administrative agencies must occasionally act alone and devise "rules and regulations" so that the administrative process would not break down when implementing public programs. Administrators simply must make "shall be" policies themselves if their agencies are to be effective. It is difficult to imagine a practical administrative situation where all details, procedures, and so on, were anticipated and accounted for by Congress so that an administrator's sole task was to follow the prescribed course of action.

Since Schechter: Toward Broad Delegation

Today, various applications of doctrines limiting delegation are yielding to doctrines permitting broad delegation; the latter take into account the limited capabilities of legislators in watching over administrative activities and the problems of administering public programs if the administrator's hands are tied. Only twice in American legal history did the courts find it appropriate to invalidate absolutely the delegation of power to public officials by Congress. And in both cases unusual circumstances prevailed because power was not delegated to a normal administrative agency which functioned according to established procedures. In *Panama Refining Co.* v. *Ryan,* 293 U.S. 388 (1935), unusual administrative chaos prevailed, while in *Schechter Poultry Corp.* v. *United States,* 295 U.S. 495 (1935), an unreasonable, excessive amount of delegated authority was involved. Nevertheless, in these cases the Supreme Court did declare the National Industrial Recovery Act of 1933 unconstitutional, arguing that it authorized the unconstitutional delegation of legislative powers to the president and an executive agency. At this point there was significant confusion over how far Congress could go in delegating its powers to the administrative branch.

Starting with the *United States* v. *Curtiss-Wright Export Co.,* 299 U.S. 304 (1936), the courts have ruled consistently in favor of Congress's right to delegate authority, as long as Congress sets forth some meaningful standards to guide administrators in their efforts to implement governmental policies. For example, in *Sunshine Anthracite Coal Co.* v. *Atkins* 310 U.S. 381; (1940), the court noted that Congress must delegate some of its legislative powers to escape legislative futility. In *SEC* v. *Chenery Corp.,* 332 U.S. 194 (1947), the Court took the position that the delegation of legislative power is acceptable if administrators "strive to do as much as they reasonably can to develop and to make known the needed confinements of discretionary power through standards, principles, and rules." In *United States* v. *Southwestern Cable Co.,* 392 U.S. 157 (1968), the Court vaguely interpreted "standards" in terms of administering in a manner which is consistent with law as "public convenience, intent, or necessity requires."

It is interesting to acknowledge that frequently the courts bend to allow the inevitable to happen with legal sanctioning. During the New Deal days governmental bureaucracy was expanding rapidly to respond to public demands caused by the Great Depression. While the courts initially fought the trend, which involved a major transfer of public policy-making power from the legislative to the executive branch and the creation of an enormous, powerful public service system, they eventually yielded. It has often been said that courts tend to lead and shape society, but here was a vivid example of where the courts were induced to follow.

On the question of delegation, the reasoning behind the *Chenery* and *Southwestern Cable Co.* decisions has by now been widely accepted by the courts. These decisions, without doubt, have allowed administrative power to reach new heights in American society because although judges paid lip service to proper standards, their holdings did not define standards in a way which could effectively control abuses of administrative discretion. This has caused many legal scholars to worry over the possible emergence of uncontrollable, irresponsible, and oppressive administrative power, especially in light of a federal district court's upholding of the constitutionality of the Economic Stabilization Act of 1970. This act gave to the president sweeping powers to "issue such orders and regulations as he may deem appropriate to stabilize prices, wages and salaries at levels not less than those prevailing on May 25, 1970." On August 17, 1971, President Nixon did freeze all prices in the absence of any significant standards laid down by Congress. Believing that Nixon's actions were without precedent and clearly unconstitutional, the Amalgamated Meat Cutters Union brought suit, but the suit was flatly rejected by the court on the grounds that Congress had provided sufficient standards (*Amalgamated Meat Cutters* v. *Connally,* 337 F.Supp. 737, D.D.C.; 1971).

In 1974, in *National Cable Ass'n* v. *United States,* 415 U.S. 336, the Court felt that delegation of legislative power to administrative agencies was acceptable as long as "an intelligible principle" is attached. In this case Justice Thurgood Marshall seemed to even want to bury the nondelegation idea forever when he commented that nondelegation "was briefly in vogue in the 1930s, has been virtually abandoned by the Court for all practical purposes," and today "is surely as moribund as the substantive due process approach of the same era" (at 352–53). The spirit of Marshall's position was reiterated in *Algonquin SNG, Inc.* v. *Federal Energy Administration,* 518 F.2d 1051, 1063 (1975): "Here the delegated power is broad, and Congress has had repeated opportunities to limit it or withdraw it altogether. It has not done so, and I think this court should not do so." Although this was said by Judge Robb in dissent, the United States Supreme Court later upheld the wisdom of this opinion in overturning the appeals court's majority (426 U.S. 548; 1976).

Justice Marshall is unquestionably right. The nondelegation doctrine is and has been dead since 1935. In fact, fifteen years after Marshall pronounced the nondelegation definitely "very dead," the Supreme Court reaffirmed Marshall's pronouncement by noting: "After invalidating in 1935 two statutes as excessive delegations, . . . we have upheld, again without deviation, Congress' ability to delegate power under broad standards" [*Mistretta* v. *United States,* 109 S.Ct. 647, 655 (1989)].

Ironically, however, despite the "deadness" of the nondelegation doctrine, the Supreme Court agreed to hear several cases which focused upon the basic constitutional issues pertaining to delegation and the directly related issue of separation of powers. Presumably, the high court heard such cases because the conservative political climate during these years encouraged such old, basic constitutional questions pertaining to the very legitimacy of administrative power to be asked once again. The Supreme Court responded, but even this quite conservative court could not bring itself to reverse a well-established legal trend in complete support of broad delegation.

In *Mistretta,* for example, the Supreme Court upheld a broad delegation of discretionary legislative power to a Sentencing Commission, consisting of three federal judges, three academics, and one prison warden, all appointed by the President subject to Senate confirmation. Prisoners (Mistretta and other) argued that the Sentencing Reform Act (18 U.S.C.A., Sec. 3551 et.seq.) allowed Congress to delegate excessive legislative or policy-making discretion to the Commission in violation of Article 1, Section 1 of the U.S. Constitution, which prohibits Congress from delegating such basic law-making powers to another branch. But the Supreme Court disagreed, arguing ". . . that the separation-of-powers principle, and the nondelegation doctrine in particular, do not prevent Congress from obtaining the assistance of its coordinate branches" (at 654). As long as an "intelligible principle" is attached to congressional delegations, the Court asserted, the delegation, however broad, is constitutional (at 654). The Court concluded ". . . that in creating the Sentencing Commission . . . Congress neither delegated excessive legislative power nor upset the constitutionally mandated balance of powers among the coordinate Branches" (at 675).

In 1991 in *Touby* v. *United States,* 111 S.Ct. 1752, the Supreme Court upheld another broad delegation which allowed the Attorney General, under the provisions of the Comprehensive Drug Abuse Prevention and Control Act of 1970 [21 U.S.C.A., Sections 811(h), 812(b)], the discretionary authority to temporarily designate new controlled substances or "designer drugs" in order to avoid an "imminent hazard to the public safety." Petitioners argued that ". . . more than an 'intelligible principle' is required when Congress authorizes another Branch to promulgate regulations that contemplate criminal sanctions." However, the Supreme Court concluded that the "intelligible principle" ". . . passes muster even if greater congressional specificity is required in the criminal context" (at 1756). Reiterating what it said in *Mistretta,* the court argued that ". . . the nondelegation doctrine does not prevent Congress from seeking assistance, within proper limits, from its coordinate branches. Thus, Congress does not violate the Constitution merely because it legislates in broad terms, leaving a certain degree of discretion to executive or judicial actors" (at 1756).

Systems analysis can help us understand what happened to the nondelegation doctrine. In 1831 Justice Story exclaimed in *Shankland* v. *Washington,* 5 Pet. 390, 395 (U.S. 1831), that "[T]he general rule of law is, that a delegated authority cannot be delegated." In 1892, Justice Harlan noted similarly "[T]hat Congress cannot delegate legislative power . . . is a principle universally recognized as vital to the integrity and maintenance of the system of government ordained by the Constitution" (*Field* v. *Clark,* 143 U.S. 649, 692). And in 1989 Justice Scalia, dissenting in *Mistretta,* stressed that the Courts ". . . must be particularly rigorous in preserving the Constitution's structural restrictions that deter excessive delegation. The major one . . . is that the power to make law cannot be exercised by anyone other than Congress, . . ." (at 678).

Bernard Schwartz points out that "[T]he law on delegation has moved from the theoretical prohibition against any delegation of legislative power . . . to a rule against unrestricted delegations (i.e., those that are not limited by *standards*)."[28] But the question remains, how could such a basic constitutional principle of nondelegation reach a point where it plays virtually no role in our constitutional system? Actually, the reasons are quite clear and, from a systems perspective, very understandable. One reason is that the judiciary really cannot practically develop meaningful tests to distinguish permissible delegations from nonpermissible ones. But secondly, and much more importantly, is that our governmental system simply could not and cannot function efficiently and effectively unless broad delegations of legislative powers are permitted. In other words, broad delegations are upheld by the courts, not because they are technically constitutional, but because practicality or sound government requires such broad delegations to administrators. Possibly Justice Blackmun, writing for the majority in *Mistretta,* said it best when he wrote that ". . . our jurisprudence has been driven by a practical understanding that in our increasingly complex society, replete with ever changing and more technical problems, Congress simply cannot do its job absent an ability to delegate power under broad general directives" (at 654).

Delegation of Judicial Powers

Most delegation cases deal with the issue of whether Congress can delegate legislative power to administrative agencies, but agency power has increased through Congress's delegation of adjudicative powers as well. Article 3, Section 1 of the Constitution clearly states that "the judicial power of the United States shall be vested in one Supreme Court and in such inferior Courts as the Congress shall from time to time ordain." In this light, can Congress legally bestow judicial powers on nonjudicial bodies or administrative agencies? The answer is yes. Actually, the delegation of judicial power to administrative agencies has never caused the same intense concern as when legislative powers have been delegated, despite the similar encroachment upon the separation-of-powers doctrine. This is probably largely due to the fact that legislative acts, whether by Congress or public agencies, have normally and traditionally had a much greater impact on society than have judicial acts. It is true that although federal appellate and United States Supreme Court holdings have had profound social consequences (for example, in the areas of education, housing, criminal procedure, and civil rights), agency-adjudicated decisions in general have had comparatively minor impact. This is not to suggest that agency adjudications have not significantly affected some industries. But agency rule making is macro-oriented, while order making is more micro-oriented. Thus, as methods for promulgating public policies, the former would likely cause more public concern than the latter.

However, it is also important to emphasize that agency rules are generally less reviewable than agency orders. This makes the delegation of judicial power much less threatening to those concerned about the undermining of the separation-of-powers principle. As long as judicial review is not precluded, the Court argued in the precedential case *Cromwell* v. *Benson,* 285 U.S. 22 (1932), the delegation of judicial power to administrative agencies seems both reasonable and necessary. In judging the constitutionality of delegated judicial power to public agencies, the Court held that "Congress did not attempt to define questions of law, and the generality of the description leaves no doubt of the intention to reserve to the Federal court full authority to pass upon all matters which this Court has held to fall within that category. There is thus no attempt to interfere with, but rather provision is made to facilitate, the exercise by the court of its jurisdiction to deny effect to any administrative finding which is without evidence, or 'contrary to the indisputable character of the evidence,' or where the hearing is 'inadequate,' or 'unfair,' or arbitrary in any respect" (at 49–50). In *City of Waukegan* v. *Pollution Control Board,* 57 Ill. 2d 170 (1974), Justice Ward argued that the U.S. Supreme Court has never found it appropriate to rule that judicial power had been vested improperly in a public agency. In addition, he contended, citing several administrative law experts, any delegation of authority, whether legislative or judicial, does not violate the separation-of-powers doctrine as long as effective legislative or judicial checks exist. He maintained that "it may be irrelevant if an agency has legislative or judicial characteristics so long as the legislature or the judiciary can effectively correct errors of the agency" (at 175).[29]

However, in *Northern Pipeline Construction Co.* v. *Marathon Pipe Line Co.,* 458 U.S. 50 (1982), the Court handed down a decision that created some confusion regarding the delegation of adjudicative powers to administrative agencies. In *Northern Pipeline* the Court's plurality applied the old public rights/private rights test to agency adjudicative authority vaguely, apparently arguing that questions of public rights can be heard in agency adjudications, but those involving private rights must be heard before a regular court established under Article 3 of the U.S. Constitution. Parenthetically, although not always easy to distinguish, an issue involving a public right involves the government and another party (for example, the Federal Communications Commission and a TV station), while a private right involves a question between only private parties (for example, TWA and a mechanic's union). Administrative law critic Professor Bernard Schwartz, as well as many others, severely criticized this decision, arguing that the employment of the public rights/private rights test to determine adjudicative authority was rejected nearly a century ago. "It is too late in the development of our administrative law for there to be any question of the legislative power to delegate adjudicatory power to agencies. Adjudications of both public and private rights may be committed to administrative agencies, as long as their decisions are subject to judicial review. To indicate otherwise, as *Northern Pipeline* did, is to go back almost a century in administrative law development."[30] Fortunately, three years later in *Thomas* v. *Union Carbide Agricultural Products Co.,* 105 S.Ct. 3325 (1985), the Supreme Court rectified its apparent error in judgment by flatly rejecting the public rights/private rights test and reaffirming the long-established judicial opinion that the legislature has the authority to delegate adjudicative powers to administrative agencies, regardless of whether public or private rights are involved, as long as agency adjudicative decisions are subject to judicial review.

A year later the high court reaffirmed its position in *Union Carbide* in *Commodity Futures Trading Commission* v. *Schor,* 478 U.S. 835 (1986).

However, in 1989 the Supreme Court in *Granfinanciera S.A.* v. *Nordberg,* 109 S.Ct. 2782, relied again on the public right/private right distinction, causing more confusion regarding when agency adjudications are unconstitutional because a party is entitled to a jury trial in an Article III court and when agency adjudications are constitutional because no jury trial is required. In *Granfinanciera* the court held that the Seventh Amendment's jury trial requirement applies because the disputes pertaining to a bankruptcy involve only private parties. Thus, as a result of inconsistent reliance on the public right/private right test by the Supreme Court when reviewing the constitutionality of agency adjudicative authority, it is not clear today exactly what delegations of judicial powers to agencies are constitutional. Nonetheless, as a general rule, as developed in *Crowell,* it can be said that most agency adjudications are constitutional, under the separation-of-powers doctrine, as long as the delegation of judicial power to administrative agencies in the statutory scheme permits judicial review [*Glenborough New Mexico Assoc.* v. *Resolution Trust,* 802 F.Supp. 387, 391 (D.N.M. 1992)].

In concluding, it should be noted that the courts will continue to permit agencies to adjudicate a variety of disputes, even when involving only private parties, because our courts simply don't have the time or expertise to settle such disputes. The fact is that the Social Security Administration alone adjudicates more than 280,000 cases each year, or more than ten times the total caseload of all federal judges. According to Kenneth C. Davis and Richard J. Pierce, Jr., agency adjudications are preferable because they: 1) cost far less than court trials; 2) yield more consistent and accurate results; and 3) relieve the courts of an enormous burden that they could not possibly handle.[31]

Delegation at the State Level

As suggested, the judiciary has in general significantly contributed to the growth of administrative power by upholding broad delegations of power from legislatures to administrators. Although for a few decades after *Curtis-Wright* (1936) the courts timidly espoused that broad delegation was acceptable only if meaningful standards were attached, by the 1970s the federal courts seemed to have abandoned any serious efforts to make legislators comply with the meaningful standard requirement. Even though the prevalent judicial mood appears to indicate that the nondelegation doctrine is dead, there are definite signs at the state level that some questions pertaining to the legitimate limits of delegated authority still exist.

State courts, following the trend set by the federal courts, have normally upheld broad delegations, but occasionally they have refused to uphold the constitutionality of broad delegations when the legislative body failed to attach any meaningful standards to guide administrative actions. The fact is that state judges are more likely than federal judges to question the competence of state and local administrators and trust them. Of course, most states, particularly the more rural states, have simpler regulatory problems and can afford to insist that state legislatures attach more meaningful standards. Also, state courts have invoked a fundamental administrative law principle that agencies, including municipalities, are mere creatures of state statute powers delegated to them by the legislative branch since they have no inherently independent or common-law powers. To cite some examples: In *Biomedical Laboratories, Inc.* v. *Trainor,* 370 N.E. 2d 223 (1977), the Illinois Supreme Court made it clear that it would not uphold administrative authority in the total absence of standards set by the legislature, because standards are necessary to indicate the scope of authorized administrative power. In *Subcontractors Trade* v. *Koch,* 62 N.Y. 2d 422 (1984), a New York court held that Mayor Koch was not delegated the legislative power to mandate that "locally based enterprises" must get at least 10 percent of all construction contracts awarded by New York City. "In order for the executive to lawfully mandate the award of construction contracts to a particular group or category of business enterprise, the legislature must *specifically* delegate the power to him and must provide adequate guidelines and standards for the implementation of that policy" (at 429). While in *State Dept. of Env. Reg.* v. *Puckett Oil,* 577 So. 2d 988 (Fla. App. 1 Dist. 1991), a Florida court struck a blow against broad delegation by overruling a state agency's actions which were ". . . in excess of any express or reasonably implied delegated legislative authority" (at 991). The court noted that "[I]t is well recognized that the power of administrative agencies are measured and limited by statutes or acts in which such powers are expressly granted or implicitly conferred" (at 991).

Subdelegation

No doubt all administrative practitioners know that, as a matter of necessity, authority granted to those at the top of the organizational hierarchy must be delegated to subordinates. If this were not done, little could be accomplished, simply because the chief executive officer, the person at the top, is technically the only nonsubordinate in the pyramidal structure. This chief could not be expected to carry out all functions. The justification for subdelegating authority to subordinates was stated decades ago by Commissioner Eastman of the Interstate Commerce Commission: "Sound principles of organization demand that those at the top be able to concentrate their attention upon the larger and more important questions of policy and practice, and that their time be freed, so far as possible, from consideration of smaller and less important matters of detail."[32] Presidents, state governors, agency heads, and the like, clearly cannot be expected to personally handle all tasks legally delegated only to them.

As early as 1839 the Supreme Court upheld the rights of a president to informally subdelegate powers to his department heads, even though the statutes did not technically permit such a delegation. For decades during the nineteenth century, presidents did not push the subdelegation doctrine too far, mostly because the mood of the day seemed to forbid irresponsible subdelegation to those to whom legislators did not formally grant power. In 1887 the United States Supreme Court ruled that a president cannot subdelegate a power to a subordinate if a statute requires a president to employ his personal judgment *(Runkle* v. *United States,* 122 U.S. 543). However, for many decades now ". . . subdelegation has become a mainstay of government operation."[33] For example, in *United States* v. *Cottman Co.,* 190 F.2d 805, 807 (1952), the court reasoned: "It is manifestly necessary that he (Secretary of the Treasury) delegate duties of this sort (remitting custom duties) to subordinate officials."

The general rule pertaining to subdelegation is that the subdelegation is allowed if the legislative body has specifically authorized the subdelegation or if the statute is silent on subdelegation. For instance, in *In Re Advisory Opinion To Governor,* 627 A.2d 1246 (R.I. 1993), the Supreme Court of Rhode Island opined that "[T]he test for determining whether a subdelegation is valid is primarily a question of statutory interpretation. . . . Our obligation is to determine whether the General Assembly fairly intended to grant the director of the DOT the power to subdelegate. . . ." (at 1250). In this case the court upheld the subdelegation not only because the statute in part specifically permitted it, but also because even where the statute was silent on the subdelegation question, at least the statute did not prohibit the subdelegation (at 1250).

On occasion, a statute may prohibit subdelegation because the legislature believes that the specific duty is too important to subdelegate to subordinates. For example, in *United States* v. *Giordano,* 416 U.S. 505 (1974), the Supreme Court ruled against a subdelegation by the United States Attorney General to his executive assistant. The court held that a fair reading of the statute limited the power ". . . to the Attorney General himself. . . ." (at 514).

Subdelegation Issues   Most legal scholars argue that it makes little sense to continue to debate whether powers should be subdelegated, but they do voice serious concern over how effectively and responsibly authority is subdelegated to subordinates by superiors. Kenneth C. Davis, who is known best in the administrative law field for his research into the proper limits of administrative discretion, believes that subdelegated authority not accompanied by meaningful standards poses a threat to rational administrative processes and should therefore be forbidden: "When the discretion of officers in individual cases is insufficiently confined and insufficiently guided by standards, a subdelegation which fails to do what reasonably can and should be done to confine and to guide discretion may well be held invalid."[34]

Subdelegation of authority to those who are technically not supposed to wield such power raises other serious questions for legislators, administrators, and the American public. If you were a legislator held politically accountable for your actions, would you feel uneasy about delegating law-making powers to agency heads, knowing that these public policy-making powers will quite possibly be subdelegated to those far down in the agency's decision-making pyramid? If you were an agency administrator, would you feel comfortable delegating vital policy-making assignments to those who are not ultimately responsible for seeing to it that the job tasks are handled properly? On the other hand, should the public feel content with a subdelegation process in which important public policy decisions are sometimes made by lower-level personnel? Do you think it is wise for relatively low-ranking agency officials with less training and relevant experience in, say, the U.S. Department of Housing and Urban Development to draft housing policies which affect millions? Do such things happen, in fact, and not just at one agency? Do you believe that it is sensible for lowly administrators in the field to employ their subdelegated authority under existing legislation to propose (that is, virtually to make) rules and regulations which will eventually govern industry behavior, knowing their rules will probably be accepted in a pro forma manner only by their superiors? How adequately can superiors be expected to supervise and scrutinize the work of their subordinates when it involves reviewing relatively important informally promulgated rules or adjudicated decisions? How far down the organizational ladder should subdelegation authority pass before democratic decision-making processes are threatened, thus jeopardizing democratic accountability in the American political system? Regardless of the democratic accountability problems posed by subdelegation, do we have any practical choice but to subdelegate powers to our public administrators and trust them to act responsibly?

Conclusion

In sum, the extremely permissive position taken by the courts regarding the delegation, as well as the subdelegation, of legislative power to administrative agencies since the mid-1930s has expanded the scope and powers of administrators beyond limitations that the founding fathers would have perceived as tolerable. The typical administrative agency today makes, administers, and adjudicates its own policies, and these agency policies frequently have significant social consequences. Theodore Lowi, like many others, looks with disfavor on this development because he holds that it is irresponsible for Congress to delegate broad legislative powers without attaching clear and useful guidelines. This present trend toward broader and broader delegation, Lowi maintains, cannot but reduce the policy-making input and impact of Congress to a relative insignificance.[35] Joseph Harris, however, argues that Congress should grant vast policy-making powers to public agencies, leaving the authority broad and vague enough that administrators can make appropriate policies to resolve particular program problems.[36] Despite the extensive policy-making powers of agencies today, administrative actions are no longer so carefully scrutinized, either by legislators or judges. Neither the courts nor legislative bodies seem to have the time, will, or expertise to do the supervising. This seems to leave the United States in a potentially dangerous position.

Administrators cannot be led to believe that just about anything they may do may be considered acceptable. Discretionary power must be controlled if freedom is to survive. However, at the same time we cannot turn back the clock to days when life was simpler. No longer are there only a few million Americans living in the United States; the population is approaching 260 million. Such a large population and the problems which go with a vast and complicated technological society necessitate an enlarged government to operate and coordinate needed programs in a complex society. Administrators need to have enough freedom and flexibility to implement programs successfully. The solution is to seek a sensible and viable balance that will permit administrators to function without crippling handcuffs, yet still work under the watchful eyes of legislators, judges, or newly created watchdog agencies—administrative courts or ombudsmen—who have the power to provide realistic vital checks. Because legislators cannot possibly be expected to draft legislation and attach meaningful standards to every phase (unanticipated and critical policy questions will always be left for administrators to resolve), less emphasis should be placed on seeking standards. More attention, however, should be placed on training public officials in and sensitizing them to principles of democratic accountability and on developing broad institutional safeguards to aid in preventing unnecessary, uncontrollable, and abusive administrative discretion.

THE POWER OF ADMINISTRATIVE OFFICIALS AND AGENCIES

At least in a formal sense, the powers originally assigned to the administrative system were quite limited. Informally, of course, administrative agencies have always exercised more power than the statutes seemed to permit. Nevertheless, public agencies had a very limited role in the legislative and judicial areas of policy formation. Today, however, administrative agencies literally make more public policies than the legislative branch and decide more legal issues than the courts. It was once popular to suggest that administrative agencies possess quasi-legislative and quasi-judicial powers in addition to their normal executive powers. But in recent years it has been commonly argued among legal scholars that the prefix *quasi* is a misnomer because it creates a misconception regarding the real authority administrative agencies have in the legislative and judicial areas. *Quasi* implies that administrators have only the appearance of possessing such powers. Although a case can still be made for calling the legislative and judicial powers of administrative agencies quasi legislative and quasi judicial, it is no longer realistic to do so. For all practical purposes, administrators nowadays are allowed to make significant public policies in some areas, to judge the merits of their laws, and even to hand out penalties to those who do not comply with their policies. James Burnham has referred to bureaucrats as the new ruling class of all advanced nations, while Eugene P. Dvorin and Robert H. Simmons have argued that misguided and inhumane public administrators have inherited so much power that the traditional, tripartite model of government, with its powers divided among the legislative, executive, and judicial branches, has lost its functional meaning.[37]

Examples of the Power of Administrators

And why should people not cry out against the expanding role of bureaucratic power? After all, with the odds greatly against any administrator's being stopped by legislators or judges from executing some action (implying that administrators may in certain cases actually possess *de facto* rather than *de jure* powers), bureaucrats have relatively broad discretionary power. For example, they can (1) give or deny persons welfare benefits; (2) grant or deny licenses involving great financial investment and careers; (3) prosecute or not prosecute felonious crimes; (4) expel students from public schools; (5) deport persons from the United States; (6) close down businesses; (7) seize a person's parked car for payment of back taxes; (8) take certain children away from their parents; (9) decide to demand or dismiss taxes that they consider due the government; (10) take away individually owned land and homes and build highways on their sites; (11) hold innocent people in jail cells as material witnesses for long periods of time; (12) strip people down at airports without genuine probable cause to carry out humiliating searches of their naked bodies; (13) prevent families from moving into their newly purchased homes until they comply with "occupancy permit" demands which frequently involve minor, yet expensive and inconvenient repairs; (14) forbid homeowners from changing such things as a simple electrical switch in their own houses until they purchase permits; (15) prevent persons from parking particular motor vehicles in their own driveways; (16) forbid entrepreneurs from placing advertising signs beyond a certain size in their store windows; (17) prevent landlords from raising rents or even from expelling tenants; (18) fine companies for not complying with safety or antipollution standards; (19) require certain private businesses to hire minority-group persons as employees; (20) force parents to send their children to schools far away from their own neighborhoods; (21) demand that local governmental officials include housing opportunities for low-income families in their community growth plans; and (22) make firms do business with persons or groups with whom they would not ordinarily conduct business.

It should be acknowledged that some of these powers rightfully belong to legislators and judges, but the point is that administrators, for all practical purposes, possess sufficient discretionary power to give practical meaning to laws and orders. For example, if an administrator states to a judge that a child has been so terribly abused by his or her parents that the child should be protected by removing the child from the parents' care, and the administrator reasonably documents his or her expert judgment, chances are high that the judge will yield to the administrator's recommendation.

Do Administrators Possess Too Much Power?

Some people feel no surprise when the United States today is characterized by many scholars as an administrative state. Legal experts have estimated (see Chapter 1) that more than 90 percent of the laws which regulate life in the United States are made by nonelected career bureaucrats with extreme job security. Is our democratic heritage threatened by the emergence of the administrative state? Is America sacrificing democratic political controls for administrative efficiency? These very critical questions need serious attention, especially in view of such statements on democracy as this one by Lewis Mainzer: "Elected officials rightly claim to be, more truly then bureaucrats, in the democratic stream. In formulating a democratic theory of political control of bureaucrats, the first rule must be that any fundamental rejection of political control is antidemocratic."[38]

The power of elected administrators (the president, state governors, state attorney general, sheriffs, auditors, and so on) and top administrative appointees, as well as that of career civil servants, has also increased dramatically in recent decades. Although the voters have more direct control over elected officials and their appointees, problems of control exist here also. Methods such as the recall to unseat irresponsible elected officials are not very effective. Elected officials who direct powerful administrative apparatus can do much harm if they abuse their positions of power. Presidents, of course, serve four-year terms and some state officials serve as long as six years before they have to run for reelection. It is easy to find instances in which presidents have strengthened their power positions, potentially threatening the constitutional system of democratic checks and balances they are sworn to uphold. Presidents can increase their positions of power (and have done so) in the American system simply by stepping a little further than previous presidents who had also exceeded their formal, constitutional powers. In the political science classroom today it is next to useless to try to explain presidential power to students by way of the U.S. Constitution. Professors must instead talk in terms of the president's informal powers. The president now initiates most legislation in the domestic sphere and drafts practically all bills in the foreign policy area. Treaties, which were once the exclusive domain of Congress, are now made by the president, under the name of executive agreements.

Examples of the Impact of Administrative Decisions: The FAA's Decision to Ground and NASA's Decision to Launch

Federal Aviation Administrator Langhorne Bond stated publicly on June 5, 1979: "Overnight my certitude has switched from the position of high likelihood of no risk to sufficient likelihood of risk and that's enough to put the planes on the ground."[39] Bond's decision to ground DC-10s for an indefinite period after investigations into the airworthiness of this aircraft helps to demonstrate the mighty, although frequently justifiable, powers regulatory administrators may wield. Eleven days before Bond issued the temporary order, a DC-10 had crashed in Chicago killing 279 persons, making it the worst air disaster in the history of U.S. aviation. The DC-10 had also been involved in other serious accidents in the 1970s, including a major crash that killed 346 people near Paris. Nevertheless, despite these human tragedies and Bond's obligation as FAA chief to protect the public's safety, complaints about his decision to ground the DC-10s were heated and plentiful.

Bond was criticized by those who had to cope with inconveniences caused by flight cancellations but most by those who stood to suffer great financial losses as a result of the DC-10s' being declared not airworthy. The McDonnell Douglas Corporation, manufacturer of the DC-10, stood to lose hundreds of millions of dollars in decreased sales and millions more for repairs, as well as costly damage to its image as a reputable aircraft company. Bond's decision would also place a hardship on domestic and foreign airlines, although these were technically out of his jurisdiction. U.S. airlines were expected to lose millions of dollars daily, based on 1978 airline profits which showed earnings of approximately $6 million dollars per day in gross revenues from operating DC-10s. Since a significant percentage of passenger seat miles would be affected by the grounding, the loss estimates indeed appeared to place these U.S. airlines under financial stress, possibly jeopardizing their ability to stay in business. Shippers, travel agents, the hotel and motel industry, and many other businesses that depend upon the transportation of air passengers would undoubtedly also feel the effects of Bond's grounding order.[40]

Top-level public administrators frequently find themselves caught between a rock and a hard place. NASA administrators found themselves in such a precarious position in the weeks before they gave the fatal okay to launch the space shuttle *Challenger* on that cold, icy Florida morning of January 28, 1986. About seventy-three seconds after ignition, combustion gas leaked through faulty O-ring seals in the right booster rocket and caused the shuttle to blow up, killing the entire crew, destroying the costly spacecraft and its valuable payload, severely damaging the image of U.S. space technology, and indefinitely postponing America's space program.

As said so often after a tragedy, this was an accident just waiting to happen. In a situation similar to Bond's, Arnold Aldrich, the space shuttle program manager, and other top NASA officials were constantly pressured to place financial and political considerations before safety concerns. According to the Report of the Presidential Commission on the Space Shuttle Accident (popularly known as the Rogers Commission Report), pressure to produce in a cost-effective manner and NASA's accommodating "can-do" attitude led NASA to increase its flight rate schedule unrealistically, compromising safety standards.[41] Testifying before the Rogers Commission, Leonard Nicholson, manager of Space Transportation System Integration and Operations at Johnson Space Center, said that attempts were made to voice concerns about the shuttle launch, "but the political aspects of the decision are so overwhelming that our concerns do not carry much weight" and the "political advantages of implying those late changes outweighed our general objections."[42] In response, the Rogers Commission recommended: "It is important to determine how many flights can be accommodated, and accommodated safely. NASA must establish a realistic level of expectation, then approach it carefully. Mission schedules should be based on a realistic assessment of what NASA can do safely and well, not on what is possible with maximum efforts."[43]

It is clear that the space shuttle *Challenger* disaster was caused more by administrative shortcomings than by design or mechanical failures, since technical problems can be resolved through thoughtful administrative actions. The Rogers Report concluded "that there was a serious flaw in the decision making process leading up to the launch. . . . A well structured and managed system emphasizing safety would have flagged the rising doubts about the Solid Rocket Booster joint seal," making the launch unlikely. "The waiving of launch constraints appears to have been at the expense of flight safety."[44]

It is easy to criticize NASA officials in retrospect for succumbing to the political and financial pressures to launch, but the pressures were severe. NASA's budget was lean, shuttle missions were behind schedule and the *Challenger*'s launch had already been delayed three times, important future missions faced long delays, grumblings were heard from legislators, impatient private clients wanted their satellites placed in orbit, and President Reagan was scheduled to deliver his State of the Union message that evening and comments about the *Challenger* mission were in his speech.[45] Given these acute demands, it is not hard to understand why administrators often take risks that compromise safety, especially when questions of safety involve speculative judgments. The statistical odds of a serious accident's happening "this time" are normally very low, while economic and political realities are usually quite clear. Given so many environmental demands, it is also easy to understand, as mentioned previously, why the procedural due process dictates of administrative law are sometimes not given the attention they should have by administrators desperately trying to survive.

As these two tragic cases demonstrate, public administrators sometimes make decisions that have an enormous impact on various interests in our society. Obviously, agency heads such as FAA's Langhorne Bond and NASA's Arnold Aldrich make billion-dollar decisions, ones that can lead to jubilant celebrations or mournful funeral processions. Some, usually those who have suffered the consequences of adverse agency decisions, feel that billion-dollar and life-or-death decision-making power should not be left to agency regulators who often function relatively independently of viable political oversight. But the hard truth is that someone or some decision-making body must make these tough decisions if public policy goals are to be reached. Thus far Congress has found it appropriate to delegate such decision-making authority to agency administrators because legislators believe that agency experts are in the best position to reach intelligent decisions.

Some Serious Concerns about Administrative Power

Elected, appointed, and regular career administrators have inherited vast powers through one channel or another. Administrative powers, compared with those of the past, have expanded in scope and intensity. Despite all the attempts to limit and control the power of administrators through various pieces of legislation and court decisions, there has undoubtedly been a significant net gain in power for administrative agencies. This enormous growth in the power of governmental agencies has without doubt upset the traditional constitutional power allocations between governmental branches and increased the probability of oppressive and unpopular government.

Regardless of these contentions, Walter Gellhorn argues that the power of administrators has been exaggerated and that it is not nearly so great as many observers suspect. Actually, Gellhorn noted to me, most administrators he has known over the decades who have left Washington posts did so because they felt they had too little power and were frustrated in their efforts to perform their jobs adequately.[46] Gellhorn may be right, but if questions are posed that put administrative power in perspective, it is easier to assess the relative power of administrators. Compared with the powers of individual congress persons and judges, how would you rank the power position of administrative chiefs today? How has the power of individual administrators grown since 1789, as compared with the power of legislators and judges? In light of the historical facts, it would be difficult to argue credibly that individual legislators or judges are, on the whole, more powerful and influential than top-level administrators, especially in view of the impact these administrators have today on determining the content of social programs. Also, it would be virtually impossible to argue credibly that growth in administrative power since 1789 has not far outstripped gains in power among legislators and judges. In short, it may be correct to hold, as Gellhorn does, that administrators are frequently frustrated by checks which tend to undermine their authority, but it is probably also true that the powers of legislators and judges are checked even more rigorously.

Some readers may be thinking that the U.S. is not so bad and that they have not been treated very unfairly, if unfairly at all, by public administrators. Because most administrators have a sense of right and wrong, adhere to a professional code of conduct, and are reviewed or at least feel the threat of review, administrative behavior in America has probably been relatively honorable. However, in this frank discussion of administrative power, what is being mainly addressed is not how administrators have performed, but how they could function if they had no scruples or public conscience. As it stands right now, the potential for abuse by administrators is great because our political system has thus far probably granted too much power to administrative agencies. This is so only because power has been extended without arranging for adequate checks or taking the time to consider seriously the grave consequences of allowing so much power to pass to the administrative branch.

There are additional reasons for concern over the potential for executives and administrative agencies to misuse their powers. Much administrative behavior is protected under various interpretations of the sovereign and official immunity doctrines. Even if the questionable behavior of administrative agencies is challenged in the courts, the odds of a successful, appeal are statistically low. Also, despite the unfair treatment a person may experience from a public administrator, it is virtually impossible to get an incompetent and irresponsible civil service employee dismissed. Classified civil service employees are well protected by a so-called merit system, which needs fundamental revision if these administrators, as contrasted to politically appointed administrators, are to be made more responsible to the public.

ADMINISTRATIVE GROWTH, THE PUBLIC INTEREST, AND ADMINISTRATIVE LAW CONSIDERATIONS

Introduction: Growth, Administrative Law, and the Public Interest

The central purpose of government is to promote the public interest. This point is made extremely clear in the writings of most political theorists over the centuries. American administrative law deals essentially with the propriety of the procedures used by public administrators to implement policies designed to promote the public interest. More specifically, administrative law provides the standards that must be incorporated into the methods employed by regulator agencies in their attempts to regulate societal activities in the public interest. As discussed earlier in this chapter, dramatic changes in the complexity of social functions have caused the demands on government to increase at an accelerated pace, thus giving birth to the reality of the administrative state in our political system. But this new administrative state has needed to be controlled. Consequently, administrative law surfaced as a pervasive legal check to help ensure that the rise of the administrative state would not be accompanied by the demise of democratic institutional practices necessary to protect the general welfare.

However, despite the emergence of procedural due process protections stemming from the growth of administrative law, many citizens, some of them scholars, have questioned the legitimacy of the major role played by the administrative system in public policy making, as well as the ability and willingness of public agency officials to represent the general public fairly and to regulate in the public interest in a democratically responsible fashion. Consequently, in the 1970s a reform movement began, aimed at forcing public agencies to act more within the public interest. In a 1977 issue of the *Public Administration Review* devoted primarily to the problem of public interest representation in the federal bureaucracy, symposium editor Edgar

Shor commented: "In a remarkably short time, the remedy of public interest representation has gained wide acceptance as a way of increasing administrative responsiveness and accountability to the public. Indeed, for the persistently suspect administrative process, and recurrently questioned bureaucratic exercise of vast discretionary power, the representativeness of agency proceedings conceivably could become a touchstone of their legitimacy. At any rate, political and executive leaders, along with administrators, can expect continuing demands for the further institutionalization of public interest advocacy."[47] Although the institutionalization of public interest advocacy has continued, a more conservative political climate, continuing even into the Clinton era, and the diminished capacity to fund public interest advocacy, have stunted the movement.

Defining the Public Interest

In order for administrative agencies to work toward fulfilling the public interest, the public interest must be reasonably identified. Public interest goals must be defined clearly enough so that agencies can pursue understandable and relatively concrete objectives (for example, the reduction of environmental pollution to "acceptable" levels), while genuine public interest groups must be recognizable. But can this be done? Arguments over definitions of the public interest have bothered social scientists for literally centuries and in the past fifty years have severely hampered the positive development of administrative law and governmental regulatory practices. The root of the definitional problem seems to be buried in the fact that the term *public interest* has been defined in radically different and often contradictory ways. Several definitions of the concept have been attempted, but it appears that no definition has been broadly accepted. In what is, nonetheless, something of a classic definition, Walter Lippman has been quoted as defining public interest as "what men would choose if they saw clearly, thought rationally, and acted disinterestedly and benevolently."[48] J.A.W. Gunn believes that the public interest is similar to what Jeremy Bentham meant by *utilitarianism,* while J.W.R. Coy believed that majority will was the guts of public interest.[49] However, many have argued, including Robert Miewald, Frank Sorauf, and Glendon Schubert, that the concept of public interest is much too vague to have any practical utility for public administrators.[50] In fact, Miewald poses this disturbing question: "But what about the possibility that there is no such thing, at least not in the sense of an operational standard against which specific administrative acts can be measured before the fact?"[51] Miewald humorously adds: "It should be quite clear that on the bureaucrat's first day on the job, the orientation officer is not able to say, 'There's the washroom, there's the water cooler, and over there in the corner is the public interest.'"[52] Despite Miewald's strong feeling that it would certainly be helpful if agency rule makers could be guided by an identifiable public interest, he concludes, as do most public interest group theorists, that "there is no public interest—not in the sense of an identifiable, enduring 'thing.' The closest one can come to it is the will of the majority of voters at any particular time."[53]

Maybe those who argue that the public interest cannot be operationalized meaningfully so that the concept can provide worthwhile guidance for agency regulators in promulgating rules (public policies) are right, but it appears silly to argue that nothing exists that American administrators can understand and appreciate as the public interest. Although it is difficult to talk about the public interest in the abstract, just as it is to discuss the concept of justice in the abstract, it appears that the public interest, like justice, begins to come into sharper focus when one deals with specific social issues (for example, environmental pollution). To determine what is or is not in the public interest requires that one employ reason—sometimes plain, logical, insightful common sense. If Leo Strauss, one of the most famous neo-Platonic thinkers of the twentieth century, were alive today, he would force students of administration to employ platonic reasoning in order to improve the understanding of public interest. Strauss would pose some provocative questions, such as: Should we have to question whether allowing industries to pollute the environment is offensive to the public interest? Employing commonly accepted moral and ethical democratic values, would America as a society have to question whether promulgating agency rules, which tend to favor only a select few at the expense of the vast majority of Americans, promotes or fails to promote the public interest? Are not certain business activities obviously contrary to what the public interest would demand? In even modern behavioralist terms, cannot systems analysis be employed by agency evaluators to detect activities which will obviously have a negative impact on our entire social system? Should not these activities be considered by U.S. governmental regulators as activities which should be banned because they threaten the public interest? Would it be in the public interest for FDA administrators to allow obviously deadly foods to be sold by businesses to consumers?

For many specific regulatory problems, though admittedly not all, probably a simple cost-benefits formula could be used by systems evaluators to determine the public interest content of some actions or some product. Only a few vital questions would have to be posed in the context of a basic democratic value framework. What are the costs? To whom? What are the comparative benefits? These questions need not imply a zero-sum game, because virtually all could gain or lose from some activities or products. However, when special interest groups would obviously benefit at high costs to the general public, administrators should be able to draw the reasonable conclusion without any difficulty that the activity or product would be detrimental to the public interest. Too often in our society common agreement on what is consistent with the public interest is frustrated by only a few, speaking for only a tiny percentage of the American public, frequently only a single industry or company. Unanimous agreement on anything is virtually impossible to attain, given human nature. But this should not imply that a clear consensus cannot be obtained. Unfortunately, in the U.S. political system special interest group lobbyists have been allowed to have a disproportionate say in determining what is in the public interest. An important challenge for agency regulators is to discover what is genuinely in the public interest versus what interest group lobbyists claim is in the public interest but really favors only their selfish interests.[54]

The Impact of Administrative Growth on Democratic Ideals and Administrative Law

What are the democratic ideals that Americans apparently cherish so dearly?[55] Have they been threatened by the emergence of the modern administrative state? If so, how and to what extent? In particular, have particular agency practices helped to destroy the functional meaning of U.S. democratic tradition? What relevance do these questions have to students of administrative law?

The democratic ideals embodied in the Constitution of the United States reflect the thinking of countless political theorists who contributed in various ways over the centuries to the development of democratic theory. However, the U.S. Constitution appears to most reflect the writings of Aristotle, John Locke, Lee Baron de Montesquieu, Jean Jacques Rousseau, John Stuart Mill, James Madison, Thomas Jefferson, and Alexander Hamilton. Together, these great theorists designed and refined the basic democratic principles of the U.S. Constitution, namely, (1) constitutionalism, (2) shared governmental powers, (3) popular government, (4) individualism, and (5) political equality. Actually, it is very difficult to separate these democratic principles into neat categories because of their obviously interrelated character. Constitutionalism, in particular, naturally implies the other four democratic ideals listed. Nevertheless, for the sake of clarity, these five democratic ideals are reviewed separately. Administrative law, an offspring of constitutional law, also reflects these democratic ideals.

Constitutionalism   Constitutionalism is the most basic, as well as the broadest, democratic ideal. Aristotle was probably the first political theorist to discuss the concept in great depth. Constitutionalism is rooted in the Aristotelian principle of the rule of law. This concept provides the basic underpinning for democratic constitutionalism. The rule of law stresses the supremacy of the law (constitutional law and all other lesser laws sanctioned by the constitution), thus prohibiting illegal actions, especially arbitrary and capricious behavior, by all public officials. Not unexpectedly, an obvious outgrowth of the rule of law, developed quite well by John Locke and other social contract theorists, is the notion of limited government. Basically, the contract theorists held that a contractual agreement was created among members of a society who sought to establish an orderly society. The contract, usually in the form of a written document (for example, a constitution), forms the basis of the government. In the contract the rights and powers of the government and the citizenry are enumerated and implied. A constitutional government such as ours passes one test of political legitimacy because it is based upon popular consent. It is also a limited government because U.S. governmental officials have specified powers; thus the breadth of their activities and power is limited. Governmental regulation has therefore been viewed as illegitimate, because many believe government's regulatory activities go beyond the scope of our government's limited and legitimate role. American constitutional government was developed by persons who found obnoxious the unlimited and tyrannical powers of governmental dictators. In a constitutional governmental system, the people, not the government, are regarded as sovereign. U.S. federal courts ideally serve to preserve this constitutional principle of limited government by reviewing acts perceived by petitioners to be beyond the scope of the government's restricted powers.

Shared Powers   Another democratic ideal in the American political system is the idea that governmental powers should be shared. The concept of shared powers also serves as a protection against excessive and illegitimate governmental power. The shared powers principle is rooted in the compatible doctrines of separation of powers and checks and balances. The separation-of-powers doctrine demands, of course, that governmental powers be divided among different governmental branches and units. Thus, a concentration of governmental power in the hands of one or a few is prevented by distributing governmental decision-making power not only among the chief executive, administrative, legislative, and judicial branches, but among the different governmental levels as well. Governmental powers are still further divided in several ways within the specific political branches and units; for example, congressional powers are separated by the House and the Senate, while specific administrative powers are divided between independent agencies. In theory, this diffusion of powers allows governmental powers to be checked and balanced because each political entity has a limited check over the powers of other authoritative actors in the governmental system (for example, judicial review of agency actions; legislative oversight of agency behavior; presidential veto of congressional bills). James M. Burns believed that a decisional deadlock was created because this system of checks and balances worked too well.[56] To most American government experts, the notion of shared powers, incidentally, is preferable to the notion of a separation of powers because it is more accurate to perceive the government's powers as shared since the Constitution does not endorse a strict separation of powers between the branches, as the courts have often pointed out.

Popular Government   The principle of popular government may be the democratic ideal cherished most by the average American. A popular government implies democratic government, which in turn implies that the ultimate political power to determine public policy directions should reside in the people. The idea of popular sovereignty is expressed in the Declaration of Independence and the United States Constitution but is seen in practice in our representative political institutions. The theory of popular government is linked closely to the attitude that all governmental officials should be held accountable to the people for their behavior because they are in reality servants of the people. This representative popular government theory clashes sharply with the theory of absolutism, under which dictators create and define the depths of their political powers with the people serving as subjects, lacking the authority to check the unrestrained powers of government. In contrast to absolutism, popular government theory stresses the role of majority will, individual rights, and liberty.

Individualism   A particularly important aspect of popular government, especially to Americans, is the concept of individualism. Individualism is a socioeconomic political concept which stresses the right of individuals to determine their own destinies. Individualism, as opposed to collectivism, emphasizes the importance of freedom, personal well-being, and the capabilities of individuals. The idea of individualism, especially before the New Deal, promoted the political and economic theories of laissez-faire. Because the doctrine of individualism has tended to reinforce certain notions which may conflict with public interest or national goals, a major governmental problem in any democratic system has always focused on how to balance societal rights with individual rights.

Political Equality   Ideally, democratic constitutionalism implies the principle of political and, to some degree, social equality. Many American government critics charge that this democratic ideal has not been achieved as well as the other ideals in our system. Political equality suggests that all persons should be treated and represented equally by government. Although identical treatment is not required by the Constitution, it does require that reasonable due process and equal protection guarantees be rendered to all persons. Because political equality is rooted in the democratic principles of equality under the law, as well as equal opportunity for all persons, arbitrary treatment of citizens by governmental officials is strictly forbidden by various laws. Legislation, court holdings, and a mass of administrative regulations have functioned in recent decades to make persons more truly equal under the law, and some of these will be discussed in later sections.

Challenges to Democratic Ideals

The growth of the administrative system in the United States, as elsewhere and throughout the history of the bureaucratization of the world, was largely a governmental response to the basic need to structure, order, and regulate society. Many social thinkers have held that the emergence of public bureaucracy in capitalist America resulted mainly because the capitalist class believed that it could benefit by having the state stabilize business activities through regulating the economic climate. This would help to reduce business risks involving vast sums of capital. Ralph P. Hummel described the growth phenomenon: "Modern bureaucracy in the public service arose out of the need of private groups—industrial entrepreneurs, financiers, and merchants—to have the state regulate the world so that the huge investments and reinvestments characterizing modern capital enterprise could be justified. Out of this came rationalized state administration of the legal system (emphasizing the enforcement of contract), the regulation of labor, the state supervision of commerce and finance, and finally state stabilization of markets. Today we criticize bureaucracy for its inflexibility, stability, and immutability in the face of change. But in the past these qualities perfectly reflected the purpose for which it was set up—to provide controls over a society that had, from the viewpoint of capital enterprises, too much change in it."[57] A less cynical viewpoint suggested earlier is that the state's administrative apparatus, as well as administrative law, grew in response to the demands placed upon American government by the citizenry. It is also possible that bureaucracy, as an institution, unfortunately expands in an effort to support its own weight. Although the precise causes of the growth of the public regulatory system will remain a mystery, there is little doubt that the expansion of administrative power has jeopardized the welfare of the five cherished democratic values just described. To what extent have these democratic ideals survived the emergence of administrative power?

Challenges to Democratic Constitutionalism   Clearly, the growth of administrative expertise has posed the greatest threat not only to democratic constitutionalism, but also to virtually all our democratic ideals. Basically, this is true because the public policy making by administrative experts, especially those who are removed from direct political controls, tends to undermine the fundamental maxims of democratic constitutionalism. Constitutionalism assumes the supremacy of the rule of law, but our public agencies hold to this principle only in theory. In practice, few written rules and regulations guide the day-to-day decisions made by administrators. In fact, it is argued, administrative discretion is so broad that the United States is ruled by public administrators. Kenneth C. Davis feels that this allows administrators to have the power of choice, thus permitting them to select and determine important public policy directions, as well as to render injustices to individuals contrary to what sensible rule of law dictates would demand.[58] Specifically, observers have discovered that public administrators can jeopardize rule of law precepts by informally promulgating rules and orders in the absence of a clear, written, and reviewable record.

Constitutional democracy is additionally compromised by the undemocratic character of administrative experts. James O. Freedman, in "Crisis and Legitimacy in the Administrative Process," acknowledged that possibly too much reliance is placed upon agency experts at the expense of more open and democratically controlled decision making.[59] To some scholars, this new class of governmental experts constitutes an administrative elite—a new oligarchical structure that appears to be democratically irresponsible. This evolution is justified, according to Felix Frankfurter, because the framers believed the power of administrative expertise could be controlled by demanding (1) high professional-performance standards; (2) the use of elaborate procedural safeguards; (3) open criticism of expert opinions and decisions; and (4) that important decisions be reserved for the elected leaders.[60] But the public's refusal to believe that these experts can be adequately controlled, as well as the public's refusal to believe that these experts are indeed experts, has caused the public to question, according to Freedman, the very legitimacy of the power of these regulatory experts in a political system which is supposed to be guided by the principles of democratic constitutionalism.[61]

Challenges to the Concept of Shared Powers   The constitutional framers established a tripartite system of government specifically designed to make public policy decision making a shared governmental function. The purpose of this plan was to ensure that decision-making power was not monopolized by a single governmental branch, but shared among three branches. This separation-of-powers idea was intended to promote democratic decision making by balancing governmental decision-making powers among legislators, justices, and the president. However, the rise of the administrative system as the fourth branch of government has possibly destroyed the tripartite decision-making system beyond repair, especially since this fourth branch is likely the most powerful. "By 1970," Eugene P. Dvorin and Robert H. Simmons claimed, "any pretense by public servants of maintaining their former disclaimers to dominance could only border on the ludicrous. Possibly the only faith in the traditional idea of a balanced, tripartite government remained in those civics courses taught by home economic teachers and football coaches."[62]

Despite the apparent threat to the traditional democratic decision-making model, experts hold that the expansion of administrative policy-making powers has actually been encouraged by the other branches. Past presidents, legislators, and court judges have asked public administrators to do more and more. Dvorin and Simmons believe that the new powers and responsibilities which have been inherited by administrators have caused a crisis of imbalance. These critics question in particular whether U.S. public administrators have accepted the moral responsibilities that come with the new powers that have destroyed what was left of tripartite power: "The combination of power and responsibility now vested in the executive branch contrasts dangerously with the scant attention paid by public administrators to questions of moral principles."[63]

The erosion of the doctrine of shared powers symbolized by the tripartite model represents to many people the end of a democracy. A long list of cynics and fatalists compete in the public administration and administrative law literature to convey in the most eloquent prose how the consolidation of powers in the administrative branch is causing the fall of democracy. While Dvorin and Simmons point to the amoral or even immoral character of administrators who have obtained such vast powers in recent times, Hummel has concluded in the most pessimistic tone that the growth of administrative power threatens democratic decision-making processes because he believes the public administration system is a closed, a political system, as contrasted to the open decision-making structure forged by the constitutional framers. Hummel contends that no matter how hard people may argue that the administrative system is open, it is unquestionably and exceptionally undemocratic and closed, a condition he perceives as a very poor substitute for the more democratic political process: "In combination with science, bureaucracy can calculate the cost of pursuing certain society-wide goals against others. In combination with technology, bureaucracy can administer most efficiently the pursuit of one set of goals against others. But there is nothing in the social relations, culture, psychology, language, and thought of the bureaucrat that gives him the capacity to replace the political philosopher or the political process. Unfortunately, there is, of course, all the power in the world available to him and no reason to think that the bureaucrat will restrain himself from the use of power any more than any of the rulers who preceded him."[64]

However, Louis L. Jaffe and Nathaniel L. Nathanson regard such pessimism as an overreaction to the nation's increasing reliance on agency experts. They do not believe that the shared powers doctrine has been seriously threatened by the growth of administrative expertise. In fact, Jaffe and Nathanson argue that those who contend that the separation-of-powers doctrine has been eroded by the new policy-making role given to administrators fail to understand the intended purpose of the doctrine: "We should in sum keep in mind that the great end of the theory is, by dispersing in some measure the centers of authority, to prevent absolutism. It is not eternally to stratify our governmental arrangements in the particular mold of 1789, or any other date."[65]

Challenges to Popular Government   Naturally, the trend toward depoliticizing the public policy-making process, as Hummel suggests, would have to challenge the democratic ideal of popular government as conceptualized by our founding fathers. But the growth of administrative expertise has created a question: How popular can a government be if public policy choice is largely left in the hands of administrators, not popularly elected political leaders? Clearly, according to the principles of popular government theory, public policy decisions should be made by political leaders under the watchful eye of the public. But Freedman holds that the arena for political debate and political decisions has shifted from true political institutions to administrative agencies.[66]

However, even if policy decisions have been transferred to nonelected governmental officials as the administrative state has developed, the popular government ideal could still remain in salvageable condition as long as the public could exert reasonable influence and retain sufficient control over the policy-making processes of public administrators. But scholarly opinion raises great doubt about such a possibility. In general, they hold that despite the efforts to promote public participation and control over administrative decision making so that democratic accountability can be preserved, public bureaucracy has been successful in resisting attempts by freedom-lovers to open the administrative process to the public. Indeed, the critics claim, the Freedom of Information Act, "sunshine" laws overall, citizen groups, liberal politicians condemning closed-door bureaucratic decision making, efforts to create effective ombudsman offices, notice and comment rule-making, even including subsidized citizen commentary, and the like, have all failed to keep open the doors of bureaucracy.[67] To Robert Alford, efforts to make public agencies an open forum for debating public policy issues have failed simply because "the principles of bureaucracy and participation are to some extent incompatible."[68] He contends, in what is basically an old Weberian insight, that public participation tends to undermine administrative expertise: "Bureaucratization implies the insulation of decision-makers from outside influences, by definition not as competent as experts are to judge the relevant range of facts, nor to balance the objectives desired. Participation implies the right and duty of the public to intervene in the determination of decisions."[69]

However, in *The Politics of Expertise,* Guy Benveniste made clear that the public is largely to blame for promoting what has become known as "anemic democracy," a condition in which the people distrust their government, yet create a "demand overload" situation for it by expecting government to tackle and cure all conceivable social ills.[70] Benveniste says this places administrative experts in a no-win situation because their regulatory expertise is demanded, but the use of their apolitical expertise is considered illegitimate (echoes of Freedman). A real challenge for our political system, if it is in fact possible—and some observers feel it is not—is to develop a capacity for limited and meaningful public participation in the administrative process without destroying the obvious advantages of expertise. Weber's insight that specialists have been employed by bureaucracy because of their expert knowledge should not be played down; if it is, another brand of spoils government will emerge which will be even more democratically irresponsible.

Challenges to Individualism   Americans have always, at least in spirit, cherished the principle of individualism. As children, we were taught that rugged individuals built the United States from nothing. Individualism is what has made this nation great! We were told further that dependence on others is a sure sign of weakness. We should learn to go it alone and to stand tall, on our own two feet. The mark of a successful individual has been one who has found financial independence by no later than age twenty-five. Americans have traditionally condemned socialism and communism for various reasons, but probably a major reason was that these economic and political systems restrict individual choice. (Administrative law in the American political system cannot be understood clearly unless its applications to administrative regulatory behavior are perceived within the capitalist, free-market ideals which Americans still endorse.) At least in principle, Americans still support capitalism, the theory of which emphasizes the virtues of individualism. No wonder, in this light, the American people in general are so afraid of what governmental regulations may do to them as individuals. In such a capitalist country as the United States, regulatory agencies represent nothing much more than an assault on individualism and, if not on private individuals, certainly on private businesses.

It should not be forgotten that bureaucracy emerged out of the need to regulate society. Control is what regulatory agencies seek. Thus, administrative agencies may pretend to be otherwise, but they are control agents which must, in order to reach their regulatory goals, to some extent destroy the freedom of individuals. Defenders of the growth of the public administrative system argue that public agencies are needed to protect individuals from stronger and potentially tyrannical forces. To a certain extent administrative agencies do accomplish this end, but governmental efforts to protect individuals from others (for example, from airplane hijackers) have simultaneously, and often justifiably, encroached upon the freedom and privacy of individuals (in the case of hijack prevention, annoying, inconvenient, and sometimes embarrassing airport preboarding body searches are employed). The Reagan administration created controversy by demanding that federal employees submit to mandatory urine tests to check for drug use. To Ralph Hummel, governmental regulation has succeeded in destroying an individual's ability to regulate himself or herself. The regulators in bureaucracy, he asserts, have caused individuals to lose their integrity: "The bureaucratic relationship has trained us to look always upward toward superiors. Culturally, what we look to them for is the answer to the question what is good or bad for us; bureaucracy has made it impossible to maintain personal norms. Psychologically, the process of bureaucratization has destroyed the integrity of the individual, made him into a being of dependency, and opened up his reservoir of human needs (the id) to direct manipulation from the outside."[71]

Lewis Mainzer also entertains the possibility that administrative agencies have tended to destroy the democratic ideal of individualism. Focusing mostly on the effects of rules and regulations upon agency employees themselves, he notes that "regulations replace judgment in bureaucracy, thereby permitting equal treatment of citizens and lessening the talent or experience required for reaching a judgment. Reliance on precedent and rules seems to deprive the bureaucrats of creative possibilities, of personal judgment."[72] The bureaucratic hierarchy, as well as bureaucracy's rules and regulations, may be functioning to the detriment of individualism, but Mainzer concludes that the charges against bureaucracy have been greatly exaggerated.

Mainzer is most likely correct. Despite talk about how the government's regulatory machinery has destroyed the minds of America's rugged individualists, hard evidence does not suggest this to be true. The regulated have in general been able to exert their individual preferences and manipulate the regulators. Private businesses are still quite independent, despite some successful regulatory efforts, and individual citizens still remain quite free to do what they like as far as should be permitted in any society which places some reasonable emphasis on the worth of social order.[73]

Challenges to Political Equality   Political equality does not imply that the polity must or should treat everyone identically under law. Obviously, various forms of political inequalities have been sanctioned by U.S. political leaders (some very sensitive to democratic values), upheld by the courts, and given tacit approval by the general public. Clearly, our federal income tax system, which is based roughly upon one's ability to pay, runs contrary to the equal protection principle. That is, in a sense, some must pay more than others for equal political representation. The U.S. governmental system has also denied political equality to certain groups. For example, those under eighteen and convicted felons are forbidden the right to vote in federal elections.

However, denial of equal protection under law (originally, the concept only applied to the states under the Fourteenth Amendment, but in several consistent decisions the courts applied the concept to the federal government through the due process clause of the Fifth Amendment) has been prohibited by the courts if unreasonable classifications of people are used to deny persons or groups equal protection due process rights. Consequently, while the government has been allowed to place taxpayers in different income categories so that they can be taxed unequally, according to their different tax classifications, the courts have forbidden the government (for example, public administrators) from classifying persons into groups according to race, religion, national origin, sex, or social class for the purpose of subjecting particular groups of people to unequal treatment. Some critics consider such classifications unreasonable whether devised by legislators or administrators, since they are related neither to legitimate governmental functions nor to the proper ends of government in this constitutional democracy.

Although political inequality has been outlawed as an unconstitutional principle, in practice U.S. governmental institutions, including administrative agencies, have historically not granted complete political equality to all persons or groups. The history of sexual and racial discrimination in the United States is well known and has tarnished the image of America as a nation that should be respected for upholding the principle of political equality. Even a cursory examination of the latest *Statistical Abstract of the United States* clearly reveals that, despite efforts to reverse the historical trend, the impact of discriminatory practices against women, blacks, and other underrepresented groups has placed them in inferior positions today, as compared with other groups which have historically enjoyed a favored position in our society. For example, the employment, job status, and pay of women, blacks, and other groups that have historically been discriminated against show poorly compared with those of white males, especially outside the federal civil service system.[74]

Inequality under the law led to the development of various plans aimed at eliminating political and social inequality in our society. Affirmative action programs today are specifically aimed at rectifying past sexual and racial discriminatory practices by government and by society in general. In sum, affirmative action programs, administered by a variety of governmental agencies, require all governmental agencies or any private institutions receiving public funds (for example, large companies on governmental contracts or universities receiving governmental grants) to design, implement, and evaluate in good faith a program aimed at compensation for past discriminatory practices. Affirmative action should not be confused with equal opportunity legislation, an example of which is fair housing laws, since equal opportunity laws only prohibit unequal treatment, while affirmative action calls for special compensatory measures aimed at correcting past mistreatment of certain groups. Affirmative action has been vehemently opposed by those who argue that the concept is based upon the erroneous assumption that two wrongs make a right. Specifically, opponents of affirmative action hold that affirmative action programs amount to nothing more than what they call reverse discrimination, which violates the due process and equal protection clauses of the Fifth and Fourteenth Amendments. By the 1996 presidential election, given the lackluster support for affirmative action by both Republican and Democratic nominees, Robert Dole and Bill Clinton, it appears that the end is near for affirmative action, evidently because most Americans oppose the "political inequality" that it has created.

Administrative Law and Political Equality: A Concluding Note   Although administrative law focuses frequently on the procedural problems pertaining to equal protection provisions of statutes and internal agency rules and regulations, considerable attention is devoted to how equally agency administrators treat those who deal with their agencies. The democratic ideal, eloquently set forth in the writings of Max Weber, is that administrators should treat all persons having business with their agencies in an objective, professional, and impersonal fashion.[75] According to democratic theory, in the context of modern bureaucracy, the paying of special favors to individuals or groups is not only unprofessional and unethical, but it is also flatly illegal. According to Victor A. Thompson, this is so because modern bureaucracy is not a compassionate human system, but an impersonal formal system rooted in the rule of law. The rule-of-law principle compels bureaucrats to treat all individuals equally, thus making the granting of a favor an illegitimate act.[76]

However, administrators do not always act impartially but in fact favor certain parties over others. James Freedman has commented that the preferential treatment given to special interests, commonly leading to eventual control by specific industries over particular agencies, has long been recognized and, unfortunately, "has had a deleterious effect on the legitimacy of the administrative process by calling into question its independence and integrity."[77]

Political scientists have held since day one that the social inequality so blatant in our society stems largely from the inability of certain groups to influence the governmental decision-making process to their benefit. As the argument goes, groups in society cannot logically expect to be given a fair shake unless they are allowed an equal opportunity to influence our government's decision makers. Formally, of course, the U.S. political system seems to allow relatively equal access and participation in the decision-making processes. But as Jeffrey L. Jowell stressed in *Law And Bureaucracy*, "the mere existence of formal channels does not itself ensure democratic decision making. Rule-making procedures, for example, ideally allow consultation of affected interests and an implicit assurance that the rules will substantially reflect the merits of the arguments presented."[78] He concluded that "rule-making procedures may be used by an administrative agency to give an impression of participation, whereas no more than *pro forma* adherence to an empty democratic ritual was involved."[79] Jowell's contention that the rule-making process is not very open in reality is supported by Murray Edelman's thesis that the myth of open rule-making represents just another "symbolic reassurance" employed by our government to deceive the public into believing that the U.S. political system is functioning in a more democratic manner than it really is.[80]

Jowell asked, "How can the opportunity of access to bureaucracy be equalized in fact?"[81] This is a crucial question which the United States must address as a society in the future—one which poses special challenges for students of administrative law as agency power increases in power and scope—because it will remain highly unlikely that the social benefits can be expected to be fairly and equally distributed if de facto equal access to the politicoadministrative decision-making process remains closed.

REGULATING IN THE PUBLIC INTEREST: REGULATION VERSUS DEREGULATION

No one living in the United States today could truly imagine what it would be like to live in a society where no form of governmental regulation existed, for it was popular demand for an orderly society that gave rise to the proliferation of governmental regulations. In the absence of any state regulation, all reasonable persons should conclude, a society would be in a constant chaotic condition. Obviously, a degree of governmental regulation serves the public interest, and the promotion of the public interest is the most basic reason that can be given to justify state regulatory activities. It should be quite clear by now that the administrative system's growth was largely due to government's efforts to regulate those activities that society believed should be regulated.

But precisely what is governmental regulation, and what are the chief goals of our regulators? Governmental regulation basically consists of any efforts aimed at resolving various defects or failures in the open, or free, marketplace. Governmental regulation is especially concerned with protecting businesses from ruthless, cutthroat competition, blocking the emergence of monopoly power, and protecting consumers from rip-off prices for merchandise (especially due to price fixing among producers and sellers), unsafe products, and unfair and illegal business practices in general. But all governmental regulation is directed to some extent at controlling the selfish interests of private parties in the social system so that the larger public interest will not be placed in serious jeopardy.[82] Louis M. Kohlmeier, Jr., acknowledged that governmental regulation is quite varied and can mean many things, but he stressed that "all regulation is government direction of private economic endeavor and all regulation tends to produce similar economic consequences which are in conflict with the basic definitions of competition and with antitrust law."[83] To Kohlmeier, the original purpose of federal regulation in the United States was to keep prices lower, but this modest objective was soon abandoned for more comprehensive and ambitious regulatory goals. Consequently, according to Kohlmeier, individual freedoms guaranteed in the Bill of Rights have been compromised by congressional and judicial approval of regulatory expansionism: "Thus has the Constitution been read and reread over nearly two hundred years to gauge the power of the federal government to regulate the nation's commerce and to discipline the exercise of that power within the government. As it turns out, there are in the Bill of Rights no absolute guarantees of freedom of private conduct from government interference."[84] Although governmental regulation in the United States has been more confined to the control of the ownership and management of private property, particularly in connection with business endeavors, virtually all social activities have come under government's regulatory sphere. Nevertheless, as Kohlmeier recognized, "Freedom of private conduct is a relative matter. Freedom of speech, of the press and of religious practice were and are relatively more absolute than freedom to own and manage private property."[85] To many persons this may appear ironic since so many scholars have held that the Constitution was designed largely by the economic elite, influenced heavily by the leading capitalist theorists, primarily to protect and promote private property rights. However, others do present credible arguments supporting the contention that business people seeking a relatively stable and predictable marketplace from the very beginning favored a constitutional system which permitted at least limited regulation of business use of private property.

However, despite the belief during the late 1700s that government should play a restricted regulatory role, the laissez-faire philosophy, symbolized by the expression *caveat emptor* (let the buyer beware), dominated the thinking of that era.[86] But by the 1960s the *caveat emptor* philosophy had been replaced by the functional doctrine of *caveat venditor* (let the seller beware). *Caveat venditor,* in many respects a symbol of the modern welfare state, stands in firm opposition to the principles of laissez-faire capitalism which promoted relatively free-swinging, selfish, exploitive, and cruel business practices during the nineteenth century. At least according to public opinion, *caveat venditor* is presently a broadly accepted ideology that embraces the attitude that economic life is too critical to society's general well being to be left unregulated. For example, even though during the Reagan years a less preregulatory attitude existed than just years before, toward the end of the Reagan era only a minority of Americans (38 percent in 1987), probably shaken by what deregulation apparently caused in the savings and loan industry, believed we had "too much" governmental regulation. During the 1992 presidential year, polls were showing that Americans strongly favored expanded regulation in various socioeconomic and political areas.[87] It is apparent that for many decades, now, most Americans have generally favored rather widespread governmental regulation. But what over the years brought on the eventual replacement of the *caveat emptor* philosophy with the prevailing proregulatory attitude epitomized by *caveat emptor?*

Arguments for Governmental Regulation

Historically speaking, governmental regulation has, of course, always existed because, as recognized by Carol Tucker Foreman and Maureen S. Steinbruner, ". . . almost every human activity has the potential to injure someone . . . ."[88] As nations developed at different times in world history, governmental regulation expanded to order the increasing complexities in society. Thus, although the colonists came to America largely to escape the various regulatory controls imposed on them in their native countries, as America matured, this nation also was destined to follow the same historical course. Societal complexity simply requires relatively comprehensive governmental regulation; Henry Jacoby has written at some length on the phenomenon of increased governmental regulation as an inevitable outgrowth of a developing society.[89] Certainly, expanding governmental regulation can be witnessed in developing Third World nations today. Like it or not, modern life demands some national, centralized control and organization; this translates into governmental regulations. For a sophisticated argument on the need for governmental regulations, one does not need to consult the writings of contemporary political scientists or administrative law scholars. Plato, in the *Republic,* presented a superb argument for the absolute necessity of governmental regulation if the polity is to achieve at least some degree of vital social harmony. Plato reasoned that the parts of the state must be coordinated for the good of whole (that is, the public interest).[90]

Kaufman on Regulation   In *Red Tape: Its Origins, Uses, and Abuses,* Herbert Kaufman presents an ardent argument in defense of the need for governmental regulation, or red tape. Kaufman asserts that while everyone seems to abhor their existence, regulations are everywhere. This mystery led him to pose and research the question: "How can any product of the human mind be so unpopular yet so widespread and enduring?"[91] In general, Kaufman concluded, as have so many, that popular demand justified comprehensive governmental regulation. Specifically, Kaufman discovered that regulations can be justified because governmental regulatory efforts have increased the compassion, fairness, and democratic accountability of American government.[92]

Kaufman believes a compassionate government cannot sit back and allow members of society to exploit one another. Selfish acts by individuals can cause harm to come to other persons, especially those who are not capable of protecting themselves. Consequently, a compassionate government must devise and employ regulations to protect people from other members of society. He emphasizes in particular that red tape should be used to regulate relations between buyer and seller with an eye toward "preventing injuries *before* they occur."[93] The FAA and the NRC are just two highly visible federal regulatory agencies which are largely responsible for preventing dangerous accidents from occurring in the future. Regulations were also promoted by the government's interest in protecting people from hardships—many due to circumstances beyond the control of the affected individuals. Thus, regulatory government grew because the government has tried to help, for instance, the victims of natural disasters (for example, the flood victims in the midwest in 1993 and the earthquake victims in Los Angeles in 1994); farmers who have become victims of shifting economic policies; handicapped veterans; and mothers with dependent children. The government's efforts to prevent such painful disruptions to the social system as worker strikes, inflation, and unemployment have also required the institution of certain regulations.[94]

The public demand that government act in a fair manner when executing its tasks provides still another reason for the existence of governmental regulations. Due process procedures (regulations), an admirable and vital trait of democratic government, fill seemingly endless volumes in the *Federal Register* and the *Code of Federal Regulations.* (The Administrative Procedure Act of 1946 requires federal agencies to publish, among other things, their rules and regulations. These rules and regulations are then codified in the *Code of Federal Regulations.*) But these regulations provide essential safeguards for persons interacting with government and for those who may be affected by the implementation of certain public policies, thus justifying their usefulness. Of course, Kaufman contends, the demand for an open, representative, and democratically accountable government has increased the regulatory burden of government. Nevertheless, fundamental fairness, he holds, must bow to implementation simplicity in a pluralist society: "Old or new, the methods of interest group representation generate more directives and controls, more steps in the forging of governmental policies, more bargaining before decisions are reached, and more postdecision litigation than would otherwise develop. Fairness, comprehensiveness, and community acceptance of policy decisions obviously rate higher than administrative simplicity and speed."[95]

Gellhorn on Regulation   In a memorial lecture presented at Saint Louis University entitled "Deregulation or Delusion," the eminent administrative law scholar Walter Gellhorn persuasively argued for the need for governmental regulations by sharply attacking the proponents of deregulation.[96] Gellhorn noted that most deregulation arguments stem from a simplistic holding that the United States can feasibly return to a laissez-faire governmental process. Bureaucrats have grown in number, he stressed, because they are needed to assist government in coping with the various social problems that have emerged. He was quick to point out that more societal problems emerge when regulatory controls are absent than when they exist. Our administrative agencies are unlikely to win popularity contests, Gellhorn asserted, despite the fact that they are very necessary. To Gellhorn, administrators are the consequence of our society's problems, certainly not the cause.

In this lecture Gellhorn conveyed his great respect for the capabilities of public administrators and the positive contributions of U.S. regulatory agencies. He essentially argued that administrative experts have been given a bum rap and have not been appreciated, despite their successful regulatory accomplishments. But Gellhorn was not blind to the problems which prevail in our administrative system. Obviously, he acknowledged, some regulations are ill-designed and archaic. Such regulations should be either abandoned or redesigned so that they are up-to-date. From the very first year of the republic, Gellhorn maintained, public administrators have been called upon to cope with social problems. A systems theorist would say that Gellhorn argued that public dissatisfactions led to the demand for regulatory control; thus our regulatory agencies indeed reflect a responsible and appropriate democratic response to popular demands on government. Unquestionably, he implied, U.S. public agencies are legitimate, democratically sanctioned institutions supported by a popular mandate. Gellhorn believes that administrative tinkering has brought more overall good than harm to this country. The Great Depression, he noted, was so severe because governmental manipulation of the economy was virtually nonexistent. But since the government's regulators have been tinkering with the economy, he exclaimed, the United States has not had very steep inflations or deep recessions, despite claims to the contrary.

"Should we allow the market to regulate itself naturally?" Gellhorn asked. In some cases he feels the market should be permitted to regulate freely, but he urged that society must be selective in what the market is allowed to control. Surely, Gellhorn asserted, we cannot safely rely on the market to regulate in society's best interest. Too many horror stories remind us of how special interests have acted selfishly and in a fashion contradictory to the nation's general welfare (for example, the reckless dumping of toxic waste, environmentally destructive strip-mining, and owner-caused mine disasters). Unfortunately, Gellhorn noted, businesses have assumed the dangerous attitude that what isn't forbidden by agency regulation should be left to free market decisions. But he warned that private entrepreneurial decisions normally focus on the short run, while governmental planners tend to focus on the long-term consequences of contemplated actions. Free market regulation cannot work, Gellhorn argued, if essential information required for intelligent social planning is held in secret by various private enterprise. Even consumers cannot make wise market choices if they cannot obtain the necessary information about services and products. Consumer advocates such as Ralph Nader have done much to protect consumer interests, but more pervasive governmental regulatory activities are necessary to defend people against sometimes selfish business operations. It cannot be forgotten, Gellhorn underscored, that businesses are primarily concerned with making high profits. Strip-mining businesses were not run by evil people, he pointed out, but by people who did what was natural to get coal out of the ground as cheaply as possible. Governmental regulation is needed to check such short-term business ventures. Gellhorn does not want selfish business motives to determine, for example, the future condition of this nation's environment. Regulation, he insisted, is required before irreparable damages occur.

Breyer on Regulation   Walter Gellhorn, in his St. Louis lecture, clearly presented some credible justifications for governmental regulation. Stephen Breyer also defends the need for governmental regulation, although he argues, like Gellhorn, that there is much room for improving traditional regulatory methods.[97]

Breyer's starting point in justifying the need for regulation is not unique. His framework for examining various regulatory methods assumes "that regulation is *justified* only if it achieves without too great a corresponding cost policy objectives that a consensus of reasonable observers would consider to be in the public interest."[98] Breyer is open to the question of what should be considered to be in the public interest. In analyzing the worth of regulatory approaches (programs), he holds that they should ultimately be evaluated on the basis of their public interest content, even if they also happen to benefit special interests. In his analytical framework, Breyer assumes that the unregulated marketplace should be considered the norm. Thus it becomes essential for all governmental regulation to be justified by demonstrating that the regulatory activity can accomplish important public policy objectives that the unregulated market cannot bring about. However, certain market failures have justified to Breyer the need for governmental intervention because the regulatory action appears clearly to promote the public welfare.[99]

Controlling monopoly power can be justified on the grounds that regulation can keep prices and profits of the "natural monopolists" within reasonable public interest limits. Specifically, regulation here is aimed at achieving "allocative efficiency," where the costs of producing the product or service are linked to the price of these products or services if they were sold in the competitive marketplace. Despite arguments by free market advocates that natural monopolists would keep prices and profits down naturally by charging only what the market would tolerate, thereby maximizing allocative efficiency, Breyer is not convinced that the public would be protected. But, he says, "Nonetheless, as long as one believes that, without regulation, the firm will raise prices substantially, one can reasonably argue that regulated prices will *help* achieve allocative efficiency."[100]

Breyer's second point is that preventing windfall profits is also a noble regulatory end. In essence, windfall profits are made by "lucky" changes in the marketplace which cause owners of a commodity to make "excessive" profits. Breyer points out that such windfall profits are normally allowed, but when they "are great in amount and do not reflect any particular talent or skill on the part of producers, there is sometimes a demand for regulation. The object of the regulation is to transfer these 'undeserved windfall profits' from producers or owners of the scarce resources to consumers or taxpayers."[101]

Breyer's third point is that regulation should be employed to correct spillover costs. Spillovers are really additional costs to society (for example, pollution of the air and waters) that have not been absorbed by the companies, but instead imposed on society. Why should society pay for such social costs as cleaning up rivers and lakes if private companies, not society, are responsible for them? Breyer argues that it should not. Governmental regulators such as the Environmental Protection Agency are needed to make producers include reasonable social costs (for example, the cost of anti-air pollution scrubbers) in their total costs of production.[102]

Breyer's fourth point is that regulation is necessary to force private enterprises to release certain information which the public has a right to know. To Breyer, information itself should be regarded as a valuable commodity. The public needs information to help it evaluate various services and products in the competitive marketplace. The release of information helps to keep the marketplace competitive, thus leading to more intelligent consumer purchases, which in turn should keep prices down. Disclosure of information is particularly useful to guard against the purposeful misleading of consumers by sellers. Information may also be required to be released in a certain form so that it can be more easily understood; for example, in recent years states have been requiring insurance companies to write their policies so that it doesn't take a Philadelphia lawyer to decode what is in the policy.[103]

Breyer's fifth point is that governmental regulation should also be used to prevent excessive and counterproductive competition. His chief argument is that under certain conditions it is in the public interest to protect particular firms from excessive competition so that needed businesses will not be bankrupted. For example, the railroads have often argued that their demise was largely due to the government's allowing truckers to go virtually unregulated, thus permitting the trucking industry to steal from them their most profitable business. Regulating against excessive competition, Breyer adds, has also been employed to stop predatory pricing. Predatory pricing, as seen in price wars, has been used by financially powerful and stable companies to drive competitors out of business. Regulations have also been used to keep new competition from entering the market if the regulators believed that increased competition would actually create unnecessary hardships on the existing companies (for example, public utilities with fixed operating costs and investments to protect), as well as consumers (who, in the case of utilities, might have to pay higher prices in the long run). However, Breyer does not generally feel that rigorous agency regulations should be used to prevent excessive competition. He contends that the public interest could be served better by deregulation in this one area, as long as antitrust laws are enforced to guard against the unlikely possibility that excessive competition may eventually lead to the creation of natural monopolies.[104]

Breyer's sixth point is that it has been argued that regulations should be improved to guard against "moral hazards" which occur when "someone other than a buyer pays for the buyer's purchases."[105] Because the buyer is not responsible for the payment, the buyer may irresponsibly purchase goods and services. Breyer notes that soaring medical costs are due in part to irresponsible and excessive use of medical services. This has placed a great financial burden on government resources since the government has become increasingly obligated to pick up the tab.[106]

Breyer's last major justification for governmental regulation is that the government, through regulatory supervision and coordination, can stimulate industrywide rationalization. Breyer's main contention here is that the public would benefit if the government in general managed industrywide development. Governmental intervention could lead to sensible cooperative planning and growth, which inevitably could yield increased efficiency and lower costs.[107]

In summary, Breyer enthusiastically supports traditional governmental regulatory methods, as long as they further the promotion of the public interest. He concludes that regulatory reform is required and that the reform measures should entail generally "less restrictive alternatives" to classical regulatory approaches, including in some cases partial deregulation.[108]

Antiregulation and Deregulation Arguments

Few today, whether scholars or everyday citizens, believe that governmental regulation is not essential. Evidently, experience and the weight of proregulation arguments have been persuasive. Nevertheless, some still argue that governmental regulation is not necessary or at least hold that only very limited regulation of the private sector is warranted. Even the most vocal supporters of governmental regulation would have to admit that governmental regulation has not always served this nation well. According to Herbert Kaufman, our regulatory processes have been generally criticized for imposing too many pointless, irrelevant, duplicative, contradictory, and inconsistent constraints. Some frustrated business executives have even exclaimed that it is impossible to comply with one agency's regulations without violating another's requirements. Once more, Kaufman acknowledges, many outdated regulations are kept alive by simple bureaucratic inertia. Regulations are also linked to program failures and perceived as awkward, too slow, and oppressive. Kaufman states that regulation horror stories are so commonplace among the regulators and the regulated that sound regulations are not noticed or appreciated.[109] Even if some worth is seen in the regulations, critics frequently charge that the regulations are too costly to justify it. James G. Cook, a specialist in technological development, has been quoted as arguing that regulations have stifled creativity and innovation in American business, thus making it difficult to justify the cost-effectiveness of the regulations. Cook believes governmental regulations have hindered individual and corporate creativity at a time when "our country's continued prosperity depends on a renewed leadership in technology and science to keep pace with strides being made by other nations."[110] However, Robert B. Reich does not blame public administrators for the voluminous, nit-picking regulations. "The underlying problem has nothing to do with nefarious forces hidden within regulatory agencies; it is inherent in the American regulatory process itself."[111] He specifically contends that businesses, employing their lawyers to take advantage of every loophole in governmental regulations, cause agencies to respond with more detailed regulations year after year in an effort to close the loopholes.[112] For example, in 1992 the government, upset with soaring cable television rates under deregulation, reregulated the cable television industry, improving new regulations to curb "runaway" basic cable rate hikes. However, exploiting the regulatory loopholes, the cable industry shocked most cable subscribers by raising their cable rates even more. In response, the regulators in 1994 promulgated more elaborate regulations to close the loopholes to stop the "excessive" charges.

Private Property Should Not Be Regulated   Since the first attempts to regulate the use of private property, there have been people who opposed such regulation on the grounds that it violates Bill of Rights guarantees, especially as found in the Fourth and Fifth Amendments. To these people, private property is sacred, and as far as they are concerned, the Constitution was originally drafted to protect property rights. The argument that the regulation of private property is sometimes necessary to protect the public interest means virtually nothing to them, for they strongly believe that private property rights should not be sacrificed for public welfare goals. They also tend to cling to Adam Smith's notion, articulated in the eighteenth century, that the pursuit of private interests is consistent with the public interest.[113] Foreman and Steinbruner concluded that the Reagan administration seemed to think that society's needs could ". . . be served by the unfettered pursuit of private interest," thus it opposed ". . . the very idea of regulation."[114] Today, a relatively small but vocal percentage of Americans even associate government regulation with communism. It is from this extreme position that some particularly emotional protests against governmental regulation must be understood.

The courts, however, have not been very sympathetic with the claim that private property rights should come before the welfare of the general public. In an early case, *Charles River Bridge* v. *Warren Bridge*, 11 Peters 420, 548 (1837), the U.S. Supreme Court did maintain that property rights should be "sacredly guarded," but concluded, nevertheless, that "we must not forget that the community also have rights, and that the happiness and well being of every citizen depends on their [the community's] faithful preservation." Chief Justice Roger Tandy's position in the *Charles River Bridge* case was affirmed in *Munn* v. *Illinois*, 94 U.S. 113 (1876). According to Louis Kohlmeier, Jr., the *Munn* case represents a "major decision in the definition of private property and public rights," and this precedential decision has supported "all the regulation of business that has come after."[115] In *Munn*, the Court also emphasized the primary importance of the public welfare, arguing that the Granger laws were justified because they sought to regulate private property rights (the business operations of elevators and railroads) that were crucially linked to public interest rights. Particularly disturbing to those who opposed the regulation of private interests was the Court's opinion that states should be able to regulate any business operations significantly affecting the public interest, regardless of the monopolistic status of the enterprise or state franchise laws. This holding expanded *Charles River Bridge* since in this case Chief Justice Roger Tandy only upheld the constitutional power of a state to regulate businesses because they were monopolies or franchises. In *Cottonwood Mall Shop Ctr., Inc.* v. *Utah Power and Light Co.*, 440 F.2d 36, 43, 1971 (*certiorari denied*, 404 U.S. 857), the court once again relied upon

Munn to justify the legislative trend, which has given to regulatory agencies "almost limitless power to regulate private commercial activity" over the years. Thus, happily or unhappily, the regulation of private property rights for the purpose of prompting the public interest has had strong consistent court support for about a century and a half.

The Free Market Is the Best Regulator   It is difficult for me, as well the vast majority of social scientists, to retain objectivity when discussing the contentions of those who argue that the free market system can provide regulations which are in the best interests of our society. Clearly, governmental regulators have not always served us well, but the natural regulatory failures of the free market system have been demonstrably worse, bringing terrible hardships and suffering to Americans, as seen in cases of child abuse, exploitation of adult workers, consumer ripoffs, formation of tyrannical commercial enterprises, pollution of our environment by selfish profiteers, and the like. Few social scientists are convinced that the free (that is, unregulated) competition between selfish interests could yield anything but chaos in a nation as large and complex as ours, or accept the patently absurd argument, epitomizing free market economics, that what's good for GM is good for America. Peter L. Kahn maintains that antiregulation arguments are rooted in the assumption that free market competition can produce desirable results for society. However, he asserts, when the free marketplace fails to produce attractive results, governmental regulation becomes suddenly quite appealing. Kahn concludes that governmental regulation may not be always perfect, but it may on occasion serve society better than the sometimes "flawed alternative" of the free market.[116]

It should be made clear that some of the antiregulation arguments do make theoretical and practical sense, especially on a micro level, but they generally fail to adequately consider the broader implications for the entire social system. That is, one could concede that free market competition would eventually provide checks against fluctuation in the natural business cycle (between inflations and depressions), but what effects would the extremes of the natural business cycle have on the people? One could also find plausible the free market theorists' argument that protective tariffs, Federal Reserve Board monetary controls, the imposition of price ceilings, and so on, simply provide artificial checks, as opposed to natural free market controls, which can only forestall the inevitable—for example, inflation—from occurring. Nevertheless, governmental tinkering with the economy, as Walter Gellhorn asserted, seems to prevent the cruel excesses of the economic cycle.

One of the most popular and basic arguments in favor of deregulation has always been that open market competition will naturally lead to the most efficient production of quality merchandise or services at the lowest competitive cost to consumers. In 1958, in *Northern Pacific Railway Co. v. U.S.*, 356 U.S. 1, 4, Justice Hugo Black wrote in defense of the free market system that it "rests on the premise that the unrestrained interaction of competitive forces will yield the best allocation of our economic resources, the lowest prices, the highest quality and the greatest material progress, while at the same time providing an environment conducive to the preservation of our democratic, political and social institutions." It is doubtful that any empirical evidence could be offered to support the claim that free market competition leads "to the preservation of our democratic, political and social institutions," especially since free market competition inevitably tends to lead to the development of monopoly power by those who have survived the forces of free-wheeling, cutthroat competition over the decades. Social Darwinism suggests that the end of survival-of-the-fittest-type competition among competitive firms in an industry produces monopoly control or at least oligarchical control over goods production or service delivery. Since monopoly or oligarchical power means power by one or a few, respectively, the ends of free market competition could hardly be consistent with democratic or social principles. Also, history has shown that once markets are dominated by one or a few companies, prices soar while service and product quality tend to decline because, it is suspected, the necessary competitive forces do not exist to keep prices down (informal price fixing can easily take place among a few competitors). Ironically, Justice Black, despite his praise for the free market system, held that regulation is required to keep the free market free! Of course, the implication here is that the free market is not capable of keeping itself free. Thus, Justice Black upheld the regulatory powers of the Sherman Act, declaring the act to be "a comprehensive charter of economic liberty" (at 84). Black thus echoed the wisdom of Jean-Jacques Rousseau who in essence argued in *Social Contract* that men must be forced (regulated) to be free.[117]

Free market competition advocates argue that governmental regulation has unfortunately promoted the welfare of special interests by allowing the regulated industries to capture and dominate the regulatory agencies. Peter Kahn summarizes quite well the argument of the antiregulation advocates. "In the gritty real world, the theory goes, democratic government serves the interests of whichever interest group turns out to be the most powerful. Unfortunately, the dominant interest group is unlikely to be the general public. Economic regulation, as a result, . . . will not serve the public interest because it is not designed to do so."[118] No doubt this argument has some teeth because the typical life cycle of a regulatory agency seems to end in the capture of the agency by the industry. Much to the dismay of the general public, this has allegedly permitted regulated industries to increase prices unjustifiably and with the protective blessings of the regulatory agency. Legislation presented for the deregulation of the airline and trucking industries, sponsored by a unique and powerful liberal-conservative coalition, was rooted in the fundamental contention that deregulation would help encourage healthier competition once free of the anticompetitive clutches of the CAB and the ICC.

Airline Deregulation: An Assessment   Almost two decades have passed since the airlines were deregulated in 1978, giving us enough time to evaluate the impact of deregulation. I concluded in my last edition, in 1988, that airline deregulation had met with "moderate success." This tentative conclusion was reached because, despite many existing problems, the airline industry's profits were showing healthy profits during the mid-1980s, air fares had generally fallen, and flights to at least the major cities had increased.

However, much has changed in the airline industry since the mid-1980s, causing most critics to conclude that reregulation of the industry is needed because airline deregulation has been a clear failure. For example, in probably understating the case, Marc Eisner remarks that failures in the airline industry, as well as in other industries that have been deregulated, ". . . have stimulated debates concerning the need for regulation,"[119] while in probably overstating the case in forceful rhetoric, Paul Dempsey concludes that the airline industry must be reregulated ". . . since deregulation has been a catastrophic failure, for creditors, stockholders, labor, and yes, consumers."[120]

Figure 2.3 shows airline operating profits from 1975 to 1994. Note that immediately after deregulation profits dropped sharply due to cutthroat competition among different airlines. However, by the mid-1980s the surviving airlines began to show impressive profits. Healthy profits continued for a few years, reaching a peak profit of $3,437 million in 1988. But since 1988 operating profits for the airline industry have dropped sharply, debt has increased dramatically, and the financial resources needed to re-equip aging aircraft suggest that the airlines will be facing serious future problems. Dempsey, points out that the troubled airline industry ". . . has lost all the profits it earned since the Wright Brothers' flight at Kitty Hawk in 1903, plus $2 billion more" and that Americans are flying in ". . . the oldest and most repainted fleet of aircraft in the developed world."[121] Industry analysts claim that losses have been caused mostly by destructive unregulated competition which has forced some airlines to charge patently unprofitable low fares to compete with Chapter 11 airlines, which can charge ridiculously low rates because they are protected from their creditors by Chapter 11 bankruptcy provisions. Also, megacarriers have been allowed under deregulation to engage in predatory pricing to drive the smaller and financially weaker airlines into bankruptcy.[122] And of course the shaky financial condition of the airlines in recent years has caused many to be concerned about aircraft maintenance and safety.[123]

The impact deregulation has had on air fares is difficult to assess because the proliferation of so many "special" fares has confused not only travelers, but analysts as well. It is true that most passengers today obtain discounted fares, yet discounted fares are based upon full fare rates, which increased 156% in only the first decade after deregulation (twice the rate of inflation) and have continued to rise dramatically. Unquestionably, discount fares can be terrific bargains, but various restrictions usually apply, involving restricted flight times and destination cities, Saturday night stayovers, "no-frills" flights, and prepurchase of tickets with nontransfer and nonrefund stipulations which can prove inconvenient and sometimes very costly to travelers. Such restrictions under deregulation have made flying today complicated at times and not necessarily a great travel bargain when cost and inconveniences are considered.[124]

Many industry analysts predict that air fares will likely increase dramatically in the coming years; competition between the airlines is on the decline since few airlines are left to compete. Since deregulation, there have been more than 150

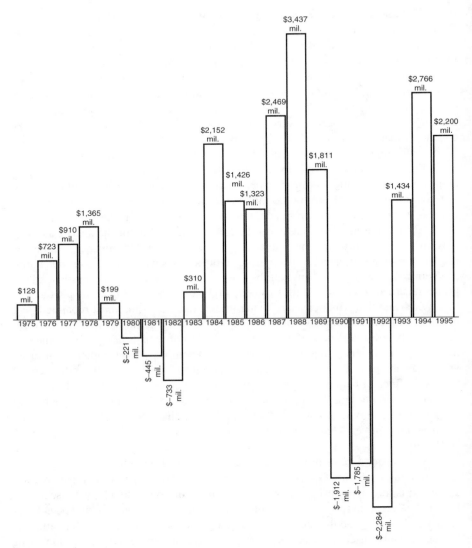

FIGURE 2.3   *Airline Operating Profits (in millions of dollars)*

Source: Air Transport, 1993 (Washington, D.C.: Air Transport Association of America, 1993), p. 3. The 1995 profit is based upon unpublished statistics obtained from Air Transport Assoc. in 1996.

bankruptcies and about fifty mergers, leaving only four airlines controlling approximately two-thirds of the market. Dempsey notes that "[B]y 1992, nearly 20 percent of the nation's fleet capacity was in bankruptcy. Of the 176 airlines to which deregulation gave birth, only one remains (America West) and, sadly, it too is in bankruptcy."[125]

'Back To The Drawing Board'

Source: Reprinted with permission of Tom Engelhardt and the *St. Louis Post-Dispatch,* March 15, 1991.

The impact of deregulation on smaller airlines and on "nonhub" cities has been tragic. Over the years since deregulation, cutthroat competition caused the weaker airlines to collapse, give way to hostile takeovers, or operate in the red for as long as they could. To meet the competition, airlines dropped their unprofitable routes to medium-sized and smaller cities, inconveniencing passengers and businesses dependent upon air service. Later, some of these cities would be serviced, at least for a while, by the smaller surviving airlines, but usually at a cost far above what passengers paid before deregulation.[126]

Supporters of airline deregulation believe that in the long run free market competition will strengthen and stabilize the airline industry and consumers and businesses will benefit from lower fares. They hold that airline users will not have to worry about having to pay excessive fares because other airlines will always be ready to "steal" dissatisfied customers. However, skeptics claim that history has shown repeatedly that ruthless, unregulated competition eventually serves only the remaining few, not the public interest. Whether airline deregulation has caused the problems the airline industry faces today is certainly debatable. It is possible, of course, that the airlines could have fared even worse if the industry had never been deregulated. However, it is true that the airline industry, almost twenty years after deregulation, is in much worse shape today than it was before deregulation. Is regulation the answer?

Regulatory Reform and the Future of Regulation

Several attempts at regulatory reform have been made since the New Deal. The deregulation experiment represented the last major reform movement, but deregulation failures have recently given rise to the reregulation movement which started during the Bush administration and has continued into the Clinton administration.

Over the decades regulatory forms have taken many broad forms. Thomas O. McGarity has classified regulatory forms into four types: substantive, procedural, structural, and cognitive.[127] *Substantive regulatory reform* aims at changing public policy outputs in administrative agencies through law making and rule making. Since the 1960s substantive changes in regulatory policy had the objective of making more progress in civil rights, consumerism, and environmental protection. An example of substantive reform was when in 1994 the Environmental Protection Agency issued a rule, authorized by the 1990 Clean Air Act, which will reduce air toxins more than ever before by severely limiting the amount of toxic air that can be released from chemical plants.[128] *Procedural regulatory reform* has focused on improving agency procedures in implementing regulatory policies. For example, procedural reform has led to negotiated rule making. *Structural reforms* have stressed restructuring agency decision making to allow environmental political actors greater or lesser influence over agency decision making. Such restructuring allowed President Reagan, and now President Clinton, to use the Office of Management and Budget to exert more control over agency rule making. *Cognitive regulatory reform* focuses on the way agencies perceive and assess regulatory problems. For example, cost-benefit analysis has been used in recent decades to determine the potential costs and benefits of proposed agency rules.[129]

So how should we evaluate regulatory reform leading to deregulation? McGarity holds that one lesson that can be learned from the deregulation movement "is that there is no inevitable march forward of the positive state."[130] However, the reality is that deregulation represents only a temporary retreat from the onward march of the positive state which, out of necessity, will inevitably become a more pervasive regulator. The deregulation movement is best characterized as reduced regulation anyway because virtually no socioeconomic or political activities go totally unregulated. And Paul Teske has noted that the reduced regulatory role played by federal regulators during deregulation ". . . led to an even more prominent role for the states in many regulatory arenas."[131]

Most observers predict that in the foreseeable future we can expect increased regulation and reregulation in most regulatory areas because of the alarming and well-publicized deregulation failures in such industries as communications, transportation, securities, and finance. For example, deregulation has caused havoc in the airline industry and it has allowed cable television customers to be charged rip-off rates by monopolistic cable companies in the communications industry. And as James Barth argues, deregulation in the savings and loan industry allowed corrupt and greedy savings and loan officers to irresponsibly manage savings and loan institutions, causing within only a few years the biggest business failure in American history, unfortunately sticking the American taxpayer with the bill of over $500 billion dollars.[132]

Inspired by the renewed reality that huge industries that have the potential to undermine the public interest must be regulated, a significant number of new regulatory and reregulatory laws and rules were passed during the Bush administration. This trend has continued at an accelerated pace under President Clinton, a proponent of positive, regulatory government. Clinton has pushed for substantive regulatory reforms in virtually everything from health care to the spotted owl.

Most ordinary people and businesses have learned to accept the "necessary evil" of government regulation. We should expect that in the future a stronger regulatory alliance will be formed between the government and the regulated businesses. Individuals will also be subjected to more red tape as government's obligation to promote the public interest intensifies. The courts will continue to complain about how big the government is and how un-American the regulators are. Yet the public will not, as individuals or groups, stop demanding that the government regulate the annoying behavior of the "other guy."

SUMMARY

The administrative system President Bill Clinton inherited is enormous, complex, and costly, especially when compared to the bureaucratic apparatus under President George Washington. But much has changed in America since the late 1700s which has necessitated the growth of public bureaucracy and the eventual maturation of administrative law. Systems theorists provide a solid conceptual framework for understanding why the administrative system developed as it did. Although there are many specific reasons which can be cited to explain administrative growth, these theorists contend that the administrative system grew largely in response to the increasing demands placed upon government by various interests in society that were concerned about various social and economic problems which troubled them. Government tried to resolve the different problems by creating public agencies. As U.S. socioeconomic institutions became more complex while American society matured, an increasing number of administrative agencies were created to regulate in the public interest.

The demand for more public services at both the national and state levels created a demand overload situation for legislators, who initially tried to handle in vain most of the regulatory problems themselves. It soon became apparent that legislators had to delegate the regulatory function to public administrators. At first administrators were given very limited powers to shape and implement public policies during the 1800s and early 1900s, but as pressures on Congress continued to mount, especially as a result of the massive socioeconomic problems of the 1930s, legislators expressed a strong desire to delegate significant policy-making powers to agency administrators, including vast authority to design, adjudicate, and implement agency policies. In *Curtis-Wright,* 299 U.S. 304 (1936), the United States Supreme Court permitted Congress to delegate broad powers to administrators as long as they attached meaningful standards to guide agency actions. However, for the past several decades the courts have allowed Congress to delegate broad policy-making powers to public administrators without the requirement of attaching meaningful standards. Although some state courts have been reluctant to permit such delegation, most have followed the path of the federal courts by upholding the constitutionality of standardless statutes which allow state administrators to assume powerful policy-making roles.

Consequently, administrative power in the 1990s is awesome. To some, the emergence of the new administrative state has eroded the principles of democratic governance and usurped individual liberties. Probably the hottest political topic today centers on what role government should play in regulating socioeconomic activities. This issue has been a major campaign issue in the political campaigns of the 1980s and 1990s and will continue to dominate political debates for the foreseeable future. Defenders of widespread governmental regulation basically argue that the regulators are necessary to protect and promote the public interest in modern society, especially by protecting the public from the selfishness of the large and mighty special interests. Those opposed to governmental regulations espouse a modified laissez-faire philosophy. They hold that the free market system is capable of providing the necessary regulatory controls. Besides, they maintain that the government has no right to encroach upon private property interests protected by the Constitution. Although there are few left who advocate no governmental regulation of private life, there are many who believe that governmental regulation is too extensive, too expensive, and too threatening to individual liberties. These people were successful in pushing for deregulation during the late 1970s and in the 1980s, and were at least partly responsible for the Republicans' taking control of Congress in 1994.

The complexities of modern living have made extensive governmental regulation necessary. But the question of how extensive governmental regulation should be will continue to be hotly debated in the years to come. Nevertheless, the future will likely bring additional bureaucratic growth, reregulation, and more regulations. It will also bring stronger ties between the business community, especially big business, and government since tomorrow's problems will demand that government and business resolve challenging socioeconomic problems together.

NOTES

1. *Historical Statistics of the United States, Colonial Times to 1970* (Washington, D.C.: Government Printing Office, 1976), pt. 1, Specs. A, F, H: pt. 2, Sec. Y; and *Statistical Abstract of the United States, 1987,* 107th ed. (Washington D.C: U.S. Government Printing Office, 1987), Specs. 1, 9, 11, 14.

2. Peter Woll, *American Bureaucracy,* 2nd ed. (New York: W.W. Norton, 1977), 1.
3. This department ceased to be a part of the President's cabinet on July 1,1971, when it was made into a quasi-independent nonprofit corporation.
4. Herbert Kaufman, *Are Government Organizations Immortal?* (Washington, D.C.: Brookings Institution, 1976).
5. Ibid., 11.
6. Ibid., 7.
7. Ibid.
8. Ibid., 11. The literature is replete with organizational theorists making this contention. See John Marini, *The Politics of Budget Control: Congress, the Presidency, and the Growth of the Administrative State* (Washington, D.C.: Crane Russak, 1992); and Glen O. Robinson, *American Bureaucracy: Public Choice and Public Law* (Ann Arbor: University of Michigan Press, 1991), 9–17.
9. Kaufman, *Are Government Organizations Immortal?,* 73–77.
10. Robinson, *American Bureaucracy: Public Choice and Public Law,* 18–19.
11. William L. Morrow, *Public Administration: Politics, Policy and Political Systems,* 2nd ed. (New York: Random House, 1980), 10.
12. John Kenneth Galbraith, *The New Industrial State,* 4th ed. (Boston: Harvard University Press, 1985).
13. James Q. Wilson, "The Rise of the Bureaucratic State," *The Public Interest,* 41 (Fall 1975); reprinted in Rourke, *Bureaucratic Power in National Policy Making,* 143.
14. For a thorough treatment of a deregulation failure, see James R. Barth, *The Great Savings and Loan Debacle* (Washington, D.C.: American Enterprise Institute, 1991).
15. Edwin W. Tucker, *Administrative Law, Regulation of Enterprise, and Individual Liberties* (St. Paul, Minn.: West Publishing Company, 1975), 1–2. (Also see George Berkeley and John Rouse, *The Craft of Public Administration,* 6th ed. (Brown and Benchmark, 1994), 41–47.
16. David H. Rosenbloom, *Public Administration: Understanding Management, Politics, and Law in the Public Sector* (New York: Random House, 1986), 62–68; David H. Rosenbloom, "The Judicial Response to the Bureaucratic State," *American Review of Public Administration,* 50 (Spring 1981), 29–51; and Harold Seidman and Robert Gilmour, *Politics, Position, and Power: From the Positive to the Regulatory State,* 4th ed. (New York: Oxford University Press, 1986), chap. 7.
17. Stephen G. Breyer and Richard B. Stewart, *Administrative Law and Regulatory Policy,* 3rd ed. (Boston: Little, Brown, 1992), 18.
18. Ibid., 22.
19. Michael Herz, "Deference Running Riot: Separating Interpretation and Lawmaking Under *Chevron,*" *The Administrative Law Journal* 6 (1992), 187.
20. Ibid.
21. Ibid., 187–233.
22. Ibid. Also see, Peter H. Schuck and E. Donald Elliott, "To the Chevron Station: An Empirical Study of Federal Administrative Law," *Duke Law Journal* (1990); Cass R. Sunstein, "Law and Administration after *Chevron,*" *Columbia Law Review,* 90 (1990); and Bernard Schwartz, "Administrative Law Cases During 1992," *Administrative Law Review,* 45 (Summer 1993), 277–278.
23. Schwartz, "Administrative Law Cases During 1992," 648.
24. Henry Jacoby, *The Bureaucratization of the World,* trans. Eveline Kane (Berkeley: University of California Press, 1973), especially Introduction and chap. 6.
25. Robinson, *American Bureaucracy: Public Choice and Public Law,* 70.

26. See, for example, Robinson, *American Bureaucracy: Public Choice and Public Law,* chap. 3; Richard B. Stewart, "Beyond Delegation Doctrine," *American University Law Review,* 36 (1987); and Richard J. Pierce, Jr., "Political Accountability and Delegated Power: A Response to Professor Lowi," *American University Law Review,* 36 (1987).
27. Kenneth C. Davis, *Administrative Law: Cases-Text-Problems,* 6th ed. (St. Paul, Minn.: West Publishing Company, 1977), 34.
28. Bernard Schwartz, *Administrative Law,* 3rd ed. (Boston: Little, Brown and Company, 1991), 44.
29. For a good analysis of *Waukegan* in the perspective of other related cases, see Davis, *Administrative Law,* 28–32.
30. Bernard Schwartz, "Administrative Law Cases During 1985," *Administrative Law Review,* 38 (Summer 1986), 295.
31. Kenneth C. Davis and Richard J. Pierce, Jr., *Administrative Law Treatise,* 3rd ed. vol. 1 (Boston: Little Brown and Co., 1994), 90–91.
32. Eastman, testimony at the hearing on H.R. 7432, before House Committee on Interstate and Foreign Commerce, 72nd Congress, end Session 7 (1933).
33. Davis and Pierce, Jr., *Administrative Law Treatise,* 87.
34. Davis, *Administrative Law,* 51.
35. Theodore Lowi, *The End of Liberalism,* 2nd ed. (New York: W.W. Norton, 1979), 92–127.
36. Joseph Harris, *Congressional Control of Administration* (New York: Doubleday, Anchor Press, 1965), especially chap. 10.
37. James Burnham, *The Managerial Revolution: What Is Happening in the World* (New York: Praeger, 1960); and Eugene P. Dvorin and Robert H. Simmons, *From Amoral to Humane Bureaucracy* (San Francisco: Canfield Press, 1972).
38. Lewis C. Mainzer, *Political Bureaucracy* (Glenview, Ill.: Scott, Foresman, 1973), 72–73.
39. "DC-10 Grounding: The Ripples Spread," *U.S. News and World Report,* (June 18, 1979), 126.
40. Ibid., pp. 25, 26; and Jane See White, "FAA Role Questioned in Aftermath of Mishaps, Disasters," *St. Louis Post-Dispatch* (September 23, 1979), 44D.
41. William P. Rogers, *Report of the Presidential Commission on the Space Shuttle Challenger Accident* (Washington, D.C., 1986), 171–73.
42. Ibid., 173.
43. Ibid.
44. Ibid., 104.
45. Also, rumor was that a live communication hookup with the *Challenger* crew was to take place during the State of the Union message. However, the Rogers Commission could not substantiate this rumor. Ibid., 176.
46. Walter Gellhorn, personal interview, Saint Louis University, March 5, 1980.
47. Edgar Shor, "Public Interest Representation and the Federal Agencies: Introductory Comments," *Public Administration Review,* 37 (March-April 1977), 132.
48. J. D. Williams, *Public Administration: The People's Business* (Boston: Little, Brown, 1980), 532.
49. Ibid., 532–33.
50. Robert Miewald, *Public Administration: A Critical Perspective* (New York: McGraw-Hill, 1978), 68–70.
51. Ibid., 69.

52. Ibid.
53. Ibid.
54. For a brief review of cost-benefit analysis, see, David H. Rosenbloom, *Public Administration: Understanding Management, Politics, and Law In the Public Sector,* 3rd ed. (New York: McGraw-Hill, Inc., 1993), 413–414.
55. It should be noted at the outset that public opinion polls have consistently shown that Americans fail to understand the meaning of democratic ideals in practice. They may embrace democratic ideals in theory, but they reject them in practice. For example, Americans would likely indicate, if asked, that they believe in free speech but would then in the same questionnaire state that they feel it is wrong to allow avowed Communists to speak at public meetings in the United States. See William H. Flanagan and Nancy H. Zingdale, *Political Behavior of the American Electorate,* 8th ed. (Boston: Allen and Bacon, 1994).
56. James M. Burns, *Deadlock of Democracy: Four-Party Politics in America* (Englewood Cliffs, N.J.: Prentice-Hall, 1967).
57. For an update, see Ralph P. Hummel, *The Bureaucratic Experience,* 4th ed. (New York: St. Martin's Press, 1994).
58. Kenneth C. Davis, *Discretionary Justice in Europe and America* (Urbana, Ill.: University of Illinois Press, 1976), 1–4.
59. James O. Freedman, "Crisis and Legitimacy in the Administrative Process," *Stanford Law Review,* 27 (April 1975), 1056–64.
60. Felix Frankfurter, *The Public and Its Government* (New Haven, Conn.: Yale University Press, 1930), 160.
61. Freedman, "Crisis and Legitimacy in the Administrative Process," 1056–64.
62. Dvorin and Simmons, *From Amoral to Humane Bureaucracy,* 1.
63. Ibid., 4.
64. Ralph P. Hummel, *The Bureaucratic Experience,* 2nd ed. (New York: St. Martin's Press, 1982), 207–8.
65. Louis L. Jaffe and Nathaniel L. Nathanson, *Administrative Law,* 4th ed. (Boston: Little, Brown, 1976).
66. Freedman, "Crisis and Legitimacy in the Administrative Process," 1063.
67. Frederick C. Mosher, Democracy and the Public Service, 2nd ed. (New York: Oxford University Press, 1982); and Francis E. Rourke, *Bureaucracy, Politics and Public Policy,* 3rd ed. (Boston: Little, Brown, 1984).
68. Robert Alford, *Bureaucracy and Participation: Political Culture in Four Wisconsin Cities* (Chicago: Rand McNally, 1969), 52. Also see Seidman and Gilmour, *Politics, Position and Power,* 76; and Bernard Rosen, *Holding Government Bureaucracies Accountable,* 2nd ed. (New York: Praeger, 1989), chap. 5.
69. Ibid.
70. Guy Benveniste, *The Politics of Expertise,* 2nd ed. (San Francisco: Boyd and Fraser Publishing, 1977), 228–39.
71. Ibid., 220.
72. Mainzer, *Political Bureaucracy,* 9.
73. For an insightful analysis of the regulatory process today, see, Sidney A. Shapiro, "Political Oversight and The Deterioration of Regulatory Policy," *Administrative Law Review,* 46 (Winter 1994), 1–40.
74. *Statistical Abstract of the United States,* 1995, sec. 13.

75. Max Weber, *The Theory of Social and Economic Organization,* trans. A.M. Henderson and Talcott Parsons (London: Oxford University Press, 1947), especially sec. 3, chaps. 4, 5, and 6.

76. Victor A. Thompson, *Bureaucracy and the Modern World* (Morristown, N.J.: General Learning Press, 1976), 111–15.

77. Freedman, "Crisis and Legitimacy in the Administrative Process," 1056.

78. Jeffrey L. Jowell, *Law and Bureaucracy: Administrative Discretion and the Limits of Legal Action* (New York: Irvington, 1984), 199.

79. Ibid.

80. Murray Edelman, *The Symbolic Uses of Politics* (Urbana, Ill.: University of Illinois Press 1967), 56–61.

81. Jowell, *Law and Bureaucracy,* 199.

82. For an overview of the issues of governmental regulation, see Peter L. Kahn, "Regulation and Imperfect Democracies," in Carol Tucker Foreman, ed., *Regulating for the Future* (Washington, D.C.: Center for National Policy Press, 1991).

83. Louis M. Kohlmeier, Jr., *The Regulators: Watchdog Agencies and the Public Interest* (New York: Harper and Row, 1969), 83–84.

84. Ibid., 25–26.

85. Ibid., 26.

86. Thomas O. McGarity, "Regulatory Reform and the Positive State: An Historical Overview," *Administrative Law Review,* 38 (Fall 1986), 399–425; and Stephen G. Breyer, *Regulation and Its Reform* (Cambridge, Mass.: Harvard University Press, 1982), chap. 1.

87. Lowi and Ginsberg, *American Government: Freedom and Power,* 666.

88. Carol Tucker Foreman and Maureen S. Steinbruner, "Righting the Record On Regulation: An Introduction," in Foreman, *Regulating for the Future,* 12.

89. Jacoby, *Bureaucratization of the World,* especially chaps. 10–13.

90. For an excellent commentary on Plato's emphasis on social harmony and its application to modern America, see William T. Bluhm, *Theories of the Political System,* 3rd ed. (Englewood Cliffs, N.J.: Prentice-Hall, 1978), chap. 3.

91. Herbert Kaufman, *Red Tape: Its Origins, Uses, and Abuses* (Washington, D.C.: Brooking Institution, 1977), 1.

92. Ibid., chap. 2.

93. Ibid., 31.

94. Ibid., 39–41.

95. Ibid., 49.

96. Walter Gellhorn, Richard J. Childress Memorial Lecture, March 4, 1980.

97. Stephen G. Breyer, "Analyzing Regulatory Failure: Mismatches, Less Restrictive Alternatives, and Reform," *Harvard Law Review,* 92 (January 1979), 549–609. For updates, see Stephen G. Breyer and Richard B. Stewart, *Administrative Law and Regulatory Policy,* 3rd ed. (Boston: Little, Brown and Company, 1992), 5–31.

98. Breyer, "Analyzing Regulatory Failure," 553.

99. Ibid., 549–60.

100. Ibid., 554.

101. Ibid., 555.

102. Ibid., 555.

103. Ibid., 556.

104. Ibid., 556–57.

105. Ibid., 557.
106. Ibid., 558.
107. Ibid.
108. Ibid., 604–9.
109. Kaufman, *Red Tape,* 4–28.
110. Bill Bogota, "Is the U.S. in an Innovative Recession?" *St. Louis Post-Dispatch,* (July 24, 1979), 8A.
111. Robert B. Reich, "How Nit-Picking Regulations Get That Way," *Harper's Magazine* (February 1987), 18.
112. Ibid., 18–22.
113. This perspective is very well expressed by the Supreme Court in *Boyd* v. *United States,* 116 U.S. 616 (1886).
114. Foreman and Steinbruner, "Righting The Record On Regulation: An Introduction," 19 and 24.
115. Kohlmeier, *The Regulators,* 22.
116. Peter L. Kahn, "Regulation and Imperfect Democracies," in Carol Tucker Foreman, ed., *Regulating for the Future,* 31.
117. Jean Jacques Rousseau, *Social Contract,* trans. Maurice Evanston (1762); Baltimore: Penguin Books, 1980, 49–50.
118. Kahn, "Regulation and Imperfect Democracies," 29–30.
119. Marc Allen Eisner, "Economic Regulatory Policies: Regulation and Deregulation in Historical Context," in David H. Rosenbloom and Richard D. Schwartz, eds., *Handbook of Regulation and Administrative Law* (New York: Marcel Dekker, Inc., 1994), 113.
120. Paul Stephen Dempsey, "Deregulation and Reregulation: Policy, Politics, and Economics," in Rosenbloom and Schwartz, 198.
121. Ibid., 180–181.
122. Paul Stephen Dempsey and A. Goetz, *Airline Deregulation and Laissez-Faire Mythology* (Westport, Conn.: Quorum Books, 1992).
123. Dempsey, "Deregulation and Reregulation: Policy, Politics, and Economics," in Rosenbloom and Schwartz, 177.
124. For a related story, see Christopher Carey, "Free and Not So Easy: Airlines Make Bonus Flights Harder to Win," *Saint Louis Post-Dispatch,* February 27, 1994, 1E.
125. Dempsey, "Deregulation and Reregulation: Policy, Politics, and Economics," in Rosenbloom and Schwartz, 177.
126. Mary Kihl, "The Impacts of Deregulation On Passenger Transportation in Small Towns," *Transportation Quarterly,* vol. 42 (1988), 243–268.
127. Thomas O. McGarity, "Regulatory Reform in the Reagan Era," *Maryland Law Review,* 45 (1986).
128. AP, "EPA Issues Cleaner Air Regulations," *Saint Louis Post-Dispatch,* March 2, 1994, 3A.
129. Bruce D. Fisher, "Controlling Government Regulation: Cost-Benefit Analysis before and after the Cotton-Dust Case," *Administrative Law Review,* 36 (Spring 1984).
130. McGarity, "Regulatory Reform and the Positive State," 411.
131. Paul Teske, "The State of State Regulation," in Rosenbloom and Schwartz, chap. 3.
132. Barth, "The Great Savings and Loan Debacle."

CHAPTER THREE

LEGISLATIVE ATTEMPTS TO ACHIEVE DEMOCRATIC ACCOUNTABILITY IN THE ADMINISTRATIVE PROCESS

KEEPING ADMINISTRATORS ACCOUNTABLE

Forces in the U.S. political system have naturally led to the development of a gigantic public service system. Most informed observers agree that an extensive regulatory network is necessary but disagree over the feasibility of specific regulatory approaches and the proper scope of regulatory activities. Administrative growth and regulatory powers will inevitably continue to increase because this modern nation can no longer rely on obsolete institutional structures and processes not designed or equipped to handle the demands placed upon government by a society about to enter the twenty-first century. In the insightful words of the famed statesman Elihu Root in an address to the American Bar Association in 1916: "We shall go on; we shall expand them, whether we approve theoretically or not, because such agencies furnish protection to rights and obstacles to wrongdoing which under our new social and industrial conditions cannot be practically accomplished by the old and simple procedures of legislatures and courts as in the last generation."[1] But Root emphasized that it would be democratically irresponsible to allow this newly emerging administrative power to go unchecked. To preserve popular government, he maintained, public administrators must be held democratically accountable for their actions: "If we are to continue a government of limited powers, these agencies of regulation must themselves be regulated. . . . The rights of the citizen against them must be made plain. A system of administrative law must be developed, and that with us is still in its infancy, crude and imperfect."[2]

Although Elihu Root warned in 1916 that the United States should work on methods to keep administrative power accountable, the early general reaction was simply to resist the growth of administrative power. Not until after World War II was any serious attention given to the problem of keeping administrators democratically responsible. The administrative law field in the United States has developed primarily since 1945, and the concern with controlling the behavior of public administrators since that time has been well documented in the professional literature.[3] It should not be inferred from this that public administrators are any more or any less unethical or corrupt than other workers, but that their jobs are unique. Democratic theory demands that all public servants, elected or nonelected, be accountable to the people. Obviously, this requires the creation of certain oversight mechanisms so that administrative behavior can be watched and controlled.

Control Mechanisms

A great variety of control mechanisms exists. Some controls can be categorized as informal, internal, or natural, while others can be classified as formal, external, or artificial. Internal checks mostly originate from within an agency or its employees. Some idealists, who place great faith in the virtues of human nature, believe that a person's own desire to perform according to ethical, moral, and professional codes of conduct can provide the best check against administrative misconduct. But others, especially those realists who take a dimmer view of human nature, feel that more formal, institutionalized checks are absolutely necessary to force employees to perform in an honest, professional, and efficient manner. The framers of the Constitution were realists about human nature because our constitutional democracy seems at times plagued by a crippling system of frustrating checks and balances which tend to hinder decision-making capabilities. Traditionally, legislators, judges, and presidents have exerted external controls over public administrators in our political system, although other institutionalized checks exist. (For example, communications media, which obtain most of their formal powers from the First Amendment, have played a powerful role in overseeing and checking administrative action.) This chapter examines congressional attempts to keep public administrators democratically accountable. Other formal and informal checks over the bureaucracy are reviewed in subsequent chapters.

When we say we want our public administrators to be controlled, what should we have in mind? First, we should be prepared to admit, as James Madison did in *The Federalist,* No. 51, that "if men were angels no government would be necessary. If angels were to govern men, neither external nor internal controls on government would be necessary."[4] However, it does not follow that we should seek more controls over public officials than are absolutely necessary. Too many controls can be counterproductive because they can serve to frustrate attempts by dedicated public servants who are simply trying to do their jobs. Needless controls can waste the time of everyone involved, thus creating morale problems and adding to the taxpayer's burden. Unnecessary checks can disrupt the administrative process, making it unable to handle vital governmental tasks effectively. Ideally, controls should be aimed at simply promoting responsible behavior and guarding against irresponsible behavior.[5]

Seeking Democratically Responsible Behavior

One could generalize that democratically responsible behavior by public agency employees is any legally and procedurally proper action that leads to the efficient accomplishment of publicly sanctioned and desired goals. Responsible administrative behavior by public administrators could be conceptualized as moral, ethical, honest, lawful, courteous, and productive actions aimed at conscientiously serving the public. While negative controls (forms of punishments) are aimed at checking irresponsible employee or agency actions, positive controls (various reward and incentive measures) are used to promote responsible conduct. Critics have maintained in recent years that entirely too much emphasis has been placed on checking administrative behavior through the use of various negative micromanagement control mechanisms, while not enough attention has been given to how agency administrators can be kept accountable and productive through positive approaches.[6]

Possibly one reason for this criticism is that irresponsible conduct is more striking or detectable than responsible behavior. We expect responsible behavior from employees. As a somewhat paradoxical consequence, we have concentrated on devising mechanisms to prevent irresponsible behavior. Irresponsible conduct has many faces. Generally, according to various statutes, those civil servants who are guilty of nonfeasance, malfeasance, or misfeasance of office are guilty of irresponsible behavior, thus justifying their removal from office. In practice, *nonfeasance* translates into doing nothing. Since few employees simply do nothing at all, claims of irresponsibility due to nonfeasance are rarely made against civil servants. Charges of *malfeasance* (evil or wrongful behavior which is wholly unlawful) are also made infrequently, simply because few employee acts can be classified as evil or positively unlawful. Allegations of *misfeasance* (improper performance of duties which a person may do lawfully) are much more common, although only seldom do such charges lead to dismissals. *Misfeasance* is not only difficult to define in context, but employee incompetence, or misfeasance, is also very difficult to substantiate in practice, largely because civil service procedures seem to function more to protect employee rights than to combat worker incompetence and promote overall efficiency and effectiveness in the public service system.[7]

In practice, irresponsible administrative behavior can be seen when an administrator (1) abuses discretionary powers; (2) reaches arbitrary and capricious decisions; (3) grossly ignores facts and reason when making decisions; (4) acts contrary to constitutional and statutory dictates; (5) violates established due process standards; (6) goes beyond lawful authority; and (7) fails to act or respond in a reasonable time. All of these irresponsible administrative actions fall into the category of malfeasance. The Administrative Procedure Act in Section 706, "Scope of Review," specifically prohibits, as do many other statutes and agency rules and regulations, such unlawful administrative conduct. It should be understood that, because of the evidentiary problems involved in making misfeasance charges stick in the public service system, efforts at holding public administrators accountable have mostly centered around preventing obviously illegal and corrupt administrative practices. Indeed, administrative law focuses almost exclusively upon illegal—not unethical, unprofessional, or poorly performed—administrative actions. It appears tough enough to keep agency officials functioning within the law. Practitioners of administrative law feel that it is up to others (perhaps political scientists, public administration scholars, organizational theorists, or management experts) to solve the problems associated with misfeasance.

Because this is an administrative law book, it is concerned primarily with how well public administrators uphold the law when serving the public. However, I have given particular emphasis to the problem of controlling the discretionary power of administrators, not only because abuses of discretion tend to be the root cause of all irresponsible administrative acts, but also because discretionary practices seem to conflict so blatantly with rule-of-law and democratic accountability maxims.

The Congressional Watchdog Role: An Overview

Despite frequent criticisms of the watchdog functions of Congress, probably the most effective external controls over administrative agencies come from there. According to James W. Fesler, Congress, in its watchdog role, has the duty to identify all errors and irresponsible administrative actions and, when possible, the obligation to correct them.[8] This is the ideal. In reality, Congress does not have the resources to carry out day-to-day supervision of administrators. Close daily monitoring of administrative work would be undesirable anyway, since it would likely disrupt normal administrative processes. Thus, the monitoring of administrative behavior must be done on a selective basis.

Fesler believes that legislators have adopted three general supervisory approaches, employing them as they deem appropriate. The first is *reactive monitoring*. Reactive monitoring is a passive approach; the legislators react only when some administrative wrongdoing is somehow called to their attention, often through complaints. Reactive monitoring seems to work best for responding to specific charges of illegal administrative acts. The second approach is *sampling monitoring*. Sampling monitoring is aimed at discovering through various sampling procedures the reasons for the poor administration of particular agency functions. Therefore, to find out why welfare cases are being mishandled, Congress may decide to sample a certain number of the cases administered randomly and periodically. The third approach is *concentrated monitoring*. Concentrated monitoring works well for close supervision of administrative functions or programs that pose higher than normal risks for corrupt or unethical activities.[9]

Despite the existence of these monitoring approaches, the possibility is always present that Congress may fail in its watchdog role. In the first place, the supervisory methods may not be used when needed. When they are employed, they may fail to provide useful information. As a matter of fact, the problems Congress has had in controlling administrative power, especially during the 1960s and 1970s, led critics to call for Congress to reinvigorate its watchdog powers. These critics think that the dramatic rise of the administrative state has been encouraged by positive congressional action, through vast delegation, and by negative inactions, such as the failure to use constitutionally sanctioned oversight powers to thwart efforts by administrators to increase their powers. The failure of Congress to deploy necessary control efforts has caused some critics to conclude that it may be too late to attempt to regain directional control over the bureaucratic leviathan. However, other observers, such as Joel D. Aberbach, conclude that Congressional oversight ". . . is far from perfect, not even pretty or neat, but we could be far worse."[10]

A famous Latin quotation—*"Quis custodiet ipsos custodes?"*—translates colloquially as "Who is to watch the watchdogs?"[11] The answer is a lot of watchdogs. In the case of U.S. administrative agencies, the more there are, the greater the odds that effective checks over public administrators will prevail, despite the fact that some of the watchdogs will fall asleep, while others will be bribed with one bone or another.

The search for ways to promote democratic accountability in the U.S. administrative system has been both challenging and frustrating. Each watchdog institution has taken a different approach, and none has been totally successful in preventing foul administrative acts.[12] While the media, for example, have tried to check against abusive administrative activities by alerting the public to the behavior, Congress has traditionally attempted to keep administrators accountable to the democratic faith by focusing somewhat systematically upon three basic areas of responsibility in the total administrative process. Specifically, congressional controls have been aimed at achieving (1) fiscal responsibility, (2) procedural responsibility, and (3) program responsibility. In recent times Congress has been concerned with achieving a fourth goal, systems responsibility, as well. Of course, keeping the hands of public servants out of the tax dollar till has always been a fundamental legislative watchdog task. Congress has also been traditionally concerned with making sure that administrators do not waste tax dollars simply through blundering. Additionally, congress persons have been concerned with the procedures employed in the implementation of public policies. Specifically, the legislative watchdogs watch to make certain that administrative agencies perform efficiently and fairly.

Naturally, it is not sufficient for congressional watchdogs to merely monitor the fiscal and procedural practices of administrators, especially since these practices represent only a means to an end. As citizens and scholars, we are all interested primarily in evaluating the administrative agency's end product, their programs. When Congress evaluates administrative programs, it is interested particularly in the effectiveness of these programs. That is, Congress seeks primarily to answer the question: Do these programs fulfill the policy goals intended by Congress? In relatively recent times, policy evaluation has taken a sensible additional step. Programs have been assessed not only in terms of the successes and failures of particular programs, but also in terms of how the programs affect the entire system.

With every passing year the watchdog role of Congress expands, as does the corps of public administrators it must supervise. Traditional controls were originally established to monitor a relatively small group of regular public administrators. However, Congress today is responsible for holding accountable to the public a large variety of administrators who have joined the public administration system, even those in private industry who are linked to the public sector by governmental contracts and grants. With such changes from the original administrative system, it is conceivable that the traditional legislative control mechanisms may be inadequate to keep the various public and quasi-public administrators democratically accountable.

Richard E. Neustadt writes that the Constitution has provided Congress with four specific oversight powers: "organization, authorization, financing, and investigation. Departments and agencies—the operating arms of the 'executive branch'— are created by acts of Congress. They gain operational authority, programmatic jurisdiction, from laws passed by Congress. They gain funds to pay for personnel and programs from congressional appropriations. And their use of both authority and money is subject to 'oversight,' to inquiry in Congress."[13] Are these constitutionally sanctioned oversight powers effective? This chapter breaks down each congressional oversight power into similar functional areas in order to evaluate the capabilities of each to monitor and control administrative behavior in the public interest.

TRADITIONAL CONGRESSIONAL OVERSIGHT POWERS

Three traditional congressional oversight powers are (1) the power to create and organize, (2) the power to control agency budgets, and (3) the power to investigate agency activities. A fourth legislative oversight mechanism, the power to control agency performance through general guidance legislation (the Administrative Procedure Act is an example), is given separate treatment later in the chapter. Because of the relevance to administrative law, separate coverage is also given to the legislative power to create and organize. In evaluating the overall worth of these congressional oversight functions, it is unwise to use snap judgments. As the systems model makes quite evident, actions by any actor in the political system must be assessed on the basis of their impact upon the whole system. Thus, the method is always to evaluate the effectiveness of a control or the extent to which an oversight method is used by our legislators from the perspective of total costs and benefits to society.

Of course, each examiner weighing the costs and benefits of various congressional oversight measures would undoubtedly reach different conclusions about their appropriateness; we all have different value systems. For instance, some Americans feel that it is very important for Congress to watch administrators closely, to limit administrative discretion severely, and, in general, to keep the scope and powers of regulators stunted. However, other Americans believe that it is of utmost importance to free administrators from close supervision, to allow administrative specialists broad discretionary powers, and to increase the scope and strength of regulatory activities. Generally speaking, the politically conservative would most likely adopt the former attitude, and the politically liberal would probably share the latter view. Such differences in our open, pluralist system of politics led to political debate and to the formation of political parties. Since the 1930s, these basic viewpoints regarding the proper relationship between Congress and the bureaucracy, conservative and liberal, have provided one fundamental division between most Republicans and most Democrats. Therefore, within reasonable democratic constitutional standards, many conclusions regarding the adequacy of legislative controls over administrative officials can have more to do with a person's politics than with what appears to be right or wrong. However, constitutional democracy does demand reasonable use of oversight powers by Congress so that the public service system can be held at least minimally accountable to the people.

With this in mind, it should be mentioned that there are plenty of critics who feel that legislators have not even performed up to minimal standards. Stephen K. Bailey, a scholar of the Congress, noted in 1970 that a whole generation of political scientists believe that Congress has performed its watchdog function very poorly.[14] Since the early 1970s, Congress, reacting to harsh criticism, has tried to reinvigorate its watchdog role, but its efforts have received mixed reviews. Some scholars suggest that the reason the watchdog role is weak is because legislators care little about strengthening it. "For many legislators, however, the oversight role has never been a high priority task, because it does not contribute to their re-election nearly as much as nursing a constituency—being an effective 'errand-boy' congressman."[15] In fact, critics maintain that legislators have contributed to the runaway growth of bureaucracy by responding to constituent demands. Since such legislative responses normally necessitate more bureaucratic action, it can "be argued that Congress itself has a vested interest in the continued growth of bureaucracy. The more agencies there are for constituents to deal with, the more important becomes the Congressional role as intermediary between the citizen and bureaucracy. From this perspective Congress becomes the protagonist rather than the antagonist of bureaucracy in government."[16]

However, other observers feel that Congress is performing its watchdog function well. For instance, Cathy Marie Johnson believes that it simply is not true that Congress is unable to control the federal bureaucracy. She holds that "[T]he legislature has the necessary control devices to prevail in any dispute with the bureaucracy."[17] Once more, she feels that increasing ". . . legislative control could be detrimental to the political system because the ability of the bureaucracy to contribute to policy making would be curtailed."[18] In an interview with veteran Congressman William Clay (D-Mo.) in 1987 he noted that the congressional oversight function was not working very well in checking administrative actions.[19] However, in a follow-up interview in 1994, Congressman Clay stressed that "[A]lthough the system isn't perfect, in just the past five years appreciable improvements have been made [in the watchdog function] and Congress has been doing a progressively better job in undercovering waste and mismanagement."[20] Today, in the mid-1990s, many scholars agree with Clay's revised assessment. Kenneth R. Mayer contends that Congress's new micromanagement approach may constitute some unwarranted intrusions into agency behavior, but such micromanagement may nevertheless have made the federal bureaucracy more efficient and accountable.[21]

The Power to Create and Organize

Probably the most rudimentary congressional oversight powers stem from Congress's authority to create and organize agencies, departments, and the like, as it sees fit. In Article 1, Section 8 of the Constitution, Congress is given the power to create agencies congress persons believe to be "necessary and proper" to help with the tasks of government. This basic constitutional power to create agencies allows Congress to become the sole architect of an agency's power structure in its enabling legislation. This further permits Congress, to reiterate an earlier point, the design flexibility necessary to make some agencies stronger or more independent than others. Such power can be perceived as a fundamental, pre-oversight power, since it provides Congress with the opportunity to structure agencies so that they can be made more or less vulnerable to various legislative oversight controls. Ideally, the power to create, if properly employed by Congress, should prevent Congress from giving life to uncontrollable Frankenstein monsters because wise legislators should be able, with foresight, to eliminate from the very beginning or restrict potentially dangerous agency powers. For example, Congress, in the statutes which enable agencies to be born, can limit agency jurisdiction, attach appropriation ceilings to discourage agency expansionism, dictate specific procedural steps to be followed when implementing legislated policies, limit administrative discretion, and spell out program content and expected policy goals in detail. Because it perceives Internal Revenue Service activities as of critical importance to Congress, Congress has, in fact, done a fairly good job through enabling statutes (original and subsequent) to keep the discretionary power of IRS administrators within limited and equitable bounds, thus making effective legislative oversight a reality in this case. However, this type of motivation among legislators probably should be considered atypical. In other cases, and in probably too many cases, Congress has created administrative agencies too hastily and in the absence of sufficient thought. The result has been the creation of poorly developed, skeletal enabling legislation that tends to encourage the development of irresponsible administrative power—power which quickly becomes too well fortified to be realistically challenged by any legislative oversight mechanisms.

Authorization Committees   Both the House and Senate have autonomous standing committees which specialize in substantive policy areas. Most of the legislative work in Congress is done in these committees, but their primary tasks center upon the establishment of initial programs and agencies to run them and assuring, through subsequent statutory review, that the programs and agencies are being run up to expectations. Because these substantive committees have the power to authorize, kill, modify, amend, or alter program directions and agency operations in any way, these committees were labeled *authorization committees* in the Legislative Reorganization Act of 1946 (60 Stat. 24, Sec. 138). This same act also described the role of two other congressional committees with watchdog functions: the *government operations committees* and the *appropriation committees,* to be treated shortly.

Authorization committees have at least six specific watchdog powers: (1) authorize, (2) reauthorize, (3) amend, (4) confirm appointments, (5) conduct investigatory research, and (6) veto proposed administrative actions. It should be clear by now that the power to authorize potentially carries great clout. Agencies cannot act without congressional authorization; thus, if the authorization committees choose to do so, they can detail in their authorization legislation specific courses of action for agency administrators to follow. Even if legislators fail to provide the proper mandates while drafting the initial legislation, they are provided with another opportunity to reflect upon the adequacy of the original enabling law during the reauthorization process. Although agencies are not always subject to routine renewal or reauthorization procedures, those agencies which are subject to periodic reauthorization can be placed in precarious positions because legislators, with the advantage of hindsight, have a second chance to impose restrictions upon the power of administrators.

Some agencies have the questionable luxury of functioning under permanent statutory authorization. Statutory legislative oversight can also be implemented through amending the initial legislation. Lawrence C. Dodd and Richard L. Scott have described the process: "In situations where agency or program mandates are too broad, where agencies implement programs in ways that Congress did not intend, or where evidence exists that initial statutory language is producing undesired consequences, the authorization committees can propose that Congress change statutory language by amendments to the original act."[22] Some critics argue that just the threat of the authorization committee's being able to propose amending the current enabling legislation is enough to scare agency administrators and cause them to use their power responsibly. In reality, however, it is hard to believe that the threat to amend legislation could serve as an effective oversight check, especially since most administrators realize how difficult it is for amendments to be approved by Congress. Commenting on the viability of the amending process as an effective oversight weapon, Dodd and Scott asserted that "despite its potential significance, the amending process has real limits as an oversight technique. It is time-consuming, and necessitates considerable agreement within Congress on specific matters of agency behavior. Without general congressional consensus, it may be difficult to pass amendments because a small fraction can filibuster them in the Senate or often delay committee or subcommittee action. For these reasons, members of Congress seeking to exert control or influence on administration in particular areas often prefer less time-consuming and more informal methods."[23]

Authorization committees have still other watchdog powers. Senate authorization committees have the power to screen persons nominated by the president to head various departments and agencies. In the confirmation hearing, committee members can obligate nominees to honor certain procedures, goals, and the like. Even so, the plain truth is that the confirmation process has turned out to be a practically useless oversight tool because legislators do not have the time to scrutinize nominees, thus making the confirmation process, with rare exceptions, a mere formality. But one may ask how it could be anything else, since presidents may submit over one hundred thousand military and about eight thousand civilian nominations during a single congressional session. Nominations for major governmental posts may receive more attention, but evidence indicates that even these nominees receive only scant review. Since the passage of the Ethics in Government Act of 1978, 92 Stat. 1824–1836, the Senate has spent a little more time evaluating at least the more important senior-level nominees for possible conflict-of-interest, outside-income violations, and "problem" backgrounds. However, Presidents Reagan, Bush, and Clinton have had virtually all of their nominees quickly and routinely confirmed.[24]

Another power of all standing committees is the power to conduct research to obtain information necessary to the performance of their functions. Legislators are concerned especially with whether or not their constituents have been treated fairly by governmental agencies. If they find that problems exist through their casework probing, authorization committee members can compel agencies to respond to the problems.

The Legislative Veto   Because of its extremely controversial nature, the legislative veto oversight technique deserves special attention. Although controversy over its use has been brewing for decades, since the late 1970s the legislative veto issue has been the focus of increased attention and hot debate, even though some scholars feel the Supreme Court ended the debate in 1983 when it ruled a legislative veto provision unconstitutional in *Immigration and Naturalization Service* v. *Chadha*, 462 U.S. 919 (more on this case later). It is highly debatable whether the legislative veto can be considered a traditional legislative oversight approach, especially since it has been plagued by hostile attacks since it first appeared in a federal statute in 1932 (Legislative Appropriations for Fiscal Year 1933, 47 Stat. 382;1932). Despite its late and slow start, use of the legislative veto as a control device increased steadily. Between 1932 and 1975, 295 legislative vetoes were imposed.[25] From the mid-1970s to around the time of the *Chadha* decision, about half of the legislative veto provisions were enacted.[26]

During the 1970s efforts were made to expand the use of the legislative veto by amending the Administrative Procedure Act so that all agency rule making would be subject to a legislative veto. However, since it was first employed to oversee agency decision making, opposition to the legislative veto has remained fierce. The strongest resistance to the veto's use seems to come from those who contend that the legislative veto is unconstitutional, although it is attacked on many other grounds. For reasons to be discussed, virtually all presidents have assailed the legislative veto, since they have held that the legislative veto represents an unconstitutional legislative encroachment upon the domain of the executive branch.

What is a legislative veto, and why all the fuss? Basically, a legislative veto provision in a statute requires that certain agency actions, usually rules, be subject to the review of Congress before they can take effect; thus Congress is given the opportunity to veto any planned activity. The general purpose of the legislative veto is to provide Congress with an opportunity to block agency or presidential actions which legislators feel exceed statutory authority or are unsound. The legislative veto gives legislators flexibility to void administrative actions by cutting corners (by allowing legislators to bypass those formal processes many believe to be required by the Constitution). Legislative vetoes have been used to overturn virtually all administrative acts, but not adjudicative decisions, since such direct legislative intrusions in the administrative process appear to be clearly unconstitutional (see *Pillsbury Co.* v. *FTC*, 354 F.2d 952;1966). There are four basic versions of the legislative veto: (1) veto by both houses; (2) veto by only one house; (3) veto by a single committee (rare); and (4) veto by just a single committee chairman (very rare).[27] Although the legislative veto has been attacked in general, critics become more critical as the veto power is exercised by a decreasing number of the entire membership of Congress.

What have been the major arguments in support of the legislative veto as a tool for overseeing agency conduct? Proponents of the legislative veto argue that its purpose is a noble one—to keep administrators democratically accountable by making them more answerable to Congress. A specific objective of the legislative veto, supporters assert, is to ensure that promulgated rules are in line with congressional intent. The legislative veto, it is held, helps to compensate for the trend toward broad delegation. Proponents hold that the legislative veto represents an honest attempt by Congress to reinvigorate its oversight powers—something critics of Congress have urged for a decade or more.

In regard to the constitutional status of the legislative veto, proponents contend that the Constitution never imposed a rigid legislative-administrative relationship. Therefore, it cannot be validly argued that the Constitution prohibits the use of the innovative oversight measure. Supporters counter the claim that the legislative veto violates the separation-of-powers doctrine by pointing out that the Constitution calls for shared powers, not strict separation. Proponents further assert that Congress has every right to attach strings (that is, the legislative veto provision) when delegating legislative powers to nonelected administrators who serve in agencies created by Congress. After all, they maintain, a president has the opportunity to meddle in the affairs of Congress in the exercise of presidential veto power. The fact that the whole Congress may not participate when administrative action is vetoed should not imply that the legislative veto is undemocratic, proponents contend. For the whole Congress to delegate veto authority to a single chamber or committee only reflects current and sensible managerial practices. Congress, it is maintained, is already too busy and certainly does not have time to scrutinize every administrative action subject to the legislative veto as an entire assembly.

But critics of the legislative veto charge that this power is in fact unconstitutional, especially when only a single authorization committee has the power to veto an agency action. Opponents argue that Congress should not have the right to circumvent the channels for amending legislation established by the framers of the Constitution. The legislative veto function violates the separation-of-powers and checks-and-balances doctrines by permitting Congress to encroach upon the powers of the president and the courts. By use of the legislative veto Congress fails to provide the president with an opportunity to use his constitutional power to veto an act of Congress. Since opponents insist that the legislative veto power can be employed to change policies and previous legislative intent they argue that the president's constitutional role in the public policy-making process should not be bypassed. The critics charge that the legislative veto also undermines the role of the courts; if administrative rules exceed statutory authority or are inconsistent with legislative intent, then, say critics, the courts should have the power to review the legality of the promulgated rules.[28]

Aside from the opposition stemming from the alleged unconstitutionality of the legislative veto generally, opponents note that it provides only a negative force against public policy making through rule making, failing to show how to improve rule-making procedures and thus also failing to encourage rule makers.[29] This negativism, it is maintained, can discourage agency administrators from proposing new and needed rules, to say nothing about what the legislative veto does to the morale of conscientious agency rule makers.

When campaigning in the 1980 presidential primaries, President Carter charged that the legislative veto would destroy regulatory enforcement, turning it "into an endless process of capricious negotiation with special interests."[30] Others argue that the legislative veto causes unnecessary delays in program implementation; adds to administrative legislative and social costs; burdens both legislators and administrators; and inconveniences the beneficiaries of agency rules.

The Chadha Decision: A Critical Analysis   Exactly fifty years after the first legislative veto provision took effect the Supreme Court in *Chadha* finally ruled on the constitutional status of the legislative veto. In writing the majority opinion, Chief Justice Warren Burger admitted that the Supreme Court felt compelled to rule on the constitutionality of the legislative veto because so many legislative vetoes had been added to statutes in recent years. The high court ruled that the one-house legislative veto provision in the Immigration and Nationality Act of 1952, Section 244(C)(2), was unconstitutional because it generally violates the separation of powers doctrine (at 951–959). Claiming that the framers of the Constitution regarded legislative tyranny as a possibility, the Court specifically argued that the legislative veto constitutes an unconstitutional encroachment on the executive branch by the legislative branch because it essentially permits Congress to legislate activities outside its constitutional domain. In this particular case, the Court noted that the one-house legislative veto allowed the House of Representatives to override a decision by the Attorney General, working with the INS, not to deport Chadha. This legislative action, the Court asserted, altered Chadha's deportation status. Justice Burger held that such action by the House violated the separation-of-powers doctrine because it voided the constitutional principles of bicameralism (Article 1, Section 1) and presentment (Article 1, Section 7). That is, in simple language, before Congress can take such action against the president or an administrative agency, Congress must pass a bill by a majority of both houses and present it to the president for his approval or disapproval. "Disagreement with the Attorney General's decision on Chadha's deportation—that is, Congress' decision to deport Chadha—no less than Congress' original choice to delegate to the Attorney General the authority to make that decision, involves determination of policy that Congress can implement in only one way; bicameral passage followed by presentment to the President" (at 954–955). In explanation, the Court noted further: "The bicameral requirement, the Presentment Clauses, the President's veto, and Congress' power to override a veto were intended to erect enduring checks on each Branch and to protect the people from the improvident exercise of power by mandating certain prescribed steps. To preserve those checks, and maintain the separation of powers, the carefully defined limits on the power of each Branch must not be eroded. To accomplish what has been attempted by one House of Congress in this case requires action in conformity with the express procedures of the Constitution's prescription for legislative action: passage by a majority of both Houses and presentment to the President" (at 957–958).

In reaching its 7–2 decision in *Chadha*, the Supreme Court also made a few other points. The Court acknowledged that the framers only authorized one of the houses to act alone under four clear circumstances, and specific procedures for such unicameral actions were made explicit (provisions allowing the House to initiate impeachment, the Senate to conduct impeachment trials, the Senate to act on presidential appointments, and the Senate to ratify treaties). Conceding that the legislative veto appears to be an efficient mechanism for checking administrative actions, the Supreme Court said that nevertheless this does not mean that efficiency measures should be ranked over constitutional principles. Thus, the Supreme Court concluded: "With all the obvious flaws of delay, untidiness, and potential for abuse, we have not yet found a better way to preserve freedom than by making the exercise of power subject to the carefully crafted restraints spelled out in the Constitution. . . . We hold that the Congressional veto provision . . . is severable from the Act and that it is unconstitutional" (at 959).

How important was the *Chadha* decision? Some legal scholars believe that *Chadha* was the most significant decision handed down in the areas of constitutional and administrative law in many years, because the ruling struck at the basic constitutional relationship between Congress and the administrative branch. In particular, some thought it would affect the way Congress delegates discretionary administrative powers to administrative rule makers, including the president, and how Congress oversaw administrative actions. The *Chadha* holding led one analyst to conclude soon after the decision that it "stands out as the most significant of the last 10 years."[31] In dissent, Justice Byron White argued that the majority decision was irresponsible because it overruled "nearly 200 separate laws over a period of 50 years" (at 977). He added: "Today's decision strikes down in one fell swoop provisions in more laws enacted by Congress than the Court has cumulatively invalidated in history" (at 1002). The *Chadha* holding also casts doubt on the constitutionality of major acts such as the War Powers Resolution of 1973 (500 U.S.C., Section 1544[C]), the Congressional Budget and Impoundment Control Act of 1974 (31 U.S.C., Section 1403), the National Emergencies Act (50 U.S.C., Section 1622), and the International Security Assistance and Arms Export Control Act (22 U.S.C., Section 2776[b]), which were designed to resolve serious conflicts between Congress and the president over the president's exercise of broad powers in the areas of impoundment, war, national emergency, and international security and arms exports.[32]

In *Chadha* the Supreme Court declared unconstitutional only the legislative veto section of the Immigration and Nationality Act, thus upholding the validity of the rest of the act on the grounds that the specific legislative veto provision is "severable." However, legal scholars assert that the *Chadha* decision has made the legal and functional status of entire acts questionable, because certain legislative veto provisions cannot be easily severed from the rest of an act without destroying the functional effectiveness of the act. That is, in some cases Congress allowed administrators to exercise certain powers under an act only as long as such powers could be checked through the legislative veto provision (i.e., recognition is given to a dependent association between practically unseverable sections of the act). Many scholars claim that this is especially true for the War Powers Resolution. Regarding this act, Daniel Franklin commented: "The Court determines the severability of a provision by determining if the deletion of that unconstitutional part alters legislative intent. Even a cursory examination of the legislative history of the War Powers Resolution shows that Congress would have never delegated the authority for unilateral presidential actions without some kind of veto."[33]

In the *Administrative Law Review* in 1991 Bernard Schwartz wrote: "The Legislative Veto may turn out to be an administrative law version of Hamlet's father—a ghost that refuses to remain in repose."[34] The fact is that Congress has virtually ignored the *Chadha* ruling, relying upon legal loopholes and a very narrow interpretation of *Chadha* to honor existing legislative vetoes in legislation and to enact new legislative vetoes that do not blatantly violate *Chadha*.[35] In fact, Schwartz notes that approximately 102 additional legislative vetoes became law only three years after with no sign in sight that Congress will ever stop passing them.

Of course, it is important to note that *Chadha* does not apply to the states, so many states use legislative vetoes as an oversight tool. In *Mead* v. *Arnell,* 791 P.2d 410 (1990), the Idaho court relied heavily upon Justice White's dissent in *Chadha* to uphold the constitutionality of a legislative veto under Idaho's constitution, holding basically that the legislative veto does not violate presentment or the separation-of-powers doctrine.

SEEKING ADMINISTRATIVE ACCOUNTABILITY THROUGH GUIDANCE LEGISLATION

This section examines the effectiveness of general statutes passed by Congress to guide and compel certain administrative behavior. By and large, these laws have proved quite effective in keeping administrative actions consistent with the democratic rules of the game. However, legislated statutes are hard-core laws. Although legislators, politicians, interest groups, and agency administrators may play selfish games with vague authorization statutes (often those which inform administrators that they must simply act in the public interest), agency budgets, and politicized investigatory committees, they cannot take the same liberties with certain laws which clearly dictate which administrative acts are or are not legally permissible. Of course, all laws contain some loopholes, and the Administrative Procedure Act certainly has its share. Nevertheless, many laws like the APA, which are aimed at controlling administrative behavior, consist of provisions which leave little room for interpretation. For the most part, in U.S. politics tactical political maneuvers to gain a power advantage have usually stopped short of flagrantly breaking the law. Well-documented exceptions exist, such as in the infamous Teapot Dome, Watergate, Iran-Contra, and saving and loan scandals that rocked the Harding, Nixon, Reagan, and Bush administrations. In short, laws have been at least modestly successful in curbing wrongful administrative conduct because rule-of-law restrictions have been generally honored by all the players. Also, the courts have been available to punish those who want to play by different rules.

A great number of laws order and restrict administrative behavior. In general, these laws are directed toward restraining democratically irresponsible and illegal administrative practices. To achieve this end, legislation has been aimed specifically at achieving procedural due process, limiting administrative discretion, making the administrative process more efficient and meritorious, insulating administrators from corruptive political pressures, terminating unwanted agencies and programs, and opening administrative decision making to public scrutiny. The forthcoming brief review considers only two types of laws: those believed to have had the greatest impact on structuring and controlling administrative behavior, and those most relevant to administrative law.

Legislative Efforts Aimed at De-Politicizing and Professionalizing the Administrative Process

As has been previously acknowledged, the field of administrative law developed rather recently in political history, not getting significantly started until after World War II. But public administration as a recognized profession and academic discipline also received a very late start. Although George Washington was elected as first U.S. president in 1789, it was nearly a century before any serious attempt took place to structure a professional public administration or civil service system in America. Somewhat illogically, the public administration profession, once it started to take on a professional character, existed for close to a half century before any clear indications appeared that public administration had emerged as a distinct field of study. In 1926 Leonard D. White published *Introduction to the Study of Public Administration,* the first book devoted solely to the study of the principles of public management.[36] The first comprehensive administrative law casebook did not appear until 1940.[37]

Our government's early administrators were well educated but certainly not in public administration and administrative law. By and large, early presidents hired persons as civil servants on the basis of their fitness credentials: that is, on the basis of how well they reflected the president's political views. Although political historians have generally credited President Andrew Jackson as the designer of the spoils system in American politics, the practice of presidents' appointing those to office who agree with them was a common custom long before the Jackson presidency. In fact, appointing and removing persons to administrative posts on grounds of shared political beliefs was so common in Thomas Jefferson's administration that Paul Van Riper, a renowned civil service political historian, has claimed that Jefferson could easily be "considered the founder of the spoils system in American politics."[38]

However, the administrative personnel system, which developed under administrations before Jackson's presidency began in 1829, was radically different. While President Jackson was an egalitarian, Presidents Washington, John Adams, Jefferson, Madison, Monroe, and John Quincy Adams appointed to administrative positions only persons who had socioeconomic status similar to their own. Appointing commoners to governmental jobs at the federal level was unthinkable before Andrew Jackson's administration. But Jackson's brand of spoils, or patronage politics, buried elitist public administration forever in America. Since Jackson's time there has been an unabated movement toward opening up the civil service system to virtually all classes.

Because President Jackson so deeply loathed what he perceived as the decadent traits of the Federalist civil servants, who still occupied many administrative positions at the time he assumed office, his spoils politics probably evolved into an overreactive force directed at purging the federal bureaucracy of all Federalist remnants, especially leftover Federalist employees. Assuming that governmental work was easy and anyone could handle the simple tasks of government, Jackson proceeded to replace the remaining well-educated upper-class Federalist administrators with his friends, relatives, and supporters, placing little emphasis on their educational merits or professional experience, especially if they had helped in his bid for the presidency. Such personnel recruitment practices soon gave great popularity to the phrase, "to the victor belongs the spoils," which epitomizes spoils politics.

For the record, however, it is worth noting that Jackson did not believe that patronage jobs should be filled only by loyal supporters. He felt that these people should also be reasonably capable. It was really his successors who employed the spoils system in its worst form.

In any event, versions of the Jacksonian meritless spoils system soon became quite popular. Jackson's successors engaged in spoils politics to staff the federal bureaucracy after their election triumphs. The spoils system idea spread rapidly to state and local governments as well, although spoils administrations had been functioning on a limited basis before Jackson's presidency. By the 1860s, spoils politics had become so pervasive, yet inefficient and corrupt, that President Abraham Lincoln was motivated to declare to a group of eager patronage seekers who had assembled in his outer office that this "spoils system might in the course of time become far more dangerous to the Republic than the rebellion itself."

The Pendleton Act of 1883   The pertinent point is that before the Civil War's end there had never existed a systematic and relentless attempt to professionalize public administration. Specifically, there had been no concerted effort to seek efficiency, effectiveness, integrity, and procedural due process (the chief focus of administrative law) in governmental administration. However, after the Civil War, reform-oriented persons set out to destroy machine government, which had achieved its strength and cohesiveness from the spoils system. The reform movement quickly picked up momentum as the press began to wage an unyielding attack against various political machines—the most notable being the one against the Tweed machine of the late 1860s and early 1870s which had thoroughly corrupted municipal administration in New York City.[39]

Generally, the reformers' central goal was to make government more democratically accountable to the people. However, they were concerned in particular with governmental administration since patronage politics had succeeded in filling national, state, and local governments with blatantly unqualified administrators. These administrators, more loyal to the machine than to constitutional principles, had little understanding of the significance of due process and equal protection under the law. Consequently, those who came before them were likely to be treated in an arbitrary and capricious manner. Friends of the machine may have benefited, but others tended to be denied their rights and privileges.

Past attempts by reformers to obtain reform civil service legislation had failed at the federal level. In 1881 the contention by the reformers that patronage politics was severely out of control obtained instant credibility when Charles Guiteau, angered because President Garfield had not given him the patronage job he sought, shot and killed Garfield. "Enough is enough!" cried the reformers. Civil service reform, which for years had drawn only modest attention, suddenly became a national issue. Less than two years later, the Pendleton Act, or the Civil Service Act of 1883 (22 Stat. 403), represented an attempt by reformers to depoliticize and professionalize the administrative process at the national level. Endorsed enthusiastically by the newly formed National Civil Service Reform League, the Pendleton Act became the first civil service law enacted by Congress. Congress had taken its first major step toward making public administration a professional and respectable profession. However, during the decades to follow, similar civil service acts were enacted in states and municipalities.

The original Civil Service Act, which has been amended several times since 1883, contained many provisions aimed at promoting a more professional federal administrative system by making administrative work more politically neutral, but especially more independent of the corruptive influences of spoils politics. Accordingly, the act's major provisions required that (1) employees be selected through open and competitive examinations; (2) civil service workers be protected from various outside political influence-peddling and solicitations; (3) civil servants be given meaningful job tenure and protected against removal for political reasons; (4) allocation of federal civil service jobs to the states and U.S. territories be done according to population (thus geographically spreading the influence of merit employees); (5) a three-member Civil Service Commission responsible for regulating the civil service system be created (replaced in 1979 by the Merit Systems Protection Board), on which only two could be from the same political party; and (6) the president determine through executive order the administrative employee classifications under the commission's authority. Also evident in these provisions is an attempt to encourage careerism and administrative expertise in the federal civil service. The reformers felt this was needed if governmental administrators were to become more efficient and responsive.

In actuality, however, the Pendleton Act had only a limited impact on federal administrative practices. Stiff opposition from spoils politicians, who struggled to retain the personal advantages of the patronage system, caused the original Civil Service Act to be limited to less than 11 percent of all civilian federal employees. Although states, cities, and counties began to pass civil service legislation (New York in 1883, Massachusetts in 1884, Albany and New York City in 1884, and Cook County, Illinois, in 1895), even cursory observation of American politics showed that in all of these areas machine politics flourished, despite the existing civil service legislation.

Woodrow Wilson was probably the first distinguished scholar to condemn public administration at all governmental levels in America, even after civil service reform had started. Wilson exclaimed: "The poisonous atmosphere of city government, the crooked secrets of state administration, the confusion, sinecurism, and corruption ever and again discovered in the bureau of Washington forbid us to believe that any clear conceptions of what constitutes good administration are as yet very widely current in the United States." To Wilson, it was essential that a science of public administration be developed, especially since the tasks of public policy making and execution were growing more complex with each passing day. He believed a science of administration was vital "to straighten the paths of government, to make its business less businesslike, to strengthen and purify its organization, and to crown its duties with dutifulness."[40] More specifically, Wilson argued that it was necessary to discover a science of administration "to rescue executive methods from the confusion and costliness of empirical experiment and set them upon foundations laid deep in stable principle." Accordingly, he maintained, "we must regard civil-service reform in its present stages as but a prelude to a fuller administrative reform."[41]

To build a democratically responsible administrative network, Wilson contended that administrators must be placed in their proper role in the political system. But what the proper role of public administrators should be is a tough question, one which has not yet been resolved by public administration and administrative law scholars. Despite the complexity of the issue, Wilson agreed with the reformers that governmental administration could be improved if administrative and political functions were separated from each other. For him it was patently obvious that "administration lies outside the proper sphere of *politics.* Administrative questions are not political questions. Although politics sets the tasks for administration, it should not be suffered to manipulate its offices."[42] Consequently, Wilson concluded with the assertion that "this discrimination between administration and politics is by now, happily, too obvious to need further discussion."[43]

Wilson's basic claim that administration could be made more scientific, and thus more professionally efficient, if it were separated from politics gained broad support from the reform-oriented public during his day. Max Weber, in particular, described as ideal a public bureaucracy that recruited and promoted personnel on the basis of merit examinations and that is subject to only general political controls. Weber also suggested, as did Luther Gulick years later, that there were certain discoverable administrative principles which tended to promote administrative expertise.[44] Daily political meddling in administrative affairs would tend only to disrupt technical, nonpolitical administrative operations. In numerous decisions the courts have generally upheld the notion that needless political meddling serves only to disrupt the administrative process.

By the 1940s the ideas of these reformers began to come under severe attack, especially their notion that administrators should be separated from politics. Now the claim was that administrators had become too powerful and too independent of traditional democratic controls; for example, nonelected city managers had replaced elected mayors, while independent regulatory commissions were now performing legislative tasks once carried out by Congress. Some critics today continue to believe reform has gone too far. The most prevalent arguments presented against reform government today are: (1) administrators now have too much neutral power, which cannot be held democratically accountable; (2) administrative discretion is so broad that it challenges the principles of democratic constitutionalism; (3) administrators are cold, aloof, and insensitive; and (4) it is patently absurd to argue that politics can be separated from administration since administration is inherently a part of the political process. No doubt there is some validity in the contention that administration cannot be functionally separated from politics, but students of administrative law are confronted with the problem of figuring out just how much interplay should exist between politicians and administrative experts.[45]

In any event, the arguments presented by the reformers have been largely persuasive and have inspired Congress to enact legislation aimed at upgrading the original 1883 act. Major revisions include: (1) the 1912 Lloyd-LaFollette Act,[46] which allowed civil service workers to join labor unions, while it also permitted employees certain rights in challenging attempts to remove them from their jobs (although these rights were originally weak, Executive Order 10988 by President John F. Kennedy significantly strengthened employee bargaining rights in general); (2) the 1920 Civil Service Retirement Act, as amended, which provides retirement and survival benefits to former civil service employees and their families;[47] (3) the Classification Act, as amended, which initiated a method for classifying employees and establishing salary scales;[48] (4) the 1939 Hatch Act, which essentially attempts to protect civil service employees from being subjected to political pressures from their employers;[49] (5) the Ramspeck Act (Civil Service Act of 1940), which placed about 90 percent of all civilian federal employee classifications under the civil service system;[50] (6) the 1949 Veterans' Preference Act which gives special scoring advantages on the civil service examinations to veterans;[51] (7) the Federal Salary Reform Act of 1962, as amended, which established that federal salaries should be comparable to those in private enterprise;[52] and (8) the Civil Service Reform Act of 1978 (92 Stat. 1111), which further clarified veterans' preferences on merit examinations; created a Senior Executive Service; a Federal Labor Relations Authority to deal with unfair labor practices in the federal service; and, by dividing it into the Office of Personnel Management and the Merit Systems Protection Board, responded to employee doubts about the objectivity of the Civil Service Commission, which had performed conflicting management-oriented and employee-oriented functions.[53]

However, despite specific attempts by reformers to eliminate patronage politics in public employment, as well as two Supreme Court decisions, *Branti* v. *Finkel* 445 U.S. 507 (1980) and *Rutan* v. *Republican Party of Illinois,* 110 S.Ct. 2729 (1990), which essentially prohibits nonmeritorious patronage hiring and firing practices for virtually all public employees unless they are in high policy-making positions requiring "trust" and "confidentiality," politicians, especially at the state and local levels, have somehow kept patronage politics healthy. In studying the persistence of patronage politics in Illinois, David K. Hamilton noted that ". . . a personnel code with rules and regulations to foster merit and a supposedly independent commission to monitor compliance are no match for a determined assault on merit hiring by the political leadership of the government."[54]

Legal Challenges to the Civil Service System: Merit versus Employee Rights

The development of the federal civil service system based upon meritorious service, as contrasted with a public administration system rooted in patronage, has not evolved free from legal challenges that questioned the merit system's constitutional and statutory legitimacy. Vehement protests have been made over the years by various activist groups who have charged that federal civil service policies serve to restrict constitutionally sanctioned participation in politics, prohibit equal opportunity in federal agencies, prevent effective collective bargaining, and in other ways deny public employees certain rights and privileges. Similar charges have been lodged against state civil service systems. The claims against the merit system raise some interesting constitutional-administrative law questions in regard to how far legislators can go in passing restrictive legislation engineered to make civil service more professional and accountable.

Restricting Political Activities   The Hatch Act of 1939 has been by far the most controversial piece of civil service legislation passed since the Pendleton Act. As Karl T. Thurber, Jr. asserts, "[T]he Hatch Act long has represented contentious public policy, public administration, constitutional, and political participation issues."[55] In 1907 President Theodore Roosevelt, a progressive who was sympathetic to the struggles of the reformers to free public service employment from undesirable political influence, issued Executive Order 642. In this order Roosevelt stated that civil service employees should be restricted from playing any active role in campaign management or campaign politics, although they were entitled to retain their constitutional rights as citizens to vote freely and to express privately their political beliefs. The executive order had limited impact, so in 1939, during Franklin Roosevelt's term, the Hatch Act was passed as a more forceful effort to take politics out of administration. The original Hatch Act prohibited civil service employees from using their "official authority or influence for the purpose of interfering with or affecting the result of an election" and from taking "an active part in political management or in political campaigns," but it allowed such an employee to retain "the right to vote as he chooses and to express his opinion on political subjects and candidates." However, the 1939 Hatch Act allowed employees to participate in nonpartisan political activities. Violation of the act's prohibitions could result in removal from office.

Basically, the Hatch Act, since its initial enactment, has been controversial because it did, in fact, forbid certain political activities of employees simply because they happened to work for the federal civil service system. The courts did not deny that the act actually takes away political rights held by noncivil service employees, but the justices argued that such denials were a reasonable price to pay to protect the civil service system from political pressures that could undermine professional public administration practices. In *United Public Workers v. Mitchell,* 330 U.S. 75

'LOOK—NOW YOU CAN GET INVOLVED IN POLITICS!'

Source: Reprinted with permission of Tom Engelhardt and the *St. Louis Post-Dispatch,* October 8, 1993.

(1947), the Supreme Court upheld the act's provisions that allowed civil service employment to be terminated if an employee chooses to participate in political activities in violation of the act. Again in 1973, in *United States Civil Service Commission* v. *National Association of Letter Carriers, AFL-CIO,* 413 U.S. 548, 567, the Court upheld the validity of the Hatch Act, concluding that "plainly identifiable acts of political management and political campaigning on the part of federal employees may constitutionally be prohibited." In reaching this decision, Justice Byron White, writing the Court's opinion, noted that the act's purpose is to ensure the government's noble end—"the impartial execution of its laws." Although Congress has placed some restrictions on free speech, the Court maintained that the act does not "seek to control political opinions or beliefs, or to interfere with or influence anyone's vote at the poll." Further, the Court held that Congress should have the right to strike a balance between the interests of employees as citizens and the interests of the government as an employer determined to promote efficiency in the federal civil service. The Court cited five justifications of the act's restrictions, thus enabling this reasonable balance to be achieved. The Court argued that: (1) civil service employees "should administer the law in accordance with the will of Congress, rather than in accordance with their own or the will of a political party"; (2) it is essential that the civil service remain in fact, as well as in appearance, politically neutral "if confidence in the system of representative Government is not to be eroded to a disastrous extent"; (3) given the large number of governmental employees on tap, it is imperative that they not be manipulated by political parties wanting to "build a powerful, invincible and perhaps corrupt political machine . . . paid for at public expense"; (4) employment and promotional opportunities should "not depend on political performance"; and (5) such employees should remain "free from pressure and from express or tacit invitation to vote in a certain way or perform political chores in order to curry favor with their supervisors rather than to act out their own beliefs." In *William M. Broadrick* v. *Oklahoma*, 413 U.S. 601 (1973), a companion case to the *Letter Carriers'* case, the Court upheld restrictions placed upon Oklahoma's state employees which were similar to the limitations placed upon federal workers under the Hatch Act.

In 1990 President Bush vetoed a Hatch Act reform bill, contending that the bill would undermine meritorious employment in the federal service. While the Republicans argued that the existing Hatch Act served to protect federal employees from political pressures, the Democrats held that the Hatch Act unfairly and unconstitutionally restricted unnecessarily the right of their employees to participate in political activities.[56]

The persistence of the Democrats, led by Senator John Glenn (D-Ohio) and Congressman William Clay (D-Missouri), finally prevailed once Bill Clinton was elected president. On October 6, 1993, President Clinton signed into law PL 103–94, a new law which significantly alters the old 1993 Hatch Act. The 1993 revised Hatch Act actually tightens on-the-job restrictions placed upon most federal and postal employees, but lifts many restrictions previously placed upon these employees while they are off duty. Under the amended 1993 Hatch Act, most federal employees and postal workers, while on the job, may not engage in any political activities. This includes even wearing campaign buttons, which the old Hatch Act actually allowed. Yet when off duty, these employees may actively participate in partisan politics. Specifically, for example, they can now participate in political campaigns; manage campaigns; organize and participate in political meetings, fundraisers, and rallies; carry posters, distribute campaign literature, and solicit votes; run and participate in phone banks; publically support and endorse candidates; and solicit contributions for the political action committee of the employee's organization from the organization's other members, as long as the employees targeted are not subordinates of the employee doing the soliciting. The 1993 Hatch Act does prohibit these employees from soliciting contributions from the general public; running for partisan political office; using their official position to influence the results of an election; and soliciting or discouraging any political activities with any persons having business with the employee's office or with any persons under investigation, audit, or enforcement action by the employee's office. The 1993 Hatch Act also does not apply to many senior executive officials (for example, those in the Executive Office, departmental heads and assistants, and presidential appointees requiring senate confirmation), or to federal employees in "sensitive positions" (for example, Federal Elections Commission, Defense Intelligence Agency, Merit Systems Protection Boards, and Administrative Law Judges).[57]

The real irony is that most surveys showed that federal employees overwhelmingly opposed Hatch Act reform, fearing increased political pressures and compromises to meritorious job performance.[58] Additionally, in a Merit Systems Protection Board survey of personnel specialists, 36 percent believed that Hatch Act reform would have a negative impact on federal employment, only 11 percent felt it would have a positive effect, and the rest thought it would have no impact or were undecided.[59] Consensus opinion seems to be that the 1993 Hatch Act is a step backward because it has the potential of exposing federal workers once again to political coercion and undermining the professionalism in the federal civil service. Only time will tell.

Labor Grievances   Consistent with the purposes of civil service legislation in general, and the Lloyd-LaFollette Act in particular (5 U.S.C., Section 7501a), "an individual in the competitive service may be removed or suspended without pay only for such cause as will promote the efficiency of the service." The Lloyd-LaFollette Act, under Section 7501(b), outlines the extent of procedural due process rights that must be accorded when an employee is dismissed or suspended without pay. When such actions are taken, a civil service employee "is entitled to reasons in writing and to: (1) notice of action sought and of any charges preferred against him; (2) a copy of the charges; (3) a reasonable time for filing a written answer to the charges, with affidavits; and (4) a written decision on the answer at the earliest practical date." The act also makes clear that "examination of witnesses, trial, or hearing is not required but may be provided in the discretion of the individual directing the removal or suspension without pay" (Sec. 7501, b, 4).

In *Arnett* v. *Kennedy,* 416 U.S. 134 (1974), Wayne Kennedy, a dismissed civil service employee who had been accorded the rights he was entitled under the Lloyd-LaFollette Act, charged that the act's protections failed to provide him with the due process protections guaranteed to him under the Constitution. Specifically, Kennedy claimed that he should be given a pretermination "trial type hearing before an impartial hearing officer before he could be removed from his employment." His employment constituted a property interest, which entitled him to elaborate due process rights under the Fifth Amendment. The practical question for the Court was whether Kennedy should be entitled to constitutional protections beyond those granted to him by statutes. Because the Court acknowledged that property rights are not determined by the Constitution, but only protected by it once the property rights have been created by statutory entitlement or rules, the Court ruled that civil service employment should not be considered a property right unless Congress wants to make it one. The Court reasoned that Congress is entitled to establish the procedures which can be used to determine the cause for a civil service employee's dismissal or suspension. Pretermination hearings are not mandated by the Constitution, the Court held. Although an employee's interest may be in job security, the government's interest is in promoting efficiency in the administrative system. Accordingly, Congress had the authority, in the interests of administrative efficiency, to legislate procedures to provide for fair dismissal review without placing a detrimental burden on the administrative process (at 152).

However, two cases in the 1980s flatly overruled the reasoning employed by Justice Rehnquist's plurality opinion in *Arnett* that a property interest (right or entitlement) can be conditioned by a statute that places restrictions on due process protections. In holding that a state employee had a property interest in using the Illinois Fair Employment Practices Act's adjudicatory procedures that was protected by the due process clause of the Fourteenth Amendment, the Supreme Court in *Logan* v. *Zimmerman Brush Co.*, 102 S.Ct. 1148 (1982), rejected the Arnett-based contention that the state legislature has the prerogative to limit due process protections connected with property entitlements simply because state statute had created the property interest in the first place. The Court reasoned that once the legislature confers a property interest entitlement, it must safeguard the property interest with the mandated constitutional due process protections." Indeed, any other conclusion would allow the State to destroy at will virtually any state-created property interest" (at 1156). Quoting from *Vitek* v. *Jones*, 445 U.S. 480, 490–491(1980), the Court noted: "While the legislature may elect not to confer a property interest, . . . it may not constitutionally authorize the deprivation of such an interest." Three years later in *Cleveland Board of Education* v. *Loudermill,* 105 S.Ct. 1487 (1985), the Supreme Court reiterated its legal position taken in *Logan* by holding that Loudermill, an employee dismissed by the Cleveland Board of Education for filling out his employment application dishonestly, had a property interest in continued employment and, therefore, had a right to due process protections. The Court said that minimum due process in this case would not require a full evidentiary hearing, but at least "some kind of hearing" so that Loudermill would not be deprived of a significant property right without an opportunity to be heard. At the very least, the Court asserted, Loudermill "is entitled to oral or written notice of the charges against him, an explanation of the employer's evidence, and an opportunity to present his side of the story" (at 1495).

Loudermill is an important precedential decision, yet it should not be interpreted as a liberal decision since it provides for extending only minimum due process hearing protections even when property or liberty interests are involved. In some cases, the informal "some kind of hearing" rights extended bordered on being practically meaningless. For example, in *Goff* v. *Dailey,* 991 F.2d 1437 (8th Cir. 1993), citing *Loudermill,* the court held that a prisoner's due process hearing rights may be satisfied by simply providing ". . . notice and an opportunity for the claimant to tell the decisionmaker his side of the story. No more is required here . . . . Inmates are certainly not constitutionally entitled to the level playing field created by a fully adversarial proceeding . . ." (at 1441).

Probably the greatest complaint voiced by public employee unions against civil service employment in the past several decades is that public employees have been generally deprived of the most persuasive collective bargaining tool—the right to strike. In the private sector, however, the Taft-Hartley Act (National Labor Relations Act of 1947; 61 Stat. 136) gave workers the right to strike. Because strikes by public employees have been thought to jeopardize the public interest, such strikes have been traditionally prohibited by common law. On the state level, strikes by public employees have been outlawed by state statutes. Some states, however, have passed laws allowing restricted strike powers to public employees, usually in those service areas perceived as nonessential. On the federal level, all public employee strikes are strictly forbidden, and consequently, civil service employees feel discriminated against. These workers argue that effective collective bargaining negotiations cannot be carried out if the government's managers know that employees cannot actually strike to win their demands. On the other hand, others contend that public employees are, in fact, different from workers in the private sector. Public employees, they maintain, should not be given the power to strike because strikes by civil servants could throw government and society into chaos. It is also maintained that public employee strikes would cause the costs of running a government to skyrocket because government would eventually have to surrender to the strikers' pay demands to stay in business. In contrast, in the private sector labor unions know that they cannot ask for demands which the company cannot afford in the competitive marketplace. Thus, demands are limited by natural market forces. Unrealistic demands would simply put companies out of business. But unrealistic public employee demands could be placed on government because the government provides vital public services which must be continued. Further, the government is not perceived to be constrained by the normal competitive market forces.

In *United Federation of Postal Clerks* v. *Blunt,* 404 U.S. 802 (1971), the Court rejected the contention of public employees that the right to strike was a constitutionally protected right. Specifically, the United Federation of Postal Clerks held that their constitutional rights had been violated by federal statutes prohibiting strikes because antistrike clauses take away public employees' rights of free speech and assembly and deny them equal protection under law since private employees have the statutory right to strike. However, the district court asserted that neither private nor public employees have a constitutional right to strike under common law doctrine. Private workers were given a specific statutory right to strike when Congress legislated the Taft-Hartley Act. Congress's legislative intent was clear. But Congress has never found it appropriate to provide federal employees with the strike power. Given the reality that the power to strike is not a fundamental right, plus the fact that no statutes exist which grant this right to federal employees, the Court failed to see how it could rule against congressional intent.[60]

Other Questions Pertaining to Public Employment Rights   In the 1990s questions regarding the rights of public employees appear endless. Public employment rights concerns range from equal opportunity in obtaining public service employment to issues of proper dress or to the rights of sexual minorities in the civil service. Because the issues seem numerous, and since many of the merit v. employee rights disputes are treated elsewhere in the book, only a few issues are noted here.

To combat the ruination of public administration by spoils politics, Congress initially proceeded in the late 1800s to make the civil service system more professional by simply legislating measures designed to promote meritorious administrative behavior in public agencies. One way to accomplish this task was to make certain that the best-qualified applicants were permitted to enter public service. Merit examinations seemed to provide a safe path to this goal. Test results allowed governmental recruiters to screen and select applicants on the basis of their performance on the examinations. Promotions were also based almost solely upon past performance and new testing. Tests seemed to be the solution to virtually all staffing problems, while democratic accountability in administration was measured almost exclusively in terms of efficiency criteria.

But starting with the 1960s, this all began to change as different groups challenged the legitimacy and fairness of the merit system's values and procedures. The fundamental claim was made that the merit system discriminated unfairly against various social groups. Women charged that the system discriminated against them because of their sex, while minorities, especially African-Americans, claimed that institutional racism prevented them from having equal access to public employment. Minorities, particularly blacks and Latinos, held that even the civil service examinations were unfair because they had a class and subculture bias.

Minority group and women's rights activism succeeded in persuading legislators, agency rule makers, and judges at the national and local governmental levels that civil service personnel policies were discriminatory. Congress passed the Civil Rights Act of 1964 (78 Stat. 241), the Equal Employment Opportunity Act of 1972 (86 Stat. 103), and a host of affirmative action legislation, while administrative rule makers promulgated rules intended to equalize employment and promotional opportunities in public jobs. Special federal attention was focused on placing minorities and women in higher classification levels, and state governments and local communities tended to follow suit.

The courts generally affirmed the legality of the actions taken by legislators and administrators. In *Griggs* v. *Duke Power Company,* 401 U.S. 424 (1971), the Supreme Court held that employers must not use selection criteria that discriminate in regard to race, religion, or national origin. Any screening or testing methods must be demonstrably job related. In this case the Court emphasized that selection criteria are illegal if they have a negative discriminatory *effect* in regard to race, sex, religion, or national origin, even if the selection methods did not have that *intent*. Legal experts point out that an effects test is a considerably stronger measure than an intent test for the simple reason that it is difficult to prove intent (for example, to prove that racial discrimination was the intent), but relatively easy to show the effects of some policy (for example, that measurable discrimination regarding race resulted). However, in *Washington, Mayor of Washington, D. C. et al.* v. *Davis,* 426 U.S. 229 (1976), the Court modified the Riggs holding in ruling on the constitutionality of recruiting practices employed by the District of Columbia. Here, the justices argued that the Court did not embrace "the proposition that a law or other official act, without regard to whether it reflects a racially discriminatory purpose is, unconstitutional *solely* because it has a racially disproportionate impact" (at 239). However, in *U.S. v. Paradise,* 107 S.Ct. 1053 (1987), Justice Brennan made clear in writing the plurality opinion that promotion procedures will likely be overruled as unconstitutional if they are found to have an "adverse impact on blacks" (at 1067). In recent affirmative action cases, it is quite evident that the courts have not taken a firm and definitive stand on the extent to which the merit principle should be compromised where the federal government has jurisdiction, in order to provide greater opportunities in employment, school admissions, and the like, to those who are less qualified and have been discriminated against, as a class, in the past.

Some critics, although they believe that compensatory programs for women and minorities may be justified on humanitarian grounds, nevertheless fear what may happen to governmental performance because of the apparent replacement of the merit system with an affirmative action-distributive justice patronage system. In rejecting the merit system, one also rejects the strong and credible argument, espoused by Max Weber and others, in regard to the advantages of a meritorious civil service system over all other forms. And it should be remembered that the argument for a merit system is not an argument against equal opportunity in Weber's thinking. In fact, Weber and his followers have maintained that an administrative system rooted in the principles of merit tends to be more open and classless (more consistent with democratic ideals) because opportunities are based upon objective performance measures, not on the basis of social class.

Still another public employees' rights question pertains to the role an employee's personal behavior should play in agency decisions regarding recruitment, promotion, and dismissal. The courts have been fairly clear on this issue, having taken the general position in recent years that employees' personal lives should be separated from their professional lives as far as the public employer is concerned. In *Norton v. May,* 417 F.2d 1161, 1165 (1969), in a precedential decision, the Court of Appeals for the District of Columbia ruled that proof must be given to substantiate the charge that an employee's personal conduct has "an ascertainable deleterious effect on the efficiency of the service." Otherwise, the court maintained, the Constitution protects the right of an individual in personal affairs. Thus, this decision places the burden of proof on the agency to show that a person's dress, personal appearance, sexual preference, and so on has such a negative effect on agency operations that the individual should not be employed, promoted, or retained by the agency. Public employers have had limited success in demonstrating such.

As old issues involving public employee rights are settled, new issues will always surface. As we approach the twenty-first century, public agencies will continue, for example, to face questions pertaining to sexual harassment, testing employees for drugs and AIDS, and evolving new issues. Such issues require the courts to balance individual privacy rights against the rights of society. Unquestionably, society has a right to prevent conditions which can have a "deleterious effect on the efficiency of public service," yet public employees also have fundamental privacy rights under the Fourth and Fifth Amendments that need to be reasonably protected.

THE ADMINISTRATIVE PROCEDURE ACT:
AN OVERVIEW OF ITS ROLE IN CONTROLLING
ADMINISTRATIVE BEHAVIOR

An administrative agency may be referred to as an administration, an agency, a board, a bureau, a commission, a corporation, a department, a division, an office, an officer, and so on. The titles have been applied casually and rather arbitrarily. Consequently, no substantive differences exist between, say, the Office of Family Services and the Division of Family Services, especially from the perspective of administrative law. They are both welfare agencies providing the same basic services to the public and obligated by statutes to follow prescribed procedures. Thus, the names assigned to them are inconsequential. What is important, as noted in Chapter 2, is that these agencies have been born at an increasing rate since July 31, 1789, when the first administrative agency was created at the federal level. Before 1900 only about one-third of present federal agencies existed; within another thirty years, supposedly during an era of conservatism, another third of our present number was added.[61] A similar proliferation took place on the state level, although the number of state and municipal agencies has really soared in recent decades, while the rate of growth on the national level seems to have declined somewhat.

But counting heads is not enough. It provides only one side of the story. Not only have agencies increased in sheer number, but public agencies have also expanded in size, scope, and procedural complexity, especially since 1932. Because of the rapid expansion of the administrative system, many Americans became alarmed during the New Deal. Pressured to investigate the possible exploitations of unchecked administrative power, FDR in the late 1930s was moved to form a commission to deal with the problems of procedural reform in public administration at the federal level. The Brownlow Commission prepared a comprehensive report on procedural problems confronting the federal administrative system. The Brownlow Commission's 1937 recommendations for procedural reform, along with reports by the American Bar Association on the state of administrative law, and the 1941 report of the Attorney General's Committee on Administrative Procedure, inspired Congress after World War II to draft and unanimously pass the Administrative Procedure Act of 1946.[62] Although by 1959 only five states followed the 1946 Model State Administrative Procedure Act, today about two-thirds of the states follow wholly or in part the Revised Model State Administrative Procedure Act of 1981 or the original 1946 Model State Administrative Procedure Act, or its amended 1961 version, while other states follow administrative plans of some kind.[63] The federal APA, as amended, is in the Appendix.

According to Kenneth Culp Davis and Richard J. Pierce, Jr., "[T]he major effects of the Act were to satisfy the political will for reform, to improve and strengthen the administrative process, to enhance uniformity in the administrative process, and to preserve the basic limits upon judicial review of administrative action."[64] In many respects, the federal APA symbolizes American commitment to fair administrative processes. Or, in the words of the court in *Riverbend Farms, Inc.* v. *Madigan,* 958

F.2d 1479 (9th Cir. 1992), "[T]he Administrative Procedures Act ensures that the massive federal bureaucracy remains tethered to those it governs or so the theory goes" (at 1483–84). Actually, much of what is said in the APA simply reiterates and elaborates on fair governmental standards already in the Constitution, especially under the due process clauses of the Fifth and Fourteenth Amendments. The act also reflects the attitudes toward administrative due process, as reflected in prior court decisions involving questions of due process, particularly the famous *Morgan* cases.[65]

Despite the APA's weaknesses, mostly attributed to its vagueness and loopholes that tend to protect agency interests, the act does represent the most meaningful piece of federal legislation in the field of administrative law. The APA is the most comprehensive, authoritative, and enduring legislation governing administrative practice in the United States today. To preserve the probity of the APA, the courts, ad hoc committees, and Congress (the act has been amended several times) have spent considerable time since its passage attempting to resolve inherent legal difficulties and generally upgrading and refining its functional effectiveness. Critics of the APA have charged that the act needs additional overhauling. However, the latest revised APA shows that no drastic revisions have been made to the act.

In general, the Administrative Procedure Act is a legislative weapon employed by Congress to promote democratic responsibility in administrative agencies, especially by limiting arbitrary and capricious agency actions and generally opening the administrative process to public view and scrutiny. Basically, the intent of Congress was to apply rule-of-law principles to the administrative process. Thus, the APA is aimed largely at making administrative behavior consistent and predictable over time and doing away with whimsical, unpredictable, and constitutionally repulsive administrative decision making. More specifically, major provisions in the APA are aimed at making the administrative process more democratically accountable. Some examples of methods follow: (1) requiring administrators to make public their proposed procedures and activities; (2) permitting those affected by rules and orders to testify in their own defense; (3) allowing persons who are compelled to appear before an agency to be represented and advised by counsel; (4) forcing agency administrators to disclose to concerned parties designated "unclassified" materials for inspection; (5) placing the burden of proof on administrators in specific cases; (6) allowing affected persons the right to submit reasonable information and arguments for the purpose of influencing agency decisions; (7) demanding that agencies keep adequate records so that agency decisions can be easily reviewed if appealed to higher levels; (8) providing for appellate remedies within the agency; (9) creating a quasi-independent status for administrative law judges to better ensure impartial hearings; (10) allowing for judicial review of agency actions; and (11) generally limiting unnecessary and undesirable administrative discretion.

Each of these procedural safeguards is described and evaluated in some detail in later chapters. However, it should be acknowledged here that there exists much criticism regarding the effectiveness of the APA in practice, although on the whole the act has done a reasonably good job of preventing flagrant violations of administrative due process norms. Probably the chief general criticism that has been lodged against the APA is that the act has numerous loopholes which allow determined administrators to use the letter of the law to avoid having to uphold the spirit of the law. But one thing is for certain: If the APA is to control administrative behavior in a respectable fashion in the 1990s, it will have to be modernized so that it can realistically respond and adjust to the many changes taking place in public administration and administrative law over the past decade. The most notable recent changes in public administration, which have obvious administrative law implications, are these: (1) increased reliance on administrators to resolve socioeconomic crises; (2) greater administrative roles in public policy making; (3) increased openness in agency activities; (4) the new demands placed on domestic administrative decision making by the pressures of international politics; (5) the blurring of the line between what may be considered rightfully public versus private administration; (6) the intensifying controversy between public versus private rights; (7) the frustrating pressures to accommodate the simultaneous demands for equal rights and opportunities, affirmative action, and meritorious administrative service; (8) experimental deregulation and reregulation in selected industries (e.g., transportation, communications, and banking); (9) new statutory demands for administrators to employ complex, sophisticated, and controversial evaluational techniques to determine the worth (costs and benefits) of proposed agency rules; and (10) growing problems associated with regulating new technologies (e.g., nuclear power and chemicals) that, frankly, our public administrators do not fully understand. Dramatic developments have also occurred in recent decades in administrative law, including (1) the rapid increase in the number of rules promulgated by governmental agencies; (2) the emergence of new conflicts due to the passage of the Freedom of Information, Privacy, Sunshine, and Ethics Acts; (3) new statutory provisions sanctioning more public participation in agency decision making; (4) the increasing vulnerability of federal agencies to lawsuits following the abolition of sovereign immunity status once enjoyed by federal agencies and the erosion of official immunity for public officials; (5) closer judicial oversight in most administrative areas; (6) the new judicial challenge to competently review cases involving extremely complicated technological questions of fact; and (7) sweeping and abrupt doctrinal changes (e.g., the presumption in favor of hearing rights for those exercising new "property" and "liberty" interests; the invalidation of the legislative veto; and the startling, although inconsistent, return to a stricter judicial application of the separation-of-powers doctrine).

The Freedom of Information Act

Despite the fact that disclosure of information about governmental operations is consistent with democratic theory, apparently public administrators feel an almost instinctive need to resist any efforts by those who wish to make administrators disclose any more information than they must to information-seeking parties. On July 4, 1966, President Lyndon B. Johnson signed into law the Freedom of Information Act (80 Stat. 383), which constituted a progressive amendment to the public information section of the 1946 APA. In signing the legislation, President Johnson declared (as quoted by Harold C. Relyea): "I have always believed that freedom of information is so vital that only the national security, not the desire of public officials or private citizens, should determine when it must be restricted."[66]

In passing the Freedom of Information Act (FOIA), the only general goal of Congress was to ensure that any person could obtain information from public agencies about the operations of the government. Congress did not demand in the act that genuinely sensitive or personal information be released. Why were administrators so upset about the prospect that they would have to live with such a constitutionally sanctioned measure as the FOIA? Could they not see that a viable democratic system cannot function if the people are unable to obtain the information necessary to intelligently scrutinize governmental operations? Does not popular government theory rest on the assumption that in order for the people to maintain popular control over their government, they must be able to know what their government is doing? Does not the viability of the First Amendment ultimately depend upon reasonably open access to governmental information? In a letter on August 4, 1822, to W. T. Barry, James Madison placed the need for open disclosure in vivid perspective: "A popular government without popular information, or the means of acquiring it, is but a Prologue to a Farce or a Tragedy, or perhaps both. Knowledge will forever govern ignorance: And a people who mean to be their own Governors, must arm themselves with the power which knowledge gives."[67]

Reasons for Administrative Resistance to the FOIA   Regardless of the persuasive popular government arguments in support of freedom of information legislation, the FOIA was, and continues to be, resisted by some agency administrators, although in recent years there has been some evidence that an increasing percentage of administrators has learned to accept it.

In investigating the reasons for opposition to the FOIA by administrators, it appears that fear of what this new legislation would bring constituted their fundamental concern. Specifically, some administrators felt that the act would: (1) cost them too much time in handling FOIA requests; (2) reduce their position of importance and authority because it would force them to release bureaucratic secrets, the real source of their power; (3) open their files and their own work to public scrutiny; (4) prevent them from hiding from public view any of their mistakes, especially their procedural errors and wrongdoings—probably justification enough for the FOIA as far as administrative law scholars are concerned; (5) in light of reasons three and four above, threaten their job security; and (6) place agency behavior in a fish bowl, thus inviting unnecessary trouble, especially in the form of bothersome FOIA lawsuits.[68]

Major Provisions of the Freedom of Information Act   In the spirit of open government and joint administrative procedure, a provision was attached to the 1946 Administrative Procedure Act which was aimed at preventing administrators from operating in unnecessary secrecy. Because governmental secrecy is the antithesis of democratic government, this provision almost had to be attached to the 1946 APA, especially since people at that time dreaded the consequences of the growth in administrative power. The thought of such awesome administrative power being wielded outside the view of the public eye and its control was even more alarming. However, Congress's original attempts to guarantee that nonsensitive administrative action be kept aboveboard failed miserably because the legislators were either naive or never intended for the provisions to accomplish the task of curbing secrecy in public agencies. According to the 1946 APA, agency officials were obligated to make available all agency records for public inspection unless they believed there was good cause for keeping records or information confidential.[69] But how could any realistic person expect this provision to work if administrators were left with the total discretion to determine good cause? Obviously, the 1946 Administrative Procedure Act had to be amended."[70]

The 1967 FOIA (80 Stat. 383) amended Section 552 of the 1946 APA. The FOIA's major provision is found in Section 552(a)(3) where Congress intended, except for limited exceptions, that "each agency, on request for identifiable records made in accordance with published rules stating the time, place, fees to the extent authorized by statute, and procedure to be followed, shall make the records promptly available to any person." Also, in Section 552(a)(4)(B) Congress placed the burden of proof on the agency to justify why information should not be released and provided for court review of unsatisfied requests for information by persons and punishment for agency noncompliance with FOIA dictates: "On complaint, the district court of the United States in the district in which the complainant resides, or has his principal place of business, or in which the agency records are situated, has jurisdiction to enjoin the agency from withholding agency records improperly withheld from the complainant. In such a case the court shall determine the matter de novo and the burden is on the agency to sustain its action. In the event of noncompliance with the order of the court, the district court may punish for contempt the responsible employee, and in the case of a uniformed service, the responsible member."

But the 1967 Freedom of Information Act, plagued by enfeebling political compromise measures, was doomed to fail from the start. Section 552(b) contained nine exemptions to the seemingly strong disclosure provision of Section 552(a)(3). The exemptions were so plentiful that they offered administrators who did not wish to disclose information under Section 552(a)(3) a golden opportunity to use one of the exemptions to avoid disclosing any information. Three exemptions were popularly used to avoid disclosure because they could be rationalized by administrators to relate: (1) "solely to the internal personnel rules and practices of an agency"; (2) to "trade secrets and commercial or financial information obtained from a person and privileged or confidential"; and (3) to "personnel and medical files and similar files the disclosure of which would constitute a clearly unwarranted invasion of personal privacy" [Section 552(b)(2)(4)(6)]. Other problems also emerged as administrators strengthened their resistance. In general, even if they knew that they would eventually have to release the requested information, many administrators tried their best to make it as difficult and expensive as possible for persons to obtain such information. Cherishing so-called official secrets, administrators commonly responded very slowly to requests for information. They often refused to release information which was not *specifically* requested. This made it very difficult for investigative reporters and academic researchers to obtain information since, never having been able to study it, they often could not identify the specific information which they sought. Excessive fees for copying data could be charged, also for the purpose of discouraging the disclosure of information. Stubborn administrators could even force those requesting information to go to court to obtain the information.

Upgrading the FOIA   Within a half-dozen years or so after the FOIA became law on July 1, 1967, it was obvious that the act had to be revised. Originally, Congress had intended the FOIA to be used by the press, scholars, and other citizens in the

'I Can See Better From Here'

Source: Reprinted with permission of Tom Engelhardt and the *St. Louis Post-Dispatch,* March 25, 1979.

spirit of popular and open government; but the great inconveniences, delays, and costs discouraged this. Consequently, the primary users of the FOIA became businesses seeking to obtain confidential information that they could use to gain an advantage over their competitors.[71] By the early 1970s several official reports had severely criticized the effectiveness of the FOIA and urged major revisions. The Library of Congress Task Force study, which had examined the act's successes and failures from its inception through 1971, and a 1972 House Committee Report emphasized the FOIA's general inability to compel administrators to release requested information.[72]

Congress responded in 1974 by making major revisions to the FOIA in Public Law 93–502 (88 Stat. 1561). Key amendments: (1) forced agencies to respond to requests for information within ten days, to answer all administrative appeals within twenty days, and permitted agencies to take on ten extra days to respond in extreme cases (Section 552[a][6][A][B]); (2) forbade agencies from charging research and copying fees above actual costs of the services, while requiring agencies to charge no fee if the general public would benefit (Section 552[a][4][A]); (3) allowed the district court, upon complaint, to determine through *in camera* (private) inspection whether classified agency materials should be kept classified, and to order improperly classified (held) materials to be disclosed (Section 552[a][4][B]); (4) reduced exemptions to only six categories of information which the agencies could withhold (Section 552[b][7]); (5) made the agency liable for court costs and attorneys' fees if it lost its FOIA dispute (Section 552[a][4][E]); and (6) allowed a court to order the U.S. Civil Service Commission to compel disciplinary measures to be taken against any administrators who arbitrarily and capriciously withhold information which should have been released (Section 552[a][4][F]).

But Congress did not stop its efforts to open the files of all federal administrators, including presidents, with Public Law 93–502 in 1974. In that same year Congress passed the Privacy Act (88 Stat. 1896; 5 U.S.C. 552[a]) to help ensure that disclosures of information would not unnecessarily encroach upon persons' right to privacy. In 1976 Congress drafted the Government in the Sunshine Act (90 Stat. 1241; 5 U.S.C. 552[b]), which requires, although with many exceptions, for all portions of all meetings of an agency, where the meetings are led by a collegial body and where most of the members have been appointed by the president and confirmed by the Senate, to "be open to public observation." And in 1978 Congress approved the Presidential Records Act (92 Stat. 2523), which provides for the preservation of presidential records and public access to them. This act, for example, afforded the public opportunity to gain access to the much-sought Watergate tapes, a source of information about the Nixon presidency that former President Nixon tried in vain to keep from the public eye.

Amendments to the FOIA in 1986 included waivers for attorney fees and the costs of obtaining information for noncommercial, educational, and media requesters. Congress's assumptions behind these amendments were that commercial requesters have ample resources and seek "selfish" information (e.g., trade secrets), while noncommercial requesters (e.g., reporters, scholars, and public interest groups) generally have limited resources, yet seek information (e.g., scandals within public agencies) that, if disclosed, could promote the public interest.

The FOIA has received mixed reviews. By 1980 most critics were applauding the FOIA. Kenneth C. Davis noted: "The Act as amended and interpreted has become a highly successful piece of basic legislation."[73] Samuel Archibald asserted that ". . . information may not be completely free but it is much more reasonably accessible."[74]

However, by the mid-1990s the FOIA had attracted many harsh critics. Davis now pointed out that one basic problem is that Congress seriously underestimated the burden FOIA requests would place upon federal agencies. "Agency compliance costs have been estimated at 50 to 200 million dollars per year, about 100,000 times Congress' original estimate."[75] Responding to this burden, many agencies just started ignoring the twenty- to thirty-day legal time limit for responding to FOIA requests. In turn, the courts responded to this practical problem by employing a balance doctrine, which essentially allowed agencies to take a very long time to respond as long as the agency showed "due diligence" and the requester could not show "exceptional circumstances" or an "urgent need" for the information. Robert G. Vaughn contends that "[U]sers of the FOIA face delays that limit the usefulness of the FOIA."[76] Vaughn claims that delays discourage requesters, cost them too much time and money, and cause hostility to develop between the requesters and the agency, as well as toward the FOIA's noble goals.[77]

Although not anticipated when the FOIA first became law about three decades ago, the FOIA has developed into a very complicated law attracting a variety of lawsuits. Most of the legal challengers focus upon: (1) what constitutes an agency record; (2) what constitutes an agency; (3) what constitutes an exemption to the disclosure requirements; and (4) how long an agency can take in responding to a FOIA request. Taking a few recent FOIA cases, in *National Sec. Archive* v. *Archivist of the United States,* 909 F.2d 541, 545 (D.C. Cir. 1990) the Court held that ". . . the White House Counsel Office is not a FOIA agency" because it is part of the president's "immediate personal staff" which only advises and assists the president, but does not function independently. Independence seems to be the key because in *Meyer* v. *Bush,* 981 F.2d 1288, 1297 (D.C. Cir. 1993), the court ruled that the Task Force on Regulatory Relief, which serves the president through advising the Office of Management and Budget, is also not an FOIA agency because it is ". . . not a body with 'substantial independent authority' to direct executive branch officials." In *Department of Justice* v. *Tax Analysts,* 492 U.S. 136 (1989), the court decided that FOIA disclosure requirements apply only if the agency creates or retains materials and is in "control" of the records at the time of the request. An agency may be in control even if it must direct the requester to another source which actually holds physical possession of the records. While in *U.S.* v. *Landano,* 955 F2d. 1064 (1993), the Supreme Court held that the FBI can not use "ease of administration" to justify nondisclosure, Justice Sandra Day O'Connor, writing for the court, noted that the FBI is not entitled to a blanket exemption from disclosing sources it uses when conducting criminal investigations. She argued that circumstances or a "more particularized approach" should be taken into account in deciding whether sources should be disclosed because FBI communications ". . . range from the extremely sensitive to the routine" (at 1138).

Freedom of Information versus Privacy: An Administrative Dilemma

The general praise for the FOIA as amended should not suggest that problems do not exist. In fact, as we near the end of the twentieth century, legislators, administrators, and the courts will face a difficult challenge in trying to reconcile the somewhat conflictual goals of the Freedom of Information Act and the Privacy Act of 1974 (88 Stat. 1897; amended into the Administrative Procedure Act, 5 U.S.C. 552[a]). The legal dilemma created by the seemingly conflictual acts was addressed by the Supreme Court in *Department of Air Force* v. *Rose,* 425 U.S. 352 (1976), shortly after the Privacy Act took effect. Although the Court's majority ruled in favor of disclosure regarding the records of air force cadets, Chief Justice Burger in dissent argued that insufficient weight had been given by the Court's majority to the cadets' privacy interests. Specifically, Congress must attempt to achieve "a proper balance between the protection of the individuals' right to privacy and the preservation of the public's right to Governmental information by excluding those kinds of files the disclosure of which might harm the individual."[78] However, for years some administrators tried to use the Privacy Act to hold back information, so in 1984 Congress amended the Privacy Act to promote a presumption of disclosure under Section 552 when questions arise about whether an agency should hold back or disclose information. "No agency shall rely on any exemption contained in Section 552 of this title to withhold from an individual any record which is otherwise accessible to such individual under the provisions of this section" (98 Stat. 2209, 2211).

The 1984 amendments to the Privacy Act favoring disclosure of nonexempt information under the FOIA provided agency administrators with a meaningful policy guideline, yet still administrators face frustrations trying to decide whether certain information should be disclosed or withheld. Parenthetically, the Privacy Act does not apply to corporations or other business organizations, but only to records kept on individuals. The FOIA and the Privacy Act embrace two cherished, yet conflicting American values which administrators must protect. While the FOIA essentially calls for disclosure of information, the Privacy Act pleads for agency protection of an individual's personal privacy by requiring agency officials to restrict the collection, maintenance, and release of information that is in clear violation of a person's privacy rights. Specifically, subsection (e) of the Privacy Act requires agencies to maintain only "necessary" records on individuals; obtain as much information from individuals as practical when the information may be considered adverse; explain to individuals how the information will be used; try to maintain accurate and fair records; and preserve the security and confidentiality of records on individuals, among other requirements. A still valid insight by David O'Brien is that problems exist because the requirements of each act, which they are entrusted with upholding, "are in many ways discordant: legitimation only of rights of access would require disclosure of all information, whereas maximum privacy protection would require that personal information never be disclosed."[79] Obviously then, administrators, who must comply with the dictates of both acts, become frustrated when, as they see it, compliance with one act appears to violate the provisions of the other.

Each act gives administrators broad discretionary powers to resolve the dilemma, but neither act provides them with meaningful guidelines to be used in resolving apparent contradictions found in these acts. Not only are statutory guidelines conspicuously absent, but even the Constitution fails to provide any clear clues for administrators. "Moreover," says O'Brien, "the particular problems which confront an agency when determining whether to grant or deny access to personal information are exacerbated by the ambiguous nature of the problem of information control and the absence of any specific constitutional guarantee of either a right of access or personal privacy." In his opinion, "without a perspicuous view of an individual's interests in both access to government records and personal privacy, development of a comprehensive policy framework for reconciling both interests and regulating agencies' information practices is impossible."[80]

According to the old Privacy Protection Study Commission, no serious conflict exists between the FOIA and the Privacy Act, if only administrators understand their proper discretionary powers under each act. The commission believed that agency administrators were most bothered by the exemption in the FOIA which prohibited disclosure of information if such disclosure would clearly "constitute an unwarranted invasion of personal privacy" (Section 552[b][7][c]). The commission pointed out that before the Privacy Act was passed, administrators under the FOIA *could* use their discretion to withhold information which they believed constituted an obvious "unwarranted invasion of personal privacy." But under the Privacy Act "an agency is still *required,* by the Freedom of Information Act, to disclose information that would *not* constitute a 'clearly unwarranted invasion of personal privacy,' but now an agency no longer has the *discretion* to disclose information it believes would constitute such a clearly unwarranted invasion."[81]

This commission failed to focus on the real problem. The chief problem for administrators is defining what constitutes a clearly "unwarranted invasion of personal privacy." This problem is not new to administrative law, nor to law in general. In the absence of meaningful guidelines, administrators will continue to be frustrated in their attempt to define and implement statutory phrases as nebulous as "for good cause," "unwarranted invasion of personal privacy," "the public interest," and the like. If Congress refuses to provide more meaning for these vague standards, and legislative intent is difficult to determine, the courts will also be unable or unwilling to provide helpful guidance. Not only do courts tend to interpret vague standards differently, but judges frequently refuse, in the absence of clear legislative standards, to go further than Congress in clarifying those standards. Witness, for example, this unhelpful Supreme Court riddle: "Exemption six ('constitutes a clearly unwarranted invasion of personal privacy') does not protect against disclosure of every incidental invasion of privacy—

only such disclosures as constitute 'clearly unwarranted' invasions of personal privacy" (*Department of Air Force* v. *Rose,* 425 U.S. 352, 382; 1976).

Many experts feel that injustices will occur if administrators are not provided with standards that can be used to guide their discretionary decisions when they are asked to release information. Despite the conflict which appears to exist between the Freedom of Information Act and the Privacy Act, the administrative and legal problems resulting from the apparent conflict should not be exaggerated. Indeed, administrators who employ common sense should in most cases have little difficulty deciding whether requested information should be released or withheld under these acts. Nevertheless, the government and concerned citizens should still try in the future to minimize the conflict. Virtually all states today have followed the federal example and have adopted freedom of information and privacy legislation.[82]

SUNSHINE AND SUNSET LEGISLATION

Sunshine Laws

In 1976 Congress drafted the Government in the Sunshine Act (90 Stat. 1241) as an amendment to the Administrative Procedure Act (5 U.S.C., Section 552b). To allow the sun to shine in at official meetings where important public policy decisions are made (for example, state hearings regarding the proposed construction of a nuclear power plant, or a city planning board meeting involving zoning issues), states have also passed sunshine legislation. In fact, in an unusual occurrence, states led the way because by the time the federal Sunshine Act was enacted by Congress in 1976, every state had passed sunshine laws.[83] *Sunshine laws* are aimed chiefly at keeping administrative decisions aboveboard. The underlying assumption of sunshine laws is that it is unwise to permit our administrators to make public policy decisions behind closed doors. In the more specific words of a scholar on the Sunshine Act: "The assumptions underlying the Sunshine Act were that increased openness would improve public knowledge of government programs, encourage higher quality work by government officials, stimulate public debate about government policies, and enhance public confidence in government actions. In short, open meetings were viewed as an integral part of the democratic process."[84]

Opponents of sunshine legislation, however, contend that such laws impede governmental decision making and drive up the costs of government. Although they concede that some decisions are important enough to involve the public, they hold that it is a waste of time and money for administrators to have to consult the public (hold open meetings) on minor policy issues. After all, they maintain, administrators are held accountable for their decisions by the appropriate legislative bodies. Supporters of sunshine laws concede that requiring decisional meetings in the sunshine may slow down the decision-making process somewhat, but they argue that this is a small price to pay for keeping governmental decision making open and democratically accountable. Besides, they point out, open decision making can expose problems which would not have been revealed if the decisions were not made in public. Proponents argue that a thorough ventilation of relevant issues early in the game will reduce the odds of running into major unanticipated problems later, thus saving the government money in the long run. It should be noted that specific provisions in statutes and ordinances already require open meetings in regard to certain issues. Sunshine laws, which differ from state to state, have had the effect of opening up some meetings which used to be closed to the public.

The courts have had to resolve some problems created by some of the vague provisions in the otherwise detailed Sunshine Act. Although the act established the presumption that agency meetings should be held in the open, ten exemptions (see 552b[c]) allow federal agencies to avoid holding meetings in public when "sensitive matters" are at stake (for example, national defense and foreign policy, internal personnel rules, trade secrets, police records under certain circumstances, information regarding the regulation and supervision of financial institutions). Parenthetically, some critics maintain that failure to hold open meetings on the financial status of the savings and loan industry, as well as exemptions from disclosure of financial information under the FOIA, helped a great deal to cause the savings and loan crisis of the late 1980s and early 1990s. In *Common Cause* v. *Nuclear Regulatory Commission,* 674 F.2d 921 (D.C. Cir.; 1982), the D.C. Circuit Court had to settle a controversy pertaining to when an agency can legally use one or more of the exemptions. But the two most common legal challenges have stemmed from what is meant under the act by *agency* and *agency meeting.* The act states that an *agency* is one which is "headed by a collegian body composed of two or more individual members, a majority of whom are appointed to such position by the President with advice and consent of the Senate, and any subdivision thereof authorized to act on behalf of the agency" (Section 552b[2][1]). In *Symons* v. *Chrysler Corporation Loan Guarantee Board,* 670 F.2d 238 (D.C. Cir.; 1981), the D.C. Circuit Court accepted the argument by the Chrysler Loan Guarantee Board, created by Congress to help monitor the government loan given to Chrysler Corporation, that it should not be subject to the Sunshine Act because, even though members of the board consisted of members appointed by the president to certain governmental posts (for example, secretary of the treasury), they served only as ex officio members on the board and were not specifically appointed to this board by the president. The court noted: "When Congress wishes to extend Sunshine coverage to ex officio agencies, it will do so" (at 244).

In *Federal Communications Commission* v. *ITT World Communications, Inc.,* 104 S.Ct. 1936 (1984), the Supreme Court focused on the question of what constitutes a meeting under the Sunshine Act. Specifically, the Court had to decide on whether certain preliminary, consultative meetings held by the FCC's Telecommunications Committee could include representatives of foreign telecommunications-governing authorities but exclude ITT World Communications, Inc. ITT charged that their exclusion violated the Sunshine Act. The Supreme Court ruled that preliminary meetings held by agency "subdivisions" that produce only general background information and do not play "an integral role in the . . . policy making process" or "effectively predetermine official actions" cannot be considered a meeting under the Sunshine Act (at 1941).

In their 1994 *Administrative Law Treatise,* Kenneth Culp Davis and Richard J. Pierce, Jr. argue that, unfortunately, the Sunshine Act has had the effect of preventing frank, insightful, and productive discussions at multimember agency meetings because the act prohibits "pre-decisional deliberations." They hold that commissioners ". . . often make important decisions through rotational voting with no prior deliberation; and communications at open meetings are grossly distorted by the presence of the public. Commissioners are reluctant to express their true views for fear that they will expose their ignorance or uncertainty with respect to issues of fact, policy and law."[85] But wait a minute! Isn't the obvious rebuttal to this criticism that commissioners, to avoid showing ignorance at open meetings, would be compelled to do their "homework" so that they would come to meetings more prepared so, in fact, the deliberations would be more substantive and fruitful? In sum, despite criticism, overall the Sunshine Act has helped to democratize agency decision making by bringing the decision-making process from behind closed doors into the "sunlight."

Sunset Laws

Dismayed at the inability to determine effectively whether certain public agencies and programs were worth funding for still another year, political leaders, trying to live within a reasonable budget, have searched desperately in the past few decades for a way to make budgetary decisions easier and more rational. As Georgia's newly elected governor, Jimmy Carter thought he had found the solution to his problems in zero-based budgeting, a budgetary technique created by Peter Pyhrr, a treasurer for Texas Instruments, who presented his idea in the *Harvard Business Review*.[86] Very simply, the zero-based budgeting technique requires a systematic evaluation of agencies and programs, usually once each fiscal year, to determine whether continued funding is justified, especially in light of the need to finance other agencies and programs within a limited budget. The approach is given the name *zero-based budgeting* (ZBB) because, before the agency or program can be considered worthy of continued funding, it is assumed that *no* monies have been budgeted for the agency or program. Soon after bringing Pyhrr to Georgia and implementing ZBB, Carter claimed that the budgetary technique was a huge success. When Carter became president, he brought ZBB with him, and it was widely publicized and tried at all governmental levels.

The ZBB concept was implemented in the form of sunset laws at a great pace in the states, especially between 1976 and 1981, yet only a few sunset laws were passed at the federal level.[87] Sunset laws, as ZBB practices, require agencies and programs to be evaluated, usually at set intervals (for example, every four years), to ascertain whether they should be given new life through continued financial support. Specifically, sunset laws provide for the automatic termination of an agency or program (the sun to set on the agency or program) unless new funds are appropriated at the end of the specified period of years. Therefore, sunset laws, in effect, provide the legislature with potent veto power. In theory, sunset laws compel legislators to give serious consideration to the worth of agency functions and programs to society before funding is reauthorized. Sunset laws are also supposed to force legislators to review the adequacy of agency procedures and the overall performance of agency administrators. Thus, the sunset review process provides legislators (different legislative committees are assigned specific agencies and programs) an opportunity to scrutinize agencies and programs at regular intervals and propose necessary changes, termination, or unaltered continuance.

The threat of having their agencies abolished or their programs suddenly cut is supposed to cause administrators to act more responsibly. However, many observers are convinced that sunset laws will not prove effective. One reason given is that many statutes already provide for programs to be terminated after a certain number of years unless new funds are appropriated. Another reason is that the legislature has always reserved the right to investigate and terminate agencies and programs; sunset laws are just a new way to do an old thing. But pressure groups have usually been very effective in persuading legislators to preserve existing agencies and programs. Should legislators be expected to respond differently under sunset legislation? For example, Colorado's limited experience with sunset laws has shown that they are not very effective. The Colorado legislature reviewed thirteen state agencies during the first year its sunset legislation was in effect. Although it did eliminate three agencies, the $11,000 this saved was offset by the $212,000 in reviewing costs (the total annual budget for three agencies).[88] Rosalie Schiff, director of Colorado's Common Cause at the time, contended that Colorado's sunset law had proved ineffective thus far because influential lobbyists were able to convince legislators that their particular agencies and programs should be retained.[89] Nevertheless, proponents insist that sunset laws require systematic program evaluation to take place after a certain number of years, keeping administrators on their toes. Without sunset laws, they assert, legislators can always elect to avoid the chore of taking the time to review agency performance and the costs and benefits of agency programs.

Kenneth J. Meier concludes that sunset legislation was supposed to stop the "forces of inertia" and eliminate unnecessary governmental agencies and programs, but "[S]unset's performance . . . has been less than its promise."[90] He claims that probably the best indication of sunset legislation's failure ". . . is that 11 states have repealed their sunset laws or allowed them to atrophy."[91]

SUMMARY

In the early years of the twentieth century, Elihu Root, speaking to the American Bar Association, declared that the public administration machinery had to expand to meet the growing demands of modern government, but he warned that Congress had to keep administrative power democratically accountable to the people. It does not appear that Congress heeded Root's warning because, since at least the mid-1930s, congressional controls over the emerging administrative state have become weaker and weaker, despite some honest congressional attempts to keep administrative activities under its firm control. However, this is not to suggest that Congress does not provide the best check against possible abuses of administrative power. The congressional watchdog may not be as powerful as it once was, but it still seems better equipped to preserve the democratic character of administrative action than any other watchdogs in the American political system, and there are signs in the 1990s that Congress is using micromanagement to better oversee the bureaucracy. It may be that bureaucratic power has become so strong that it is now beyond the realistic control of all existing external systemic checks.

The vast majority of critics argue that the traditional congressional controls over bureaucracy have become conspicuously less effective as the scope and strength of the administrative state has developed. All these control mechanisms have been found to be fairly inadequate for effectively controlling administrative behavior. Specifically, Congress's ability to create agencies and organize administrative business through enabling legislation provided Congress with the potential to restrict administrative power from the beginning. However, since the 1930s, Congress has tended to draft skeletal statutes that have provided agency administrators with vast discretionary powers to mold and implement public policies as they like. Realizing in the 1970s and early 1980s that it had not used its "pre-oversight" power very well, Congress increasingly turned to the legislative veto so it could check administrative actions it believed to be unacceptable. Unfortunately for Congress, the Supreme Court declared the legislative veto unconstitutional in 1983, yet Congress has largely ignored the decision, continuing to include "more constitutional" legislative veto provisions in new laws.

The purse-string power used to be considered Congress's strongest weapon against public agencies' stepping out of line. However, controlling agency expenditures is much more difficult than it would seem. The huge size and complexity of most agency operations work in favor of the agency. Congress does not have time to study complex agency operations and budgets in detail. Consequently, Congress usually does not know where to begin in slashing agency appropriations. Besides, all agencies have friends inside and outside Congress who will fight hard to make certain that funds for their particular programs are not cut. Virtually the same reasons can be given for why Congress's investigatory power has also proved quite ineffective in discovering and checking misuses of administrative power. Ideally, congressional investigations are used to discover administrative problems in various governmental agencies. However, even with the help of the General Accounting Office, legislators do not have the time to conduct many congressional investigations or to carry out thorough investigations after they do decide to investigate certain agency practices. GAO reports are frequently very good, but Congress typically has very little time to study the hundreds of reports that GAO conducts every year, each one focusing on a problem which probably needs considerable attention.

In an attempt to make public administration more democratically responsible to the American public, Congress passed various pieces of guidance legislation. The Pendleton Act of 1883 represented a modest effort to take unnecessary and disruptive politics out of public administration at the federal level. Later acts were also aimed at professionalizing the federal civil service system. The states passed similar legislation. However, legislative attempts to make public service more responsible and meritorious have created some problems. The most serious problem has stemmed from the charge that the merit system has encroached upon the constitutional rights of individuals in various ways. Reacting to past criticism of procedural problems in the administrative system, Congress passed the Administrative Procedure Act in 1946.

The APA is the most comprehensive statute in administrative law. It is designed to make administrative procedures more fair. More specifically, the APA functions to make administrators honor constitutional due process and rule-of-law principles, especially by prohibiting arbitrary and capricious administrative behavior. On the whole, the APA is a reasonably sound law that has probably done much to improve the quality of administrative practices in the United States, despite the fact that it fails to apply to roughly 90 percent of informal, discretionary, administrative actions. Several major amendments, including the Freedom of Information Act, have done much to improve the original APA. Nevertheless, the APA has come under attack from critics who hold that vague standards and numerous exemptions have done much to weaken the authoritative potential of the law by allowing determined administrators to use the broad discretionary powers granted to them under the act to escape having to uphold the true spirit of many of its provisions.

In recent decades state legislatures and, infrequently, the U.S. Congress have implemented new ideas aimed at keeping the administrative process more democratically responsible. Sunshine laws have been employed to keep administrators from making important policy decisions in private, while sunset legislation has been used to force legislators to evaluate agencies and programs to determine at specified intervals whether they are satisfactory enough to warrant continued funding. Although sunshine laws have attracted criticisms, overall they have proved relatively successful in making agency decision making more open and democratic. Sunset legislation, on the other hand, has produced dismal results and has been seen by most critics as a failure. Several states have even repealed their sunset laws.

NOTES

1. American Bar Association Bulletin, 355, 368–69 (1916).
2. Ibid.
3. Kenneth C. Davis and Walter Gellhorn, with Paul R. Verkuil, moderator, "Present at the Creation: Regulatory Reform Before 1946," *Administrative Law Review*, 38 (Fall 1986), 511–33. In remarks originally presented to the Spring 1986 American Bar Association Council's meeting, administrative law section, it was made clear that, although regulatory groundwork was laid before 1945, serious regulatory reform efforts came after 1945. Also see David H. Rosenbloom, "The Evolution of the Administrative State and Transformations of Administrative Law," in David H. Rosenbloom and Richard D. Schwartz, *Handbook of Regulation and Administrative Law*, eds. (New York: Marcel Dekker, Inc., 1994), 3–36.
4. Jacob F. Cooke, ed., *The Federalist*, no. 51 (Cleveland: World Publishing, 1961), 349.
5. Cathy Marie Johnson, *The Dynamics of Conflict between Bureaucrats and Legislators* (New York: M.E. Sharpe, Inc., 1992), 138–159.
6. Kenneth R. Mayer, "Policy Disputes as a Source of Administrative Controls: Congressional Micromanagement of the Department of Defense," *Public Administration Review*, 53 (July/August, 1993), 293–301.
7. Ronald D. Sylvia, *Public Personnel Administration* (Belmont, California: Wadsworth Publishing Company, 1994), chaps. 2, 7, and 17.

8. James W. Fesler, *Public Administration: Theory and Practice* (Englewood Cliffs, N.J.: Prentice-Hall, 1980), 311.
9. Ibid., 313–14.
10. Joel D. Aberbach, *Keeping a Watchful Eye: The Politics of Congressional Oversight* (Washington, D.C.: The Brookings Institution, 1990), 213.
11. Juvenal, *Satires,* 347; and Fesler, *Public Administration,* 315. Neither Fesler nor I give the literal translation of the Latin, but the purpose is served.
12. Kenneth F. Warren, "The Search for Administrative Responsibility," *Public Administrative Review,* 34 (March-April 1974), 176–82. Also, see Terry L. Cooper, *The Responsible Administrator* (San Francisco: Jossey-Boss Publishers, 1990).
13. Richard E. Neustadt, "Politicians and Bureaucrats," in *Current Issues in Public Administration,* ed. Frederick S. Lane (New York: St. Martin's Press, 1978), 51.
14. Stephen K. Bailey, *Congress in the Seventies* (New York: St. Martin's Press, 1970), 92.
15. Francis E. Rourke, *Bureaucracy, Politics, and Public Policy,* 3rd ed. (Boston: Little, Brown, 1984), 72.
16. Ibid.
17. Cathy Marie Johnson, *The Dynamics of Conflict Between Bureaucrats and Legislators,* 159.
18. Ibid.
19. Congressman William Clay, personal interview, February 17, 1987.
20. Congressman William Clay, personal interview, March 10, 1994.
21. Kenneth R. Mayer, "Policing Disputes as a Source of Administrative Controls: Congressional Micromanagement of the Department of Defense," 293–301.
22. Lawrence C. Dodd and Richard L. Scott, *Congress and the Administrative State* (New York: Wiley, 1979), 163.
23. Ibid., 163–64.
24. Randall B. Ripley and Grace A. Franklin, *Congress, the Bureaucracy, and Public Policy,* 5th ed. (Pacific Grove, California: Brooks/Cole Publishing Co., 1991), 66–68.
25. Richard Cohen, "Junior Members Seek Approval for Wider Use of the Legislative Veto," *National Journal* (August 6, 1977), 1228–32.
26. Michael Saks, "Holding the Independent Agencies Accountable: Legislative Veto of Agency Rules," *Administrative Law Review,* 36 (Winter 1984): 42; and Joseph Cooper and Patricia Hurley, "The Legislative Veto: A Policy Analysis," *Congress and the Presidency,* 10 (Spring 1983), 1–24.
27. The one- and two-house legislative vetoes are common, but legislative vetoes from a committee in one house are rare. The Future Trading Act of 1978, 7 U.S.C., Sec. 6c(c), provides an example of a committee veto, while the Supplemental Appropriations Act of 1953, Ch. 758, 66 Stat. 637, allowed the chairman of the House Appropriations Committee to exercise a legislative veto.
28. Harold H. Buff and Ernest Gellhorn, "Congressional Control of Administrative Regulation: A Study of Legislative Vetoes," *Harvard Law Review,* 90 (May 1977), 1373–75. Also, see Cornelius M. Kerwin, *Rulemaking: How Government Agencies Write Law and Make Policy* (Washington, D.C.: Congressional Quarterly, Inc., 1994), 225–229.
29. Ibid., 1373–97.
30. *Wall Street Journal,* February 8, 1980, 7.
31. Rowland L. Young, "Supreme Court Report: The Court Vetoes the Legislative Veto," *American Bar Association Journal,* 69 (September 1983), 1288.

32. Incidentally, President Reagan was charged with violating the International Security Assistance and Arms Export Control Act by having arms shipped to Iran and the Nicaraguan Contras without notifying Congress in the Iran-Contra affair.

33. Daniel P. Franklin, "Why the Legislative Veto Isn't Dead," *Presidential Studies Quarterly,* 26 (Summer 1986), 486.

34. Bernard Schwartz, "Administrative Law Cases During 1990," *Administrative Law Review,* 43 (Summer 1991), 477.

35. Randall B. Ripley and Grace A. Franklin, *Congress, the Bureaucracy and Public Policy,* 5th ed. (Pacific Grove, California: Brooks/Cole Publishing Co., 1991), 63–64.

36. Leonard D. White, *Introduction to the Study of Public Administration* (New York: Macmillan, 1926).

37. Walter Gellhorn, *Administrative Law: Cases and Comments* (Mineola, N.Y.: Foundation Press, 1940).

38. Paul Van Riper, *History of the United States Civil Service* (New York: Harper and Row, 1958), 23.

39. Van Riper, *History of the United States Civil Service,* 43–44; see also Ronald D. Sylvia, *Public Personnel Administration* (Belmont, California: Wadsworth Publishing Co., 1994), 15–21.

40. Woodrow Wilson, "The Study of Administration," *Political Science Quarterly,* 16 (December 1941): 485–86.

41. Ibid., 485.

42. Ibid., 484.

43. Ibid., 495.

44. Fesler, *Public Administration,* 26–29.

45. See, for example, the *President's Advisory Council on Executive Organization: A New Regulatory Framework* (Washington, D.C.: Government Printing Office, 1971), Roy L. Ash, Chairman (Known as the Ash Council Report); American Bar Association's Administrative Law Section's Report, reprinted in Peter L. Strauss and Cass R. Sunstein's "The Role of the President and OMB in Informal Rulemaking," *Administrative Law Review,* 38 (Spring 1986), 206–7; and Marianne K. Smythe, "An Irreverent Look at Regulatory Reform," *Administrative Law Review,* 38 (Fall 1986), 451–70.

46. 37 Stat. 555.

47. 41 Stat. 614.

48. 63 Stat. 954.

49. 53 Stat. 1147.

50. 54 Stat. 1211.

51. 63 Stat. 666.

52. 78 Stat. 412.

53. For an excellent description of the provisions in the Civil Service Reform Act of 1978 see, Rosen, *Holding Government Bureaucracies Accountable,* 141–147.

54. David K. Hamilton, "The Staffing Function in Illinois State Government after *Rutan,*" *Public Administration Review* 5 (July/August 1993), 381–386.

55. Karl T. Thurber, Jr., "Revising the Hatch Act: A Practitioner's Perspective," *The Public Manager* (Spring 1993), 43.

56. Ibid., 46. Republicans also feared that Democrats would benefit the most from Hatch Act reform because more federal workers are Democrats, thus creating the potential to increase public union control over the federal government.

57. Jenne Ponessa, "The Hatch Act Rewrite," *Congressional Quarterly* (November 13, 1993), 3146–3147.
58. Thurber, Jr., "Revising the Hatch Act," 43–46.
59. Ibid., 45.
60. For a good summary of the rights to strike of public employees, see Sylvia, *Public Personnel Administration,* chap. 15.
61. Herbert Kaufman, *Are Government Organizations Immortal?* (Washington, D.C.: Brookings Institution, 1976), 34–63.
62. For a most enlightening informal discussion of the events leading up to the passage of the APA by two of the key participants in its creation, Walter Gellhorn and Kenneth C. Davis, see remarks delivered at the Spring 1986 Council Meeting of the American Bar Association in celebration of the fortieth anniversary of the APA by Walter Gellhorn and Kenneth C. Davis with Paul R. Verkuil, moderator, reprinted under the title of "Present at the Creation: Regulatory Reform before 1946," *Administrative Law Review,* 38 (Fall 1986), 511–33.
63. Arthur Bonfield, "The Federal APA and State Administrative Law," *Virginia Law Review,* 72 (March 1986), 297–336. The states that have adopted the Revised Model State Administrative Procedure Act of 1981 (13 Uniform State Laws Ann. 347) in whole or in part, or the original Model State APA or its 1961 revision include Alabama, Arkansas, Connecticut, Georgia, Hawaii, Idaho, Illinois, Iowa, Louisiana, Maine, Maryland, Michigan, Mississippi, Missouri, Montana, Nebraska, Nevada, New Hampshire, New York, North Carolina, Oklahoma, Oregon, Rhode Island, South Dakota, Tennessee, Vermont, Washington, West Virginia, Wisconsin, and Wyoming.
64. Kenneth Culp Davis and Richard J. Pierce, Jr., *Administrative Law Treatise,* 3rd ed., vol. 1 (Boston: Little, Brown and Company, 1994), 14.
65. *Morgan* v. *United States,* 298 U.S. 468 (1936); *Morgan* v. *United States,* 304 U.S. 1(1938); and *United States* v. *Morgan,* 313 U.S. 409 (1941).
66. Harold C. Relyea, "The Freedom of Information Act," *Public Administration Review* (July-August 1979), 310.
67. Gaillard Hunt, ed., *The Writings of James Madison* (New York: G.P. Putnam's Sons 1910), 9:103.
68. Frances E. Zollers, "The Implementation of the Consumer Product Safety Act Section 6(b) and the Conflict with Freedom of Information Act Policies," *Administrative Law Review,* 38 (Winter 1987), 61–81.
69. Ibid., 311–15.
70. Ibid., 314.
71. Russell M. Roberts, "Faithful Execution of the FOI Act: One Executive Branch Experience," *Public Administration Review,* 39 (July-August 1979), 318–23.
72. House Committee on Governmental Operations, *United States Governmental Information Policies and Practices-Administration and Operation of Freedom of Information Act, Hearings,* 92nd Cong., 2nd sess. (Washington, D.C.: Government Printing Office, 1972), 8, 15.
73. Kenneth Culp Davis, Administrative Law Treatise, 2nd ed., vol. 1 (San Diego: K.C. Davis Pub. Co., 1979), 309.
74. Archibald, "Freedom of Information Act Revisited," 316.
75. Davis and Pierce, Jr., *Administrative Law Treatise,* 3rd ed., vol. 1, 194.

76. Robert G. Vaughn, "Federal Information Policy and Administrative Law," in David H. Rosenbloom and Richard D. Schwartz, eds., *Handbook of Regulation and Administrative Law* (New York: Marcel Dekker, Inc., 1994), 479.

77. Ibid., 478–481.

78. House Report 1497, 89th Cong., 2nd sess., 11.

79. David M. O'Brien, "Freedom of Information, Privacy, and Information Control: A Contemporary Administrative Dilemma," *Public Administration Review,* 39 (July-August 1978), 324.

80. Ibid., 323–24.

81. U.S. Privacy Protection Study Commission, *Personnel Privacy in an Information Society* (Washington, D.C.: Government Printing Office, 1977), 520.

82. Arthur Earl Bonfield and Michael Asimow, *State and Federal Administrative Law* (St. Paul, Minn.: West Publishing Co., 1989), 589–90.

83. Howard I. Fox, "Government in the Sunshine," *1978 Annual Survey of American Law,* (1979), 305–6.

84. Larry W. Thomas, "The Courts and the Implementation of the Government in Sunshine Act," *Administrative Law Review,* 37 (Summer 1985), 260.

85. Davis and Pierce, Jr., *Administrative Law Treatise,* 3rd ed., vol. 1, 221.

86. Peter A. Pyhrr, "Zero-Base Budgeting," *Harvard Business Review,* 48 (November-December 1970), 111–21.

87. Kenneth J. Meier, *Politics and the Bureaucracy: Policymaking in the Fourth Branch of Government,* 3rd ed., (Pacific Grove, Calif.: Brooks/Cole Publishing Company, 1993), 158–59.

88. Kenneth J. Meier, *Regulation: Politics, Bureaucracy, and Economics* (New York: St. Martin's Press, 1985), 296.

89. George E. Berkley, *The Craft of Public Administration,* 3rd ed. (Boston: Allyn and Bacon, 1981), 291–92; and Meier, *Regulation: Politics, Bureaucracy, and Economics,* 296–97.

90. Kenneth J. Meier, *Politics and the Bureaucracy,* 3rd ed., 159.

91. Ibid.

CHAPTER FOUR

Protecting Administrators from Undue Interference and Harassment

LEGITIMATE VERSUS ILLEGITIMATE MEDDLING IN THE ADMINISTRATIVE PROCESS: AN OVERVIEW

Public administrators should not be insensitive to all pressures from their environment. Popular government and democratically accountable public administration require that public officials be reasonably responsive to the legitimate demands placed upon them by various political actors. Systems theory makes clear that all public administrators, whether in totalitarian or democratic governments, must be somewhat responsive to environmental demands to survive. Because of the openness in democratic administrations, their administrators are placed under even more pressure to respond to external demands. In fact, a vital function of administrative law is keeping open the channels of communication and influence between public administrators and concerned individual and group interests and their political representatives. For example, when promulgating administrative rules, agency rule makers are required to provide an opportunity for interested parties to submit comments on the proposed rules under the Administrative Procedure Act.

However, while democratic government is enhanced by a certain degree of input in the administrative process, administrative actions are harmed by undue interference. Undue interference in the administrative process takes many forms, but in general any intervention that is inappropriate, improper, excessive, unethical, or illegal can be classified as undue. Civil service reformers, elected political officials, court justices, public administration scholars such as Max Weber and Woodrow Wilson, and public administrators themselves have all noted how administrative behavior can be undermined by unnecessary and counterproductive intrusions. Edwin

Tucker stressed about two decades ago that for public administrators to perform their jobs in a democratically proper and professionally objective manner, "it is imperative that an administrator's actions be determined by the Constitution, legislative mandates, judicial pronouncements, agency rules and practices, and the administrator's personal impartial judgment."[1] Accordingly, Tucker concluded, "The shaping of administrative behavior by corrupting extra-legal interference, however beneficent the motivation of the corrupter may be, disparages government and denies justice to the party who is adversely affected because of covert tampering."[2]

The vast majority of public administrative theorists have argued persuasively that although general political controls should guide administrative decision making, daily and routine administrative work is best handled by objective and professional administrators. To prevent the disruption of normal administrative processes, our political leaders have structured the administrative system so that administrators can enjoy a certain degree of independence from outside forces, particularly interest group and political pressures. The underlying assumption, challenged to a degree by the Ash Report as discussed earlier, is that structural independence can help to promote efficient, effective, and responsible public administration through generally reducing biases, costs, and malfeasance in the planning and execution of public policies. In this chapter the focus is on the thin line that separates acceptable influence (oversight) by political actors from unacceptable and illegal harassment of administrative officials. Attention is paid to how interest groups, legislators, and presidents have tried to peddle influence to gain special favors from administrators. The legitimacy of such transactions is assessed from the perspective of what administrative law and democratic government permit.

PROTECTING ADMINISTRATORS FROM THEMSELVES AND OTHERS: CONFLICT-OF-INTEREST LAWS

Most public administrators seem to be honest, but are they honest because they want to be or because they have to be? This philosophical question deserves the special attention of organizational theorists. However, it is true that the vast majority of political theorists, in contemplating the nature of man, have concluded that because people are inherently selfish creatures, they probably would commit dishonest and profitable acts if given the opportunity. Generally, these political theorists have pointed out that genuine moral character can be tested only under very unrealistic circumstances. For instance, Plato, in the *Republic,* essentially posed this question: How honest would a person be if he had the opportunity to act as he wished, in the absence of laws, and with the absolute knowledge beforehand that, if he acted dishonestly, he would not be caught or punished for his actions?[3]

Only extremely naive idealists could structure a governmental system upon the assumption that if unchecked by laws and the threat of punishment, people would instinctively act in consistent honesty. Successful laws are based on fear and can remain effective only as long as they are respected. If laws are perceived by people to pose no real threat to them, whether because they are not enforced or only feebly enforced, fear of the consequences of violation diminishes, along with the effectiveness of those laws.

Laws are designed with the specific intention of reducing the risk that social disruption will occur because people left to their own devices will act in ways contrary to the interests of others and thereby jeopardize the public interest. Simply, laws are employed to establish order. Conflict-of-interest laws have been legislated to better ensure that actions by public officials are objective, untainted by personal interests. Herbert Kaufman contends that conflict-of-interest laws are necessary "to keep the government from turning into an instrumentality of private profit for those in its employ or those with private fortunes at their disposal."[4] Specifically, Kaufman believes that conflict-of-interest laws are needed to control administrative behavior because administrative officers possess so much power and are confronted with so many temptations. And some scholars argue that conflict-of-interest laws are needed even more in modern American society than when our Republic first began because as a society we have increasingly devalued the public sector and have unfortunately become obsessed with promoting our selfish financial and career interests.[5] ABC correspondent Sam Donaldson, in response to the seventeen corruption charges faced by Representative Dan Rostenkowski (D-Ill.) in 1994 actually noted on "Weekend with David Brinkley" that misusing public office for private gain has become so commonplace that part of Rostenkowski's defense will probably be to claim that he only did "what everyone is doing."[6]

What Are Conflicts of Interest?

Conflicts of interest for governmental employees, according to various federal, state, and local statutes and ordinances, as well as agency rules and regulations in general, exist when a public servant uses an office for personal gain by paying special favors to private interests in exchange for payments of some kind (money, products, or services). A conflict of interest also exists when a public official uses a governmental position to benefit individual private interests (commonly private business interests) or the interests of the government worker's family or friends. Administrators, although largely unelected public officials, still represent one segment or another of the public interest. Accordingly, public administrators must avoid real as well as apparent conflicts of interest. A person does not have to benefit personally from a conflict-of-interest situation for a conflict of interest to exist. Getting into a position where one could potentially benefit from the conflict-of-interest is enough to make a person guilty of violating a conflict of interest law. For example, in *United States* v. *Mississippi Valley Generating Co.* (364 U.S. 520; 1961), the Supreme Court held that a conflict of interest existed between a consultant for the government and the consultant's regular employer because an atmosphere was created which tended to invite unnecessarily biased and dishonorable decisions: "The statute does not specify as elements of the crime that there be actual corruption or that there be any actual loss suffered by the Government as a result of the defendant's conflict of interest. This omission indicates that the statute establishes an objective standard of conduct, and that whenever a government agent fails to act in accordance with that standard, he is guilty of violating the statute, regardless whether there is positive corruption. The statute is thus directed not only at dishonor, but also at conduct which tempts dishonor. This broad proscription embodies a recognition of the fact that an impairment of impartial judgment can occur in even the most well-meaning men when their personal economic interests are affected by the business they transact on behalf of the Government" (at 549–550). In *re Berger Co. Util. Auth.*, 553 A.2d 849, 853 9 (N.J. Super.; 1989), the New Jersey Superior Court held that a hearing official should have disqualified himself from hearing a utility case because a clear conflict of interest existed since he had inquired about a job possibility with the very utility company before his commission where he was acting as an adjudicator. In *Sanjour v. E.P.A.*, 984 F.2d 434 (D.C. Cir. 1993), the court upheld a government ethics law which prohibited E.P.A. employees from receiving reimbursement and pay for unofficial writing and speaking engagements, even though they related to their official duties, because such created at least the appearance of a conflict of interest.

The Court in *Mississippi Valley* acknowledged that biased judgments, leading possibly to personal gain, can occur among even "the most well-meaning men." In so holding, the court answered the question posed by Plato, which was noted previously. Plato, of course, answered his own question in the *Republic*. He believed that the conflict-of-interest problem among governmental decision makers, at least the top-level administrators responsible for making important public policy decisions, could be eliminated by taking away all of their private property. Plato believed that private property interests tended to corrupt governmental administration because such interests generated too much temptation.

Of course, Plato's solution to the conflict-of-interest problem in government would hardly be acceptable in a private-property-oriented country such as the United States. However, it should be noted that U.S. Lawmakers have realized that private property interests are at the root of the conflict-of-interest controversy because conflict-of-interest laws in this country are aimed primarily at preventing public servants from using their offices to secure unethical and illegal economic advantages.

Specific examples of economic conflicts of interest are numerous. They are directed more at benefiting a public official personally than the public. Nonelected administrative officials, because they hold so much discretionary power and commonly serve out of the limelight, are likely to be exposed to the most tempting conflict-of-interest situations. The range of conflicts of interest among public administrators is so great that U.S. conflict-of-interest laws are not even aimed at eliminating all such instances, but only those which appear to pose potentially significant threats to fair and objective governmental decision making.[7] It seems clear that all persons possess conflicts of interests of some kind in their jobs. For example, people of different religious and ethical beliefs work for public agencies where they are entrusted with implementing public policies which may conflict with their beliefs (an emotional example is that of a prolife advocate working for a public hospital that provides abortion services). In numerous decisions the courts have said that the government does not seek to regulate, through the conflict-of-interest laws, the role that public employees' religious or personal beliefs may play in their performance as governmental employees.[8] But the government does seek to regulate blatant conflict-of-interest situations, especially where unscrupulous administrative officials solicit favors of value in exchange for, to cite a few examples: (1) approving permits and licenses; (2) overlooking license violations; (3) awarding contracts or grants; (4) giving tax breaks; (5) not enforcing code violations; (6) releasing privileged information; (7) approving applications from aliens seeking permanent residency; and (8) granting any other special requests and privileges that would probably be denied on the basis of the facts by objective and honest administrative decision makers.

Conflict-of-interest problems have plagued government in America since its beginning. The first widespread scandal was the Yazoo Land Fraud of 1795 in Georgia. During the past decade or so, disclosures of such conflicts of interest appeared frequently on the front pages of the newspapers. Watergate, involving numerous conflict-of-interest violations in the Nixon White House, was, of course, the most publicized governmental scandal of the 1970s. Recent examples of conflict-of-interest scandals plagued the Reagan and Bush administrations involving the military, the Environmental Protection Agency, Housing and Urban Development, and the regulators of the savings and loan industry. Accusations regarding Whitewater have plagued President Clinton's administration, while one of Clinton's aids was forced to resign after using a presidential helicopter to take him on a golf trip. Conflicts of interest have been historically worse on the local level.[9]

Official Attempts to Control Conflicts of Interest

Without much question, blatant conflicts of interest among public employees were more prevalent decades ago, especially during the heyday of machine politics, but widespread publicity given to conflict-of-interest scandals in our media age has prompted renewed efforts by legislators, presidents, and rule makers to squelch conflicts of interest in government. A few major efforts warrant mention. Under federal law, it is a crime for a public official to "directly or indirectly, corruptly . . . (ask, demand, exact, solicit, seek, accept, receive or agree) to receive anything of value for himself or for any other person or entity, in return for 'being influenced' in the performance of his official duties, or for 'being influenced' to commit or aid in committing, or to collude in or allow, any fraud, on the United States; or . . . being induced to do or omit to do an act in violation of his official duty." Violation of this section is punishable by a fine of "not more than $20,000 or three times the monetary equivalent of the thing of value, whichever is greater, or . . . (imprisonment) for not more than fifteen years, or both, (disqualification) from holding any office of honor, trust, or profit under the United States" (18 U.S.C., Section 201[c]). In Section 201(e), it is a crime if anyone "directly or indirectly, corruptly gives, offers or promises anything of value to any public official or person who has been selected to be a public official, or offers or promises any public official or any person who has been selected to be a public official to give anything of value to any other person or entity, with intent—(1) to influence any official act; or (2) to influence such public official or person who has been selected to be a public official to commit or aid in committing, or collude in, or allow any fraud or make opportunity for the commission of any fraud, on the United States; or (3) to induce such public official or such person who has been selected to be a public official to do or omit to do any act in violation of his lawful duty."

During the Carter administration, the Ethics in Government Act was passed.[10] This 1978 act was aimed primarily at restricting postemployment contacts between former top-level administrators now working in the private sector and their former agencies, in an attempt to reduce the revolving door syndrome. Title 5 of this act makes it unlawful for ex-agency executives to *ever* try to influence any "particular matters" in the former agency where they were "personally and substantially" involved, either formally or informally. Other bans prohibit them from getting involved in certain matters for one- and two-year periods after they have left their particular agencies. The act also includes financial disclosure provisions for all GS-16 and higher-level GS employees, to guard against blatant economic conflicts of interest. However, under the act former employees may appear and participate in business matters before their former agencies as long as their business does not involve the "particular matters" excluded by the act, and as long as the former employees are not subject to the one- and two-year bans precluding employees from engaging in any business dealings with the agency. And since the act applies only to the particular former employee, it does not prevent a business associate of the former employee from dealing with his or her former agency; nor does it stop the former agency employee, when his or her one- or two-year ban has expired, from assisting a business associate in dealings with the former agency even when they concern "particular matters" (ah—there's the loophole!).

In 1987 Michael K. Deaver, a friend and former aide to President Ronald Reagan, became the first high-ranking White House official to face criminal charges under the Ethics in Government Act after a special prosecutor's investigation. The investigation evidently disclosed that Deaver had violated conflict-of-interest provisions of the Ethics in Government Act, especially by making contacts with top White House officials, including President Reagan, on behalf of his clients less than one year after leaving the White House on January 4, 1985.[11] The Deaver Case has stimulated thought on the usefulness of the Ethics in Government Act. That is, it must be made clear that ironically, after the special prosecutor's office spent 4200 work days on the Deaver investigation, Special Prosecutor Whitney Seymour, Jr., was unable to convince the grand jury to indict Deaver on violations of the Ethics in Government Act. He had to settle for two counts of perjury. According to rumors from the special prosecutor's office, "loose" provisions under the Ethics in Government Act made it difficult to obtain indictments on specific violations of the act. To William Safire, a noted Washington columnist, this strongly suggests that the Ethics in Government Act has no teeth, and in the future the act will prove feeble in deterring influence peddling.[12] Safire's prophetic insight proved to be accurate. As a result in 1989 Congress tried to strengthen the 1978 Ethics Act by passing the Government Ethics Reform Act of 1989. This Ethics Reform Act: (1) limited outside income for members of Congress and noncareer executive branch officials; (2) placed greater restrictions upon postemployment lobbying activities; (3) created uniform acceptance rules per-

Source: Reprinted with permission of Tom Engelhardt and the *St. Louis Post-Dispatch,* October 5, 1994.

taining to gifts; (4) established stricter financial disclosure laws; and (5) authorized significant salary increases for high executive branch officials and House members, presumably to reduce the reliance upon outside income too often cultivating conflict-of-interest situations which tend to undermine the public interest.

Executive orders have also been used in attempts to improve ethics in governmental service. President Lyndon B. Johnson's Executive Order #11222, known as "Standards of Ethical Conduct for Government Officers and Employees," states: "Where government is based on the consent of the governed, every citizen is entitled to have complete confidence in the integrity of his government. Each individual officer, employee, or advisor of government must help to earn and must honor that trust by his own integrity and conduct in all official actions" (Section 201).[13] (This order was updated by President Richard Nixon's Executive Order #11590.)[14] The Johnson order also prohibits any governmental official or advisor from soliciting or accepting in either a direct or indirect manner "any gift, gratuity, favor, entertainment, loan, or any other thing of monetary value, from any person, corporation, or group which—

(1) has, or is seeking to obtain, contractual or other business or financial relationships with his agency; (2) conducts operations or activities which are regulated by his agency; or (3) has interests which may be substantially affected by the performance or nonperformance of his official duty" (Section 201[a]). Under Section 201(b), agencies, with the approval of the Civil Service Commission, are allowed to make exceptions to the requirements of Section 201(a) as long as they are "necessary and appropriate in view of the nature of their agency's work and the duties of their employees."

Because of the unique regulatory situation of some agencies, agency rule makers have promulgated rules directed at preventing conflicts of interest among their employees. Some of these conflict-of-interest regulations appear stricter than the general federal statutes. Enabling legislation which gives birth to the agency may contain provisions focusing on conflicts of interest that would probably be peculiar to the agency. For example, federal trade commissioners are not permitted to engage "in any other business, vocation, or employment" (15 U.S.C., Section 41).

The Effectiveness of Conflict-of-Interest Prohibitions

Conflict-of-interest statutes, executive orders, and agency rules generally call for severe punishments for those governmental employees who are found guilty of violating conflict-of-interest prohibitions. Punishments range from stiff fines and lengthy prison sentences to simple removal from office. Overall, conflict-of-interest laws appear to be comprehensive, clear, and well written. Few loopholes can be found, and the courts have generally given strong support to their usefulness. Therefore, if governmental employees in fact read and believed the documents stating that violators would be discovered and punished, the completeness and forcefulness of the conflict-of-interest rhetoric would surely scare employees into dutiful compliance.

The problem is that the conflict-of-interest bark has historically been much greater than its bite. What is worse is that many public employees are not very frightened by this dog any more. The truth is that conflict-of-interest laws are virtually impossible to enforce unless governmental employees flagrantly violate them. Elaborate, time-consuming, and expensive schemes to catch those who are using their public office for such personal gains as payoffs (e.g., the Deaver case) have demonstrated how difficult it is to catch and prosecute those who have violated conflict-of-interest prohibitions. From a systems perspective, the additional time and costs to the political system would probably preclude the guilty employee's being prosecuted and punished in full accordance with the law.

In sum, laws can remain effective only as long as they are feared. Because conflict-of-interest laws are difficult to enforce, they should not be perceived as the most effective instruments for combatting unethical and illegal employee conduct. Most critics feel that in the final analysis honorable public employee behavior must be motivated from within. From Confucius and Plato to more modern democratic theorists such as Thomas Jefferson, the thinking has been that a person's inner attitudes toward governance, not conflict of interest or other similar statutes, provide the best guidance for proper conduct. The National Academy of Public Administration's report quotes a 1785 letter to Peter Carr, in which Thomas Jefferson wrote: "Whenever you are to do a thing, though it can never be known but to yourself, ask yourself how you would act were all the world looking at you, and act accordingly."[15] To obtain responsible behavior in governmental administration, it is necessary to place less emphasis on restrictive laws and more emphasis on the early ethical training of children, conveying the importance of upholding ethical standards in professional degree programs where future public servants are educated, and on careful public service recruitment. All this is much easier to advocate than to accomplish.

CONGRESSIONAL INFLUENCE PEDDLING

Obviously, congresspersons have a right to try to influence the directions of the administrative branch. The Constitution, especially in Article 1, Section 8, clearly provides certain formal and informal powers to Congress so it can exert its influence in shaping the administrative system. When legislators act within these constitutionally sanctioned powers, no ethical or legal problems emerge. But too often legislators believe that they own administrators and thus can manipulate the administrative process in any way they see fit to accomplish their goals. The famed Speaker of the House, Sam Rayburn, made this point so clear when he embraced Newton Minow, who had just been appointed to the Federal Communications Commission, and said to him: "Just remember one thing, son. Your agency is an arm of the Congress; you belong to us. Remember that and you'll be all right."[16] There is a sense in which Rayburn could not have been more wrong, but it is necessary to recall his immense success and longevity in office and the vast numbers of legislators and other officials who emulate him. If the constitutional checks and balances system, which is rooted in the separation-of-powers doctrine, is to function properly, other governmental branches must remain relatively independent of one another. In short, influence peddling among the governmental branches must have its limits.

There are proper and improper ways for legislators to influence administrative actions. Authorized methods for shaping and controlling administrative behavior include the legislating of enabling statutes that include policy and procedural guidelines, confirming key administrative appointments, making appropriations, investigating agency activities, and other such orthodox techniques which the Constitution regards as necessary and proper legislative intrusions in administrative business. But fortunately, this constitutionally democratic system frowns upon congressional attempts to influence administrative decisions in unethical ways and outlaws congressional influence peddling, which is in blatant violation of separation of powers mandates, besides being flatly dishonest.

Illegal legislative influence peddling before administrative agencies is rather easy to define, understand, and analyze, but it is very difficult to pinpoint what constitutes such action. Consequently, those who are determined to stop legislators from using unethical means to influence administrators are frustrated. Using bribes, blackmail, and physical threats to motivate administrators to make them comply with a legislator's will are clearly illegal criminal acts which are prohibited by criminal and administrative law statutes. But virtually all other legislative methods for pressuring administrators to meet the demands of legislators fall into a huge gray area where it is frequently very difficult to distinguish illegal from unethical acts and unethical acts from those which are acceptable within the democratic rules of the game.[17]

Influence Peddling as Part of Representative Democracy

These gray areas are of considerable interest. In the first place, it should be recognized that in the U.S. democratic system politics plays a crucial role in governmental decision making. Nothing in this open political system prohibits legislators or other politicians from representing the interests of their constituents. Indeed, as delegates of their constituencies, they have a democratic commitment to represent their concerns and to try to fight for their interests. In the words of former Senator Paul Douglas (D-Ill.), the American people "distrust and dislike a self-perpetuating bureaucracy, because they believe that ultimately it will not reflect the best interest of the people. They therefore turn to their elected representatives to protect their legitimate interests in their relationship with the public administrators.[18]

What is wrong, then, with legislators who want to do the best job they can to represent in Washington those interests which were primarily responsible for sending them to Congress? Why shouldn't they persuade administrators to make decisions which help promote the welfare of their constituents? Is anything wrong with this attitude by Senator Mike Mansfield (D.-Mont.): "I would be remiss in my duty if I did not try to do for my constituents everything I possibly could to comply with their legitimate requests. I certainly think this is a part of the job of being a Senator."[19] The answer is that probably nothing is wrong with legislative influence peddling as long as it does not undermine ethical and constitutional principles of due process and equal protection and if legislators represent their entire constituency fairly. In theory, at least, this sort of representative democracy makes sense.

In practice, unfortunately, legislative influence peddling commonly falls far short of the normative standards set forth in the ideal model of representative democracy. In reality, the motives of the legislators may not be as innocent and noble as implied by the previous quotations. Too much evidence exists to suggest that sometimes legislators seek to influence administrative action for the most selfish and irresponsible reasons. That is, some legislators must obey the commands of special interests (for example, the oil industry) because they owe their past electoral success and their continued political survival to them. Retired Senator Thomas F. Eagleton (D.-Mo.) has charged that control over congresspersons by special interests, especially as a result of campaign contributions, has become an ever-increasing accountability problem, as the costs of political campaigns continue to skyrocket.[20]

How gray are the democratic ethics of a situation in which legislators selfishly peddle influence before administrative agencies as loyal lobbyists for special interests, and not as representatives striving to serve their constituents' general welfare?

For instance between 1964 and 1969, Russell Long, a Democrat and an "oil senator" from Louisiana, had a $1,196,015 income from oil interests. Of that amount, $329,151 was nontaxable because of the oil depletion allowance tax laws Long helped to write and push through Congress as chairman of the mighty Senate Finance Committee.[21] But in lobbying for the oil interests before administrative officials and his fellow congresspersons, Long did not believe he was peddling influence in a manner that denied his constituents equal representation, because he equated oil interests with the general interests of the people of Louisiana. Nor did he perceive any conflict of interest between his oil holdings and his role as a senator.[22]

Congressional influence peddling assumes many forms, and it is sometimes very difficult to judge, and especially to prove, whether it is carried out in the best interests of a legislator's constituency or not. To achieve their objectives, legislators have on occasion misused congressional committees, have purposely seen to it that legislation is vague and filled with loopholes, have misused their investigatory powers to harass and threaten administrators, have made unethical and sometimes illegal *ex parte* contacts with administrators to promote special interest causes, and have used other means to manipulate the administrative process.[23] In so doing, they have violated the separation-of-powers doctrine by getting involved in matters which should be decided by administrative experts, not by politicians. A 1979 Nader report argued that congressional partisan politics has made a shambles out of administrative decision making, especially in the Federal Trade Commission (the focus of the report): "Even more destructive to the sense of purpose and nonpolitical ideals of the Commission are the Congressional politics that permeate it. Congressional pressures have made nonsense of priorities for action which related only in theory to the importance of the social issue involved."[24] The 1993 Gore Report concluded similarly that professional, efficient administration is too often compromised by illegitimate influence peddling.[25]

The Courts on Congressional Meddling in the Administrative Process

Some legislators use their personal legislative powers to cajole, harass, and pressure administrators in other ways in an attempt to win administrative decisions favorable to the special interests to which they owe their political careers. But Congress as a whole may also occasionally overstep its constitutional powers in an effort to influence specific administrative action. The systems model of the administrative system vividly conveys that certain demands other than the constitutional kind place pressures on legislators which help to mold their perceptions and decisions. Thus, the decisions of legislators are on occasion motivated by their personal convictions. These may be particularly rooted in their religious and nationalistic beliefs, in their attitudes that special circumstances warrant such decisions, or possibly in a feeling that modern demands justify particular action. But when legislative decisions are motivated by such forces, too frequently the actions are found to be unconstitutional by the courts.

'You Don't Mind If I Look Over Your Shoulder, Do You?'

Source: Reprinted with permission of Tom Engelhardt and the *St. Louis Post-Dispatch,* March 26, 1982.

It can be said at the outset that the courts have often permitted Congress to intervene in the business of public administrators. Judging from what has been said in court decisions over the years, especially since the 1930s, one might say the courts perceive Congress as the creator and caretaker of the administrative machinery. Consequently, the courts have allowed Congress to do what it believes is necessary and proper in regard to delegating power to administrators and even judges. In general, in the past half century the courts have not ruled that a sharp separation of powers should exist between the administrative branch and its creator, the Congress. However, in the past few years, the Supreme Court has occasionally surprised the legal community by employing a rather strict interpretation of the separation-of-powers doctrine to prevent Congress from encroaching on the administrative branch (*INS* v. *Chadha,* 462 U.S. 919; 1983, *Bowsher* v. *Synar,* 106 S.Ct. 3181; 1986; and *Metropolitan Washington Airports Auth.* v. *Citizens,* 111 S. Ct. 2298; 1991). Despite the high court's occasional rulings which apparently endorse a rather strict application of the separation of powers doctrine, the Supreme Court's prevailing position is in support of a flexible, shared powers doctrine as exemplified in *Mistretta* v. *U.S.,* 109 S.Ct. 647 (1989) and *Touby* v. *U.S.,* 111 S.Ct. 1752 (1991). In *Mistretta,* for example, the Court argued that James Madison had a "flexible approach to separation of powers" because he rejected, as did the Framers in general, ". . . the notion that the three Branches be entirely separate and distinct" (at 659). Consequently, the court held in *Mistretta* that Congress did not violate the separation-of-powers doctrine when it established a Sentencing Commission where sentencing power is shared by federal judges and nonjudges.

Placing Congressional Influence Peddling into the Perspective of Legislative and Administrative Roles: ***D.C. Federation of Civic Associations* v. *Volpe***   The case of the *D.C. Federation of Civic Associations* v. *Volpe,* 459 F.2d 1231 (1972), is an excellent case for understanding how the courts view the different roles played by legislators and administrators in the U.S. political system, especially in light of their roles as political actors under the influence of virtually omnipresent political pressures.[26] In this case, the U.S. Court of Appeals for the District of Columbia Circuit essentially held that legislators are free to exert strong persuasive political pressure on administrative officials—short, of course, of illegal pressure—but administrators are not free to yield to such political influence when making administrative decisions.

The *Volpe* case involved a situation in which Representative William Natcher (D.-Ky.), then an influential member of the House Appropriations Committee and the District of Columbia subcommittee, threatened Secretary of Transportation John Volpe with withholding funds for a much-needed District of Columbia subway transit system unless Volpe approved the construction of the proposed Three Sisters Bridge. Because the proposed bridge would affect the Georgetown Historic District and would also use part of Overton Park, Volpe was required by statute to carry out an environmental impact study to determine the extent to which the building of the bridge would harm the historic site and parkland (23 U.S.C.A., Section 138). However, in the absence of any environmental impact data or any record (a record is required by the APA, Sections 556 and 557), Volpe bowed to the political pressures of Representative Natcher and his supporters and announced on August 12, 1969, that he had approved the construction of the proposed Three Sisters Bridge project. The case presents two interesting questions. One, could Representative Natcher, playing the role of a legislator, legally exert such political pressure on an agency administrator? Two, could Volpe, playing the role of an agency administrator, allow his decision to be influenced by political pressures?

In the first place, agreeing with the district court's findings, Chief Judge Bazelon, writing for the appellate court, acknowledged "that the pressure exerted by Representative Natcher and others did have an impact on Secretary Volpe's decision to approve the bridge" (at 1246).[27] Despite the strong political pressures placed on

Volpe by Natcher, the court did not find that Natcher acted beyond the scope of his powers as a congressman. Evidently, such influence peddling by Natcher was viewed by the court as a natural function of the political process: "To avoid any misconceptions about the nature of our holding, we emphasize that we have not found—nor, for that matter, have we sought—any suggestion of impropriety or illegality in the actions of Representative Natcher and others who strongly advocate the bridge. They are surely entitled to their own views on the need for the Three Sisters Bridge, and we indicate no opinion on their authority to exert pressure on Secretary Volpe" (at 1249). It is important to note, however, that if the court believed that Volpe was acting in a quasi-judicial capacity in reaching his decision on the bridge, as contrasted to a legislative-administrative capacity, Representative Natcher's *ex parte* communications (contacts) with Volpe would likely have been condemned by the court since the court earlier noted (at 1246) that such influence peddling was prohibited in *Sangamon Valley Television Corp.* v. *United States,* 106 U.S.App.D.C. 30 (1959). (Later the D.C. Circuit Court condemned *ex parte* contacts with quasi-judicial officials in *Professional Air Traffic Controllers Organization* v. *Federal Labor Relations Authority,* 685 F.2d 547; 1982.)

On the other hand, the court held that Volpe, as an administrator bound by statutory obligations, could not let his decisions be swayed by political considerations. In testifying before the district court, Volpe asserted that his "decision was based on the merits of the project and not *solely* on the extraneous political influence" (at 1246). However, Judge Bazelon ruled that Volpe's decision must be made "strictly on the merits and completely without regard to any consideration not made relevant by Congress in the applicable statutes" (at 1246). The court did acknowledge that the error in decision making would have been "more flagrant, of course, if the Secretary had based his decision solely on the pressures generated by Representative Natcher. But it should be clear that his action would not be immunized merely because he also considered some relevant factors" (at 1248). Bazelon believed such political pressures were not intended by Congress to be considered in reaching such decisions (at 1247). However, the court confused its decision somewhat by noting that if Volpe's action had been *purely* legislative, the court might have reached a different conclusion. Judge Bazelon perceived Volpe's decision as one involving a mixture of legislative, judicial, and administrative functions.

It is worth noting that in *United States ex rel. Parco* v. *Morris,* 426 F.Supp. 976 (1977), District Court Judge Becker, citing Bazelon's decision in the *Volpe* case, ruled against petitioners who maintained that an administrator's decision should not stand because it violated the separation-of-powers doctrine since it rested on a congressman's influential recommendation. But Judge Becker emphasized that his holding was consistent with Bazelon's decision because here the administrator was performing a purely legislative act, thus making it irrelevant that the administrative decision may have been motivated by a legislator's weighty recommendation. In so holding, Becker noted that "when the agency action is purely 'legislative,' as in the informal rulemaking involved here, the decision 'cannot be invalidated merely because the . . . action was motivated by impermissible considerations' any more than can that of a legislature" (at 982). Furthermore, Judge Becker found "no Constitutional violation in a Congressional attempt to influence the regulatory interpretation of statutes. Interrogation of agency officials at Congressional hearings often serves such a purpose and is part of the give and take of democratic government. We think that the contention the Parcos seek to raise is really one of administrative law, i.e., that an agency decision may be invalid if induced by secret or otherwise improper influence" (at 982).

The *Volpe* decision still stands as law today. Recently, in *Town of Norfolk* v. *U.S. Army Corps of Engineers*, 968 F.2d 1438 (1st Cir. 1992), the First Circuit Court relied heavily upon *Volpe* in upholding a controversial decision by the Army Corps of Engineers pertaining to discharge of fill at an artificial wetland site. Reflecting back upon the *Volpe* case, the court in *Town of Norfolk* condemned Volpe's reliance upon the political influence peddled by Representative Natcher, concluding that "[T]he defects in the Secretary's decision in *Volpe* were colossal, including his failure to compile an administrative record . . . ." (at 1459).

In concluding, it should be stressed that the courts since *Volpe* have been insisting that administrators reach decisions on the basis of the merits and in the context of a written, reviewable record, even indicating the date and nature of any *ex parte* contacts. Judges note that agency decision making cannot be reviewed properly unless a meaningful, complete record is kept. A comprehensive record would show the role played by political influence peddling in agency decision making.

The Limitations of the Speech or Debate Clause   The Speech or Debate Clause found in Article 1, Section 6(1) of the U.S. Constitution grants certain liberties to congresspersons in their role as legislators, but some congresspersons have on occasion abused these liberties to meddle in the administrative process. When this has happened, the courts have objected. The Constitution is very vague as to exactly how the Speech or Debate Clause should be applied to legislators. All that is written is that "Senators and Representatives . . . for any speech or debate in either House . . . shall not be questioned in any other place." However, court opinions have clarified its meaning. In *Gravel* v. *United States*, 408 U.S. 606 (1972), the Supreme Court contended that the Speech or Debate Clause "was designed to assure a coequal branch of the government wide freedom of speech, debate and deliberation without intimidation or threats from the Executive Branch. It thus protects members against prosecutions that directly impinge upon or threaten the legislative process" (at 616). But the Court was quick to point out that senators and representatives are not protected in acts which are nonlegislative in nature. That is, wrote Justice Byron White: "Members of Congress are constantly in touch with the Executive Branch of the Government and with administrative agencies—they may cajole, and exhort with respect to the administration of a federal statute—but such conduct, though generally done, is not protected legislative activity" (at 625). The purpose of the clause, White argued, is not to protect legislators who try to influence agency decisions. Rather, the purpose of the clause is to protect normal legislative functions or those "deliberative and communicative processes by which . . . [congresspersons] participate in committee and [congressional] proceedings with respect to the consideration and passage or rejection of proposed legislation or with respect to other matters which the Constitution places within the jurisdiction of either House" (at 625). Only on rare occasions have the courts extended the scope of the Speech or Debate Clause, Justice White noted, and then only out of an effort to preserve necessary legislative proceedings. This clause, according to the 1972 Court, gives immunity to legislators and their aides in regard to speech, voting, and various other legislative functions, but it does not permit legislators or their assistants "to violate an otherwise valid criminal law in preparing for or implementing legislative acts" (at 622).

In *United States* v. *Brewster,* 408 U.S. 501 (1972), the Supreme Court rejected Senator Daniel B. Brewster's argument that he should be immune from prosecution on bribery charges because he was protected from prosecution under the Speech or Debate Clause. Specifically, Brewster was charged with soliciting and accepting a bribe in exchange for promising to carry out a legislative function which would violate federal law. But Chief Justice Warren Burger, evidently outraged by such an abuse of the Speech or Debate Clause, wrote: "The immunities of the Speech or Debate Clause were not written into the Constitution simply for the personal or private benefit of Members of Congress, but to protect the integrity of the legislative process" (at 507). Burger emphasized that the clause applies only to "those things 'generally done in a session in the House by one of its members in relation to the business before it,' . . . or things 'said or done by him as a representative, in the exercise of the functions of that office'" (at 512). Burger noted that the clause does not extend immunity to those acts which cannot be considered proper functions of the legislative process, but its purpose is certainly not "to make Members of Congress super-citizens, immune from criminal responsibility" (at 516). The Speech or Debate Clause immunity privilege, Burger concluded, is "broad enough to insure the historic independence of the Legislative Branch, essential to our separation of powers, but narrow enough to guard against the excesses of those who would corrupt the process by corrupting its members . . . taking a bribe is, obviously, no part of the legislative process or function; it is not a legislative act" (at 526).

In recent cases the courts have built upon *Gravel* and *Brewster* to expand the scope of qualified immunity for legislators under the speech or debate clause to immunize ". . . members of Congress against both criminal and civil liability based on their legislative conduct, whether the action is for prospective relief or damages." [*Montgomery County* v. *Schooley,* 627 A.2d 69, 74 (Md. App. 1993)]. Clearly, the key is to determine the boundaries of legislative conduct because there is legal precedent now to protect legislators from being held liable for criminal acts if somehow the conduct can be construed as "within the sphere of legitimate legislative activity" (at 75). Hopefully, the courts in the future will not find forms of illegal influence peddling by legislators before our public administrators, such as bribery, conduct that is within the scope of "legitimate legislative activity."[28]

The Use and Misuse of Loyalty Oaths   Basically, loyalty oaths have been used to force individuals to disavow certain associations, beliefs, and principles. Although the use of loyalty oaths at the national and state levels has been on a general decline in recent times because of many serious legal challenges to their constitutionality, they nevertheless have a long history in America, being first employed to compel allegiance during the Revolutionary War.[29] They were also used extensively during the Civil War and during the Red Scare of the 1920s. During the 1940s and 1950s, in response to Cold War mania, people were forced to sign loyalty oaths in exchange for privileges such as governmental jobs, swearing that they did not advocate the violent overthrow of the American government or belong to any organization that did. Some loyalty oaths, especially at the state and local levels, were directed more toward making people disavow any attachment to Communism.

The general purpose of the loyalty oath in public personnel practices is to ensure that governmental employees, paid out of the public treasury, will not use their employment to undermine the American government. Various loyalty and security programs have been used in conjunction with loyalty oaths since 1947 in an effort to purge the government of disloyal persons who pose unnecessary security risks. For example, in 1947 President Harry S Truman, in initiating a federal government security program, ordered that governmental workers should be dismissed if evidence existed which cast doubt on their loyalty. This security program applied to governmental employees as well as to many quasi-governmental workers (employees working for private companies under governmental contract). It is of special interest to students of administrative law that the various governmental security programs allowed discharged persons the right of appeal, yet did not always permit them to confront and challenge the sources of the incriminating evidence.

During the late 1940s and early 1950s, the misuse of loyalty oaths and security programs reached its peak. The word *McCarthyism* symbolizes the shame of this era in American history, an era in which real or imagined Communist threats caused some of our governmental leaders to place on the back burners the constitutional principles which they claimed they wanted to preserve. The leader behind this movement was Senator Joseph R. McCarthy (R.-Wis.), a man who recklessly charged numerous public employees and private citizens with being Communists without being able to substantiate the charges. (McCarthy, by the way, used the Speech or Debate Clause's immunity privilege to protect himself from lawsuits.) Americans who were more truly American than McCarthy finally brought the senator down. However, this is not to suggest that traces of McCarthyism do not still persist. Eventually, McCarthy was charged by his Senate colleagues with acting in a manner unbecoming of a senator. On December 2, 1954, a special senate committee officially condemned his conduct in two senatorial committees. With that, Senator McCarthy, as a major force, faded rapidly.

But before this, even the courts tended to uphold the constitutionality of very questionable loyalty oaths and security programs. For example, in 1951, in *Garner* v. *Board of Public Works,* 341 U.S. 716, the Supreme Court ruled that compelling prospective public employees to sign a noncommunist affidavit constituted a reasonable public employment prerequisite. In 1952, in *Adler* v. *Board of Education,* 342 U.S. 485, the high Court held that a state law can be used to disqualify from public service employment any person who advocates the overthrow of the American government by violence or any other illegal means or is a member of any organization which advocates such. Three years after the Senate censured Senator Joseph McCarthy, the Supreme Court began a dramatic reversal of its previous position. In *Yates* v. *United States,* 354 U.S. 298 (1957), a case which did not directly involve loyalty oaths, the Court, drastically modifying its decision in *Dennis* v. *United States,* 341 U.S. 494 (1951), ruled that a distinction must be recognized between believing in something and acting upon those beliefs. The *Yates* ruling had immediate practical significance for those who had held that forcing people to take loyalty oaths violated the First Amendment guarantees of freedom of speech, association, and assembly. Because the *Yates* decision in effect requested that a "clear and present danger" should be established between beliefs and the threatening use of these beliefs (for example, acting on held communist beliefs by trying to violently overthrow the American government), it now became very difficult for the government to require loyalty oaths which essentially asked if prospective governmental employees or those in public employment advocated the violent overthrow of the American government or belonged to any organizations that did.

Beginning with *Speiser* v. *Randall,* 357 U.S. 513 (1958), the Supreme Court, under Chief Justice Earl Warren, started to hand down a series of decisions aimed at eliminating the unconstitutional use of loyalty oaths. In *Speiser* the Court ruled, in a related matter, that loyalty test oaths could not be required as a condition for obtaining governmental benefits. In *Baggett* v. *Bullitt,* 377 U.S. 360 (1964), the Supreme Court struck down a loyalty oath because it was too vague. In 1966 in *Elfbrandt* v. *Russell,* 384 U.S. 11, the so-called Warren Court overruled the 1951 *Garner* decision by holding that a state loyalty oath which forbade state employees becoming Communist Party members was unconstitutional on the grounds that the law was not related to specific illegal actions and, in addition, was rooted in the unconstitutional doctrine of guilt by association. The *Elfbrandt* case established that loyalty oaths may not abridge First Amendment freedoms. A year later, in *Keyishian* v. *Board of Regents of New York,* 385 U.S. 589 (1967), the Warren Court struck down a loyalty-security law which was directed at disqualifying from state governmental employment any person who advocated the overthrow of the government by force or by any other illegal means or belonged to any association that did. In overturning the 1952 *Adler* holding, the Court in *Keyishian* determined that such loyalty security laws violated First Amendment protections guaranteeing persons freedom of speech and association. In *Keyishian,* the Court stressed that a person should not be expected to give up his or her constitutional rights to obtain governmental employment.

However, the unpopular Vietnam War, chaotic student demonstrations, violent minority protest movements, and other such occurrences identified with the 1960s evidently caused a conservative shift in the electorate, which apparently helped Richard Nixon reach the White House. Within a few years, given his unusual opportunity to appoint so many justices to the high Court, President Nixon turned the relatively liberal Warren Court into the relatively conservative Burger Court. Before long the new Court started reversing some earlier Warren Court decisions. In regard to loyalty oaths, for example, the Burger Court shocked many constitutional and administrative law experts by upholding, in *Cole* v. *Richardson,* 405 U.S. 676 (1972), a Massachusetts loyalty oath that required state employees to swear that they would "uphold and defend the Constitution of the United States of America and the Constitution of the Commonwealth of Massachusetts" and "oppose the overthrow of the government of the United States of America or of this Commonwealth by force, violence, or by any illegal or unconstitutional method" (at 677). As to the first requirement of the oath, the Court held that the oath, similar to the oaths required by the U.S. Constitution in Article 2, Section 1, Clause 7 (applicable to the president) and Article 6, Clause 3 (applicable to federal and state public officials), is constitutional because it simply asks "for an acknowledgement of a willingness to abide by 'constitutional processes of government'" (at 682). In writing the decision, Burger reasoned that a state oath "need not parrot the exact language of the constitutional oaths to be constitutionally proper" (at 682). Regarding the more controversial part of the Massachusetts loyalty oath, which required an employee to swear that he or she "will oppose the overthrow of the government of the United States of America or of this Commonwealth by force, violence, or by any illegal or unconstitutional method," the Court found that such was a reasonable extension of the first part of the oath, requiring only that Massachusetts public employees were "willing to commit themselves to live by the constitutional process of our system" (at 682). The oath did not, Burger argued, "require specific action in some hypothetical or actual situation" (at 683).

Furthermore, the Court held that the oath was sufficiently clear and thus could not be overturned on the grounds that it was too vague, as was the situation in the 1964 *Baggett* case, 377 U.S. 360. Also, the Court recognized that since no evidence existed to show that the oath had been used to harass public employees since its enactment in 1948 (in fact, nobody had been prosecuted under the oath), there existed no real cause to exaggerate its role. If the oath had been employed to harass public employees, Burger noted, the Court would have been confronted with a different issue.

Using Bills of Attainder and *Ex Post Facto* Laws to Punish Administrators   In drafting the Constitution, the founders of this country's government gave broad powers to the legislative branch, apparently because they believed that if tyrannical power were to emerge within a branch, it would most likely be in the administrative branch, not within an assembly where so many voices are heard. In *Fletcher* v. *Peck,* 6 Cranch 87, 136 (1810), the Court noted that this reasoning might be valid. Nevertheless, Congress was "not so numerous as to be incapable of pursuing the objects of its passions," and thus "barriers had to be erected to ensure that the legislature would not overstep the bounds of its authority and perform the functions of the other departments." Accordingly, the constitutional framers, among other restrictions they imposed on congressional power, prohibited the U.S. Congress and state legislatures from legislating any bills of attainder or *ex post facto* laws: "No bill of attainder or ex post facto law shall be passed" (Article 1, Section 9, Clause 3).[30]

But what is a *bill of attainder* or an *ex post facto* law? Simply, a *bill of attainder* is a legislative act directed toward an individual which pronounces the person guilty of an offense without the benefit of due process procedures (a trial). But in *Springfield Armory, Inc.* v. *City of Columbus,* 805 F. Supp. 489, 493 (S.D. Ohio, 1992), the Ohio court noted that "[A] legislative act does not automatically violate the prohibition against bills of attainder merely because it places some burden upon an identified individual or group. That is, specificity alone does not establish that a law is an unconstitutional bill of attainder. Rather, the burden imposed by the legislature must constitute punishment." Historically, bills of attainder were directed at serious offenses, especially treason, with sentences usually resulting in death. Milder forms of bills of attainder, not resulting in death sentences, are known as *bills of pains and penalties,* but both forms are strictly prohibited by the Constitution (*Losier* v. *Sherman,* 157 Kans. 153; 138 P.2d 272; 1943). If legislators had the power to employ bills of attainder to convict persons of crimes, such power would encroach upon the rightful powers of the judiciary, thereby undermining the democratic forces believed to exist in the separation-of-powers doctrine. In *Fletcher* v. *Peck,* the Court asserted that "the Bill of Attainder Clause not only was intended as one implementation of the general principle of fractionalized power, but also reflected the Framers' belief that the Legislative Branch is not so well suited as politically independent judges and juries to the task of ruling upon the blameworthiness of, and levying appropriate punishment upon, specific persons" (6 Cranch 87,136). The constitutional ban on bills of attainder has generally been considered essential to the preservation of liberty.

But the constitutional prohibition of *ex post facto* laws has likewise been regarded as absolutely necessary to the promotion of liberty and justice in a free society. In banning the use of *ex post facto* legislation, the constitutional framers guaranteed that a person would be able to perform activities which are not prohibited by existing laws without the fear of being punished under new laws at sometime in the future. In *People of U.S. ex rel. Umbenhowar* v. *McDonnell,* 11 F.Supp. 1014, 1015 (1934), the court defined an *ex post facto* law as "one which renders an act punishable in a manner in which it was not punishable when it was committed, or which deprives accused of any substantial right or immunity possessed by him before its passage to prior offenses." In *Strong* v. *State,* 1 Black, Ind., 196 (1822), the court noted that "the plain and obvious meaning of prohibition is that the legislature shall not pass any law, after a fact done by any citizen, which shall have relation to that fact, so as to punish that which was innocent when done; or to add to the punishment of that which was criminal; or to increase the malignity of a crime; or to retrench the rules of evidence, so as to make conviction more easy." In *Ethics Com'n* v. *Cullison,* 850 P.2d 1069, 1079 (Okla. 1993), the court stressed that the Oklahoma constitution's *ex post facto* clause ". . . prohibits the punishment of an act which was not defined as criminal at the time of the act." Although *ex post facto* legislation may strike today's Americans as obviously unfair, they have been used throughout history by many dictators, who did not question their character. However, these dictators were not bound by rule-of-law dictates, which under the U.S. Constitution, place law above the arbitrary and capricious personal decisions of whimsical leaders. *Ex post facto* laws are inconsistent with rule-of-law principles and, accordingly, cannot be tolerated in a nation which cherishes due process of law. In American society the *ex post facto* principle is so commonly accepted that virtually any law, rule, or the like applied in an *ex post facto* manner is simply regarded as patently unfair.

Despite the relatively respectable due process of law tradition in the United States, on occasion national and state legislators have trespassed upon the domain and rights of administrators by passing unconstitutional bills of attainder and *ex post facto* laws. In 1866, the Supreme Court ruled that laws legislated to prevent former Civil War Confederate soldiers from obtaining governmental benefits were bills of attainder (*Cummings* v. *Missouri*, 4 Wallace 277; 1866; and *Ex parte Garland*, 4 Wallace 333; 1866). In *United States* v. *Lovett*, 328 U.S. 303 (1946), the Supreme Court found a congressional act to be an unconstitutional bill of attainder because Congress specifically intended for three named individuals, whom Congress regarded as subversives, to be punished by removing them from governmental employment without a trial. Speaking for the Court, Justice Hugo Black maintained that the clear goal of Congress was to "permanently bar" the three named individuals from further governmental employment because Congress, not the courts, decided that they were "unfit." Ruling that the issue at hand was justifiable because the Constitution prohibits the passage of any bills of attainder, Justice Black held that the act must be regarded as an unconstitutional bill of attainder if it applies "to named individuals or to easily ascertainable members of a group in such a way as to inflict punishment on them without a judicial trial" (at 315), as was the situation here.

In *United States* v. *Brown*, 381 U.S. 437 (1965), Chief Justice Earl Warren ruled that a provision in the Landrum-Griffin Labor Act was an unconstitutional bill of attainder because it made it a crime for Communists to hold office in labor unions. The Court found that this provision violated the separation-of-powers doctrine by promoting the "legislative exercise of the judicial function, or more simply—trial by legislature" (at 442). Chief Justice Warren stressed that the separation-of-powers doctrine "was obviously not instituted with the idea that it would promote governmental efficiency. It was, on the contrary, looked to as a bulwark against tyranny" (at 443).

In a highly publicized case, *Hiss* v. *Hampton*, 338 F.Supp. 1141 (1972), Circuit Judge Robb (U.S. Dist. Ct., D.C.) ruled that a 1954 federal statute, popularly known as the Hiss Act, was unconstitutional on the grounds that it was an *ex post facto* law.[31] Alger Hiss and Richard Strasburger had applied for retirement annuities under the Civil Service Retirement Systems, but they were informed that under the Hiss Act they were ineligible to receive benefits because they were in violation of specific provisions of the act. However, Judge Robb, citing the opinion in *Cummings* v. *Missouri*, argued that "a statute is an *ex post facto* law, and invalid, if its purpose and effect are to punish for past conduct and not to regulate a profession, calling or present situation" (at 1148). According to the legislative history of the Hiss Act, Judge Robb concluded that without any question the purpose of the act was to punish specific former federal employees and not to regulate future conduct: "There is substantial evidence in the 'objective manifestations of congressional purpose' that the primary target of the Act was Alger Hiss and not general regulation of the federal service" (at 1149).

Judge Robb scolded Congress for legislating a law with no apparent legitimate regulatory purpose: "Neither Hiss nor Strasburger was a federal employee at the time the Act was passed, and we do not understand how the conduct of federal employees could be regulated or their moral standards elevated by imposing a financial penalty for their prior conduct upon men who were not federal employees or likely ever again to become federal employees. Retroactive punishment of former employees for their past misdoings has no reasonable bearing upon regulation of the conduct of the presently employed. The proper function of regulation is to guide and control present and future conduct, not to penalize former employees for acts done long ago" (at 1149). In summary, Judge Robb concluded, the only important question to decide in this case "is simply whether the Constitution permits Congress to deprive them of their annuities by retroactive penal legislation. We conclude that it does not. We hold that as applied retroactively to the plaintiffs the challenged statute is penal, cannot be sustained as regulation, and is invalid as an *ex post facto* law prohibited by the Constitution" (at 1153).

TINKERING WITH ADMINISTRATORS: THE PRESIDENT'S APPOINTMENT AND REMOVAL POWERS

If a U.S. president could at will appoint and remove administrators, the president would virtually have the capacity to destroy the efficiency and effectiveness of the administration process through reckless manipulation of agency administrators. A president is entrusted with controlling and leading the administrative system and should possess reasonable powers over it, along with the freedom to appoint and remove administrators as seems advisable. The complete freedom to appoint and remove, at the president's personal pleasure, would undoubtedly prove extremely disruptive to normal administrative operations. Consequently, presidential appointment and removal powers have been restricted by various constitutional provisions, federal statutes, and court holdings. Generally, the limitations which have been placed on the president's appointment and removal powers have been directed at stabilizing the administrative process, professionalizing its character, and protecting public administrators from undue interference and harassment. Of course, efforts aimed at confining the president's power to appoint and remove administrative officials are consistent with the constitutional framers' chief objective of keeping all governmental powers shared and limited.

The President's Appointment Power

The Constitution states in Article 2, Section 1, Clause 1 that "the executive power shall be vested in a President of the United States of America." In order that the president could function as the chief executive, the constitutional framers in Article 2, Section 2, Clause 2 provided that the president "shall nominate, and by and with the advice and consent of the Senate, shall appoint ambassadors, other public ministers and consuls, judges of the Supreme Court, and all other officers of the United States, whose appointments are not herein otherwise provided for, and which shall be established by law; but the Congress may by law vest the appointment of such inferior officers, as they think proper, in the President alone, in the courts of law, or in the heads of departments."

As interpreted by the courts, this constitutional provision vests exclusive powers in the president to appoint persons to all major executive posts in the government, so long as the nominees meet with the approval of the Senate. Essentially, this appointment power provides presidents with the authority to select those high-level administrators whom they want in their administrations. Generally, high-level administrators are distinguished from those lower down in that the former normally possess considerably greater policy-making discretionary powers than the latter. Consequently, most lower-level governmental administrators, as permitted by Article 2, Section 2, Clause 2, have been placed by Congress under the civil service system. With the expansion of the administrative system, presidents have been given the rightful authority to appoint members to the independent and quasi-independent regulatory commissions. The appointment powers of governors and mayors are similar, although their appointment powers are generally considerably more limited.

In *Buckley* v. *Valeo,* 424 U.S. 1 (1976), the Supreme Court, reaffirming the holding in *Springer* v. *Philippine Islands,* 277 U.S. 189 (1928), held essentially that the Constitution did not permit Congress to usurp the president's appointment powers. In *Buckley,* it was charged, *inter alia,* that the Federal Election Campaign Act of 1974 (2 USC, Section 437h) violated Article 2, Section 2 Clause 2, of the Constitution because the act permits Congress, not the president, to appoint four members to the six-member Federal Elections Commission. The Court ruled that although the Constitution does not call for a rigid separation of powers between the governmental branches, it does forbid Congress from appointing its own members to administrative positions (those in which officers perform the normal administrative functions, including rule making and order making within the scope of Article 2).

In 1991 the Supreme Court in *Freytag* v. *Commissioner of Internal Revenue,* 111 S.Ct. 2631, held that Congress could use its discretion under the Appointments Clause to allow the chief justice of the Tax Court, not the President, to appoint special trial judges (formerly called commissioners) because the court said they were "inferior officers," not "officers of the United States." This decision has proved very "difficult to interpret," according to administrative law scholars Kenneth C. Davis and Richard J. Pierce, Jr., because ". . . its reasoning could require major restructuring of the administrative state."[32]

The reason legal scholars are bothered by the Court's holding in *Freytag* is because the Court's majority, to justify permitting the Tax Court's chief justice appointment power, argued that the Tax Court was *not* an agency, but a "court of law." Of course, by labelling the Tax Court a "court of law," the appointment of "inferior officers," according to Article 11, Section 2, Ch. 2, could be assigned to the Tax Court's chief justice by Congress since Congress has the discretion to delegate this appointment power to the President alone, courts of law, or heads of departments. In this case the Congress elected to give the appointment power to the "court of law."

The problem is, however, that few legal and political scholars appear to regard the Tax Court as a constitutionally sanctioned court of law for the purpose of applying Article 11, Section 2, Ch. 2, including even the four justices concurring in this case. Ironically, both sides in the case even argued that the Appointments Clause applied only to Article III courts. It was only the Supreme Court's majority that held that "Congress' consistent interpretation of the appointments clause evinces a clear congressional understanding that Article I courts could be given the power to appoint" (at 2645).

The point is that most scholars still regard the Tax Court as an agency similar to many other agencies in the Executive Branch which exercise judicial or quasi-judicial powers such as the Occupational Safety and Health Regulatory Commission, all of which are under the president's appointment authority. *"Freytag* illustrates the surprising extent to which the entire modern structure of government rests on an uncertain and controversial constitutional footing," Davis and Pierce maintain. Since the Tax Court is similar to hundreds of other agencies in our administrative system which exercise judicial power, the *Freytag* decision seems to call into question the broad applicability of the president's appointment powers, especially regarding quasi-judicial, independent regulatory agencies.[33]

The Appointment Power's Limitations

Despite the broad presidential appointment powers, it would be a mistake to assume that the president could blatantly abuse this power to the flagrant detriment of the administrative process. As noted previously, presidents have almost routinely managed to obtain confirmation of those they have nominated, although confirmation is certainly not automatic.[34] Remember recently the problems Presidents Bush and Clinton had with some of their nominees. The president's appointment power is limited by the Senate's negative confirmation power. The president may have absolute power to appoint, but the Senate has absolute power to not confirm.

Arthur S. Miller, in *Presidential Power,* points out that the president's appointment power is also restricted by congressional statutes, thus forcing the appointment power to be shared."[35] Justice Louis Brandeis, Miller acknowledged, cited many examples of times when Congress placed restrictions on whom presidents could appoint to administrative positions. In a dissenting opinion, in *Myers* v. *United States,* 272 U.S. 52 (1926), Brandeis noted that Congress in the past had limited the appointment power by requiring appointees to: (1) be citizens; (2) be residents of specific geographical regions; (3) possess particular professional qualifications and experience; (4) pass qualification tests; and (5) be representatives of various political, professional, age, sex, race, and property groupings. Under Article 2, Section 2 the president is given the authority "to fill up all vacancies that may happen during the recess of the Senate by granting commissions which shall expire at the end of their next session."

On the informal side, senatorial courtesy has always played a role in limiting presidents' flexibility in appointing anyone they wished to various administrative offices. For example, in 1789, during the very first presidential appointments, President George Washington had to withdraw an appointment to a naval post because he did not observe senatorial courtesy.[36] "Failure of the Executive to follow the wishes of a Senator (or Senators) of the state from which a nominee is selected or where he will serve will usually defeat the appointment."[37]

Nevertheless, the power to make appointments has allowed presidents to change the bureaucratic perspective. In regard to the judiciary, for example, President Richard Nixon changed the philosophical perspective of the Supreme Court in a short time. Presidents Ronald Reagan and George Bush also left their mark on the high Court as well as the lower courts through their many appointments. Of course, President Bill Clinton, being the only Democrat to hold the presidency since 1969, except for Jimmy Carter, is trying his best to replace the relatively conservative Republican appointees with more liberal Democrats. Likewise, key top-level appointments throughout a president's administration can dramatically shift the philosophical position of the administration.

The President's Limited Removal Powers

In a sense, presidential appointment power is restricted most by the limitations placed upon the president's removal powers. That is, in order to appoint persons to administrative posts, the president must first remove those already occupying the positions. If the president had unlimited appointment and removal powers in combination, these powers over the administrative apparatus would be awesome, but presidential appointment and removal powers are limited by both formal and informal checks. However, in regard to removal powers, the president's authority is curtailed considerably more. From the administrators' perspective this is fortunate because, if presidents were allowed to remove administrators and appoint replacements at their whim, administrators could never function without worrying about whether their actions would lead to their dismissal by an irate president. In the words of Justice Felix Frankfurter, they would have to fear being removed "by the Damocles sword . . . for no reason."[38]

The Constitution is silent on the president's role in regard to removing administrative officials. Of course, according to the Constitution, any federal administrator, including the president, can be removed by impeachment, but the impeachment process is strictly a legislative function.[39] In *Myers* v. *United States,* 272 U.S. 52 (1926), President William Howard Taft, at the time Chief Justice of the Supreme Court, argued that under Article 2 of the Constitution the president had the power to remove those "executive officers appointed by him," and Congress had no constitutional authority to prohibit such presidential action. Although Meyers was a purely executive officer (a postmaster), Taft contended that the Constitution gave the president the power to remove even those administrators who "perform duties of a quasi-judicial character . . . whose decisions after a hearing affect interests of individuals, the discharge of which the President can not in a particular case properly influence or control" (at 135). If this decision stood today, the relationship between the president and the administrative regulatory system would be radically different, especially because the president would be able to remove commissioners from the independent regulatory agencies at will.

The Precedential *Humphrey* Case   Court sanctioning of the legitimacy of the headless governmental branch came less than a decade after *Meyers* in *Humphrey's Executor* v. *United States*, 295 U.S. 602 (1935), with the Court holding that the president could not remove independent regulatory commissioners except for good cause. Since the president could not control (head) such regulatory commissions, these agencies became known as headless.

Unlike Meyers, Humphrey was not a purely executive official but rather a member of the Federal Trade Commission. As a member of this independent regulatory agency, Humphrey performed quasi-judicial functions in hearing and deciding cases. To protect the independence of these quasi-judicial officials, Congress specifically prohibited the president from removing these commissioners except "for inefficiency, neglect of duty or malfeasance in office" (Federal Trade Commission Act of 1914, Section 1, 15 U.S.C., Section 41). Therefore, the question for the Court became whether Congress, under the Constitution, could validly place such a restriction on the president's removal power.

In delivering the opinion of the Court, Justice George Sutherland stressed that a regulatory agency such as the FTC, which performs quasi-legislative and quasi-judicial functions "cannot in any proper sense be characterized as an arm or an eye of the executive. Its duties are performed without executive leave and, in the contemplation of the statute, must be free from executive control" (at 628). The Court argued that it is plain that the Constitution did not assign illimitable removal powers to the president, especially in the case of administrators performing quasi-legislative and quasi-judicial tasks. Consequently, Congress has the power to restrict the president's removal powers in regard to independent regulatory agencies (at 629).

Once again, the perceived supreme importance to democratic government of keeping governmental powers comfortably separated played a major role in the Court's holding in *Humphrey*. Justice Sutherland contended that the necessity of preserving a separation of powers between the governmental branches had never been challenged seriously. Sutherland considered that the principle of separation of powers would be violated if presidents were permitted to remove independent regulatory commissioners without sound cause since such removal authority would threaten "the independence of a commission, which is not only wholly disconnected from the executive department, but which, as already fully appears, was created by Congress as a means of carrying into operation legislative and judicial powers, and as an agency of the legislative and judicial departments" (at 630).

In concluding, Justice Sutherland made very clear that the removal powers of the president depend upon the specific functional classification of the administrators in question. Sutherland expressed the emphatic point that the Myers decision applied only to those administrations performing purely executive functions. However, as to quasi-legislative and quasi-judicial administrators such as *Humphrey*, the Court held that "no removal can be made during the prescribed term for which the officer is appointed, except for one or more of the causes named in the applicable statute" (at 632).

Today, the *Humphrey* decision stands on firmer turf than it did when the decision was handed down in 1935. This is true because in *Wiener* v. *United States*, 357

U.S. 349 (1958), the Court, praising the wisdom of Justice Sutherland in *Humphrey,* gave solid endorsement to the *Humphrey* ruling. Although the Court noted that the Humphrey's case was a *cause celebre* (at 353), it felt that it should hear the *Wiener* case "because it presents a variant of the constitutional issue decided in *Humphrey's Executor* v. *United States*" (at 351). In *Wiener,* Justice Frankfurter, writing the unanimous opinion, made clear that the circumstances surrounding the removals of both Humphrey and petitioner Wiener, both quasi-legislative and quasi-judicial officers, were virtually the same: "The ground of President Eisenhower's removal of petitioner was precisely the same as President Roosevelt's removal of Humphrey. Both Presidents desired to have commissioners, one on the Federal Trade Commission, the other on the War Claims Commission, 'of my own selection.' They wanted these Commissioners to be their men." However, one notable difference distinguished the two cases. While Humphrey's removal without good cause (for political reasons) was prohibited by statute (15 USC, Section 41), Wiener was not specifically protected from removal by the War Claims Act of 1948 (62 Stat. 1240). Nevertheless, the Court asserted, since Congress created the War Claims Commission to adjudicate claims, it became a quasi-judicial body with officials to be protected from removal by the president, except for good cause. Thus, the Court concluded: "Judging the matter in all the nakedness in which it is presented, namely, the claim that the President could remove a member of an adjudicatory body like the War Claims Commission merely because he wanted his own appointees on such a commission, we are compelled to conclude that no such power is given to the President directly by the Constitution, and none is impliedly conferred upon him by statute simply because Congress said nothing about it. The philosophy of Humphrey's Executor, in its explicit language as well as its implications, precludes such a claim" (at 356).

The Impact of *Humphrey* The significance of the *Humphrey* decision, as upheld and expanded in *Wiener,* must not be underestimated. Few decisions in American history have had more of an impact on administrative structure than these two decisions. And, of course, court decisions regarding structure carry with them meaningful procedural implications. If the Courts in *Humphrey* and *Wiener* had upheld Taft's broad interpretation of presidential removal powers in *Myers,* which permitted quasi-legislative and quasi-judicial administrators to be subject to unrestricted presidential removal as long as the president had authority to appoint them, the entire independent regulatory system would have developed much differently. For one thing, actually independent regulatory commissions would not exist today, except in a nonindependent, politicized capacity with status similar to that of the executive departments. Obviously, this would tend to make these regulatory commissions highly partisan agencies, filled with the sitting president's own supporters. As a result, the public policy perspective of the regulatory administrators would be expected to change dramatically and suddenly from one presidential administration to the next. Whether impartial adjudicative proceedings could take place would be highly questionable since the influence and pressures of partisan politics would tend to bias agency proceedings and decisions.

But the Courts in *Humphrey* and *Wiener* did not uphold the *Myers* decision. Consequently, a rather large and powerful independent regulatory system has developed since the 1935 *Humphrey* decision, and it has not been very vulnerable to White House political pressures or controls. But is this necessarily good? Was Justice Sutherland right in *Humphrey* when he asserted unequivocally that an agency such as the FTC "cannot in any proper sense be characterized as an arm or an eye of the executive" (at 628)? But many, especially in the field of public administration, question the insightfulness of Sutherland's contention because such regulatory agencies are obviously very much a part of the administrative system, which the president is held responsible for administering.[40] Do these regulatory administrators not make significant public policy decisions that influence the directions of presidential administrations in attempting to resolve this nation's socioeconomic problems? How can a president be expected to tackle complex public policy problems like inflation successfully if top-level administrators in the administrative system (for example, the chairman of the Federal Reserve Board) can make major policy decisions (such as a monetary decision causing banks to drop their interest rates) that are independent and frequently contrary to the policy directions taken by the president? Can an administrative system be efficient and effective if all the independent regulatory agencies are pulling in opposite directions under no central or authoritative leader?

Recent Supreme Court Cases Uphold the Wisdom of *Humphrey* and *Wiener*

After *Wiener* the Supreme Court entertained no serious challenges to the constitutional legitimacy of independent regulatory agencies or to the limitations placed upon the president's removal powers for about three decades. However, the appointment of new conservative justices to the Supreme Court by Presidents Reagan and Bush evidently encouraged new challenges. But despite the rehashing of essentially the argument presented by Chief Justice Taft in the *Meyer* case, the Supreme Court ended up reaffirming the legitimacy of the independent agencies and the president's limited removal powers.

In *Bowsher* v. *Synar*, 106 S.Ct. 318 (1986), the Supreme Court upheld the right of Congress to delegate powers to independent regulatory agencies and to protect their independence. However, the Court refused to permit Congress to use the removal powers by allowing Congress to use the removal power to manipulate executive officials. In *Morrison* v. *Olson*, 487 U.S. 654 (1988), the high Court once again affirmed the Constitutional status of independent agencies, as it did in *Mistretta* v. *United States*, 488 U.S. 361 (1989). In *Morrison* the Court's majority ruled that the Congress did not violate the separation-of-powers doctrine by drafting an independent counsel provision which allowed the president to remove the independent counsel only for cause. The Court did agree that the investigative and prosecutional functions were inherently executive functions normally under a president's control, but the Court reasoned that since the independent counsel was assigned the task of investigating for prosecution any wrongdoing in the Executive Branch, it only made sense to not allow the president to exercise "at will" removal powers. Concurring, Justice Antonin Scalia charged that the Court's majority ignored established law which placed limits on what Congress could do to limit presidential power over the Executive Branch.

Kenneth C. Davis and Richard Pierce, Jr. sympathize with Scalia's criticism because they assert that "[T]he opinion does not state any justifiable standard for determining the limits on Congress's power to limit presidential control of Executive Branch officers." Specifically, they maintain, the Court has not specified ". . . the type of Executive Branch officers that must be subject to presidential power to remove 'at will' or what constitutes adequate 'cause' for removal of officers who can be removed only 'for cause'." Davis and Pierce, Jr. conclude: "Without some judicially enforced limit on Congress' power to limit the President's power to control Executive Branch officers, Justice Scalia's concern that Congress will emasculate the presidency seems plausible."[41]

Justice Scalia's major concern is with accountability. His basic argument is that if the president is going to be held accountable for activity in "his" Executive Branch, he should be placed in a position to control it. To Scalia, administrative agencies and the public policies they promulgate should be under the direction and control of the president. To Scalia, it is that simple! The president should have the power to appoint and remove all administrative officials in the Executive Branch who make public policy. To Scalia, the Court made a grave mistake in *Humphrey,* so grave in fact that he suggests strongly in his concurring opinion in *Freytag* v. *Commissioner of Internal Revenue,* 111 S.Ct. 2631 (1991), that the *Humphrey* decision should be reversed. He argues that the consequence in *Humphrey* was to create a 'headless Fourth Branch' which prevents the president from diminishing the very officers the president appointed to the Federal Trade Commission or other such "independent" agencies. To Scalia, such a scheme makes ". . . agencies less accountable to him, and hence he less responsible for them" (at 2660). And Scalia adds: "Depending upon how broadly one reads the President's power to dismiss 'for cause,' it may be that he has no control over the appointment of inferior officers in such agencies; and if those agencies are publicly regarded as beyond his control—a 'headless Fourth Branch'—he may have less incentive to care about such appointments" (at 2660–2661).[42] In concluding, Justice Scalia suggests that the Court should admit to being wrong in *Humphrey's Executor* because ". . . adjusting the remainder of the Constitution to compensate for *Humphrey's Executor* is a fruitless endeavor" (at 2661).

Even though Justice Scalia raises some points worthy of more scrutiny, his viewpoints on agency independence and presidential removal powers are definitely in the minority because most scholars and practitioners apparently believe that independent regulatory agencies should remain fairly independent of presidential manipulation. Specifically reacting to Scalia's comments in *Freytag,* Bernard Schwartz concludes: "To most of us, on the other hand, *Humphrey* was correctly decided and remains under *Freytag* and other recent decisions, the bastion of the necessary independence of agencies such as the FTC, which can be insulated from political pressures because they are not subject to direct presidential control."[43]

SUMMARY

Responsive and accountable public administration in a democratic country demands that the administrative process be kept reasonably open to those who want to influence administrative decision making. Nevertheless, the integrity of democratic administration can be jeopardized if public administrators are not protected from undue interference and harassment from those special interests in their environment. Specifically, unethical and illegal influence peddling tends to bias administrative decisions in favor of those special interests who are peddling the influence. This chapter gave special attention to various kinds of meddling in the administrative process that undermine the ability of agency officials to develop and administer public policies in an objective, fair, efficient, and effective manner.

The lines between permissible, unethical, and illegal tampering with the administrative apparatus are often very thin, but steps have been taken to make unlawful influence peddling which is obviously disruptive to the administrative machinery and contrary to the public interest. To protect administrators from themselves, various conflict-of-interest statutes have been legislated. Conflict-of-interest laws make it illegal for public officials to accept things of value in exchange for preferential treatment. These laws also make it a crime for parties to offer gifts to public administrators.

To protect the independence and righteousness of the administrative process, some modest limits have been placed upon legislative influence peddling. For example, in *D. C. Federation of Civic Associations* v. *Volpe*, 459 F.2d 1231 (1972), the Supreme Court held that administrators cannot make policy decisions based upon political influence pressures alone but must reach decisions in light of relevant facts. Recently, the wisdom of *Volpe* was emphatically upheld in *Town of Norfolk* v. *U.S. Army Corps of Engineers*, 968 F.2d 1438 (1st Cir. 1992). In *Gravel* v. *United States*, 408 U.S. 606 (1972), and *United States* v. *Brewster*, 408 U.S. 501 (1972), the Court argued that the Constitution's Speech or Debate Clause cannot be used to protect illegal legislative influence peddling, especially such activities as are not legislative in function or are criminal in character (for example, soliciting, accepting, or offering bribes). The courts have also struck down bills of attainder and *ex post facto* laws (for example, the Hiss Act of 1954 and the Urgent Deficiency Act of 1943), which have no regulatory purpose but which have been passed to harass and punish administrators [e.g., *Hiss* v. *Hampton*, 338 F. Supp. 1141 (1972); *Ethics Com'n* v. *Collusion*, 850 P. 2d 1069 (Okla. 1993); and *Springfield Armory, Inc.* v. *City of Columbus*, 805 F. Supp. 489 (S.D. Ohio 1992)]. In addition, the courts have overruled the constitutionality of loyalty oaths, which have been required by legislators, especially at the state level, as a condition of employment and used, in general, to keep administrative officials in line. In 1970 the Civil Service Commission dropped the loyalty oath requirement for federal employees.

In the final analysis, these measures have done little to protect administrators from undue congressional meddling in the administrative process. Democratic procedures permit legislators to lobby administrators, but unethical *ex parte* contacts are discouraged. The distinction between unethical and ethical legislative lobbying practices is extremely nebulous, and this has allowed legislators to manipulate administrative actions unfairly. Congress is unlikely to pass meaningful legislation that would tend to restrict its influence over administrative conduct. Political scientists for decades have asserted that the big interest groups in America "own" legislators and, as a result, compel their congress persons to pressure administrators to make decisions that favor their respective special interests.

To prevent the president from being able to harass and politically manipulate certain administrative officials at personal discretion, the Supreme Court has ruled that the president's power to appoint major "officers of the United States" is virtually absolute (*Buckley* v. *Valeo,* 424 U.S. 1; 1976), yet Congress has the discretion to delegate the appointment of "inferior officers" to the president alone, courts of law, or heads of departments (*Freytag* v. *Commissioner of Internal Revenue,* 111 S.Ct. 2631; 1991), while presidential removal powers are limited to the removal of those administrators who perform purely executive functions. In *Humphrey's* v. *United States,* and *Wiener* v. *United States,* 357 U.S. 349 (1958), the high Court held that a president cannot remove, except for good cause, administrators who perform quasi-legislative and quasi-judicial functions. These decisions have made administrators in independent and quasi-independent regulatory agencies (the Federal Trade Commission and the War Claims Commission are respective examples), in which legislative and judicial functions are performed, virtually unremovable until their set terms expire.

In *Freytag* v. *Commissioner of Internal Revenue,* 111 S.Ct. 2631, 2660 (1991), Justice Scalia attacked the *Humphrey* decision, arguing vehemently that *Humphrey* created a "headless Fourth Branch" which made independent ". . . agencies less accountable to him, and hence he less responsible for them." Many sympathize with Scalia's argument that *Humphrey* has created serious accountability problems, yet *Humphrey* has survived a recent flurry of legal challenges because most seem to believe that, all things considered, independent regulatory agencies should remain fairly protected from corruptive, political pressures.

NOTES

1. Edwin Wallace Tucker, *Administrative Law, Regulation of Enterprise, and Individual Liberties* (St. Paul, Minn.: West Publishing Company, 1975), 1975.
2. Ibid.
3. *The Republic of Plato,* trans. Francis M. Cornford (New York: Oxford University Press 1945), chap. 5. Plato entertained the thought that even good men may not have the will to resist evil acts if they have no fear of being punished. He pondered: "Surely this would be strong proof that men do right only under compulsion; no individual thinks of it as good for him personally, since he does wrong whenever he finds he has the power" (at 45).
4. Herbert Kaufman, *Red Tape: Its Origins, Uses, and Abuses* (Washington, D.C.: Brookings Institution, 1977), 50.
5. Terry L. Cooper, *The Responsible Administrator,* 3rd ed. (San Francisco: Jossey-Bass Pub., 1990), 109.
6. Sam Donaldson, "Weekend with David Brinkley" (June 12, 1994).

7. Walter Gellhorn, et al., *Administrative Law: Cases and Comments,* 8th ed. (Mineola, N.Y.: Foundation Press, 1987), 982–984.

8. Ibid.

9. Robert Roberts, "The Public Integrity Quagmire," in Carolyn Barr and Norma M. Riccucci, eds., *Public Personnel Management: Current Concerns—Future Challenges* (New York: Longman Publishing Group, 1991), 144.

10. Public Law 95-521; 18 U.S.C. Section 207.

11. "Deaver Named in Indictment," *St. Louis Post-Dispatch,* March 19, 1987, 1 and 16.

12. William Safire, "A Weak Indictment against Mike Deaver," *St. Louis Post-Dispatch,* March 24, 1987, sec. B, p. 3.

13. 30 Fed. Reg. 6469, May 8, 1965.

14. 36 Fed. Reg. 7831, April 23, 1971.

15. Ibid., 126.

16. Newton Minow, Review of *Politics and the Regulatory Agencies* by William Cary, *Columbia Law Review,* 68 (February 1968), 383–84.

17. For an article that puts this into context see "The Other Scandal," *The New Republic,* March 23, 1987, 6.

18. Paul H. Douglas, *Ethics in Government* (Cambridge, Mass.: Harvard University Press, 1952), 85–88.

19. Ibid., 12883.

20. Senator Thomas Eagleton on "How the Senate Works," conference at Clemson University aired on C-Span, November 11,1986.

21. Carl E. Lutrin and Allen K. Settle, *American Public Administration Concepts and Cases,* 3rd ed. (Palo Alto, Calif.: Mayfield Publishing, 1985), 336.

22. Ibid.

23. Stephen G. Breyer and Richard B. Stewart, *Administrative Law and Regulatory Policy: Problems, Text, and Cases,* 3rd ed., (Boston: Little, Brown and Company, 1992), 660–685.

24. E. Cox, R. Fellmeth, and J. Schultz, "The Consumer and the Federal Trade Commission," in *Administrative Law and Regulatory Policy,* ed. Stephen G. Breyer and Richard B. Stewart (Boston: Little, Brown, 1979), 773.

25. Al Gore, "Creating a Government That Works Better and Costs Less," (Washington, D.C.: U.S. Government Printing Office, 1993).

26. *Certiorari denied,* 405 U.S. 1030 (1972).

27. *D.C. Federation of Civil Associations, Inc.* v. *Volpe,* 140 U.S. App. D.C. 162, 434 F.2d 436 (1970).

28. See also, *Virginians Against a Corrupt Congress* v. *Moran,* 805 F. Supp. 75 (D.D.C. 1992); *Bardoff* v. *U.S.,* 628 A.2d 86 (D.C. App. 1993); *U.S.* v. *Vasquez,* 985 F.2d 491 (10th Cir. 1993); and *Ethics Com'n* v. *Cullison,* 850 P.2d 1069 (Okla. 1993).

29. In 1970 the Civil Service Commission dropped the loyalty oath as a requirement for federal employment. Loyalty oaths have also been eliminated for Job Corps members, Medicare recipients, and students receiving federal financial assistance.

30. Article 1, Section 10, Clause 1 specifically prohibits states from passing any bill of attainder or *ex post facto* law.

31. The Hiss Act (Pub.L. No. 83-769; 68 Stat. 1142) was originally enacted on September 1, 1954, but amended on July 31, 1956 (Pub.L. No. 84-854; 70 Stat. 761), and again on September 26, 1961 (Pub.L. No. 87-299; 75 Stat. 640). On September 6, 1966, the whole act was codified as 5 U.S.C. Secs. 8311 8322 (Pub.L No. 89-554; 80 Stat. 557).

32. Kenneth C. Davis and Richard J. Pierce, Jr., *Administrative Law Treatise,* 3rd ed., vol. 1 (Boston: Little, Brown and Company, 1994), 65.

33. For other reviews of *Freytag,* see Marshall J. Breger, "Colloquium: The Supreme Court's Administrative Law Docket," *The Administrative Law Journal,* vol. 6 (1992), 269–277; and Bernard Schwartz, "Administrative Law Cases during 1991," *Administrative Law Review,* vol. 44 (Summer 1992), 629–635.

34. Norman C. Thomas, Joseph A. Pika, and Richard A. Watson, *The Politics of the Presidency,* rev. 3rd ed. (Washington, D.C.: Congressional Quarterly, 1994), 256–258.

35. Arthur S. Miller, *Presidential Power in a Nutshell* (St. Paul, Minn.: West Publishing Company, 1977), 42.

36. Ibid., 41.

37. Ibid., 44.

38. *Wiener* v. *United States,* 357 U.S. 849, 349–356 (1958).

39. Federal judges can also be removed by the impeachment procedure.

40. Once again, the Ash Report provides an excellent argument in defense of the position that independent regulatory commissions are part of the administrative system and, therefore, should be under presidential control.

41. Kenneth C. Davis and Richard J. Pierce, Jr., *Administrative Law Treatise,* 3rd ed., vol. 1, 52–53.

42. Marshall J. Breger, *op. cit.,* notes that since Scalia was joined by three other justices and Clarence Thomas was joining the Court, Scalia's comments should not be taken too lightly. However, since Breger made those comments at the time of Thomas' confirmation, David Souter, Ruth Ginsberg, and Stephen Breyer have joined the Supreme Court. Although Justice Souter concurred with Justice Scalia in *Freytag,* Justices Ginsberg and Breyer will most likely oppose Scalia in this legal area.

43. Bernard Schwartz, "Administrative Law Cases during 1991," 632.

CHAPTER FIVE

RULE-MAKING: AGENCIES AS LEGISLATIVE BODIES

THE GROWING IMPORTANCE OF AGENCY RULE-MAKING

If the field of administrative law has a primary focal point, it would have to be rule-making. Rule-making is at center stage among other administrative topics since virtually every discussion involving administrative law issues would almost have to be rooted in the rule-making process. This is so because the vast majority of agency policies are the product of the rule-making process. To Cornelius M. Kerwin, who has written many scholarly works on the rule-making process, "[R]ule-making is the single most important function performed by agencies of government."[1]

The legislative branch, with the blessing of the courts, has transferred much of its lawmaking powers to administrators simply because legislators felt compelled to delegate such power to meet the increasing demands placed upon government by the citizenry. But regardless of why lawmaking powers were so delegated, the fact is that administrative agencies have been created and expanded at an accelerated pace. For over the past half century, legislative bodies at all governmental levels were eager to allow administrators to have primary responsibility for making all decisions they deem necessary for implementing general public policies. In reality, lawmaking by agency administrators has become so prevalent that some scholars assert that the change constitutes de facto amendments to the U.S. Constitution and state constitutions that we must recognize and accept, and as best we can let this new reality of the administrative state work for us.[2]

The subtitle of this chapter, "Agencies as Legislative Bodies," was selected because I felt that it best encapsulates the role of modern administrative agencies. Although public administrators also perform adjudicative and purely administrative functions, probably their most important task is making rules to govern society. When making rules, public administrators in fact interpret general congressional statutes and assign them their real meaning by giving them life in society. Or, as Kerwin asserts, "[P]ut simply it is rules, not statutes, that tell us how to order our affairs."[3] Although some laws are more precise in their language and intent than others, legislatures are increasingly cranking out pieces of legislation that leave the precise intentions of their public policy statements quite unclear. In fact, the courts have recognized this trend but have refrained, in general, from compelling Congress or state legislatures to draft legislation with clearer standards. Of course, these developments have placed administrators in a very powerful position; they can design and execute public policies according to what within reason they perceive as being good or bad for society. Actually, if a top-level administrator opposes a certain piece of legislation, for whatever reason, the odds are low indeed that that agency will take efforts to see that the particular public policy is successfully implemented. Many instances of this can be seen, but one example should illustrate the point.

It should be stressed that administrative power is determined largely by the amount of rule-making authority delegated to administrators by legislators. Congress remains the primary source of administrative power and the chief watchdog overseeing agency behavior. If legislators are content with delegating away the most fundamental governmental power, that of lawmaking, to administrative agencies, and if the courts continue to give their approval, this change in governmental structure will simply have to be accepted.[4] No other authoritative vehicle in our system is capable of reversing this trend. However, most scholars in the field believe that despite the fact that the delegation of significant lawmaking powers to public administrators represents a threat to traditional democratic practices,[5] such delegation seemed almost inevitable, given the mounting demands on modern government, especially since rule-making practices can prove advantageous to the system of government. Some scholars also maintain that rule-making be kept within the democratic limits if determined efforts are made to carefully structure and check rule-making so that the process complements democratic government. This chapter examines rule-making in relative detail, especially with an eye on how fair and democratic rule-making procedures are in molding U.S. public policies.

WHAT IS RULE-MAKING?

Actually, answering this question in a definitive manner presents quite a challenge, mostly because of problems in both rule-making terminology and the way rule-making processes are implemented by various governmental agencies. Administrative law is a relatively new field, which has not developed in a very logical or systematic way. Actually, the laissez-faire attitude prevalent in America before the New Deal played an instrumental role in deterring the development of a set of administrative laws designed to regulate the behavior of public agencies. Consequently, and predictably, during the 1930s and 1940s when New Deal challenges and World War II demands stimulated the rapid growth of bureaucracy, public agencies began to function chaotically in the absence of a comprehensive body of laws designed to regulate administrative procedure. By the time the Administrative Procedure Act was passed in 1946 in response to the obvious need to control and regularize agency actions in the public interest, administrative law nomenclature had already been developed in a random and unstructured way by individual public agencies and through common law, which reflected the inconsistent usage and application of administrative law terminology by both administrators and judges.

Because of America's administrative law history before the passage of the Administrative Procedure Act, the APA's attempt to standardize administrative law terminology has met with only partial success. Today administrative law scholars and practitioners are still frustrated by the inconsistent meanings given to administrative law terms, especially when clear distinctions and applications are considered very crucial, as with rules and orders. Since orders and rules normally carry different weight before the courts and their penalties for noncompliance may be very different, it is necessary that the distinction between rules and orders be more definitive and useful. For example, in a frequently cited case, an automobile driver argued that his speeding ticket conviction should be overruled by the court because the speed limit in question had been set by an "order" of the New York State Traffic Commission, not filed as a rule, and therefore was not applicable to him. The court ruled that despite the fact that the commission called it an "order," it was really a rule because it was a "legislative or quasi-legislative norm or prescription which established a pattern or course of conduct for the future" (*People* v. *Cull,* 10 N.Y.2d 123, 126; 1961).

Despite the acute need to make a sharper distinction between the meanings and significance of rules and orders, public agencies, courts, and legislators continue to employ the terminology inconsistently, thus causing confusion for outsiders and themselves. For instance, the Treasury Department has a tradition of referring to rules as decisions, which it publishes as "Treasury Decisions," while regulatory commissions such as the FTC and FCC like to shape public policy through "orders," which they apply as general rules or regulations.[6] The state of confusion over the status of rules and orders motivated Bernard Schwartz to write: "Today the administrative law student too often feels like Alice after going through her looking glass; he yearns for that *other* room where chairs are actually chairs and tables, tables—and rules and regulations are rules and regulations and orders, orders."[7] However, Kenneth C. Davis and Richard J. Pierce, Jr. acknowledge the definitional problem, but play it down, remarking: "Notwithstanding the theoretical difficulty of distinguishing between rulemakings and adjudications and unsatisfactory APA definitions, agencies and courts have experienced little difficulty in practice."[8]

Despite the terminological problems, administrative law terms and processes are defined by the federal APA. Although definitions of rule-making, order making, and the like, must be employed when the act specifically applies, APA terminology and procedures are not considered mandatory outside the APA's specific jurisdiction. Since the APA's jurisdiction is largely limited to situations involving formal administrative decision making, agencies have a great many opportunities to simply ignore

APA definitions and requirements. Judging from the large number of suits filed against public agencies for flagrantly violating APA requirements, many public administrators evidently know little or nothing about APA's requirements, or they choose to ignore them. Nevertheless, it appears that with each passing year, APA terminology and procedures are becoming more accepted, especially as the APA is refined by further amendments.

According to the Administrative Procedure Act, "rule-making" means an "agency process for formulating, amending, or repealing a rule," and the act defines a "rule" to mean "the whole or a part of an agency statement of general or particular applicability and future effect designed to implement, interpret, or prescribe law or policy or describing the organization, procedure, or practice requirements of an agency" (Sec. 551). In simple language, a rule is a law made in an administrative agency. When an administrative agency engages in rule-making, it is legislating policy. In fact, Kerwin notes that "[T]he history of rule-making is the history of American public policy."[9] Rules are designed to regulate both the internal operations of administrative agencies and to help implement the broad public policies assigned to government agencies by the legislature.

Depending upon the statutory base of agencies, some agencies have potent rule-making strength, while others are severely limited in their rule-making powers. Congress, in the process of creating administrative agencies over the decades, allocated some agencies, such as the Environmental Protection Agency, vast lawmaking powers, while it severely restricted the legislative function of others, such as the Internal Revenue Service. The IRS may be one of the most-feared agencies in the federal government; yet IRS employees actually have fewer rule-making and discretionary powers than most government departments.

Frequently, Congress has actually specified the kind of weight the rules should carry, as well as whether the courts should have the right to review the rules made by agencies. Because of this, Congress has, in effect, created first-class and second-class agencies in governmental bureaucracy. Consequently, public agencies have unequal status, powers, and influence in the American political system.

Although the distinction is often blurred and the courts frequently fail to recognize it, it is nevertheless valuable to note the difference in status between legislative (substantive) and interpretative rules. As one might suspect, legislative rules carry much more clout than interpretative rules. "First-class agencies," because of their statutory foundation, have been given the legal and undisputed authority to draft *legislative rules,* which carry the thrust of law (*New Jersey* v. *Department of HHS,* 670 F.2d 1262, 1282 [3rd Cir. 1981]). Normally, legislative rules are not open to interpretation or invalidation by the courts, as are interpretative rules. Commenting on the status of legislative rules, as long as they are otherwise constitutional, Kenneth C. Davis wrote that: "a court may no more substitute its judgment as to the content of a legislative rule than it may substitute its judgment as to the content of a statute."[10] Because *interpretative rules* (also spelled *interpretive*) are made by agencies without the advantage of direct statutory sanctioning to make rules with the force of law, such rules are weaker and considered open to the courts. The courts can readily interpret and invalidate these rules, thus interpretative rules receive less deference or respect by the courts than legislative rules (*Frank Diehl Farms* v. *Secretary,* 696 F.2d 1325, 1329 [11th Cir. 1983]). However, the strength of interpretative rules increases the more they are: (1) backed by demonstrated legislative intent; (2) long standing; (3) supported by agency expertise; and (4) supported by any other factors which strengthen their reasonableness before the courts (*National Muffler Dealers Association, Inc.* v. *United States,* 99 S.Ct. 1304, 1307; 1979). Theoretically, interpretative rules are only supposed to *interpret* existing provisions in statutes, not to add to or make new substantive law [*Nat'l Family Planning and Reproductive Health Assn* v. *Sullivan,* 979 F.2d 227, 237 (D.C. Cir. 1992)].

For example, the court in *Rocky Mountain Helicopters, Inc.* v. *F.A.A.,* 971 F.2d 544, 547 (10th Cir. 1992), ruled that an interpretative rule must satisfy three requirements: "(1) the factual findings underlying the interpretation must be supported by substantial evidence, . . . (2) the agency must offer a satisfactory explanation for its actions, . . . and (3) the interpretation must be consistent with the statute, rule, or regulation being interpreted, . . ."

The Supreme Court in *Chevron* v. *Natural Resources Defense Council,* 467 U.S. 837 (1984), has probably given more strength to interpretative rules because some courts have applied *Chevron* to interpretative rules, even though apparently most legal scholars think that *Chevron* should apply only to legislative rules.[11] In *Chevron,* the court held basically that courts should defer to an administrative interpretation of a statute in the event that legislative intent is ambiguous or silent, as long as the statute does not clearly prohibit it.

Despite the fact that legislative bodies have granted some agencies stronger rule-making power than others, legislative assemblies at every level in American government have allowed all agencies to make rules the public must obey. The rule-making function is probably the most basic power of any public agency. Surely, no agency could operate if it had to obtain congressional clearance before it could ever act. But because agency-made laws have the potential to be arbitrary, capricious, or unjust in a number of ways, steps have been taken to guard against administrators who may abuse their rule-making powers and draft rules which rub abrasively against the American spirit of fairness and due process. Not only are all rules ultimately subject to legislative oversight and judicial review, but various acts, especially the Administrative Procedure Act, and court decisions have also established legal guidelines for administrators to follow in legislating rules.

APA Notice and Comment Rule-Making

Section 553 of the APA in essence requires administrative agencies to follow fair and reasonable procedures when they make rules. Although liberal exceptions exist for particular agencies and under certain conditions (mostly foreign affairs agencies working with sensitive national security data or domestic agencies dealing with "private and secret" information), the APA requires administrators to follow several important procedural steps when making rules. First, administrators are required to give public notice of proposed rule-making by publishing the proposal in the *Federal Register* (an official daily government publication). To be proper, the notice should include: (1) the "time, place, and nature" of the proposed rule-making proceedings; (2) the legal basis on which the rules are proposed; and (3) a general description of the proposed rule along with an explanation of the issues involved. Second, agencies are compelled to provide opportunities for "interested persons" to take an active part in the rulemaking process by allowing them to submit "written data, views, or arguments with or without opportunity for oral presentation." Third, the act specifies that a "substantive rule" should not be allowed to take effect until at least thirty days after its public notice. Fourth, administrators are legally obligated to grant concerned parties "the right to petition for the issuance, amendment, or repeal of a rule." Figure 5.1 visually demonstrates this process.

Formal Rule-Making

Only three kinds of rule-making are acknowledged by the Administrative Procedure Act: informal (notice and comment rule-making), formal (trial-like hearing rule-making) and a new rule-making approach, called Negotiated Rule-Making, codified into sections 561–583 of the APA in 1990 (Negotiated Rule-Making is an experimental approach with limited application and is discussed later in the chapter). Informal notice and comment rule-making, which simply provides notice and an opportunity for interested parties to make comments on the proposed rule, is by far the more common procedure. However, the APA provides for formal rule-making to be employed "when rules are required by statute to be made on the record after opportunity for an agency hearing" (Sec. 554). When formal rule-making is required by statute, the APA sections governing adjudications must be followed. In *Vermont Yankee Nuclear Power Corp.* v. *Natural Resources Defense Council*, 435 U.S. 519, 547 (1978), the Supreme Court noted that when formal rule-making is required administrative agencies are expected to promulgate rules employing "the full panoply of procedural devices normally associated only with adjudicatory hearings." Among other things, this entails the submission of evidence and opportunity to cross-examine it.

In reality, however, very few statutes call for trial-like hearings in the making of rules. The most-known statute requiring formal rule-making procedures is the Food, Drug, and Cosmetic Act of 1938, 21 U.S.C. Section 371(e)(3). Under the act, before issuing a rule the Food and Drug Administration must (1) hold a public hearing affording interested parties an opportunity to be heard; (2) base decisions on substantial evidence in light of the record; (3) structure the order (rule) to include findings of fact based upon the formal hearing record; and (4) provide for review of adjudicatory proceedings before agency findings of fact substantiating the rule can be considered conclusive or final. These elaborate formal rule-making procedures have been sharply criticized because such procedures tend to cripple the rule-making process. One critic of formal rule-making, Bernard Schwartz, asserts in vivid prose that formal trial-like procedures "are out of place in rulemaking. They imprison a legislative process within a formal strait jacket designed for an entirely different type

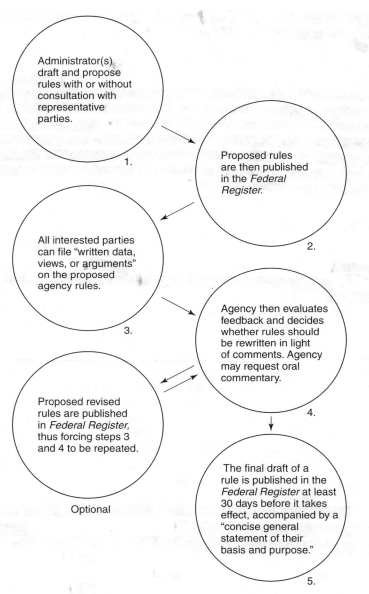

FIGURE 5.1   *The Normal APA Rule-making Process: Notice and Comment Rule-making*

of proceeding and may produce a virtual paralysis of the administrative process."[12] Criticizing the Food, Drug, and Cosmetic Act in particular, he claims that the formal rule-making requirement has caused long delays, with all rules taking at least two years to promulgate and with some taking over ten years. One hearing, which focused on whether peanut butter should contain 87.5 percent or 90 percent peanuts, produced a weighty 7,736-page transcript and lasted about nine years.[13] Kenneth C. Davis and Richard J. Pierce, Jr. are just as direct, concluding that there is "solid evidence" proving ". . . that the formal rulemaking procedure simply does not work."[14] Also citing the fiasco of the long peanut butter proceedings, Davis and Pierce note that most issues are much more complex than determining the percentage of peanuts that should be in peanut butter. They claim that the typical controversy involves more difficult questions of fact and policy, thus creating the real possibility that many formal rule-making proceedings could last even longer than the peanut butter case. To these scholars, "[I]t is simply impossible to complete a major rulemaking in a timely manner through the use of formal adjudicatory proceedings."[15]

The reality is that legislators, as well as judges, realize that formal rule-making normally "does not work"; consequently legislators have tried to write legislation which does not statutorily require formal rule-making, while judges have handed down decisions which have allowed agencies to escape having to employ formal rule-making. *United States* v. *Florida East Coast Railway Co.,* 410 U.S. 224 (1973), has had the greatest impact on severely limiting agency use of formal rule-making because the court held essentially that informal notice and comment rule-making could usually be substituted for the formal rule-making hearing requirement. Specifically, the Supreme Court in *Florida East Coast* applied the hearing requirement very loosely, arguing that a "proper hearing" could result from the written comments submitted in the notice and comment process, thus establishing a record and satisfying the APA's "on the record after hearing" requirement. Despite the questionable legal rationale employed in *Florida East Coast,* this case has set a strong precedent because of the almost universal agreement that the formal rule-making process is not viable in most rule-making situations [e.g., *Bell Telephone Co. of Pennsylvania* v. *FCC,* 503 F.2d 1250 (3rd Cir. 1974); *United Airlines* v. *CAB,* 766 F.2d 1109 (7th Cir. 1985)].

As a result of *Florida East Coast,* courts very rarely compel an agency to employ formal rule-making except when: (1) a specific statute clearly requires formal rule-making; (2) an oral, evidentiary hearing is mandated by statute; and (3) adjudicative facts specific to an individual involving "property" or "liberty" interests must be resolved through a due process, formal rule-making agency hearing.[16]

RULE-MAKING: LOOPHOLES AND THEIR SIGNIFICANCE

Some may be disturbed by the apparent burden placed upon administrators by certain APA requirements, yet others may be encouraged by such rule-making requirements that seem to compel administrators to promulgate rules in an open, fair, and democratic manner which encourages public participation. After all, as one prominent scholar of rule-making stresses, rule-making has inherent democratic problems simply because rule-makers are not elected and, therefore, not directly accountable to the American people. Thus, "[T]he legitimacy of the rulemaking process is clearly linked to public participation."[17]

However, despite these APA requirements, most rules are made behind closed doors by administrative agencies without any input at all from interested persons. Lewis Mainzer once noted, even during the alleged height of the participatory movement in rule-making during the 1970s, "[A]gencies no doubt make vast numbers of rules day by day with nothing but internal procedure, but others affect outsiders as well or primarily."[18] And Kenneth C. Davis has concluded: "Probably most rule-making is still done with little or no party participation of any kind."[19]

The problem is that the APA simply permits its general requirements too many exceptions, which have the effect of permitting administrators to take the easy way out by interpreting vague clauses in the act so that they will not have to be inconvenienced. Unfortunately, some administrative officials seem to have a natural instinct to protect agency operations from public view by unnecessarily classifying material and functions from public scrutiny, thereby avoiding uninvited headaches. However, if government is to be democratic and accountable, as many operations as reasonable should be conducted in the open. Because of APA loopholes, rule-making and other important administrative activities have sometimes been kept too secretive.

In 1967 the Freedom of Information Act, an amendment to the APA, was passed to help force public agencies to become more public. Amendments have strengthened the originally rather weak FOIA over the years, although critics still contend that serious loopholes effectively prevent it from accomplishing its lofty objective of keeping *public* policy in the public eye. In a democracy public policy decisions should ideally involve the public. Delegating lawmaking powers to administrators is acceptable under most circumstances, but allowing administrators to make laws in secrecy appears contrary to popular government theory. Democratic theorists maintain that secretive decision making tends to encourage the growth of tyranny in government. Critics claim the Central Intelligence Agency and Federal Bureau of Investigation, two American public agencies, have for decades managed to operate quite undemocratically outside the public eye. Because of the nature of these public institutions, it seems that a certain degree of operative secrecy should be considered tolerable. For example, a spy can't spy if everything is known about the spying agenda. But it has been alleged that these agencies have frequently abused their privileged position and that lessons should be drawn from their abuses. It is true that the FBI and CIA have been successful in keeping their policies and practices not only from the American people, but also from interested congress persons and presidents (away from popular governmental machinery).

Pressure on these agencies to disclose publicly some of their controversial involvements—agency-head turnovers, leaks to the press, and books published by former CIA and FBI agents—have combined to force these agencies' doors open just a bit to allow us to at least peek at some of the activities of the CIA and FBI, with shocking results. Evidently, these agencies have: (1) carried out political assassinations (CIA); (2) acted to overthrow foreign governments (CIA); (3) blackmailed presidents (FBI); (4) worked as partners with the Mafia (FBI); (5) had prior associations with Lee Harvey Oswald, the assassin of President Kennedy (CIA and FBI); (6) sabotaged the 1972 presidential election (FBI); (7) illegally invaded the privacy of persons by breaking into their homes and private offices to obtain personal information (FBI), and secretly helped build up the political and military power of President Saddam Hussein of Iraq, who later used this power against the United States in the Gulf War in 1991.[20]

The Rule-Making Power Rationale

How can the delegation of vast rule-making powers to public administrators who are not subject to direct check by the voters be justified in a democratic nation? Although the extensive legislative powers granted to administrative agencies are feared by those who believe that administrative processes in a democratic country should closely reflect the prescriptions of democratic theory, an overwhelming majority of onlookers persuasively argue that modern government could not possibly handle the burdens placed upon it by a demanding public if legislators had to call all the shots or even most of them. There is some evidence that Americans expect their government to cope with the problems which plague their daily lives but really don't seem to care how this is done.[21] By and large, administrative regulators have been accepted as legitimate by a public whose attitudes are rooted in a pragmatic philosophy. The pragmatic character of the American people has yielded the commonly accepted belief that theory is fine but only as long as it is as practical as it is elegant.[22]

Because the public tends to uphold democratic theory in the abstract but not altogether on practical grounds, it was easy for democratic theory to be compromised over the decades for better or for worse, so that it supports a modern, technological society which demands a fleet of regulators to guide and protect the public interest. Despite the fact that the United States Constitution does not, at least literally, allow administrators to act as legislators, the public has been quite willing to rationalize the granting of these legislative powers to public administrators. Probably the most basic insight offered to justify the rule-making function of administrative agencies is that rule-making, in fact, cannot be equated with the lawmaking function of legislators. Lawmaking is lawmaking and rule-making is rule-making—and that's that! While lawmaking is the drafting of basic public policies or laws by democratically elected legislators, it is held that rule-making constitutes, in actuality, only a quasi-legislative power and not a genuine legislative power which can lead to the formation of fundamental public policies. Contrary to fact, proponents of the delegation doctrine suffer from the illusion that rule-makers do not engage in basic public policy making, but only in the making of those rules necessary to order the internal administrative procedures in their agencies and to make operational general congressional legislation already entrenched in legislative standards.

Practical considerations tend to dominate the reasons for allowing administrators to play such an assertive legislative role in the governmental system. A trite contention, yet valid, is that legislators simply do not have the time, will, or expertise to draft detailed legislation. Thus, public policies are purposely left vague by legislators so that administrators in the field and close to the action can have the flexibility to make any rules to implement public policies, as long as those quasi-legislative measures are consistent with legislative intent and proper procedure. It is also believed by many critics that administrators, not legislators, are in the best position to make meaningful public policies because administrators can employ their plentiful field experiences to mold abstract, congressionally mandated public policies into practical public programs that stand a realistic chance of working in the field. It is also maintained that administrators, by virtue of their positions, are the real experts in their specialized areas and, therefore, should be accorded the power and flexibility they need to administer public policies in an insightful and responsive manner. Overall, administrators are perceived by many scholars, especially political scientists and sociologists, as being in a better position than legislators to make rules (policy statements) that reflect rational adjustments to environmental pressures.

But aside from the practical aspects of rule-making for society, most observers probably do not see the rule-making function as being particularly threatening to the U.S. democratic system. In the first place, as noted, administrators are not free to make general, or even rather specific, public policies as they see fit. Agency activities are watched not only by the Congress, the courts, and the president, but also by the public, guided by the news and editorial opinions in the newspapers and on television and radio. CBS's "60 Minutes" news magazine show is an enlightening example of the impact such a show can have on shaping public opinion and checking agency behavior.[23] Despite the occasional scandal and discoveries of mismanagement, critics generally think that government administration is basically sound and responsible, especially at the national level. Political scientists have traditionally been more critical of public administration at the state and local levels.[24] It is held that professionalism, reflecting both expertise and a professional code of ethics, seems to keep most administrators accountable to the public. Rule-making, especially notice and comment rule-making, is thought by many to be a reasonably fair and open process.

Various pieces of legislation, especially the Administrative Procedure Act, help to define and structure rule-making procedures so that the process is fair to the citizenry. Such amendments to the APA as the Freedom of Information Act, the Privacy Act, the Sunshine Act, and the Negotiated Rulemaking Act of 1990 were all passed, it is argued, to guarantee administrative due process in rule-making, as well as in other areas. The APA in Sections 552, 553, and 706 also compels agencies to obey their own rules, while other sections require agencies to reach decisions based on "substantial evidence" (556, 557, and 706) and not to make "arbitrary and capricious" decisions (706[2][a]). Although all these sections do not apply to rule-making specifically, they represent basic principles which pervade rule-making, tending to make rules reasonable and dependable from the public's standpoint.

However, these arguments used to justify the very powerful legislative role played by administrators are not accepted as valid by many critics. Such experts assert that those who support the trend toward increased delegation of legislative powers to administrative agencies without worry are closing their eyes to rather blatant realities. It is foolish to suggest, these critics contend, that when agencies make rules, they are only carrying out the will of the legislators. The legislators do not attach meaningful guidelines (standards) to their mandated public policies; in recent years the trend has been for the legislature to pass public policy statements on to public agencies virtually without any meaningful guidelines in terms of their guidance capabilities (indicating clearly legislative intent). Consequently, rule-makers have been given the awesome power to design and implement fundamental public policies which have a profound impact on the American way of life, and Congress has not been reluctant to provide administrators with this authority.

In *The End of Liberalism,* Theodore Lowi held almost thirty years ago that legislators had delegated irresponsibly too broad lawmaking powers to agency rule-makers.[25] By the mid-1990s, he argued more vehemently that such irresponsible delegation, the source of power for rule-makers, constitutes a clear "derangement" of our Constitution.[26]

Another argument espoused by those who endorse a liberal application of the delegation doctrine asserts that administrators, because they are close to people and happenings in the field, are in the best position to obtain information and develop the insights necessary to shape wise public policies. But the critics maintain that these administrators frequently get too close to the field operations to regulate in the public interest objectively, thus failing to take the needs of the whole system into account. This charge is highly debatable, especially since no conclusive evidence exists suggesting that it is contrary to the intent of the system for people to fight and protect, to the best of their abilities, for their programs and clients. [27] It is also true that many of the regulatory agencies are obligated by statute to oversee, as well as promote, the welfare of those regulated. For example, the Federal Trade Commission promotes private business interests by dedicating itself not so much to protecting consumer interests, as many seem to believe, but to defending the right of business to function in the marketplace in relative freedom. Thus, in many instances, unless evidence is clearly to the contrary, it is difficult to contend that if rules favor the healthy development of an industry (for example, airlines), these rules necessarily are detrimental to the public interest.

However, in the absence of a convincing amount of evidence, a more credible charge is that field administrators use informal rule-making processes to make rules that benefit, at least in the short run, the regulated interest at the expense of the public. Close ties, even friendship associations, can impair administrators' objectivity and cause them to grant to the industry concessions that can jeopardize the public safety. Evidence suggests, for example, that such was a contributing factor in the DC-10 air disasters and the ill-fated launch of the *Challenger,* as discussed in Chapter 2.

Opponents of the exaggerated application of the delegation doctrine also attack the proponents' contention that the public welfare is protected from irresponsible rule-making because the rule-makers are adequately checked through both internal and external controls. But how effective are these controls? Norton Long argued long ago that administrators are ultimately checked by themselves—that is, by prior training and a professional code which provides them with a value framework which guides their behavior.[28] However, rule-of-law advocates have always felt particularly uneasy with this position, especially since history has shown that people are not always capable of governing themselves. Besides, these critics maintain, what is honorable and professional to one public servant may not be perceived as honorable and professional to another. Surely, the 1973 Senate Watergate hearings give much credibility to this viewpoint, as well as testimony given before the Rogers Commission (regarding the Iran-contra affair) in 1987. Thus, it does not seem illogical to hold that those who believe that administrative behavior can be effectively checked through administrators' adherence to professional codes of conduct are only engaging in wishful thinking. Responsibility in governmental administration cannot rest securely over time on the hope that civil servants will act responsibly, guided largely by an abstract professional code in, say, drafting rules to promote the public interest. The problem is that professionalism cannot be concretely defined and thus is incapable of providing the clear guidelines necessary to guarantee democratically responsible agency action.

Professionalism guided by concrete and elaborate external and internal statutes and rules would be consistent with the notion of "officialdom" as developed in Max Weber's famous and respected classical model on the ideals of bureaucracy. In Weber's thinking, professionalism should be guided by rigid and comprehensive statutes and rules that define the duties and obligations of the office. In this way, professionalism would be confined and structured and thus safer and more useful for governing administrative behavior. However, in the American administrative system, flexibility in administration has been wholeheartedly promoted as a virtue, thus preventing the development of essential statutes and rules necessary to prohibit the sometimes outrageous interpretations given to the professional code by irresponsible public administrators. To some, the argument that rule-makers should be granted great flexibility in administration is basically rooted in a lazy unwillingness on the part of legislators and administrators to become involved in the hard work vitally necessary to provide reasonable structuring of and limitations on delegation and rule-making. Theodore Lowi, for example, acknowledges that it is unwise to handcuff administrators unnecessarily with inflexible statutes and rules. Nevertheless, he notes that the need-for-flexibility argument, although basically sound, has been "overused as an alibi for malfeasance in legislative drafting. Social pressure for some kind of quick action also interferes with drafting of a proper rule, even though this too is a much overused alibi."[29] Kenneth Culp Davis, condemning the broad discretionary flexibility given administrators in the absence of meaningful legislative guidelines and agency rules, tersely wrote: "Perhaps nine-tenths of injustice in our legal system flows from discretion and perhaps only one-tenth from rules."[30] Davis has always had a way of making his words count. This leading administrative law scholar has spent much of his academic career probing the ways in which discretion in decision making, especially rule-making, can be "confined, structured, and checked." Davis is very critical of those who assert that present rule-making procedures represent a fair and open process in the American government system. Formal rule-making procedures are relatively fair and open, Davis admits, but most rule making is very informal. Unfortunately, this too often leads to gross abuse of the rulemaking power and the drafting of informal rules (public policy statements) in the absence of meaningful input by the public.[31] Lowi agrees, adding that the ideal of formal procedures leading to orders and rules in administrative agencies is largely a myth: "In practice, agencies end up with the worst of case-by-case adjudication and of rule-making."[32]

THE DEMOCRATIC CHARACTER OF RULE-MAKING PROCEDURES AND PUBLIC POLICY OUTPUTS

How democratic is the rule-making process? In answering this question, the most popular approach, taken mostly by law-oriented writers, has been to analyze the nature of rule-making procedures. Their focus would essentially be on the legislative statutes and agency procedures outlining rule-making steps and centering on the question: How closely do these steps follow prescribed democratic standards? Realizing that attention to only formal or ideal requirements and procedures of rule-making would be shortsighted, these scholars also spend considerable time examining informal aspects of rule-making. As far as these critics go, they do an admirable job, particularly when they point to the notable differences between what formal rule-making demands and the actual rule-making procedures practiced by administrators.

Unfortunately, the analysis of the democratic character of rule-making normally stops here. An in-depth analysis of the democratic character of rule-making requires that the ends and means of rule-making be meaningfully linked to each other. That is, legal scholars seem to become so involved with the technical legal requirements of rule-making (the means) that they either ignore or fail to emphasize the vital social purpose of rule-making (the ends). It is absolutely impossible to reach intelligent conclusions regarding how democratic our current rule-making practices really are unless rule-making procedures are carefully scrutinized in the context of the actual public policies they produce. Thus, two additional questions need to be stressed: Who participates meaningfully in the rule-making process? And, probably of greater social importance, who really benefits from the public policies created by rule-makers? For certain, democratic theorists are most interested in the answers to these two questions. They would contend that formal and informal procedures mean very little in a democratic country if, in the final analysis, the general public is not provided with ample and genuine opportunity to influence public policy making, while it must nonetheless stand to become the chief beneficiary of implemented public programs (the product of final rules in our case). Before addressing the issues surrounding these questions, it is appropriate to address some other points related to this question: Is rule-making consistent with democratic government?

Are Rule-Making Procedures Developed and Structured Enough?

A popular argument has been made that rule-making is safe for democracy because the delegation of this law-making function by legislators to administrators has not been done in the absence of reasonable checks. It appears that despite the importance of the rule-making power, legislative assemblies were content to delegate the most fundamental governmental power (the legislative power) without attempting to confine this power by limiting its use through viable restrictions. As Robert S. Lorch points out, despite the vital importance of the rule-making function to the preservation of democratic procedures in governance, only about one-tenth of the Administrative Procedure Act focuses on rule-making standards. The agencies themselves do not devote much attention to developing rule-making standards either, although the time devoted to developing standards depends upon the nature and purposes of each agency.

The relatively unstructured condition of rule-making has been further compounded by the steadfast reluctance of the courts to demand that agencies develop and structure rule-making procedures, especially when Congress has not requested agencies to do so through statutes. Although rule-making procedures lack meaningful structural guidelines at the national level, the situation is even worse at the state and local levels. Although the situation is improving, some states have not even passed a basic administrative procedure act to give general guidance to administrative procedures in their respective states. Local governments, although often compelled to follow the federal APA and their state's administrative procedure acts when they have jurisdiction (for example, federally funded programs in a local community normally require the recipient communities to honor federal procedures such as notice), have developed virtually no rules governing administrative procedure. This is unfortunate because democracy probably acquires its most practical meaning at the local governmental level, where the average citizen has the most frequent confrontation with administrators. Yet citizens are most likely to be denied administrative due process by rather undistinguished local officials who are more geared to personalized administration than their typically more qualified federal counterparts. In this sense, impersonalization is regarded as a virtue in administration because it implies that all those who come before an administrative agency are given the same equal treatment according to established rules and regulations.

Of course, many vehemently argue that democracy would not be well served by rigidly structured rule-making procedures that were too inflexible for quick and decisive responses to problems which plague the democratic state. Generally, these critics hold that a simple and flexible rule-making system avoids procedural arthritis, which can stifle administrative efforts to generate needed public programs in response to public demands. They also maintain that complex procedures can confuse the public, thus discouraging citizens from participating in the rule-making process altogether.

These arguments have some validity and point to a serious problem unique to democratic, as opposed to totalitarian, countries. They are, nevertheless, not convincing. They are not convincing because democratic countries, if democratic practices are to be preserved, must resolve democratic problems with democratic solutions. The streamlining of rule-making procedures may make it easier for administrators to propose, draft, and implement rules, but if the procedures are undemocratic, the likelihood that the resulting public policies would reflect majority will would diminish. There seems to be little question among democratic theorists that, logically, democracy is best preserved by the continuance of democratic decision making. Consequently, those who cherish democratic institutions must seek a way to allow essential flexibility in rulemaking while simultaneously guaranteeing that rulemakers remain democratically accountable to the public.

Public Participation in Rule-Making: Myth versus Reality

Ideally, the public can meaningfully participate in the rule-making process. On paper, rule-making is a relatively open process. In *Riverbend Farms, Inc.* v. *Madigan,* 958 F.2d 1479, 1483–1484 (9th Cir. 1992), the court exclaimed: "The Administrative Procedure Act ensures that the massive federal bureaucracy remains tethered to those it governs—or so the theory goes." According to the APA (Sec. 553), as well as state APAs, proposed rules are announced to the public by being published in the *Federal Register* or a similar governmental news source on the state level. After such notice, agencies are required under "normal" circumstances to "give interested persons an opportunity to participate in the rule-making through submission of written data, views, or arguments with or without opportunity for oral presentation" (Sec. 553[c]). Agencies are also required to "consider relevant matter presented" before drafting their final rules, and such adopted "substantive" rules shall not become effective for at least thirty days after passage (Sec. 553[d]). Finally, to protect against the possibility of unsound rules being kept in force, "each agency shall give an interested person the right to petition for the issuance, amendment, or repeal of a rule" (Sec. 553[e]). It would appear that even a devout cynic would have to admit that rule-making is fair and open to democratic participation after reading Section 553 of the APA.

Unfortunately, however, this rule-making section is so plagued with exceptions and loopholes that it turns out to be a cynic's paradise. For example, after evaluating the difference between what ought to be and what is in rule-making, Jeffrey F. Jowell concluded that formal rule-making prescriptions, as developed in the APA, amount to not much more than what Murray Edelman several years ago referred to as "symbolic reassurances," where myths, symbols, rituals, and the like, are used by states to appease the public.[33] Jowell wrote summarily: "In other words, rule-making procedures may be used by an administrative agency to give an impression of participation, whereas no more than pro forma adherence to an empty democratic ritual is involved."[34]

These cynical perspectives on the openness of rule-making to meaningful participation by interested persons is shared by many, and apparently for good reasons. Careful examination of all exceptions or loopholes in the rule-making section of the prototypical APA shows that there are enough loopholes in the legislation to allow administrators ample opportunities to undermine what the section ideally promotes. A leading administrative law scholar supports this insight by his assertion: "The strength of 553 may lie in the procedure marked out for rule-making when the exceptions do not apply. Experience for a quarter of a century or more fully confirms that strength. The weakness of 553 may lie in the extensive exceptions."[35] For instance, although on the surface public notice of rule-making is required, notice does not apply to "interpretative rules, general statements of policy, or rules of agency organization, procedure, or practice" (Sec. 553[b][3][A]).[36]

This means that agencies have broad discretion. They can select from various rule types, as well as rule-making methods which do not require notice. Rules may be promulgated by a variety of informal and formal methods where: (1) absolutely no participation by affected or interested persons is involved; (2) participation is limited to consultation or conferences between the interested persons and the agency; (3) consultation takes place with advisory committees; (4) formal written arguments and facts are solicited and submitted to the agency; or (5) trial-like hearings are conducted. Any of these rule-making procedures can be used more or less formally. But the bottom line is that by promulgating interpretative rules and policy statements, rule-makers can quite easily avoid the making of substantive or legislative rules where the granting of notice is much more common, but not necessarily required. Notice is never absolutely required. There are enough loopholes in the rule-making legislation that notice can almost always be avoided by an administrator determined not to comply.

But why should certain rules be exempt from requiring notice and allowing interested parties to participate? Anyone who is familiar with administrative law understands that interpretative rules may carry considerable weight. It was noted earlier in this chapter that interpretative rules (agency "laws" which have resulted from interpretations of legislative statutes entrusted to the agency), in fact, constitute agency policy, and such policy is normally upheld by the courts. The application of an interpretative rule by an agency could cause an industry, for example, to incur substantial unanticipated expenses (for example, the EPA decides that dangerous waste includes certain substances and, therefore, they cannot be emitted into the atmosphere). Consequently, it seems only fair that affected parties be given notice and provided an opportunity to present arguments in their behalf.

The problem is further compounded by the failure of the Congress to pass clear and well-developed legislation. It has been especially the case in recent decades that Congress passes the most general legislation, allowing administrative agencies great latitude in giving functional meaning to legislative policies through their interpretations. Consequently, most rules made by administrators can be regarded as interpretative rules, although distinguishing between an interpretative rule and a legislative rule, as indicated previously, is not always an easy task.[37] The charge has been made that administrators are too often abusing their rule-making powers by relying too heavily on the interpretative rule loophole, thus weakening the democratic fabric of rule-making by eliminating notice, an obvious prerequisite to meaningful participation in the shaping of public policy. Also of importance, the wisdom of excluding interpretative rules from notice requirements is also suspect on the grounds that interpretative rules are very likely to be durable as well as unreviewable. In criticizing case law on interpretative rules, Michael Asimow concluded: "Interpretative rules are usually neither tentative nor temporary. Finally, even if their effect on the regulated parties is subject to a probably illusory administrative reconsideration, their effect on others, such as consumer or competitors, may be definitive and virtually unreviewable."[38]

Policy statements by administrative agencies are also issued without the benefit of notice, despite the fact they, too, carry great clout. It is sometimes difficult to distinguish between legislative and interpretative rules; yet it is no less a chore to distinguish policy statements from legislative rules. *Policy statements* are supposed to be more tentative than legislative rules; yet policy statements are expected to be developed enough to provide a genuine guide for agency behavior in executing public policy. Critics have held that policy statements are to be both tentative and concrete, but this, they acknowledge, is a contradiction. Nevertheless, policy statements, as exempted interpretative rules, can play and have played a significant role in shaping public policies which determine in part the way Americans can live. Therefore, agency policy statements also should not be exempt from the notice requirements, and healthy democratic participation should not be blocked.

Notice is also not required when agencies issue rules pertaining to agency procedure, organization, and practice. Such appears to be an unjustifiable exemption, even if notice involves inconveniencing agency officials somewhat. Max Weber reasoned decades ago that the operating procedures of public bureaucracies should be made known to the public. In a democracy, this guarantees that bureaucracy functions in the context of the rule of law. Fundamental fairness, Weber argued, demands that the public be notified about the rules and regulations which govern administrative procedure so that the public is protected from arbitrary and capricious agency practices that can promote unreliable, irresponsible, and unstable agency behavior. To Weber, the importance of properly drafting and publicizing bureaucratic rules and regulations in a "legal-rational" system of government, such as that of the United States, could not be overemphasized.[39] It seems only fair that people who come before administrative agencies should be able to rely on relatively consistent agency practices over time. Surely, agencies must be allowed to make necessary procedural adjustments from time to time, but such changes in operational procedures should be made public so that persons counting on certain established procedures are not unfairly inconvenienced.[40]

Although the APA does not require notice to be given when agencies issue interpretative rules, policy statements, or rules regarding agency organization, procedures, and practices, some federal agencies give notice anyway. However, democracy will not be properly served unless the APA is amended to require all federal agencies, except for those involved in sensitive policy areas, such as the CIA, to issue notice for such proposed rules. In a democracy, the first impulse should be to open the door to participation in the making of virtually any kind of public policy, not to close it. If genuine public policies in the form of rules are to be generated by rule-makers, the rule-makers should be compelled to open rule-making to interested parties as much as possible. It is reasonable to assume that public policy outputs will generally reflect the public policy-making inputs. Thus, undemocratic inputs will yield undemocratic outputs.[41]

The APA requirement that requires public agencies to solicit and consider all relevant material in the drafting of a final substantive rule has attracted considerable criticism, not so much because of what Section 553(c) says but for what actually goes on in practice. The consensus is that participation in the rule-making process is far from equitable and democratic. It is important to emphasize that Section 553(c) requires administrative agencies only to consider relevant materials presented. It does not require administrators to actually be influenced by submitted data and arguments.

Under this section agency officials are also given the discretion to decide what constitutes relevant submitted information. This gives agency officials great power because, as organizational theorists have long pointed out, those who control the information can control the situation. To Weber, this was the real source of power for bureaucracy.[42] Thus, for all practical purposes, when making rules, administrators have absolute discretionary power to ignore or honor any or all inputs from interested parties attempting to shape the rules in their favor. (It must be said, however, the Congress had no real choice but to give administrators such discretion because realistically it would create a potentially chaotic, disruptive, and inefficient situation if rule-makers were legally obligated to respond formally to every "comment" and submitted "relevant materials.") And the courts have been quite willing to accept the expertise of administrators in determining the relevancy of submitted data. Obviously, then, two intriguing questions emerge: One, to whom do agency rule-makers tend to listen and respond? Two, why?

A preponderance of credible evidence presented by social scientists suggests strongly that rule-makers are influenced much too much by the powerful special interest groups and not enough by those forces which are more representative of the public interest.[43] This reality was acknowledged in *Riverbend Farms* when the court said that "usually special interest groups influence the rulemaking process, even though the process is open to 'members of the public'" (at 1484). One problem in interest group theory has always been the inability of the observers to define the public interest definitively enough so general agreement could be reached on its meaning. Trying to block the merger of the International Telephone and Telegraph Corporation with the Hartford Fire Insurance Company in the early 1970s, Ralph Nader and Reuben B. Robertson (D.-Conn.) argued before the court that the merger, among other things, was contrary to the public interest. District Judge Blumenfeld, however, did not sympathize with the claim of Nader and Robertson that they represented the public interest, especially since the public interest could not be satisfactorily defined.[44] But if the public interest cannot be defined, why does Congress assign regulatory agencies to the task of regulating within the public interest?

But only a naive observer of the American system could conclude that all interest groups have equal access and influence on U.S. decision makers, whether they are lawmakers or rule-makers. Real pluralist politics in America tends to substantiate the realist's belief that life is unfair. It only makes sense, despite the obvious inequities, that the most powerful interests are in the best position to influence policy decisions so that they can become even more powerful and secure. This reality is well documented and is even justified by social Darwinists, who hold that the social system is strengthened by allowing the strong to survive and the weak to perish.

This is the key point. For all practical purposes, the power game that started during the colonial period is now over. Victors and vanquished, so to speak, have emerged. The big, rich, powerful interests are the winners. These interests, exerting their great influence, have been able to change the original rules of the game to favor their privileged position, thus ensuring no serious threat from competitors and, thereby, effectively destroying what was left of the free marketplace in the United

States. Therefore, weaker interests today (many small businesses, consumer groups) have very little chance of influencing, say, rule-making in their favor over the wishes of the powerful interests (for example, IBM, General Motors, ITT, or the AMA), because virtually all the wild cards in the game have already been dealt to the big interests. That is, in this context already-powerful interest groups could be accused of cheating because they are playing with a stacked deck that makes fair competition among pluralist interests impossible. This stacked deck has given the powerful interest groups the cards they need to make them formidable lobbyists before the rule-makers. As compared to lesser opponents in this modern influence-peddling game, the big interests are in an advantageous position because they have well-organized, well-financed, stable lobbying organizations that are staffed by well-paid, full-time professionals who are able to tap a stockpile of in-house information. According to Robert S. Lorch, this gives the powerful interests strong teeth with which to bite agency rule-makers. Although he somewhat overstates himself here, Lorch claims "teeth are all that count in politics."[45]

Some observers of the power game argue that the big interests are not only too much for their competitors, but too much for the regulatory agencies as well. Lack of personnel and necessary technical knowledge and data and legal obstacles, particularly when some interests have seemingly endless resources with which to fight agencies with limited budgets, inspired at least one federal rule-maker to say, in a remark quoted by Caroline E. Mayer, "We're no match for the people we're supposed to regulate."[46] Summarizing the chief argument of the critics, Robert A. Kagan noted that there exists a serious problem in achieving democratic rule-making in America because "regulatory agencies are not too stringent but overly accommodative to the businesses they are supposed to control; they become 'captives' of the dominant firms in the regulated industry, protecting their interests rather than preventing or redressing injuries to the public."[47]

In a card game, the players could start over again after throwing out the cheaters, but real-life contenders cannot start over; they must cope with the players already in the game and do their best to make the game more fair. Davis contends that "probably most rulemaking is still done with little or no party participation of any kind."[48] But this seemingly undemocratic practice should not be taken that pessimistically. Formal party participation is certainly excluded from the making of most rules, but one should not infer that rule-makers are not listening or are insensitive to the pressures coming from their environment through the normal feedback cycle. Systems theory makes clear that all capable decision makers read in and respond to input from their respective environments. In this case, rule-makers are normally informed enough to anticipate at least the basic reactions to their proposed and final rules from various interest groups. A plethoric number of studies of interest group politics by social scientists over the past few decades have demonstrated that most governmental decision makers, including agency rule-makers, tend to favor the powerful interest groups in their policy outputs, even in the absence of any evidence of formal participation in the decision-making process by the always pervasive big interests.[49] In regard to agency rule-making, this happens if for no other reason than that the rule-makers do not want to ruffle the feathers of those who can relentlessly fight back.

In summary, if the rule-makers feel pressured more by the well-organized, well-financed, and determined special interests, then it is only logical to assume that agency policies will tend to favor these special interests. But when decision makers (rule-makers) in a political system favor special interests over the public interest, the system ceases to be a democratic one rooted in the rule of law. Plato argued in *Laws* that such politics function more like parties than governments because parties normally favor special interests, but governments should not.[50] Jean Jacques Rousseau argued similarly in *Social Contract* that democracy is undermined when special interests dominate the general will.[51] In *The Federalist Papers* James Madison argued that democratic liberty allows for the pursuit of selfish interests by private parties—but not to the point where the public interest is placed in jeopardy. Madison considered the preservation of relative freedom by preventing any single or few interests from destroying the larger public interest a critical role of government.[52] Thus, the consensus among theorists seems to be that promoting the public interest, not special interests, is government's rightful role. Therefore, Americans should seek to equalize group inputs in the rule-making process and design rule-making techniques so that the public interest is better represented and democracy can be preserved. But is it naive to assume, given the tremendous influence big interests already have over agency policy-making today, that this goal can be achieved? Only in fantasy do things get better and does life always continue happily ever after. Maybe this country will never be able to release the tightening grip the powerful interests already have on our rule-makers. In this era of corporate takeovers and mergers, it appears that the most powerful interests are becoming even more powerful, promising to make it even more difficult for agency administrators to protect and promote the public interest over the wants of the newly emerging "super special interests."

But maybe this rhetoric is too alarmist since Kerwin concludes that although 80 percent of the interest group lobbyists report that their participation influences rule-making 84.1 percent of the time, ironically agency rule-makers claim in another survey that they make few changes to proposed rules because of interest group participation and do not show any significant preference for comments by special interests over the general public.[53]

More Exemptions to the APA

There are still more exemptions to Section 553 of the APA; they also tend to close rule-making from open, democratic participation. Although these exemptions deserve comment, what has just been said about the interactions between rule-makers and various interest groups helps to explain the whys of these exemptions, too. Most, if not all, the exemptions tend to favor administrators and certain special interests, but probably not the general public. Administrators benefit directly from the freedom they are given to draft rules, thus sparing themselves many headaches. The powerful interest groups, on the other hand, benefit indirectly because they are the most capable of dealing with the complex, time-consuming, and expensive rule-making process, with its confusing and inconsistent procedures.

Section 553(e) allows interested persons "the right to petition for the issuance, amendment, or repeal of a rule." However, the APA does not require agencies to do anything more than *receive* these petitions. Administrators are given total discretion in deciding what attention they should give certain inputs. Systems theory suggests that administrators would unlikely ignore those inputs which could pose serious problems to the agency. It should be recalled that it is very important in systems theory that agency leaders respond properly to feedback from their environment so that the smooth continuance of agency operations can be assured. But it is logical to conclude that the rhetoric of Section 553(e) creates another significant loophole. The loophole is certainly reasonable in that administrators should not be compelled to act on every petition submitted, but the loophole nevertheless permits agencies to treat submitted petitions unequally. It is only sensible to assume, especially in the context of systems theory, that agencies would likely honor most of those petitions, regardless of their objective merits, which place the greatest demands upon the agencies.

Military or foreign affairs functions (Sec. 553[a][1]) and matters relating to "agency management or personnel or to public property, loans, grants, benefits, or contracts" (Sec. 553[a][2]) are also exempt from the general APA rule-making requirements. While some of these exemptions seem justified, others are questionable, especially since the exemptions are allowed to apply under all circumstances, regardless of the democratic fairness and reasonableness of their application. Probably those military and foreign affairs functions actually linked to national security interests, especially in legitimate classified areas, should be excluded from the Section 553 requirements. But what about those military and foreign affairs activities which cannot reasonably be considered sensitive or meaningfully related to national security? It is true that the defense of the United States should be given high priority, but the importance of defense matters should not blind the country so that it is able to allow the Defense Department to carry out any business matters in the absence of public comment. There is no reason to exclude the public from rule-making leading to important, nonsensitive policy decisions. For example, should not the public have a right to object to a proposed rule that calls for nuclear missile tests or the dangerous dumping of nuclear wastes close to large population centers? Has this nation not learned decades earlier that certain DOD decisions placed the lives of innocent persons in jeopardy (for example, bomb tests in the 1950s in Utah leading to radiation sickness in the 1980s and 1990s) when an open airing of the proposed test sites could have prevented unnecessary risks? These past decisions are costing taxpayers millions of extra dollars today in tort liability suits against the federal government.

It would seem democratically justifiable to amend Sec. 553(a)(1) of the APA so that only those military and foreign affairs matters considered sensitive or those which place in jeopardy national security interests are exempted from normal rule-making procedures established in the act. In addition, it might even be a good idea to request the rule-makers taking the exemption to note in writing, for the record, why taking the exemption is justified.

Similarly, why should the public not be allowed to express opinions regarding matters related to "agency management or personnel or to public property, loans, grants, benefits, or contracts" (Sec. 553[a][2])? Under certain circumstances, it would be unwise and unethical for agencies to open the rule-making process in these areas to the public, especially if by doing so, they would disclose business secrets or endanger the public interest. For instance, under special circumstances, it would be detrimental to the public interest, in a financial sense, for an agency to disclose prematurely the intention of building a road through a particular area because such notice would undoubtedly cause speculators to buy key property so that they could make it difficult for the government to obtain the needed property at a reasonable price.

For purposes of privacy, there are reasons to keep personnel records secret, but possibly not when employee performance becomes a significant factor. The business of awarding loans, grants, and contracts has become quite controversial, especially since so much money is involved. Although Congress has dealt with some of these matters in such transactions as the Lockheed and Chrysler loans, most are negotiated directly with administrative agencies. Richard P. Nathan pointed out that during the Nixon presidency Nixon reached the conclusion that the bureaucracy had tremendous powers to influence public policy directions because these agencies were directly responsible for awarding billions of dollars in federal loans, grants, and contracts each year.[54] On a lower level, state and local agencies also yield such power. Does not the public have a right during rule-making to question, for example, the intention of public agencies to award costly contracts? Or, as Robert S. Lorch sarcastically asserted in this regard, "I can imagine that some people might be interested in knowing in advance that the Park Service is about to sell Old Faithful to a steam generating company."[55]

Finally, the APA, under Sec. 553(b)(A), allows agencies to prevent participation by not giving notice if agency officials believe that to do so would be "unpracticable, unnecessary, or contrary to the public interest." However, the agency must show "good cause" when invoking this exemption, stating the reasons. In 1992 in *Riverbend Farms,* op. cit., the court recognized the importance of the good cause exception, but stressed that the ". . . exception goes only as far as its name implies: It authorizes departures from the APA's requirements only when compliance would interfere with the agency's ability to carry out its mission" (at 1485). Despite the fact that this loophole could be abused by those administrators determined to limit participation by using an unreasonably broad interpretation as to when notice seems "unpracticable, unnecessary, or contrary to public interest," the exemption is acceptable since the abuse could not likely be carried too far. Justifying "good cause" too often could muster suspicion and create cause for investigation.

Another consideration is that there are times when inviting unnecessary participation through notice may be disruptive to the administrative process; for example, notice could lead to time-consuming participation at a time when administrators need to respond quickly to alleviate a serious social problem. But to reiterate, the exemption does not seem to be contrary to democratic principles as long as the withholding of participation is modest and truly within the public interest—an expediency in the administrative process, particularly in times of emergency, seems to be within the public interest.

SENSIBLE SUGGESTIONS FOR MAKING RULE-MAKING MORE DEMOCRATIC

One thing becomes evident from reading the literature pertaining to rule-making: an increasing number of administrative law critics are quite displeased with the state of rule-making today. They argue that rule-makers have essentially been given carte blanche discretionary powers to implement and eventually judge the appropriateness, effectiveness, and fairness of their own administratively constructed public policies, under which the public must live. These scholars are particularly upset with the position taken by the spokespersons for another point of view who hold that public administrators should be given the necessary flexibility (discretion) to implement and adjudicate public policies since they are real experts. Because external checks on administrative actions have proved to be quite ineffective in practice, these critics are quick to point out that the future of democratic policy making in the United States is in real jeopardy. They claim that any semblance of democratic procedure in rule-making today is missing.

Basically, the scholars advocate three chief suggestions for improving the democratic character of rule-making. One is to improve the delegation of lawmaking or rule-making powers to administrative agencies by attaching standards and guidelines which can be effective in guiding rule-makers. The second is to confine and structure internal rule-making procedures so that procedural due process and rule-of-law principles are honored in the making of rules. Third, the scholars advocate that better review of agency actions be provided in general, in the area of rule-making in particular, by improving supervisory methods that can be employed by legislative assemblies, courts, and the public. The ideas of Theodore Lowi and J. Skelly Wright on rule-making reform tend to encapsulate very well the opinions of many others.[56]

Lowi: Today's Rule-Making Is Undemocratic

In his classic work, *The End of Liberalism,* Theodore Lowi set forth a forceful, scholarly argument that holds basically that our rule-making practices are undemocratic and contrary to the public interest. His argument is as valid today in the 1990s as it was when he first made it in the 1960s, especially since overall delegation has become broader. He contends that administrators have written very poor laws, laws so vague and inconsistent that they cannot convey legislative intent to administrators. Although Lowi is opposed to the practice of legislators' delegating broad legislative powers to administrative agencies through undeveloped, skeletal statutes, he nevertheless feels that improving delegation through designing better laws is one way to make rule-making more consistent with juridical democracy. Lowi contends that rule-making could be made more democratic if increased "administrative formality" were in practice, by which he means, simply, the adherence by administrators to internal agency rules and regulations governing the promulgation of substantive agency policies (rules). More specifically, administrative formality in rule-making would obligate rule-makers to follow more prescribed written rules. Such rule-making formality would curtail the use of administrative discretion and produce more formalized, written rules. Lowi contends that the present rule-making process encourages bargaining between agency leaders and privileged interests, ending in rules that are implicit or in reality even nonexistent but in any event, crippling to the public interest.[57]

Lowi further maintains that "early and frequent administrative rule-making" is a necessary requisite in administrative formality.[58] In other words, the frequent making of needed rules tends to formalize administrative procedure because it leads to a body of written rules that provides general guidelines for future internal or external agency policy stands. In short, such formalization tends to give the public agency structure and consistency. According to the Supreme Court, structure and consistency must be promoted in public agencies so the agencies act reliably (*Heckler* v. *Community Health Services of Crawford,* 104 S.Ct. 2218; 1984). Formalization also necessarily limits discretionary actions since agencies, by law, are compelled to comply with their own rules. Lowi submits that the promulgation of "early rules" (those drafted by an agency early in the life of a mandated statute) is in the best interests of democratic government because the procedure permits a relatively quick evaluation of whether legislative intent is reasonably represented by agency interpretations of specific statutes. Early rule-making also is sensible, according to Lowi, because it facilitates legislative and judicial review of agency rule-making and the relevance of agency actions.[59]

Lowi believes administrative formality, fostered by "early and frequent rule-making," promotes administrative centralization. He believes that this makes sound managerial sense because it provides "unity of direction" to rule-making. He contends that if enough procedural and substantive rules to form a "guiding light" are promulgated by an agency, administrative decision making at all hierarchical levels within the agency could reflect prescribed general organizational goals in a more consistent manner. This would not only make agency decisions quicker and more decisive, but it would also make them more reliable and responsible and, thus, more in line with democratic accountability in decision making.[60]

Lowi holds that the democratic nature of rule-making could also be improved significantly through codification. He asserts that present administrative law is in such a mess that codification could serve to clarify ambiguities, remove inconsistencies, and generally resolve many of the administrative law problems due chiefly to disorganization. Essentially, *codification* is a process whereby centralized organization is achieved through systematic categorization. In administrative law, the systematic recording and indexing of pertinent statutes, rules, judicial decisions, and the like, into a comprehensible and accessible source would help to make administrative law in general, but rule-making in particular, more consistent and accessible. In addition, Lowi argues that codification would help to restore democratic control over agency practices. In particular, it would tend to restore healthy legislative dominance over administration by presenting administrative law in a practical, understandable, and useful package. A unified code of administrative law would allow legislators to delegate powers, such as rule-making powers, more broadly to administrators, yet still retain basic control over administrative actions because legislators would be left with a current, comprehensible, and practical administrative law code which they could employ to manage and oversee administrative behavior. Lowi thinks codification could eventually evolve into an adequate substitute for what he perceives as "the futile oversight process."[61]

Judge Wright: Rule-Makers Must Keep Adequate Records, Especially Recording *Ex Parte* Contacts

J. Skelly Wright, Chief Judge of the U.S. Court of Appeals for the D.C. Circuit, argues persuasively that rule-making could be made more equitable and democratic if rule-makers only kept a reasonable record during informal rule-making. Informal rule-making, which is also commonly known as the notice and comment approach, is the most popular APA-sanctioned rule-making procedure used by administrative agencies, except when specific agency statutes require rule-making "to be on the record after opportunity for hearing" (Sec. 553[c]).

Wright is appalled at the way rule-making is carried out by federal agency officials, especially since the APA's rule-making requirements are so simple. He notes that "the procedure under the APA for informal rulemaking is so simple that it is unfortunate what has been done to it by the agencies and by the courts. All that is required by the statute is that the proposed rules and supporting data be published in the *Federal Register* with notice that comments and counter-comments on the proposed rules will be received by the agency during a stated limited period."[62] Unfortunately, Wright adds, agencies frequently make rules in the complete absence of adequately kept records.

Wright asserts that surely there should be no question as to what should constitute a proper record for informal rule-making. A proper record should simply include: (1) the published proposed agency rule with its relatively detailed description; (2) the final rule with written agency justification for it; and (3) the comments and counter-comments, documents, and so on, submitted as a response to the proposed published rule. Such would constitute a proper record unless testimonial transcripts or special hearing records are involved.

Despite the fact that in the 1971 Volpe case the Supreme Court decided to require agencies in the future to keep a proper record, most agencies in the 1990s still do not do so, although improvements have been made. What agency administrators must understand, Wright exclaims, is that agencies are now compelled to keep a record in informal rule-making. He asserts: "We are not mind readers; nor are we unduly impressed by pretensions of agency expertise unsupported by the record. . . . It is with respect to this record that we must review the reasons given by the agency for proposing the rule initially, and approving it finally."[63]

However, Wright argues, not only does the failure to keep an adequate record preclude intelligent review of agency rule-making, but it is also patently undemocratic and detrimental to the promotion of the public interest. The reasons are obvious. Rule-making in the absence of a decent record keeps rulemaking, a very important policy-making process, "behind closed doors." The keeping of a record is consistent with popular government theory because it ensures that decision makers are allowed to see the light of day, in the forms of further comment, analysis, and review, if deemed necessary.[64]

Wright expresses particular concern for unethical and undemocratic *ex parte* contacts (contacts made to benefit the *present* party, usually at the expense of the *absent* party or parties), which can easily be carried out between privileged parties and agencies if all their dealings remain totally out of public view and thus off the record. If an interested party wants to influence rule-making, Wright argues that their contributions should properly be placed in the record so that all other interested parties have an opportunity to respond. Wright asks: "Why should only some parties have private access to the eye or ear of the decision-maker during rulemaking? What conceivably acceptable reason can there be for such private access during rulemaking? If there is a reason, can it be strong enough to overcome the damage to the rulemaking proceeding caused by the appearance of preference and prejudice created by the *ex parte* contacts if disclosed, and the damage to the other interested parties, to the record, and therefore to judicial review, if the *ex parte* contacts remain undisclosed?"[65]

Wright concludes that *ex parte* contacts are such one-sided affairs that they give unfair preference to the special interests and undermine the public interest. This is a dangerous practice to continue in a democratic society because public policies can be easily warped by *ex parte* contacts with our rule-makers; yet reviewing courts would never be able to determine what inputs actually shaped the final rules. Wright takes this view: "Unless *ex parte* contacts during rulemaking are avoided, in addition to keeping the public and other parties in the dark, the reviewing court is denied access, not only to the contents of the contacts, but also to whatever response those contacts would have triggered were their contacts known. How is a court to make in-depth review of the record when some parts, perhaps some important parts, have been withheld—from it, from the public, and from other interested parties? How is a court to know—how is anyone to know—whether an undisclosed *ex parte* contact with the decisionmaker tilted his decision one way or another? Whatever the law was with respect to *ex parte* contacts during informal rule-making proceedings before *Overton Park,* in my judgment a reviewing court acting under the mandate of *Overton Park* can no longer accept a record flawed by such practices. . . . Why—why the *ex parte* contacts?"[66]

It seems that the vast majority of administrative law scholars and political scientists condemn *ex parte* contacts in principle. However, there are those who argue that *ex parte* contacts constitute a legitimate aspect of pluralist, democratic politics. They argue, as Judge Wald did in *Sierra Club* v. *Castle,* 657 F.2d 298 (D. C. Cir. 1978), that Congress prohibited *ex parte* contacts on communications only in formal rule-making proceedings, not in informal rule-making. Proponents contend that rule-makers need to listen to lobbyists who make *ex parte* contact with them in order to promulgate intelligent, responsible rules. Advocates acknowledge that *ex parte* contacts could lead to biased agency rules that serve more to promote the welfare of special interests than the public interest, but they believe that if adequate records are kept on the *ex parte* contacts, reviewing courts could always judge whether biased, irresponsible decisions on rules were made. However, such may be wishful thinking because certainly agency administrators, if they wanted to hide biased agency rule-making, could easily construct a record of the *ex parte* contacts that buries the truth.[67]

Negotiated Rule-Making: An Effort to Promote Consensual Rule-Making

In 1990 Congress passed the Negotiated Rulemaking Act.[68] This reform measure was designed to bring together representatives of various organizations who agency administrators believe represent those organizations which will be impacted the most by proposed agency action leading to a promulgated rule. Ideally, these representatives would work together with agency rule-makers to negotiate a settlement on a proposed rule which all parties, having a major stake in the outcome, could "live with." Starting in the 1980s, negotiated rule-making, or what is popularly called "Reg-Neg," has been sold as a reform rule-making approach which would greatly improve the quality of participation in the rule-making process and, as a consequence, also improve the substance of the actual rules promulgated. Proponents also held that Reg-Neg would significantly reduce lawsuits resulting from the promulgation of rules because Reg-Neg participants would unlikely want to sue since they participated in the negotiation of the rule and now have a vested interest in making it work.[69]

The concept of negotiated rule-making, endorsed in the literature by a weighty consensus of scholars (practitioners, especially the rule-makers themselves, are more ambivalent about the idea) is, of course, rooted in a very old and tested technique for reaching decisions—a technique employed for many decades for mediating and resolving labor disputes. For instance, in the 1930s the Fair Labor Standards Act established a process whereby interested parties were brought together in committees to negotiate settlements to labor disputes. In the 1960s Charles Lindblom, a public administration scholar, advanced an idea for improving decision-making in public agencies by proposing the concept of Partisan Mutual Adjustment (PMA),[70] which embraces virtually all of the basic arguments for and the components of Reg-Neg. Lindblom argued, as a proponent of Reg-Neg, that decisions that are reached through negotiation or through interested parties mutually working out differences between them (i.e., through PMA) are much more likely to respect and honor those decisions than when decisions are "crammed down their throats." Philip Harter, who in 1982 wrote the article "Negotiating Regulations," is credited the most for promoting the Reg-Neg concept. In this article he applies essentially Lindblom's arguments in trying to persuade the reader why negotiated rule-making should frequently be substituted for traditional notice and comment rule-making. To Harter, traditional rule-making is characterized by an adversarial process where special interests ruthlessly pressure rule-makers to promulgate rules which favor their particular interests at the expense of the public interest, while the rule-makers create records to avoid being sued. Harter contends that traditional notice and comment rule-making usually produces long delays in the issuance of rules, substantively flawed rules, and rules that fail to gain respect and compliance from the regulated. On the other hand, Harter maintains that Reg-Neg promotes a negotiation or Lindblom's PMA type process that tends to lead to informed, intelligent rules that the regulated, whose representatives participated in the process, are willing to uphold (see Figure 5.1 for an example of Reg-Neg).[71]

On the surface Reg-Neg looks like a desirable alternative to notice and comment rule-making, particularly because it has the promise of promoting more "informed" rules which will likely enjoy wide acceptance and voluntary compliance, as well as significantly reduce lawsuits caused by the promulgation of "insensitive" rules by agency rule-makers. Reg-Neg has enjoyed initial acceptance because of its promise. By the mid-1990s most federal agencies have at least experimented with Reg-Neg, especially after President Clinton's Executive Order 12866 in 1993 encouraged the use of negotiated rule-making. However, all things considered, Reg-Neg will probably face a fatal rocky road in the future. The basic problem with Reg-Neg is that it can work only under ideal conditions, which, of course, limits its ability to be used very broadly by agencies to promulgate rules. In the first place, negotiated rule-making will succeed only if the potential exists for a negotiated settlement or rule. This means that the stakes cannot be too high or issue-conflict too intense. For example, it would likely prove futile to use Reg-Neg to promulgate a rule on abortion procedures at abortion clinics because of the intensity of the moral issue. Secondly, the regulatory objectives must be clear, yet in reality agency rule-makers themselves are often not sure what their objectives should be. Thirdly, the regulatory issues must be ripe for resolution, although a host of problems may prevent maturation (e.g., insufficient data on the issue, every participating organization may not be "ready"). Fourthly, the "right" participants must be selected as negotiators. They must be willing to compromise and have the authority to do so (i.e., they must be able to speak for their organizations). Fifthly, agency rule-makers must not select too few or too many Reg-Neg participants, yet somehow assemble an ideal number that truly reflects those interests that a negotiated rule would affect the most. Certainly Reg-Neg cannot work in a large assembly hall filled with participants, yet Reg-Neg would also fail if only, say, four participants were supposed to represent a large diversified field of organizations. Sixthly, Reg-Neg will work only if participants perceive advantages to participating in Reg-Neg, but the truth is that many organizations may rather stick with their sophisticated lobbyist network already in place rather than rely upon the risky Reg-Neg process in which each organization would have very limited control. Seventhly, organizations must not only have the will to participate, they must also have the time and resources to do so. The typical Reg-Neg process would likely take many negotiating sessions spread over a period of at least several months, if not

EVALUATION
• Identify issues and deadlines
• Identify interested parties
• Compare to selection criteria
• Confirm management interest
• Select convenor

NEGOTIATIONS
• Establish ground rules/protocols
• Define "consensus"
• Set meeting schedule
• Publish notices of meetings
• Review available information and issues
• Review draft rule or proposals if available
• Establish work groups or subcommittees as necessary
• Negotiate text or outline of proposed rule

CONVENING–PHASE 1
• Identify additional parties
• Discuss Reg-Neg with parties
• Discuss issues with parties
• Determine willingness of parties to negotiate
• Report to agency
• Obtain agency management commitment
• Preliminary selection of 15-25 participants

RULE-MAKING
• Negotiations concluded

• If consensus is reached on language of rule:
  • Agency circulates draft for international/external review
  • Agency publishes consensus as draft rule

• If consensus is reached only on issues or outline:
  • Agency drafts proposed rule
  • Agency circulates draft for internal/external review
  • Agency publishes NPRM

• If consensus is not reached:
  • Agency proceeds with rule-making using discussions as a guide
  • Agency drafts and publishes NPRM

• Draft rule is subject to public comment
• Committee notified of public comment
• Agency revises rule if necessary
• Agency publishes final rule

CONVENING–PHASE 2
• Obtain parties' commitment to negotiate
• Publish "notice of intent to negotiate"
• Process FACA charter
• Select facilitator/mediator
• Respond to public comments on "notice"
• Adjust committee membership if necessary
• Arrange organizational meeting
• Arrange committee orientation/training

FIGURE 5.2   *Negotiated Rule-Making at EPA*

years. Small organizations, therefore, may not be able to commit the time and financial resources to Reg-Neg, even though they may have a great stake in the rule eventually promulgated by Reg-Neg. Such small organizations would probably rather
participate in the much less costly notice and comment rule-making process. Eighthly,
agencies must be able to select very skilled convenors with considerable mediation
experience to handle participants who may have more advanced negotiating skills
than the convenors. Convenors must achieve a consensus among the Reg-Neg participants so a rule can be promulgated, yet this will rarely be an easy task. Ninthly, and
very importantly, agencies must be willing to accept the negotiated rule, which
means that the agency must be willing to give up a lot of its rule-making power. Undoubtedly, if participants ever suspect that their input is just a waste of time because
the agency will simply promulgate the rule it really wants, the Reg-Neg process will
immediately be perceived as a farce and break down.[72]

The main reason Reg-Neg will probably fail as a procedure for promulgating
rules or be used on a very limited basis is that most of the conditions cited above describe most rule-making situations. After acknowledging a long list of conditions that
must be satisfied for Reg-Neg to succeed, Kenneth C. Davis and Richard J. Pierce,
Jr., who are more pessimistic about the future of Reg-Neg than most scholars, conclude: "Unfortunately, most major rulemakings involve all of these conditions. Thus,
most major rulemakings are poor candidates for resolution through Reg-Neg, which
has succeeded in only about 20 percent of the rulemakings in which it has been
tried."[73] Davis and Pierce stress that Reg-Neg has little chance of succeeding because
it is virtually impossible to get all parties to agree on anything when "[T]he stakes are
high, and a large number of parties will be affected in disparate and complicated
ways."[74]

But possibly the worst criticism of Reg-Neg comes from Derek McDonald because he actually attacks the very legitimacy of the process. McDonald acknowledges that only one Reg-Neg rule by 1993 had been challenged in court. However, he
holds that this fact should be "viewed with concern" because Reg-Neg has introduced ". . . some of the problems that Congress today now faces—especially the crisis of interest group politics that have served to discredit much of the product of the
national legislature."[75] McDonald argues that Reg-Neg will turn out to be an illegitimate democratic rule-making procedure if agencies passively serve as brokers for
conflicting special interests, while failing to make certain that the resulting rules actually serve to promote the public interest.[76]

Cornelius Kerwin is much more optimistic about the future of Reg-Neg. Although he recognizes the many problems associated with Reg-Neg, he nonetheless
concludes that ". . . participation in the form of regulatory negotiation is a permanent
part of contemporary rulemaking."[77] He is right that it is a part of today's rulemaking, but it is and will remain only a very small part. Reg-Neg can be used only under
ideal conditions and, even when used, has reportedly an 80 percent failure rate. Given
the time, energy, and expense that must be devoted to Reg-Neg, this is an alarming
failure rate, which will raise plenty of eyebrows. Consequently, as time passes, we
can expect Reg-Neg to drift into oblivion.

SUMMARY

The lawmaking power is the most basic of governmental powers. Although the constitutional framers originally assigned this function to Congress, Congress eventually delegated away much of the authority to public administrators. A similar course of action has taken place at the state level. In agencies, lawmaking is called *rule-making*. It would be wrong to assume that promulgated rules do not often carry the same force as laws drafted by legislators. In fact, the courts have insisted that they would not set aside a legislative rule any more than they would overturn a law passed by Congress. Interpretative rules are also quite authoritative, although they stand more of a risk of being overruled by the courts when challenged. The truth, even though it might gravely shock those who wrote the Constitution, is that more than 90 percent of modern American laws are rules (public policies) promulgated by agency administrators.

To guide the rule-making process, Congress has drafted specific provisions in the Administrative Procedure Act. Basically, these provisions have been designed to make agency rule-making fair by opening up the process to all interested parties. But critics charge that the democratic character of rulemaking procedures under the APA is more apparent than real. They point to major loopholes in the APA rule-making requirements that permit agency rulemakers the discretion to favor certain interest groups over others. Systems theorists contend that public administrators would have a tendency to favor those powerful interests in the political system which could jeopardize agency security because agency leaders are naturally concerned about responding appropriately to those environmental demands which pose the greatest threat to agency well-being.

Social scientists' consensus is that present agency rule-making practices do, in fact, favor the powerful interests at the expense of the weaker interest groups and the general citizenry. If an effects test is applied, the interest group theorists argue, it is clear that agency rules have mostly benefitted the *haves* to the detriment of the *have-nots*. To improve the democratic nature of rule-making, several suggestions have been proposed. Most notably, it has been suggested that more formal procedures should be incorporated into the rule-making process to further structure rule-making so that the uncertainties and inequities associated with agency discretion could be minimized. In an attempt to make rule-making more substantively sound and fairer to the parties who ostensibly would be most affected by agency rules, reformers managed to get passed the Negotiated Rulemaking Act of 1990. This new law encourages rule-makers, using agency intervenors working with representatives from "key" organizations, to negotiate proposed rules. Reg-Neg, as it is called, shows some promise, but skeptics believe it will ultimately fade away as a viable rule-making approach, mainly because the process is too costly and time-consuming and can be employed only under ideal conditions. Also, cynics claim that Reg-Neg is structured better to serve special interests than the general public. Reformers in general have argued that agency rule-making could be improved if rule-makers limited *ex parte* contacts with outside parties or at the very least kept a record of any *ex parte* contacts.

NOTES

1. Cornelius M. Kerwin, "The Elements of Rule-Making," in David H. Rosenbloom and Richard D. Schwartz, ed., *Handbook of Regulation and Administrative Law* (New York: Marcel Dekker, Inc., 1994), 345.
2. Susan Sommer, "Independent Agencies As Article One Tribunals: Foundations of a Theory of Agency Independence," *Administrative Law Review,* 39 (Winter 1987), 83–100. Also see Donald E. Elliott, *"INS* v. *Chadha:* The Administrative Constitution, the Constitution, and the Legislative Veto," Supreme Court Review 183 (1983), 166–76.
3. Cornelius M. Kerwin, "The Elements of Rule-Making," 345.
4. Ibid., 350–351.
5. Theodore J. Lowi, "Two Roads to Serfdom: Liberalism, Conservatism and Administrative Power," *American University Law Review,* vol. 36 (Winter, 1987), 295–322.
6. This regulatory agency practice has been severely criticized by administrative law scholars since both "rules" and "orders" yield public policies. Yet participation in rule-making is generally considered more consistent with democratic norms since in theory the processes are much more open to interested parties seeking to influence the content of the final rule.
7. Bernard Schwartz, *Administrative Law,* 3rd ed. (Boston: Little, Brown, 1991), 162.
8. Kenneth C. Davis and Richard J. Pierce, Jr., *Administrative Law Treatise,* 3rd ed., vol. 1 (Boston: Little, Brown and Company, 1994), 227.
9. Cornelius Kerwin, "The Elements of Rule-Making," 348.
10. Kenneth C. Davis, *Administrative Law and Government,* 2nd ed. (St. Paul, Minn.: West Publishing Company, 1975), 119. Also see Robert A. Anthony, "'Interpretive' Rules, 'Legislative' Rules and 'Spurious' Rules: Lifting the Smog," *The Administrative Law Journal of The American University,* 8 (Spring, 1994), 1–22.
11. Robert Anthony, "Which Agency Interpretations Should Bind Citizens and Courts?" *Yale Journal on Regulation,* vol. 1 (1990); and Kenneth C. Davis and Richard J. Pierce, Jr., *Administrative Law Treatise,* 3rd. ed., vol. I, 119–123.
12. Schwartz, *Administrative Law,* 3rd ed., 193.
13. Ibid., 170–71, Also, Kenneth C. Davis and Richard J. Pierce, Jr., *Administrative Law Treatise,* 3rd ed., vol. 1, 290–291.
14. Kenneth C. Davis and Richard J. Pierce, Jr., *Administrative Law Treatise,* 3rd ed., vol. 1, 290.
15. Ibid., 291.
16. Ibid., 294.
17. Cornelius M. Kerwin, *Rulemaking: How Government Agencies Write Law and Make Policy* (Washington, D.C.: Congressional Quarterly, 1994), 161.
18. Lewis Mainzer, *Political Bureaucracy* (Glenview, Ill.: Scott, Foresman, 1973), 39.
19. Davis, *Administrative Law and Government,* 121.
20. See, for example, David Wise and Thomas Ross, *The Invisible Government* (New York: Random House, 1964); Frederick C. Mosher et al., *Watergate: Implications for Responsible Government* (New York: Basic Books, 1974); Dan Rather and Gary P. Gates, *The Palace Guard* (New York: Harper & Row, 1974); Philip Agee, *Inside the Company: CIA* (New York: Stonehill Publishing, 1976); David Nachmias and David H. Rosenbloom, *Bureaucratic Government: USA* (New York: St. Martin's Press, 1980).
21. Pollsters have found that Americans do not condone unethical behavior in their public officials but seem to be more concerned with officials' possessing strong leadership than

high personal morals and ethics. For example, exit poll data after the 1992 presidential election showed that George Bush won the "morality" vote, yet lost because Bill Clinton was perceived as the more capable leader. Likewise, in the 1996 campaign Clinton was perceived as having more "morality" problems than Bob Dole, yet Clinton led in the polls because he was still perceived as more capable.

22. For a fascinating and enlightening behavioral analysis showing how Americans seem to support various democratic ideas only in the abstract, see William H. Flanigan and Nancy H. Zingale, *Political Behavior of the American Electorate,* 8th ed. (Boston: Allyn and Bacon, 1994), chap. 8.

23. Russell H. Weigel and Richard Jessor, "Television and Adolescent Conventionality: An Exploratory Study," *Public Opinion Quarterly,* 37 (Spring 1973), 76–90.

24. Ira Sharkansky, *The Maligned States,* 2nd ed. (New York: McGraw-Hill, 1977), esp. chap. 1–2, tries to defend the states against the criticisms of the political science community.

25. Quoted in Theodore Lowi, *The End of Liberalism* (New York: W. W. Norton, 1969), 302–303.

26. Theodore J. Lowi, "Two Roads to Serfdom: Liberalism, Conservatism and Administrative Power," *American University Law Review,* 36 (Winter 1987), 295–322; and Theodore J. Lowi, "Legitimizing Public Administration: A Disturbed Dissent," *Public Administration Review,* 53 (May/June 1993), 261–264.

27. Aaron Wildavsky, *The Politics of the Budgetary Process,* 4th ed. (Boston: Little, Brown, 1983), argues that it is healthy for the system when each department, agency, or interest has to fight for its own welfare. The net result, he maintains, is stronger parts that contribute to a stronger whole.

28. See Norton E. Long, "Bureaucracy and Constitutionalism," *American Political Science Review* (September 1952), 808–18.

29. Theodore Lowi, *The End of Liberalism,* 2nd ed. (New York: W. W. Norton, 1979), 302.

30. Kenneth C. Davis, *Discretionary Justice: A Preliminary Inquiry* (Urbana, Ill.: University of Illinois Press, 1969), 25.

31. Ibid., chap. 1.

32. Lowi, *End of Liberalism,* 2nd ed., 303.

33. Murray J. Edelman, "Symbols and Political Quiescence," *American Political Science Review,* 54 (September 1960), 195–204.

34. Jeffrey J. Jowell, *Law and Bureaucracy: Administrative Discretion and the Limits of Legal Action* (New York: Dunellen, 1984), 199.

35. Davis, *Administrative Law and Government,* 122.

36. Florence Heffron, with Neil McFeeley, *The Administrative Regulatory Process* (New York: Longman, 1983), chap. 9.

37. Kenneth C. Davis and Richard J. Pierce, Jr., *Administrative Law Treatise,* 3rd ed., vol. 1, 233–248. For a dated, but good, treatment of this issue, see Michael Asimow, "Interpretive Rules and Agency Statements," *Michigan Law Review,* 75 (January 1977). It should be noted that the words *interpretative* and *interpretive* (for the rules) have been used interchangeably in the literature. The word *interpretative* appears in the Administrative Procedure Act, but since it is grammatically incorrect, *interpretive* has been substituted by many scholars.

38. Asimow, "Interpretive Rules and Agency Statements," 531–32.

39. See Reinhard Bendix, Max Weber: *An Intellectual Portrait* (New York: Doubleday Anchor Books, 1978), chaps. 12 and 13.

40. Robert A. Leone, *Who Profits: Winners, Losers, and Government Regulation* (New York: Basic Books, 1986), esp. chap. 3.

41. Jack H. Knott and Gary J. Miller, *Reforming Bureaucracy: The Politics of Institutional Choice* (Englewood Cliffs, N.J.: Prentice-Hall, 1987), esp. chaps. 2 and 3.

42. H. H. Gerth and C. Wright Mills, ed., *From Max Weber: Essays in Sociology* (New York: Oxford University Press, 1946), chap. 8.

43. See Thomas R. Dye, *Who's Running America?: The Conservative Years* (Englewood Cliffs, N.J.: Prentice-Hall, 1986); and William F. Kent, "The Politics of Administrative Rulemaking," *Public Administrative Review,* 42 (September/October 1982), 420–26; and Cornelius M. Kerwin, *Rulemaking: How Government Agencies Write Law and Make Policy,* chap. 5.

44. *United States* v. *International Telephone and Telegraph Corp.* and the *Hartford Fire Insurance Co., 349F.Supp.* 22 (1972).

45. Robert S. Lorch, *Democratic Process and Administrative Law* (Detroit: Wayne State University Press, 1969), 103.

46. Lorch, *Democratic Process and Administrative Law,* 103. See also Caroline E. Mayer, "Too Much Regulation? Not as Regulators Tell It," *U.S. News & World Report* (October 8, 1979), 74.

47. Kagan, *Regulatory Justice,* 74.

48. Davis, *Administrative Law and Government,* 121.

49. Some good sources are Philip Selznick, *TVA and the Grass Roots* (Berkeley: University of California Press, 1949); Marver Bernstein, *Regulating Business by Independent Commissions* (Princeton, N.J.: Princeton University Press, 1955); C. Wright Mills, *The Power Elite* (New York: Oxford University Press, 1959); Murray Edelman, *The Symbolic Uses of Politics* (Urbana: University of Illinois Press, 1964); Peter Woll, *American Bureaucracy,* 2nd ed. (New York: W. W. Norton, 1977); Lowi, *The End of Liberalism,* 2nd ed.; James E. Anderson, *Public Policy Making,* 2nd ed. (New York: Holt, Rinehart and Winston, 1979); Martha Derthick and Paul J. Quirk, *The Politics of Deregulation* (Washington, D.C.: Brookings Institution, 1985); Leone, *Who Profits: Winners, Losers, and Government Regulation*; B. Guy Peters, *American Public Policy: Promise and Performance,* 2nd ed. (Chatham, N.J.: Chatham House, 1986); Randall B. Ripley and Grace A. Franklin, *Congress, The Bureaucracy and Public Policy,* 4th ed. (Chicago: Dorsey Press, 1987); and Kenneth J. Meier, *Politics and the Bureaucracy: Policymaking in the Fourth Branch of Government,* 3rd ed. (Pacific Grove, California: Brooks/Cole Publishing Company, 1993).

50. Plato, *Laws, in the Dialogues of Plato,* trans. Benjamin Jowell (London: Oxford University Press, 1953), 4: 284–85.

51. Jean Jacques Rousseau, *Social Contract,* trans. Maurice Cranston (Baltimore: Penguin Books, 1968), esp. books 2 and 3.

52. James Madison, Alexander Hamilton, and John Jay, *The Federalist Papers,* no. 10 (New York: Random House, 1937), 48–51.

53. Cornelius M. Kerwin, *Rulemaking: How Government Agencies Write Law and Make Policy,* 205–210. Kerwin notes that both interest group lobbyists and agency rule-makers have probably given biased responses. Lobbyists want to convey that they are effective, while rule-makers want to be recognized as fair and impartial.

54. Richard P. Nathan, *The Plot That Failed: Nixon and the Administrative Presidency* (New York: Wiley, 1975), esp. chap. 5.

55. Lorch, *Democratic Process and Administrative Law,* 104. Although Lorch says this, he is technically incorrect (and he probably knows it; the irony was the point). Because Old Faithful is located in a national park, the Park Service would probably have to obtain congressional approval before the sale. For an excellent analysis of the problems of government by contract, see Bruce L. R. Smith and D. C. Hague, ed., *The Dilemma of Accountability in Modern Government: Independence versus Control* (New York: St. Martin's Press, 1971).

56. See Lowi, *End of Liberalism,* 2nd ed.; Lowi, "Two Roads to Serfdom: Liberalism, Conservatism and Administrative Power," Schwartz, *Administrative Law,* 3rd ed., chaps. 2 and 4; Davis and Pierce, Jr., *Administrative Law Treatise,* 3rd ed., vol. 3, 97–103; and J. Skelly Wright, "Rulemaking and Judicial Review," *Administrative Law Review 30* (Summer 1978), 461–466.

57. Lowi, *The End of Liberalism,* 2nd ed., 36–38, 302–5.

58. Ibid., 302–3.

59. Ibid., 304.

60. Ibid., 304–5.

61. Ibid., 305–07.

62. Wright, "Rulemaking and Judicial Review," 465.

63. Ibid.

64. Ibid.

65. Ibid., 466.

66. Ibid.

67. See Davis and Pierce, Jr., *Administrative Law Treatise,* 3rd ed., vol. 1, 333–339, for a good legalistic review of how the courts have regarded *ex parte* contacts.

68. 5 U.S.C. Sections 581–590 (Renumbered by Congress to Sections 561–570 in the Administrative Procedure Technical Amendments Act, Pub. 2. No. 102–354, 106 Stat. 944 1992).

69. Cornelius M. Kerwin, *Rulemaking,* 185–191.

70. Charles E. Lindblom, *The Intelligence of Democracy* (New York: Free Press, 1965).

71. Phillip Harter, "Negotiating Regulations: A Cure for the Malaise, *Georgetown Law Review, 71* (1982).

72. Cornelius M. Kerwin, *Rulemaking,* 185–191.

73. Kenneth C. Davis and Richard J. Pierce, Jr., *Administrative Law Treatise,* 3rd ed., vol. 1, 374–375.

74. Ibid., 375.

75. Derek Raymond McDonald, "Judicial Review of Negotiated Rulemaking," *The Review of Litigation,* vol. 12 (1993), 487.

76. Ibid.

77. Cornelius M. Kerwin, *Rulemaking,* 191.

CHAPTER SIX

ORDER-MAKING: AGENCIES AS JUDICIAL BODIES

WHAT IS ORDER-MAKING?

Public administration agencies today, as a result of broad delegation of both rule-making and order-making powers, have the legal authority to make "laws" or the public policies that govern socioeconomic and political activities in the United States. In fact, scholars estimate that well over 90 percent of the laws that regulate our lives, whether at work or at play, are now made by our public administrators, not by our legislators or our traditional lawmakers. These administrators promulgate public laws or policies through either rule-making or order-making (adjudication), although frequently a combination of the processes is employed to make and fine-tune agency policies. Agency policies may target the whole society (e.g., general environmental regulations), an entire industry (e.g., passive safety restraints for all automobiles), particular companies or a single company (e.g., safety regulations directed at a specific nuclear power plant), or even an individual (e.g., a termination hearing decision involving a public employee).

Agency policy decisions may grant or deny benefits (e.g., permit an industry to operate or not operate under certain conditions; grant or deny a license to a business or an individual; grant or deny a welfare recipient, farmer, or veteran a benefit). Whether benefits are given or taken away, agency actions are ideally supposed to be guided by due process considerations. In agency rule-making, due process may mean allowing all interested parties ample opportunity to respond to a proposed rule, while in an agency adjudication it may mean allowing a person in a termination hearing sufficient time to examine and respond to allegations of misconduct.

As noted, our public administrators make public policies through agency rule-making and agency adjudications (order-making). Formally, or according to the language of the Administrative Procedure Act (APA), P.L. 404, 60 Stat. 237, Sec. 551 (1946), as amended, "rule-making means agency process for formulating, amending, or appealing a rule," while "adjudication means agency process for the formulation of an order." While rule-making is a quasi-legislative process, adjudication is a quasi-judicial process. In technical terms, when a public agency engages in rule-making the result is a rule. When the agency employs adjudication (order-making), the product is an order. According to the specific language of the AAP,

> [a] rule means the whole or part of an agency statement of general or particular applica-
> bility and future effect designed to implement, interpret, or prescribe law or policy or de-
> scribing the organization, procedure or practice requirements of an agency and includes
> the approval or prescription for the future of rates, wages, corporate or financial struc-
> tures or reorganizations thereof, prices, facilities, appliances, services or allowances
> thereof or valuations, costs, or accounting, or practices bearing on any of the foregoing.

In contrast, the APA states that an "order means the whole or a part of a final dispo-sition, whether affirmative, negative, injunctive, or declaratory in form, of an agency in a matter other than rule making but including licensing."

When a public agency adjudicates (judges), the agency issues an order that rep-resents a judgment in favor of one party or the other in a dispute. Just as Supreme Court decisions establish policies to be followed (e.g., court-ordered school desegre-gation), agency orders also set policies and establish precedents that commonly have the impact of laws. The need for agency adjudication arises normally when a dispute touches on a policy area within the regulatory jurisdiction of a particular public agency. The dispute may be between the agency and a private party (e.g., the Federal Communications Commission and a television station), between private outside par-ties (e.g., two television networks) seeking new policies or policy clarifications af-fecting operations in their industry, or between an intervenor or "party of interest" in a hearing involving an agency and a regulated company (e.g., an environmental group such as Union of Concerned Scientists intervening in a licensing hearing in-volving the Nuclear Regulatory Commission and a utility company).

Adjudications are mostly retrospective in focus. That is, agency adjudicative actions are aimed at trying to settle unresolved past conflicts between specific parties. Because participation is limited only to those parties involved in the agency's adju-dicative proceedings, order-making is not supposed to lead to the development of broad public policies for the future. However, despite widespread criticism, some regulatory agencies have preferred to employ order-making to make prospective agency orders of general applicability. When orders play this role, they are made to function more like rules than orders. Critics claim that orders should be restricted in their application so that they are not used simultaneously as retrospective orders and broad prospective rules. That is, critics feel that administrators should not try to use the order-making process to kill two birds with one stone. Order-making is designed to deliberate adjudicative facts, not legislative facts. When an agency is considering adjudicative facts during adjudicative proceedings, either informal or formal, it is concerned with determining who did what to whom and for what reasons in order to settle a dispute between specific parties. Under normal conditions it would be inappropriate during adjudication to entertain *legislative* facts, which relate only to general public policy considerations but are irrelevant to the specific dispute. (An example of legislative facts is public attitudes toward subsidized housing. An example of a specific dispute about legislative facts is a determination of a housing agency's illegally denying subsidy payments to a claimant.)

In sum, since administrative orders are supposed to be directed toward particular parties involved in a controversy, participation excludes the general public, and only adjudicative facts should be seriously entertained. The vast majority of administrative law experts, among them Kenneth C. Davis, Henry J. Friendly, David Shapiro, J. Skelly Wright, Richard K. Berg and Cornelius M. Kerwin, believe that it is foolish under most circumstances to promulgate general public policies through the order-making process.[1]

DIFFERENTIATING ORDER-MAKING FROM RULE-MAKING

Definitive guidelines to determine when issues appear appropriate for the adjudicative process simply do not exist. However, a few very rough guidelines that administrative agencies and courts have generally endorsed may be helpful. In general, the order-making process (frequently referred to as the case-by-case approach to formulating regulatory policies) is used in lieu of the rule-making process when (1) the issue in question involves specific parties in a dispute; (2) the matter concerns past behavior and is not future oriented (although orders do set precedents); (3) the issues or problems could not have been reasonably anticipated by the agency; (4) the agency wants to reach only a tentative decision because its administrators lack sufficient knowledge, experience, and confidence at the time in the specific area; and (5) the matter is simply too esoteric, complex, and varied to be resolved by the formulation of a general rule.

It is not always easy to differentiate between order-making and rule-making, nor is it easy to judge when order-making or rule-making should be employed to promulgate regulatory policies. The truth is that the legislative rule-making and judicial ordermaking functions in administrative agencies are frequently juxtaposed in practice. Adding to the confusion, asserts Edwin J. Madaj, ". . . is the anomaly that formal rule making is in many ways more procedurally like an adjudication than an informal adjudication."[2] Trying to differentiate between the two processes often turns out to be a futile academic exercise. For example, when the Federal Trade Commission (FTC) reviews the advertising practices of a certain company, concludes that the practices are deceptive, and orders the company to retract its earlier contentions publicly, is the agency functioning in a purely judicial capacity? The fact is that FTC decisions or orders (such as forcing a company to carry out corrective advertising) almost always shape FTC policy toward certain business practices. In many instances FTC hearing decisions establish rules that businesses dare not overlook.

In 1908, in *Prentis* v. *Atlantic Coast Line Company,* 211 U.S. 210, the Supreme Court tried to make a practical distinction between rule-making activities and order-making activities. The Court said that "the establishment of a rate is the making of a rule for the future, and therefore is an act legislative, not judicial in kind" (at 226). But only a year later the New York Court of Appeals, in *People ex rel. Central Park, N. and E.R.R. Company* v. *Willcox,* 194 N.Y. 383 (1909), complicated the definitional problem by contradicting the Supreme Court's interpretation of rule-making. The appeals court contended respectfully that the Supreme Court's definition ran contrary to established judicial authority in New York and added that it was not "convinced that the function of prescribing a rate is necessarily nonjudicial solely because it enforces a rule of conduct for the future" (at 386). Thus, because of the definitional problems, the courts have made a common practice of deciding administrative law cases, especially if the functions are hazy, without ever attempting to differentiate between judicial and legislative activities.

The failure to draw a distinction presents legal problems and causes some confusion because the APA specifies the procedural obligations of administrative agencies under sections of the act labeled "Rule-making" and "Adjudications." It may be difficult to establish an authoritative position and reach a respected decision based on certain procedural requirements or points of law in the APA if the courts cannot decide which sections of the act to apply, because they are uncertain as to which agency processes are in question.

Two simple tests have been used to try to determine whether agency decisions should have followed rule-making or order-making processes. Both tests fail as reliable measures, although they should not be discarded as useless since most agencies probably try to comply with the test requirements in general when promulgating policies. The first is the *past-future test,* which poses the question: Is the agency policy concerned with regulating past or future practices? If the regulatory policy is aimed at controlling future conduct, the policy should have been promulgated through rule-making procedures. However, if the policy is directed primarily at resolving a dispute involving past behavior, the policy position should have been the consequence of adjudication. The second test, called the *specific-general test,* seeks essentially to discover whether the promulgated agency policy is directed toward a specific or a general audience. If agency policy is aimed at regulating the activities of no specific parties, but parties in general, the policy should have been generated through rule-making. If the policy decision is directed toward specific parties (frequently even named parties in a controversy) the policy should have been developed through adjudication.

Unfortunately, however, agency policies almost never tend to be wholly past-specific or future-general in content or application. What compounds this problem further is that agencies have the legal, discretionary authority to decide whether they should employ the rule-making or order-making approach when making agency policies. Agency discretion is especially well respected by reviewing courts if agency officials take care to rationalize their approach selection as necessary to achieve a particular agency goal. About the only time courts would find an abuse of agency discretion in this matter would be in a situation in which an agency promulgated a policy through adjudication and then applied the new policy in such a way that serious adverse consequences resulted or the retroactive application obviously caused more harm than good (*SEC* v. *Chenery Corp.,* 332 U.S. 194; 1947; *NLRB* v. *Bell Aerospace Co.,* 416 U.S. 267; 1947; *First Bancorporation* v. *Board of Governors,* 728 F.2d 434, 10th Cir.; 1984; *District Lodge 64* v. *NLRB,* 949 F.2d 441 [D.C. Cir. 1991]).

For all practical purposes, such agency discretionary power has allowed agencies to ignore the general-specific and past-future tests when making policies, although most agencies do take these tests into account because of external pressures to conform to what is expected. Nevertheless, agency leaders frequently decide to choose either rule-making or order-making procedures to promulgate agency policies, not because one procedure may be more appropriate, but because one process may be perceived as more convenient by the agency officials. For instance, some agency administrators believe they can control the development of their regulatory policies better if they use the more flexible case-by-case approach, since the courts have generally allowed agencies to change policy directions with each case. On the other hand, the courts have been much more insistent that policies resulting from rule-making be honored by agencies for the purpose of keeping these policies consistent over time (*Vitarelli* v. *Seaton,* 359 U.S. 535; 1959; *Motor Vehicle Mfrs. Ass'n* v. *State Farm Mutual,* 463 U.S. 29; 1983; *South Cent. Terminal Co.* v. *U.S. Dept. of Energy,* 728 F.Supp. 1083, 1096 [D. Del. 1990]).

PROS AND CONS OF ORDER-MAKING AND RULE-MAKING IN AGENCY POLICY-MAKING

It is very important to comprehend the character of order-making and rule-making if one is to develop conceptually strong insights into the agency policy-making process. After all, formal agency policies, which essentially represent the regulatory role played by an agency, are made through either the rule-making or order-making process. Consequently, a great deal can be learned about agency behavior and its relationship to its external environment if these basic processes are contrasted. This section compares the more important features of order-making and rule-making, with an eye to their relative merits in generating sound regulatory policies rooted in democratic procedures fundamental to the maintenance and promotion of administrative due process. Special attention is devoted to how the public, regulated industries, and agency administrators perceive the comparative advantages and disadvantages of rule-making and order-making. Justifications are then presented to explain why a large number of administrative law critics prefer rule-making to order-making for the promulgation of most regulatory policies, and why they frequently become irritated at regulators who keep insisting on promulgating policies through adjudication.[3]

Procedural Differences

There are several basic procedural differences between rule-making and order-making. Although some of the these differences have been made apparent in previous discussions, a brief review is helpful. The basic procedural difference between the two is that the rule-making process is legislative in character, and order-making is judicial in nature. Of course, this basic procedural difference makes these two approaches to administrative policy formation fundamentally distinct. While rule-making typically involves the notice and comment approach, order-making procedure is supposed to be trial-like, meaningfully reflecting procedures followed in regular court trials. Thus, unlike rules, hearing orders impose penalties and rewards directed at particular parties involved in the hearing proceedings. Hearing decisions (orders) must be based wholly on the hearing record. Specifically, this means that administrative law judges who preside over agency hearings must root their orders in evidence presented at the hearings. The bulk of hearing evidence results from written and oral testimony and cross-examinations involving specific questions pertaining to a particular dispute.

Final rules do not have to be based on the varied information and arguments submitted to the rule-makers as a response to publication of a proposed rule in the *Federal Register.* Rule-makers have only the legal obligation to accept comments. They do not actually have to be influenced by these comments and data in drafting rules, although the courts, especially since *Overton Park,* have been insisting that rule-makers avoid "arbitrary and capricious" rule-making by rooting their decisions in substantial evidence based "on the record," especially after holding public hearings. The Court's position has probably forced many agency decision makers to pay more attention to submitted comments, but still discretion remains a powerful instrument on the side of administrators because it takes very little in practice for rule-makers to defend their rules against charges that they were arbitrarily and capriciously drafted.

Differences in Uniformity and Consistency

Because rule-making procedures are designed to facilitate the making of generally applicable rules that help to shape an overall regulatory game plan, attempts have been made to promote uniformity and consistency in agency policies. As a result of agency attempts to develop policies that can be applied in a uniform and consistent manner to those who will come under their regulatory umbrella, little effort is made to address unique objections and problems some of those to be regulated might have. Thus, rule-making procedures are designed primarily to produce broad, sweeping regulatory policies that are not particularly sensitive to individual cases or problems. In contrast, order-making, which utilizes the case-by-case approach, has the advantage of developing policies incrementally over time by addressing individual cases. Therefore, the real strength in the order-making approach lies in its emphasis on tailoring decisions (policy outputs) to special circumstances. In this sense, order-making is more compassionate than rule-making, at least for the individual parties involved. In fact, adjudicative procedures are much more elaborate than rule-making procedures simply because sincere efforts have been made to promote administrative due process during adjudication so that the rights of individuals are protected. The obvious disadvantage, however, is that this case-by-case approach may cause agency policies to fluctuate in an unpredictable manner over time, preventing the development of a stable and uniform policy climate for the regulated.

One serious problem with making policies through the order-making process is that resulting agency decisions come without warning, sometimes creating great hardships for those who must comply with the orders even though they were not parties in the dispute and who therefore did not have the opportunity to present data and arguments. Rules, on the other hand, are proposed in the *Federal Register* before they become law (a final rule). Despite the fact that some rule-makers give little attention to comments by outsiders on proposed rules, all interested parties are at least afforded the opportunity to provide input.

In addition, because agencies are compelled under Section 553(b) of the APA to publish their proposed agency rules in the *Federal Register,* agencies are obligated to spell out their policy intentions rather clearly for all to scrutinize. This has the obvious advantage of forcing agencies not only to clarify their policy positions but also to justify them in anticipation of challenges to their position. Many people think this prevents rule-makers from hiding the ball from interested parties, helping to ensure democratically accountable agency actions.[4] Such an open policy-making process, as contrasted to adjudication, allows judicial review of proposed agency policy before it is too late, as long as the petitioning party can show the court that it would suffer unfairly if the proposed action were carried out. The order-making process clearly fails to provide these advantages to affected parties.[5]

Policy Planning

Intelligent administrative policy-planning for the future demands that agency regulators develop a comprehensive game plan so that rational actions can be taken by the regulatory agency for the purpose of reaching desired goals. Agencies can rely on either rule-making or order-making approaches to achieve their regulatory ambitions. When facts and arguments are considered, rule-making appears to be preferable to order-making for policy planning by an administrative agency. The most persuasive reason, noted previously, is that in general rule-making tends to be general-future oriented, while order-making is more specific-past in focus. Planning through rule-making allows agency planners to obtain varied feedback from a diverse environment every time the agency proposes a rule. This ability to build a comprehensive database to aid future planning decisions is one of the key advantages of rule-making over adjudication in the area of policy planning.[6]

In contrast, the adjudicative process in administrative agencies is poorly designed for wise agency planning, not only because the process has a past-specific orientation but because the focal policy areas are left too much to chance selection. That is, some agencies (for example, the NLRB) cannot adjudicate unless outside parties raise the issue in a dispute. This causes agency planning, Shapiro once wrote, to "depend [more] on the accident of litigation than on conscious planning."[7] In fact, this largely causes agency planning to be left somewhat randomly to outsiders who are in no way concerned about an agency's efforts to develop sensible, long-range regulatory policies. It is true, however, as noted previously, that some agencies, like the FTC and the Environmental Protection Agency (EPA), do possess the power to initiate cases for the purposes of settling disputes and/or making and clarifying policies. This is considered overall to be a haphazard, inefficient, and ineffective way to approach agency policy-making, especially in view of the fact that the typical regulatory agency must confront massive regulatory problems with its very limited resources. In "Policy Oscillation at the Labor Board: A Plea for Rulemaking," Samuel Estreicher argues that the adjudicative approach to policy-making by the National Labor Relations Board has turned labor law into a "nightmare." He concludes by noting that the NLRB should "take its policymaking responsibility more seriously" by relying on the rule-making approach. Its use "should improve the quality of the Board's decision, its success rate in the courts, and, ultimately, its institutional standing."[8]

Rule-Making or Order-Making? Perspectives from the Regulated, the General Public, and Agency Officials

It is accurate to say that the perceived advantages and disadvantages of rule-making or order-making as policy-making approaches depend largely on how particular parties believe specific rule-making or order-making practices will benefit or harm their interests. Three broadly defined groups have a stake in agency policy-making procedures, and each perceives the pros and cons of rule-making and order-making procedures quite differently. This should be expected since the regulated, the general public, and the agencies themselves have radically different selfish interests to protect and promote.

The Regulated.   Of course, the regulated seek to secure their position in society by attempting to influence administrative policy-makers to see things their way. Big, wealthy, and powerful interest groups have been successful in persuading rule-makers to see it their way. For this reason, the regulated industries generally prefer rule-making to order-making. Rule-making provides the regulated with advance notice and a chance to submit viewpoints for the purpose of altering a proposed rule more to the industry's liking. Since rule-makers do not want to promulgate policies that might meet with forceful resistance, including lawsuits, agencies frequently respond to the so-called "suggestions" of the regulated.

The regulated also favor rule-making over adjudication because the process generally leads to quickly promulgated rules, uniformly applied in the industry. This has the advantages of minimizing unnecessary delays in the implementation of policies deemed necessary by a regulated industry and reducing business uncertainties and promoting fair competition among industry competitors. In sharp contrast, adjudication is generally perceived by the regulated as a closed, expensive, time-consuming process leading to uncertain and sudden policy stands. In the view of the regulated, the incremental order-making process excludes the general industry from agency policy decisions, leads to unnecessary litigations, and tends to promote instability and industrywide inequities. However, at times particular industry competitors may prefer adjudication to serve their special interests. For example, companies with vast financial resources may want to delay the implementation of agency policies they believe to be unfavorable, particularly those they feel will prove costly or give their competitors a better relative position in the marketplace. Individual corporations, or groups of them, have been known to delay agency implementation efforts for many years, sometimes a decade or more.

The General Public.   The general public, who frequently regard the regulated as their nemesis and perceive the regulators as captives of those that they are entrusted with regulating, also favor administrative rule-making to administrative adjudication. In the first place, if policy-making through adjudication is perceived as expensive, unpredictable, and impractical by the regulated, one can imagine how the general public would react. The public, probably best represented by underfunded and understaffed consumer groups such as Common Cause and Nader's Raiders, do not commonly look with favor on fighting for their interests via the agency order-making process. Agency adjudicative processes are simply too complex, costly, and time-consuming; and the resulting orders frequently have limited applicability or social impact.

The resources of consumer or citizen action groups are generally so scarce that these organizations have learned that they can usually be more cost-effective in shaping agency policy development if they concentrate their efforts on influencing agency rule-making. The rule-making process ideally permits any interested party to present information and arguments for or against a proposed agency rule. Compared with agency adjudicative procedures, rule-making steps are simple and easily understood. For example, after reading the proposed rule in the *Federal Register*, all a party has to do is write or call the contact person at the agency cited along with the proposed rule. The example from the *Federal Register* shown here displays the apparent simplicity and openness of rule-making, naturally making it appealing to the general public, especially since access appears as open to the little person as to corporate giants.

Big money or a high-priced lawyer does not appear to be necessary to influence agency rule-making decisions. This public perspective is true as long as agency decision makers do not play favorites when weighing submitted comments. It should be noted, however, that in reality the average person is very unlikely to read the *Federal Register* or even to be aware of its existence, a fact that works to the advantage of special interests, which pay much more attention to proposed rules published in the *Federal Register*, thus placing themselves in a better position to react to proposed agency rules they oppose.

Nevertheless, on its face, the rule-making process, as contrasted with order-making, seems to embrace the democratic principles of fair play more than agency

---

Federal Register/Vol. 61, No. 65/ Wednesday, April 3, 1996/Proposed Rules

Department of Health and Human Services
21 CFR Parts 71, 170, and 171

Substances Approved for Use in the Preparation of Meat and Poultry Products; Reopening of Comment Period

AGENCY: Food and Drug Administration, HHS.

ACTION: Proposed rule; reopening of comment period.

SUMMARY: The Food and Drug Administration (FDA) is reopening for 60 days the comment period for a proposed rule that appeared in the **Federal Register** of December 29, 1995 to amend FDA's regulations governing the review of petitions for the approval of food and color additives and substances generally recognized as safe (GRAS) to provide for joint review of such petitions by the Food Safety and Inspection Service (FSIS), U.S. Department of Agriculture (USDA), when meat or poultry product uses are proposed. The closing date for submission of comments was March 14, 1996. This action is being taken in response to a request for additional time to answer comments.

DATES: Written comments by June 3, 1996.

ADDRESSES: Submit written comments to the Dockets Management Branch (HFA-305), Food and Drug Administration, 12420 Parklawn Dr., Rm. 1–23, Rockville, MD 20857.

FOR FURTHER INFORMATION CONTACT: George H. Pauli, Center for Food Safety and Applied Nutrition (HFS-200), Food and Drug Administration, 200 C St. SW., Washington, DC 20204, 202-418-3090.

---

adjudication. Rule-making is comprehensible, relatively quick, and democratically accountable, especially in the sense that decision making is kept aboveboard and equal access is provided to all. As Professor Estreicher asserted while making his plea for the use of the rule-making process at the NLRB: "Rulemaking ensures a level of public participation in the policymaking process not currently available. The opportunity for public participation is automatic with each notice of rule-making, and open to all concerned."[9] Pluralist interests are fairly represented also. Despite political interest group realities that suggest otherwise, the general public is probably correct in assuming that public policies are more fairly promulgated through rule-making than order-making and that their interests will probable be best represented by agency rule-making.

Agency Officials.   It is difficult to state generally whether most agencies prefer rule-making or order-making for formulating agency policies. From the perspective of agency officials, there are obvious advantages and disadvantages of each approach. Rule-making allows agencies to propose and implement rules rather quickly; yet only under ideal circumstances is the process free from headaches for agency rule-makers. If the proposed rules are significant or controversial, agency administrators can expect vehement commentary protests from interests in their environment, some of which are very powerful and influential. Despite the total discretionary power of agency officials to consider or ignore submitted comments, agency leaders are always fearful of powerful protests to proposed agency actions that might jeopardize the stability and welfare of their agency.

Agency officials also see the difficulty of promulgating general policies through rule-making that will be fair to all affected parties. One chief advantage to rule-making, as contrasted with agency adjudication, is that it is quite cost-effective in the sense that it allows an agency to make efficient use of its limited resources, since blanket rules are made that can be applied, for example, industrywide to resolve many questions all at once.

Because of the inequities inevitably involved in the promulgation and implementation of general policies, some agencies have preferred to use adjudication or the case-by-case approach. On the whole, this approach provides agency administrators with more flexibility and thus the potential to avoid unnecessary and disruptive regulatory battles. The adjudicative process allows agency officials to assess the entire regulatory picture and to focus on specific problems they perceive as most troublesome. This is especially true if agencies possess the statutory authority to initiate cases. Agency administrators may also prefer the adjudicative approach because it allows them greater flexibility in reversing previous policy directions quickly, without having to advertise and defend their new policy decisions before all interested parties. As mentioned earlier, the courts are more tolerant of agencies reversing previous orders than they are of sudden agency rule reversals.

Agency administrators may also prefer the order-making approach over rule-making because they might be undecided on just what course of regulatory action to take. By proceeding by the case-by-case approach, agency decision makers have the flexibility of cautiously building regulatory policies at the same time when insufficient data and technical knowledge should rightfully preclude risky, comprehensive policy stands.

In reality, because circumstances differ significantly from one agency to another, the reasons for one agency's preferring rule-making over order-making vary greatly. But systems theory does suggest that agency administrators would not only evaluate their choice of policy-making tools on the basis of perceived short- and long-range consequences but also consider which approach appears to be politically best. Since systems theorists maintain that agency survival needs must be considered first, the chances are good that agency officials will normally prefer the policy-making method that can best help them reach their statutory obligations without jeopardizing agency stability or causing any unnecessary headaches.

SERVING DUE PROCESS IN AGENCY HEARINGS

Earlier comments in this chapter on the difficulty of differentiating rule-making from order-making should not be interpreted to mean that it is never obvious which function is being performed by an administrative agency. When an agency is required by statute to hold a full hearing under specified conditions, the APA outlines how the hearing should be conducted. Section 554 of the act, "Adjudications," simply sets forth steps and features to be included in formal order-making (that is, in a fair hearing). Each year federal agencies conduct literally millions of hearings, with the Social Security Administration alone conducting 1.2 million, although well over 90 percent are not elaborate formal hearings. If state agencies are included, we can say that public agencies conduct many millions of cases each year.[10] The agency hearing, even a formal hearing, is not expected to be a copy of a formal trial, but hearings should reflect basic court procedures. One fundamental reason for this is that the courts have found that it is easier to review legal points and procedures if the agency hearing process closely resembles actual court proceedings. Judges have found it difficult to review the fairness of hearing procedures when hearings have been "too informal."

Hearings should be conducted in such a way that due process is served. Because administrative agencies decide questions that may place heavy financial or personal hardships on persons who might lose, agency hearings are expected to uphold constitutional principles of fair play by not denying anyone freedoms, rights, or property without due process of law. Although due process is mentioned in the Constitution, it is not defined. But over the years the term has been given some meaning by legislatures and courts, although no clear meaning has been reached. In *Snyder* v. *Commonwealth of Massachusetts,* 54 S.Ct. 330 (1934), the Court held that due process should meet standards of "fundamental fairness"; in *Rochin* v. *California,* 342 U.S. 165 (1952), the Court argued that any governmental activity that is "shocking to the conscience" contradicts due process, or, as Edwin W. Tucker noted, "The constraints of due process are generally shaped by the contemporary collective intuitive sense of what is right and what is wrong."[11] More recently, the Supreme Court in *Cleveland Board of Education* v. *Loudermill,* 105 S.Ct. 1487, 1493 (1985), stated: "The point is straightforward: the Due Process Clause provides that certain substantive rights—life, liberty, and property—cannot be deprived except pursuant to constitutionally adequate procedures. The categories of substance and procedure are distinct. Were the rule otherwise, the Clause would be reduced to a mere tautology." The *Loudermill* decision makes clear that once "certain substantive rights" are granted by the legislature, they become "property interests" that cannot be taken away unless minimum due process procedures are employed. Consequently, since Congress and state legislatures have been granting persons more and more legal entitlements or property interests under law, we can expect to see in the future the granting of more hearings to persons, extending to them at least the minimum due process protections.[12] On the other hand the Supreme Court has held emphatically that *only* administrative or procedural due process (a step down from more elaborate constitutional due process protections) need to be provided when property rights are not at stake. In *Board of Curators* v. *Horowitz,* 435 U.S. 78 (1978) and *Pension Benefit Guar. Corp.* v. *L.T.V. Corp.,* 110 S.Ct. 2668 (1990), the Court ruled that due process in the form of normal adjudications was not required because property interests were not involved. Thus, in administrative law the meaning of due process shifts with the kinds of interests at stake. Administrative agencies must be certain about the interests at stake so that they can extend to persons the appropriate due process procedures.

In an attempt to achieve due process in agency hearings, the major provisions of the APA require agencies to: (1) provide appropriate persons proper notice as to the "time, place, and nature of the hearing," "the legal authority and jurisdiction under which the hearing is to be held," and "the matters of fact and law asserted"; (2) take into consideration "the convenience and necessity of the parties or their representatives" when scheduling the time and place of the hearing; (3) afford all concerned parties (normally limited to litigants in the dispute) the opportunity to submit and consider all relevant facts, arguments, and proposed settlements or adjustments as time and public interest may permit; and (4) forbid agency employees who have acted as investigators or prosecutors in a case to participate in a hearing decision, except as counsel or a witness in the public proceeding. In addition to these provisions, sections subsequent to 554 strengthen the effort to achieve a fair hearing by legally obligating agencies to: (1) allow persons in hearings to be represented by counsel; (2) conclude hearing business "within a reasonable time"; (3) promptly inform interested parties as to the action taken or intended and, in the case of denied requests, the reason why the request was denied; (4) arrive at decisions, rules, or orders in light of the "whole record" or part of the record which is based on "substantial evidence"; (5) provide unbiased and quasi-independent administrative law judges (formerly known as hearing examiners), who can reach decisions fairly and impartially; (6) permit persons to dispute and challenge agency evidence and opinions by providing adequate time and opportunity for persons to present conflicting data, conduct cross-examination, and so on, "as may be required for a full and true disclosure of the facts"; (7) keep a complete transcript of the hearing proceedings to constitute the "exclusive record," or reviewable basis for decision; (8) state and substantiate in the record all findings and conclusions; (9) provide for within-agency appeal; and (10) permit and prepare for judicial review of agency actions.

A few relevant cases put contextual meaning and life into the statutory prescriptions of how public agencies ought to perform and dramatize the importance of administrative due process in the making of public policies through order-making. *Morgan* v. *United States,* 304 U.S. 1 (1938), is a classic administrative law case that focuses on some fundamental requisites that should be included in any fair hearing process. The judicial wisdom displayed in the case was influential in shaping the 1946 APA. The appellant, Morgan, a stockyard operator, argued in this case that the secretary of agriculture had set the maximum rate he could charge in his business without due process of law. The Packers and Stockyards Act of 1921 extended to the secretary of agriculture the power to "determine and prescribe" maximum and reasonable rate charges, but only after a "full hearing." Because Congress realized that it was granting the secretary vast discretionary powers, which could be abused by irresponsible secretaries, the Congress emphasized its intention that rates should never be imposed on stockyard operators without the benefit of a fair hearing. Morgan charged that: (1) the secretary's decision was made behind closed doors; (2) Morgan was not given proper notice; (3) specific charges were not made against him; (4) he was not given reasonable time to respond to the general charges made against him; (5) he was never able to see and examine agency evidence to be used against him; (6) he was not allowed to see and make a rebuttal to the department's findings and conclusions; and (7) he was denied an appeal or rehearing within the agency. Originally, Morgan appealed the secretary's order to the district court, which refused to hear the complaint. Morgan then appealed to the Supreme Court. Chief Justice Charles Evans Hughes, speaking for the majority, reversed the district court's decree and declared invalid the secretary's order, arguing that his decision could not stand "as the hearing was fatally defective" on several grounds (at 22).

In the first place, the Court held that administrative agencies must respect and uphold specific directions and intentions of Congress when executing congressional policies if liberty is to be retained:

> The vast expansion of this field of administrative regulation in response to the pressure of social needs is made possible under our system by adherence to the basic principles that the Legislature shall appropriately determine the standards of administrative action and that in administrative proceedings of a quasi-judicial character the liberty and property of the citizen shall be protected by the rudimentary requirements of fair play. These demand 'a fair and open hearing,' essentially alike to the legal validity of the administrative regulation and to the maintenance of public confidence in the value and soundness of this important governmental process. Such a hearing has been described as an "inexorable safeguard" (at 15).

The Court elaborated further on the nature of a fair hearing:

> The right to a hearing embraces not only the right to present evidence, but also a reasonable opportunity to know the claims of the opposing party and to meet them. The right to submit argument implies that opportunity; otherwise the right may be but a barren one. Those who are brought into contest with the Government in a quasi-judicial proceeding aimed at the control of their activities are entitled to be fairly advised of what the government proposes and to be heard upon its proposals before it issues its final command (at 18).

The Court was particularly disturbed by the secretary's choice to accept and make "as his own the findings which have been prepared by the active prosecutors for the Government, after an *ex parte* discussion with them and without according any reasonable opportunity to the respondents in the proceedings to know the claims thus presented and to contest them. That is more than an irregularity in practice; it is a vital defect" (at 22).

It is important to emphasize that due process entitles parties only to an *opportunity* to be heard, but it does not require a hearing to be held if the right to a hearing is waived.

In *Reno* v. *Flores,* 113 S.Ct. 1949, 1450–51 (1993), the Supreme Court, in rejecting the claim that automatic review should be provided in deportation cases, held that "[D]ue process is satisfied by giving the detained alien juveniles the *right* to a hearing before an immigration judge" even if the hearing does not take place because the right is waived.

In sum, although in America the meaning of due process has remained relatively stable over time, unquestionably what constitutes precisely due process in, say, agency hearings at a given point in our history depends upon a lot of things. In posing the question, "what process is due," Supreme Court Justices, Souter, White, O'Connor, and Rehnquist, dissenting in *Burns* v. *U.S.,* 111 S.Ct. 2182, 2192 (1991), quoted cases to make this point. "Due Process unlike some legal rules, is not a technical conception with a fixed content unrelated to time, place, and circumstances, . . . but is 'flexible (calling for such procedural protections as the particular situation demands.'" In a sociopolitical context, the meaning of due process in general, but in agency adjudications specifically, changes with our political moods as we shift back and forth from relative conservativism to relative liberalism.[13]

ADMINISTRATIVE HEARINGS VERSUS COURT TRIALS

Overview

The agency hearing process is usually less elaborate or formal than typical court trials. Since parties may suffer substantial losses if they come out on the short end of agency hearings, adjudicative procedures must be elaborate enough to protect persons from blatant or gross denials of due process. However, since only administrative law matters are the subject of agency hearings (for example, license renewals or rate adjustments), it has been commonly argued that agency adjudicative procedures need not approach the rigorous and complex procedures demanded in court trials, in which the litigants may have much to lose. Of course, in criminal cases defendants sometimes literally have their lives at stake. Due process procedures in such cases, especially in a nation that cherishes human rights doctrines, are expected to be quite elaborate.

In fact, some observers have argued that many agency disputes involve privileges, not rights, and that the adjudicative procedures should therefore be informal, if granted at all. These critics think it is highly questionable whether hearings should be granted by agencies at all, since persons are not legally entitled to something if only privilege is in question. They feel that an agency is only being generous when it grants a hearing to a party who has a dispute involving a privilege.

However, because agencies could avoid confrontations with parties by regarding the matter in question as a privilege instead of a right, thus escaping the obligation of holding an inconvenient and time-consuming hearing, the courts in the past few decades have been placing an increasing number of areas of controversy in the rights category to protect persons against possible agency abuses. In *Goldberg* v.

Kelly, 397 U.S. 254 (1970), the Supreme Court flatly rejected the value of the rights-privileges distinction, arguing essentially that the right to a hearing should depend not so much on whether the claim is considered a right or a privilege, but on the extent to which a person might be expected to suffer a "grievous loss."

Hearings can be more or less formal, but most agency adjudications are quite informal, frequently amounting to nothing more than discussions involving the concerned parties, which lead to a mutually acceptable settlement. However, to protect those involved, Congress has required minimum due process procedures. Specifically, the Administrative Procedure Act, the most rudimentary law governing administrative procedure, has set forth basic uniform standards that must be followed by agency administrators when conducting hearings. Not only has Congress, through various statutes, compelled agency administrators to honor certain procedural safeguards in adjudications, but pressures to comply with the principles of due process have also come from constitutional provisions, especially the Fifth and Fourteenth Amendments, as well as from the public, the media, the regulated, the courts, and even the agencies themselves. Some of the strictest rules to ensure fundamental fairness in agency adjudications stem from agency rules and regulations governing procedure.

Even so, many agencies have not done a very good job in ensuring that parties in disputes are accorded fair treatment in agency hearings. Some agencies, according to the court, have been content to allow adjudicative procedures that, even in the light of the existence of APA requirements, "are shocking to the conscience" (*Rochin* v. *California,* 342 U.S. 165 [1952]). As a result, the courts in recent decades have tried to ensure reasonable fairness in agency adjudications by imposing their collective will on agency administrators. In *John R. Gagnon* v. *Gerald H. Scarpelli,* 411 U.S. 788 (1973), a precedential case, the Supreme Court outlined what it believed should constitute *minimum* due process standards, especially in cases in which severe penalties may be attached to a decision (for example, a revocation of probation resulting in return to prison). In the *Goldberg* case the Supreme Court tried to place into perspective the weights that should be assigned to the obligation of the agency to extend procedural due process to "clients" versus agency needs to reduce the demands on its limited resources. Although it appears that the Supreme Court would apply the principle more broadly, at least in the context of welfare claimants, the Court held: "Thus, the interest of the eligible recipient in uninterrupted receipt of public assistance, coupled with the State's interest that his payments not be erroneously terminated, clearly outweighs the State's competing concern to prevent any increase in its fiscal and administrative burdens" (at 266). But three years later, in *Gagnon,* the Court felt that some procedural protections (for example, the agency's having to provide counsel to a party) go beyond minimum due process entitlements and tend to place a heavy burden on the limited resources of a public agency and that such procedural safeguards therefore need not always be granted.

In 1976 in *Mathews* v. *Eldridge,* 424 U.S. 319, the Supreme Court created a three-point analysis test that it felt should be used to determine what due process procedures should be extended to parties under various circumstances.

First, the private interest that will be affected by the official action; second, the risk of an erroneous deprivation of such interest through the procedures used, and the probable value, if any, of additional or substitute procedural safeguards; and finally, the Government's interest, including the function involved and the fiscal and administrative burdens that the additional or substitute procedural requirement would entail (at 335).

This three-pronged test demands that agency administrators take a practical approach to agency hearings, realizing that providing certain due process procedures may cost far more than they are really worth.

This cost-conscious approach to due process in agency hearings has survived into the 1990s.[14] In *Cleveland Board of Education* v. *Loudermill,* 105 S.Ct. 1487 (1985), the Court argued that once a property right is granted, the state has the legal obligation to protect it by extending "some kind of hearing" (i.e., at least minimum due process procedures that need not be very elaborate or expensive). In this particular situation the Court held that allowing the employee at least the opportunity to respond to charges against him in a pre-termination hearing ". . . would impose neither a significant administrative burden nor intolerable delays" (at 1495). In 1991 in *Burns* v. *U.S.,* 111 S.Ct. 2182, it was noted that the *Mathews* approach to the application of due process is still applied—and very broadly: "Although *Mathews* itself concerned the adequacy of administrative fact-finding procedures, we have not confined the *Mathews* approach to administrative contexts. . . . The *Mathews* analysis has thus been used as a general approach for determining the procedures required by due process whenever erroneous governmental action would infringe [on] an individual's protected interest . . ." (at 2192–2193).

The cost-conscious standards espoused by the Court in *Mathews* have unquestionably caused agency administrators to avoid having to provide elaborate hearing procedures or trial-like procedures where they felt they could get away with it. However, over the past two decades or so, as noted, legislative bodies and the courts at the national and state levels have conferred upon persons certain due process rights that they once did not have. This extension of rights, frequently making statutory entitlements property rights, has legally obligated administrators to resolve conflicts involving such rights through elaborate due process hearings. Even applying the cost-reduction analysis recommended in *Mathews,* it cannot be ignored that the Court in *Mathews,* in two of the three points in its three-point analysis test, stressed that the interest at stake must be considered along with the procedural impact upon that interest. Since the interests at stake are now frequently property interests, elaborate trial-like procedures are often granted by administrators to protect them.

Also, judges have often urged administrators to make many hearings more trial-like for selfish reasons. Judges have contended that sensible judicial review of administrative hearings cannot occur if agency hearing procedures fail even to resemble court trials. Judges have maintained that it is next to impossible to determine whether proper due process procedures have been extended in a hearing if no reasonable procedural structure is followed.

Should Agency Hearings Be More Trial-Like?

There is strong reason to suspect that despite the problems associated with the varied interpretations and applications of due process in agency adjudications, it probably would be wise not to formalize the agency hearing process too much. In many respects, the argument that agency adjudicative procedures should become more formalized or more trial-like makes only limited sense. If agency hearing procedures were made more trial-like, judicial review of hearings actions would be facilitated simply because all procedures leading to agency rulings would be clearly spelled out for the reviewing judges to see. However, the costs of achieving due process in this kind of agency adjudication may be too high, especially when there is no significant evidence to suggest that very many parties participating in administrative hearings are denied fair treatment.

In the precedential case, *Mathews* v. *Eldridge,* 424 U.S. 319 (1976), the Court reflected on the practical costs of extending hearing rights, especially in making hearing procedures trial-like. The Court noted:

> Financial cost alone is not a controlling weight in determining whether due process requires a particular procedural safeguard prior to some administrative decision. But the Government's interest, and hence that of the public, in conserving scarce fiscal and administrative resources is a factor that must be weighed. At some point the benefit of an additional safeguard to the individual affected by the administrative action and to society in terms of increased assurance that the action is just, may be outweighed by the cost. . . . The ultimate balance involves a determination as to when, under our constitutional system, judicial-type procedures must be imposed upon administrative action to assure fairness. . . . The judicial model of an evidentiary hearing is neither a required, nor even the most effective, method of decisionmaking in all circumstances. The essence of due process is the requirement that "a person in jeopardy of serious loss (be given) notice of the case against him and opportunity to meet it" (at 348).

Professor Todd Rakoff contends that essentially three models have been used to determine what sort of due process is due in agency hearings.[15] The first model or approach basically requires that administrators provide "some kind of hearing" procedures that minimally satisfy due process requirements as mandated by legislation. That is, administrators employ the minimum process due hearing rights and then ask: "What's wrong with this? Do we need to provide anything else or are these procedures O.K.?" The second model starts from the opposite position and assumes that due process can be obtained only in trial-type hearings which employ the adversary approach. This model poses the question: "Is there justification for departing from a trial-type hearing in deciding the matter?" The third model, adopted by the Supreme Court in *Brock* v. *Roadway Express, Inc.,* 107 S.Ct. 1740 (1987), applies an unacceptable risk standard, which asks: "Are the procedures used so out of line that due process will be subjected to unacceptable risks," or in the Court's language ". . . contain an unacceptable risk of erroneous decision?" (at 1749).[16]

This unacceptable risk standard is the new applicable standard and, when applied, would rarely require that administrators must provide trial-like hearing procedures even when property or liberty interests are at risk. At this point in the 1990s, the Court's position is that trial-type hearings should normally not be granted, balancing the interests of the state against property interests, unless they are absolutely sanctioned by specific statutory provisions. Ultimately, due process is protected by making agency hearing procedures subject to judicial review.[17]

Some have argued that the Supreme Court since *Goldberg* has gone too far to reduce the procedural protections in agency hearings. Certainly, the High Court's decisions starting with *Mathews* have made it much easier for agency administrators to avoid having to provide elaborate trial-type hearings. But is this necessarily the wrong course to take? The plain truth is that administrative hearings should not be expected to provide formal, court-like procedural protections to litigious parties because administrative agencies are not supposed to act like courts. The sole function of courts is to hear and decide controversies. This is their only constitutional obligation. On the other hand, the primary role of an administrative agency is to see to it that legislative statutes are faithfully executed. Agencies are not courts of law, and to expect that they should function like courts is to expect too much from the administrative system. It should be understood that lawmakers decided in the 1940s to require agencies to provide hearings so that affected parties could question the procedural soundness and fairness of agency actions. Such a legislative measure was taken to help ensure administrative accountability, but clearly legislators never intended to turn administrative agencies into trial courts.

Agency versus Court Compassion

Despite the less elaborate due process standards of typical administrative adjudication compared with court trials, some critics believe that persons stand a better chance of receiving fairer, more compassionate treatment from administrative agencies than from courts. According to Victor A. Thompson, this is so because administrative agencies have the luxury of being able to make more "particularistic," as contrasted to "universalistic," decisions than the courts. Therefore, Thompson concludes, administrative agencies tend on the whole to be more compassionate toward individual parties than do the courts. In explanation, Thompson notes:

> A belief persists that an individual can get personalized, compassionate treatment in the courts if it is denied to him by the bureaucracy. Although the belief seems plausible because of the large amount of time and money spent by courts on individual cases, it is not well-founded. In the first place, court treatment is so expensive and time-consuming that most people forego it. Bad as it is, an administrative appeal, or a letter to a congressman, and especially the latter, gives the average individual a better chance of success.[18]

Thompson argues that judges, unlike public administrators, feel compelled to make universalistic decisions or decisions that largely ignore or sacrifice the individual for the sake of upholding the law:

More important is the fact courts are institutionalized to seek the general principle in the individual case. Justice is blind. The individual is unimportant; only the principle counts. One of the hardest lessons for a young law student to learn is that he must give up his natural, compassionate interest in the outcome and dispositions for the actual persons involved in the cases he studies and that he must concentrate solely on the principle of the law involved.[19]

Therefore, Thompson reasons, "Since courts are staffed with law students grown older and professionally successful, courts are among our least compassionate institutions. They rule by deduction from general principles. . . . Decision by deduction from rules is the least compassionate kind there is."[20] Thompson does not deny that administrative agencies also make impersonal, insensitive, universalistic decisions that are patently unfair to individuals, but he does suggest that due process, when measured in terms of compassion instead of the degree of procedural formality alone, is less likely to be experienced in the courts.

Professors Ernest Gellhorn and Ronald M. Levin argue an opposing view. In sharp contrast, they contend that court decisions are "essentially personal." They hold that agency decisions are bureaucratized because they are "institutional decisions" made by technical experts or bureaucrats way down in the hierarchy where power has been "subdelegated" to them. They maintain that the impersonal adjudicative decision tends to serve the bureaucracy more than the individual because ". . . it is the product of a bureaucracy rather than of a single person or a group of identifiable people."[21]

A survey of Administrative Law Judges (ALJs) reported in 1994 in the *Administrative Law Review* tends to support Gellhorn and Levin's view. Respondents answered that trial judges make more personal decisions affecting a "person or a few people," while ALJs make decisions which usually affect "many people" and are "national in scope."[22]

In summary, court trial procedures are more elaborate than those normally employed in agency hearings, but one should not necessarily conclude from this that court trials are more apt to reflect the principles of fundamental fairness than are agency hearings. But the most important point to reiterate is that administrative agencies are not supposed to function like courts. The chief task of an agency is to administer public policies. Also, agencies are required by statute to handle and resolve many disputes daily. Also, unlike courts, they do not have the luxury of being able to reject cases. As a result, agencies must routinely resolve disputes while attending to their administrative tasks. Thus, agency administrators are frequently forced to forego elaborate hearings for the sake of administrative expediency. Given the limited human and financial resources characteristic of virtually all governmental agencies in the 1990s, as well as the much publicized failure of our federal government to curb the runaway budget deficit successfully, it is reasonable to assume that Congress does not realistically expect anything else. These realities should be kept in mind in the next few sections, which focus on specific features that characterize administrative adjudications, especially formal hearings.

BIAS, DUE PROCESS, AND REGULATORY EFFECTIVENESS

Administrative Law Judges: The Independence Issue

There are critics who are concerned over the apparent lack of independence of ALJs from agency control and political influence, yet others play down the independence problems as not serious. These defenders of the present regulatory system stress the importance of maintaining an agency adjudicative system that provides for fair hearings, yet simultaneously does not seriously undermine the effectiveness of the regulatory process. Norman Abrams, for example, voices concern about agency influences that might unfairly bias an ALJ's judgment, but nonetheless he understands why an agency would not want to see hearings conducted by adjudicators who are oblivious and insensitive to agency policies, "goals, special regulatory problems, and political considerations." He asks: "Is this inconsistent with the notion of an independent hearing officer?"[23] Also sympathetic to the real problems that agencies face in their efforts to regulate fairly and effectively, Kenneth C. Davis argues especially that the independence of ALJs helps to serve the promotion of objectivity and fairness in agency adjudications, but independence should not be so extreme that it frustrates the policy-making efforts of agency administrators.[24]

It should be understood that administrative agencies, boards, and commissions are not politically neutral institutions. Their leaders are political appointees and they serve, to a greater or lesser extent, political causes. Eleanor M. Fox acknowledges the political nature of agency adjudications in her study of two very different political personalities who chaired the Federal Trade Commission: Michael Pertschuk and James C. Miller, III. Chairman Pertschuk, President Carter's appointee and a liberal who tended to side with the underdog and believed that government should do its best to protect individuals from abuse, especially from big business, reached decisions in agency adjudications that reflected clearly his philosophical perspective. Chairman Miller, on the other hand, was President Reagan's appointee and a conservative who sided with the successful, believed that government tended to be the enemy of big business, and felt that governmental intrusion in the private sector tends only to protect the inefficient and weaken society. Chairman Miller's decisions also reflected his predispositions. "At every turn, Mr. Miller drew the inference against the intervention and Mr. Pertschuk drew the inference for it."[25] Regardless of the facts, Fox concluded, ". . . one sees what one is predisposed to see."[26] Commenting on the value of her own research, she noted: "An understanding of the political nature of the FTC chairmanship helps the student of judicial decisionmaking to pierce the myth of the neutral judge applying economic principles dispassionately."[27] It is important to stress that Fox's study serves to acknowledge the political realities of agency decision makers, even those serving in a quasi-judicial capacity. She, in actuality, did not condemn the fact that these men let their political philosophies guide them in their jurisprudential role.[28] Possibly Bernard Schwartz summarizes the bias of the prejudgment situation best: "If freedom from bias is taken in the broad dictionary sense of absence of preconceptions, no one can ever have a fair trial. The judicial mind is no blank piece of paper; the judge or administrative adjudication starts with inevitable preconceptions. In this sense there is a prejudgment in every case."[29]

Obviously, then, the practical legal question is: How independent should hearing officers be from agency politics, philosophical orientations, outside political pressures, and any other potentially prejudicial influences, if agencies are to provide hearings that are "fair enough"? Predispositions should not bias hearing decisions to such an extent that a mockery is made of due process. To Norman Abrams, for an agency to conduct a reasonably fair hearing, only sufficient impartiality and fairmindedness should prevail, but not so much that ALJs must separate themselves from agency policy positions or their political ideas.[30] This viewpoint is upheld in a famous bias case, *American Cyanamid* v. *F.T.C.*, 363 F.2d 757 (1966), in which the court ruled that hearing officers should not be disqualified simply because they express strong attachment to agency policies. In *Rombough* v. *F.A.A.*, 594 F.2d 893 (2nd Cir; 1979), the court held that it is not inappropriate for agency officials to make hearing decisions that are simply consistent with state agency policy positions. In a more recent case, *Alma* v. *United States,* 744 F.Supp. 1546 (S.D. G.A.; 1990), the court argued that a hearing official should not normally be disqualified from hearing a case even though the official publicly stated his or her position on the issues.[31]

Closed Mind Rule

The courts have generally been guided by the "closed mind" rule in bias or prejudgment cases. To prevail before the court the petitioner must prove through "clear and convincing evidence" that the adjudicator has ". . . an irrevocably closed mind on matters critical to the disposition of the proceedings" (*Housing Study Group* v. *Kemp,* 736 F.Supp. 321, 332 [D.D.C.; 1990]). For example, in *Northwestern Bell Telephone* v. *Stofferahn,* 461 N.W.2d 129, 131 (1990), the South Dakota Supreme Court held that a public utility commissioner should have recused himself because "clear and convincing evidence" showed that he had an "unalterably closed mind." This commission had previously been ". . . a zealous and active opponent of the deregulation legislation . . ." under question and South Dakota law provides that "[N]o commissioner shall participate in any hearing or proceeding in which he has any conflict of interest . . ." (S.D.C.L., Sec. 49–1–9; 1983).

Prejudgment of Legislative versus Adjudicative Facts

In deciding bias or prejudgment cases, courts often make a distinction between prejudgment of *legislative facts* and prejudgment of *adjudicative facts.* Legislative facts are general facts pertaining to law or public policy that help officials at the hearing understand the content of the policy or law. Legislative facts have a general and future orientation since disputes involving legislative facts often focus on the likely impact of certain policies. Normally, courts will not rule that hearing examiners or ALJs should have to disqualify or recuse themselves simply because they have taken or prejudged a prior position on laws, policies, or legislative facts unless, as mentioned, the prejudgment is so severe that it is certain that the adjudicator has an "irrevocably closed mind." Thus, the standard for disqualifying hearing officers who have prejudged legislative facts is not tough because it is assumed that virtually all adjudicators, as public officials, have expressed opinions on public policies.

One of the most famous cases involving prejudgment of legislative facts is *Federal Trade Commission* v. *Cement Institute,* 333 U.S. 683 (1948). In this case the Supreme Court did not feel that the commissioners on the FTC had to have disqualified themselves simply because they had clearly expressed grave doubts about the legality of the Cement Institute's pricing scheme prior to a hearing before the FTC. The Court opined that due process was not violated, because the Cement Institute was afforded the opportunity to defend its pricing system before the FTC's commissioners, who did not necessarily have an "irrevocably closed mind" on the pricing method (at 701). In *Stofferahn,* involving prejudgment of legislative facts, the Court upheld standards for determining bias as established in *Cement Institute,* but clear and convincing evidence showed that this particular commissioner has "an unalterably closed mind."

In cases involving alleged prejudgment of adjudicative facts, however, courts have generally applied a much tougher standard to ensure due process. Adjudicative facts, in contrast to legislative facts, do not pertain to general policy-oriented facts, but to the more specific facts in a particular dispute relating to the "who, what, where, and how" questions. Adjudicative facts are the kind of particular and immediate facts that judges and jurors decide (e.g., Did television station KZZZ-TV violate FCC Rule XX by broadcasting such and such a program on such and such a date?). Of course, prejudgment of adjudicative facts in administrative hearings would virtually guarantee that due process would not be served. As a consequence, courts have usually ruled that hearing officials must be disqualified if they have prejudged adjudicative facts.

Possibly the most frequently cited case involving the prejudgment of adjudicative facts is *Cinderella Career and Finishing School, Inc.* v. *FTC,* 425 F.2d 583 (D.C. Cir.; 1970). In this case the D.C. Circuit Court argued that Chairman Dixon prejudged not only legislative facts in his public speeches about the finishing school prior to the school's hearing before the FTC but also specific adjudicative facts, precluding any semblance of fair hearing.

In a highly publicized case former baseball star Pete Rose, who was accused of gambling on baseball games including his own team, argued successfully that baseball Commissioner Bart Giamatti had prejudged adjudicative facts by deciding that Rose's involvement in betting on baseball games had occurred. Giamatti had written a favorable letter to a judge or a convicted felon who was to act as an informer against Rose. In the letter Giamatti said he believed that what the informer said about Rose's gambling on games was true. In light of such prejudgment of accusations against Rose (adjudicative facts), the Ohio court ruled that a hearing conducted by Giamatti would deny Rose his procedural due process rights to a fair, unbiased tribunal free from "improper prejudice" (*Giamatti* v. *Rose,* 1989 W.L. 111386, 111447 [Ohio Misc., 1989]).

Personal Bias

Prejudice or personal bias for or against a person by an ALJ or hearing examiner also normally constitutes grounds for disqualification of the adjudicator(s). *Personal bias* (also called *actual bias*) is directed toward the person, not the issue. Personal bias can be established by showing that an adjudicator or adjudicators, possibly the whole administrative tribunal, have expressed a strong personal bias either for or against a party that would make a fair and impartial hearing virtually impossible. For example, personal bias was charged in a Colorado case because a hearing examiner had in the past called the plaintiff's lawyer a "nasty little fellow" and a "smart ass" (*Neopolan U.S.A. Corp* v. *Industrial Claims Appeals Office,* 778 P.2d 312 [Colo. Ct. App; 1989]). Such bias need not be enough to disqualify an adjudicator, however, if a reviewing court believes that otherwise the hearing officer allowed "thoughtful and discriminating evaluation of the facts" (*NLRB* v. *Pittsburgh S.S. Co.,* 337 U.S. 656, 660; 1949). Personal prejudice may also be demonstrated if it can be shown that an adjudicator consistently rules against one side (*NLRB* v. *Miami Coca-Cola Bottling Co.,* 222 F.2d 341 [5th Cir.; 1977]).

Conflict of Interest

Courts have held that hearing proceedings may be biased and violate procedural due process standards when conflicts of interest, *ex parte* contacts, or an appearance of unfairness can be shown. The most blatant conflict of interest can be seen when a hearing official stands to gain or lose something of value personally from the hearing decision. In New Jersey the superior court ruled that a public utility commissioner should have disqualified himself because he had entered into a clear conflict of interest when he had inquired about possible employment with a utility company involved in a hearing in which he was an adjudicator (*In re Bergen Co. Util. Auth.,* 553 A.2d 849, 853 [N.J. Super.; 1989]).

Ex Parte Contacts

Bias or prejudice may also compromise fair hearings as a result of *ex parte* contacts or communications. *Ex parte* contacts tend to undermine procedural due process in agency hearings because they allow a particular party or party's representatives to communicate with hearing officials about adjudicative or legislative facts in the absence of the other parties in the dispute, thus giving the party making the contact an unfair opportunity to influence the adjudicator(s). Such *ex parte* contacts are normally prohibited whether court judges or agency administrators are involved, although *ex parte* contacts are not necessarily prejudicial if matters related to the case were not discussed (*Romey* v. *Landers,* 392 N.W. 2d 415,421 [S.D.; 1986]). Nonetheless, *ex parte* contacts are normally frowned upon because such contacts give the appearance of impropriety.

Appearance of Fairness Doctrine

An old doctrine known as the *appearance of fairness doctrine* is rooted in common law. Although this standard was at first applied to court trials, the Supreme Court of Washington applied the appearance of fairness doctrine to administrative hearings as far back as 1898 in *State ex rel. Barnard* v. *Board of Educ.*, 52 P 317 (Wash; 1898). The appearance of fairness doctrine is made quite clear in *Mordhorst* v. *Egert,* 223 N.W.2d 501, 505 (S.D.; 1974), where the court, quoting a prior case, wrote:

> A fair and impartial tribunal requires at least that the trier of fact be disinterested . . . and that he also be free from any form of bias or predisposition regarding the outcome of the case. . . . Not only must the procedures be fair, "the very appearance of complete fairness" must also be present. These principles apply not only to trials, but equally, if not more so, to administrative proceedings.

But the truth is that courts are very reluctant to require hearing officers to disqualify themselves because of any appearance of bias alone. Plenty of lip service is paid to violations of the appearance of fairness doctrine, but courts are much more likely to enforce this standard when it is coupled with findings of concrete bias.[32]

However, in *1616 Second Ave. Rest* v. *Liquor Auth.,* 550 N.E.2d 910 (N.Y.; 1990), the New York court of appeals held that the chairman of the state Liquor Authority violated Second Avenue Restaurant's due process rights by failing to disqualify himself after making public statements against the restaurant, thus giving the "appearance of impropriety" that any "disinterested observer" (a popular standard applied by the court) could readily see. Judge Wachtler wrote:

> But whether or not he had actually prejudged the matter, his statements nonetheless gave the impression that he had, and that impression lent an impermissible air of unfairness to the proceeding. More importantly, those statements and the message they conveyed to a "disinterested observer" established the Chairman's public position on the issue (at 913).[33]

Despite the fact that Judge Wachtler wrote for the majority in this case, Judges Simons, Alexander, and Hancock, writing in dissent, probably reflect better the opinion of most courts today when they held that simply an appearance of impropriety due to alleged bias is not sufficient to justify disqualification; existing law requires, quoting from *Matter of Warder* v. *Board of Regents,* 53 N.Y.2d 186 (1981), a "factual demonstration to support the allegation of bias and proof that the outcome flowed from it" (at 914).

Combination of Functions

One other major source of possible bias is from hearing officials who perform a combination of functions. A combination of functions occurs when an administrative agency allows a hearing official or body to perform not only the adjudicatory function but also the investigatory and possibly even the prosecutory function.[34] According to Stephen R. Miller and Larry T. Richardson, "[T]his practice compromises the objectivity of the administrative inquiry, favoring the interests of the agency."[35] They contend further that the "combination of functions is the most obvious source of bias in administrative hearings."[36] Critics, as well as many courts, have argued that combining the investigatory, prosecutory, and adjudicatory functions in the same hearing official or body present a blatant conflict of interest, violating the appearance of fairness principle, and, of course, procedural due process. Realizing the procedural due process problems presented by the combination of functions problem, many agencies have in good faith tried to separate the investigatory, prosecutory, and adjudicatory roles within their agencies, but some observers charge that this still is not enough to save due process in agency hearings. The reality is, these critics assert, that all these functions are being performed by the same agency's personnel, leading the public to believe that agency officials are working together in a biased manner.

Technically, the federal Administrative Procedure Act, Section 554(d), as well as many state APAs, prohibit agency hearing officials (decision makers) from also serving in a prosecutory and investigatory role. However, Section 554(d), as well as the section's counterpart in most state APAs, applies only to certain formal hearings, thus allowing the combination of functions to be practiced when formal hearing procedures do not have to be observed, which, of course, accounts for most agency hearings.

Today, although combination of functions practices are apparently condemned by most legal scholars and practitioners, the courts have generally not ruled against the use of combination of functions in agency hearings for mostly practical reasons. Courts have normally been sympathetic to agency administrators who have argued that separating functions is costly because it (1) prevents hearing officers from consulting with those who are the most knowledgeable about the case (i.e., those who participated in the investigation); (2) forces the use of more staff to handle cases; (3) causes confusion over what communications among staff are permissible; (4) delays hearing officials from hearing and disposing of cases rapidly; and (5) defies overall practical considerations of administrative efficiency and effectiveness.

In reviewing *In re Deming,* 108 Wash.2d 82 (1987), Stephen Hobbs concluded that one of the reasons that the Washington supreme court applied the "weaker" appearance of fairness doctrine to rule that due process was not violated by the state's Judicial Qualifications Commission when it combined investigatory, prosecutory, and adjudicatory powers was because practical administrative factors had to be weighed, specifically, a ruling against the commission would require a basic and costly restructuring of the Commission.[37]

A petitioner must overcome not only concerns of administrative practicality to prevail in a combination of functions charge, but also the presumption of honesty and integrity. In other words, the petitioner must overcome the presumption that professional and honest administrators cannot serve due process even if they combine functions.

Rule of Necessity

A controversial doctrine related directly to bias or prejudice cases is the *rule of necessity*. The rule of necessity, based in common law, is controversial because the doctrine appears blatantly to defy common sense. It precludes the disqualification of a hearing examiner, even though the adjudicator may in fact be biased, because no one else is eligible to hear the case. The rule of necessity applies to a single hearing official or an entire administrative tribunal. To many critics, denying due process to a party in an agency hearing this way is wrong, and it certainly points to a problem within the administrative law system. Does it make sense to say "Allowing such bias is clearly unfair and will very likely deny the party procedural due process, but let's do it anyway"? To some courts, the rule does make sense and they have not hesitated to apply it. In *Brinkley* v. *Hassig,* 83 F.2d 351 (10th Cir.; 1936), the court reasoned that when disqualification means that no tribunal will be eligible to hear the case, the public interest must be upheld, even though the individual's rights may be compromised somewhat, by employing the rule of necessity. "From the very necessity of the case has grown the rule that disqualification will not be permitted to destroy the only tribunal with powers in the premises" (at 357).

It is true that the courts do not like to use the rule of necessity, but certain situations apparently give them little choice. Take, for example, the Federal Trade Commission's situation. Joseph E. Edwards contends that the full FTC would probably never be disqualified, despite prevailing prejudice, because no provision in the Federal Trade Commission Act provides for a change in venue.[38] This means that some commissions could be disqualified because of bias (as was Chairman Dixon in the *Cinderella* case), but never the entire FTC. In fact, in *Marquette Cement Mfg. Co.* v. *Federal Trade Commission,* 147 F2d 589 (1945), and *FTC* v. *Cement Institute,* 333 U.S. 683 (1948), the courts said exactly this. In *Cement Institute,* for example, the Court, applying the rule of necessity, concluded: "Had the entire membership of the Commission [been] disqualified in the proceedings against the respondents, this complaint could not have been acted on by the Commission or any other government agencies" (at 701). It appears, then, that possibly the best way to do away with having to use the rule of necessity, which clearly undermines attempts to achieve due process in agency adjudications, is to make legislators provide sensible hearing alternatives when bias becomes an issue.

CONSIDERING EVIDENCE IN AGENCY HEARINGS

Overview: Common Body of Rules of Evidence Apparently Needed

The issues and questions surrounding the case of evidence in reaching decisions in agency hearings are often very technical and contradictory and thus quite confusing, even to legal experts. A major reason for this is that an accepted body of rules of evidence, which would govern all formal administrative hearings, has not made its debut into administrative law just yet. In contrast, in 1975 federal rules of evidence (FRE) were enacted to govern the handling of evidence by federal courts. The FRE provided common rules of evidence that helped to restructure and order the submission and use of evidence. Michael H. Graham, who believes that modified FRE should be used to guide the handling of evidence in agency hearings, contends that FRE have greatly benefitted federal courts and could also benefit agency adjudications. "The enhancement provided by the FRE of predictability and consistency in rulings on admissibility, along with explicit recognition of considerations of waste of time, fosters preparation and orderly conduct of trials."[39] Graham points out that hearings in our federal agencies are somewhat chaotic because they "are governed by more than 280 different sets of regulations controlling the admissibility of evidence."[40] Lack of a common body of rules of evidence also plagues hearings in state agencies. Graham admits that some critics have opposed applying FRE to agency adjudications because they feel that agency proceedings are significantly different from court trials, but he disagrees. "However, the fact is that the FRE apply in federal civil non-jury trials where the need to develop and control an evidentiary record is functionally indistinguishable from the analogous need in administrative adjudications."

Numerous cases have made it clear that a common body of rules of evidence does not apply to administrative hearings at the federal or state level, for example, *Goodridge* v. *Director,* 337 N.E.2d 927 (Mass., 1978); *Manhattan Scene* v. *SLA,* 397 N.Y.S.2d 495 (4th Dept., 1977). *Murphy* v. *Department of Public Welfare,* 480 A.2d 382 (Pa. Commw. Ct., 1984); *IHC Hospitals* v. *Board of Comm'rs,* 108 Idaho 136; 1985; and *Walter N. Yoder and Sons* v. *NLRB,* 754 F.2d 531 (4th Cir., 1985). Agreeing with Graham, Richard J. Pierce maintains that the fact that over 1100 federal ALJs apply 280 different evidentiary rules of evidence has made a mess out of the adjudicatory system. He claims that the ". . . evidentiary procedures now used in agency adjudications vary substantially along a spectrum from no reference to evidentiary rules at all, to hortatory reference to the FRE as a source of guidance, to mandatory incorporation of the FRE."[41] As does Graham, Pierce concludes that steps should be taken to incorporate uniform codes of evidence into agency hearings, but he urges that newly developed standards should not be so rigid that they would prevent adjudicators from employing their discretion to exclude "unreliable evidence."[42] Unreliable evidence pertains mostly to questions involving the reliability of hearsay evidence. Issues surrounding hearsay are discussed later in the chapter.

For public administration, probably the central point regarding evidence is that in a free and open society, evidence employed to justify conclusions in trials or hearings should be gathered, presented, and evaluated in a manner that does not undermine the principles of fair procedure. Focus in the following sections is on how fairly evidence is presented and judged. To provide meaningful insights, once again some comparison are made between procedures employed in administrative adjudications and court trials.

Introduction to Procedural Due Process Issues Concerning Evidence

Both administrative hearings and court trials have as an ideal reaching decisions that are both rational and fair. But how can one determine whether adjudicative findings (findings are decisions rooted in adjudicative facts) are rational and fair? Surely there are no foolproof tests, but common sense can play a significant role in assessing whether adjudicative decisions are based upon reasonable review and use of the facts and whether procedural due process has been accorded to the disputing parties. In *Bean* v. *Unemployment Ins. Comm'n,* 485 A.2d 630 (Me., 1984), the court stated that agency findings do not have to be very detailed or technical, but they must be elaborate enough to explain the basis for the decision. Therefore, it is not enough to summarize findings in a single sentence (*Ship Creek Hydraulic Syndicate* v. *Department of Transportation,* 685 P.2d 715 [Alaska, 1984]) or in statutory language in the absence of relevant facts (*Gibson* v. *Municipal Retirement System,* 683 S.W.2d 882 [Tex. Ct. App., 1985]) or cause a court to inquire into the thinking of agency adjudicators because they based their finding on a record ". . . so bare as to frustrate effective judicial review" (*Community for Creative Non-Violence* v. *Lujan,* 908 F.2d 992, 998 [D.C. Cir., 1990]).

It would be a mistake even to lose sight of the immediate and chief purpose of agency adjudications: to resolve disputes. However, it must also be remembered that in agency hearings where "final decisions" resolve disputes, important public policy decisions are often developed as well. This dual purpose in administrative adjudications undoubtedly causes some ALJs to pay more attention to creating public policies they consider worthwhile than to resolving disputes in the most fair manner. ALJs are cognizant of the reality that agency chiefs can overrule their adjudicative decisions if their decisions rule blatantly contrary to agency policies and goals.

Fairness and rationality in adjudicative proceedings depend not only on the factual quality of the evidence entered into the record but also on how the evidence is actually submitted, employed, and evaluated. Thus, the procedural steps used in employing evidence frequently become the main focal point of critics. Most experts agree that it is not the presentation of evidence by each party per se that is most crucial in allowing any tribunal to reach a fair and rational decision; rather it is providing parties in a dispute with the opportunity to scrutinize and challenge the reliability of the evidence the opposing party presents. Kenneth C. Davis, for example, holds that "the central feature of a trial is not affirmative presentation of evidence by each side; it is the opportunity for each side to attack the evidence presented by the other side."[43] Parties can use various tactics in an attempt to diminish the probative worth of the other disputant's evidence, including (1) written and oral arguments; (2) rebuttals; (3) explanatory statements; and (4) cross-examinations. These due process protections apply to agency hearings as much as to court trials.

Proper Notice

A hearing notice is equivalent to a complaint issued in a civil suit. The importance of providing proper notice when a procedural due process calls for a full evidentiary hearing or formal hearing ". . . with live witnesses and cross-examination and all the rest of the procedural hoopla . . . ."[44] cannot be underestimated. In fact, as Bernard Schwartz exclaims, "[T]he first requirement of such 'procedural hoopla' is that of notice."[45] This is because the quality of evidence presented in one's defense would clearly suffer if proper notice is not given. Put simply, proper notice provides the party with essential and specific information about the complaint and sufficient time to prepare a defense. Under the federal APA, Section 554(b), "Persons entitled to notice of an agency hearing shall be timely informed of (1) the time, place, and nature of the hearing; (2) the legal authority and jurisdiction under which the hearing is to be held; and (3) the matters of fact and law asserted."

Courts have long noted that a part of the right to be heard includes proper notice. In *Goldberg* v. *Kelly,* 397 U.S. 254 (1970), the Supreme Court regarded notice, specifically "timely and adequate notice detailing the reasons for a proposed (action), as a fundamental requisite of due process." Two decades later a New York court held that "Fundamental due process requires reasonable notice sufficient to allow a party to adequately prepare and present a defense to charges that will be the subject of a hearing" (*Diamond Terminal Corp.* v. *New York State Dept. of Taxation and Fin.,* 158 A.D.2d 38, 41; 1990).

In a 1978 administrative law case the Supreme Court placed the role of notice in clear perspective when it said that the "purpose of notice under the Due Process Clause is to apprise the affected individual of, and permit adequate preparation for, an impending 'hearing'" (*Memphis Light, Gas, and Water Division* v. *Craft,* 436 U.S. 1, 14, 1978). This ruling was in reference to termination of utility service to a customer. The Court argued that the municipal utility company violated due process requirements when it failed to inform the customer of the availability of procedures designed to protect against a termination of utility service. In other situations, due process does not necessarily obligate a public agency to tell parties how to complain. That is, due process does not always require an administrative agency to tell someone specifically how to use the protest procedures, as long as they are available. However, in this case the Court felt that because of the importance of utility termination and the varied educational levels of utility customers in general, due process should have entailed a rather specific explanation to the customer on how to complain (for example, where and when to complain, and to whom, specifically).

Proper notice also means that actual fundamental fairness must be accorded, not just the appearance of fairness. In other words, the form of the notice, even though technically correct, may not constitute proper notice in actuality if common sense dictates that the notice did not convey in meaningful terms what should have been conveyed in the notice. That is, procedural due process regarding notice means ideally that the notice should actually or meaningfully notify and not deceive. Of course, courts differ considerably on what constitutes proper or actual notice. Nothing in administrative law seems very certain, even something as apparently so simple as notice. For instance, normally the courts hold that formal, written notice is appropriate, yet some judges have ruled that if it can be shown that parties actually were notified by other means so that they understood the essential facts, "the requirement of notification purposed to inform may be satisfied by actual knowledge, especially when it is acted upon" (*McLay* v. *Maryland Assemblies, Inc.,* 269 M.D. 465, 477; 1973). In *Landover Books, Inc.* v. *Prince George's County,* 566 A.2d 792 (1989), the Court ruled that an adult bookstore owner had received proper notice because he ". . . appeared and participated in the hearing on the appeal, thus indicating that it (Landover Books) knew the contents of the notice. . . . Under the circumstances presented, we hold that service as in compliance with the substantive requirements of the ordinance despite the technical irregularity since Landover had actual knowledge of the violation . . ." (at 798).

The truth is that courts will usually uphold the adequacy of notice if they believe that the record of the hearing clearly indicates that the party knew enough about the charges against him or her and had sufficient time to prepare an adequate defense. Nevertheless, courts have on occasion, possibly too often, upheld notices as proper when they have fallen far short of what a reasonable person would consider proper due process standards. Possibly this is so because proper notice in administrative hearings does not have to be as elaborate or detailed as in criminal complaint, although proper notice for administrative hearings still must be fair enough to allow a party a *sufficient opportunity* to protect his or her rights. Sufficient opportunity is stressed because parties are not guaranteed a right to an adequate defense, but only an opportunity through proper notice to prepare an adequate defense. In *Diamond Terminal* v. *Dept. of Taxation,* 557 N.Y.S.2d 962 (A.D. 3 Dept.; 1990), a person went unprepared at his hearing because he contended that he did not have time to prepare, even though the record showed that the hearing officer had offered to give him a thirty-day adjournment to prepare. The Court felt that the fact the petitioner was given the opportunity to prepare for his defense, even though he did not take advantage of it, "supports a finding that the notice given was sufficient under those circumstances" (at 963).

Burden of Proof

In criminal proceedings the burden of proof is always on the state. That is, criminal defendants are presumed innocent until the state proves them guilty beyond any reasonable doubt. However, in administrative adjudications the burden of proof does not always rest on the agency, although it often does. The federal Administrative Procedure Act incorporates the traditional common law practice that places the burden of proof on the party bringing the action (for example, a person applying for a government benefit must prove that he or she is eligible or an agency charging a company with a rule violation must prove the violation. In short, the mover under the APA normally has the burden of persuading the administrative tribunal that the evidence supports his or her position. The APA, Section 556(d), states: "Except as otherwise provided by statute, the proponent of a rule or order has the burden of proof."

Common sense should suggest that, as a practical matter, it makes a significant difference which side has the burden of proof at a hearing. It is frequently considerably more difficult to prove a charge than to defend against one. Thus, as Barnard Schwartz asserts: "All too often, determining where the burden of proof lies determines who prevails in the case."[46] When the APA does not apply and/or statutes are not clear as to which party has the burden of proof, courts have usually held that agency adjudication should follow customary common law, which assigns the burden to the initiator. However, often court rulings have required agencies to assign burden of proof in such a way that vital liberty and property interests are protected.

In *Esposito* v. *INS*, 936 F.2d 911 (7th Cir., 1991), the court maintained that Esposito, an alien who had entered the United States through fraudulent and willful misrepresentation, had the burden of proof before the Board of Immigration appeals to show why the board should exclude from consideration its hearing a murder conviction by an Italian court. "The burden of course, is on him to point to exceptional procedural infirmities in the proceedings leading to his convictions, and he has failed to do so" (at 915). In *Tyra* v. *Secretary of Health and Human Services,* 9886 F.2d 1024 (6th Cir.; 1990), the court acknowledged how the burden of proof can shift from the claimant to the agency. Parenthetically, under some circumstances the burden of proof may shift back and forth several times before a resolution is reached. In *Tyra* the court pointed out that under the Social Security Act, Section 223(d), as amended, 42 U.S.C.A., section 423(d), the "claimant has the ultimate burden to establish an entitlement to benefits by proving the existence of a disability" (at 1028). In this case Tyra had the burden of proving that he had a severe impairment that prevented him from returning to his previous work. The ALJ ruled that Tyra was impaired enough that he could not return to his past job. However, with this finding the Court noted that the burden of proof shifts to the agency to show what kind of work, if any, the claimant can perform. "At this step in the analysis it becomes the secretary's burden to establish the claimant's ability to work. The secretary must prove that . . . the claimant retains the capacity to perform a different kind of job" (at 1028–1029).

Hearsay Evidence and Its Controversial Status

Hearsay ("heard saying")[47] is discussed by many, but my experience has been that few really understand the meaning and uses of hearsay. What is hearsay or hearsay evidence? Hearsay evidence is second-hand evidence, either oral or written, because it does not come directly from those who made the original statement, but from those on the witness stand who claim that they heard another person say it (*Stockton* v. *Williams,* 1 Doug., Mich. 546, 570; 1845). Under the New Jersey Rules of Evidence, Rule 63(1)-63(33), which is very similar to Rule 801(c) of the Federal Rules of Evidence, hearsay evidence is defined as "[E]vidence of a statement offered to prove the truth of the matter stated, which is made other than by a witness while testifying at the hearing . . . ."

Hearsay evidence carries weaker probative force (i.e., weight in tending to prove something as true) than nonhearsay because it stands either wholly or partly on the credibility and competence of people other than the witnesses (*State* v. *Klutz,* 206 N.C. 726, 804; 1927). Such evidence is not subject to cross-examination because the people who originally made the statements are not present at the hearing. An example of evidence considered hearsay is helpful in clarifying the suspicious nature of such evidence. Imagine that there are three people involved: Green, Black, and White. Green, who is on the witness stand, tells the tribunal that he was told by Black that she saw White, who is on trial for murdering her boyfriend, kill her boyfriend while engaged in a violent argument. Green's statement must be considered hearsay because it is indirect evidence coming from Black who is not present to offer direct testimony. In such a criminal case, the hearsay rule would be applied, thus excluding Green's statement. However, under special circumstances such inferior hearsay evidence has been allowed. In our case, for example, let us say that the court could not subpoena Black to testify, because she had died prior to the trial; yet her dying words to Green were that she saw White kill White's boyfriend. Dying declarations have been allowed a hearsay exception by some courts in the past. Beyond the dying declaration exception, thirty-nine other hearsay exceptions have been noted for criminal law alone (e.g., recorded recollections; entry in public record; assertion of pedigree).[48] Nonetheless, hearsay evidence is seldom admitted into evidence in criminal trials because of its obvious inferiority (*State* v. *Ah Lee,* 23 P.2 424 [Or. 1890]); *State* v. *Shaw,* 847 S.W.2d. 768 [Mo. banc 1993]).

Despite the fact that hearsay evidence is rarely allowed to enter the record in court trials, such evidence is accepted in agency hearings. For those of us who want hearing decisions to be based on sound and conclusive evidence, permitting hearsay evidence to be included in the official record, which is used ultimately to substantiate the hearing decision, may seem like kangaroo court nonsense. Hearsay evidence can be reliable and steer tribunals to accurate and just decisions, especially if a preponderance of hearsay all seems to support the same conclusion (*Woolsey* v. *Nat'l Transportation Safety Bd.,* 993 F.2d 516, 521 [1993]). However, hearsay evidence can also be completely inaccurate. The worst thing about hearsay, as implied earlier, is that it is evidence that cannot be tested for its reliability through cross-examination (*Wulfkuhle* v. *State Dep't of Revenue,* 234 Kan. 241; 1983; and *Pacific Gas & Electric Co.* v. *FERC,* 746 F.2d 1383 [9th Cir., 1984]). Since cross-examination appears to most legal scholars to be the single best instrument for bringing the truth to light in disputes, hearsay evidence must be considered far inferior to presented facts that have survived the grueling test of cross-examination unshaken.

Nevertheless, despite the weak probative content of hearsay evidence, the Administrative Procedure Act and the courts have allowed hearsay to be presented and used as evidence in administrative hearings. In *Tyra* v. *Secretary of Health and Human Services,* 896 F.2d 1024, 1030 (6th Cir., 1990), the court said "relevant evidence not admissible in court, including hearsay, is admissible at an administrative hearing." Section 356 of the APA fails to exclude the use of hearsay evidence by stating that "any oral or documentary evidence may be received." However, although Section 556 allows hearsay evidence to be accepted at the discretion of the hearing examiners, it does obligate the agency to exclude as a "matter of policy" all "irrelevant, immaterial, or unduly repetitious evidence," thus discouraging the use of hearsay. Another provision in the same section also discourages hearing examiners from relying too much on hearsay evidence in reaching decisions: "A sanction may not be imposed or rule or order issued except on consideration of the whole record or those parts thereof cited by a party and supported by and in accordance with reliable, probative, and substantial evidence." Since hearsay evidence is rarely considered reliable or probative in content, this section in a sense contradicts its other provision that "Any oral or documentary evidence may be received." Is this section suggesting that hearsay evidence can be received but not used to support hearing decisions?

The controversy surrounding hearsay evidence focuses on two basic questions. Should hearsay be admissible? If it is admissible, what weight should the hearsay evidence be given by agency adjudicators. In criminal law the focus is more on the first question, while in administrative law the focus is more on the second question. That is, because administrative hearings are less formal than court trials, many critics believe that attention should not focus so much on whether the hearsay should be admitted into the hearing record, but on how much weight the hearsay evidence should be given by hearing examiners of ALJs when using it to reach decisions. Courts tend to agree. In *Requero* v. *Teacher Standards and Practices,* 7889 P.2d 11, 14 (Or. App.; 1990), the court noted that "[T]he hearsay nature of evidence . . . may affect the weight that a fact finder chooses to give it, but does not in itself make it inadmissible. Similarly, the nonexistence of corroborating or independent evidence that tends to prove the same fact as the hearsay evidence is not a prerequisite to admissibility of the hearsay, but bears instead on the weight or sufficiency of the evidence offered."

Common sense must be emphasized to answer both questions. Since hearsay is automatically somewhat suspect or questionably reliable, common sense should dictate whether it should be admitted into the record or not. Without question, the quality of hearsay differs substantially. Some hearsay may amount to wild and false rumor spread by an unreliable person, while other hearsay may be "the kind of evidence on which responsible persons are accustomed to rely in serious affairs" (*NLRB* v. *Remington Rand, Inc.,* 94 F.2d 862, 873 [2d Cir.; 1938]). Courts have normally upheld the admissibility of hearsay "in administrative proceedings, so long as the admission of evidence meets the tests of fundamental fairness and probity" (*Bustos-Torres* v. *INS,* 898 F.2d 1053 [5th Cir.; 1990]).

In sum, it makes practical sense to use hearsay evidence in agency hearings even though the use of such evidence presents certain problems. However, the problems with hearsay evidence can be drastically minimized if agency adjudicators act professionally and in good faith to see to it that all evidence, including hearsay, is introduced and weighed in a responsible manner so that due process is honored.

Making Sense of Hearsay in Light of the Residuum Rule, the Perales Rule, and the Substantial Evidence Test

The *residuum rule* requires that a finding cannot stand unless it is supported by evidence that would be acceptable in a jury trial. When the residuum rule is applied to hearing decisions, it means that hearsay evidence can be used in helping to reach a decision; however, the decision itself must not be supported by hearsay evidence alone but by substantial, nonhearsay evidence. Thomas R. Mulroy, Jr., and Douglas

G. McClure provide a frank descriptive definition of the residuum rule: "In other words, hearing officers cannot base their findings on hearsay unless they could have legitimately reached the same result without the hearsay evidence."[49] In *Carroll* v. *Knickerbocker Ice Co.,* 113 N.E. 507, 509 (1916), the district court, in rejecting a death benefit claim, noted: "Still in the end, there must be a residuum of evidence of legal (i.e., non-hearsay) evidence to support the claim before an award can be made." In *Requero* v. *Teacher Standards and Practices,* 789 P.2d 11, 14 (Or. App. 1990), the court, quoting Kenneth C. Davis, made clear that

> [T]he residuum rule requires a reviewing court to set aside an administrative finding un-
> less the finding is supported by evidence which would be admissible in a jury trial . . .
> no matter how reliable the evidence may appear to the agency and to the reviewing
> court, no matter what the circumstantial setting may be, no matter what may be the ev-
> idence or lack of evidence on the other side, and no matter what may be the conse-
> quences of refusing to rely upon evidence.

The residuum rule has frustrated and angered many agency adjudicators from the very beginning because it prevents them from reaching decisions based solely upon hearsay evidence, which can be difficult for hearing officials with hefty case-loads who want to reach quick decisions on the basis of what they believe are reliable documents pertaining to the cases in their files (such documents technically consti-tute only hearsay evidence).[50]

Beyond the practical reasons for rejecting the residuum rule, opponents offer other criticisms. Most of their criticism focuses on the perceived illogical nature of the residuum rule. Critics argue that the residuum rule illogically classifies all hearsay evidence as incompetent regardless of the equality of the hearsay. In legal terms, the residuum rule makes even the highest quality hearsay technically incompetent, and this contradicts reliability standards associated with the admission of evidence. That is, it is argued that properly admitted hearsay (hearsay allowed because any reason-able person would accept it as reliable) must still be considered incompetent or non-substantial evidence incapable of supporting a hearing finding. Kenneth C. Davis claims that the most illogical problem with the residuum rule "is the lack of correla-tion between reliability of evidence and the exclusionary rules of evidence. The ex-clusionary rules were designed for guiding admission or exclusion of evidence, not for weighing its reliability, and were designed for juries, not for administrators."[51]

However, the attacks on the worth of the residuum rule come mostly from those who believe that its application simply causes unnecessary and costly administrative inconveniences and delays. The residuum rule is not just another stupid rule that makes no sense. In the spirit of justice, it makes a lot of sense. It simply requires that at least some evidence used to reach a hearing decision should be based upon more than just hearsay, upon at least a residuum of substantial evidence (i.e., nonhearsay evidence). Is that too much to ask to help guarantee fair hearing decisions? However, it appears that residuum rule opponents are not really saying that the residuum rule will not serve administrative justice in agency hearings better. They contend, at least implicitly, that our administrative system cannot afford the luxury of using the residuum rule because its use will increase administrative costs even more in an age when supporting even vital governmental services has become increasingly difficult.

The 1971 Supreme Court decision that stands apparently as the most outspoken word against the value of the residuum, *Richardson* v. *Perales,* 402 U.S. 389, encapsulates the prevalent sentiment of critics that the residuum rule is too impracticable to apply during a time when the administrative burden is so heavy. The *Perales* Court reasoned in rejecting strict reliance upon the residuum rule that

> There is an additional and pragmatic factor which, although not controlling, deserves mention. This is what Chief Judge Brown has described as "the sheer magnitude of the administrative burden," and the resulting necessity for written reports without "elaboration through the traditional facility or oral testimony." With over 20,000 disability claim hearings annually, the cost of providing live medical testimony at those hearings . . . would be a substantial drain . . . (at 406).

Ever since the *Perales* decision was handed down in 1971 there has been a lively debate over whether the residuum rule is still applicable law. The controversy is very much alive today because some legal scholars and court justices insist that the residuum rule is dead, while other scholars and justices argue that it is still governing law. For example, in 1990 in *Requero,* the Oregon court rejected the use of the residuum rule by arguing essentially that hearsay evidence can be "sufficiently trustworthy" and constitute "substantial evidence" (at 15). Many other state and federal courts have also rejected the residuum rule for the same or similar reasons. On the other hand, many other courts have held that the residuum rule has merit and must still be applied. In *Trujillo* v. *Employment Sec. Comm'n,* 610 P.2d 747, 748 (1980), the court stated emphatically that "[I]n many circumstances hearsay is reliable and probative, and at times it may be the only evidence available. Nevertheless, we believe that the residuum rule should be retained in those administrative proceedings where a substantial right, such as one's ability to earn a livelihood, is at stake. In those instances . . . hearing decisions . . . must be based upon . . . substantial evidence." In *Foust* v. *Leijan,* 942 F.2d 712, 719 (10th Cir.; 1991), the court held that Department of Interior hearing decisions involving land rights must be supported by "substantial evidence."

Confusion about applicability of the residuum rule has prevailed since the *Perales* decision over two decades ago because the *Perales* holding conveyed mixed messages about the legal status of the residuum rule. Many legal scholars felt that the *Perales* Court rejected the residuum rule because it upheld a Social Security hearing examiner's decision that was totally rooted in hearsay evidence, not "substantial evidence." The key to understanding the Court's decision, however, is in understanding how the Court justified its decision. It then becomes clear that the Court did not in fact reject the residuum rule, but only added some flexibility in its use.

In many respects the circumstances in the *Perales* case are unique, and these help explain why the *Perales* Court reached the decision it did. Pedro Perales, a thirty-four-year-old truck driver, claimed that he had become permanently disabled by lifting an object while working. He applied for disability benefits under the Social Security Act. On the whole, his medical records indicated that he was not disabled and could resume work in a matter of months, although one doctor concluded otherwise. In fact, one doctor, Dr. Langston, who had great credibility before the hearing examiner and eventually the *Perales* court, concluded that Perales was clearly not disabled and was faking in order to collect undue disability payments. In fact, Dr. Langston recommended that he should see a psychiatrist. Later, Dr. Bailey, a psychiatrist, and Dr. Mattson and Dr. Leavitt all agreed with Dr. Langston's diagnosis. Beyond this, several other doctors' reports supported Dr. Langston's diagnosis. Only Dr. Morales, a former fellow employee of *Perales* perceived as biased by the hearing examiner and eventually the *Perales* court, reached an opposite conclusion.

Given these facts, it is clear from a careful reading of the *Perales* decision that the Court's majority was predisposed to rule against Perales. But the Court also felt that Perales was really treated very fairly by the hearing examiner. What became important to the Court was the fact that Perales, represented by counsel, was given an opportunity to subpoena the doctors so that they could be cross-examined, but that Perales declined the opportunity to do so. The court noted: "Notice was given to claimant Perales. The physicians' reports were on file and available for inspection by the claimant and his counsel. And the authors of these reports were known and were subject to subpoena and to the very cross-examination that the claimant asserts he has not enjoyed" (at 407).

Given these hearing conditions, then, the *Perales* Court had to decide when and how the residuum rule should be applied and what should really constitute substantial evidence. The Court made a practical decision. It reasoned that it makes sense to suspend the strict application of the residuum rule when the opportunity is given to subpoena documents and witnesses so that the hearsay evidence can be cross-examined. If Perales took advantage of this opportunity, the hearsay evidence would have been transformed into substantial evidence. In effect, the spirit of the residuum rule was not really undermined by the *Perales* Court because Perales was given the opportunity to subpoena and cross-examine the "hearsay evidence." To the *Perales* Court this failure to take advantage of this opportunity made the hearsay evidence tantamount to substantial evidence.

It is also important to acknowledge that in *Perales* the Court noted that "[C]ourts have recognized the reliability and probative worth of written medical reports even in formal trials and, while acknowledging their hearsay character, have admitted them as an exception to the hearsay rule" (at 405). Is the Court not saying, then, that such medical records really constitute substantial evidence, consistent with the residuum rule, since such evidence, because of its reliability and probative value, is accepted in court trials under a hearsay exception? If so, this is just one more reason to doubt whether the *Perales* Court ever meant to reject the residuum rule.

In sum, the Supreme Court in *Perales* probably did not intend to abolish the residuum rule, but it evidently did intend to develop a new flexible standard for applying it. This new standard has become known as the "*Perales* rule." Under the new *Perales* rule, the residuum rule still largely applies, which means that hearing officials can use hearsay evidence to substantiate their rulings, but the decision must still be supported by some substantial evidence. This sounds identical to the residuum rule requirements, but the different twist is that the substantial evidence test under the new *Perales* standard can be more easily satisfied. Reviewing courts must now look at the unique circumstances that surround the use of the hearsay evidence.

The Exclusionary Rule's Applicability in Administrative Hearings

From approximately the beginning of President Ronald Reagan's administration until the present, the exclusionary rule, as applied to criminal law, has come under constant and vehement attack mostly by conservatives. They believe that the rule has been used too often to prevent otherwise good evidence from being admitted into evidence just because the evidence was seized illegally by police, thus allowing many criminals to get off on mere "procedural technicalities." Simply stated, the exclusionary rule has been used in criminal trials to exclude illegally seized evidence, which has given rise to the "fruit of the poisonous tree" doctrine. In criminal law the doctrine, although it may apply in administrative law, has had the practical effort of making all evidence and all secondary obtained evidence stemming from it) inadmissible ". . . because procedural steps in obtaining the evidence violated constitutional due process" (*Wong Sun* v. *United States,* 371 U.S. 471 [1983]). Opposition to the exclusionary rule has evidently influenced the courts because recent decisions have tended to weaken the clout of the exclusionary rule.

The status of the exclusionary rule in administrative hearings is not clear.[52] Some courts have upheld the relevance of the exclusionary rule in agency adjudications, while other courts have not. For example, in a New York case in 1979 the court argued that the exclusionary rule should apply to administrative hearings as well as to criminal trials (*Piccarillo* v. *Board of Parole,* 48 N.Y. 2d76, 81). Some federal courts have agreed (e.g., *Knoll Assoc.* v. *FTC,* 397 F.2d 530 [7th Cir.; 1968] and *Navia-Duran* v. *INS,* 568 F.2d 803 [1st Cir.; 1977]). Supporters of the exclusionary rule often maintain that the Fourth Amendment's privacy protections, as well as the Fifth Amendment's protection against self-incrimination, should be upheld whether the government is prosecuting a person for burglary or deciding whether to revoke someone's medical license.

Nevertheless, as in criminal cases, the courts have been increasingly very reluctant to compel agency adjudicators to honor the exclusionary rule. Of course, agency hearings are normally much less formal than court trials, thus making the admission of evidence more flexible. In fact, the federal APA, Section 556(d), says "Any oral or documentary evidence may be received," and it is well established in administrative law that virtually all admitted evidence, no matter how irrelevant or incompetent, cannot cause "reversible error" or fatally flaw the decision as long as the decision is otherwise supported by substantial evidence.

Exclusion of Privileged Evidence

This does not mean, however, that agency adjudicators can normally go so far as to require that privileged evidence be admitted. As the Revised Model State Administrative Procedure Act, Section 10, states: "Agencies shall give effect to the rules of privilege recognized by law." Privileged evidence is protected either by the

Constitution or by statute or, sometimes, by common law. Privileged evidence, for example, consists of attorney-client, husband-wife privilege and other recognized constitutional and statutory testimonial privileges, as well as specifically the privilege against self-incrimination and the use of illegally obtained evidence. As expected, then, in *Southern Cal. Gas Co.* v. *Public Utils. Comm'n,* 784 P.2d 1373 (1990), the California court upheld the attorney-client privilege in a public utility commission hearing.

It may seem contradictory and confusing to note that illegally seized evidence is considered privileged evidence, yet at the same time point out that the trend, as noted, has been against compelling public agencies to honor the exclusionary rule, thus making them exclude from hearing proceedings illegally obtained evidence that should be considered privilege. The truth is that the situation is contradictory and confusing, but this is not unique to law, especially administrative law. Due to conservative political pressures and other factors, the vast majority of decisions since the early 1980s, although the trend against the exclusionary rule started earlier, have rejected the application of the exclusionary rule under most circumstances. In 1984 the U.S. Supreme Court in *INS* v. *Lopez-Mendoza,* 468 U.S. 1032, held that the exclusionary rule did not apply to civil deportation hearings, even though, it should be added, losing parties normally suffer a grievous loss. In *Lopez-Mendoza,* employing the most popular reason for throwing out the exclusionary rule, the Court opined that enforcing the use of the exclusionary rule would only minimally deter officials from conducting illegal searches. In *Finkelstein* v. *State Personnel Board,* 267 Col. Rptr. 133 (Cal. App. 3 Dist.; 1990), a California Court assumed for the sake of argument that the briefcase search in question was illegal under both federal and California constitutions, yet nevertheless rejected the application of the exclusionary rule, allowing the illegally seized evidence to be used to terminate a government employee's employment. Comparing *Finkelstein* to a prior ruling by the same court in which the court upheld the exclusionary rule, the court concluded that ". . . in this case there was no search for evidence of crime and no motive to use such evidence for disciplinary purposes. Because of this factual difference, the deterrent effect of the exclusionary rule . . . is lacking here" (at 138).

What is clear from *Finkelstein* and other cases is that courts are very unlikely to apply the exclusionary rule if they feel that the officials who illegally seized evidence did not know how it would be used later. The logic employed by the courts is that excluding illegally obtained evidence from, for example, an employee termination hearing, is not going to deter police officers from conducting illegal searches where they had no idea that such evidence may be used later in a noncriminal termination proceeding. Do you accept this rationale? This rationale appears more like an excuse to toss out the exclusionary rule than a sensible reason to reject its use. It seems that the best way to discourage any governmental official from conducting illegal searches is to make certain that any illegally seized evidence is excluded from criminal trials or administrative hearings. This makes even more sense when one considers the other chief reason for using the exclusionary rule: the government should not benefit in a criminal trial or an agency adjudication from its own unlawful acts that produced the illegal evidence.

Right to Counsel in Agency Hearings

Courts have insisted that a fair hearing should offer several procedural due process protections, but does the call for fairness require agencies to permit persons in hearings to be represented by counsel, even appointed counsel (paid for by the government)? In 1963 in the now famous *Gideon* v. *Wainwright* case, 372 U.S. 335, the Supreme Court ruled that in criminal cases defendants have the right to appointed counsel if they cannot afford to pay a lawyer. Later, in 1972, the Court held that the *Gideon* decision applies even to misdemeanor trials from which a possible jail sentence could result (*Argersinger* v. *Hamlin*, 407 U.S. 25).

The right-to-counsel issue has been settled comfortably in criminal cases, but the right to counsel in agency hearings leaves many questions unanswered. During the 1970s a significant number of courts and legal scholars argued that unless legal counsel is actually provided to indigents across the board, blatant inequities in applying administrative justice in agency hearings will inevitably occur. In a sense, it would be simpler and fairer to apply the *Gideon* rule to all administrative hearings than to try to choose the hearings to which it would apply. On the other hand, given the millions of minor hearing cases heard each year by administrators, it became just as clear that it would be very impractical to apply the *Gideon* solution to agency adjudications. The cost to taxpayers would be prohibitive, not only because of the added costs for lawyers but also because these lawyers would unquestionably provide legal defenses that would delay case settlements and place extra financial and staff burdens on agency efforts to prepare, present, and defend their positions.

In *Goldberg* v. *Kelly*, 397 U.S. 254 (1970), the most influential right to counsel case during the 1970s, the Supreme Court stressed the crucial significance to the right to counsel by reiterating an earlier position that "the right to be heard would be, in many cases, of little avail if it did not comprehend the right to be heard by counsel."[53] However, although some applauded the decision as a giant step forward in extending the right to counsel to indigent parties in agency hearings, in fact, the *Goldberg* holding only confirmed a right that the federal Administrative Procedure Act has already granted to federal employees unless specific provisions in federal statutes placed restrictions on the right. Section 555(b) of the APA read: "A person compelled to appear in person before an agency or representative thereof is entitled to be accompanied, represented, and advised by counsel or, if permitted by the agency, by other qualified representatives." But it was also made clear in *Goldberg* that the welfare claimant did not have the right to government-appointed *free* counsel. Many legal scholars and social scientists became irritated by the obvious Catch-22 situation posed by the *Goldberg* decision. That is, what good is it to be allowed to obtain counsel if you can't afford to pay for such representation?

Three years after *Goldberg*, in *John R. Gagnon* v. *Gerald H. Scarpelli*, 411 U.S. 778 (1973), in which the right-to-counsel question was discussed in the context of a revocation of parole hearing, the Court methodically reviewed what should be considered the minimum due process rights in administrative law hearings. Drawing from the precedential case, *Morrissey* v. *Brewer*, 408 U.S. 471 (1972), the Court acknowledged that even the right to counsel, let alone paid counsel, had not been established in a de facto sense as a minimum right. Nonetheless, the Court suggested that the right to government-provided counsel may be advisable under very rare circumstances and when deemed appropriate by the hearing officials.[54] The court did provide guidelines to help hearing officers decide when counsel should be provided, considering, for example, "whether the probationer appears capable of speaking effectively for himself."[55] With great reservation, the Supreme Court in *Gagnon* opened the door just slightly to allow for appointed counsel in cases where very serious consequences (for example, return to prison, loss of life-sustaining welfare benefits, or deportation) would occur to financially and/or educationally deficient persons if adverse rulings were reached.

At the same time, however, the Supreme Court presented in *Gagnon* a strong case for why counsel should not be provided in virtually all administrative hearings, contending that to do so would place a tremendous and unjustifiable burden on administrative tribunals: "Certainly, the decision making process will be prolonged, and the financial cost to the State—for appointed counsel, counsel for the State, a longer record, and the possibility of judicial review—will not be insubstantial" (at 788). In placing the right to counsel in the context of balancing due process entitlements with agency responsibilities, the Court reasoned that "due process is not so rigid as to require that the significant interests in informality, flexibility, and economy must always be sacrificed" (at 788).

Despite efforts by the Court to review systematically questions pertaining to the right to counsel, particularly the right to state-supported counsel, the *Gagnon* case left many questions unanswered by creating a vague circumstances test to be applied at the discretion of the hearing officials. Since it is understandable that such hearing officials probably identify somewhat with agency interest, how fair does it seem for the Court to leave the decision on whether persons in hearings should be provided with paid counsel to the very people who will be hearing the case? Would it not take exceptionally fair-minded hearing examiners to grant the request for appointed counsel to parties, knowing the extra time, expense, and headaches it will undoubtedly bring?

A related point is also noteworthy. The APA generally requires agency adjudicators to respect a person's right to obtain legal counsel. However, a loophole in section 555(b) does not obligate agencies to advertise that this right exists. As a consequence, some agencies have, as a matter of official policy, actively discouraged parties from being represented by counsel. At least one state court has spoken out against the administrative practice of not notifying parties that they have the right not only to counsel, but also possibly to free or low-cost counsel (provided by various publicly and privately supported legal service units). For example, the Tennessee Supreme Court in *Simmons* v. *Troughber,* 791 S.W. 2d 21, 24 (Tenn. 1990), ruled that the Tennessee Department of Employment Security's failure to inform an employee of the possible availability of free or low-cost legal representation violated her statutory right to a fair hearing.

Beyond agencies' simply keeping silent about the right to counsel, the most popular step to discourage representation by counsel is to place a fee limit on what attorneys can charge. For example, the Social Security Administration long ago adopted a rule that placed an absurdly low ten-dollar fee limit on how much an attorney could earn while representing Social Security claimants in disability claims. In 1954 Congress set a ten-dollar fee limit on the amount an attorney could receive for representing a veteran in a death or disability claim.[56]

Sympathetic to veterans' inability to secure counsel under this fee limitation rule, a district court in 1984 held this fee to violate due process protections (*National Ass'n. of Radiation Survivors* v. *Walters*, 589 F.Supp. 1302 [N.D. Cal.]). However, the Supreme Court reversed the decision, arguing that due process or "fundamental fairness" had not been violated by the ten-dollar fee limitation (*Walters* v. *National Ass'n of Radiation Survivors*, 106 S.Ct. 3180 [1985]). Speaking for the High Court, Justice Rehnquist asserted that the costs and benefits of extending certain "extra" procedural safeguards must be given serious consideration. Employing the balance test developed in *Mathews* v. *Eldridge*, 424 U.S. 319 (1976), which basically calls for weighing the costs and benefits of applying the present governmental procedures to the government against the costs and benefits of applying the existing or alternative procedures to the government against the costs and benefits of the existing or alternative procedures to the private party, Rehnquist wrote: "We have emphasized that the marginal gains from affording an additional procedural safeguard often may be outweighed by the societal cost of providing such a safeguard" (at 3189).

The Supreme Court upheld the *Walters* decision in 1990 in *U.S. Dept. of Labor* v. *Triplett*, 110 S.Ct. 1428, by holding that even though fee limitations may make attorneys unavailable to claimants, this in itself does not deny claimants due process since they still have the right to counsel. Thus, in reviewing the state court's ruling, the Supreme Court concluded that ". . . the evidence . . . did not remotely establish *either* that black lung claimants are unable to retain qualified counsel or that the cause of such inability is the attorney's fee system administered by the Department. The Court therefore had no basis for concluding that the system deprives claimants of property without due process of law" (at 1435).

Agencies have also tried to prevent parties from employing counsel by arguing that the use of counsel impairs agency business, especially its investigations. However, this argument has been rejected by most courts since Section 555(b), even acknowledging the section's loopholes, allows agencies to forbid the employment of counsel only under exceptional circumstances. For example, in *Professional Reactor Operator Soc.* v. *U.S. NRC*, 939 F.2d 1047, 1051–1052 (D.C. Cir. 1991), the Court held that the NRC's exclusion of subpoenaed witnesses' counsel during NRC's investigations violates the APA's more weighty right-to-counsel provision.

The right-to-counsel controversy in administrative law cases has been brewing for many years. Scholars seem to be divided on whether this "extra" procedural safeguard would prove too burdensome to the hearing process in our public agencies. Knowing the adversarial character of lawyers, no doubt the pressure of legal counsel at administrative hearings would slow things down—in the name of proper legal representation, of course! Several years ago, after examining the right-to-counsel debate, Judge Henry J. Friendly presented a fascinating and provocative idea to resolve the problem. Judge Friendly agrees that administrative hearings, handling routine questions pertaining to welfare benefits, school suspensions, and so on should not be turned into elaborate criminal adversary proceedings. In a now-famous administrative law article entitled, "Some Kind of Hearing," he argues that the adversary hearing approach should be abandoned in many administrative law areas that he categorizes as "mass justice" areas.

> These problems concerning counsel and confrontation inevitably bring up the question whether we would not do better to abandon the adversary system in certain areas of mass justice, notably in the many ramifications of the welfare system, in favor of one in which an examiner—or administrative law judge if you will—with no connection with the agency would have the responsibility for developing all the pertinent facts and making a just decision.[57]

In so arguing, Judge Friendly attacks the basic need for counsel on the grounds that the provision of counsel in many administrative law areas cannot be justified in a cost-benefit sense: "The appearance of counsel for the citizen is likely to lead the government to provide one—or at least to cause the government's representative to act like one. The result may be to turn what might have been a short conference leading to an amicable result into a protracted controversy."[58]

Judge Friendly largely rests his call for experimentation in administrative mass justice (that is, doing away with the adversary process in many administrative law areas) on the legal argument that there exists "no constitutional mandate requiring use of the adversary process in administrative hearings unless the Court chooses to construct one out of the vague contours of the due process clause."[59] His nonadversary, investigative model would have the advantage of settling disputes informally and quickly in a conference-like environment. Although Judge Friendly acknowledges that the experiment would represent "a sharp break with our tradition of adversary process," he claims that "that tradition . . . was not formulated for a situation in which many thousands of hearings must be provided each month."[60]

The whole question of whether claimants actually benefit from having counsel at administrative hearings, the resolution of which would be quite helpful in aiding our decision on whether the Friendly experiment should be tried, was addressed in "Effect of Representation on a Claimant's Success Rate—Three Study Designs," published several years ago in the *Administrative Law Review.*[61] Although only a few studies are cited, the preliminary data tend to cast great doubt on whether claimants in administrative hearings win more favorable decisions at a greater rate because they are represented by counsel. For example, one empirical study cited revealed that welfare claimants in Wisconsin won at "'about the same' rate without counsel as claimants represented by counsel."[62]

In sum, the status of the right to counsel in agency hearings is much clearer in the 1990s than it was in the 1970s. Federal and state courts have made it fairly clear in the past two decades that parties generally have a right to legal counsel, but not guaranteed government-supported counsel. However, the possibility of free or low-cost legal representation is available on a limited basis to indigents through various legal services operations. Courts have normally insisted that proper notice includes informing parties that they have the right to be represented by legal counsel at agency hearings, but courts have been reluctant to push the advertising of legal representation too far, especially requiring agencies to inform parties about the possible availability of free or low-cost counsel. In a few instances the courts have ruled that certain circumstances, usually practical situations upholding a state interest (e.g., an excessive administrative burden), necessitate that public agencies not permit parties to be represented by counsel, particularly if the disputed issue is considered minor.

DECISION MAKING IN AGENCY ADJUDICATIONS

It has been made quite apparent by now that agency hearings are normally much more informal than court trials at every stage in the proceedings. Evidence is not only accepted and used in a more informal manner in agency adjudications than in court trials, but the process employed in reaching decisions is also considerably more informal in agency hearings. In fact, hearing proceedings are often so informal that evidence may be presented to and evaluated by the hearing officials and a decision reached in a matter of ten to twenty minutes. However, as noted, some hearings have been very formal and elaborate and have continued for several years. Although court trials can also be short, it is unusual, except in matters involving small claims, for decisions to be reached so quickly because of the more formal requirements associated with handling evidence and reaching decisions in light of the evidence. In this last section, principles, doctrines, and rules associated with hearing decision-making are reviewed. And, it must be stressed, as it was in *Vollstedt* v. *City of Stockton,* 269 Ca.Rptr. 404, 408 (Ca. App. 3 Dist.; 1990), that ". . . the question of whether the trial was 'fair' encompasses post-hearing actions of the agency as well" (i.e., the post-hearing decision-making process).

Applying Standards of Proof in Decision-Making

There is a qualitative difference between decision-making in court trials and agency adjudications. As contrasted with agency hearings, judges or jurors in court trials should root their decisions in more weighty evidence than ALJs in agency hearings. Simply stated, the standard of proof should be higher for court decisions than for agency hearing decisions. In criminal cases decisions must be based upon the highest possible standard, or the *beyond a reasonable doubt* standard. In an ideal situation, judges or juries cannot convict a person of a crime if a reasonable doubt exists as to whether the person is guilty of the crime. This high standard has posed some problems because either some guilty parties have not been prosecuted or the prosecutors have failed to win their case under this lofty standard, thus allowing guilty parties to go free. On the other hand, many legal scholars contend that this is a small price to pay for a justice system that honors freedom and individual rights.

There are those who hold that while the criminal justice system is "too fair," permitting many "guilty" parties to escape prosecution or conviction because of "due process technicalities," the administrative justice system is "too unfair," denying parties procedural due process rights while agency administrators rush to dispose of huge caseloads as quickly as possible. Critics point out that the failure to honor reasonable due process protections in agency hearings can sometimes cause parties guilty of no crime to suffer more harm (e.g., loss of a professional license or business, revocation of parole, or deportation) than they would have if convicted of certain criminal acts. This reality motivated Justice Brandeis to conclude many decades ago that deportation decisions, for example, may prove more harmful to persons in deportation hearings than verdicts in criminal trials because adverse deportation rulings may "result . . . in loss of both property and life; or all that makes life worth living" (*Ng Fung Ho* v. *White,* 259 U.S. 276, 284; 1922).

Most agency hearing officials have the unenviable task of having to resolve an enormous volume of cases, thus justifying to a certain extent why agencies must restrict procedural due process protections. It is understandable, then, that the standard of proof for reaching hearing decisions falls short of the higher standard of proof required in criminal trials. When reaching decisions in agency hearings, the burden of persuasion is satisfied if the *preponderance of the evidence* supports the decision.

In *Steadman* v. *SEC,* 450 U.S. 91 (1981), the leading case in this area, the Supreme Court clearly established the application of the preponderance-of-the-evidence standard for administrative hearings governed by the APA. A brief review of this case helps to clarify how the preponderance-of-the-evidence standard became law, especially since the APA does not use the specific rhetoric "preponderance-of-the-evidence." In 1971 the Securities and Exchange Commission (SEC) began disciplinary action against Steadman, charging that he had violated many federal securities laws. After a lengthy on-the-record (evidentiary) hearing before an ALJ and after review by the SEC, which employed a preponderance-of-the-evidence test to assess the weight of the evidence, the Commission concluded that Steadman was guilty of violating several antifraud, conflict-of-interest, proxy, and reporting provisions of federal security statutes. As a result, it ordered that Steadman be banned permanently from affiliating with any investment companies or associating with any investment companies or associating with any investment advisors, thus prohibiting him from practicing his profession. Steadman sought judicial review, arguing that because of the potentially severe penalties, the SEC should not have used the preponderance-of-the-evidence standard, but should have employed the stricter *clear-and-convincing-evidence* standard to weigh the evidence to substantiate the very serious intent to defraud charges.

However, both the appeals court and the Supreme Court disagreed. The High Court reasoned that the substantial evidence requirement in the APA requires that a decision must be supported by a certain "quantity of evidence." The Court was not persuaded by Steadman's argument that the substantial evidence requirement pertains to the "quality" of evidence only. The Court argued that legislative intent was clear from the ". . . House Report, which expressly adopted a preponderance-of-the-evidence standard: Nor is there any suggestion in the legislative history that a standard of proof higher than a preponderance of the evidence was ever contemplated, much less intended" (at 101–102). The Court went on to say that "Congress was primarily concerned with the elimination of agency decision making premised on evidence which was of poor quality—irrelevant, immaterial, unreliable and non-probative—and of insufficient quantity—less than a preponderance" (at 102). Consequently, the Court concluded that through APA provisions Congress has "expressed its intent that adjudicatory proceedings subject to the APA satisfy the statute where determinations are made according to the preponderance of the evidence" (at 104).

Although the APA preponderance-of-the-evidence standard normally governs agency adjudicators when reaching hearing decisions, specific statutory provisions may override the APA requirement calling for a higher standard of proof. For example, in deportation cases today, as long as the alien had entered the country legally, decisions are governed by the higher clear-and-convincing-evidence standard. In *Bustos-Torres* v. *INS,* 898 F.2d 1053, 1057 (5th Cir.; 1990), the petitioner contended that evidence used against him ". . . is not the clear and convincing evidence necessary for deportation." The court acknowledged that "[A]lthough the government has the ultimate burden of providing deportability by clear and convincing evidence, in a Section 125 (a)(2) case charging deportability of an alien who entered the country without inspection, the government need only show alienage."[63]

There are many critics of the preponderance-of-the-evidence standard. The most prevalent criticism is that the weak standard is applied when common sense should suggest that ALJs should employ stricter or higher due process standards when serious deprivations may result. Justices Lewis Powell and Potter Stewart, the dissenters in *Steadman,* present this criticism well. They argue that when potential penalties are equivalent to or greater than criminal penalties, our common law tradition should supersede the APA, especially since the APA does not specifically state that the preponderance-of-the-evidence standard must be applied.

Another criticism is simply that these standards of proof are confusing because they are not clearly distinct. These different standards are used in agency hearings and in court trials to support decisions. But how useful or practical are these tests? Can these standards be applied meaningfully in different situations? Are you convinced that a person of reasonable intelligence could tell you the difference between, say, substantial evidence, preponderance of the evidence, clear and convincing evidence, and evidence that leaves no reasonable doubt? These standards all apply to the *weight* of the evidence, but do you think clear and meaningful distinctions and applications of these standards can be made? When it comes to weighing any evidence, whether in an agency hearing or court trial, the weighing process and the accompanying decision process are quite subjective. What is clear and convincing evidence to one person is not clear and convincing evidence to another. Nonetheless, the preponderance-of-the-evidence standard is the basic standard of proof test used in agency hearings, whatever this standard really means in practice.[64]

Making Decisions on the Basis of the Whole Record

The APA, Section 556(d), requires ALJs to make hearing decisions leading to the issuing of any order only after ". . . consideration of the *whole record* or those parts thereof cited by a party and supported by and in accordance with the reliable, probative, and substantial evidence" (my emphasis). Requiring agency adjudicators to base their decisions on the whole record and not just part of the record seems like a very reasonable and patently fair requirement; however, before the APA was passed in 1946, hearing adjudicators were allowed to substantiate their decisions upon only part of the record. Of course, this permitted hearing decision-makers to ignore parts of the hearing record that may have contradicted the evidence they used to substantiate their decision. In fact, it clearly gave unscrupulous adjudicators the opportunity to reach outrageously unfair decisions by totally ignoring facts in the record that would cause any reasonable person to reach an opposite decision. Nevertheless, this practice of having to look at only part of the record to satisfy the "one-sided substantial evidence" test was upheld by the courts before the passage of the APA. In *Marzacco* v. *Lowe,* 58 F.Supp. 900, 903 (D.N.J., 1945), the court remarked: "Under the present prevailing system of administrative law, all evidence to the contrary . . . is a closed book into which this court dare not peek, at least not effectively."

Louis J. Jaffe, among many others, found this narrow and absurd application of the substantial evidence rule horrifying. Rightfully, Jaffe insisted that it is very hard to believe that any truly reasonable and responsible person could, in good conscience, reach rational conclusions by looking at only part of the record.[65] The court reached the same conclusion in *Holo-Krome Co.* v. *NLRB,* 947 F.2d 588 (2d Cir.; 1991), when the court scolded the NLRB for ignoring important parts of the record (e.g., an ALJ's finding) to justify an unreasonable decision not substantiated by the whole record. The court noted that the whole record must be used in searching a decision, including weighing ". . . evidence opposed to the board's view" (quoting from *Local One, Amalgamated Lithographers* v. *NLRB,* 729 F.2d 172, 175 [2d Cir.; 1984]) (at 593). In fact, the court concluded that the NLRB's refusal to consider a critical part of the whole record made ". . . the evidence supporting the Board's decision . . . less than substantial" (at 592). Consequently, the court ruled that "(T)he Board's decision regarding this evidence was in no way justified by the record before it" (at 595). In so holding, this federal court relied heavily upon the arguments set forth in the classic case on the whole record requirement, *Universal Camera Corp.* v. *NLRB,* 340 U.S. 474 (1951), in which the Supreme Court stressed that hearing decision-makers must base their decisions on the whole record, including conflicting evidence. "The substantiality of evidence must take into account whatever in the record fairly detracts from its weight. This is clearly the significance of the (APA) requirement . . ." (at 488).

The question of what constitutes the whole record has also been disputed. The dispute is based generally on problems pertaining to definitions of formal and informal evidence and questions over which evidence needs to be included in the "whole" record. Of course, agencies have been charged with keeping incomplete records, failing to note *ex parte* communications that may influence adjudicators and should therefore be part of the record, and failing to admit certain kinds of evidence (e.g., hearsay or documents and testimony that are "too costly" or "too inconvenient" to obtain). Nevertheless, the whole record requirement is generally honored by responsible ALJs and does not present a significant problem in administrative law. The whole record rule has unquestionably greatly improved the quality of decision-making in agency hearings. Probably the best description of the whole record requirement in the context of the substantial evidence rule that agency adjudicators should follow is found in *300 Gramatan* v. *Human Rights Division,* 45 N.Y. 2d 176, 181 (1978): "In the final analysis, substantial evidence consists of proof within the whole record of such quality and quantity as to generate conviction in and persuade a fair and detached fact finder that, from that proof as a premise, a conclusion or ultimate fact may be extracted reasonably—probatively and logically."

Hearing Decisions Must be Based upon the Exclusive Record

One of the most fundamental principles in administrative law is the *exclusiveness-of-the-record* principle. It is simple and easy to understand, but these simple principles normally carry the most practical weight in law because they are easy to comprehend, follow, and enforce. The exclusiveness-of-the-record principle means that hearing examiners must base their decisions *only* on the evidence produced during the hearing proceeding that constitutes the exclusive record. There are only a few exceptions to this principle. The exclusiveness-of-the-record principle is stated clearly in the federal APA, Section 556(e): "The transcript of testimony and exhibits, together with all papers and requests filed in the proceeding, constitutes the exclusive record for decision . . . ."

As noted, the exclusive record principle is and should be a basic maxim that must be followed in a judicial proceeding, whether an agency hearing or a court trial. How absurd it would be if parties in an agency adjudication presented and responded to evidence on the record and then the adjudicators later reached a decision based on evidence not entered as evidence during the hearing when parties had an opportunity to rebut it. The Court in *Mazza* v. *Cavicchia,* 105 A.2d 545, 554 (N.J.; 1954), noted how ridiculous and unfair such adjudicative behavior would be: "Unless the principle is observed, the right to a hearing itself becomes meaningless. Of what real worth is the right to present evidence and to argue its significance at a formal hearing, if the one who decides the case may stray at will from the record in reaching his decision."

Of course, problems develop when agency adjudicators in fact do rely upon information to reach decisions that are not a part of the exclusive record. *Ex parte* contacts or communications may unduly prejudice hearing decisions because such contacts may provide hearing decision-makers with information not noted on the record. *Ex parte* communications are patently unfair and tend to undermine due process in hearing decision-making because the information tends to be one-sided, almost always favoring one party at the expense of the other. And since the *ex parte* information is not included as part of the record, a rebuttal to it could not be given by the other party in the dispute. Besides, since *ex parte* evidence is not part of the exclusive record, reviewing courts could never judge the weight adjudicators gave to it when making the decision. It is for these reasons, the court acknowledged in *Portland Audubon Soc.* v. *Endangered Species,* 984 F.2d 1534 (9th Cir. 1993), that the Administrative Procedure Act, Sec. 557(d)(1), prohibits off-the-record *ex parte* contacts.

Ex parte communications, contacts, or pressures can easily bias or severely contaminate a hearing decision; thus courts have found *ex parte* influence peddling generating *ex parte* evidence to be flatly illegal under most conditions. In a leading case, *Sangamon Valley Television Corp.* v. *U.S.,* 269 F.2d 221 (D.C. Cir.; 1959), the court overturned a decision by the FCC allowing a television station to relocate in St. Louis because of improper *ex parte* influence peddling. The court noted that such *ex parte* contacts struck at the core of the Commission's quasi-judicial powers, corrupting the process. Fundamental fairness, the court argued, requires that the proceeding be conducted in the open, with all the evidence becoming part of the exclusive record. In *English* v. *Long Beach,* 217 P.2d 22 (Col.; 1950), the court held that the exclusiveness-of-the-record rule prohibits talking to a doctor about the extent of injury off the record and outside the hearing, while in *Cowart* v. *Schweiker,* 662 P.2d 731 (11th Cir.; 1981), the court concluded that the exclusiveness-of-the-record principle had been violated because hearing examiners considered medical reports by doctors submitted after the close of the hearing.

The exclusiveness-of-the-record principle is also violated by the gathering and use of "secret evidence" by hearing officials to help aid their decision. In an old state case, *Carstens* v. *Pillsbury,* 158 P. 218, 220 (Col.; 1916), the court held that to gather secret evidence ". . . and to consider it without even giving the parties an opportunity to . . . meet it in any reasonable way, is contrary to all principles of justice and fairness. It cannot be entertained for a moment." *Ex parte* "views" or inspections also violate the exclusiveness of the record rule by allowing the viewer (agency adjudicator) to view something (e.g., accident site) outside of the record, preventing the "view" from being cross-examined. Of course, the *ex parte* view could cause injustices in hearing decisions, especially if the view happened to be a mistaken or incorrect one. In *Feinson* v. *Conservation Comm.,* 429 A.2d 910 (Conn.; 1981), an *ex parte* view was found to undermine the exclusiveness of the record because it was not noted on the record and no opportunity was given to rebut the view. But in *Zuniga* v. *San Mateo Dept. of Health Serv.,* 267 Cal. Rprt. 755, 761 (Cal. App. 1 Dist.; 1990), the court upheld the *ex parte* view because no prejudice from the viewing was identified and the other party was given sufficient opportunity to respond to the *ex parte* viewed evidence.

The *Zuniga* decision is rooted in a controversial application of the exclusiveness-of-the-record principle regarding the use of *ex parte* evidence. *Ex parte* evidence is sometimes allowed by courts, especially if it can be shown that no prejudice resulted and an opportunity was given to rebut it. In *Market Street Ry* v. *Railroad Commission,* 324 U.S. 548, 562 (1945), the Supreme Court argued that in addition to showing that *ex parte* evidence was received, prejudice must be demonstrated to show that due process violations occurred. The basic criticism of the *Market Street* ruling is that it tends to require opposing parties to prove that *ex parte* evidence or any extra-record evidence has somehow prejudiced the hearing decision. Since demonstrating prejudice is frequently very difficult to do, critics contend that such a requirement would really take the thunder out of the exclusiveness-of-the-record rule. Consequently, many courts have totally rejected the controversial ruling on the exclusiveness-of-the-record principle espoused in *Market Street,* which is not that difficult since the *Market Street* Court spoke before the federal APA became law. Probably most courts follow the approach adopted in *First Savings and Loan Assn.* v. *Vandygriff:* "It is not the burden of the complaining party to demonstrate harm by showing the extent, if any, to which the official was persuaded by the secret information" (at 742).

Use of Official Notice in Reaching Decisions

Closely linked to the principle of exclusiveness-of-the-record is the doctrine of *official notice.* In fact, official notice constitutes the most significant exception to the exclusiveness-of-the-record requirement because officially noticed facts (i.e., "very obvious" facts) are permitted to be used by adjudicators to help substantiate their hearing decisions as "extra-record" evidence after the hearing is over. Let us put the use of official notice into perspective.

In reflecting on the appropriateness of evidence employed to justify judicial decisions, Justice Louis Brandeis concluded: "Nothing can be treated as evidence which is not introduced as such." If taken literally, and it never has been, Brandeis's holding would preclude the use of *judicially noticed facts* in court trials and *officially noticed facts* in administrative hearings. To avoid confusion at the outset, it should be made clear that judicial or official notice is not the same as "notice provided" to a party. Judicial and official notice refer simply to when a tribunal accepts a fact as obvious and notorious without further proof. When a court notices (recognizes) a fact as indisputably true, the court is judicially noticing the fact. Official notice is the administrative tribunal's counterpart to judicial notice. Therefore, when hearing officers accept facts as unquestionably true, these officials are giving official notice to these facts. Officially noticed facts are normally supposed to be so indisputable or obvious that reasonable people would accept them as common knowledge (for example, Christmas falls on December 25). Officially noticed facts, if they cannot be acknowledged as true on the spot, should at least be easily verified by consulting, say, a telephone book or public records. Because of the nature of such facts, officially noticed facts are normally not entered into the record; yet they do form part of the extra-record used by hearing examiners to reach their decisions (*Citizens of the State of Florida* v. *Florida Public Serv. Comm'n.,* 440 So.2d 371 [Fla. Appl., 1983]; and *Dionne* v. *Heckler,* 585 F.Supp. 1055 [D.Me., 1984]).

It is easy to justify the use of official notice; for Brandeis's standard to be applied literally would create unnecessary and counterproductive hardships for all tribunals. In administrative agencies, it would slow down to a crawl the disposition of cases. Surely it would be silly not to recognize and use facts that are obvious and helpful to those hearing officials wanting to make fair, reasonable, and practical decisions. It would be a serious mistake for independent regulatory commissioners, for example, to ignore practical and obvious facts when deciding public policy questions that, when implemented in the real world, will have significant social impact.

It would be just as absurd to permit unreasonable and time-consuming challenges to indisputable facts employed responsibly by hearing officials to reach decisions. Although there has been some scholarly and judicial debate over how flexibly official notice should be applied by administrative tribunals, in general, reviewing courts have allowed hearing examiners to officially notice facts that are not obvious to the general public, yet are readily accepted as common knowledge to agency experts who have acquired considerable expertise in specialized areas.[66] The Supreme Court has acknowledged that hearing decisions cannot always be totally supported by the evidence in the record; nor is such support required. Therefore, decisions must ultimately rest in part on facts that are officially noticed by agency experts.[67] But expertise should not be irresponsibly used by agencies to notice facts which cannot be given such status legitimately. This would constitute an abuse of the function of official notice, thus causing the appropriate employment of official notice to "become lost in the haze of so-called expertise."[68]

Although there is no evidence to indicate that official notice has been misused to any significant extent in agency hearings, problems could arise to undermine the extension of fair adjudications if hearing officials acted irresponsibly. Most notably, they could use official notice to recognize facts that are not obviously true, even to the experts. When highly complex, technical questions are involved, giving official notice to facts is less convincing and inappropriate. Even worse, hearing examiners could use facts that are officially noticed only after the hearing proceedings have ended to help substantiate their findings. This practice has bothered reviewing courts because it unfairly prevents any challenges to the validity and use of the officially noticed facts. In *Heckler* v. *Campbell*, 103 S.Ct. 1952, 1953 (1983), the Supreme Court said that it is a basic administrative law principle "that when an agency takes official or administrative notice of facts, a litigant must be given an adequate opportunity to respond."

Also, the agency that initiates the action normally has the burden of proof. If hearing officers place significant weight on officially noticed facts to substantiate their decisions, even if they allow parties the opportunity to challenge these facts, in effect, the agency is illegitimately shifting the burden of proof from itself to the parties before it. This is so because now the facts are assumed to be accurate unless the parties before an agency show the facts to be untrue.

In sum, few seem to have any serious reservations about the use of official notice, as long as its use does not jeopardize procedural due process protections in agency hearings. For fair procedures to be honored, most experts believe that official notice must be kept limited in its application. According to scholars, responsible employment of official notice would involve: (1) making certain that all officially noticed facts are actually obvious and well known to the average person; (2) noticing technical facts not considered common knowledge to the average person only if the facts are recognized as indisputable knowledge by experts in the field (for example, that recklessly disposing radioactive waste poses a serious health hazard); (3) informing all relevant parties in regard to the officially noticed facts considered to help reach the decision; (4) providing sources to officially noticed facts (for example, agency files); (5) the exclusion of *litigation facts* (facts that have emerged in the pending dispute since such facts are presently in question); (6) prohibiting the use of officially noticed facts for establishing principal evidence on which the decision rests; (7) likewise, the preclusion of any officially noticed facts from becoming part of the substantial evidence; and (8) sufficient opportunity to contest all officially noticed facts that could be reasonably challenged (for example, facts in agency files cited but not brought forth). The last limitation seems to be the most vital in preserving fair use of official notice.

Concluding the Hearing Business

The final actions taken by ALJs to conclude hearing business involves the issuance of the written decision. Before the hearing officials write or issue a "recommended, initial, or tentative decision" ("final" decision of the ALJ, but tentative since it can be rejected by the agency head), Section 557(c) of the APA requires that all parties be given "reasonable opportunity to submit . . . (1) proposed findings and conclusions; (2) exceptions to the decisions or recommended decisions . . . ; and (3) supporting reasons for the exceptions or proposed findings or conclusions." Such is normally submitted in the form of legal briefs to the ALJ.

Section 557(c) also specifically requires that the record should ". . . show the ruling on each finding, conclusion, or exception presented." The Section also requires that "all decisions including initial, recommended, and tentative decisions" be part of the formal written record and ". . . include a statement of (A) findings and conclusions, and the reasons or basis therefore, on all the material issues of fact, law, or discretion presented on the record; and (B) the appropriate rule, order, sanction, relief, or denial thereof."

Regarding formal adjudicative decisions, the APA provisions are quite specific and demanding, but evidently the intent of Congress was to force adjudicators to act responsibly in making hearing decisions. Specifically, by compelling ALJs to justify in detail the factual and legal reasons for their findings, Congress in effect is forcing hearing officials to think seriously about their hearing decisions. Of course, this also tends to promote responsible and democratically accountable hearing decisions, as well as a justification for agency orders (public policies) that will make it easier for all affected parties to follow and understand. Possibly most important from a legal standpoint is that detailed justifications for findings and conclusions make judicial review considerably easier and much more effective.

Despite the specific requirement regarding the documentation of hearing decisions, hearing records too often are woefully inadequate, resulting in poorly

documented decisions. Many judges still complain that they cannot conduct competent judicial review of agency adjudications because of inadequate hearing records,
despite repeated attempts by the courts over the years to make agency adjudicators
keep adequate hearing records by complying with APA record-keeping requirements.
Observers have maintained that adjudicators still keep poor hearing records because
agencies conduct too many hearings and the actual drafting of the decisions has been
delegated to lower-level bureaucrats ("opinion writers"). Such opinion writers end up
justifying decisions in vague, generic legal reasons, failing to justify in specific legal
terms the particular case. Consequently, "the opinion becomes more of a rationalization for the decision than an explanation."[69]

It must be stressed that ALJs do not make final decisions for the agency.
Agency heads have the authority to make "institutional decisions" for their particular
agency or bureaucracy by overruling the decision reached by an ALJ. This is a legally
sanctioned agency right and it is considered legitimate because agency heads, almost
always political appointees, have the obligation of promoting policies that are consistent with the administration's views (i.e., the presidential administration on the
federal level and the governor's administration on the state level). As a consequence,
an ALJ's decision technically constitutes only a tentative decision or an advisory
opinion subject to being overruled by the agency chief. As a practical matter, most
hearing decisions are quite routine and "apolitical" and, therefore, become the
agency's final decision. However, hearing decisions that are politically sensitive may
be reversed by the agency head to make agency policy consistent with the administration's policy. Courts urge that reasonable justifications be given to justify reversing
an ALJ's decision, but reasonable justifications are not always given since political
reasons do not always seem reasonable in light of the specific facts and law pertaining to a particular case (*Central Transport Inc.* v. *National Labor Relations Board,*
997 F.2d 1180 [1993]).

The current practice of permitting agency heads inevitably to decide a hearing
decision bothers some practitioners and scholars because the practice rejects an
old, commonsensical legal principle established in *Morgan* v. *U.S.,* 298 U.S. 468,
481 (1936), that "[T]he one who hears must decide." In this case Chief Justice Hughes argued that responsible and fair decision-making ". . . cannot be
performed by one who has not considered evidence or argument" (at 481). However, increasing hearing caseloads forced a more practical, flexible approach, so
in a follow-up case, *Morgan* v. *U.S.,* 304 U.S. 1, 18 (1938), known as *Morgan II,*
the Supreme Court held that the decision-maker need not be present at the hearing,
as long as he ". . . dipped into (the record) from time to time to get its drift." *Morgan
II* had the effect of allowing subordinates to hear and decide cases. Today, and for
many decades now, agency heads only casually review the tentative decisions
reached by ALJs, rejecting those decisions that staffers recommend should be
changed to suit administrative policy. As noted, even the ALJs assign the writing
of the decisions to their assistants or "opinion writers," bureaucratizing and im-
personalizing the whole process, which at times causes due process to be undeter-
mined.

SUMMARY

It was noted in Chapter 5 that many critics believe that agency rule-making procedures are not very democratic and, as a result, rules are promulgated which tend to benefit the more influential groups in our society. But this chapter stressed that, by comparison, most scholars hold that rule-making is a far better method for making public policies, especially those policies aimed at large groups, than is the order-making process. Basically, rule-making is preferred because it is perceived as a much more open, democratic process than order-making. That is, while agency adjudications are normally closed to outside interested parties who are not specific litigants in the dispute, the rule-making process is open to all interested parties who want to influence the drafting of rules. Rules, the product of agency rule-making, are also favored over orders for promulgating general policies because they are future-general in nature, while orders have a past-specific orientation. Although the rule-making process is generally considered to be the best approach for agencies to employ when making public policies, some agencies such as the NLRB have, nevertheless, relied heavily upon order-making. Administrators in these agencies have found order-making very convenient, especially when they have felt that it is desirable to make policies gradually and cautiously on a case-by-case basis.

Before the passage of the Administrative Procedure Act in 1946, the courts conveyed the clear message, especially in *Morgan* v. *United States,* 304 U.S. 1 (1938), that public agencies needed to improve their hearing procedures to make them more consistent with constitutional due process standards. Provisions in the APA, however, helped to make agency hearings more fair. Although APA requirements stopped short of demanding that agencies conduct hearings like court trials, court decisions since 1946 have had the impact of making formal agency hearings come close to mirroring court procedures, especially in regard to giving notice, keeping records, presenting evidence, weighing evidence, and reaching decisions based upon substantial evidence. Since *Goldberg* v. *Kelly,* 397 U.S. 254 (1970), the courts have been pondering the question of whether agencies, under certain circumstances, should even be compelled to provide persons paid counsel in hearings.

The trend toward making administrative hearings more trial-like has bothered many critics who claim that, although moves to make hearings more like court trials have generally improved due process protections in agency hearings, these steps have placed an unduly heavy and costly burden on agency officials and taxpayers. They maintain essentially that public agencies were not designed to act as courts in our political system. They assert also that excessive legal formalism in agency hearings has precluded the possibility of efficient public administration and that it has caused injustices because it has created unnecessary administrative delays.

NOTES

1. See Kenneth C. Davis, *Discretionary Justice: A Preliminary Inquiry* (Chicago: University of Illinois Press, 1969), chap. 3; Henry J. Friendly, *The Federal Administrative Agencies: The Need for Better Definition of Standards* (Cambridge, Mass.: Harvard University Press,

1962), chap. 1; David L. Shapiro, "The Choice of Rulemaking or Adjudication in the Development of Administrative Policy," *Harvard Law Review,* 78 (March 1965), 921–72; J. Skelly Wright, "Rulemaking and Judicial Review," *Administrative Law Review,* 30 (Summer 1987), 461–66; Richard K. Berg, "Re-examining Policy Procedures: The Choice Between Rulemaking and Adjudication," *Administrative Law Review,* 38 (Spring 1986), 149–80; and Cornelius M. Kerwin, *Rulemaking: How Government Agencies Write Law and Make Policy* (New York: Congressional Quarterly Press, 1994), 50–51, 161–213.

2. Edwin J. Madaj, "Agency Investigations: Adjudication or Rulemaking?—The ITC's Material Inquiry Determinations under the Antidumping and Countervailing Duty Laws," N.C.J. Int'l and Com. Reg., V. 15 (1990), 445.

3. For one critic's analysis, see William Funk, "Rationality Review of State Administrative Rulemaking," *Administrative Law Review,* vol. 43 (Spring 1991). Funk does a good job of comparing the use of the rule-making approach for making public policies at the state and federal levels.

4. Shapiro, "Choice of Rulemaking or Adjudication in the Development of Administrative Policy," 940–41; Kerwin, *Rulemaking,* 161–213.

5. Bernard Schwartz, *Administrative Law,* 2nd ed. (Boston: Little, Brown, 1984), 145–49, 191–96; also Berg, "Re-examining Policy Procedures," 160–76.

6. It should be acknowledged that agency decisions, which have great impact on the shaping of regulatory policies, are so informal that they cannot be discussed in the context of the more formalized rule-making and order-making procedures. Nevertheless, basic agency policies are normally made through one or the other, order-making or rule-making. Informal discretionary decisions made outside rule-making and order-making tend only to refine and define basic agency policies.

7. Shapiro, "Choice of Rulemaking on Adjudication in the Development of Administrative Policy," 932.

8. Estreicher, "Policy Oscillation at the Labor Board: A Plea for Rulemaking," *Administrative Law Review,* 37 (Spring 1985), 181.

9. Ibid., 177.

10. Kenneth C. Davis and Richard J. Pierce, Jr., *Administrative Law Treatise,* 3rd ed., vol. 1 (Boston: Little, Brown, 1994), 377–378.

11. Edwin W. Tucker, *Administrative Law, Regulation or Enterprise,* and *Individual Liberties* (St. Paul, MN: West Publishing Company, 1975), 108.

12. See *Reeve Aleutian Airways, Inc.* v. *U.S.,* 982 F.2d 594, 598 (1992).

13. Recent works have noted such shifts. See Jeremy Rabkin, *Judicial Compulsions: How Public Law Distorts Public Policy* (New York: Basic Books, 1989); Christopher F. Edley, Jr., *Administrative Law: Rethinking Judicial Control of Bureaucracy* (New Haven: Yale University Press, 1990); and Davis and Pierce, Jr., *Administrative Law Treatise,* 3rd ed., vol. 2, chap. 9.

14. The obsession with the cost-conscious approach is epitomized by cost-benefit analysis, which became very "popular" during the Reagan presidency. See Christopher M. Heiman et al., "Project: The impact of cost-benefit analysis on federal administrative law," *Administrative Law Review,* vol. 42 (Fall 1990), 545–654.

15. Todd D. Rakoff, "*Brock* v. *Roadway Express,* and the New Law of the Regulatory Due Process," *The Supreme Court Review,* vol. 4 (1987), 157–200.

16. Ibid.

17. For an analysis of risk standards in administrative law, see Frank B. Cross, Daniel M. Byrd III, and Lester B. Lave, "Discernible Risk—A Proposed Standard for Significant Risk in Carcinogen Regulation," *Administrative Law Review,* vol. 43 (Winter 1991), 61–88.

18. Victor A. Thompson, *Bureaucracy and the Modern World* (Morristown, NJ: General Learning Press, 1976), 114.

19. Ibid.

20. Ibid., 114–15.

21. Ernest Gellhorn and Ronald M. Levin, *Administrative Law and Process in a Nutshell,* 3rd ed. (St. Paul, MN: West, 1990), 270.

22. Lloyd Musolf, "Administrative Law Judges: A 1948 Snapshot," *Administrative Law Review,* vol. 46 (Summer 1994), 265. For an updated study, see Charles H. Koch, Jr., "Administrative Presiding Officials Today," *Administrative Law Review,* vol. 46 (Summer 1994), 271–295.

23. Norman Abrams, "Administrative Law Judge Systems: The California View," *Administrative Law Review,* 2 (Fall 1977), 490–92. Non-ALJs or administrative judges (AJs) also preside over agency hearings. Although ALJs must hold law degrees, AJs may not have law degrees, yet may be technical experts (e.g., physicists adjudicating a Nuclear Regulatory Commission case). Theoretically, AJs are supposed to be used in "less serious" adjudications (e.g., when basic liberties or severe penalties are not at stake), but this is not always true in practice. In 1992, the Administrative Conference of the United States made recommendations for the use of ALJs and AJs (57 Fed. Reg. 61,760).

24. Kenneth C. Davis, *Administrative Law Treatise,* 2nd ed. (St. Paul, MN: West Publishing Company, 1980), 3: 325–27.

25. Eleanor M. Fox, "Chairman Miller, the Federal Trade Commission, Economics, and *Rashomon,*" *Law and Contemporary Problems,* vol. 50 (Autumn 1987), 35.

26. Ibid.

27. Ibid., 34.

28. Ibid., 34–35.

29. Bernard Schwartz, *Administrative Law: A Casebook* (Boston: Little, Brown and Company, 1988), 510.

30. Abrams, "Administrative Law Judge Systems," 491.

31. For a comprehensive review of the independence question and other issues pertaining to the role and performance of ALJs, see Jeffrey S. Lubbers, "The Federal Administrative Judiciary: Establishing an Appropriate System of Performance Evaluation for ALJs," *The Administrative Law Journal of the American University,* vol. 7 (Fall/Winter 1994), 629–657.

32. For a solid discussion of the appearance of fairness doctrine, see Van Noy, "The Appearance of Fairness Doctrine: A Conflict in Values," *Washington Law Review,* vol. 61 (1986).

33. Also, see *Grant* v. *Shalala,* 989 F.2d 1332, 1345 (1993), in which the court stressed that all tribunals ". . . must be unbiased but also must avoid even the appearance of bias." For a critique of *Grant,* see Bernard Schwartz, "Administrative Law Cases During 1993," *Administrative Law Review,* vol. 46 (Summer 1994), 311–312. For a thorough analysis of this case, see Edward McGonagle, "Administrative Law," *Syracuse Law Review,* vol. 42 (1991).

34. Stephen Hobbs, "Judicial Discipline and Due Process in Washington State," *Washington Law Review,* vol. 63 (1988), 732–737.

35. Stephen R. Miller and Larry T. Richardson, "A Central Panel System for Mississippi's Administrative Law Judges; Promoting the Due Process of Law in Administrative Hearings," *Mississippi College Law Review,* vol. 6 (Spring 1986), 133.

36. Ibid.

37. Hobbs, op. cit., 737.

38. Joseph E. Edwards, "Disqualification of Federal Trade Commission or Members Thereof," *American Law Reports,* vol. 8 (1991).

39. Michael H. Graham, "The Case for Model Rules of Evidence in Administrative Adjudications," *Federal Bar News and Journal,* vol. 38 (May 1991), 189.

40. Ibid.

41. Richard J. Pierce, Jr., "Use of the Federal Rules of Evidence in Federal Agency Adjudications," *Administrative Law Review,* vol. 39 (Winter 1987), 2–3.

42. Ibid.

43. Davis, *Administrative Law and Government,* 192.

44. *Altenheim German Home* v. *Turnock,* 902 F.2d 582,584 (7th Cir.; 1990).

45. Bernard Schwartz, "Administrative Law Cases During 1990," *Administrative Law Review,* vol. 43 (Summer 1991), 481.

46. Bernard Schwartz, *Administrative Law: A Casebook* (Boston: Little Brown and Company, 1988), 553.

47. Hearsay represents the modern grammatical construction of the eleventh-century Old English expression, "saying-hear" and the twelfth century's version, "heard saying." "Hear-saying" was noted by the year 1340, and by the sixteenth century, the term *hearsay* first came into use in the practice of law. By the close of the seventeenth century, rules governing hearsay had become firmly established in English law. See Dennis Murphy, "Hearsay: The Least Understood Exclusionary Rule," *Journal of Criminal Justice,* vol. 17 (1989).

48. Murphy, op. cit., 269. Because of all the exceptions to the hearsay rule and the controversy pertaining to its use, Eleanor Swift in "Abolishing the Hearsay Rule," *California Law Review,* vol. 75 (1987) discusses the consequences of abolishing the hearsay rule. She concludes that we should consider further many assumptions and values on the hearsay rule before thinking of abandoning it.

49. Thomas R. Mulroy, Jr., and Douglas G. McClure, "The Case for Allowing Hearsay in Illinois Administrative Proceedings," *Illinois Bar Journal* (June 1989), 556.

50. It is not uncommon for courts to maintain that reliable documents such as medical reports are technically only hearsay, but for all practical purposes should be considered substantial evidence because of their high quality and probative value. For example, the Supreme Court in *Richardson* v. *Perales,* 402 U.S. 406, 407–408 (1971), noted that "[A]lthough the reports are hearsay in the technical sense, because their content is not produced live before the hearing examiner, we feel . . ." that such evidence can constitute "substantial evidence" because of its "reliability and probative value."

51. Kenneth C. Davis, *Administrative Law Treatise,* vol. 3, 242.

52. For a lengthy discussion of the exclusionary rule in administrative law, see Scott Meacham, "Evidence: The Exclusionary Rule in Civil Administrative Hearings: *Turner* v. *City of Lawton,*" *Oklahoma Law Review,* vol. 40 (1987), 321–337.

53. *Powell* v. *Alabama,* 287 U.S. 45, 68–69 (1982).

54. A parole revocation seems to many people to be a criminal law matter, not an administrative one, but it is administrative because it involves the question of what to do administratively about a person's prison sentence after that individual has been convicted

in a criminal court. Questions concerning the granting or revoking of parole are handled by an administrative tribunal, usually called a parole board.

55. Tucker, *Administrative Law, Regulation of Enterprise, and Individual Liberties,* 127.

56. For a review of legal representation at the SSA, see William Justin DeLoenardis, "Representing Your Client at the Social Security Disability Hearing," *Washington State Bar News* (October 1987), 21–23; Prentice Cox, "Social Security Netting Regulations: Balancing Administrative Convenience with the Rights of Beneficiaries," *Minnesota Law Review,* vol. 73 (1989), 1143–1174.

57. Henry J. Friendly, "Some Kind of Hearing," *University of Pennsylvania Law Review,* 123 (June 1975), 1289.

58. Ibid., 1288.

59. Ibid., 1290–91.

60. Ibid., 1290.

61. William D. Popkin, "Effect of Representation on a Claimant's Success Rate—Three Study Designs," *Administrative Law Review,* 31 (Fall 1979), 449–61.

62. Ibid., 451.

63. Despite exceptions to the preponderance-of-the-evidence standard, the courts are very reluctant to require a higher standard of proof than the federal APA or state APAs minimally require. In *SEC* v. *Savoy Industries,* 587F.2d 1149 D.C. Cir.; 1978), (issuing an injunction); *Walters* v. *Lucas,* 497 F.2d 1230 (9th Cir.; 1979) (revocation of pilot's license); and *In re Revocation of License of Polk,* 449 A2d7 (N.J., 1982) medical disciplinary hearing), the preponderance-of-the-evidence standard was found to be sufficient.

64. In *Woodby* v. *INS,* 385 U.S. 276 (1966), the Supreme Court reviewed standards of proof but did not discuss how the standards actually differed.

65. Louis J. Jaffe, "Administrative Procedure Re-examined: The Benjamin Report," *Harvard Law Review,* vol. 54 (March 1943), 732.

66. For a review of this debate, see Stephen G. Breyer and Richard B. Stewart, *Administrative Law and Regulatory Policy,* 2nd ed. (Boston: Little, Brown, 1985), 625–33.

67. *FCC* v. *Nat'l. Citizens Commission,* 98 S.Ct. 2096.

68. *Baltimore & O.R. Co.* v. *Aberdeen & R.R. Co.,* 303 U.S. 87, 91–92 (1986); and *Carson* v. *Department of Employment Security,* 376 A.2d 355 (Vt., 1977).

69. For an in-depth review of the politicalization of medicare adjudications, see Eleanor D. Kinney, "In Search of Bureaucratic Justice—Adjudicating Medicare Home Health Benefits in the 1980s," *Administrative Law Review,* vol. 42 (Spring 1990).

ADMINISTERING PUBLIC POLICIES: DISCRETIONARY AGENCY ACTIONS

In this book it has been stressed that administrative agencies, much to the dismay of those who endorse a clear separation of powers in government, have legislative, judicial, and administrative powers. We have just concluded a discussion regarding agency order-making functions, while in Chapter 5 the rule-making authority of public agencies was examined. In this chapter, emphasis is on administrators in their traditional role as administrators of congressionally sanctioned public policies. We want to describe and assess the policy implementation powers of agency officials, especially in light of their broad discretionary authority. Because of the major role administrative discretion plays in administrative law, virtually the entire chapter is devoted to discussion of the use and misuse of discretionary power, with special attention paid to how sound discretionary actions can be promoted and abuses of discretion can be minimized.

FORMAL VERSUS INFORMAL AGENCY ACTIONS

Agency officials can follow either relatively formal or informal procedures. Of course, agency actions are not wholly formal or informal, but a mixture of the two. That is, formal action would consist of decision-making processes based solely on the book, in which detailed steps are followed when arriving at decisions. However, since the Administrative Procedure Act or other acts or rules always allow administrators some freedom of choice (discretion) when making decisions, even under the most formalized or structural decision-making situations, complete adherence to formal procedures becomes both impossible and undesirable.

Actually, only about 10 percent of all administrative action can be properly classified as formal.[1] A formal agency action normally consists of those actions by administrators which fall well within prescribed (usually written) procedures, as dictated by legislative statutes, court rulings, and/or agency rules and regulations. Formal administrative action, as contrasted to informal administrative action, is characterized by the limited role an administrator's discretion can play in determining what procedures can be followed and what decisions can be reached as the result of following specified procedures. The clearest example of formal agency behavior can be seen when agencies make orders through the holding of formal hearings, which are similar to trial-like proceedings. Agency rule-making can also be quite formal if administrators follow the elaborate provisions for making rules as required in Sections 556 and 557 of the APA, discussed previously. Generally speaking, informal action refers to any administrative action or inaction (for example, a decision not to act) that does not use a trial-like hearing. Formal rule-making requires a trial-like hearing and is governed by Sections 556 and 557 of the APA, while informal rule-making, which does not require a formal hearing, is governed by Section 553 or not by the APA at all. Likewise, adjudications which require a formal trial-like evidentiary hearing are considered formal, while adjudications that occur without a trial-like hearing are considered informal.

As an academic exercise, it would be futile to try to classify all administrative actions into neat categories as either formal or informal because in practice administrators interchange formal and informal procedures. For example, hearings range from the very informal to the very formal, but at what exact point does formality begin and informality end? That is, at what precise point does an administrative hearing become formal enough to be considered trial-like? When some traits of a trial are present, yet others are not, it becomes quite difficult to judge just how formal or trial-like the administrative hearing is.

As noted, informal administrative actions are characterized by a broader use of administrative discretion than are formal administrative activities. As the formal-informal agency action continuum in Figure 7.1 illustrates, the more agency actions are controlled by administrative discretion, the more informal the agency action is. Conversely, the more formal the procedural codes (statutes, rules, court orders) that dictate agency actions, the more formal the agency action is considered to be. Of course, agency actions would never, in practice, be completely controlled by formal procedural codes or totally dominated by an administrator's discretion. The extreme ends in the continuum represent only the theoretical extremes. Although at times one may not perceive any evidence that an administrator's discretionary decisions are being modified by prevailing legal sanctions, in reality administrators, at least sane ones, are always cognizant of the need to give in somewhat to environmental pressures to conform to expected patterns of behavior. Systems theory conveys the point that it would be unrealistic to think that administrators could expect to survive in office for long by totally ignoring all prevailing legal and professional sanctions when employing their discretionary powers. An appropriate response to systemic demands would entail keeping the use of discretion within at least minimally tolerable bounds.

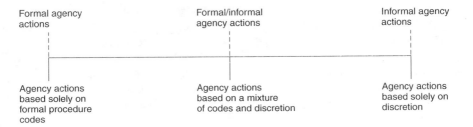

FIGURE 7.1   *Discretion in Formal-Informal Agency Actions*

But this is not to suggest that administrative discretion is not abused. In fact, much of this chapter studies abuses of discretion and methods for controlling them. However, it is maintained that the vast majority of discretionary acts by our public administrators are reasonable because they are guided by numerous legal, ethical, and professional standards of conduct forced upon them by the system in which they function. Even when reviewing court cases involving the use of discretion, one finds that most allegations of discretionary abuse rest on technical legal arguments.

DEFINING ADMINISTRATIVE DISCRETION

Discretionary actions by administrators are informal administrative acts, even though they may be within an administrator's formal authority. According to Kenneth C. Davis, the most authoritative source on the concept of administrative discretion, a public administrator "has discretion whenever the effective limits on his power leave him free to make a choice among possible courses of action or inaction."[2] To Davis, it is important to stress, as it is implied above, that "discretion is not limited to what is authorized or what is legal but includes all that is within 'the *effective* limits' on the officer's power."[3] Davis adds that the specific phraseology he employs to describe discretion "is necessary because a good deal of discretion is illegal or of questionable legality."[4]

Davis holds that the lifeblood of the administrative process "is informal discretionary action."[5] Further, he emphasizes that informal discretionary power is enormous, especially when compared to an administrator's quite limited formal powers.[6] Scholars have noted that although vague and general statutes give rise to discretionary power, these statutes do not effectively control or limit discretion. Consequently, all willful administrators can use their discretionary authority to make themselves far more powerful than their creators, the Constitutional framers and legislators, probably originally intended.[7]

When examining the breadth of informal discretionary power, it is easy to understand why it is considered to be the lifeblood of the administrative process. Informal discretionary powers include such positive functions as "initiating, prosecuting, negotiating, settling, contracting, dealing, advising, threatening, publicizing, concealing, planning, recommending and supervising."[8] But the most awesome discretionary power is the "omnipresent power to do nothing."[9] That is, administrators may simply decide not to initiate, prosecute, negotiate, settle, contract, deal, and so on. These negative discretionary powers in practice provide administrators with more discretionary clout than do positive discretionary powers, because it is far more difficult to check the former than the latter. That is, action, simply because it is action, is more easy to control than inaction, since checks are designed mostly to cope with abusive action, not abusive inaction.

For those of us interested in the problems of implementing public policies, the above has obvious implications. Through failing to act, or acting very feebly, administrators can use their discretionary powers to help ensure the failure of certain duly authorized public programs under their jurisdiction which they disfavor. Although courts have ruled that administrators are not free to use their discretionary authority to block the implementation of programs authorized by Congress, or to prevent persons from receiving their statutory entitlements, strong-willed administrators may nevertheless have their way in most instances, especially since forcing administrators to comply with statutory demands through court action is so difficult.[10] As Davis and Pierce, Jr. conclude: "Judicial review of agency action can never be more than a partial solution to the problem of discretion.[11] Federal agencies take millions of actions every year. . . . It is unrealistic to expect courts to identify or to deter each of the occasional cases in which agencies abuse their discretion."[12] Besides, courts work too slowly, frequently acting after the damage has been done (after the administrator has achieved his or her purpose).

When we think of the discretionary power of administrators, we probably think in terms of how administrative officials may employ their broad discretion to say yes or no to certain major program proposals. For example, in Chapter 4, in *D.C. Federation of Civic Associations* v. *Volpe*, 459 F.2d 1231 (1971), we reviewed a situation where John Volpe, then secretary of transportation, used his discretion to approve construction of the Three Sisters Bridge, a very controversial project vehemently opposed by many civic associations and environmentalists. Although Volpe's decision essentially constituted an abuse of discretion in the eyes of Judge Bazelon, the *Volpe* case served, *inter alia,* to demonstrate the vast discretionary powers administrators possess to make final decisions, thus very likely determining the fate of major public programs. It is true that administrators possess great discretionary powers in making final decisions, but Davis holds that an administrator's interim decisions may actually carry more weight than his or her final decisions.[13] Interim actions may be more subtle, but they can nevertheless make or break programs. In essence, interim decisions determine what steps, if any, should be taken to reach some end. Of course, an administrator's interim decisions play a significant role in determining the possible ends which will result. Typically, agency administrators use their discretion to make interim decisions in response to such key questions as: "Shall we investigate the X Company? Shall we institute an investigation proceeding? Shall we make it a prosecutory proceeding? Or shall we make it somewhat one and somewhat the other, allowing its nature to change as it progresses? Shall we give X a chance to escape by agreeing to comply? Or shall we make an example of X? Shall we start a cease-and-desist order proceeding, or shall we recommend a criminal prosecution to the Department of Justice?"[14]

Such interim questions appear to be endless; yet how each question is answered may make a big difference to, say, company X: "X may be vitally affected at every step. Even if it is found guilty of nothing the investigation may cost half a million. Or its license worth millions may be jeopardized. Adverse publicity may cripple its business."[15] Discretionary interim decision making may also play a critical role in determining the fate of public policies. In *Implementation*, Jeffrey Pressman and Aaron Wildavsky held that success in implementing public policy programs depends heavily upon whether administrators make the vital discretionary interim decisions which permit programs to pass the crucial "clearance points" necessary for program survival.[16] In sum, dramatic final actions by public agencies may make front-page news headlines ("Fed hikes interest rates against Clinton's wishes"), but the daily, routine, non-newsworthy interim decisions (Fed decides to discount Labor Department's projection on unemployment) are largely responsible for preventing such agency headline stories from ever occurring.

Thus far, administrative discretion has been defined in the context of substantive decision making, but the scope of informal discretion extends much further. Says Davis: "Discretion is not limited to substantive choices but extends to procedures, methods, forms, timing, degrees of emphasis, and many other subsidiary factors."[17] Actually, because administrative law focuses on procedure, administrative law scholars and the courts are not so much interested in what substantive choices were made, but in how discretion was used by administrators in making their choices. Figure 7.2 illustrates how an administrator can ideally exercise his or her discretion in resolving an administrative problem. The model conveys that to resolve an administrative problem, an administrator would first have to employ discretion to discover the relevant facts and then use discretion to search for those applicable laws, rules, and so on, which would settle the matter. But this ideal conceptualization is grossly complicated in reality. In the real world, administrators may use their discretionary powers to deny that a problem even exists. This action in itself must be regarded as a powerful exercise of discretion.

But even if an administrator acknowledges the existence of the problem, discretion may be exercised to define it in a particular way. Naturally, the discretion to define the problem in various ways provides administrators with the flexibility to arrive at different possible solutions. In addition, administrators can use their discretion to determine what facts are relevant and what laws, rules, and so on, are pertinent. Of course, the discretion to include and exclude facts which are perceived as relevant or irrelevant allows administrators the opportunity to apply or not apply various laws, rules, and so on, since the facts of a situation obviously determine what laws and rules should be applied. Discretionary decisions are also clouded by administrators' past experiences, present environmental circumstances and pressures, politics, and personal values. Regarding police discretion, Joel Samaha comments: "Discretion

FIGURE 7.2   *Ideal Exercise of Discretion*

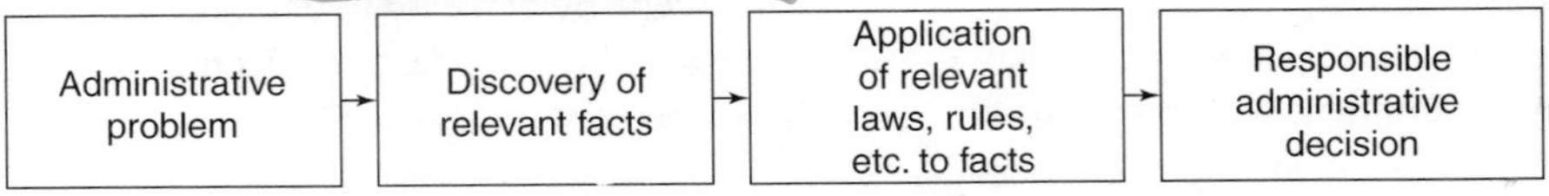

creates an enormous gap between what law books say and what law officers actually do, because class, race, economics, and politics influence discretion."[18] Uncertainty also plays an intervening role: "A decision as to what is desirable may include not only weighing desirability but also guessing about unknown facts and making a judgment about doubtful law, and the mind that makes the decision does not necessarily separate facts, law, and discretion. Furthermore, the term 'discretion' may or may not include the judgment that goes into finding facts from conflicting evidence and into interpreting unclear law; the usage is divided."[19] In sum, discretionary decisions are very complicated informal administrative actions which involve factors and processes which are extremely difficult to pinpoint and assess. It is partly for these reasons that abuses of administrative discretion are hard to prove, especially if bad faith must be shown to substantiate the charge that an administrator abused his or her discretionary authority when reaching a decision.[20]

A HISTORICAL GLANCE AT DISCRETION: RULE OF LAW VERSUS DISCRETIONARY POWER

In an enlightening article entitled "Some Reflections on the Anglo-Saxon Heritage of Discretionary Justice," Joel Samaha asserts that the history of discretion is important to examine because the "discretion/law controversy extends back at least as far as 600 A.D."[21] But more important than the duration of the discretion/law dispute, Samaha contends, is the fact that the arguments for and against the use of discretion versus the strict adherence to law, as well as proposed solutions to the discretionary justice problem, have remained practically unchanged. Through the centuries the discretionary justice problem, he notes, has been to balance the need to ensure equality under law through the consistent and objective application of the laws with the need to make the law sensitive to individual cases.

In studying the use of discretion in Anglo-Saxon history, one must stress that discretion has always somewhat challenged the determined efforts by heads of state to make Anglo-Saxon justice based on the rule of law: "Discretion," Samaha has observed "has always been at war with law in Anglo-American history."[22] That is, while rule-of-law government has been associated with the fair and consistent administration of justice in constitutional democracies, the use of discretion in government has traditionally been identified with the unfair, arbitrary, and capricious decisions of absolute leaders in dictatorial systems. Our Anglo-Saxon disdain for the use of discretion may be epitomized best on the Department of Justice building, where a conspicuous engraving reads: "Where Law Ends Tyranny Begins."

But why can we not escape the use of discretion? Is it even desirable to try to abandon our reliance on discretion? Does the engraving on the Justice Department's building represent an overreaction to the possible dangers of discretionary justice? Samaha argues that history has clearly shown that we cannot help but employ discretion, and moreover, that there are sound reasons for incorporating discretion into any governmental system. Even though Samaha notes that the law/discretion controversy dates back to at least 600 A.D., the truth is that the classical Greeks, in the days of Plato and Aristotle, around 400 B.C., recognized the need for discretion to aid administrators in the application of written laws. In a nutshell, it was argued that discretion, although the specific word was not used, gave laws the necessary flexibility to make them viable.[23]

The administration of the Christian penitentials is especially helpful in describing the role of discretion in any system based upon laws. In order to control personal conduct in a manner acceptable to Christian moral principles, a set of books was developed which assigned specific penances for particular sins; these were the *penitentials.* The hope of the Church was that this penitential system could function to minimize the use of discretion by local priests held responsible for enforcing church law (moral codes). However, the priests soon found, as do all who administer regulations of some nature, that a strict adherence to the rules creates many injustices. Exceptions must be made, and the making of exceptions call for discretion.

Samaha reports that the "combination of severity, disparity, and the individualization of sentences all led to the exercise of discretion in the administration of penance."[24] The harshness of the penalties for sins caused priests to mitigate the penalties, especially for those who could not physically endure the required punishments. Priests also had to exercise discretion to resolve the many apparent contradictions in the books of penitentials. Finally, priests believed that special circumstances should be taken into consideration when evaluating the severity of the sin: "It is to the sinner and not the sin that the priest must look if he is to save a soul and restore a sinner to the congregation. Here arose the great problems posed by tailoring the penalty to suit the offender."[25]

Samaha maintains that the discretionary problems which faced these priests one thousand years ago were really eerily similar to the discretionary predicaments which plague decision makers in modern times.[26] Do not our regulatory administrators employ discretion when they decide not to impose penalties on, say, companies which have violated their standards, especially if they feel that the companies could not survive the financial strain? In light of the numerous contradictions in various statutes and rules, does not administrative discretion seem essential to keep administrative operations running smoothly? When imposing penalties, or in administration in general, is discretion not used at times by administrators to fit the regulatory action to individual circumstances? In reviewing agency actions, have not the courts acknowledged in numerous opinions over the years how vital the role of administrative discretion is to the stability of normal administrative operations?

Samaha concludes that even the priests' exercise of discretion was attacked for essentially the same general reasons that modern users of discretion are criticized. For instance, priests were charged with abusing their discretionary powers to: (1) favor special interests; (2) promote their own personal welfare; and (3) indirectly encourage an increase in violations in society through their arbitrary, capricious, and frequently corrupt administration of the rules and standards.[27] Samaha observed that "the corrupting influence of the wide powers of discretion held by the Anglo-Saxon priests is mirrored in the wholesale assault on the sentencing powers of modern-day judges."[28]

This brief historical view of the use of discretion in the past serves to make the simple point that the exercise of discretion, although absolutely necessary, has always presented a problem for societies, especially those which find rule of law principles laudable. To preserve due process under law, many societies have tried to limit the abuses of discretionary power. For example, Bishop Ebo, recognizing that the local priests had to exercise broad discretion in applying the confusing and contradictory books of penitentials, believed that the discretionary justice problem could be resolved by "giving priests proper guidelines to follow so that they would not be left to their own devices in prescribing penance. Specifically, he recommended controlling discretion by rule."[29]

DAVIS ON THE PROBLEM OF DISCRETION

No informed student of administrative law could credibly argue that Davis is not the most authoritative source on the subject of discretionary justice. Since the late 1960s, Davis has written three books on the discretionary justice theme: *Discretionary Justice: A Preliminary Inquiry, Discretionary Justice in Europe and America,* and *Police Discretion.* He has also devoted considerable space to the topic in other works, most notably his comprehensive *Administrative Law Treatise.*[30] Because his ideas on discretion have, by his own admission, changed somewhat over the years, various writings of his are consulted so that an accurate and updated review of his thinking on the subject can be presented.[31]

Davis did not decide to devote so much attention to the discretionary justice problem merely for the fun of it. He is convinced that the discretionary justice issue poses the most serious threat to individual procedural due process rights. Ten years after his publication of *Discretionary Justice,* a book written to inspire needed research efforts in the areas of discretionary justice, he noted that "the dismal fact is that . . . no major work has attempted either to build on that foundation or to create a new foundation on which to build."[32] Consequently, he still holds in the mid-1990s, as emphatically as he did when he wrote *Discretionary Justice* in 1969, that the greatest discretionary injustices are inflicted against individual parties by administrators who abuse their discretionary power when handling these cases. He stresses that ". . . unlimited agency discretion is subject to potential abuse in the form of different treatment of like cases based on impermissible motives or as a consequence of poor institution management or design."[33]

Why does the use of informal discretionary administrative action present such a serious threat to individual liberty? Before responding directly to this question, it is necessary to stress that Davis perceives discretionary justice actions by agency administrators in terms of their impact on individual parties (for example, individuals eligible for welfare, and individual associations and corporations). Public policymaking decisions are excluded from his analysis of discretionary justice because, although they involve discretionary acts (for example, to deregulate or not to deregulate the railroads), they do not involve discretionary justice decisions since the decisions are aimed at a larger group (the railroad industry) and the specific party (a particular railroad company). That is, when a bureaucrat says something is just a matter of policy to a person making an inquiry, the bureaucrat is implying that legislators and agency rulemakers set general policy. The discretionary decisions made to form such policies do not involve discretionary justice. However, in most cases when these general public policies are applied to individual cases, discretionary justice decisions are involved.

Davis thinks several reasons can be given to justify the particularly alarming nature of the discretionary justice problem. Of course, the chief reason is that administrators can easily abuse their discretionary powers when applying general public policies to individual cases. But what makes this problem severe is that the opportunity for discretionary abuses is enormous because, as mentioned before in this chapter, about 90 percent of all agency action involves informal agency action (action in the absence of trial-like procedures). Of the 90 percent of agency action which is informal, Davis holds that about 99 percent of it involves the use of discretion. If this discretionary activity were controlled, the discretionary justice issue would not attract so much attention as a problem, but the fact is that this informal discretionary action is largely uncontrolled. Therefore, the problem is really not how to eliminate discretion (although Davis argues that unnecessary discretion should be eliminated), but how to control it. The severity of the discretionary justice problem is given more weight by the reality that this largely uncontrolled discretion is also not practically subject to judicial review.[34]

But the discretionary justice question continues to remain the number one problem not only in administrative law but also in the quality of justice rendered to individuals by our government, because too many people have a negative attitude toward our human ability to resolve this very challenging legal problem. However, Davis flatly rejects the viewpoint of such a defeatist position. Such negativism, he contends, has retarded research into 90 percent of all administrative behavior.[35] Consequently, research findings in the area of informal and unreviewable discretionary actions, which could provide useful clues on how to better control administrative discretion so that injustices to individuals can be reduced, are virtually nonexistent. Davis admits that many people will find the study of discretionary justice hopeless, thus forcing them to concentrate on the aspects of administrative law which are more concrete and, therefore, easier to study: "That is why the literature of jurisprudence deals with judges and legislators, not with discretion. That is why administrative law literature has been almost entirely limited to rule-making, formal adjudication, and judicial review, with hardly any effort to penetrate the discretionary jungle."[36]

Democratizing Discretion: Confining, Structuring, and Checking Discretion

Davis sharply disagrees with William Pitt's immortalized wisdom, "Where law ends tyranny begins." Davis exclaims that "in our system of government, where law ends tyranny need not begin. Where law ends, discretion begins, and the exercise of discretion may mean either beneficence or tyranny, either justice or injustice, either reasonableness or arbitrariness."[37] To Davis, the quotation on the front of our nation's justice building, "Where Law Ends Tyranny Begins," is a patently absurd insight into the nature of governmental power. He holds correctly that there has never existed in history a government of laws without the exercise of discretionary power by men.[38] Even if we should observe the behavior of those who work within the Department of Justice, in the building on which Pitt's words are engraved, Davis insists that we would quickly discover these governmental employees using discretion to apply laws. We would even find, he continues, that these Justice Department workers would be "much more occupied with discretion than with law. Not one of them who understands his job would agree that where law ends tyranny begins. Every conscientious employee of the Department of Justice, from the Attorney General on down," Davis emphasizes, "is striving to assure that where law ends, wise and beneficent exercise of discretionary power begins."[39]

But what can be done to ensure that discretionary power does not evolve into a tyrannical force? That is, what can be done to democratize the use of discretion? To minimize injustices as a consequence of the misuse of discretionary power, Davis believes that "we should eliminate much unnecessary discretionary power and that we should do much more than we have been doing to confine, to structure, and to check necessary discretionary power. The goal," he maintains, "is not the maximum degree of confining, structuring, and checking; the goal is to find the optimum degree for each power in each set of circumstances."[40] But in holding that administrative discretion should be confined, structured, and checked, what exactly does Davis have in mind?

Confining Discretionary Power   Davis explains that sometimes discretionary power can be too restricted, while at other times it can be too broad. If administrative discretion is too limited, injustices can result from the lack of special consideration given to an individual's unique situation or problem. But when discretionary power is too broad, inequitable, and arbitrary, decisions tend to create injustices. As a general rule, in the American administrative system, discretion is rather limited at the lower administrative levels, where red tape tends to restrict severely the decision-making alternatives of those workers performing relatively routine tasks.[41] But as the administrative functions become more complex and less routine at higher and higher administrative levels, the scope of discretion broadens. Although Davis acknowledges that injustices occur to individuals because discretion may be too confined, he argues that in the American system most injustices occur because the exercise of discretion is much too broad.[42]

Consequently, discretion must be confined. When Davis speaks of confining discretionary power, he is specifically talking about eliminating and limiting its use. Under ideal conditions, he points out, all necessary discretionary power would be confined within specified boundaries, and all unnecessary discretion would lie outside these parameters. Statutes and rules would ideally provide the guidance needed to keep the exercise of discretion absolutely within these confined boundaries, thus preventing administrators from abusing their discretion by stepping beyond their clear scope of legitimate discretionary authority (see Figure 7.3).

However, Davis holds that this ideal is seldom realized, and consequently, injustices result because administrators exceed their reasonable discretionary powers.[43]

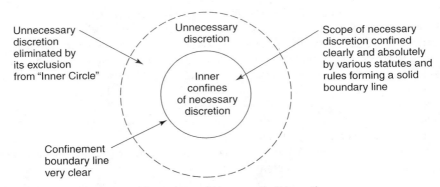

FIGURE 7.3   *Ideal Confinement of Necessary Discretion*

Unreasonable discretionary actions are not illegal, however, because administrative discretion has not been properly confined by statutes and rules. Parenthetically, it should be made clear that statutes create administrative discretion through their vague rhetoric (standards), although even the most conscientious legislators may have a tough time drafting workable statutes (i.e., statutes that do not handcuff administrators) without resorting to nebulous words. In the words of Ernest Freund, written sixty years ago: "A statute confers discretion when it refers an official for the use of his power to beliefs, expectations, or tendencies, instead of facts, or to such terms as 'adequate,' 'advisable,' 'appropriate,' 'beneficial,' 'convenient,' 'detrimental,' 'expedient,' 'equitable,' 'fair,' 'fit,' 'necessary,' 'practicable,' 'proper,' 'reasonable,' 'reputable,' 'safe,' 'sufficient,' 'wholesome,' or their opposites."[44] Thus, in the absence of clear statutes and essential rules to guide and confine discretion, unnecessary discretion becomes integrated with necessary discretion, thus opening the door for discretionary abuses (see Figure 7.4). Unless necessary discretion is reasonable, limits of discretion become dangerously confused. Such an atmosphere would not be conducive to promoting fair and consistent discretionary decision making.

Although such critics as Herman Finer, Theodore Lowi, and Richard B. Stewart have seriously questioned the virtues of the legislators' delegating vast discretionary powers to agency administrators through vague statutes, Davis contends that "the chief hope for confining discretionary power does not lie in statutory enactment but in much more extensive administrative rule-making and legislative bodies need to do more than they have been doing to prod the administrators."[45] In the last clause of this statement, Davis means that legislators need to push administrators into promulgating agency rules which can be used to confine their own discretion. Davis argues that administrators, not legislators, are in the best position to draft rules which are necessary to limit their own discretionary powers because they know best what specific administrative processes are involved in implementing public policies.[46]

However, for various reasons, administrators are reluctant to promulgate rules which they feel may later tie their hands, especially if they lack confidence in their ability to anticipate the precise consequences of their rules. But such delay in mak-

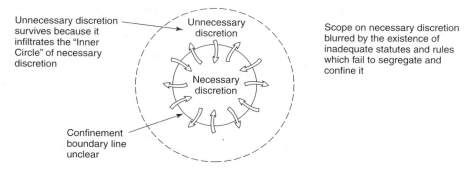

Unnecessary discretion survives because it infiltrates the "Inner Circle" of necessary discretion

Unnecessary discretion

Necessary discretion

Scope on necessary discretion blurred by the existence of inadequate statutes and rules which fail to segregate and confine it

Confinement boundary line unclear

FIGURE 7.4   *Realistic Lack of Confinement of Necessary Discretion*

ing rules causes vague statutory standards to go unclarified for too long. Davis believes this administrative problem should be and can be corrected: *"The typical failure in our system that is correctable is not legislative delegation of broad discretionary power with vague standards; it is the procrastination of administrators in resorting to the rule-making power to replace vagueness with clarity."*[47] The best corrective step is to push administrators into using their rule-making powers earlier and more assiduously so that rules can properly confine discretion.[48]

In Davis's thinking, the administrative rule-making procedure "is one of the greatest inventions of modern government. It can be, when the agency so desires, a virtual duplicate of legislative committee procedure. More often it is quicker and less expensive."[49] It is also fair, efficient, and democratic, and thus ideally suited to confining administrative discretion, especially when compared to the less democratically sensitive order-making process.[50]

Structuring Discretionary Power, Especially through Openness   We cannot hope to democratize administrative discretion by simply confining it, although this is an essential initial step. In searching for ways to confine discretionary power, we are basically looking for ways to encapsulate discretion within specified boundaries. This can be accomplished, Davis suggests, "through statutory enactments, through administrative rules, or by avoiding the development of discretionary power beyond the boundaries."[51] However, structuring discretion is aimed toward a different objective. In our attempts to structure discretion, Davis holds, our purpose "is to control the manner of the exercise of discretionary power within the boundaries, and this, too, can be accomplished through statutory enactments, through administrative rules, and by other means."[52] Once again he emphasizes the marvelous attributes of the rule-making process, noting that rules can be employed to confine discretion as well as to help structure discretionary power (that is, to aid in directing its use within its defined limits). Specifically, according to Davis, structuring discretion involves the tasks of regularizing it, organizing it, and ordering it with the goal in mind of improving discretionary actions toward individual parties so that discretionary justice prevails.[53]

Davis believes that discretionary injustices could be reduced significantly if administrators only cared to take the time to develop viable methods for structuring their discretionary decisions. But just as administrators have been dragging their feet in regard to finding ways to confine their discretionary power, they have also shown great reluctance to take the steps necessary to structure their discretionary actions. Davis perceives most agency decision making as relatively unstructured and, therefore, democratically repulsive. He thinks agency actions tend to violate the canons of democratic government because they are often wantonly inconsistent. Agency decisions tend to be inconsistent, Davis holds, because procedures and standards are applied arbitrarily and capriciously by administrators in reaching decisions from case to case. Employing different methods and criteria allows agency officials to arrive at dramatically different decisions in situations in which the facts and circumstances of the cases seem to be quite similar. Unfortunately, this practice tends to make discretionary agency decisions distastefully unreliable.[54]

What compounds the problem for democratic decision making is that the bases for agency decisions are frequently kept secret. For example, in reference to the unstructured manner in which the Internal Revenue Service reaches decisions, Davis points out that the IRS relies on secretive reasons (for example, unpublished rulings) to make decisions which affect the welfare of individual parties. But what is even worse about this *"IRS practice is that it often gives different treatment to two taxpayers who have identical problems, without explanation."*[55] And further, he notes that the IRS has always held the attitude "that it has no duty either to follow its own unpublished rulings or to explain why it departs from them. Its public position is that unpublished rulings may not be used as precedents."[56] In reality, however, the IRS uses unpublished rulings freely as precedents on which to base future decisions.

The IRS may provide the worst example of inconsistent decision making through its failure to structure its decision-making procedures, but the IRS is by no means the only federal agency, or state agency for that matter, which is guilty of employing secretive and nonstandardized procedures to reach inconsistent and, consequently, unpredictable determinations. Such practices are, unfortunately, common throughout the administrative system. The challenging task, then, is to structure agency decision-making processes so that similar situations in cases tend to generate similar and expected agency responses. To accomplish this structural goal, Davis recommends that agency discretion should be controlled more by the use of "open plans, open policy statements, open rules, open findings, open reasons, open precedents, and fair informal procedure."[57] He commented that he emphasized the word *open* for an important reason: "Openness is the natural enemy of arbitrariness and a natural ally in the fight against injustice."[58] Davis contends that open procedures should be sought to help structure discretionary power, especially since openness is very consistent with what democratic government demands. However, Davis acknowledges that open methods may sometimes be quite inappropriate for certain governmental tasks, such as decisions involving security secrets or trade secrets. He maintains that openness allows discretionary actions to be placed in the spotlight so that they can stand a better chance of being controlled. How can abuses of discretion be detected and controlled if the reasons justifying discretionary determinations are kept secret?

When agencies have developed policies and rules, Davis argues that it is necessary for the agency administrators to keep us informed by telling us what they are. Publicizing agency policies and rules helps to structure discretionary action simply by keeping open the lines of communication between agency administrators and outsiders, thus allowing healthy and corrective feedback. Also, by placing themselves on public record, administrators would not necessarily commit themselves to certain actions, but they would create for themselves an obligation to follow their publicized courses of action unless they state and publicly justify why they want to change directions. Thus, public disclosure of agency policies and rules would aid in the structuring of discretion by helping to prevent administrators from employing their discretionary power to alter their policies and procedural stands suddenly, secretively, and without sound reasons.[59]

Before formal trial-like hearings, agency officials are required by the APA, in reaching decisions, to state systematically their findings of fact and to note in writing their reasoned opinions (why they reached the decisions that they did). But to structure the use of discretion, Davis holds that it would be a good idea to have administrators openly state their findings and reasons in support of their informal discretionary decisions whenever practical. Presently, he asserts, discretionary decisions are too often made without any reasons given for the actions taken.

In introducing Davis's plea for across-the-board openness as a method for controlling possible abuses of discretion, I have presented the fundamental arguments for compelling agencies to follow open precedents. But to reiterate, his chief contention was that consistency can be promoted better if agency officials are obligated to follow established and publicized precedents. Consistency, he maintains, is a highly desirable administrative trait in any government because it tends to reduce arbitrariness while simultaneously promoting equal treatment under law. Nevertheless, Davis should not be accused of striving for a rigid application of openness in regard to the use of open precedents or any other call for agency openness. The general objective, he asserts, should never be to seek an extravagant application of the rule of law or excessive use of discretion. The goal should be to seek a reasonable balance between the two.[60]

Checking Discretionary Power   The idea that any form of governmental power should be checked must retain the highest respect in every society which cherishes freedom. But, Davis asserts, the hard reality is that our liberty is threatened by the prevalence of too much administrative discretion which is, for all practical purposes, absolute. Absolute discretionary power, he points out, may not always be employed invidiously, but the potential for evil acts is ever present.[61] He regards such absolute discretionary power as out of character with the principles of democratic government. For Davis, discretionary power is absolute when it is both unchecked and unreviewable: "Absolute discretion means unchecked and unreviewable discretion. When no other authority can reverse the choice made, even if it is arbitrary and unreasonable, discretion is absolute."[62]

The threat absolute discretion poses to our free and democratic system of government is perceived by many others. In *United States* v. *Wunderlich,* 342 U.S. 98, 101 (1951), Justice William O. Douglas exclaimed: "Law has reached its finest moments when it has freed man from the unlimited discretion of some ruler, some civil or military official, some bureaucrat. Where discretion is absolute, man has always suffered. . . . Absolute discretion . . . is more destructive of freedom than of man's other inventions." In the same year, in *New York* v. *United States,* 342 U.S. 882, 884 (1951), Douglas wrote: "Absolute discretion, like corruption, marks the beginning of the end of liberty." In an insightful dissenting opinion in *SEC* v. *Chenery Corp.,* 332 U.S. 194, 215 (1947), Justice Robert Jackson, in direct reference to the need for the Court to keep the administrative leviathan from exercising absolute discretionary powers, argued that the need for administrative discretion cannot "support action outside of the law. And what action is, and what action is not, within the law must be determined by the courts, when authorized to review, no matter how much deference is due to the agency's fact finding. Surely an administrative agency is *not* a law unto itself" (my emphasis). And decades later D.C. Circuit Judge J. Skelly Wright wrote that Davis's concern for the need to check "unchannelled, unreviewable, and untrammelled discretion" is unmistakably legitimate.[63]

Davis holds that the democratic principle of checks and balances is a valuable and practical democratic idea that should be implemented from top to bottom in our governmental system. To him, the principle of check is conceptually simple: "What may be called 'the principle of check' means simply that one officer should check another, as a protection against arbitrariness."[64] He believes that checks are most effective when they are aimed directly at stopping discretionary injustices resulting from arbitrary and illegal administrative behavior. Checks are not very effective when they are indirect, as in *de novo* review. The problem with *de novo* review (a new hearing/review) is that it constitutes a fresh or second attempt to check abuses. For this reason *de novo* review does not check directly. Davis considers *de novo* review of discretionary action inferior because such review may introduce arbitrariness or illegal actions for the first time. Frequently, these *de novo* actions are not checked because they are perceived as final agency actions.[65] Therefore, one could say that *de novo* reviews create only an illusion that misuses of discretionary actions in agencies are ultimately being checked. According to Davis, genuine checks should properly be directed at preventing abuses of discretion in final actions "so that almost all final action is subject to a check for arbitrariness or illegality."[66]

Compared with our very modest successes in confining and structuring discretion, Davis contends, our successes in checking discretion have been much greater, although we must work harder to develop better checks.[67] But how should administrative discretion be checked so that discretionary abuses leading to injustices can be minimized? Davis discusses five methods for checking discretionary power. Discretion can be checked by: (1) supervision and review by supervisors; (2) administrative tribunals; (3) legislative committees; (4) ombudsmen; and (5) judicial review of agency action.[68]

A CRITIQUE OF KENNETH CULP DAVIS' DISCRETIONARY JUSTICE

In "Beyond Discretionary Justice," a classic analysis of Davis' *Discretionary Justice,* Judge J. Skelly Wright expressed strong support for Davis's struggle to see to it that administrative discretionary power is appropriately confined, structured, and checked.[69] Wright agrees with Davis that discretion must be controlled if we are to make any significant progress in curbing and eliminating abuses of administrative discretion. Further, Wright acknowledges that Davis has done a brilliant job in placing the American legal system in perspective with the role played by administrative discretion, as well as proposing a tentative scheme for controlling the most outrageous abuses of discretionary power.[70] However, Wright detected serious flaws in Davis' "powerful manifests." Wright's central criticism is simply that Davis's approach is unrealistically and unjustifiably optimistic: "The underlying tone of Discretionary Justice is optimistic."[71] He specifically rejects Davis's thinking that "if we have the will to create an effective system of law to guide and channel administrative decisionmaking, then the monster can be tamed."[72]

"The real question," Wright says, "is whether we have the will."[73] He doubts that we do, especially if we are going to rely upon the will of administrators to take the initiative to confine and structure their own discretionary powers. Wright finds Davis surprisingly naive in his belief that administrators will be willing to curtail the use of their own discretionary powers without being forced to do so. This difference in viewpoints between Davis and Wright over possible ways to control behavior represents a classic clash between the perspectives of an idealist and a realist. That is, Davis is essentially arguing that administrators can eventually be relied upon to write their own rules to confine and structure their own discretion, while Wright is asserting that this is utter nonsense since people cannot be expected to surrender their powers voluntarily—in this case, through drafting rules limiting their own discretionary powers.

It is not that Wright does not believe that agency rule-making cannot help to limit and structure administrative discretion. Clearly, he feels that rule-making can serve this end. For instance, Wright asserts that Davis is "most convincing when he argues that 'the procedure of administrative rule-making is . . . one of the greatest inventions of modern government" and that it can be employed to combat unnecessary and abusive uses of discretion.[74] But Wright deeply disagrees with Davis's main contention that "the chief hope for confining discretionary power lies in voluntary agency rule-making."[75] Against this holding by Davis, Wright asserts in typical realistic rhetoric: "If that is true, there may be no hope at all. For the sad fact is that powerful forces are at work which inclines agencies toward an ad hoc case-by-case mode of operation. The first of these is simply the bureaucratic imperative of keeping the wheels turning."[76] To keep the wheels turning, administrators generally feel that they need the necessary flexibility in which to function properly. Rules limiting discretion are normally viewed by administrators as irritants which restrict their alternatives. If given the choice, administrators would rather have the freedom to muddle through by making *ad hoc* decisions.[77] In Wright's view, "ad hoc decisions tend to leave the agency freer to change direction at will and allow it to avoid the risks inherent in advance commitments."[78]

Thus Wright concluded that, given the historical struggle by determined administrators to keep the discretionary powers as broad as possible, "it is unrealistic to suppose that many agencies will dramatically move to confine their own discretion."[79] Emphasizing that "it would be foolish to rely too heavily on voluntary conversion" because, in the final analysis, that is an "unrealizable ideal," he argues that fortunately there are more feasible methods which can be employed to make the control of administrative discretion a realizable goal.[80] Wright's solution is rooted in force, however, and not in the blind faith that administrators will be their own reformers. To think that reform can come from within appears ridiculous to Wright. Specifically, he holds that administrators can write their own rules to curb their discretionary power, but only if they are compelled to do so by Congress and the courts, although he believes that the courts must lead the way. In capsular fashion, he notes: "But while all branches of government must join in the fight to limit discretion, I believe it is the courts which will have to bear the primary burden. Not only must the courts, on occasion, formulate rules of their own which will limit discretion. They must also resuscitate the legal principles which will force sometimes reluctant congressmen and administrators to take action. The courts cannot bear the burden alone; they are not equipped to act as superadministrators, formulating individual rules to govern the thousands of cases heard daily by agencies. But they can reestablish the doctrines which were designed to compel or encourage other branches of government to assume their parts of the task."[81]

Wright holds that "More and more legislators have come to realize that the so-called 'expertise' of the executive branch is in reality no more than a cloak which hides the raw exercise of untrammeled power. Whereas once it was believed that administrative 'experts' could magically provide a 'scientific' solution to public policy problems, many congressmen now realize that most questions of policy are questions of values, and that the people must determine for themselves the values which they favor. In time, the movement for greater balance between the legislature and the executive promises to bring about the first substantial reallocation of power in almost two generations."[82] Wright now seems to have been idealistic himself. Since the writing of this article in 1972, Congress has shown some modest, but not unusual, efforts to reinvigorate its controls over the administrative machinery, but with extremely limited success. Most experts, as was pointed out previously in Chapters 1 and 2, argue that given the established and increasing powers of the administrative branch, it would be exceedingly difficult for Congress to successfully reassert the powers they have surrendered to administrators for nearly two hundred years, but especially since the 1930s. Although contempt for technocracy in the 1960s and 1970s led to a call for more control over the discretion of agency experts and an emphasis on participatory, pluralistic, democratic agency decision-making, a demand for greater administrative efficiency in the 1990s has gained new respect for the technocrats and increased deference to "technocratic discretion" by legislators and judges.

In any event, Wright maintains that Congress can confine and structure administrative discretion "by reassuming its rightful role as the architect of fundamental administrative policy."[83] Wright means here that Congress should not delegate authority to administrators without attaching standards sufficient to guide agency actions. Although most scholars, including Davis, have pronounced the delegation doctrine dead, Wright believes that the delegation doctrine can still be used as an effective weapon in controlling administrative discretion. In Wright's thinking, by accepting the demise of the delegation doctrine, we are also accepting Congress's unconstitutional right "to vote itself out of business."[84] Unquestionably, he contends, there simply must be limitations placed upon how far Congress can go in transferring its constitutional powers to administrators in the absence of instructions on how these powers can be exercised.[85]

Wright attacks Davis's line of reasoning that the delegation doctrine should be rejected as a method for confining and structuring discretion because it is impractical. We should not accept Davis's position that the delegation doctrine is an impractical weapon in combatting discretionary abuses because, Wright urges, Davis interprets the history of the doctrine to mean that "the legislature either cannot or will not impose meaningful standards on administrative discretion."[86] Wright thinks that "the delegation doctrine retains an important potential as a check on the exercise of unbounded, standardless discretion by administrative agencies.[87]

Even though Davis seeks to confine and structure administrative discretion in a manner more consistent with democratic principles, Wright maintains that Davis's proposed solutions are not so democratic. Consistent with his defense of the constitutional soundness of the delegation doctrine, Wright asserts essentially that it is not in the long-range interests of democracy to argue that administrators should be permitted to make fundamental policy decisions simply because legislators themselves seem unable to set clear policy courses: "An argument for letting the experts decide when the people's representatives are uncertain or cannot agree is an argument for paternalism and against democracy."[88]

Moreover, Wright points out that support for delegating broad powers to administrators is based on the erroneous assumption that conflict over policies can be avoided if policy problems are passed on to administrators. But how can throwing a policy mess into the laps of administrators resolve any problems? He emphasizes that such action can lead to only two unfortunate results: "On the one hand, if the problem is really intractable, it is unlikely that the agency, with all its expertise, will do any better with it than Congress. Indeed, if there is political opposition to any contemplated action, the agency may actually be more vulnerable than Congress."[89] This can only cause an agency to keep blundering along without any real direction or purpose, using discretion in a haphazard way.[90]

Agency actions can be given direction if Congress cares to take the time to perform its constitutional duty by attaching prospective guidelines and standards when delegating powers to administrators. And rule-making, Wright maintains, can still serve a crucial function in controlling discretionary power, but we should not expect administrators to confine and structure their own discretion. Congress and the courts must force administrators to draft those rules which will help to curtail discretionary abuses. Wright thinks rules, as Davis suggests, can serve to structure discretion by making the intentions of administrators clear to the public. Rules shall be employed in an open political system to give individual parties "fair warning" regarding agency policies and procedures. Wright acknowledges that the purpose of a democratic regulatory system "is presumably to bring primary conduct into conformance with agreed upon social norms. Yet a system operating without rules cannot possibly achieve this goal, since the people being regulated are not informed of what the societal norms are."[91] In the end, the use of discretion in any governmental regulatory operations will inevitably be irrational and arbitrary. Yet the sad reality is, he admits in support of Davis, that we have failed to make our administrators live by rules which force them to exercise their discretionary powers within a due process framework."[92]

While Davis plays down the role the courts can play in helping to confine, structure, and check discretion, Wright, as mentioned, feels that the courts must assume primary responsibility for forcing administrators to limit the application of administrative discretion: "The courts should control discretion by vigorously reasserting their inherent role as the interpreters of legislative enactments and guardians against invidious and irrational exercises of governmental power."[93] More specifically, he believes that the courts must take the initiative and pick up the ball after legislators and administrators have fumbled their attempts to provide the necessary vehicles for placing administrative discretion under safe control. Ironically, Wright notes, in some cases this may require that the courts develop the appropriate standards and guidelines for Congress to attach to statutes when delegating powers to administrators. Wright believes that if we want to take giant steps toward resolving the discretionary justice problem, the courts will have to swing a big judicial stick in the future. Wright, like Davis, wants administrators to possess necessary discretionary powers, but he wants the courts to vigorously oversee and overrule discretionary agency actions which are not within their reasonable authority: "If the agency acts beyond its statutory authority as the relevant statute is interpreted by the courts, the agency action must be reversed."[94] In so doing, Wright concludes that "judges can narrow the scope of agency discretion even if the administrators are unwilling to narrow its scope themselves."[95] But the reality is that the judiciary has evidently largely ignored the advice of Wright because the courts, especially since the famous *Chevron* ruling in 1984, *op. cit.*, have handed down decisions which have had the impact of allowing administrators to exercise even broader discretionary powers.[96]

REACTING TO DAVIS: GIFFORD'S MODEL OF DISCRETIONARY DECISION MAKING

To reiterate, Kenneth Culp Davis believes that administrative discretion is insufficiently confined, structured, and checked. To control discretion for the purpose of curtailing abuses of discretion (arbitrary and capricious decision making made illegal by the Administrative Procedure Act, Section 706[2][A]), Davis urges that agency administrators promulgate standards and rules based on past agency experiences in handling similar factual situations in cases to guide future discretionary administrative decisions. To Daniel J. Gifford, Davis's position is rooted in five basic assumptions:

1. The administration of a statute is a learning process for an agency.
2. Repeated application of the statute to differing situations forces that agency to evaluate specifically the various problems faced by regulated subjects.
3. This repeated contact with the regulation in a variety of circumstances helps the agency develop an overview of the problems.
4. The needed narrowing of discretion comes from rules, standards, and precedents that gradually emerge as the agency acquires more information about its tasks.
5. This information comes, in part, from the repeated decisionmaking.[97]

However, Gifford, among many others whom he cites, seriously doubts whether agency decision making consists of enough recurring common "factual components" to allow standards and rules to be developed within agencies to set precedents for future agency decisions. He points out that many scholars challenge Davis's position, describing "agency work as resolving numerous cases in which the particular factual components rarely repeat themselves. Under this approach, precedents or rules play a smaller role in administrative decisions than in judicial decisions. This is due to the factual variety of cases coming before an agency decision."[98] In particular, Gifford cites an old study by Professor I.L. Sharfman of the Interstate Commerce Commission that found that cases coming before the ICC were almost always so factually unique that they had to be resolved on a case-by-case basis, making virtually impossible the development of general standards and rules to be used as guiding precedents for future resolution of ICC cases.[99] Gifford asserts that this does not mean that Sharfman rejects Davis's pursuit of common rules to confine and structure administrative discretion to promote decisional consistency in public agencies. "Rather, Sharfman's deprecation of rules, precedents, standards, consistency, and predictability results from his different perception of the kinds of cases which form the bulk of the agency workload. The nonrepetitious nature of these cases accounts for his emphasis upon the importance of 'the special facts of each controversy' and his belief in the unimportance of precedent in that agency's work."[100] In short, the assumptions of Sharfman and Davis are radically different and miles apart. Simply put, Davis believes that enough repetition of relevant facts occurs in cases in our public agencies to allow our administrators to develop standards and rules to be employed in the future to help confine and structure unnecessary discretion. Sharfman feels such thinking is idealistic and unrealistic, given the great diversity of dissimilar factual cases coming before agencies. Gifford believes that the Sharfman-Davis perceptions regarding the nature of agency caseloads are at opposite ends of a continuum (Figure 7.5).[101]

So the question is: Do relevant facts recur in agency cases frequently enough to permit agency administrators to promulgate those standards and rules worthwhile in

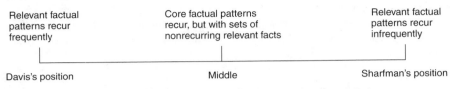

FIGURE 7.5   *Sharfman-Davis Perceptions on Agency Caseloads*

curbing unnecessary discretionary actions and thereby promoting fairer, predictable, nonarbitrary and noncapricious decision making? Attempting to answer this question, Gifford developed a set of criteria to analyze the situation:

1. The proper guiding, structuring, or confining of discretionary decision making must be related to the agency's information collection and evaluation processes because authoritative rules or guides ought to be imposed upon decision makers only when these rules or guides produce decisions of higher quality than would be the case without them.
2. Better informed people tend to make higher quality decisions.
3. The decision-making process itself is often a major source of agency information.
4. The value of agency experience in deciding cases and as sources of relevant information for the formulation of standards governing the disposition of future cases is affected by the nature of the agency caseload.[102]

From the application of these criteria, Gifford designed a descriptive model (Figure 7.6)[103]

Of the variety of cases that come before agencies, only a limited percentage fall into the NE quadrant and thus provide the essential "recurring relevant factors" that promote the development of general standards and rules to guide the exercise of discretionary decision making. As Figure 7.6 illustrates, only in the NE sector are the cases important enough to warrant elaborate justification or to be "class justified" because they have a sufficient number of common factual recurrent situations; these cases are appropriate sources of the information needed to develop useful standards and rules to guide administrative discretion. In the SW corner, just the opposite situation exists. Here the agency cases are nonrecurring and perceived as unimportant to the development of agency rule-making. These cases do not require the attention of top administrators; they simply need to be "managed" or settled (unique justifications are given to dispose of the cases quickly) by lower level administrators. In the NW quadrant, the cases are perceived as important enough to justify the attention of top-level administrators, but the cases are too unique in character to provide the necessary commonalities absolutely essential to allow for the development of general standards and rules to guide future agency decision-making. The cases in the SE quadrant do recur enough to allow for the formation of general standards and rules to confine discretion, but the cases are regarded as unimportant to the development of agency policy and the fulfillment of agency regulatory goals. Therefore, these cases require only quick decisions with simple to no justifications by lower-level agency officials.

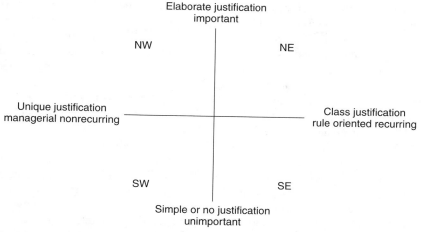

FIGURE 7.6   *Gifford's Model on Agency Cases*

So what does this all mean? The model reveals the complexities of discretionary decision making. It also discloses that the potential to confine administrative discretion through general standards and rules is limited by the kind of cases handled within an agency and by the types of cases various agencies must typically settle. While some agencies may handle a large percentage of cases that could be placed in the NE quadrant, other agencies may find few cases that could appropriately be placed in the NE sector. Gifford concludes that the techniques suggested by Davis for confining, structuring, and checking administrative discretion (namely, rule-making) have limited application. "The several techniques for confining, checking, and guiding the exercise of discretionary power which he has proposed may be more suitable to some categories of administrative caseloads than to others, and to some levels of bureaucratic hierarchy than to others."[104]

THE COURTS' ROLE IN CONTROLLING DISCRETIONARY AGENCY ACTIONS

As noted in Chapter 2, for the sake of expediency the courts since *Schechter Poultry Corp.* v. *United States,* 295 U.S. 495 (1935), have generally allowed Congress to delegate increasingly broader discretionary powers to administrators without compelling Congress to limit an agency's administrative discretion by attaching meaningful standards (standards that can be used to guide and restrict the exercise of discretion). However, by the early 1970s some observers detected that a judicial attitude had started to emerge, echoing the mood of many Americans, that the discretionary powers of administrators had grown too threatening for democratic processes and, therefore, had to be better controlled. In 1980, looking back over the 1970s,

Bernard Schwartz summarized why the Supreme Court under Warren Burger started to reverse the attitude of earlier Courts toward the power position of administrative agencies: "The changed approach of the Burger Court reflects both the society of the past decade and the period through which it has been passing. Inevitably the malaise about administrative agencies and the manner in which they operate that has increasingly spread through the society has had its effects within the Marble Palace. The present Court's changing administrative law jurisprudence may be seen as a direct response to growing distrust of agencies and their failure to protect that very public interest they were created to serve."[105]

According to Schwartz, the Burger Court took a tough new stand against broad and abusive uses of discretionary power by administrative agencies. He contends that while previous Courts had tolerated vague delegated statutes, which allowed administrators to write their own tickets in regard to what Congress intended, the Burger Court adopted a stricter approach. Schwartz asserts that the Burger Court showed an unwillingness "to look beyond the black letter of delegating statutes and read in implied powers in the light of presumed congressional intent to confer broadside authority."[106] In short, the Burger Court began to reassert the old democratic idea, emphasized by J. Skelly Wright in "Beyond Discretionary Justice," that delegated authority must be transferred in a democratically responsible fashion.

Davis agrees with Schwartz that the overall judicial attitude toward discretionary administrative power changed, but not as much in the high Court. Davis claims that this altered judicial perspective since 1970 has increased the potential for petitioners to win cases in agency or judicial appeals on the grounds that administrative discretion has not been properly restrained. Many cases can be cited to substantiate this judicial reversal; but Davis notes that the courts in the immediate future will not necessarily rely upon past precedential decisions but will seek to confine, structure, and check discretion by handing down new precedential rulings of their own: "Judicial disapprovals of uncontrolled discretion often are not based on precedents; judges often create precedents. In the coming years, many questions of first impression about uncontrolled discretion will arise and much new law, not based on specific precedents, will be created.[107]

These views about the present and future efforts of the courts to control discretion seem to be based more on high hopes than on actual case law. It is true that the courts in the past few decades have apparently started to rethink their position on what the judicial role should be in controlling discretion. But in too many cases, their *obiter dicta* (comments not necessary to support the holding) denouncing discretionary actions which were encouraged by the existence of virtually standardless statutes ultimately failed to motivate the courts to override the same discretionary activities that they had just denounced. Even Schwartz acknowledges that the courts have too often attacked the discretionary justice problem with mere rhetoric rather than with hard rulings aimed at invalidating illegitimate discretionary behavior. Martin Shapiro asserts that although judges became lay heroes during the 1960s and 1970s when they attacked technocratic administrative discretion in response to public distaste for "rule-by-administrative experts," during the 1980s the courts began to develop a new respect for technocratic administration and once again began deferring to agency expertise. Decisions handed down by the Supreme Court in particular in the past decade or so, starting with the famous precedential case, *Chevron, U.S.A., Inc.* v. *Natural Resources Defense Council, Inc.*, 467 U.S. 837 (1984), have substantiated Shapiro's observation [*Heckler* v. *Chaney*, 470 U.S. 821 (1985), and *Lincoln* v. *Vigil*, 113 S.Ct. to 2024 (1993)]. Ironically, the courts, especially the Supreme Court, has decided to defer broadly to agency expertise/discretion during the same period when suddenly the president and Congress have made efforts to micromanage the actions of public agencies to make them more democratically accountable.

CASES OVERRULING DISCRETIONARY ACTIONS

Cases pertaining to the use and misuse of discretion by administrative agencies are numerous, since virtually all administrative law disputes fundamentally involve judgments rooted in discretion. Whether our focus is on formal or informal rule-making, order-making, and so on, discretionary decisions must play a significant role since laws and rules must be interpreted and applied. Thus, if we look hard enough, we can discover legions of cases where the courts apparently tried to limit an agency's use of unlimited discretion by specifically noting instances where an agency had exceeded and/or abused its discretionary authority. In *Germania Iron Co.* v. *James,* 89 F.2d 811, 818 (8th Cir. 1898), a case involving the breadth of administrative discretion in adhering to standard procedures in adjudications, the court stated: "What a force the attempt to secure rights in any judicial tribunal must become, if its rules and practice are ignored or applied at the arbitrary will of the judge." In *Vitarelli* v. *Seaton,* 359 U.S. 535 (1959), the Supreme Court held that administrators are not free to follow agency rules arbitrarily. As Justice Felix Frankfurter succinctly expressed: "He that takes the procedural sword shall perish with that sword" (at 547). In *Hammond* v. *Lenfest,* 398 F.2d 705, 715 (2d Cir., 1968), the appellate court emphasized that a clear abuse of administrative discretion occurs when agency administrators choose to ignore basic rule-of-law principles by arbitrarily violating their own established rules.

In *Environmental Defense Fund, Inc.* v. *Ruckelshaus,* 439 F.2d 584, 598 (D.C.Cir., 1971), the court insisted that when administrative actions affect the "life, health, and liberty" of individual interests, the judiciary must subject agency behavior to "strict judicial scrutiny." Specifically, according to the court, close supervision of agency actions in cases involving such personal interests should function to "require administrative officers to articulate the standards and principles that govern their discretionary decisions in as much detail as possible" and "to ensure that the administrative process itself will confine and control the exercise of discretion" (at 598). A year earlier the same court in *Greater Boston Television Corp.* v. *FCC,* 444 F.2d 841, 850 (1970), held the courts have a legal obligation to scrutinize agency decisions to make certain that agency determinations are based upon "reasoned discretion."

In *Citizens to Preserve Overton Park, Inc.* v. *Volpe,* 401 U.S. 402 (1971), Secretary of Transportation John Volpe decided to use public funds to build a highway through a public park (Overton Park) even though a statute forbids such construction if a "feasible and prudent" alternative route is available. Volpe argued that his decision to approve construction of the highway was not subject to judicial review because he had sole discretionary authority to determine whether a "feasible and alternative" route existed. The Supreme Court rejected Volpe's argument, holding that his informal discretionary action was reviewable under the "arbitrary, capricious" or "abuse of discretion" standards (at 413–14). (The courts often make no distinction between these two standards or tests, reasoning that if an administrator acts "arbitrarily and capriciously," the administrator is necessarily abusing his or her administrative discretion). In *Overton Park* the Court asserted that Volpe's decision should be overruled if "a clear error of judgment" (a new standard) could be found, thus making his informal discretionary action "arbitrary, capricious" or constituting an "abuse of discretion" (at 416). The high Court found such a clear error in his judgment. Recently, the courts have used the "clear error" test as a convenient way to defer more readily to agency discretion. For example, in *Kisser* v. *Cisneros,* 14 F.2d 615, 618–619 (1994), the court argued that when applying the "arbitrary and capricious" standard to determine whether the agency has abused its discretion, the court should be "highly deferential," presuming "the validity of agency action. . . . We may reverse only if the agency's decision is not supported by substantial evidence, or the agency has made clear error in judgement."

Of course, the courts have held that agencies need to record their "reasoned opinions" to help the reviewing courts decide whether discretion was abused in the decision-making process (*Dunlop* v. *Bachowski,* 421 U.S. 560, 571; 1975). In *Portland Cement Ass'n.* v. *Ruckelshaus,* 486 F.2d 375, 393 (1973), the appellate court argued that fundamental fairness in rule-making requires that discretion cannot be employed to allow rules to be promulgated in the absence of inadequate data or on secretive data.[108] A year later, in *National Cable TV Ass'n.* v. *United States,* 415 U.S. 336, 342 (1974), the Supreme Court, while ruling in favor of the agency's use of discretion, at least paid lip service to the need for discretion to be defined and guided by standards. In *Loyola Univ.* v. *FCC,* 670 F.2d 1222 (1982), the D. C. Circuit Court ruled that an agency acts arbitrarily when the agency can show no reasonable basis for its actions. Discretion is also abused when extraneous considerations (i.e., factors that should have played no role in the decision) are used to support an agency decision, *P.P.G. Corp.* v. *State Liquor Auth.,* 52 N.Y.2d 886 (1981).

Since 1975, court decisions have denounced a wide variety of discretionary agency actions, although the courts have not always found it appropriate to overrule the specific agency actions in question or to develop clear and useful standards which could be used to limit the free exercise of administrative discretion. In *White* v. *Roughton,* 530 F.2d 750, 753–754 (7th Cir., 1976), the court came down hard on an official who had been administering a township assistance program without the guidance of any written standards or rules. The court argued that standards were required to guard against potential abuses of discretion. Because administrator Roughton had established no written rules to guide his discretion, the court held that he could not apply eligibility requirements in a fair and consistent manner. As far as the court was concerned, Roughton, by not limiting his own discretion, allowed himself to possess "unfettered discretion," a clear violation of procedural due process principles.

Two 1979 Supreme Court decisions attempted to limit the use of discretion by restricting an agency's implied powers. Schwartz held that *FCC* v. *Midwest Video Corp.*, 99 S.Ct. 824, and *NLRB* v. *Catholic Bishop of Chicago*, 99 S.Ct. 1313, narrowed agency discretion by refusing to permit administrators to expand the scope of their delegated powers by freely and arbitrarily reading into legislation powers which have not been specifically conferred. For Schwartz, these two rulings represented the *McCulloch* v. *Maryland* (4 Wheat 316 U.S.; 1819) counterpart for administrative law in that the Court was saying that administrative agencies cannot exercise powers which are not specifically delegated to them unless the discretionary use of implied powers can be justified as *necessary* and *proper.*[109] In *Midwest Video Corp.*, the Court held that specific FCC rules were not reasonably necessary to maintain effective TV regulation and therefore constituted an illegitimate extension of their delegated powers, while in *Catholic Bishop* the Court ruled that the NLRB exceeded its statutory discretionary jurisdiction by expanding its regulatory arm to cover lay teachers working for church-governed schools.

In *Sharon Steel Corp.* v. *EPA*, 597 F.2d 377 (3d Cir., 1979), and *United States Steel Corp.* v. *EPA*, 595 F.2d 207 (5th Cir., 1979), the two circuit courts agreed that the EPA can abuse its discretion by using feeble excuses to suspend required notice and comment rule-making under the "good cause" or "impractical" exception of the APA. The third and fifth circuit courts ruled that the argument by the EPA that APA-required rule-making procedures had to be suspended because of the EPA's tight schedule did not by itself justify the suspension.

Although Professor Davis expresses serious second thoughts on his assessment of the importance and wisdom of *Morton* v. *Ruiz*, 415 U.S. 199 (1974), in his 1994 *Administrative Law Treatise*, 3rd edition, co-authored with Richard J. Pierce, Jr.,[110] in his 1978–1984 *Administrative Law Treatise*, 2nd edition, he argued that the Supreme Court in *Ruiz* did an excellent job in helping to confine agency discretion by establishing four important propositions which could be used by lower courts to curb the use of unnecessary and abusive discretionary power. The first was that the authority to implement a program necessarily requires rule-making (at 231). Thus, any exercise of discretion in the absence of guiding rules could easily be held invalid in the face of this proposition. Second, agency policies are "ineffective" unless they are rooted in a legislative rule or rules (at 236). This places obvious restraint on the exercise of discretion by forcing administrators to act within the limits of expressed legislative intent. Third, unpublished *ad hoc* decisions are prohibited by the APA (at 236). If honored, this proposition would have a profound impact on the future use of administrative discretion because the decision in fact requires lower courts to overturn virtually all unpublished *ad hoc* agency decisions, of which there are plenty. And fourth, agency decisions setting eligibility requirements for welfare benefits cannot be determined in an *ad hoc* manner (at 232). If this is the case, Davis asserts, "then

probably most determinations other than those relating to eligibility for welfare cannot be made on an *ad hoc* basis."[111]

The D.C. Circuit Court in *Coal Exporters Association of the United States v. United States*, 745 F.2d 76 (1984),[112] ruled that the ICC had exceeded its "executing discretion" when implementing the vague provisions of the Staggers Rail Act of 1980 (49 U.S.C., Section 10505; 1982). The court concluded: "Here we admit that the commission has substantial discretion as to how to carry out Congress's instruction concerning the accommodation of shipper and rail carrier interests, but wherever the bounds of discretion are, we have no doubt that the agency's accommodation, as announced and applied in this case, 'is not one that Congress would have sanctioned'" (at 96). In *Sang Seup Shin v. INS*, 750 F.2d 122 (1984), the same court handed down a similar ruling, holding that the Board of Immigration Appeals of the INS had exceeded the boundaries of its discretion by refusing to "individualize" discretion properly by not reopening a deportation decision even in light of crucial new facts.

The Supreme Court handed down only one major setback for broad use of agency discretion during the 1980s. In *Motor Vehicle Mfrs. Ass'n. v. State Farm Mut.*, 103 S.Ct. 2856 (1983), the high Court ruled that the National Highway Traffic Safety Administration abused its discretion by acting arbitrarily and capriciously in rescinding the passive restraint requirement, Standard 208, that required new motor vehicles manufactured after September, 1982, to be equipped with seat belts to protect the lives of passengers. Returning in this case to the "clear error in judgment" standard set forth in *Overton Park*, Justice Byron White, speaking for the majority, concluded that the agency was guilty of "clear error" because it failed to support its rescission decision with any reasonable basis and explanation. "By failing to analyze the continuous seat belt in its own right, the agency has failed to offer the rational connection between facts and judgment required to pass the muster under the arbitrary and capricious standard. . . . While the agency is entitled to change its view on the acceptability of continuous passive belts, it is obligated to explain its reasons for doing so" (at 2873).

With *Chevron* still serving in the 1990's as the chief precedential case guiding court decisions pertaining to the exercise of administrative discretion, relatively few judicial decisions have overruled discretionary agency action. However, courts have still set aside blatantly abusive discretionary acts in clear violation of the law. For example, in *ALM Corp. v. U.S. Envtl Protection Agency, Region II*, 974 F. 2d 380, 383 (3rd Cir. 1992), the court stressed that there should be "great deference" to agency discretion, but the courts should set aside clear abuses of discretion. In *Haitian Centers Council, Inc. v. Sale*, 823 F. Supp. 1028 (E.D.N.Y. 1993), the court came down hard on Attorney General Janet Reno for abusing her discretion in the handling of Haitian refugees, some having AIDS, who sought to immigrate to the United States for political asylum. The court argued that Reno was abusing her discretion by treating Haitian refugees differently from other immigrants just because they were Haitian, many with AIDS. The court held that "[T]he Attorney General has 'broad discretionary power to parole unadmitted aliens,' but she may not exercise that discretion 'to discriminate invidiously against a particular race or group or to depart without rational explanation from established policies'" (at 1048).

CASES UPHOLDING DISCRETIONARY ACTIONS

The sampling of cases above might have created the impression that the   have been busy monitoring and guarding against possible abuses of discretion, but conspicuously absent are recent cases by the Supreme Court denouncing discretionary abuses. The sad truth is, as suggested earlier, that the courts, especially the Supreme Court, have not contributed much to efforts aimed at curtailing abuses of administrative discretion. There are several reasons for this. Of course, the primary reason is that court rulings seem to touch upon only a tiny fraction of discretionary administrative actions. Second, too many court decisions seem too vague, contradictory, filled with loopholes, and, consequently, confusing and difficult to employ comfortably in guiding administrative discretion. Third, court holdings have tended to be too narrow and incomplete, applying only to very specific questions of the proper use of discretion, thus making valid generalizations for guiding discretion virtually impossible to infer. And fourth, the Supreme Court, as the judicial leader, has refused to take bold and certain steps toward controlling discretion. In fact, the high Court has too often acted as a negative force in overruling more creative lower court opinions, especially those of the relatively progressive D.C. Circuit Court of Appeals.

A Supreme Court decision which still receives intense criticism from liberal administrative law critics is *Vermont Yankee Nuclear Power Corp.* v. *Natural Resources Defense Council, Inc.,* 435 U.S. 519 (1978), which directly reversed two separate and innovative D.C. Circuit Court rulings, *Natural Resources Defense Council* v. *Nuclear Regulatory Commission,* 547 F.2d 633 (D.C.Cir., 1976), and *Aeschliman* v. *Nuclear Regulatory Commission,* 547 F.2d 622 (D.C.Cir., 1976).[113] Some critics believe the *Vermont Yankee* decision represents an unwise reversal of a progressive judicial trend which had been developing since the mid-1960s at the appellate level, led by the D.C. Circuit Court of Appeals.[114] In essence, liberal administrative law scholars and judges had perceived the trend as healthy because the appeals courts were taking a "hard look" at the use of agency discretion in various areas, especially rule-making.[115] With the *Vermont Yankee* holding, this all came to an abrupt halt.[116] But what did the Supreme Court say in the *Vermont Yankee* decision to anger the liberal administrative law establishment so intensely?

Briefly, in *NRDC* v. *NRC* the D.C. Circuit Court held invalid a rule promulgated by the NRC and also the commission's decision to grant Vermont Yankee Power Corporation a license to start construction of a nuclear plant. The court rooted its decision in the argument that the NRC's rule-making procedures were inadequate for proper "ventilation of the issues" (*NRDC* v. *NRC,* 547 F.2d 633, 654; at 644). The court reasoned that the NRC failed to employ the available rule-making methods in a responsible manner, thus precluding the possibility that an adequate representation of facts and opposing views could be presented. The court contended that it is sometimes necessary, in the interest of upholding procedural due process standards, for agencies to follow more elaborate rule-making procedures than required by Section 553 of the APA, especially when the issues are socially important and technically complex. Short of demanding that the NRC follow certain rule-making procedures, Circuit Court Judge Bazelon argued that a reviewing court has the responsibility of making sure that agencies provide "a meaningful opportunity [for participation] in the proceedings as guaranteed by due process" (at 643).

But Justice William Rehnquist, writing the Supreme Court opinion, disagreed. He maintained that if the APA granted agency officials the broad discretionary power to decide which lawful rule-making procedures to follow, the judiciary could not demand that the rule-makers follow more elaborate procedures than required, except in extremely rare situations (*Vermont Yankee Nuclear Power Corp.* v. *NRDC,* 435 U.S. 519, 543). Further, Rehnquist noted that misunderstanding and uncertainty which would undermine Section 553 of the APA would develop if reviewing courts were allowed to supplement agency procedures with additional procedures not required by existing statutes.

The Supreme Court's decision in *Vermont Yankee* has been subject to heated criticisms by those such as Wright who believe that the courts must take the initiative in devising standards which can be used to help confine and structure agency discretion. For example, Michael J. Perry and Allan F. Wichelman, in separate law review articles, argue that the federal court system is in the most advantageous position, because it is relatively free from the normal political pressures, to insist that crucial public policy issues be given more than superficial attention by regulatory agencies when drafting rules.[117] For a dozen or so years before *Vermont Yankee,* the courts were beginning to take action to limit agency discretion in rule-making to better ensure that the rule-making procedures selected were not aimed at satisfying short-run objectives but were directed more at ensuring that the long-term public interest was promoted. But, Wichelman writes, *"Vermont Yankee* calls an abrupt end to this development. Reviewing courts are warned not to 'explore the procedural format' utilized by an agency nor 'to impose upon the agency [the court's] notion of which procedures are 'best' or most likely to further some vague, undefined public good.'"[118] The hands-off principle established in *Vermont Yankee* allows agencies to continue to use their discretion irresponsibly to avoid taking more elaborate rule-making steps, perceived essential by many, for the healthy development of highly complex and socially relevant public policies: *"Vermont Yankee's* greatest significance lies in its reversal of the trend, especially apparent in the District of Columbia Circuit, toward requiring rule-making procedures that are more elaborate then those required by Section 553 of the APA when complex and sensitive issues of great public importance are involved."[119]

Kenneth C. Davis claimed, in "Administrative Common Law and the *Vermont Yankee* Opinion," that the Supreme Court's opinion in *Vermont Yankee* was so terrible that he felt it was imperative to stop the printing of the second edition of his *Administrative Law Treatise* so that he could include a commentary on how weak the *Vermont Yankee* decision was. A year and a half after Davis condemned the *Vermont Yankee* decision in his treatise, he asked: "Would words of condemnation be changed if they could be rewritten to speak as of now?" He emphatically replied: "The answer is no, but the answer is not free from doubt. And the doubt is whether the words should be even stronger, not whether they should be weakened."[120]

Davis contends that it is necessary that judge-made common law be developed so that abusive discretionary practices can be controlled. He points out that in the past the Supreme Court has been instrumental in developing common law which has been helpful in refining administrative law, as well as other legal areas. However, he claims that the *Vermont Yankee* holding *"essentially forbids lower courts to follow the Supreme Court's example."*[121] Specifically, the Court's opinion in *Vermont Yankee* is repulsive to Davis because "the main thrust of the opinion is to outlaw new common law that adds to the procedural requirements of Section 553 of the APA."[122] This opinion, Davis holds, is a bad one for many reasons, but what makes the decision particularly unpalatable is that the decision contradicts the legislative history of the APA itself. He notes that the Court's prohibition of common law development "is directly and specifically a violation of the first sentence of section 559 of the APA."[123] Davis asserts that Congress recognized the need for common law to assist the development of administrative law by stating in Section 559 of the APA (originally found in Section 12 of the 1946 APA): "Nothing in this Act shall be held to diminish the constitutional rights of any person or to limit or repeal additional requirements imposed by statute or otherwise recognized by law."[124] Logically, he concludes: "Law that is neither constitutional nor statutory has to be common law."[125]

Apart from this major Court oversight, Davis claims that the high Court was also blatantly and pathetically wrong in *Vermont Yankee* in concluding that the courts cannot impose supplemental rule-making standards because the APA has already established "maximum procedural safeguards." He makes a credible case that the Supreme Court erred in its decision simply because it was unaware of relevant passages in the APA which clearly convey that the APA had set only minimum procedural standards, not maximum standards.[126]

The *Vermont Yankee* decision still remains controversial in the 1990s. However, the passage of time has allowed to surface opinions more supportive of *Vermont Yankee.*[127] Today, many still cling to the belief that the *Vermont Yankee* decision was a poor one. Other scholars, as well as judges, maintain that the court in *Vermont Yankee* had no choice but to rule as it did because it is not up to the courts to require agencies to follow more elaborate procedures than the APA requires. As again explained by the Supreme Court in *Chrysler Corp.* v. *Brown,* 441 U.S. 281, 312 (1979): "We held in *Vermont Yankee* that courts could only in 'extraordinary circumstances' impose procedural requirements on an agency beyond those specified in the APA. It is within an agency's discretion to afford parties more procedure, but it is not the province of the courts to do so."

If the *Vermont Yankee* decision stood alone, its precedential force might be doubted. But the *Vermont Yankee* case does not stand alone. A few months after *Vermont Yankee,* the Supreme Court handed down another decision, *FCC* v. *National Citizens Committee for Broadcasting,* 436 U.S. 775 (1978), which again attracted much scorn. According to Daniel D. Polsby, the *NCCB* case must be viewed in light of *Vermont Yankee:* together they conveyed the clear message to the lower courts that the Burger Court believed that some of these courts, especially the D.C. Circuit Court of Appeals, had gone too far in their efforts to monitor and control agency actions, especially agency use of discretion.[128] In *FCC* v. *NCCB,* the Supreme Court overruled the D.C. Circuit Court opinion which had held that the FCC had abused its discretion by arbitrarily and capriciously defending an outdated grandfather clause pertaining to the licensing of television and radio stations. The Supreme Court said, in sum, that the appeals court had no business trying to limit agency discretion. Judging from the D.C. Circuit Court's clear statement on administrative discretion in *Western Coal Traffic League,* cited above, the D.C. Circuit Court must have finally received the Supreme Court's message.

In reviewing the *NCCB* case, Polsby admitted that the court of appeals ruling did constitute possibly the boldest judicial attempt to extend judicial influence over agency discretionary matters and that maybe the D.C. Circuit Court had indeed gone too far.[129] However, Polsby believes the Court's ruling served to cripple future attempts by the courts to intervene in agency discretionary matters and to develop innovative guidelines that could be used to control discretion. Polsby maintains that it is unquestionable that Congress has left the basic ordering of policy-making values in agency hands, but he holds that administrative discretion should not be so broad that it should be unreviewable and, therefore, virtually uncontrollable, as the Supreme Court appeared to suggest in the *Vermont Yankee* and *NCCB* cases. Acknowledging that the FCC's cross-ownership decision in the *NCCB* case did not constitute what one could consider a "reasoned decision," Polsby asserted that it would be "difficult to imagine how scatterbrained an administrative agency would have to be to entitle a reviewing court to remand a problematic docket for a 'hard look.'"[130]

Although the Supreme Court in 1983 ruled in *State Farm* that the National Highway Safety Administration abused its discretion in its rescission of a motor vehicle safety standard because it failed to provide an adequate explanation for the rescission, since that holding the high Court has repeatedly upheld broad discretionary actions by agency administrators. These decisions have served to establish the clear position of the Supreme Court that broad agency discretion should be honored unless Congress has instructed the courts to scrutinize administrative discretion more carefully, with an eye toward restricting it. In *Capital Cities Cable, Inc.* v. *Crisp,* 104 S.Ct. 2694 (1984), a unanimous Supreme Court held that when Congress has directed an agency, in this case, the Federal Communications Commission, to exercise administrative discretion, judicial review should be limited to only the question of whether the agency exceeded its statutory authority or abused its discretion by acting arbitrarily.

In possibly the most influential administrative law case handed down in the past few decades, *Chevron, U.S.A., Inc.* v. *Natural Resources Defense Council,* 104 S.Ct. 2778 (1984), the Supreme Court expanded on its position that agencies should be allowed to exercise broad discretion in making policy choices when executing statutes. Quoting from its decision in *Morton,* the Court stated: "The power of an administrative agency to administer a congressionally created . . . program necessarily requires the formulation of policy and making of rules to fill any gap left implicitly or explicitly by Congress. . . . If Congress has explicitly left a gap for the agency to fill, there is an express delegation of authority to the agency to elucidate a specific provision of the statute by regulation. Such legislative regulations are given controlling weight unless they are arbitrary, capricious, or manifestly contrary to statute. Sometimes the legislative delegation to an agency on a particular question is implicit rather than explicit. In such a case, a court may not substitute its own construction of a statutory provision for a reasonable interpretation made by the administrator of an agency" (at 2782). Consequently, the Supreme Court concluded that the particular policy choice by the Environmental Protection Agency to control air pollution (i.e., the adoption of the "bubble" concept, previously explained) "is a reasonable policy choice for the agency to make" (at 2783).

Consistent with its position on discretion developed in *Capital Cities Cable* and *Chevron,* the Supreme Court in *Regents of the University of Michigan* v. *Ewing,* 106 S.Ct. 507 (1985), ruled in a unanimous decision that universities should be accorded the broadest range of discretion in making decisions pertaining to the academic performance of students. Stating emphatically that this case, involving a student contesting admission to an academic program, should never have been litigated, the Court stressed that to safeguard academic freedom, the courts should stay away from reviewing academic decisions made by faculty members.

That same year the Supreme Court held in *Heckler* v. *Chaney,* 105 S.Ct. 1649 (1985), that an agency's refusal to act or take enforcement action is unreviewable unless Congress has indicated otherwise. "This Court has recognized that an agency's decision not to prosecute or enforce, whether through civil or criminal process, is a decision generally committed," unless Congress has said otherwise, "to an agency's absolute discretion" (at 1656). The justification for the Court's holding, as presented by Justice Rehnquist, writing for the majority, has attracted severe criticism. In his reasoning, Rehnquist felt it was necessary to address an apparent conflict between two provisions in the Administrative Procedure Act that has bothered legal scholars for several decades. It is important to understand Rehnquist's perception of the conflict and his resolution of it to grasp the present Supreme Court's posture on judicial review of administrative discretion.

Justice Rehnquist summarized the conflict between Sections 701(a)(2) and 706(2)(A) of the APA by exclaiming that commentators feel that tension exists "between a literal reading of Section (a)(2), which exempts from judicial review those decisions committed to agency 'discretion,' and the primary scope of review prescribed by Section 706(2)(A)—whether the agency's action was 'arbitrary, capricious, or an abuse of discretion.' How is it, they ask, that an action committed to agency discretion can be unreviewable and yet courts still can review agency action for abuse of that discretion?" (at 1654).[131] Rehnquist's answer is quite simple. He argues that Section 701(a)(1) permits judicial review of agency action only if Congress provides for judicial review, but precludes review of discretionary agency action "if the statute is drawn so that a court would have no meaningful standard against which to judge the agency's exercise of discretion. In such a case, the statute ('law') can be taken to have 'committed' the decisionmaking to the agency's judgment absolutely" (at 1655). To Rehnquist, this interpretation of Section 701(a)(1) also resolves its conflict with the "abuse of discretion" review standard found in Section 706(2)(A) because "if no judicially manageable standards are available for judging how and when an agency should exercise its discretion then it is impossible to evaluate agency action for 'abuse of discretion'" (at 1655).

This reasoning by Rehnquist in *Chaney* has baffled and irritated some judicial scholars. One such scholar is Bernard Schwartz. He vehemently argues that this "where there is no law to apply" notion only reiterates the same heresy of *Overton Park* because there is "no place for unreviewable discretion in a system such as ours."[132] As long as the case is justifiable, Schwartz asserts, "all discretionary power should be reviewable to determine that the discretion conferred has not been abused. What the English courts call the *Wednesbury* principle is just as valid in American administrative law. Under it the reviewing court should always be able to determine that the discretion has not been exercised in a manner in which no reasonable administrator would act. To this extent, there is always 'law to apply' and hence reviewable discretion, Section 701(a)(2), *Overton Park* and *Chaney* notwithstanding."[133]

Despite considerable scholarly criticisms of the *Chevron* and *Chaney* decisions, these two cases, especially *Chevron,* have established strong precedent, causing courts since the mid-1980s to defer often and probably too readily to agency expertise, unwilling to scrutinize all but the most blatant abuses of administrative discretion. In *ABF Freight System, Inc.* v. *N.L.R.B.,* 114 S. Ct. 835, 839 (1994), the Supreme Court, citing *Chevron,* again said emphatically that "When Congress expressly delegates to an administrative agency the authority to make specific policy determinations, courts must give the agency's decision controlling weight unless it is 'arbitrary, capricious, or manifestly contrary to statute.'" And specifically citing *Chaney,* the high Court in *Lincoln* v. *Vigil,* 113 S. Ct. 2024, 2031 (1993), reiterated its position that an agency decision not to act, or specifically not to enforce, is "presumptively unreviewable" because "an agency's 'decision not to enforce often involves a complicated balancing of a number of factors which are peculiarly within its expertise,' . . . and for this and other good reasons, . . . (is) 'committed to agency discretion.'"

Numerous other cases can be cited to substantiate the argument that, on the whole, the courts have done considerably more to promote the broad and potentially dangerous use of discretion than to limit discretion. In the final analysis, despite arguments to the contrary, it seems in general that the courts have thus far tried to control only the most flagrant abuses of discretionary power. This is especially true for the Supreme Court, and the Rehnquist Court is unlikely to shift direction. As we shall see in the next chapter, which focuses exclusively on the role the courts play in reviewing agency actions, judges still cling to doctrines which help them to avoid getting involved in and, according to so many court opinions, disrupting the normal administrative processes. But it seems that normal administrative procedures, unfortunately, too often include the unfair and abusive treatment of individual parties, as well as practices that lead to poorly planned major social policies. To improve administrative decision making in the future, and in particular to help prevent administrative abuses, the courts will have to watch discretionary agency behavior more closely and own those actions which reasonable persons would consider repugnant to procedural due process standards. This must be accomplished without imprisoning administrators through undue interference and placing unnecessary restrictions on their discretion.

NONTRADITIONAL ALTERNATIVES
TO CONTROLLING ADMINISTRATIVE POWER

We have discussed previously, especially in Chapter 3, methods which have been traditionally employed in the United States for monitoring and controlling administrative behavior. In concluding this chapter, it is appropriate to comment briefly on a
few nontraditional alternatives which have been proposed for checking the exercise
of administrative power, especially the use of discretion. The following methods are
considered nontraditional only because they have not been formally institutionalized
on a broad scale in the American political system. Some governmental systems have,
however, experimented with these methods with some success.

Administrative Courts

It seems that the present judicial system is ill-equipped to handle all the administrative law conflicts in modern administrative government. Once more, the burden being placed on the judicial system by administrative law questions is increasing daily,
as the administrative state continues to expand. For some, the solution would be to
develop an administrative court system which could devote its attention only to administrative controversies.

　　The idea that a special judicial system was needed, independent from agency
control, yet not connected to the regular court system either, was first given support
in America near the turn of this century.[134] In 1910 the Mann-Elkins Act (36 Stat.
539) created a judicial body which embraced the chief features of an administrative
court. The purpose of this court was to provide judicial review of actions by the ICC
in a more expeditious manner than the appellate courts could.[135] Because of political
pressures, the Commerce Court collapsed a few years later, but I.L. Sharfman, one of
the former members of the shortlived court, exclaimed: "It is by no means certain that
its failure was inherent in the premises upon which it was reared, or that the same
need for economy and expertness that led to the development of administrative agencies may not again create a well founded demand for corresponding judicial specialization."[136] The call for judicial specialization in administrative actions has continued
well into the 1990s. During the 1930s, the President's Committee on Administrative
Management and the American Bar Association pushed for an administrative court
system similar to the one which had been implemented in France, arguing that such
a system was necessary if administrative power was to be kept democratically accountable. However, their recommendations were rejected by the Attorney General's
Committee on Administrative Procedure in 1941. This committee was not sympathetic with the argument that the regular court system could not adequately handle
administrative law disputes. The second Hoover Commission in 1955 also favored an
administrative court system, as did the Ash Council in 1971,[137] the American Bar Association's Standing Committee on Federal Judicial Improvements in 1989, and the
Report of the Federal Courts Study Committee (1990).[138]

　　The Ash Council recommended the creation of a separate administrative court
which would function somewhat akin to our tax court. While the tax court hears only

specialized tax cases, the administrative court urged by the Ash Council would review only cases in the areas of energy, securities, and transportation. According to the Ash Report, the advantage of this judicial review arrangement would be that it could provide expert review of technical questions in the areas of energy, securities, and transportation, thus developing over a period of time a uniform and valuable body of administrative law. The Ash Council proposed a three-panel court consisting of fifteen judges serving fifteen-year terms. A year earlier, the Occupational Safety and Health Act (OSHA) of 1970 (84 Stat. 1590) created an administrative court-like arrangement by separating the judicial and legislative functions. While OSHA, in the Department of Labor, was given the responsibility of setting and enforcing standards, adjudicative matters were assigned to an independent agency, the Occupational Safety and Health Review Commission. According to Neil Sullivan, "the separation of adjudicative and legislative functions between the Review Commission and OSHA is consistent with the recommendations of many groups that have been concerned with improving the administrative process through creation of administrative courts to ensure a strict separation of functions."[139]

Administrative courts would have limited jurisdiction, having authority only over disputes involving governmental agencies. As conceptualized, the use of administrative courts would not preclude judicial review of agency action by the regular courts. Properly used, the administrative courts would reduce the caseload for the regular courts by hearing those time-consuming cases of lesser importance. However, according to a 1990 study by Harold Bruff, administrative courts would reduce the caseload burden only very moderately since administrative cases constituted only 14 percent of the cases in federal courts in 1989.[140] Major issues, especially those involving constitutional and statutory procedural due process questions, would be decided by the regular judiciary. Ideally, while the structural independence of administrative courts helps to ensure unbiased review of administrative actions, the expertise of the reviewing judges helps to provide for effective review of technically complicated cases. If modeled after the French design (likely, since the French administrative court system is considered to be the best), administrative courts would have other advantages over the regular courts. They would be less costly, parties would not necessarily have to retain legal counsel, the administrative court would provide some assistance in helping parties to prepare their cases, and "standing" to bring suit would be easier to obtain. All things considered, supporters of an administrative court system for America hold that it could protect citizens from abuses of administrative powers, especially misuses of discretion, while helping to promote smooth administrative operations through competent review.[141]

Since we do not have an administrative court system in the United States, although one has been variously advocated since before 1900, there may be something wrong with the idea. Lewis Mainzer notes that "British and American observers worry deeply about the divided jurisdiction of the civil and administrative courts and argue that there is great value in a single, unified system of courts."[142] Harold H. Bruff voices the same concern, arguing that the development of an administrative court system could cause the ". . . loss of the generalist perspective." He believes that this could constitute a serious loss because the wisdom behind generalist courts is that "... sound decisionmaking results from exposure to a wide range of problems. ..."[143]

Critics cite other potential problems. Some fear that interest groups would corrupt the appointment process, making sure that judges are appointed to these administrative courts who would likely hand down decisions favorable to their special interests. Administrative courts would be particularly susceptible to political pressures for favorable appointments because these specialized courts would repeatedly hear cases in specialized regulatory areas. "Capturing" judges on administrative courts, critics hold, would be most cost-effective for the special interests, yet at a tremendous cost to the promotion of the public interest.[144] On the other hand, such judges, protected by long fifteen-year terms, could shun the biased will of special interests, reaching decisions that are fair and objective.

On the whole, however, the administrative court plan has merits which should be given serious attention by our lawmakers. The French administrative court system, despite criticisms, has been at least modestly successful. In America, there is no question that our courts are overburdened, and too frequently with cases which could be much better adjudicated by judges in administrative courts who have expertise in specific administrative areas (for example, nuclear power). Undoubtedly, growth trends in public administration make it very clear that administrative law disputes will contribute to even greater caseload problems for our regular courts in the future. This will mean that unless something is done to alleviate the caseload problem, an increasing number of legitimate administrative law questions which genuinely need to be resolved will not be heard. Or if they are heard, they will be heard only routinely, without any serious effort exerted to see to it that administrative due process is upheld. A well-designed administrative court system could provide at least part of the answer.

How About an Ombudsman System?

Kenneth J. Meier points out that some observers of public bureaucracy recommend the implementation of some form of ombudsman system in the United States "[B]ecause controlling bureaucracy via other political institutions does not guarantee beneficent administration ... ."[145] Supporters of the ombudsman plan claim that it can be used to keep administrative behavior in check, especially discretionary administrative actions toward individual parties. The ombudsman concept can be traced back to where it was implemented, in Sweden in 1809. But in more recent times the Danish Ombudsman plan, instituted in 1955, has helped to provide a useful model for other nations or smaller political entities (states and cities) to follow. Since 1955 many nations have incorporated into their system, not necessarily on a national scale, some form of the ombudsman plan. Several works during the 1960s of which Walter Gellhorn's *Ombudsmen and Others* and *When Americans Complain* probably became the most popular, were quite influential, causing the ombudsman idea to gain widespread popularity in the United States. However, despite the intellectual popularity of the concept, by the 1990s the ombudsman plan has been implemented only very modestly in the United States, mostly at the state and local levels. A few states have implemented an ombudsman system statewide (e.g., Alaska, Hawaii, Iowa and Nebraska), although virtually no ombudsman plan strictly duplicates the original Danish ombudsman model.

What is an *ombudsman?* An ombudsman is simply an officer, commissioner, or the like, who is appointed by a governing authority (for example, a congressional or parliamentary body, a state legislature, a city council, a board or commission, or, less frequently, an executive official) for the chief purpose of serving as the citizens' defender. Specifically, an ombudsman's office is established so that citizens can voice complaints about public service operations. Ombudsmen are expected to listen to and investigate the complaints and act on those which are legitimate. Typically, ombudsmen are not responsible for running around and discovering the nefarious acts of administrators. Normally, ombudsmen are supposed to start their investigations only after specific complaints have been brought to their attention by citizens, although they may initiate broader investigations of administrative activities which are related to the original complaints. Supporters believe that the ombudsman could be particularly useful for detecting, exposing, and recommending remedies for discretionary injustices committed by public administrators. An excellent definition of an ombudsman is given by Davis: "An ombudsman is a high-level officer whose main function is to receive complaints from citizens who are aggrieved by official action or inaction, to investigate, to criticize, and to publicize findings, but who typically has no power to correct injustice or maladministration except by criticizing and persuading."[146]

The ombudsman concept has been criticized for many reasons. One reason is that an ombudsman system would simply add another costly layer to the already gigantic governmental bureaucracy. In fact, Meier asserts that no comprehensive ombudsman plan has ever been implemented for a government as large as the United States because, to do so, ". . . would likely require a bureaucracy as large as many bureaus it would investigate."[147] These critics contend that we already have institutional arrangements to handle citizen complaints about the public service. Specifically, they note that legislative assemblies and the courts are designed to handle such complaints. However, we have already noted that the courts are overburdened and, thus, probably incapable of responding adequately to the beefs that citizens have toward bureaucracy. Besides, to reiterate a well-known point, the courts are too expensive and generally very inconvenient to use, especially to resolve the typical complaints an ombudsman would handle (for example, repeated agency errors, slow response to citizen needs). In practice, our courts are now used primarily to resolve relatively major legal disputes, but they always must stick to actual legal controversies. Frequently, ombudsmen deal with complaints that do not involve illegal administrative behavior, but with actions which fall within the law and yet need attention to correct agency operations which inconvenience and abuse persons unnecessarily. Such matters are clearly beyond the jurisdiction of the courts.

Hans A. Linde and George Bunn also say legislators are ill-equipped to handle competently the sort of typical complaints an ombudsman's office would process:

"Overall, the congressional officers are able to provide assistance to many of the constituents who write for help. One Senator has estimated that he does about 3,000 such 'favors' for constituents in a year and a half. Nevertheless, there is much left to be desired in this process of mediating between the citizen and government. A congressional office is simply not equipped to give the type of personal attention which so many of these letters demand, for as dedicated as legislators and their staffs may be, the amount of constituent mail is staggering."[148] These scholars conclude that legislators provide inadequate substitutes for ombudsman offices because, even in responding to citizen complaints, legislators do little to correct the breakdowns in administrative operations on a regular basis.[149]

Walter Gellhorn, probably the leading American authority on the ombudsman system, basically agrees with the insights of Linde and Bunn. In an interview with this eminent scholar, Professor Gellhorn pointed out for me some of the main arguments for instituting in America an ombudsman system or any similar grievance mechanism. To Gellhorn, ombudsmen should not play an adversary role similar to the role lawyers play in our legal system when defending their clients. He simply perceives an ombudsman's office as a complaint bureau where citizens can come to voice their grievances against public service performance, or say in effect: "I'm not getting proper service and should not someone look into the matter?"[150]

Gellhorn acknowledged that we have traditionally relied upon our national and state legislators to respond to our complaints about how we have been treated by administrators. But he is convinced that legislators normally investigate complaints with only the individual's interest in mind and without proper regard to the actual merits of the complaint. That is, the legislator's approach is often expressed in the attitude that: "By God, I'm going to win this case for my constituent!"[151] But Gellhorn aptly noted that the constituent's complaint is often illegitimate and should not be defended and won. However, he exclaimed: "But from the legislator's point of view, who is trying to win 'brownie points' from his constituent, winning is the important thing."[152] What Gellhorn wants is "someone to look into the situation from the standpoint of improving administration and not merely [from the perspective of] getting satisfaction for the original complainant."[153] Unfortunately, he confided, legislators are often content with resolving the particular problem for the complainant, while allowing the administrative problem to continue for others.

Gellhorn maintained that an ombudsman would handle the complaint much differently. The ombudsman may not try to resolve an alleged administrative problem in light of a single complaint; but after hearing the same complaint several times, he would be motivated to investigate the reasons for the problem, acknowledging that the frequency of the case points to an administrative breakdown somewhere. Then the ombudsman would be prepared to ask: "Can't something be done to make sure that this problem does not occur again?"[154]

But then who is really going to act for the individual citizen when he or she is victimized by an administrator's abusive discretionary actions? If an ombudsman's office is designed to defend citizens, should the ombudsman not be concerned primarily with doing just that? It should be pointed out that some critics perceive an ombudsman system as just another typical bureaucratic response to a bureaucratic problem. Robert Miewald emphasizes that an appointed ombudsman would be "expected to be a member in good standing of the bureaucracy."[155] When a citizen has a grievance about how he has been mistreated by some public agency, Miewald exclaims that the last thing this citizen wants is to be given the same runaround by a bureaucratized ombudsman office which instinctively relates more to fellow bureaucrats than to citizens who do not speak or understand the bureaucratic tradition. Consequently, Miewald finds some merit in continuing the old system, under which biased legislators are summoned by citizens to respond to their complaints. He admits that critics such as Gellhorn are right in noting that "the greatest failure of the legislators is the lack of impartiality. But who wants impartiality? Impartiality in the bureaucracy means going along with the system. If I have a gripe about the bureaucracy, I am not particularly interested in a sober analysis of the existing rules, especially if those rules have caused my anguish. I do not need an ombudsman to provide me with another explanation of Catch-22. I want some action."[156]

The most serious charge against the viability of the ombudsman concept is that ombudsmen would be unable to alleviate administrative injustices and influence positive administrative reforms because an American ombudsman would not be expected to have any real powers (for example, the power to prosecute) except the power of persuasion. How, then, could ombudsmen's suggestions be expected to carry any weight with those in our political system who have real power? Gerald Caiden, after researching the role played by several ombudsmen offices, concluded that ombudsmen really have limited jurisdictional power, conduct mostly superficial investigations, receive little recognition, and have feeble political clout.[157] In fact, most observers contend, somewhat ironically, that ombudsmen seem to be most "effective" when the system least needs it (i.e., when the existing administrative system is already fairly competent and responsive).[158] Also ironically, Robert D. Miewald and John C. Comer, after investigating the ombudsman system in Nebraska, discovered that the typical ombudsmen clientele needs ombudsmen the least since they are middle-class, relatively well-educated citizens who are experienced and sophisticated enough to voice their own complaints.[159]

In *When Americans Complain*, Gellhorn asks: "What is it that makes a critical opinion weighty? Why should an administrator subordinate his judgment to that of a critic, when the critic is known to be toothless?"[160] His response is that opinions carry weight if they are respected in the community. In most situations, ombudsmen would have the respect of the people and, consequently, public officials would be foolish to ignore their criticisms. In light of valid criticisms, he holds that "few administrators have shown dogged devotion to errors that have been persuasively pointed out in an unrancorous atmosphere."[161] Besides, Gellhorn asserts, ombudsmen are frequently placed in the position of being the best defenders of administrative practices when criticisms are unfair. In short, Gellhorn perceptively concludes: "Powerlessness does not necessarily connote unpersuasiveness."[162] Given the apparent virtues of the ombudsman concept, Gellhorn urges America to give the system a try. However, other scholars are not convinced the ombudsman system is worth implementing in the United States in a comprehensive way.

Resorting to Whistle-Blowers

Various methods have been advanced as feasible for protecting citizens against the arbitrary and ruthless use of administrative power. Of course, the most basic check was provided by our constitutional framers when they established a political system with shared governmental powers. Through the years legislators and judges have proposed and instituted various mechanisms for controlling administrative authority. However, in spite of these efforts to control administrative power, especially the use of administrative discretion, administrators seem to have only increased their relative position of power in our governmental system.

In response to this reality, more innovative ideas, such as administrative courts and various ombudsman plans, have been proposed by those fearful of the new power of public administrators. Citizen groups, especially consumer protection organizations, have joined the battle by pushing for ways to stop administrative officials from misusing their offices. Some scholars have argued that the best general approach for controlling administrative power is to make sure administrative actions are conducted in the open so that everyone can have an opportunity to see and judge the appropriateness of administrative acts.

But of all the ideas that have been proposed to keep administrative actions democratically accountable and fair to individual parties, probably the most novel idea is to institutionalize whistle-blowing. Because some believe that traditional methods have failed to prevent administrators from abusing their administrative powers, they have argued that we should rely on those inside public agencies to blow the whistle on those whom they discover acting afoul.

The positive social value of whistle-blowing had been recognized by our governmental leaders as far back as 1899 when Congress passed the Refuse Act, which provided that a person who squealed on a polluter was entitled to receive one-half of the assessed fines, even if the squealer worked for the polluting company.[163] Judging from the discoveries of thousands of dumping sites across our land, where both private and public enterprises have dumped toxic chemical wastes presenting serious health hazards, this law makes sense and should still be enforced. Of course, police organizations, frustrated by being confined by institutionalized methods for fighting crime, have also relied heavily on inside informers to blow the whistle on fellow criminals.

In *Whistle Blowing*, Ralph Nader and others make a strong argument for employing whistle-blowers to help keep all public officials acting responsibly. The inherent problem with using external control techniques to control administrative misconduct is that the watchdogs are always outside looking in. However, Nader notes, potential whistle-blowers are inside public agencies, where they are obviously in the best strategic position to spot abuses of power. Nader holds that by detecting and blowing the whistle on nefarious official behavior, agency members can provide a valuable public service: "In the past . . . whistle blowing has illuminated dark corners of our society, saved lives, prevented injuries and disease, and stopped corruption, economic waste, and material exploitation. Conversely, the absence of such professional and individual responsibility has perpetuated these conditions."[164]

Possibly the most famous whistle-blower in recent American history was John Dean, legal counsel to President Nixon. Dean's testimony before the Senate Watergate Committee, which investigated the illegal activities of the Nixon White House, was directly responsible for the fall of the Nixon administration.[165] Nader tells the story of many more whistle-blowers who have served America well in recent years by blowing the whistle on their co-workers and bosses.[166]

Although responsible whistle-blowing can provide Americans with a valuable weapon against such official misconduct as discretionary injustices, Nader is cognizant of the probability that irresponsible whistle-blowing could render a costly disservice to virtually all parties concerned, especially by disrupting needed administrative services. Nader contends that responsible whistle-blowers must consult their consciences after spotting administrative abuses and personally decide whether the apparent misdeed should be reported. To guide their decision to blow or not blow the whistle, he recommends that all civil servants should apply the Nuremberg principle—a principle developed at the trials of Nazis charged with war crimes held during 1946 in Nuremberg, Germany. Basically, the Nuremberg principle holds that individuals, not organizations, are ultimately responsible for preventing injustices. Consequently, he places all those inside bureaucracy on notice "that the defense of 'following orders' is fundamentally defective because there exists with respect to every organization a higher law, a higher principle, a higher morality."[167]

However, Nader's advice could lead to frustrating problems. It should be recognized that morality is difficult to define and, thus, everyone marches to a different moral drummer. During the investigation into the Iran-Contra scandal in the 1980s, Colonel Oliver North lied blatantly to Congress about matters concerning the scandal, evidently believing that he should not blow the whistle on his superiors, but should instead answer to a moral authority higher than the U.S. Congress. In fact, he rooted his 1994 U.S. Senate campaign on his moral choice to defy Congress. Fortunately, he lost.

Due to repeated reports of corruption in our public agencies during the 1970s, pressures were predictably placed on Congress to do something about protecting whistle-blowers. Congress responded by placing some provisions in the Civil Service Reform Act of 1978 (92 Stat. 1111), which gave whistle-blowers limited protection. Basically, the legislation aimed at prohibiting reprisals from being taken against whistle-blowers. More specifically, the act prohibited governmental "officials and employees who are authorized to take personnel actions . . . from taking or failing to take a personnel action as a reprisal against employees who . . . lawfully disclose violations of law, rule, or regulation, or mismanagement, gross waste of funds, abuse of authority, or a substantial and specific danger to public health or safety."[168] To enforce this objective, the act created a special independent council, with members appointed to five-year terms by the president, to investigate any allegations that reprisals have been taken against whistle-blowers and to punish those who have taken reprisal actions.[169]

Critics immediately attacked this law, arguing that the protective provisions were much too weak to really protect whistle-blowers against agency retaliation. These critics predicted that the risks to whistle-blowers under this law were so clear

'After All, It's Not Just Any Old Limb He Went Out On'

Source: Reprinted with permission of Tom Engelhardt and the *St. Louis Post-Dispatch,* October 3, 1978.

that few employees would dare blow the whistle. This prediction proved true, so Congress amended the 1978 Law with the Whistleblower Protection Act of 1989 (103 stat. 16). These amendments strengthened significantly the protections for whistle-blowers by: (1) redefining retaliation, expanding the definition to include even threats of retaliation; (2) making it easier to prove retaliation by having to show only that whistle-blowing was a contributing factor to agency action against them, not a prevailing factor; (3) making it more difficult for the government to defend itself by arguing that the whistle-blower was really being punished for other reasons, not for whistle-blowing (the government now has to base its stand on "clear and convincing evidence" rather than on a "preponderance of evidence"); and (4) allowing whistle-blowers to initiate independent action before the Merit Systems Protection Board if the Special Counsel (formerly the special independent council) failed to pursue their case.[170]

Unquestionably, the Whistleblower Protection Act of 1989 constitutes a significant improvement over feeble whistle-blower protections found in the 1978 Civil Service Reform Act. However, evidence suggests that whistle-blowers still are at great risk. Common sense dictates that no whistle-blowing statute can totally protect whistle-blowers, so whistle-blowers will remain at risk.

SUMMARY

Administrative power is feared by many today because public administrators possess broad discretionary powers that do not appear to be very closely monitored by the other branches of government. Observers claim that democratic government in America is being threatened by the use of excessive administrative discretion. Specifically, they contend that administrative discretion plays too great a role in shaping and exercising public policy. But the problem of finding the proper dose of unthreatening discretion is as old as democratic government itself. Theoretically, the use of administrative discretion conflicts sharply with basic rule-of-law principles, since its use seems to place administrators above the law. The exercise of discretion is condemned by strict rule-of-law advocates who maintain that where law ends, tyranny begins. For them, the use of discretion must eventually lead to the decline of liberty and the rise of tyranny.

Kenneth C. Davis, the leading authority on the subject, stresses the seriousness of the discretionary justice problem and, consequently, urges administrative law scholars to devote considerably more attention to it. However, he does not accept the position that discretion leading to tyrannical rule must start where the law ends. He insists that when the law ends, only the use of discretion begins and that discretion can be employed to preserve democratic institutions and practices. Davis says that most discretionary injustices occur when administrators exercise their broad, informal discretionary powers which fall into their legitimate scope of authority. Such discretion represents approximately 90 percent of all agency actions. He asserts that few injustices occur when administrative actions are formal (structured) and also subject to judicial scrutiny. To guard against abuses of administrative discretion, he suggests that steps be taken to confine, structure, and check informal discretionary agency actions. He believes that administrators should draft their own rules to confine, structure, and check discretionary agency behavior.

However, critics charge that Davis is naive to think that administrators will be willing to place effective restrictions on their own discretionary powers voluntarily, especially since most administrators seek more flexibility in their work. J. Skelly Wright argues that administrative discretion will not be adequately controlled in the future unless Congress decides to reassert its authority to play its proper constitutional role as the chief architect of our laws. But in the final analysis, he feels that the courts must assume primary responsibility for compelling administrators to structure discretion so that its use is more in line with constitutional standards of fair play.

But these recommendations also seem to be rooted in naive assumptions. Recent court decisions and congressional behavior do not suggest that judges and legislators are willing to take steps to restrict the exercise of administrative discretion. While Congress has refused to attach meaningful standards to guide agency discretion, *Chevron, Chaney,* and *ABF Freight Systems, Inc.* stand as major examples of the court's willingness to defer readily to the broad exercise of administrative discretion.

Since traditional political controls have apparently not been able to adequately control the use of administrative discretion, some nontraditional ideas have been proposed for keeping discretionary agency practices within limits which would be safe for democracy. Proposals have called for administrative courts, ombudsmen, and even the institutionalization of whistle-blowing. Some of these ideas have been experimented with on a limited basis, receiving only faint support.

NOTES

1. Kenneth C. Davis and Richard J. Pierce, Jr., *Administrative Law Treatise,* 3rd ed., vol. 1 (Boston: Little, Brown, and Co., 1994), 22.
2. Kenneth C. Davis, *Discretionary Justice: A Preliminary Inquiry* (Westport, Conn.: Greenwood, 1980), 4. This book is a reprint of his classic work first published by University of Illinois Press (Urbana, 1969).
3. Ibid.
4. Ibid.
5. Kenneth C. Davis, *Administrative Law: Cases-Text-Problems* (St. Paul, Minn.: West Publishing Company, 1977), 440.
6. Ibid., 440–47.
7. Davis and Pierce, Jr., vol. 3, chap. 17.
8. Ibid.
9. Ibid.
10. For a discussion of such court rulings, see Kenneth F. Warren, "'Spatial Deconcentration': A Problem Greater than School Desegregation," *Administrative Law Review,* 29 (Fall 1977), 577–99.
11. Davis and Pierce, Jr., vol. 3, 105.
12. Kenneth C. Davis, *Administrative Law: Cases-Text-Problems* (St. Paul, Minn.: West Publishing Company, 1977), 443.
13. Ibid., 442.
14. Ibid.
15. Ibid.
16. Jeffrey Pressman and Aaron Wildavsky, *Implementation* (Berkeley: University of California Press, 1973), chaps. 1–3; see also Daniel A. Mazmanian and Paul A. Sabatier, *Implementation and Public Policy* (Glenview, Ill.: Scott Foresman, 1983), esp. chaps. 1–3; and Robert F. Durant, "EPA, TVA and Pollution Control: Implications for a Theory of Regulatory Policy Implementation," *Public Administration Review,* 44 (July/August 1984), 305–13.
17. Davis, *Discretionary Justice,* 4.
18. Joel Samaha, *Criminal Law,* 2nd ed. (St. Paul, Minn.: West Publishing Company, 1987), 14.

19. Davis, *Discretionary Justice,* 4–5.
20. See, for example, the court's arguments in defense of the broad use of discretion in *United States* v. *International Telephone Corp. and Hartford Fire Insurance Co.,* 349 F. Supp. 22 (1972). It is not as necessary to prove "bad faith" today because "good faith" cannot be used as a defense when constitutional rights are violated by public officials.
21. Joel Samaha, "Some Reflections on the Anglo-Saxon Heritage of Discretionary Justice," in *Social Psychology and Discretionary Law,* ed. Lawrence Edwin Abt and Irving R. Stuart (New York: Van Nostrand Reinhold, 1979), 4.
22. Ibid.
23. See, for example, Plato's discussion of the need for flexibility in *The Republic,* trans. F.M. Cornford (New York: Oxford University Press, 1945), Book 7, 514a-519e, and Aristotle's call for flexibility in laws in *The Politics,* trans. T.A. Sinclair (Baltimore: Penguin Books, 1962), Book 3.
24. Ibid., 8.
25. Ibid., 7.
26. Ibid., 11.
27. Ibid., 11–14.
28. Ibid. 13.
29. Samaha, "Some Reflections on the Anglo-Saxon Heritage of Discretionary Justice," 13–14.
30. Davis, *Discretionary Justice;* see also Kenneth C. Davis, *Discretionary Justice in Europe and America* (Urbana: University of Illinois Press, 1976); Kenneth C. Davis, *Police Discretion* (St. Paul, Minn.: West Publishing Company, 1975); Davis, *Administrative Law Treatise*; and Davis and Pierce, Jr., *Administrative Law Treatise,* 3rd ed., vol. 3, chap. 17.
31. In his 1979 *Administrative Law Treatise,* 2: 160, Davis wrote that the discussion of discretionary justice represents "a mixture of new ideas with ideas drawn from the 1969 book and from the writer's *Police Discretion* (1975) and *Discretionary Justice in Europe and America* (1976)."
32. Davis, *Administrative Law Treatise,* 2: 160.
33. Davis and Pierce, Jr., *Administrative Law Treatise,* 3rd ed., vol. 3, 102.
34. Davis, *Administrative Law Treatise,* 2: 158.
35. Ibid.
36. Ibid., 159.
37. Davis, *Discretionary Justice,* 3.
38. Davis, *Administrative Law Treatise,* 2: 165.
39. Davis, *Discretionary Justice,* 3.
40. Ibid., 3–4.
41. However, this is not always the case. In *Police Discretion,* Davis argues that police officers on the beat possess enormous and significant discretionary powers. Their decisions may have major consequences for individuals.
42. Davis, *Discretionary Justice,* 52–54.
43. Ibid., 55.
44. As quoted in Oscar Kraines, *The World and Ideas of Ernest Freund: The Search for General Principles of Legislation and Administration* (Birmingham, Alabama: University of Alabama Press, 1974), 104, appearing in Donald D. Barry and Howard R. Whitcomb, *The Legal Foundations of Public Administration,* 2nd ed. (St. Paul, Minn.: West Publishing Company, 1987), 248.

45. Davis, *Discretionary Justice,* 55.
46. Norton Long, "Public Policy and Administration: The Goals of Rationality and Responsibility," *Public Administration Review,* 14 (Winter 1954); Henry Friendly, *The Federal Administrative Agencies* (Cambridge, Mass.: Harvard University Press, 1962); and Davis, *Discretionary Justice,* 56–59.
47. Davis, *Discretionary Justice,* 56–57.
48. Ibid., 57.
49. Ibid., 65.
50. Ibid., 65–68.
51. Ibid., 97.
52. Ibid.
53. Ibid.
54. Ibid., 97–99.
55. Davis, *Administrative Law Treatise,* 2: 207.
56. Ibid.
57. Davis, *Discretionary Justice,* 98.
58. Ibid.
59. Ibid., 102.
60. For another viewpoint on how to control abuses of administrative discretion, see Ronald A. Carr, Colin A. Diver, and Jack M. Beermann, *Administrative Law: Cases and Materials,* 2nd ed. (Boston: Little, Brown, 1994), 279–293.
61. Ibid., 152–156.
62. Ibid., 152–153.
63. J. Skelly Wright, "Beyond Discretionary Justice, *Yale Law Journal,* 81 (January 1972), 575–577.
64. Davis, *Discretionary Justice,* 142.
65. Ibid., 142–43.
66. Ibid., 142.
67. Davis, *Administrative Law Treatise,* 2: 171.
68. Davis, *Discretionary Justice,* 142–161.
69. Wright, "Beyond Discretionary Justice," 575–577.
70. Ibid., 576–580.
71. Ibid., 577.
72. Ibid.
73. Ibid.
74. Ibid.
75. Ibid., 578
76. Ibid.
77. The expression "muddling through" was made famous in the public administration literature by Charles Lindblom; for his arguments putting "muddling through" in a favorable light, see "The Science of Muddling Through," *Public Administration Review,* 19 (Spring 1959), 79–88. More recently, Daniel J. Gifford in "Discretionary Decisionmaking in the Regulatory Agencies," 117–21, applies the concept of "muddling through" to his analysis of agency discretion.
78. Wright, "Beyond Discretionary Justice," 579. Of course, this view is not profound and is made by virtually every scholar writing on the subject. For a more recent article see, Charles H. Koch, Jr., "Judicial Review of Administrative Discretion," *The George Washington Law Review,* 54 (May 1986).

79. Wright, "Beyond Discretionary Justice," 579.
80. Ibid., 578–79.
81. Ibid., 581–582.
82. Ibid., 580.
83. Ibid., 581.
84. Ibid., 582.
85. Ibid.
86. Ibid., 584.
87. Ibid., 583–584.
88. Ibid., 585.
89. Ibid.
90. Ibid.
91. Ibid., 589.
92. Ibid., 587–93.
93. Wright, "Beyond Discretionary Justice," 581; see also Davis, *Administrative Law Treatise,* 2: 173. Basically, Davis argues that the courts provide a poor check against discretionary abuses because of the "practical unavailability" of judicial review.
94. Wright, "Beyond Discretionary Justice," 595.
95. Ibid., 596.
96. Bernard Schwartz, *Administrative Law,* 4th ed. (Boston: Little, Brown, 1994) 831–834, 890–913.
97. Gifford, "Discretionary Decisionmaking in the Regulatory Agencies," 104.
98. Ibid., 104.
99. Ibid., 105–106. See Isaiah L. Sharfman, *The Interstate Commerce Commission* (New York: Commonwealth Pub., 1931–1937).
100. Gifford, "Discretionary Decisionmaking in the Regulatory Agencies," 105.
101. Ibid. 106.
102. Ibid., 103.
103. Ibid., 122.
104. Ibid., 135.
105. Bernard Schwartz, "Administrative Law Cases during 1979," *Administrative Law Review,* 32 (Summer 1980), 411.
106. Ibid.
107. Davis, *Administrative Law Treatise,* 2: 161.
108. Certiorari denied, 417 U.S. 921 (1974).
109. Schwartz, "Administrative Law Cases During 1979," 414.
110. Davis and Pierce, Jr., *Administrative Law Treatise,* 3rd ed.
111. Davis, *Administrative Law Treatise,* 2nd ed., 161. Ironically, in their 1994 *Administrative Law Treatise,* 2nd ed., 161, Davis and Pierce, Jr. reject Davis's earlier analysis, specifically stating that agencies must be allowed to make *ad hoc* adjustments through adjudications to legislative rules because no agency can ". . . identify and answer definitively in advance all of the questions that will arise in implementing a regulatory scheme . . . ." Common sense, they assert, dictates that Ruiz's restrictions on the application of legislative rules, severally limiting discretion," is not, and cannot, be the law" (at 274).
112. *Certiorari denied,* 105 S.Ct. 2151 (1985).
113. For criticism of *Vermont Yankee,* see sources noted by Allen F. Wichelman, "Case Notes: *Vermont Yankee* v. *NRDC,*" *Santa Clara Law Review,* 19 (1979), 801–803.

114. Ibid.

115. The "hard look" standard was developed in *Greater Boston Television Corp.* v. *FCC,* 444 F.2d 841, 851 (D.C. Cir., 1970), cert. denied, 403 U.S. 923 (1971). It requires reviewing courts to make sure that the decision maker took a "hard look" at the facts before reaching a decision.

116. Ibid., 803.

117. Michael J. Perry, "Substantive Due Process Revisited: Reflections on (and beyond) Recent Cases," *Northwestern Law Review,* 71 (September-October 1976), 417–469; and Wichelman, "Case Notes," 801–803.

118. Wichelman, "Case Notes," 803–804.

119. Ibid., 807.

120. Kenneth C. Davis, "Administrative Common Law and the *Vermont Yankee* Opinion," *Utah Law Review* (1980), 17.

121. Ibid., 7.

122. Ibid. 10.

123. Ibid.

124. Ibid.

125. Ibid., 11.

126. Ibid.

127. Cass, Diver, and Beermann, *Administrative Law,* 546–547.

128. Daniel D. Polsby, *"FCC* v. *National Citizen:* Judicious Uses of Administrative Discretion," Supreme Court Review (1978), 2–3.

129. Ibid., 2–3.

130. Ibid., 36.

131. See, for example, Kenneth C. Davis, *Administrative Law Treatise,* 2nd ed., vol. 5 (San Diego; K.C. Davis Publishing Co., 1984), 274–283.

132. Bernard Schwartz, "Administrative Law Cases During 1985," *Administrative Law Review,* 38 (Summer 1986), 310.

133. Ibid., 310–311. For a discussion of the *Wednesbury* principle, as set forth in *Associated Provincial Picture Houses Ltd.* v. *Wednesbury Corporation* (1948) 1 K.R. at 229, see M.A. Fazal, "Judicial Review of Administrative Discretion: Anglo-American Perspectives," *The Trent Law Journal,* 9 (1985), 29–32.

134. Frank Goodnow, *Comparative Administrative Law* (New York: G. P. Putnam's Sons, 1903), chaps. 1–3, 5, advanced the idea that it would be wise to develop an administrative court-like system.

135. Neil Sullivan, "Independent Adjudication and Occupational Safety and Health Policy: A Test for Administrative Court Theory," *Administrative Law Review,* 31 (Spring 1979), 179.

136. Ibid.

137. Ibid., 179–180.

138. Harold H. Bruff, "Specialized Courts in Administrative Law," *Administrative Law Review,* vol. 43 (Summer 1991), 331.

139. Sullivan, "Independent Adjudication and Occupational Safety and Health Policy, 177–178.

140. Bruff, "Specialized Courts in Administrative Law," 331.

141. Stephen Breyer, *Regulation and Its Reform* (Cambridge, Mass.: Harvard University Press, 1982), 361. In 1994 President Clinton appointed Stephen Breyer to the Supreme Court.

142. Lewis Mainzer, *Political Bureaucracy* (Glenview, Ill: Scott, Foresman, 1973), 54.

143. Bruff, "Specialized Courts in Administrative Law," 331.

144. Ibid., 331–332.

145. Kenneth J. Meier, *Politics and the Bureaucracy: Policymaking in the Fourth Branch of Government,* 3rd ed. (Pacific Grove, Calif.: Brooks/Cole Publishing Company, 1993), 186.

146. Davis, *Administrative Law Treatise,* vol. 2, 172–173.

147. Meier, *Politics and the Bureaucracy,* 187.

148. Hans A. Linde and George Bunn, *Legislative and Administrative Processes* (Mineola, N.Y.: Foundation Press, 1976), 608.

149. Ibid.

150. Interview with Walter Gellhorn, St. Louis University, March 5, 1980.

151. Ibid.

152. Ibid.

153. Ibid.

154. Ibid. However, Kenneth J. Meier, op. cit., argues that the problem with ombudsmen is that they focus on individual complaints and really do not try to resolve the broader, systemic problem in the administrative process.

155. Robert D. Miewald, *Public Administration: A Critical Perspective* (New York: McGraw-Hill, 1978), 249.

156. Ibid., 250.

157. Gerald W. Caiden, *Organizational Handbook of the Ombudsman* (Westport, Conn.: Greenwood Press, 1983).

158. Meier, *Politics and the Bureaucracy,* 3rd ed., 187.

159. Robert D. Miewald and John E. Comer, "Complaining as Participation: The Case of the Ombudsman," *Administration and Society,* vol. 17 (February 1986), 481–500.

160. Walter Gellhorn, *When Americans Complain: Governmental Grievance Procedures* (Cambridge, Mass.: Harvard University Press, 1966), 229.

161. Ibid.

162. Ibid., 229.

163. Ralph Nader, Peter J. Petkas, and Kate Blackwell, eds., *Whistle Blowing* (New York: Grossman Publishers, 1972), 9.

164. Ibid., 7.

165. John Dean, *Blind Ambition: The White House Years* (New York: Simon and Schuster, 1976), chaps. 9–10, provides a fascinating, though possibly somewhat biased, account of this event.

166. Nader et al., *Whistle Blowing,* chaps. 5–15.

167. Ibid.

168. Quoted in N. Joseph Cayer, *Public Personnel Administration in the United States,* 2nd ed. (New York: St. Martin's Press, 1986), 34–35.

169. Ibid., 31–32.

170. Robert G. Vaughn, "Consumer access to product safety information and the Future of the Freedom of Information Act," *The Administrative Law Journal,* vol. 5 (Fall 1991), 699–702.

CHAPTER EIGHT

JUDICIAL REVIEW OF AGENCY BEHAVIOR

JUDICIAL REVIEW: AN OVERVIEW

Over the decades the courts have expressed their clear intolerance for administrators who displayed a conspicuous disrespect for principles of procedural due process.[1] It appears that if constitutional democracy is to be preserved, agency administrators cannot be allowed to ignore laws designed to regulate their behavior or use their discretionary powers in a reckless or wanton manner. In our relatively open system of government, as has been acknowledged, there are many formal and informal vehicles which function to help keep the exercise of administrative power under reasonable control and within the realm of minimally acceptable democratic accountability standards. Yet there are those who argue that the judicial system probably provides the best authoritative vehicle for checking administrators who act afoul. The courts hear very few cases, take a relatively long time to act, are expensive, time-consuming, and inconvenient, and are quite particular and frequently unpredictable about the kinds of cases they regard as reviewable. Nevertheless, they do have the power to overrule agency actions and always represent a threat to any administrator who may contemplate acting contrary to the demands of fair and rightful procedure. Under special circumstances, the Congress has made some agency activities unreviewable; but most agency actions are ultimately subject to judicial review, especially since judges have the final say as to what the legislature intended to be reviewable or unreviewable. The courts can also declare unconstitutional various attempts by legislative assemblies to make certain administrative actions exempt from judicial review.[2]

The power of judicial review extends awesome authority to the courts because it allows them to declare legislative and administrative actions unconstitutional, thereby making those acts null and void. *Judicial review,* in the context of administrative law, can be defined accurately as the legitimate sphere of judicial scrutiny of agency actions and the methods which the courts employ to consider the propriety of agency behavior. The power to review the constitutional acceptability of legislative and executive actions makes the courts, in effect, the chief interpreters and defenders (or destroyers) of the Constitution, the basic blueprint which controls our government's way of doing things. In our political system, there exists no higher authority than the Supreme Court on the constitutionality of official behavior. The judicial review power enables nine justices to have the last word on what constitutional and statutory provisions really mean and to have the final say over whether governmental officials, at any level of government, are acting in a way which is consistent or inconsistent with constitutional or statutory requirements. Martin Shapiro stresses that judges exercise enormous judicial discretion which allows them to actually make law. He argues that "[A]lthough many judges and a few legal scholars persist in the view that judges only 'discover' or 'interpret' rather than 'make' law, the phenomenon of judicial law-making is widely recognized." Shapiro concludes that judges simply possess the discretion to choose "what law to make."[3]

However, despite the enormous potential power of the courts, most judges have historically been wise enough to exercise their power with caution. No doubt, judges have realized from the beginning, as President Andrew Jackson once reminded them, that the courts' greatest strength is in their power to strike down acts by governmental officials; but the courts' greatest weakness is that they are completely dependent upon the officials in the other governmental branches to enforce their decisions. Consequently, unreasonable and reckless court decisions would, according to virtually all American government scholars, quickly diminish the prestige and authoritative influence of the courts. Thus, in a very real sense, the judicial review power is very precariously held because, to retain their powers, judges must watch it or their decisions will not be respected or upheld by legislators, administrators, interest groups, or the American people in general.

From a systems perspective, the courts must respond to environmental pressures as much as all other political actors in the political system. Political actors retain their power only so long as they can allocate values to society authoritatively. Power does not rest on formal sanctioning alone but on perceived legitimacy and respect. This reality contributes significantly to our understanding of the way courts use their judicial review powers. Despite those who have argued that courts have on occasion played an activist role (have been forceful in pushing for policy changes), in fact, they have almost always made rather conservative decisions. That is, fearing intense reaction to radical court holdings, courts have mostly made conservative decisions which have either upheld the status quo or pushed forward only gradually. Judges walk the same streets and watch the same news programs we do. When making decisions, judges are quite aware of the sort of decisions on social policies governmental institutions and society will tolerate. This is one of the chief reasons social reforms proceed at such an incremental pace. The courts refuse to really push hard for needed changes in the areas of civil rights, housing, environmental policy, regulation of nuclear power, and so on. Although the courts' historical conservatism can be criticized since it allows only the most gradual social change, at the same time the courts' practice of judicial self-restraint can be applauded because it has contributed significantly to the stability of the American political system—a trait traditionally valued highly by political scientists.

However, any court decisions, conservative or liberal, because of their perceived impact on society, are unquestionably likely to disturb some group and prove disruptive. Although court decisions which deviate radically from current social practices would likely prove the most disruptive, court decisions which tend to support the status quo have historically pleased the haves and angered the have-nots. Social inequities can obviously obtain further sanctioning by court decisions which support the status quo.

Of course, the Supreme Court's ruling in *Dred Scott* v. *Sanford*, 19 Howard 393 (1857), possibly the worst decision ever handed down by the high Court, was a decision that supported the status quo but proved extremely disruptive to social order in America. In this case the Court held that blacks could not become United States citizens and that blacks should not be entitled to enjoy the benefits of citizenship. This was a blatantly racist decision, even for the 1850s; it served only to ignite the controversy surrounding the slavery issue and, consequently, played a key role in making the Civil War inevitable. In an unfortunate and costly way, the *Dred Scott* case serves to demonstrate the major role the judiciary, especially the Supreme Court, plays in influencing American social history.

It should be emphasized that it is exceedingly difficult to have a federal appellate court decision overridden because the Supreme Court simply lacks the time to review very many appellate court rulings. The Supreme Court may overrule a circuit court decision, and the circuit courts may set aside district court holdings; they often do. But it takes a constitutional amendment to overturn a Supreme Court decision on the Constitution. However, if the high Court overrules a congressional statute, Congress can void the Court's decision by simply passing another statute, as long as only statutory construction is in question, not constitutional issues. Of the tens of thousands of appellate and Supreme Court decisions involving constitutional questions which have been made over the years, virtually all have been allowed to stand by Congress. Congress has amended the Constitution to overrule Supreme Court decisions only five times. For example, the precedential clout of the *Dred Scott* decision was eradicated after the Civil War by the passage of the Fourteenth Amendment. Another possible reason the courts have been reluctant to flaunt their judicial review powers is that the Constitution did not specifically assign the judicial branch this power. This power was given to the judiciary by Chief Justice John Marshall in *Marbury* v. *Madison*, 1 Cranch 137 (1803). By arguing in this case that the courts should have a right to overrule acts of the other branches of government as unconstitutional, he established for the courts the power of judicial review. Marshall's basic contention was that this right was intended by the constitutional framers and was consistent with their perception of the separation-of-powers doctrine.

Although the authority of judicial review has been accepted as a legitimate judicial power by the vast majority of Americans, it should be pointed out that some still hold, as Judge Gibson did in *Eakin* v. *Raub,* 12 S.&R. 330 (1825), that the courts should not possess such power. This old Pennsylvania Supreme Court case has become famous for Judge Gibson's repudiation of Justice Marshall's logic in *Marbury.* It is considered to be probably the best argument against the judiciary's review power. Gibson argued, essentially, that the courts should not have the authority to declare congressional acts unconstitutional because, while the courts are not a very representative (democratic) body, legislative assemblies are much more so. Courts, he maintained, should not be allowed to declare null and void acts which are representative of the wishes of the American people. The judicial review principle, he held, is essentially antidemocratic. But this viewpoint fails to recognize that democratic governments also have the obligation to protect the interests of minorities. Without judicial review, minority rights would likely be subject to the tyranny of majority will. Gibson later reversed his position and supported the concept of judicial review.

THE CHANGING ROLE OF THE COURTS

Observers have pointed out that the role the courts play in American government has changed significantly since the early days of the Republic; but the most dramatic changes have occurred since the 1930s, especially during the decade of the 1970s. Basically, it is argued that the courts once played a relatively restricted role in the American political process because they practiced judicial self-restraint. But today the courts play a major role because they are now practicing judicial activism. However, since the early 1990s the quite conservative Supreme Court, unlike most lower federal courts and state courts, has taken fewer cases and has been less active than it has in several years. Generally, however, this transition from a rather passive judiciary to an activist one has had a profound impact upon the relationship between the courts and administrative agencies.

The Courts' Traditional Role

By and large, the development of the judicial system in the United States has followed an expected course. Its evolution has largely mirrored the transformation of American government from a small, simple, and limited governing structure to a giant, complex, and pervasive governmental leviathan.[4] However, it seems valid to maintain that the court system for most of its history followed the lead of the other two branches but did not play the role as leader itself. In recent decades the courts, although the pace has slowed, have been trying to follow the torrid developmental pace set by the administrative agencies. When the administrative branch's regulatory role began to expand swiftly during the 1930s and 1940s, the courts first took the position that they should, as much as possible, try to leave administrative matters in the hands of the administrative experts. Although this attitude is not so strong now, it is argued later in this chapter that despite contentions to the contrary, the supposedly activist courts today have been noticeably restrained by this still-operative hands-off attitude. This attitude became very evident during the last few years of the Burger Court, and so far it has dominated the thinking of the Rehnquist Court into the 1990s.

The purpose of judicial review under the traditional model was simple. Basically, the job of the courts was to settle specific legal disputes between particular litigants. Typically, the issues that the courts had to resolve were quite simple, narrow, and well defined, while the solutions appeared fairly obvious and the decisions had very limited social relevance. The legal disputes centered mostly on clear procedural questions. Did Smith receive proper notice? Did the agency deny Jones benefits entitled to him by statute? Few ever denied that it was unnecessary for the courts to protect the public by resolving such questions. For fundamental due process principles to be preserved, it appeared that the courts simply had to at least monitor the procedures that agencies employed while going about the business of implementing public policies.

Under the traditional judicial review perspective, the judiciary should stay as removed as possible from stepping on administrators' toes by hearing cases pertaining to substantive administrative policy questions. During the 1930s the courts, led by the Supreme Court, attempted to avoid ruling on disputes having to do with questions of fact (substantive issues), while concentrating on questions of law. Charles W. Stewart has written: "During the New Deal, the Supreme Court chose to eschew substantive review, permitting most administrative agencies to do business relatively free from concern with court interference."[5] To accomplish this end, judges relied on several legal doctrines to discourage requests for judicial review of substantive agency decisions (discussed later).

The Courts' Modern Role

Most scholars agree that the courts today play a dramatically different role in public administration than they did in the 1930s and 1940s. Most clearly, these changes can be seen in: (1) the increased number of administrative law cases handled by the courts; (2) the courts' willingness to step in and hear a much broader variety of administrative law disputes; and (3) the major impact the courts' decisions have upon the shaping of administrative processes and substantive policies, as well as upon American social life in general. Of course, the pervasive and powerful role that the courts now play in American government has caused them to be described in textbooks as activist courts, as contrasted to their once relatively passive and meek role. To some, this new activist judicial attitude is a blessing, while to others it has created some serious problems which might prove dangerously disruptive to administrative operations and thus be harmful to the public interest. In *Judicial Compulsions,* for example, Jeremy Rabkin argues vehemently that the courts' compulsion to intervene in agency business and to often substitute its public policy-making power for the agency's public policy authority has led to the making of poor and democratically unsanctioned public policies,[6] while George Will, a noted columnist, contends that "judicial policy-making" undermines representative government by imposing undemocratically approved social policies on the people.[7]

The Increasing Number of Cases Heard   The courts have been asked to settle a growing number of disputes in all areas of law. For various reasons, the American people have turned more and more to the courts to resolve their problems. Today, it seems that few accept "no" as an answer, whether it is an employee who has been denied a promotion or a company which refuses to comply with a governmental regulation. Americans, living in a society which has grown massive and very impersonal, have, more than ever, taken on an exaggerated "what's in it for me?" litigious attitude, resulting in the filing of numerous suits with the promise of winning absurdly favorable settlements. Courts are responding by resolving disputes which judges of yesteryear, practicing judicial restraint, never dreamed they could ever litigate.

The welfare state notion that government should protect its citizens from the cradle to the grave has had its impact on the courts. While once the courts normally heard cases involving major disputes, usually between two private parties, now courts hear cases which involve relatively trivial matters, often between a private party and a public agency. In a sense, the courts have been largely responsible for increasing their own expanding caseloads. Judges have opened the judicial doors to new kinds of cases by ruling that governmental benefits, in an increasing number of situations, should be regarded as *rights* (legal entitlements), not *privileges*. Regardless of the humanitarian merits of this argument, it has encouraged a plethora of new suits to be filed during the late 1960s and into the 1990s. Increasing educational levels, the affluence of Americans today (which allows so many to afford costly legal services), legal services organizations, the availability of free legal services to some, the growing involvement of administrative agencies in the private sector, the growth of citizen and consumer action groups, the courts' new relaxed attitude on standing, and the surplus of lawyers filing nonsense suits because they need the work have all served to encourage Americans to go to court.

Steven Vago emphasizes that more than ever the American people have come to rely upon the courts to resolve their problems. "Indeed," Vago asserts, "litigation is becoming a national pastime, and more and more people are telling their troubles to a judge."[8] The number of civil cases filed in the district courts, where the vast majority of administrative law cases are heard, went from 59,284 in 1960 to 168,789 in 1980 to 228,600 in 1993, or up 286 percent from 1960.[9] The number of federal judges has also increased dramatically in response to the increasing number of cases filed in federal court. In 1900 there were only 110 federal judges (9 Supreme Court justices, 156 circuit judges, and 77 district judges), while as of June 1, 1995, there were 820 federal judges (9 Supreme Court justices, 179 circuit judges, and 632 district judges), constituting a significant increase of 533 percent, yet one that is dismally failing to keep pace with the much sharper increase in caseloads.[10] To compound this problem, this dramatic increase in civil cases has come during a period when the courts have already been overburdened by criminal law cases. Analysts contend that this caseload problem is acute and must be somehow be brought under control.[11]

The Courts' New Eagerness to Hear a Broader Range of Cases   At one time, the courts were quite selective as to the types of cases they were willing to hear. Courts generally refused to decide cases which they believed were best left to agency discretion. Under the traditional model, the courts refrained from overruling agency actions unless administrators clearly abused their discretionary authority by violating the clear constitutional and statutory procedural due process rights of citizens or reached decisions which were completely unsupported by substantive evidence. However, according to Donald L. Horowitz, this has all changed. The courts "have moved beyond protection of the rights of parties aggrieved by administrative action to participation in problem solving and protection of more general public interests against agencies accused of indifference to the public interest. Judicial review has passed from matters of procedure to matters of both procedure and substance."[12]

Today our judges have become society's handymen, available to listen and provide solutions to whatever seems to be bothering us. Consequently, the scope of the judicial review today seems to have virtually no limits. Observers contend that the courts' basic approach to public litigation has changed dramatically. They claim that the typical federal administrative law case today involves many parties seeking solutions to incredibly complex and multifaceted legal disputes which have meaningful social significance. A new twist in the cases commonly heard today is that the judges, unlike those in the past, must concentrate on the likely impact their decisions will have on future public policy directions. Judges have become deeply involved in policy planning, a task performed in the past almost exclusively by legislators and executives. Judges today get significantly involved in the making of public policy by ordering administrators, for example, to bus students to certain neighborhood schools, to perform or stop performing abortions, to leave on or turn off life support systems, and the like.

The Activist Courts' Impact on Administrators   In Horowitz's view, for the first fifteen to twenty years after the APA was passed, the courts interpreted APA provisions to avoid getting involved with the work of the federal bureaucracy, but recently the APA has been used by activist courts to enable them to play an active role in the business of administrative agencies. Although not all courts have jumped into the administrative thicket to the same extent, Horowitz holds that the tendency has been for judges to perform job tasks related to public policy which were once handled exclusively by agency administrators. He contends that many judges simply want to play, in effect, the role of chief administrator with the final say: "Increasingly, the courts insist on having the last word on the merits of public importance."[13]

Horowitz maintains that what is taking place is essentially the judicialization of the administrative process. In so many ways, he notes, administrative agencies have started to function like "second-class courts," in that the courts have insisted more and more that various agency decision-making processes should become more trial-like, reflecting more closely the procedures used by courts.[14] But this attempt to make administrative agencies function more like courts has been met with stiff opposition from those who believe that more legal formalism serves mostly to make it virtually impossible for administrators to act in a swift, efficient, effective, and fair manner. Horowitz feels the change in name from "hearing examiners" to "administrative law judges" symbolizes the extent to which agency hearings have become more trial-like.[15] To some, administrative agencies are beginning to function more like courts of original jurisdiction than administrative agencies, thus blurring the distinction between the administrative and judicial roles in our governmental system. In a sense, judicial review activities are commencing in agency hearings and continuing on appeal to the appellate courts and possibly even up to the Supreme Court. Acknowledging this basic development, Horowitz asserts: "Judicial review of substantive issues is therefore the aftershock of the judicialization of agency proceedings. Why accept the counterfeit administrative version of a just decision when one can have the real currency, robes and all? The more similar the administrative and judicial processes become, the more the same functions will be performed interchangeably."[16]

In short, courts today are more judicially active in the administrative process than they were a few decades ago. Judicial activism can probably be seen the best in the courts' growing reluctance to avoid ruling on substantive social policy questions (for example, the feasibility of using busing to achieve racial integration in our public schools) being considered by our public administrators. In numerous opinions, judges of yesteryear presented arguments as to why the courts should not unnecessarily meddle in administrative affairs. However, in the past few decades this passive attitude has been giving way gradually to a new judicial attitude which is supportive of active monitoring of virtually all administrative activities. The reasons most often cited to justify this new activist judicial role seem to be conveyed best by the new action-oriented judges themselves. In *Environmental Defense Fund, Inc.* v. *Ruckelshaus,* 439 F.2d 584, 598 (D.C.Cir., 1971), the court contended that administrative actions which have impact on such basic personal interests as "life, health, and liberty" must be closely scrutinized by the courts, while in *Calvert Cliffs* v. *AEC,* 449 F.2d 1109, 1111 (D.C.Cir., 1971), Judge J. Skelly Wright concluded: "Our duty, in short, is to see that important legislative purposes, heralded in the halls of Congress, are not lost or misdirected in the vast hallways of the federal bureaucracy." In these statements an unmistakable distrust for administrative experts appears to ring loud and clear. However, the famous 1984 *Chevron* case, op. cit., supposedly set strong precedent by establishing the principle that courts should allow agency administrators to interpret statute and defer to agency expertise/discretion unless the administrative action or inaction is clearly prohibited by statute. Despite the many court decisions which seem to follow the *Chevron* doctrine, which calls for judicial self-restraint, in 1992 Thomas W. Merrill concluded, after extensive research into the application of *Chevron,* that about half the courts fail to apply the *Chevron* doctrine to resolve deference questions. In fact, his research reveals that ". . . in recent Terms the application of *Chevron* has resulted in less deference to executive interpretations than was the case in the pre-*Chevron* era."[17]

THE AVAILABILITY OF JUDICIAL REVIEW OF ADMINISTRATIVE ACTIONS

Judicial review is commonly perceived as the most basic remedy available to those who seek relief because they feel that they have been or will be harmed by *illegal* administrative actions. However, seeking relief through the courts appears much easier than it really is. If courts refuse to review a person's plea for review, as they fre-

'Another Deft Swerve To The Right, Sandra'

Source: Reprinted with permission of Tom Engelhardt and the *St. Louis Post-Dispatch,* June 23, 1991.

quently do, the aggrieved person will simply have to learn to live with the agency decision which motivated the appeal. There are many reasons that a court will not grant review of agency actions, the principle one being that judges usually like to defer to agency authority and expertise. However, a great deal of administrative law deals with the more specific and technical justifications cited by the courts for granting or denying petitions for review of administrative decisions. In the next few sections focus is on the issues, questions, and factors which tend to determine not only what administrative actions are reviewable (*reviewability*), but also to what depths these reviewable activities should be reviewed (*scope of review*).

What Is Reviewable?

It is very difficult to answer the question: What is reviewable administrative action? Judges and administrative law scholars have always argued over what should or should not be appropriately considered judicially reviewable agency behavior. Although various legislative and judicial attempts have been made to zero in on what should or should not be subject to review, the painful truth is that the reviewability question has been uncomfortably left unsettled. It would be convenient if we could easily place some agency actions in the reviewable category and others in the unreviewable category, but this simply cannot be done, because it is too unclear as to which actions are legitimately reviewable and unreviewable as circumstances change from case to case. The complex and confusing nature of the reviewability question is possibly epitomized best in the intentionally contradictory title of Kim Morris's article, "Judicial Review of Non-reviewable Administrative Action."[18]

It has been my experience that much of the confusion over the reviewability question exists because the distinction between reviewability and scope of review questions is often not made clear. However, it is important to understand that the two concepts pose related, but nevertheless distinct, legal questions. Reviewability is identified with the basic question: Is the matter within the court's jurisdiction for review, thus, according to administrative law rhetoric, making the dispute available for judicial review? While a reviewable issue is within the legitimate jurisdiction of the courts (for example, because a statute specifically provides for review of certain agency decisions), an unreviewable issue is outside the legitimate jurisdiction of the courts (for example, because a statute specifically excludes some action from review, thereby essentially making the decision of agency officials in these unreviewable areas final).

Once a court has answered the necessary questions pertaining to whether or not the case qualifies or is available for review, the court can determine how far its legitimate scope in reviewing a reviewable case should extend. For instance once the court decides that a case pertaining to the use of discretion is within the court's proper jurisdiction for review, the court can ask: To what depth should our inquiry extend into an agency's use of discretion? Obviously, as has been stressed in earlier sections, courts respond to this question quite differently. While passive courts are reluctant to review most discretionary agency decisions, active courts like to probe deep into an agency's use of discretion.

What determines whether judicial review should be made available to petitioners in administrative law disputes? First, the court must answer *no* to the following basic question: Have applicable statutes prohibited judicial review of the specific administrative action under question? But to the following questions, the court must answer *yes:* Have the relevant statutes explicitly, or at least implicitly, permitted review? Has an eligible party petitioned for review (should the petitioner be given standing to sue)? Has a proper defendant been named in the suit? Is the case ready for review in terms of its timeliness? This question implies three important subsidiary questions. Acknowledging that administrative agencies normally have primary jurisdiction, the court must decide whether it should now intervene (assert its jurisdiction) in the dispute. In seeking relief, has the petitioner exhausted all administrative remedies made available by the agency? Is the case ripe for review (ready for review in the sense that the legal issues are definitive enough, have evolved enough, and have been presented vividly enough to allow the ruling court to reach a clear decision)? And finally, have proper forms of action (specific and technical legal methods for remedial relief, such as request for an injunction) been followed in filing for review? We will return to these questions throughout the remainder of this chapter, especially in the section entitled, "Court Reluctance to Review Agency Actions: Obstacles to Obtaining Review."

The APA and Reviewability   By 1946 when the Administrative Procedure Act was passed the presumption of reviewability was well-established administrative law. The *Stark* decision clearly had a profound impact on the drafting of the APA because the act generally endorses the *Stark* maxim of broad reviewability. Bernard Schwartz once even exclaimed that "the APA codifies the *Stark* v. *Wickard* principle."[19]

Sections 702 and 704 of the APA uphold the spirit of *Stark*. Section 702 reads: "A person suffering legal wrong because of agency action within the meaning of a relevant statute, is entitled to judicial review thereof"; Section 704 states: "Agency action made reviewable by statute and final agency action for which there is no other adequate remedy in a court are subject to judicial review." If it were not for the two exceptions to review set forth in Section 701, all federal administrative actions would be subject to review. However, Section 701 states that "Chapter 7—Judicial Review" applies "except to the extent that: (1) statutes preclude judicial review; or (2) agency action is committed to agency discretion by law." But clearly, Congress, in enacting the legislation, intended for the courts to be able to review those agency actions not specifically excluded from review by statutes. Therefore, the APA does establish a presumption of reviewability. Actually, legislative intent is very clear in regard to the presumption of reviewability when statutes are silent on the availability of review. A House committee stated that "the mere failure to provide specially by statute for judicial review is certainly no evidence of intent to withhold review."[20]

The cases which uphold the presumption to reviewability under the APA are numerous, but in no decision is the APA's presumption of reviewability better espoused than in *Abbott Laboratories* v. *Gardner,* 387 U.S. 136 (1967). Justice Harlan, writing for the majority, upheld the contention asserted in *Rusk* v. *Cort,* 369 U.S. 367, 379–380 (1962), "that only upon a showing of 'clear and convincing evidence' of a contrary legislative intent should the courts restrict access to judicial review" (at 141). Justice Harlan also maintained, citing *Shaughnessy* v. *Pedreiro,* 349 U.S. 48, 51 (1954), that the legislative record on the drafting of the APA "manifests a congressional intention that it cover a broad spectrum of administrative actions, and this Court has echoed that theme by noting that the Administrative Procedure Act's 'generous review provision' must be given a 'hospitable' interpretation" (at 140–41).[21] The general presumption of reviewability as established in *Stark* and *Abbott Laboratories* was emphatically reasserted in *Reno* v. *Catholic Social Services,* 113 S.Ct. 2485 (1993), and *Thunder Basin Coal Co.* in 1994.

The Reviewability of "Unreviewable" Administrative Actions   Under Section 701(a)(1)(2) of the APA, agency actions are unreviewable if "statutes preclude judicial review" or "agency action is committed to agency discretion by law." But what do these exclusions mean in practice? Does the first exclusion mean that no matter how absurd administrative action may be, as long as it is protected by statute, it cannot be reviewed? Does it mean that administrators can violate statutory dictates yet remain free from having their actions reviewed? Does the second exclusion mean that administrators can flagrantly abuse their discretionary powers at the expense of claimants yet feel content that their abusive use of discretion can never be reviewed? Unfortunately, the tendency of the courts has been to answer "yes" to these questions because the courts have been generally reluctant to apply the presumption of reviewability to Section 701 exclusions.

However, the illogic of absolutely precluding judicial review of agency actions under Section 701(a)(1)(2) attracted heated criticisms from the very beginning. Judges and legal scholars have argued that at times circumstances justify judicial review of these supposedly unreviewable agency decision-making areas. In 1951 Justice William O. Douglas voiced his opposition to the majority opinion in *United States* v. *Wunderlich,* 342 U.S. 98, where the Court argued that judicial review of agency action cannot take place even though an administrative determination is shown to be obviously false, as well as reached in an arbitrary and capricious manner, if statutory provisions preclude review. In his dissent, Justice Douglas severely criticized the wisdom of any "finality provisions" in statutes which preclude judicial review entirely, regardless of the circumstances. In response to a specific "finality provision" excluding review of decisions made by contracting officers, Douglas remarked that the majority opinion upholding the validity of the finality provision would have a "devastating effect" and it would tend to make "a tyrant out of every contracting officer" (at 101).

Douglas's dissenting attitude in *Wunderlich* is slowly winning acceptance, but there remains steady judicial resistance. In *Shaughnessy* v. *Pedreiro,* 349 U.S. 48 (1956), the Court held that statutory provisions barring review of administrative action should not be interpreted so strictly as to absolutely preclude review. In keeping with the *Shaughnessy* holding, the court held in *Welch* v. *United States,* 446 F.Supp. 75 (D.Comm, 1978), that a statutory provision, which made all military death benefits claims "final and conclusive" (unreviewable), could be reviewed in matters pertaining to questions of law. In *Owens* v. *Hills,* 450 F.Supp. 218 (N.D., Ill., 1978), the court ruled that a statutory provision, which made decisions by HUD's secretary "final and conclusive" and "not to be subject to review," should not be applied to totally prohibit judicial review; and in *Ralpho* v. *Bell,* 569 F.2d 607 (1977), the D.C. Circuit Court argued that despite the strong rhetoric precluding judicial review of agency decisions under the Micronesian Claims Act, the "no-review" clause does not preclude judicial intervention to review complaints that the agency has violated either statutory or constitutional mandates. In the district court's view, to absolutely preclude a person's right to seek judicial remedy to correct an agency wrongdoing which has caused the individual harm would cast in doubt how seriously our nation is committed to the promotion of human rights and basic liberties (at 626).

Although clear law has not been established because various courts have not applied Section 701(a)(1)(2) of the APA consistently, it does appear that a strong consensus of judges nonetheless feel that, despite any "absolute" preclusions of judicial review, ultimately these preclusions themselves are scrutinized by the courts and agency actions are really not final until the courts say they are. As Bernard Schwartz recently concluded, despite judicial decisions that uphold preclusions to review, there still exists ". . . the strong presumption in our law in favor of judicial review. That presumption normally prevails even in the face of statutory provisions that appear to preclude review."[22]

Several recent cases have upheld the basic presumption of reviewability even in the face of provisions precluding review, although the courts may have upheld the particular preclusion in dispute [*Franklin* v. *Massachusetts,* 112 S.Ct. 2767 (1993); *Reno* v. *Catholic Social Services,* 113 S.Ct. 2485 (1993); and *Kisser* v. *Cisneros,* 14 F.2d 615 (1994)]. However, probably no court summarizes the situation on the "unreviewability" of agency decisions better than a New York court in *New York City Dep't of Envt'l Protection* v. *New York Civil Serv' Comm'n,* 579 N.E. 2d 1385 (N.Y. 1993). In this case a New York statute made the state's Civil Service Commission's decisions "final and conclusive" and "unreviewable." The court noted that the state legislature has the right to preclude review of agency actions and it has clearly done so by statute. But citing a prior case, the court responded: "'Even where judicial review is proscribed by statute, the courts have the power and the duty to make certain that the administrative official has not acted in excess of the grant of authority given . . . by the statute or in disregard of the standard prescribed by the legislature'" (at 1387). The court held that despite the statutory preclusion of review, the courts still must look to see whether agency actions were "purely arbitrary." The court stressed that despite the explicit preclusion of judicial review of agency actions by statute, ". . . judicial review cannot be completely precluded." Courts have the responsibility of checking to see whether ". . . the agency has acted illegally, unconstitutionally, or in excess of its jurisdiction" (at 1387). Or, in the succinct words of the D.C. Circuit Court, in our administrative system agency administrators cannot ". . . expect to escape judicial review by hiding behind a finality clause" [*Dart* v. *United States,* 848 F.2d 217, 224 (D.C. Cir. 1988)].

Court Reluctance to Review Agency Actions: Obstacles to Obtaining Review

As we have seen, in recent times judges, whether liberal or conservative, have been finding it easier and easier to justify judicial intervention in the administrative process. Nevertheless, this trend should not be exaggerated because, by and large, the courts for two basic reasons still try to avoid involving themselves in the administrative thicket unless they believe that conditions "compel" judicial review of agency actions. These basic reasons should be evident by now, but their importance to the smooth operations of our governmental system justifies their reiteration. One, judges feel they simply lack the technical knowledge and sufficient time to decide technical questions of fact which they believe could be handled much more competently by agency experts specifically trained to deal with such matters. This suggests a second related reason: The courts are not interested in interfering with or disrupting normal administrative operations in any way, because undue intervention has the potential to undermine and discredit the administrative process.

Several legal doctrines have evolved over the years which have been employed to protect administrative functions from hasty, unnecessary, and disruptive judicial excursions in the administrative process. Those seeking judicial review of agency actions feel these doctrines have often proved to be tough obstacles to overcome in obtaining court review.

Standing to Sue   We have considered many complex administrative law subjects; yet possibly the easiest legal principle to comprehend is the basic law of *standing*. In the context of administrative law, fundamental standing law holds that those who are harmed by administrative action should have the opportunity to challenge the legality of the action in court, as long as the action is legitimately reviewable agency action on other grounds. The standing issue essentially asks that the court answer the vital question: Should the petitioner have the right to "stand" before the court and argue his case?

Although the basic standing issue is a very simple one, the importance of the question of standing should not be underestimated. The doctrine of standing poses a prerequisite question. That is, will the court let a person have standing so that the person can have the opportunity to argue the case on the basis of its merits? Standing must be obtained before the petitioner's dispute will be allowed to continue. Many times, especially in administrative law cases, petitioners fail to pass the entryway standing test and are thereby prevented from presenting a possibly solid case before the court on the basis of the merits. Actually, it has been argued that the courts sometimes unreasonably deny standing to petitioners so that they can avoid having to reach an unwanted decision based upon solid evidence and sound legal arguments.[23]

Since the late 1960s, the courts have become in general more lenient in granting standing. While at one time the courts interpreted injury in very narrow terms, thus precluding the possibility that many would obtain standing before the court, broad judicial interpretations of what constitutes a litigious injury have recently eroded many of the traditional barriers preventing parties from obtaining standing to sue. The relaxation of standing requirements in the past two decades has been largely responsible for a new flood of cases in such citizen-consumer areas as consumer, environmental, and housing law. This development is one of the chief reasons that administrative law has become so important to the study of public administration and public policy in recent years.

What tests must a petitioner pass in order to receive standing? The most basic standing requirement that must be satisfied is a constitutional one. That is, in Article 3, Section 2, the Constitution requires that our federal courts can decide only cases of controversy between parties. This means that a genuine dispute must exist, with the court being placed in a position to provide a judicial remedy (relief) to a legally injured party (one who has suffered an "injury of fact") (*Lujan* v. *Defenders of Wildlife*, 112 S.Ct. 2130, 1992). This constitutional requirement is designed to prevent abstract nonsense suits or to guard against what Justice Oliver Wendell Holmes referred to, in *Giles* v. *Harris*, 189 U.S. 475, 486 (1903), as "in the air" controversies.

But what constitutes a cognizable (judicially r all cases until the late 1960s, the courts would percei in which one party suffers a direct monetary loss as Thus, parties went to court to sue for financial settlem mitted against them. For example, a private company, inj ernmental agency, could sue for financial compensation under this narrow interpretation of standing law, petitione ob- tain standing because they could not demonstrate to a court ncial loss is or would be different from what others in a group would suf n *Perkins* v. *Lukens Steel Co.,* 310 U.S. 113 (1940), the Supreme Court held: "Respondents, to have standing in court, must show an injury or threat to a particular right of their own, as distinguished from the public's interest in the administration of law" (at 125). In an earlier suit by a taxpayer challenging the right of the government to spend his tax dollars on a federal program he opposed, the Court ruled that he was not entitled to standing because he could only show that he is suffering in an indefinite way in common with other taxpayers (*Frothingham* v. *Mellon,* 262 U.S. 477; 1923). Because of the consequences of ruling otherwise, standing principle as it applies to taxpayers in *Frothingham* has never been reversed. In 1984 the Supreme Court, for example, in *Valley Forge ETC* v. *American United, ETC.,* 102 S.Ct. 752, upheld the *Frothingham* rule by refusing to grant standing to the respondents, Americans United For Separation of Church and State et al., who tried to prevent the Secretary of Health, Education, and Welfare from giving surplus government property to a religious organization. The Court argued that the respondents lacked standing as taxpayers because they could not show that they had suffered or would suffer any personal injury any different from any other taxpayer. Quoting from *Frothingham,* the Court said: "The party who invokes the power [of judicial review] must be able to show not only that the statute is invalid but that he has sustained or is immediately in danger of sustaining some direct injury as the result of its enforcement, and not merely that he suffers in some indefinite way in common with people generally" (at 761).[25]

Pressures placed on the courts in the past twenty years or so by citizen, consumer, and legal action groups have been quite successful in softening standing requirements. The liberalization of standing law is probably best conveyed in a series of public housing opportunity cases during the 1970s, although this liberalization trend can be seen in a host of cases in other public policy areas. In *Warth* v. *Seldin,* 422 U.S. 490 (1975), the Supreme Court, in a 5–4 decision, denied standing to petitioners challenging a zoning ordinance which they believed discriminated against low- and moderate-income persons, thus depriving them of affordable housing opportunities in Penfield, a relatively affluent white suburban community near Rochester, New York. Although the Court's majority denied standing to the petitioners on the technical grounds that they were third parties (not the low- and moderate-income persons themselves) and, therefore, could not establish a direct, particularized, and "cognizable interest" in the zoned property in question, the majority did imply that parties with a direct stake in the zoning ordinance who could show that they have a "substantial probability" of being harmed by the ordinance's enforcement could obtain

he *Warth* decision, although generally perceived as a somewhat conserv-
cision on standing, nevertheless remains a relatively modern standing case
cause the Court did at least recognize that standing could be granted to a petitioner
on the basis of: (1) a claimed noneconomic injury; (2) a substantial probability that
the party will be injured by a governmental action; and (3) a denied statutory entitlement.

In *Resident Advisory Bd.* v. *Rizzo,* 425 F.Supp. 987 (E.D., Pa., 1976), Judge
Broderick, building on *Warth,* ruled that those being denied housing opportunities
were entitled to standing because they could both demonstrate an actual injury and
show how the Court could provide remedial measures. Regarding the Resident Advisory Board, which claimed to be composed of and representing lower-income residents eligible to live in the proposed Whitman public housing project, the court held:
"RAB is a proper plaintiff with standing to represent its members. Although there is
no allegation that RAB was injured as an organization by the termination of the Whitman project, it is clear that RAB has established actual injury to its members. . . .
Clearly, if RAB's claims are legally cognizable, its members have been injured by the
failure to build the Whitman project. Those RAB members who live in racially impacted areas of the City of Philadelphia are obviously harmed by the failure to build
a scheduled housing project in a non-racially impacted area. Those on the waiting
list, which is predominantly Black, have lost the opportunity to live in public housing in a Whitman area" (at 1012).

In *Village of Arlington Heights* v. *Metropolitan Housing Corp.,* 429 U.S. 252
(1977), the Supreme Court itself cast doubt on the conservative interpretation of *Warth*
by ruling that the Metropolitan Housing Development Corporation, a nonprofit organization wishing to build a housing project for lower-income persons, should be given
standing on both economic and noneconomic grounds. The Court also emphasized that
the MHDC should be given standing because it would likely benefit from a favorable
court ruling. In addition, the Court stressed that "it has long been clear that economic
injury is not the only kind of injury that can support a plaintiff's standing" (at 262).

In *Duke Power Co.* v. *Carolina Environmental Study Group,* 438 U.S. 59, a
nonhousing case in 1978, the Supreme Court took a bold step toward eliminating
several confusing standing requirements. In reviewing previous standing cases, it
concluded: "We . . . cannot accept the contention that, outside the context of taxpayers' suits, a litigant must demonstrate anything more than injury in fact and a substantial likelihood that the judicial relief requested will prevent or redress the claimed
injury to satisfy the 'use and controversy' requirement of Act III." In many respects,
the liberalization of standing law since the late 1960s threw standing law into terrible
confusion. Some standing tests were kept, others tossed aside, while still new ones
were invented. The confusion over what standing tests should apply under particular
circumstances caused many to call for the virtual abandonment of standing requirements.[26] In the future we can expect, as they already do in the states, that courts will
grant standing almost routinely, as long as the plaintiffs can pass the simplest standing test of showing only a fairly reasonable causal connection between an injury or
likely future injury and the defendant's action. In fact, in *Clarke* v. *Securities Indus-*

try Ass'n., 107 S.Ct. 750 (1987), the Supreme Court applied a simple "zone of interest" test to determine whether standing should be granted. The Court explained that "the zone of interest test is a guide for deciding whether, in view of Congress' evident intent to make agency action presumptively reviewable, a particular plaintiff should be heard to complain of a particular agency decision. In cases where the plaintiff is not itself the subject of the contested regulatory action, the test denies a right of review if the plaintiff's interests are so marginally related to or inconsistent with the purposes implicit in the statute that it cannot reasonably be assumed that Congress intended to permit the suit. The test is not meant to be especially demanding" (at 757).

Unquestionably, it is fairly easy today for parties to obtain standing, yet recent decisions demonstrate that courts are still quick to deny standing if basic standing prerequisites are not satisfied. For example, in *Branton* v. *FCC*, 993 F.2d 906 (D.C. Cir. 1993), the court denied standing to a listener of a radio broadcast on which variations of the "f" word were aired ten times. After the Federal Communications Commission failed to act upon the listener's complaint, he filed suit in federal court. However, the court held that he lacked standing because no request for damages or other relief for the "marginal" harm was sought, but instead he wanted sanctions imposed against the radio station ". . . in the hope of influencing another's future behavior" (at 909). In *Renne* v. *Geary,* 111 S.Ct. 2331 (1991), the Supreme Court, although it based its decision on ripeness grounds, argued that it is very questionable whether standing can be given to individual members of a committee because their third-party status does not allow them to sue on behalf of the whole committee. While in another case, *INS* v. *Legalization Assistance Project,* 114 S.Ct. 422 (1993), the high Court failed to give standing to Legalization Assistance Project, a legal help organization which had challenged an INS regulation which placed a limited amnesty on immigrants who had entered the United States illegally. The Court argued that Congress intended standing to be given to parties actually suffering from the illegal wrongs committed by the administrative agency or are "within the 'zone of interests' protected by statute," not by third parties "outside the 'zone of interests'" (at 423–424).

In sum, despite some grey areas in standing law, Justice Scalia a few years ago in *Defenders of Wildlife* did an admirable job of summarizing the basic elements of standing. He wrote: "Over the years, our cases have established that the irreducible constitutional minimum of standing contains three elements: First, the plaintiff must have suffered an 'injury in fact'—an invasion of a legally-protected interest which is (a) concrete and particularized . . . ; and (b) 'actual or imminent', not 'conjectural' or 'hypothetical'. Second, there must be a causal connection between the injury and the conduct complained of—the injury has to be 'fairly . . . trace(able) to the challenged action of the defendant, and not . . . the result (of) the independent action of some third party not before the court'. . . . Third, it must be 'likely,' as opposed to merely 'speculative,' that the injury will be 'redressed by a favorable decision.'" By *particularized,* Scalia said ". . . we mean that the injury must affect the plaintiff in a personal and individual way" (at 2136).

Primary Jurisdiction   A rather simple way for courts to avoid reviewing an administrative controversy is to invoke the doctrine of primary jurisdiction. Recently, Bernard Schwartz pronounced this doctrine ". . . one of the foundations of modern administrative law."[27] The *primary jurisdiction doctrine* serves to allow administrative agencies primary or initial jurisdiction without court intrusion in resolving disputes involving administrative agencies. When Congress has failed to define jurisdiction for a particular matter, the court is confronted with the problem of deciding whether it has primary or initial jurisdiction in the particular question brought to its attention. The court is brought into the controversy initially when an aggrieved party tries to bring legal action against another party in court. In giving consideration to the suit, the court may elect to apply the doctrine of primary jurisdiction; it usually does this, thus dismissing the case. The court will inform the interested parties that a particular administrative agency should have primary or initial jurisdiction in the case. That is, the administrative agency should have first crack at resolving the dispute before the court voices its opinion on the matter. However, a court will occasionally inform the parties that the decision reached by the agency should be considered final, thereby giving the agency both *primary* and *exclusive* jurisdiction. The primary jurisdiction doctrine acknowledges that public agencies should normally be permitted to settle disputes affecting their agencies first unless: (1) the agency has ruled previously on a similar question; (2) the regulation or issue in the dispute is patently unreasonable; or (3) the issue poses a question which is clearly within the jurisdiction and competence of the judiciary.

A few cases serve to illustrate how the courts have applied the doctrine in practice. In *Texas and Pacific R.R. Co.* v. *Abilene Cotton Oil Co.*, 204 U.S. 426 (1907), the Abilene Cotton Oil Company sued the Texas and Pacific Railroad Company because of a perceived rate overcharge. The Supreme Court ruled in essence that the ICC should be given primary jurisdiction in the overcharge dispute. In effect, the Court said that shippers with complaints about rate charges should first take their cases to the ICC and then, if necessary, file suit in the district court.

What specific reasons have the courts given for using the primary jurisdiction doctrine? In *Far East Conference* v. *United States*, 342 U.S. 570, 674–675 (1952), the Court asserted that administrative matters are best handled by administrators, not judges. This is the intent of Congress when it creates agencies. The courts should not ignore this reality. Agencies are best equipped to promote unified regulatory policies through informed opinion and flexible procedures. In *Burlington Northern, Inc.* v. *United States*, 103 S.Ct. 514 (1982), the Supreme Court ruled that the Interstate Commerce Commission has primary jurisdiction in determining the rates railroads charge shippers. In reversing the D.C. Circuit Court of Appeals, the high Court scolded the lower court for interfering with the rate-setting authority of the ICC by vacating an ICC rate order. Speaking for the Court, Chief Justice Burger noted that "the more appropriate course would have been to remand to the Commission for explanation rather than to undertake itself to construe the order, and in so doing to interfere with the Commission's primary jurisdiction contrary to important congressional policies" (at 522).

But courts do not always find it appropriate to employ the primary jurisdiction doctrine to dismiss cases involving agencies. In *Nader* v. *Allegheny Airlines,* 426 U.S. 290 (1976), Ralph Nader sued Allegheny Airlines in federal district court for compensatory and punitive damages after he was bumped from an Allegheny flight for which he had confirmed reservations. Nader specifically charged that Allegheny Airlines' secret overbooking practices were deceptive, thus inconveniencing travelers who believed they in fact had confirmed reservations. Therefore, his suit claimed that Allegheny Airlines was guilty of fraudulent misrepresentation. Should CAB be given primary jurisdiction to settle the claim? While the lower courts said yes and employed the primary jurisdiction doctrine, the Supreme Court said no. It argued: "Referral of the misrepresentation issue to the Board cannot be justified by the interest in informing the court's ultimate decision with 'the expert and specialized knowledge' . . . of the Board. The action brought by petitioner does not turn on a determination of the reasonableness of a challenged practice—a determination that could be facilitated by an informed evaluation of the economics or technology of the regulated industry. The standards to be applied in action for fraudulent misrepresentation are within the conventional competence of the courts, and the judgment of a technically expert body is not likely to be helpful in the application of these standards to the facts of this case" (at 305).

In *Farmers Ins. Exchange* v. *Superior Court,* 826 P.2d 730 (Cal. 1992), the California Supreme Court agreed with the U.S. Supreme Court's decision in *Nader,* contending that the primary jurisdiction doctrine applies when practical concerns compel courts to allow administrative agencies the initial opportunity to resolve technical regulatory questions, but not when nonregulatory issues arise such as fraudulent misrepresentation that cannot be resolved appropriately by agency experts (at 737–738). This court stressed that primary jurisdiction is a mutually beneficial and practical doctrine, concluding that it ". . . evolved for the benefit of courts and administrative agencies, and unless precluded by the Legislature, it may be invoked whenever a court concludes there is a 'paramount need for specialized agency fact-finding expertise'" (at 746).

Exhaustion of Available Administrative Remedies

Closely associated with the primary jurisdiction doctrine is the sister doctrine of *exhaustion of available administrative remedies.* The Tenth Circuit Court made this simple distinction between the two doctrines: "The exhaustion doctrine applies where the agency *alone* has exclusive jurisdiction over the case (generally premised on the agency's expertise), whereas primary jurisdiction applies where *both* a court and an agency have the legal capacity to deal with the issue" (*Mountain State Gas Co.* v. *Petroleum Corp.,* 693 F.2d 1015, 1019–19:82). The exhaustion doctrine calls for the courts to stay clear of disputes within the public agencies until the petitioner has completed (totally exhausted) all channels of appeal within and provided by the agency. According to the Supreme Court in *McKart* v. *United States,* 395 U.S. 185,193 (1969), the exhaustion doctrine "provides 'that no one is entitled to judicial relief for a supposed or threatened injury until the prescribed administrative remedy has been exhausted.'" Thus, if grievant X tries to pull rank on an agency by taking the grievance to court because he or she believes that he or she is getting nowhere with the agency's grievance procedures, the court can use exhaustion to refer the matter back to the agency unless X has exhausted all redress procedures made available to him or her by the agency. The simple exhaustion requirement is that all administrative remedies must be pursued and exhausted by the grievant, "that is, of pursuing them to their appropriate conclusion and, correlatively, of awaiting their final outcome before seeking judicial intervention" (*Aircraft and Diesel Corp.* v. *Hirsch,* 331 U.S. 752, 767;1947).

The exhaustion doctrine is not controversial. Its usefulness has been recognized since around the turn of the century.[28] Justice Oliver Wendell Holmes applied the doctrine in *United States* v. *Sing Tuck,* 194 U.S. 161 (1904), a case in which the petitioners, who had been denied entry into the United States, decided to appeal the initial agency decision to the courts, even though governing statutes had established remedies for relief within the agency. Holmes noted simply that the courts should not be made available to the petitioners until they had exhausted the administrative appellate process. To allow such petitioners to bypass the available administrative remedies would, in Holmes's view, create an unnecessary burden on the courts to resolve problems which should be decided by the governmental agencies.

The exhaustion doctrine is perceived by virtually all observers as an essential legal weapon. It is designed to prevent an unnecessary disruption of the administrative process by according agencies a certain degree of autonomy. The underlying assumption of the doctrine is that, if left alone, agencies are quite capable of working out most conflicts which arise to the mutual satisfaction of all concerned parties. Even when agencies are in obvious error, it is held that the courts should give agencies an ample opportunity to correct their mistakes. To the Supreme Court in *Bowen* v. *City of New York,* 106 S.Ct. 2022 (1986), this makes the doctrine of exhaustion "intensely practical" (at 2032). In *McCarthy* v. *Madigan,* 112 S.Ct. 1081 (1992), the Supreme Court elaborated on the practical importance of giving administrators ample opportunity to correct administrative errors. "The exhaustion doctrine also acknowledges the common sense notion of dispute resolution that an agency ought to have an opportunity to correct its own mistakes with respect to the programs it administers before it is hauled into federal court. Correlatively, exhaustion principles apply with special force when 'frequent and deliberate flaunting of administrative processes' could weaken an agency's effectiveness by encouraging disregard of its procedures" (at 1086). The Court also noted that ". . . exhaustion promotes judicial efficiency in at least two ways. When an agency has the opportunity to correct its own errors, a judicial controversy may well be mooted, or at least piecemeal appeals may be avoided . . . and even where a controversy survives administrative review, exhaustion of the administrative procedure may produce a useful record for subsequent judicial consideration, especially in a complex or technical factual context" (at 1086–1087). In employing exhaustion, the courts recognize the independent powers and obligations of the autonomous administrative branch, thus paying respect to the more basic separation-of-powers doctrine.

There are situations, however, where the courts elect not to use exhaustion, believing that circumstances justify judicial intervention before agency remedies have been exhausted. Courts have refrained from using exhaustion and have intervened when it has appeared that an agency has: (1) violated (or will surely violate) constitutional due process guarantees; (2) acted (or will act) in an unfair and biased manner; (3) provided (or will inevitably provide) only hopeless and futile remedies (sometimes in bad faith); and (4) delayed remedial relief proceedings unreasonably. For example, in 1969 the D.C. Circuit Court elected to intervene because agency remedial action was having a "chilling effect" on the petitioner's First Amendment rights (*National Student Association* v. *Hershey,* 412 F.2d 1103). In *McCormick* v. *Hirsch,* 460 F.Supp. 1337 (M.D., Pa., 1978), the court ruled that exhaustion should not be applied when an agency's remedial actions encroach upon constitutionally protected religious freedoms. In *Gibson* v. *Berryhill,* 411 U.S. 64 (1973), the Supreme Court held that it was improper to apply exhaustion when solid evidence exists showing an agency hearing to be seriously biased. In *Continental Can Co.* v. *Marshall,* 603 F.2d 590 (7th Cir., 1979), the court refused to apply exhaustion and intervened because it contended that it would be futile for the petitioner to pursue its case in the agency, since the same issues had been heard in the agency before with the same results and with the issue having not yet been satisfactorily resolved. In *Walker* v. *Southern Ry.,* 385 U.S. 196 (1966), the high Court reiterated an old but still applicable rule—that grievants should not be expected to wait indefinitely for agency relief action. In *Sioux Valley Hosp.* v. *Bowen,* 792 F.2d 715 (8th Cir., 1986), the court held that exhaustion should not be given, because the agency was applying a futile administrative remedy, while in *Luna* v. *Bowen,* 641 F.Supp. 1109 (D.Colo., 1986), the court felt that an exception to the exhaustion requirement should be made because the agency demonstrated an adamant commitment to a view against the claimants. Finally, in *Darby* v. *Cisneros,* 113 S.Ct. 2539 (1993), the Supreme Court held that the courts need not require the exhaustion of "optional appeals" within an agency beyond what is specifically required by statute or agency rules. The Court stated: "Section 10(c) (of the APA) explicitly requires exhaustion of all intra-agency appeals mandated either by statute or by agency rule; it would be inconsistent with the plain language of Section 10(c) for courts to require litigants to exhaust optional appeals as well" (at 2545).[29] In sum, the exhaustion doctrine should almost always be honored unless certain administrative actions or inactions are clearly depriving parties of adequate and deserved appeal procedures.

The Ripeness Principle   *Ripeness* implies what one would think it implies. When a contested agency determination is ripe, it is mature enough to be ready for judicial review. Just as apples need to ripen before they are edible, disputes with administrative agencies need to ripen before the courts will hear them. If the court perceives a controversy as green, it will regard the controversy as premature and deny review until it reaches maturity. In this regard, then, the ripeness principle is very much a matter of common sense (*Seafarers Int'l Union* v. *United States Coast Guard,* 736 F.2d 19 [2d Cir., 1984]).

But when does a challenged agency action become ripe enough for review? Of course, to be ripe, a controversy must satisfy the basic tests we have been discussing.

That is, a petitioner must have a legitimate justiciable dispute, must have exhausted all available administrative remedies, must have satisfied the primary jurisdiction requirements, and must have passed the test for standing. The ripeness test is a broad test which goes beyond specific reviewability tests to discover whether the case is totally ripe. Because of the general nature of the ripeness principle, it is frequently confused with other, more specific tests, particularly with standing and exhaustion tests. However, while standing and exhaustion ask specific questions, ripeness poses the broad question: What general role should the court play in light of this case? In general, is this the type of controversy which the court should decide?

As do the doctrines just discussed, the ripeness principle also serves a dual purpose. That is, the ripeness principle functions to protect the administrative process from undue interference by the courts, as well as to protect the courts from having to hear controversies which the courts were not designed to decide. In *Abbott Laboratories* v. *Gardner,* 387 U.S. 136, 148 (1967), the Supreme Court asserted that the primary purpose of ripeness "is to protect the courts, through avoidance of premature adjudication, from entangling themselves in abstract disagreements over administrative policies, and also to protect the agencies from judicial interference until an administrative decision has been formalized and its effects felt in a concrete way by the challenging parties."

When the courts test for ripeness, they want to discover, essentially, whether an agency action has had an adverse effect on the petitioner. Bernard Schwartz explains: "The tests of ripeness are adverse effect, concreteness, and imminence. Whether an agency act is sufficiently ripe for review depends primarily upon the effect of the act. If an agency act does have adverse effect upon the person or property of private individuals, then it should be reviewable at the instance of such persons. If, on the other hand, it is only a preliminary or procedural measure, which does not of itself have impact upon them, review should be denied."[30] Employing these tests for ripeness, the Supreme Court in *Thomas* v. *Union Carbide Agr. Products Co.,* 105 S.Ct. 3325 (1985), decided that the particular dispute in question indeed constituted a case in controversy that could be resolved only by the exercise of judicial powers as authorized by Article 3 of the Constitution, thus making the case ripe for review (at 3332–33). Justice O'Connor, speaking for the Court, concluded that because possible injury could occur to Union Carbide Agricultural Products Company and other pesticide chemical manufacturers because the constitutionality of a certain arbitration scheme used by the Environmental Protection Agency under the Federal Insecticide, Fungicide, and Rodenticide Act was in question,[31] the Court could provide "preventive relief" (at 3333).

As long as all means of appeal have been exhausted, it is not difficult for the courts to determine whether a case is ripe if an administrative agency simply orders a party to act or not to act in a particular manner. It is also easy to see that when a welfare agency makes a final decision to deny a person a welfare benefits claim, the dispute is ripe for review (as long as statutes do not preclude review). Schwartz notes that cases are clearly ripe for review when decisions (for example, orders, directives) have an immediate impact upon a particular person's "rights and obligations": "Their adverse effect makes them ripe as soon as they are issued, unless there are further administrative remedies to be exhausted."[32]

Problems emerge in judging whether a case is ripe, however, when contested general agency directives are issued which are not aimed at specific parties. The Supreme Court struggled with this problem in the *Abbott Laboratories* case. When the Food and Drug Administration issued a regulation which required all drug labels to carry particular information, the drug manufacturer brought suit, arguing that the commission had exceeded its authority. The government argued that the case was not yet ripe for review since the regulation had not been enforced and, therefore, the impact of the regulation upon the industry was impossible to assess. But the Supreme Court held the government's "pre-enforcement" argument to be unreasonable because the regulation created an immediate and obvious hardship on the drug manufacturers, thus making the case ripe for review. Specifically, the hardship was that the drug manufacturers had to comply with the directive or risk prosecution and costly penalties for noncompliance.[33]

However, in 1993, a more conservative Supreme Court in *Reno v. Catholic Social Services,* 113 S.Ct. 2485, apparently restricted its decision in *Abbott Laboratories* by arguing that a "benefit-conferring" rule by an administrative agency is not ripe for review until the petitioner actually has applied for the benefit and is rejected. Under *Abbott Laboratories,* the benefit-conferring rule could actually be challenged as to its fairness and/or legality before the challenger actually applied for the benefit. Bernard Schwartz believes that the Supreme Court's ruling on ripeness in *Catholic Social Services* will unfortunately now ". . . require an untold number of plaintiffs to make unnecessary expenditures of time and money before they can obtain decisions on the validity of rules that may directly affect them."[34]

The Doctrines of Comity, Abstention, and Full Faith and Credit   The comity and abstention doctrines are two other doctrines used to stop the courts from meddling into the affairs of administrative agencies. *Comity,* a popular doctrine in international law, obligates one nation to respect and uphold the laws of another; it is applied in principle to administrative law. Comity embraces the broad principle that governmental institutions should generally and initially honor the decisions or judgments of other governmental branches before they become involved. The principle, which can be perceived as a form of respect or courtesy, is an old established one which stands behind the *"full faith and credit"* clause of the U.S. Constitution, which obligates the states to honor the civil statutes of one another. As applied to administrative law, the doctrine constrains the courts to have as their first instinct the notion to honor and respect the wisdom of the decisions reached in administrative agencies.[35] Comity, although not a binding doctrine, has practical significance for administrative law because it promotes a certain mind-set in judges which has the impact of discouraging counterproductive judicial meddling in agency activities by avoiding potential conflicts. Edwin Wallace Tucker has said this: "Relying on comity, a federal court, independent of statutory directives governing its jurisdiction, may forbear taking action while a state proceeding is in progress. By doing so, conflicts are avoided."[36]

Abstention, a judge-made doctrine, supports the spirit of comity. Basically, the doctrine requires the federal courts to respect the independence of state activities. When applied to administrative law, the abstention principle largely calls for the avoidance of unnecessary conflicts between the federal judiciary and state administrative systems. It requests the courts to display "scrupulous regard for the rightful independence of the state governments"[37] by remaining removed from involvement unless there is "danger of irreparable injury."[38] The doctrine functions to prevent disruption of state administrative operations, while simultaneously freeing federal courts from having to adjudicate unnecessary and time-consuming constitutional questions.

From what has been said in this section, it becomes obvious that the courts can rely upon many legal doctrines and principles to deny reviewing contested administrative actions. However, despite the abundance and power of these legal obstacles to review, it is clear that in the past few decades the trend has been generally for the courts to rely upon these legal weapons less and less as a means to deny petitioners their day in court.

SCOPE OF REVIEW

Reviewability and scope of review are associated with each other, but each implies very different questions from the other. Once a court has decided to make review available, the court must decide what its proper *scope of review* should be (to what extent it should review complaints against administrative actions on the basis of the actual merits of the case). Obviously, it would be impossible and unwise for the courts to try to scrutinize the legality of all challenged administrative activities. To emphasize an earlier point, virtually all administrative law scholars believe that unnecessary judicial meddling into agency operations would prove disruptive and counterproductive. Further, the scholars point out, the courts do not have the time or the expertise to competently review the merits of even a tiny fraction of contested administrative actions.

However, at the same time the courts have an obligation to the American people to keep administrative behavior fair, reasonable, and accountable. In its relationship with administrative agencies, this is the judicial system's most basic job task; and it means that the courts' scope of review must be broad enough that those agency actions which exploit individuals and pose serious threats to procedural due process standards can be stopped by judicial intervention. Ideally, the courts should seek a scope of review broad enough to prevent dangerous administrative abuses, yet narrow enough that normal administrative operations are not disrupted by unwanted judicial interference. In *NLRB* v. *Brown,* 380 U.S. 278 (1966), the Supreme Court reflected upon the judiciary's proper scope of review in reviewing agency activities, in this case actions of the National Labor Relations Board. The Court was specifically addressing what it meant by its conceptualization of "limited judicial review": "When we used the phrase 'limited judicial review' we did not mean that the balance struck by the Board is immune from judicial examination and reversal in proper cases. . . . Courts should be 'slow to overturn an administrative decision' . . . but they are not left to 'sheer acceptance' of the Board's conclusions. . . . Reviewing courts are not obliged to stand aside and rubber-stamp their affirmance of administrative decisions that they deem inconsistent with a statutory mandate or that frustrate the congressional policy underlying a statute. Such review is always properly within the judicial province, and courts would abdicate their responsibility if they did not fully review such administrative decisions. Of course due deference is to be rendered to agency determinations of fact, so long as there is substantial evidence to be found in the record as a whole" (at 290).

Since the beginning of the growth of big governmental bureaucracy during Franklin D. Roosevelt's presidency, vehement arguments have developed over what the proper scope of review over administrative behavior should be. Although the focal question of the dispute is extremely challenging and remains unsettled today, serious attempts have been made to develop guidelines on what course the courts should follow when faced with the frequently raised question: *To what depth should we probe this contested agency action?* In answering this question, judges are concerned about going too far and overstepping their proper judicial role, as defined broadly in Article 3 of the Constitution. The maximum constitutional limits of review prohibit the courts from violating the separation-of-powers doctrine by performing nonjudicial tasks. Thus, reviewing courts could violate the Constitution by extending their scope of review to allow themselves to perform functions which have been duly assigned to only administrators or legislators. For example, in *Federal Radio Commission* v. *General Electric Co.,* 281 U.S. 464 (1930), the Supreme Court argued validly that a reviewing court should not take the place of administrative agencies by usurping their "purely administrative" functions. It was reasoned that reviewing courts should perform only their rightful judicial role and should not play the role of a "superior administrative agency" by acting as their administrative supervisors. This appears sound, but the guideline is certainly not easy to operationalize. For instance, the courts have always disagreed as to what are purely judicial and purely administrative functions. If the courts decided to drastically restrict their reviewing scope, they could also violate Article 3 by failing to review legitimate legal controversies. In any event, the courts have the final say in what is within their proper reviewing scope. Consequently, court opinions on scope of review vary greatly from court to court, thus making it very difficult to come to any definitive conclusions as to what agency actions are legitimately within the courts' scope of review.

Scope of Review and the APA

During the New Deal era the courts handed down many opinions which provided a fairly clear idea of what generally should be regarded as inside or outside the courts' legitimate scope of review. In fact, Section 706, the "Scope of Review" section in the APA, is largely a codification of court opinions on score of review (see Section 706 of the APA in the Appendix to this text). Although Kenneth C. Davis is very critical of many APA provisions, he believes in general that the scope of review *"provisions themselves have a good deal of clear meaning, and they are a good summary of the law of judicial review."*[39]

Considering the impossible task of trying to define absolutely what should or should not be within the courts' legitimate scope of review, Davis is probably correct in concluding that the APA framers did a laudable job in providing useful guidelines for future courts to follow in deciding how far they should go in scrutinizing disputed agency actions. To provide some focus and to avoid unnecessary confusion, we shall examine the more problematical provisions in Section 706; but it is worth summarizing here what the section generally appears to sanction, either explicitly or implicitly. Normally, administrative law scholars and the courts have agreed that agency actions are well within the courts' proper scope of review if administrators have: (1) clearly violated the constitutional rights of citizens; (2) exceeded their statutory authority; (3) acted in blatant contradiction of previous court rulings; (4) neglected to follow well-established procedures of administrative due process; (5) abused their discretionary power in a cruel and obvious fashion; (6) denied fundamental rights, not privileges, to persons; (7) committed "prejudicial error" in reaching decisions; (8) made unreasonable decisions which either have "no basis in fact" or cannot be supported by any "substantial evidence"; (9) reached reckless decisions which totally ignore or blatantly misuse facts; (10) departed for inexplicable or senseless reasons from established agency procedures and prior decisions; (11) brought to question some problem where few, if any, judicial opinions or precedents exist; and (12) otherwise violated clear questions of law.

Seeking the Proper Scope of Review over Administrative Actions

No doubt Section 706 provisions have provided guidelines to help the courts decide what they should review. Unquestionably, however, these provisions are still quite vague and, therefore, wide open to interpretation by those applying them. For example, Section 706 provisions ask the courts to override agency actions which are "arbitrary, capricious, [or] an abuse of discretion" ([2][A]); to declare unlawful administrative behavior which is "in excess of statutory jurisdiction, authority or limitations" ([2][C]); and to set aside agency decisions which are "unsupported by substantial evidence" ([2][E]). Reasonably informed people have a fairly good idea of what these provisions generally mean, but obviously there is still much room for debate over, for instance, what constitutes "an abuse of discretion"; what is "in excess of statutory jurisdiction"; or what should qualify as "substantial evidence" to support an agency conclusion.

Most of the administrative law literature pertaining to scope of review focuses on these kinds of difficult questions. Naturally we should be realistic enough not to expect anyone to arrive at an absolute conclusion as to which administrative actions are "arbitrary and capricious" and which are not and which, therefore, are within or beyond the courts' legitimate scope of review. What is clearly "arbitrary and capricious" behavior to one judge may seem within reasonable limits of administrative discretion to another. The crucial point here is that these different judicial perceptions do play a decisive role in determining whether the courts will review contested administrative actions. Consequently, each court becomes the interpreter of what Section 706 provisions really mean in practice.

Nevertheless, despite the relative vagueness of APA scope of review provisions, it is not unrealistic to expect the meaning of Section 706 provisions to be further clarified. Since 1946, courts have been particularly active in their attempts to refine the meaning of these legal requirements so that they convey a more common meaning and are applied in a more equitable and consistent manner. In so doing, the courts have developed certain rules, tests, and principles to help them employ Section 706 provisions in their efforts to determine their proper scope of review over administrative actions. The more important ones are discussed below.

The Deference Principle   The *deference principle* is such a basic doctrine in administrative law that it is touched upon in virtually every chapter in this book. It is rooted in the separation-of-powers doctrine and in plain common sense. In honor of the constitutional separation-of-powers doctrine and out of respect for the expertise of administrators, judges have relied upon the deference doctrine to guide their interpretations and applications of Section 706, "Scope of Review," dictates. Despite the tendency toward judicial activism, which has brought a general broadening of the courts' scope of review, deference to administrative authority and expertise by the courts is still the rule rather than the exception. As the 1980s began, Bernard Schwartz exclaimed: "Of course, the scope of review is normally dominated by the doctrine of deference to the agency. This has not yet been altered by the changed atmosphere that is starting to prevail in the regulatory area."[40] In the context of the Airline Deregulation Act of 1978 (92 Stat. 1075), which called for the gradual dissolution of the Civil Aeronautics Board, the D.C. Circuit Court in *Frontier Airlines* v. *CAB*, 602 F.2d 375, 378–379 (1979), nevertheless acknowledged the applicability of the deference principle by stating: "New era or old, so long as the Board continues to be entrusted by Congress with the primary responsibility for the health of air transportation, it remains true that . . . courts have no special qualifications in this area for second-guessing the Board as to the merits of its determinations, once they have been arrived at within a framework of procedural fair play."

In this assertion the court paid recognition again to the solidly established principle that the courts should normally defer problems involving questions of fact, as contrasted to questions of law, to the judgment of administrators. To recall, questions of fact basically pertain to the factual "what was" or "what is" evidence administrators need to evaluate in order to reach rational decisions. In contrast, questions of law essentially relate to the ways in which laws affect the "what was" and "what is" evidence, focusing on how laws apply to the evidentiary facts. Typical administrative law questions pertain to administrative jurisdictional and procedural due process considerations, particularly in regard to the use of administrative discretion, and in the specific context of constitutional, statutory, and common law mandates. Thus, the *Frontier Airlines* case conveys the message that the deference principle is applied to limit the courts' scope of review over administrative decision making, just as it was in the precedential case *Gray* v. *Powell,* 314 U.S. 402 (1941), where Justice Stanley F. Reed, speaking for the Court, wrote: "Where, as here, a determination has been left to an administrative body, this delegation will be respected and the administrative conclusion left untouched. . . . Although we have here no dispute as to the evidentiary facts, that does not permit a court to substitute its judgment for that of the Director" (at 412).

It was noted in the last chapter that the courts in the 1980s and 1990s, as contrasted to the 1960s and 1970s, expressed a greater willingness to defer to agency discretionary authority and expertise. This was especially true for the Supreme Court, as a few cases should make clear. In *United States* v. *Erika, Inc.,* 102 S.Ct. 1650 (1982), the Supreme Court held that it was the clear intention of Congress to have the courts limit their scope of review by deferring to agency expertise in regard to the determination of benefits under Part B of the Medicare program. In *Capital Cities Cable, Inc.* v. *Crisp,* 104 S.Ct. 2694 (1984), the high Court stressed that courts should defer to agency discretion when Congress has sanctioned such discretion. In the famous precedential case *Chevron, U.S.A., Inc.* v. *Natural Resources Defense Council,* 104 S.Ct. 2778 (1984), discussed previously, the Supreme Court deferred to the expertise of the Environmental Protection Agency, contending that "considerable weight should be accorded to an executive department's construction of a statutory scheme it is entrusted to administer, and the principle of deference to administrative interpretations" (at 2782). And in *Regents of the University of Michigan* v. *Ewing,* 106 S.Ct. 507 (1985), the Supreme Court emphasized that utmost deference should be accorded academic institutions to protect their academic freedom. "When judges are asked to review the substance of a genuinely academic decision, . . .they should show great respect for the faculty's professional judgment. Plainly, they may not override it unless it is such a substantial departure from accepted academic norms as to demonstrate that the person or committee responsible did not actually exercise professional judgment" (at 13). However, in *Bowen* v. *American Hospital Ass'n.,* 106 S.Ct. 2101 (1986), the Supreme Court acknowledged that although considerable use has been made of this deference principle, "agency deference has not come so far that we will uphold regulations whenever it is possible to 'conceive a basis' for administrative action" (at 2112).

As noted in a previous discussion of *Chevron,* the actual impact of *Chevron* on the courts' willingness or unwillingness to defer to agency discretion and expertise is open to question. However, evidence does suggest that despite so much judicial and academic rhetoric supporting the deference principle, many courts seem to ignore the *Chevron* doctrine and insist on playing an active public policy-making role. And, of course, this is the chief question raised by *Chevron.* Should courts readily defer to agency expertise when statutes seem to be ambiguous, allowing agency administrators to exercise broad discretion in interpreting statutes or the intent of Congress, or should the courts take the responsibility of interpreting vague statutes?

Despite considerable noncompliance with the *Chevron* doctrine by the lower courts, at least the Supreme Court in the 1990s has continued to uphold the wisdom of *Chevron*. In *Pauley v. Bethenergy Miner, Inc.,* 111 S.Ct. 2524 (1991), the Supreme Court argued that *Chevron* should be followed because the judiciary should play a very limited role in making public policies and that interpreting statutes is very much a part of the public policy-making process, which Congress reserved for public agencies, not the courts. Specifically citing *Chevron,* the Court summarized its position on deference: "Judicial deference to an agency's interpretation of ambiguous provisions of the statutes it is authorized to implement reflects a sensitivity to the proper roles of the political and judicial branches . . . ['(F)ederal judges—who have no constituency—have a duty to respect legitimate policy choices made by those who do'); . . . As *Chevron* itself illustrates, the resolution of ambiguity in a statutory text is often more a question of policy than of law. . . . When Congress, through express delegation or the introduction of an administrative gap in the statutory structure, has delegated policy-making authority to an administrative agency, the extent of judicial review of the agency's policy determination is limited" (at 253).

But what perplexes so many about the reasoning in *Chevron* is that it is also true that "the resolution of ambiguity in a statutory text" is often more a question of law than of policy. Such makes applying *Chevron* difficult for some judges, especially those who are predisposed to thinking that it is more up to the courts to interpret ambiguous statutes because, after all, what are the courts for?[41]

Substantial Evidence Rule   The broad deference principle logically supports the more narrow *substantial evidence rule,* which is normally applied to limit a court's scope of review over agency determinations involving questions of fact. The deference doctrine is a comprehensive principle which generally calls for the courts to leave administration to the administrative experts, but it frequently simultaneously implies the use of the substantial evidence rule. The substantial evidence rule essentially requires the courts to see whether there is any substantial evidence supporting challenged agency decisions.[42] Section 706(2)(E) of the APA requires specifically that administrative decisions must be "supported by substantial evidence" on the basis of a record. If a reviewing court asked to review a contested agency decision under Section 706(2)(A) finds that substantial evidence exists to support the agency determination, the agency has, in effect, passed the substantial evidence test, and the court should withdraw from reviewing the particular matter any further. In so doing, the court is limiting its scope of review, checking only to see whether any reasonable (substantial) evidence exists to support the agency's decision. For example, in *Arkansas v. Oklahoma,* 112 S.Ct. 1046 (1992), the Supreme Court scolded the Court of Appeals for the Tenth Circuit because it did not defer to agency expertise on the basis of the substantial evidence rule. The Court noted that the Court of Appeals ". . . disregarded well-established standards for reviewing the factual findings of agencies and instead made its own factual findings. . . . Although we have long recognized the 'substantial evidence' standard in administrative law, the court below turned that analysis on its head. A court reviewing an agency's adjudicature action should accept the *agency's* factual findings if those findings are supported by substantial evidence on the records as a whole. . . . The court should not supplant the agency's findings merely by identifying alternative findings that could be supported by substantial evidence" (at 1060).

The application of the substantial evidence rule would be easy enough if the courts only knew what constitutes substantial evidence. But as with so many administrative law principles, rules, and tests, the substantive evidence rule has become difficult for the courts to apply with dependable consistency because no clear operational definition of substantial evidence has evolved. Attempts to clarify the meaning of "substantial evidence" have proven quite futile since other nebulous terms have been used in definitions. Since the time before the passage of the APA to the present, judicial attempts to define substantial evidence sound uncomfortably similar, indicating that five decades have seen only insignificant progress toward making the substantial evidence rule more viable.

In 1938, for example, the Supreme Court, in *Consolidated Edison Co.* v. *NLRB,* 305 U.S. 197. 229, said: "Substantial evidence . . . means such relevant evidence as a reasonable mind might accept as adequate to support a conclusion." Since what different "reasonable minds" would accept to substantiate a conclusion would vary greatly, this definition seems to help very little. A year later in *NLRB* v. *Columbian Enameling and Stamping Co.,* 306 U.S. 292, 300 (1939), the Court made another attempt by noting that substantial evidence is "evidence which is substantial, this is, affording a substantial basis of fact from which the fact in issue can be reasonably inferred." The thrust of this statement is not really helpful. It simply says judges must in the future determine whether substantial evidence existed to justify an administrator's decision by determining whether the decision rested upon a reasonably substantial basis of fact. Still no help came in 1966, when the Supreme Court asserted in *Consolo* v. *Federal Maritime Commission,* 383 U.S. 607, 619, that substantial evidence is any "relevant evidence as a reasonable mind might accept as adequate to support a conclusion." For whatever reason, the Ninth Circuit in 1979, in *RSR Corp.* v. *FTC,* 602 F.2d 1317, felt that somehow the substitution of *realistic* for *reasonable* would resolve the definitional problem: "Substantial evidence means such relevant evidence as a realistic mind might accept as adequate to support the (agency's) conclusion." And in 1991 in *Foust* v. *Lujan,* 942 F.2d 712, 714, (10th Cir.), the court defined substantial evidence as ". . . something more than a mere scintilla but something less than the weight of the evidence," whatever concrete or practical meaning this has!

It may be expecting too much to feel that better operational definitions of substantial evidence can be developed. After all, some abstract concepts have escaped definitive definitions for centuries—for example, justice and love. Sometimes we must rely upon common sense and professionalism to make things work. This is particularly true in the legal field. Kenneth C. Davis suggests that what is important is that judges "generally understand that they may not properly substitute their judgment for administrative judgment except on questions of law on which they are the experts, . . . and that in most cases other factors have a much stronger influence than the words of the formula that is supposed to apply."[43]

If the courts want to expand their scope of review over administrative agencies, it will be difficult to stop them, for they have the judicial discretion necessary to apply such terms as "reasonableness" and "substantial evidence" in whatever manner they see fit. "Despite the statutory formulas," Davis asks "do not the courts continue as the architects of the scope of review?"[44] Certainly, the vague Section 706 guidelines will not function to prevent judicial meddling in administrative affairs if the courts are determined to intrude. However, it is true that unwarranted lower court intrusions in the administrative process may be overruled by higher courts.

The "Whole Record" Requirement   Before the passage of the APA, the courts in general had developed an extremely narrow version of the substantial evidence rule. Under this narrow version, any reasonable evidence that tends to support the challenged administrative action should be accepted by the courts. In practice, this application of the substantial evidence rule meant that as long as any plausible evidence was presented to support a conclusion, whether the evidence represented only one side of the picture or a tiny fraction of the whole record or all of it, the reviewing court was obliged to honor the agency's right to use such evidence (obviously one-sided) to support its conclusion. It was maintained in those pre-APA days that the courts should not be entitled to weigh the facts to determine whether a "proper" decision was reached, but only to check to see whether any reasonable facts at all were cited by an agency to support its finding. Just prior to the passage of the APA, the Court, in *Marzacco v. Lowe,* 58 F.Supp. 900 (D.N.J., 1945), commented on the practical implications of this one-sided substantial evidence test: "Under the present prevailing system of administrative law, all evidence to the contrary . . . is a closed book into which this court dare not peek, at least not effectively" (at 903).

Louis J. Jaffe found this narrow application of the substantial evidence rule horrifying. Rightfully, Jaffe insisted that it would be absurd to believe that truly reasonable and responsible individuals could, in good conscience, reach rational conclusions by looking at only part of the record: "Obviously responsible men would not exercise their judgement on only that part of the evidence that looks in one direction."[45] However, despite blatant farcical and inequitable consequences of this version of the substantial evidence test, this narrow version of the substantial evidence test managed to survive until after the passage of the APA.

The APA framers were particularly disturbed over the use of this one-sided substantial evidence test. In drafting Section 706(2) of the APA, they made certain that the courts would have to apply the substantial evidence rule in light of the *whole* record. This legislation extended the courts' potential scope of review over agency "questions of fact" determinations. Specifically, Section 706(2) created a much broader substantial evidence test for the courts to employ because the courts were now compelled to judge whether the facts of the case, taken as a whole, would lead a reasonable person to conclude that substantial evidence exists, considering all contrary evidence in the record, to support the agency's conclusion. In *Universal Camera Corp. v. NLRB,* 340 U.S. 474 (1951), the Supreme Court noted the meaning and significance of the whole-record requirement. The Court acknowledged that the APA now prohibited the courts from looking at only a part of the record to determine whether agency decisions are supported by substantial evidence and further pointed out that reviewing courts must now examine the whole record, including conflicting evidence: "The substantiality of evidence must take into account whatever in the record fairly detracts from its weight. This is clearly the significance of the (APA) requirement . . . that courts consider the whole record" (at 488). Courts today still apply the same whole-record standard as established in *Universal Camera Corp. (State of Wyo.* v. *Alexander,* 971 F.2d. 531 [10th Cir. 1992]).

Not surprisingly, the question of what constitutes the whole record has also been disputed. The dispute is generally based in problems pertaining to definitions of formal and informal evidence and questions over which evidence needs to be included in the "whole" record. Agencies have been charged with keeping incomplete records, as has been noted before; this would keep courts from being able to apply the substantial evidence rule adequately. Nevertheless, the whole-record requirement has improved the substantial evidence test by broadening the courts' scope of review so that fairer and more reasonable judicial review of agency actions can take place. For reviewing courts, what is reasonable has changed from a review of a partial agency record to a complete assessment of the facts supporting conclusions on the basis of the whole record.

The "Fundamental Rights" Requirement   The scope of review over agency determinations involving questions of fact is usually quite limited by the substantial evidence rule. However, the Supreme Court has ruled that the courts' scope of review can be expanded under certain conditions, especially when fundamental rights are at stake. *Fundamental rights,* as they have been interpreted by the courts, normally involve constitutionally guaranteed liberties; but in recent years some courts have ruled that some statutory entitlements (for example, welfare benefits) should be regarded as fundamental rights.[46]

The famous *Ben Avon* doctrine (also called the "constitutional fact" doctrine), set forth in *Ohio Valley Water Co.* v. *Ben Avon Borough,* 253 U.S. 287 (1920), established that full court review is necessary when constitutional facts are in question. In the *Ben Avon* case, the Pennsylvania Public Service Commission had set a "fair value" rate at a level Ohio Valley Water Company believed was so low that it was confiscatory in nature, thus depriving it of constitutionally protected property rights without due process. While the Pennsylvania court ruled that the court's scope of review was restricted by the substantial evidence rule, the Supreme Court held that full review should be granted and the substantial evidence test made inapplicable because a constitutional question of fact (property rights) was involved. The Court argued that "if the owner claims a confiscation of his property will result, the State must provide a fair opportunity for submitting that issue to a judicial tribunal for determination upon its own independent judgment as to both law and facts; otherwise the order is void because (it is) in conflict with the due process value" (at 289).

The *Ben Avon* doctrine has struggled for survival over the decades, but it is clear that its spirit lingers, especially in a few states where the doctrine is still cited by the courts to justify their positions on scope of review.[47] Actually, the *Ben Avon* doctrine was expanded by a precedential California decision, *Strumsky* v. *San Diego*

Employees Retirement System, 11 Cal.3d 28 (1974). The emerging *Strumsky* doctrine declares that statutory entitlements, in addition to constitutional guarantees, may qualify for full judicial review. Under the *Strumsky* doctrine, a reviewing court is obliged to grant full review when agency actions deprive persons of statutory entitlements in which they have "a fundamental vested right." As one would predict, the notion of fundamental rights has been expanded by persuasive lawyers who have been able to convince California judges, at least, that agency decisions involving motor vehicles, stockbrokers, disability benefits, age discrimination, and licenses should receive full judicial review since fundamental rights are at stake. The spirit of the *Strumsky* doctrine has received some recognition at the federal level.

Unquestionably, both federal and state courts have the tendency to expand their scope of review when fundamental rights are at stake. However, the *Ben Avon* doctrine has almost totally been ignored by federal and state courts since 1936 because, very frankly, the doctrine simply demands too much from the courts. As Kenneth C. Davis and Richard J. Pierce, Jr. assert: "The 'constitutional fact' doctrine could not long survive in a legal system in which many agencies routinely make numerous findings of fact that form the predicates for determining the constitutionality of agency actions. . . . Over time, the Court recognized that it would be absurdly inefficient to require reviewing courts to engage in *de novo* review of all 'constitutional facts.' "[48] Despite its implicit rejection by the courts, it should be noted, however, that the Supreme Court has never specifically overruled the *Ben Avon* doctrine.

The *"De Novo* Review" Requirement   *De novo* review essentially means a new trial. When a court grants *de novo* review in an administrative law dispute, it is ordering fresh judicial proceedings so that the arguments and evidence in the controversy can be weighed again by a new, independent tribunal. *De novo* review is rooted in the constitutional requirement that fundamental rights (life, liberty, and property) cannot be taken away without due process of law. In some instances, administrative action does not go far enough in protecting parties from being denied constitutional liberties without adequate due process safeguards. When this happens in the administrative process, a court may order a trial *de novo* so that the case can be heard for a second time.

In the precedential case Ng *Fung Ho* v. *White,* 259 II.S. 276 (1922), the Supreme Court contended that it is appropriate to grant *de novo* review when an agency action (in this case, a deportation order) may deprive a person of essential liberty "that makes life worth living" (at 284). In essence, the Court held that extending a court's scope of review is justified when it appears that mere reliance upon the substantial evidence test would likely threaten to deprive a person of a constitutional right without the required due process protections.

In general at least the basic wisdom of *Ng Fung Ho* still stands today. For example, in *City of St. Louis* v. *Department of Transp.,* 936 F.2d 1528, 1533 (8th Cir. 1991), the court said: "To the extent that the decisions in question rest on findings of fact, we are obliged to uphold them if they are supported by substantial evidence. The agency's interpretation of its governing statutes presents, of course, a question of law, and courts normally review questions of law de novo, . . ." However, this should not be taken to imply that *de novo* review is frequently granted by the courts.[49] If this became the case, the courts would begin to assume functions which should be performed by our public agencies. In fact, in an interesting state case, *Bentley* v. *Chastain*, 249 S.E.2d 38 (1978), a Georgia court held that statutory provisions which sanction *de novo* review of agency actions are unconstitutional because such provisions ask the courts to perform nonjudicial administrative job tasks, while in *Silwany-Rodriquez* v. *INS*, 975 F.2d 1157, 1160 (5th Cir. 1992), the court paid lip service to the *de novo* requirement stating that at least "[T]o the extent it involves a question of law, this is subject to de novo review," yet then emphasized that "[S]uch review, however, is limited.' " Bernard Schwartz poses a good question in light of this reasoning. He asks: "How can review be both de novo and limited?" He answers sarcastically: "The answer, of course, is that, under *Chevron*, review becomes 'limited' and 'de novo' becomes a ritual incantation devoid of practical content."[50] Schwartz may be exaggerating because, as mentioned, courts still generally honor the *de novo* review requirement, yet it is also true that many courts today are trying to limit their burden and one way to do it is to narrow their scope of review by restricting the application of *de novo* review.

COURT ORDERS AND THE PROBLEMS OF COMPLIANCE

Judicial review is a fundamental process in the American governmental system which makes the judiciary the guardian of the principles of fair play as set forth in statutory and constitutional law. Fortunately, judicial review has so far been used in a flexible manner; it can prevent or prohibit administrative abuses when necessary, yet also allow the administrative process to proceed in an uninterrupted fashion when it is appropriate and expedient to do so. Court decisions resulting from judicial review of agency actions carry great weight and must be honored by administrators, although administrators on occasion may resist and delay compliance with court orders they do not like. If administrators fail to comply with court orders, specific *writs* (orders) may be issued. Writs provide a means (judicial remedies) to protect parties from administrative wrongs. The most commonly issued writs are: (1) *writ of habeas corpus,* which requires an official to present the prisoner in court and justify why the person is being held; (2) *writ of injunction,* which compels or restrains actions by public officials, usually with the purpose of preventing some immediate harm caused by their performance or nonperformance; (3) *writ of mandamus,* which forces an official to carry out certain mandatory functions as required by law; (4) *writ of prohibition,* which orders officials to stop performing activities beyond their legal powers; and (5) *writ of quo warranto,* which makes an official or public agency show the legal authority under which the official or agency functions. If public administrators fail to comply with these writs, they could face fines, jail sentences, or both for contempt of court. If courts did not have this punitive threat, their power to review cases and check administrative abuses would be a hollow one. But because the courts do have this power, judicial review has proven rather effective as a regulatory weapon in our system.

Despite the success of courts in having most of their decisions and court orders carried out, administrators on occasion show flagrant disrespect for the courts by refusing to comply with court decisions and orders. Public officials are particularly apt to violate court orders when they feel that public opinion is on their side, despite the constitutionality or legality of their actions. Although the courts could impose fines or send officials to jail for contempt of court, the administrators know that, historically, the courts have been quite reluctant to take such drastic measures against officials who normally command high respect and popularity in their local areas. For example, public school administrators are not perceived by their communities as criminals. Thus, when they decide not to comply with a court order (for example, a busing order) because they believe it would not be in the best interests of their school system, courts have found it difficult to gain broad respect from the public by having these school officials rounded up and thrown into jail for noncompliance. The general attitude seems to be that jails are for genuine criminals, not for those who believe that a social issue should be handled differently from the way particular courts think it should be done.

Public administrators nationwide have an additional advantage over the courts since injunctions and other court rulings are directed against specific officials. Thus they have the effect of forcing compliance with laws and court orders only in a specific case. For example, if school administrators in Boston refuse to implement school integration plans as ordered by the court, school officials elsewhere can carry out their own segregationist policies, despite their illegality, until the courts finally focus on their school districts and start to direct actions at them. It should be recognized that every time a court decides it should employ every weapon possible to enforce compliance, it risks failure or noncompliance. Judges know failures reflect upon their power, prestige, and image. Consequently, the courts' power to demand compliance with their orders is limited by the courts' own calculation of the odds of obtaining successful compliance vis-a-vis opposition from administrators and public opinion.

It seems clear that steps should be taken to protect the prestige, power, and credibility of the courts. But this is much easier said than done. Court judges themselves could adopt a get-tough policy and hand out tough sentences for noncompliance, but the judges are already overburdened, and such a move would probably prove futile and counterproductive. The other governmental branches, jealously clinging to their power, may not be ready to create a stronger and more comprehensive court system that would enhance the opportunity for more court-made law. Elected officials are frequently reluctant to endorse an unpopular court decision, fearing that the public may take its revenge at the ballot box. But if public administrators are allowed to defy court orders at an increasing rate in the future, the ability of the courts to protect against administrative abuses will decline accordingly.

SUMMARY

Courts represent the last hope for redressing administrative injustices for those who feel that they were wronged by agency actions. Despite the inconvenience and expense of redressing wrongs through the judicial system, the courts can provide an effective remedy for persons who have become victims of illegal agency behavior, although the courts can provide no relief for parties who have been victimized by unethical agency practices. The courts' power stems from their authority to declare acts of public officials unconstitutional and/or in violation of statute. However, justices have been reluctant to overplay their judicial role since they must rely upon the other governmental branches to enforce their decisions. Most judges are unwilling to jeopardize the good health of the courts by constantly making unpopular decisions against administrators whose actions enjoy broad community support. To survive, the courts, like any other political actor in the political system, must respond appropriately to environmental demands.

It is also true that some judges believe that the courts should exercise restraint in passing judgment on agency actions unless administrators are in clear violation of the law. Actually, during the 1800s and the early 1900s, most judges presumed that administrative actions were unreviewable unless Congress specifically made certain agency actions reviewable. However, for the past half century or so the more activist courts have taken an opposing position and have functioned under the presumption that administrative actions are reviewable unless Congress specifically precludes judicial review. Congress has normally prohibited review of agency behavior when it believes that allowing review would be unnecessarily disruptive to routine administrative processes. Despite congressional prohibitions against review, the judiciary, as the chief interpreter of the Constitution, has given review anyway if it was felt that the statutory preclusion of review had the effect of somehow denying persons constitutional rights.

Simply, courts consider agency actions reviewable if they perceive administrative conduct to be within their proper jurisdiction. However, parties seeking judicial review of agency actions find that it is not always easy to obtain review. To protect the administrative process from unnecessary and counterproductive judicial meddling, the courts have required petitioners to pass several tests before they will grant review. For a dispute to be ripe for review, petitioners must satisfy at least the basic reviewability requirements of standing, primary, and exclusive jurisdiction, as well as exhaustion.

Once a court has determined whether certain agency actions are reviewable (within its jurisdiction), it must then decide whether the actions are within the court's proper scope of review. In making this determination, the court must decide how far it wants to carry out review in a particular area.

Out of deference to agency expertise, most courts have tried to limit their scope of review, thus leaving most administrative controversies to be resolved by the administrators themselves. Although Section 706 of the Administrative Procedure Act extends broad scope of review powers to the courts, judges have mostly chosen to review questions of law, avoiding questions of fact. This is because the courts do not exist for the purpose of deciding whether agency administrators reach the right decisions, in light of the facts, but whether they use proper procedures in reaching them. It is for this reason that it is said that administrative law deals mostly with questions pertaining to procedural due process in public agencies.

Judicial review is normally restricted to formal agency actions; these constitute only about 10 percent of all agency behavior. As was pointed out in the last chapter, this disturbs many administrative law scholars because they note that most administrative injustices occur when informal discretionary decisions are involved. In this light, judicial review offers parties only weak protections against abuses of administrative power.

NOTES

1. In particular, see the scolding of administrative officials by the courts in *Morgan v. United States,* 304 U.S. 1(1938); *Cinderella Career and Finishing Schools, Inc. v. FTC,* 25 F.2d 583 (D.C.Cir., 1970); *Citizens to Preserve Overton Park v. Volpe,* 401 U.S. 402 (1971); *Motor Vehicles Manufacturers Ass'n. v. State Farm Insurance Co.,* 463 U.S. 29 (1983); *Bowen v. American Hospital Ass'n.,* 10th S.Ct. 2101(1986); and *Haitian Centers Council, Inc. v. Sale,* 823 F.Supp. 1028 (E.D.N.Y. 1993).

2. Because the subject of judicial review is so crucial to the understanding of other areas of administrative law and behavior (for example, rule-making and order-making), many general aspects of judicial review have already been given brief attention, especially in Chapter 2, where the courts were introduced as political actors, with a major role in the administrative process. Nonetheless, a few important points need to be reiterated and developed before proceeding to the discussion of the more technical features (for example, standing and ripeness) and some of the more lively academic arguments.

3. Martin Shapiro, "Discretion" in David H. Rosenbloom and Richard D. Schwartz, eds., *Handbook of Regulation and Administrative Law* (New York: Marcel Dekker, Inc., 1994), 511.

4. Owen M. Fiss, "The Bureaucratization of the Judiciary," *The Yale Law Journal,* vol. 92 (July 1983), 1442–68; and Glen O. Robinson, *American Bureaucracy: Public Choice and Public Law* (Ann Arbor: University of Michigan Press, 1991), 108–110.

5. Charles W. Stewart, "Self-conscious Interest and the Democratic Process: The Case of Citizens Regulating Agencies and Federal Courts," *Law and Policy Quarterly,* 1 (October 1979), 418.

6. Jeremy Rabkin, *Judicial Compulsions: How Public Law Distorts Public Policy* (New York: Basic Books, 1989).

7. George Will, "Who Decides: Judges or People," *St. Louis Post- Dispatch,* November 2, 1994, 7B.

8. Steven Vago, *Law and Society,* 4th ed. (Englewood Cliffs, N.J.: Prentice-Hall, 1994), 190.

9. *Statistical Abstract of the United States 1994,* 114th ed. (Washington, D.C.: U.S. Government Printing Office, 1993), 211.

10. Recent statistics from *United States Government Manual, 1995–96* (Office of the Federal Register, National Archives and Records Administration, 1995), 71 and 75.

11. Steven Vago, *Law and Society,* 4th ed., 190–194.

12. Donald L. Horowitz, "The Courts as Guardians of the Public Interest," *Public Administration Review,* 37 (March-April 1977), 150. Also see the entire issue of the *Administrative Law Review,* vol. 43 (Fall 1991), which is entirely devoted to judicial review of agency actions.
13. Horowitz, "Courts as Guardians of the Public Interest," 150.
14. Ibid., 150–51.
15. Ibid., 151.
16. Ibid. Also see Charles H. Koch, Jr., "An Issue Driven Strategy For Review of Agency Decisions." Koch does an excellent job in analyzing the impact the new courts' role has had on agency administration.
17. Thomas W. Merrill, "Judicial Deference to Executive Precedent," *Yale Law Journal,* vol. 101 (March 1992), 970. Ironically, in the same year Michael Herz, in "Deference Running Riot," *Administrative Law Journal,* vol. 6 (Summer 1992), 187–233, reached the opposite conclusion, as implied by the title.
18. Kim Morris, "Judicial Review of Non-reviewable Administrative Action: Veteran's Administration Benefit Claims," *Administrative Law Review,* 29 (Winter 1977), 65–86.
19. Bernard Schwartz, *Administrative Law,* 2nd ed. (Boston: Little, Brown, 1984), 455.
20. House Judiciary Committee, in *Administrative Procedure Act: Legislative History* (Washington, D.C.: U.S. Government Printing Office, 1946), 275
21. Some cases consistent with *Abbott Laboratories* in regard to reviewability under the APA include *Airline Dispatchers Assn.* v. *National Mediation Board,* 189 F.2d 685 (D.C.Cir., 1951), *cert. denied,* 342 U.S. 849 (1951); *Association of Data Processing Service Organizations* v. *Camp.* 397 U.S. 159 (1970); *Barlow* v. *Collins,* 397 U.S. 159 (1970); *Tooahnippah* v. *Hickel,* 397 U.S. 598 (1970); *Citizens to Preserve Overton Park* v. *Volpe,* 401 U.S. 402 (1971); *Dunlop* v. *Bachowski,* 421 U.S. 560 (1975); *Chrysler Corp.* v. *Brown,* 441 U.S. 281(1979); and *Bowen* v. *Michigan Academy of Family Physicians,* 106 S.Ct. 2133 (1986). For recent cases not so consistent with *Abbott Laboratories,* see *Lindahl* v. *Office of Personnel Management,* 105 S.Ct. 1620 (1985); *Heckler* v. *Chaney,* 105 S.Ct. 1649 (1985); and *Franklin* v. *Massachusetts,* 112 S.Ct. 2767 (1992).
22. Bernard Schwartz, "Administrative Law Cases During 1993," *Administrative Law Review,* vol. 46 (Summer 1994), 321.
23. For an argument that the court denied standing to avoid "social unrest," see Kenneth F. Warren, "The Housing and Community Development Act: Two Years after Hartford," *Administrative Law Review,* 30 (Fall 1978), 549–60.
24. For example, see *Tennessee Electric Power Co.* v. *TVA,* 306 U.S. 1181 (1937); *Perkins* v. *Lukens Steels Co.,* 310 I,'.S. 113 (1940); *United States* v. *Caltex Philippines, Inc.,* 344 U.S. 149 (1952); and *Kansas City Power and Light Co.* v. *McKay,* 225 F.2d 924, *cert. denied,* 350 U.S. 884 (1955). It should be mentioned that various immunity provisions protect government officials from certain suits—a topic treated in Chapter 10 of this book.
25. The basic argument against granting standing for a generalized taxpayer grievance was upheld in 1974 in *United States* v. *Richardson,* 418 U.S. 166.
26. Regarding this position, see Justice William J. Brennan's concurring opinion in *Simon* v. *Eastern Kentucky Welfare Rights Organization,* 426 U.S. 26 (1976), where he asserts that the application of standing tests is in pathetic confusion (at 64–66). See also Mark V. Tushnet, "The New Law of Standing: A Plea for Abandonment," *Cornell Law Review,* 62 (April 1977), 663–700.

27. Bernard Schwartz, "Administrative Law Cases During 1992," *Administrative Law Review*, vol. 45 (Summer 1993), 269.

28. The first recognized use of the exhaustion doctrine by the Supreme Court was in *Cosmos Exploration Co. v. Gray Eagle Oil Co.*, 190 U.S. 301 (1903).

29. For an insightful critique of *Darby*, see Bernard Schwartz, "Administrative Law Cases During 1993," *Administrative Law Review*, vol. 46 (Summer 1994), 317–321.

30. Bernard Schwartz, *Administrative Law*, 3rd ed. (Boston: Little, Brown and Company, 1991), 563.

31. 7. U.S.C.A., Section 135a(C)(1)(D)(iii).

32. Bernard Schwartz, *Administrative Law*, 3rd ed., 563–564.

33. Curiously, a Colorado ruling contradicted the law established in *Abbott Laboratories* by holding that a general regulation has to be actually enforced against a specific part before it can be considered for review (*Colorado-UTE Electric Ass'n v. Air Pollution Comm'n.*, 591 P.7d 1323 [Colo App., 1978]). This argument, however, was rejected in *Thomas v. Union Carbide Agricultural Products Co.*, 105 S.Ct. 3325 (1985). This reasoning in the Colorado decision was essentially upheld by the U.S. Supreme Court in 1993 in *Reno v. Catholic Social Services*, 113 S.Ct. 2485.

34. Bernard Schwartz, "Administrative Law Cases During 1993," 324.

35. Before the Supreme Court reversed in *John Parisi v. Philip B. Davidson*, 405 U.S. 34 (1972), out of respect for a military proceeding, the two lower courts relied upon comity to create a "distance" between the federal judiciary and the military justice system.

36. Edwin Wallace Tucker, *Administrative Law, Regulation of Enterprise and Individual Liberties* (St. Paul, Minn.: West Publishing Company, 1975), 134.

37. *DiGiovanni v. Camden Fire Insurance Ass'n.*, 296 U.S. 64, 73 (1935).

38. *Beal v. Missouri Pacific Railroad Corp.*, 312 U.S. 45, 50 (1941).

39. Kenneth C. Davis, *Administrative Law*, 78.

40. Schwartz, "Administrative Law Cases During 1979," 435. Also see Stephen Breyer, "Judicial Review of Questions of Law and Policy," *Administrative Law Review*, 38 (Fall 1986), 363–98.

41. For further analysis on *Chevron*, see Cass R. Sunstein, "Law and Administration after *Chevron*," *Columbia Law Review*, vol. 90 (December 1990); Thomas W. Merrill, "Judicial Deference To Executive Precedent," *Yale Law Journal*, vol. 101 (March, 1992); and *ABF Freight System, Inc. v. N.L.R.B.*, 114 S.Ct. 835 (1994).

42. The substantial evidence rule had been recognized long before the 1946 APA. Its lengthy history dates back to at least 1912, when the Supreme Court, in *ICC v. Union Pacific Railroad*, 222 U.S. 541, 548, espoused the rule by maintaining that reviewing courts should "examine the facts . . . to determine whether there was substantial evidence to support the order."

43. Kenneth C. Davis, *Administrative Law*, 80.

44. Ibid., 92.

45. Louis J. Jaffe, "Administrative Procedure Re-examined: The Benjamin Report," *Harvard Law Review*, 56 (March 1943), 732.

46. See *Goldberg v. Kelly*, 397 U.S. 254 (1970).

47. Bernard Schwartz, *Administrative Law*, 4th ed., 864–872.

48. Kenneth C. Davis and Richard J. Pierce, Jr., *Administrative Law Treatise*, 3rd ed., vol. III, 158.

49. In *Chrysler Corp.* v. *Brown,* 441 U.S. 281 (1979), the government argued that *de novo* review should be reserved only for very rare cases. The Court failed to respond to the government's argument, but the position seems sound. *De novo* review should be limited so that stability in and respect for the administrative process can be maintained.
50. Bernard Schwartz, "Administrative Law Cases During 1993," 327.

CHAPTER NINE

SUING THE GOVERNMENT AND ITS ADMINISTRATORS

TORT LIABILITY ISSUES IN A DEMOCRATIC STATE: AN OVERVIEW

Because of the emergence of the administrative state, our entire political system has been affected by efforts to make governmental bureaucracy democratically responsible to the citizenry. The president has created a huge White House staff and extended the informal powers of the presidency in an attempt to keep the administrative system accountable to the national constituency. Congress has also enlarged its staff and created new control mechanisms so that it can retain political control over the administrative machinery. Congress has, in addition, passed major legislation (for example, the APA) in an effort to force public administrators to uphold democratic procedural due process standards. Citizen and consumer organizations have also played a role in checking administrative behavior. Meanwhile, the courts have become more active in recent decades in seeing to it that individual rights, at least in certain areas, are better protected from possible administrative abuses of power. To accomplish this end, the courts have agreed to review a greater variety of administrative law cases, as well as to expand their scope of review in the cases that they do decide to review. Since the 1930s the courts have gradually extended procedural due process protections to persons dealing with administrative agencies. Since the late 1960s the courts have turned many citizen *privileges* into citizen *rights,* thus providing individuals with a considerably stronger position than they have heretofore had from which to challenge agency actions toward them. The courts made judicial review of agency actions toward individuals much more available by liberalizing the standing prerequisites. However, possibly the most significant development occurred during the 1970s when Congress, with the approval of the courts, took from public officials many of the official immunity protections which for so long had made it virtually impossible for citizens to sue public agencies and their officials for grossly irresponsible and malicious conduct. Under present law, it is considerably easier for individuals to sue public administrators for damages caused by "reckless" administrative actions. But is this necessarily a good thing? Can our public administrators function efficiently and effectively as policy implementors if they must always contend with the possibility that they may be found personally liable for their administrative acts? In the implementation of public policies, is it not a given that some citizens will benefit, while others will be hurt?[1] This is a reality because governmental administrators are largely responsible for allocating the state's scarce resources. Some will always claim that the pie was divided in a manner which has seriously hurt their interests—so much so that they may be motivated to sue the administrators who caused them injury. Of course, others will want to sue administrators or the government for damages because they believe administrators have wrongfully denied them due process rights, statutory entitlements, or mistreated them in other ways.

On the other hand, is it right for a democratic state to employ official immunity to protect administrators from being held responsible for blatantly negligent, exploitative, or malicious actions which cause great harm to individuals or organizations? Should not governmental administrators be held reasonably accountable for their actions? Do not immunity protections tend to encourage irresponsible administrative behavior by eliminating the possibility of damage suits, despite how reckless and harmful the administration may have been? Given the pervasive role administrative power plays in our lives today, would it be in the best interests of ordered liberty to immunize the government and its administrators from liability claims? The central purpose of this chapter is to explore some of the major issues raised by these questions, while examining the specific rights individuals apparently have when they decide to bring tort liability claims against the government or its officers.

THE SOVEREIGN IMMUNITY DOCTRINE

What is the sovereign immunity doctrine, what are its origins, how has it been applied, what are its pros and cons, and why has the doctrine survived so long in American history? The *sovereign immunity doctrine* holds that the government is sovereign and, therefore, cannot be held liable for its actions. More specifically, the doctrine makes it impossible for parties to sue the government for civil damages unless the government permits the suit. The government can permit suits by passing legislation which allows claims to be made against the government under certain conditions. For example, the Tucker Act of 1855 (28 U.S.C.A., Sec. 1331) confers jurisdiction on U.S. district courts to hear claims against the United States involving contracts (*United States* v. *Mitchell,* 463 U.S. 206; 1983; and *Spectrum Leasing Corp.* v. *United States,* 764 F.2d 891; 1985), the Federal Tort Claims Act of 1946 (60 Stat. 842) allows persons under certain circumstances to sue the United States government for tortious acts committed against them by its officials (*Dalehite* v. *United*

States, 346 U.S. 15; 1953; *United States* v. *Varig Airlines,* 104 S.Ct. 2755; 1984; and *Barrett* v. *United States,* 845 F.Supp. 774; 1994), while Section 702 of the APA, as amended in 1988, permits the federal government to be sued for non-money damages in injunctive and mandamus actions. Overall, about forty statutes allow the federal government to be sued for tortious acts under specific circumstances, although only one, the Federal Torts Claims Act of 1946, as amended, has general applicability. But what makes the government sovereign is the very fact that no party can sue unless the government allows the suit. As the Supreme Court made clear in *Federal Deposit Insurance Corp.* v. *Meyer,* 114 S.Ct. 996, 1000 (1994), the government still enjoys Sovereign immunity because "[A]bsent a waiver, sovereign immunity shields the Federal Government and its agencies from suit. . . . sovereign immunity is jurisdictional in nature. Indeed, the 'terms of (the United States) consent to be sued in any court define that court's jurisdiction to entertain the suit.'"

From one perspective the sovereign immunity doctrine is "dead" because the federal government has waived its absolute sovereign immunity status, allowing suits against the government under restrictive circumstances. However, from another perspective the sovereign immunity doctrine is still very much alive because in most cases the government still has not allowed itself to be sued, and when it does, the kind of tort suit that can be filed is very limited, normally forbidding or placing caps on money damages and totally prohibiting punitive damage awards. In fact, Harold J. Krent asserted in a recent article that ". . . many have noted that sovereign immunity was never applied as comprehensively in the past as it is today."[2]

The sovereign immunity doctrine has been heavily relied upon by the courts for more than two centuries to stop liability suits against the United States government and its state governments. Ironically, however, the use of this doctrine has never been formally sanctioned by our lawmakers.[3] The sovereign immunity doctrine is deeply rooted in America's Anglo-Saxon legal heritage, and it was evidently just assumed that the doctrine should become part of our legal system. The mysterious emergence of the application of the doctrine was recognized by a California court: "How it became in the United States the basis for a rule that the federal and state governments did not have to answer for their torts has been called 'one of the mysteries of legal evolution.'"[4] This mystery has been acknowledged for a long time. About a hundred years ago, in *U.S.* v. *Lee,* 106 U.S. 196, 207 (1882), the Supreme Court acknowledged that "while the exemption of the United States and of several states from being subjected as defendants to ordinary actions in the courts has . . . repeatedly been asserted here, *the principle has never been discussed or the reasons for it given, but it has always been treated as an established doctrine*" (my emphasis).

Although the evolution of the sovereign immunity doctrine in American law may be perplexing, the doctrine's historical origins are very clear. As noted, the doctrine is entrenched in our Anglo-Saxon heritage. Actually, it was one of the most fundamental doctrines on which old Anglo-Saxon law was based. Specifically, the sovereign immunity doctrine rests on the medieval argument that the king (the British monarch) is sovereign and, therefore, incapable of wrongdoing. But what seems baffling to most scholars is that, although the king-can-do-no-wrong argument may have made sense for a monarchical governmental system, in which the king reigns above the law, it appears to make little-to-no sense for a constitutional political system based on the rule of law. Under a rule-of-law system, of course, no one is supposed to stand above the law. Therefore, it was argued, how could a doctrine be employed in American government—a rule-of-law political system—to place governmental officials (for example, public administrators) above the law? Surely, if public officials cannot be sued for their tortious acts because they are protected by the sovereign immunity doctrine, while others in the private sector can be sued because they are not protected by any such doctrine, the doctrine in effect places these governmental officials above the law.[5]

It should be pointed out that, technically speaking, the sovereign immunity doctrine does not necessarily protect governmental officials from tort liability suits, but only the government. Under common law doctrine, individual public officials could be sued for their tortious acts while functioning as governmental employees. However, for the most part the sovereign immunity doctrine has also been applied in such a way as to provide absolute immunity protections to individual public officials. That is, the courts have until very recently argued that governmental officers performing within their official line of duty shall be granted extensive immunity privileges, if not absolute immunity, so that they will not be vulnerable to liability suits when their official actions may have caused someone harm. For example, in *Barr* v. *Matteo,* 360 U.S. 564, 571, (1959), the Supreme Court held that public officials should have the luxury of being "free to exercise their duties unembarrassed by the fear of damage suits in respect of acts done in the course of those duties."

Bernard Schwartz is opposed to any governmental immunity system which unfairly and unreasonably prevents those hurt by the government or its officers from being able to sue for justifiable damage claims.[6] Kenneth C. Davis agrees, contending that blanket or sovereign immunity protections are patently unjust. He cites the *Lee* case, where the Court explained: "Courts of justice are established, not only to decide upon controverted rights of the citizens as against each other, but also upon rights in controversy between them and the government."[7] But Davis contends that under the sovereign immunity doctrine "the courts are barred from finding facts and applying the law; unless some other tribunal is available, the parties have no means of settling their controversy except by resort to force." He notes further: "When the government is one of the parties, it always prevails because it is always stronger; no private party has an army, navy, and air force."[8]

Davis is also convinced that the sovereign immunity doctrine is un-American and defies plain common sense. For this reason, it had to be abandoned.[9] What sense, he argued, does it make in a modern rule-of-law nation such as the United States for private persons to be subject to liability claims for recklessly running down a person on the street, while the driver of the governmental vehicle is not liable for the same act?

Davis' indictment of the sovereign immunity doctrine is harsh, yet clearly some reasonable arguments to justify the existence of the sovereign immunity doctrine must exist, especially since the doctrine has survived into the 1990s, even given some immunity waivers sanctioned by Congress.

Of course, the traditional arguments in support of the sovereign immunity doctrine are based upon the contention that it is potentially very dangerous to allow persons to sue the government for damages that it might cause because, conceivably, suits brought by enough parties could literally bankrupt and, therefore, destroy the government. For example, if a United States Air Force pilot mistakenly dropped a nuclear bomb on Boston and completely devastated the metropolitan area, should all survivors and their families, businesses, and so on, be given the opportunity to sue the federal government for damages? The humane response might be yes, but the practical response would be no.[10] Actually, the sovereign immunity doctrine has rarely been defended for any reasons other than practical ones. It has probably never been defended on the grounds that it is fair to individuals. Clearly, it is not because the doctrine in fact sanctions individual suffering so that the general public will not suffer. In the imagined Boston tragedy, because liability claims against the federal government would undoubtedly bankrupt and destroy it, the practically minded would contend that the suits should not be allowed. That is, the government should protect itself and the general public against the possibility that the government could be destroyed by massive suits by invoking the doctrine of sovereign immunity. According to supporters of the doctrine, this governmental action would be justified in the reasoning that it is far better for one or a few to suffer than for society as a whole to suffer.

During the heyday of the sovereign immunity doctrine, Justice Oliver Wendell Holmes, speaking for a unanimous court in *Kawananakoa* v. *Polyfolank,* 205 U.S. 349, 353 (1907), employed traditional logic to defend the doctrine when he explained: "A sovereign is exempt from suit, not because of any formal conception or obsolete theory, but on the logical and practical ground that there can be no legal right as against the authority that makes the law on which the right depends."

Few today believe that the government should remain totally immune from liability suits. The present perspective on sovereign immunity is epitomized by Justice Traynor's conclusion in *Muskopf* v. *Corning Hospital District,* 56 Cal. 2d 211 (1961): "After a re-evaluation of the rule of governmental immunity from tort liability we have concluded that it must be discarded as mistaken and unjust." But Kenneth C. Davis feels that the Supreme Court had made this point about a century ago in *Lee.* In reflecting on how long it has taken for the wisdom in *Lee* to become accepted as law in America as a consequence of Congress's amendments to the APA in 1976, which made the administrative state vulnerable to some kinds of tort liability suits, Davis remarked, "How strange that the Court's 1882 statement never did become clear law until 1976."[11]

The death of an absolute application of the sovereign immunity doctrine was not unexpected. Since the 1930s social reformers had been pushing to advance the rights of individuals in many areas, but particularly against the administrative state. How could the sovereign immunity doctrine survive without waivers in a new liberal social atmosphere that demanded that individuals be accorded due process protection? Surely, by the 1970s few believed that due process did not include the right of individuals to sue governmental agencies for their tortious acts, especially since it is generally recognized that the government is in a much better position to absorb losses than are individual parties. Nevertheless, the sovereign immunity doctrine still lives on in most areas, preventing injured parties in particular from being fairly compensated monetarily for tortious actions against them. Statutes are carefully written to allow only certain liability suits, but they generally preclude major liability claims against the government. Defenders of sovereign immunity argue that such statutory restrictions to liability claims against the government are absolutely necessary to guarantee our government's stability and survival. In the past few decades many states have followed the federal example by amending their sovereign immunity statutes to permit limited damage suits, yet states have also protected their survival by placing strict limitations upon liability suits, limiting financial awards and moving toward ". . . what amounts to a governmental-operated system of mutual insurance for those damaged by administrative action"[12] (discussed later).

SUING GOVERNMENTAL ADMINISTRATORS: THE ROAD TOWARD QUALIFIED IMMUNITY FOR ADMINISTRATORS

Governmental immunity and official (officer) immunity do not mean exactly the same thing. While *governmental immunity* immunizes the government (for example, public agencies) from tort liability suits because of its actions, *official immunity* immunizes the government's officers from liability claims against them because of their actions. But it seems that the courts have always had a rather difficult time making a practical and functional distinction between the two. In fact, some courts have ruled that governmental and official immunity cannot be distinguished in meaningful substantive terms. In *Larson v. Domestic and Foreign Commerce Corp.*, 337 U.S. 682 (1949), the Court ruled essentially that suits against governmental officers should be disallowed in most cases because they are protected by the government's sovereign immunity status. The Court reasoned that a suit against a government's officer was "in substance, a suit against the Government over which the court, in the absence of consent, has no jurisdiction" (at 688). This judicial opinion set the tone for many other court decisions, thus making it well-nigh impossible for persons to sue either the government or its officers in tort suits.

In an insightful article on the subject of governmental and official immunity in 1963, Louis Jaffe also concluded that "the officer's immunity is the government's immunity as well. . . ."[13] Not unexpectedly, however, when some courts began to challenge the validity and fairness of immunity protections in American government, they chipped away at both governmental immunity and official immunity at the same time because of the close relationship between governmental and official immunity. As a result, today the government enjoys only *limited* immunity, while virtually all government officers enjoy only *qualified* immunity. *Limited immunity* for the government means essentially that the government in general is protected under sovereign immunity, yet the government's immunity is limited because limited tort liability actions against the government, as authorized by statute, are permitted.[14] *Qualified immunity* for public officials means their immunity protections are not absolute, thus making some of their actions (for example, malicious acts not authorized by statutes) vulnerable to damage claims against them as individuals.[15]

Before the modern qualified immunity doctrine emerged into a position of dominance, the more traditional doctrine of official immunity emerged to dominate American administrative and constitutional law. What justifications were given to justify granting official immunity (virtually absolute immunity) to governmental administrators?

The development of the qualified immunity position for public administrators did not follow an even and clear path. To understand the development of the qualified immunity perspective, it is helpful to divide its development into roughly three stages. These stages convey that initially administrators enjoyed virtually no immunity. Then a trend started which eventually made administrators immune to tort suits. Finally a reaction to the almost absolute immunity status obtained by administrators stimulated liberal reformers to demand that official immunity should be qualified.

Immunity under Common Law

Under Anglo-Saxon common law, public officials were extended no immunity privileges simply because they worked for the government. The reason for this is rooted deeply in our democratic heritage. According to democratic theory, civil servants are perceived to be *ordinary* citizens who are taking their turn serving their government. Because they are still regarded as ordinary citizens under the rule of law, it was held that they should not be entitled to special immunity privileges different from those of any other citizens. Bernard Schwartz explains the common law logic: "If public officers are not vested with immunity greater than that of ordinary citizens, it follows that they can be sued for the damages caused by their acts, just as a private individual can be, even if the acts were performed in the course of their official work."[16] According to the great British legal scholar, A.V. Dicey, the prohibition against immunity for public servants is entrenched in the concept of legal equality under law, a concept which he noted had been implemented in Britain: "With us every official, from the Prime Minister down to a constable or a collector of taxes, is under the same responsibility for every act done without legal justification as any other citizen."[17]

It should be stressed that under common law public administrators are immune as long as the damaging act was *within their statutory authority.* But which official acts are clearly within the administrator's statutory authority is a subject frequently open to debate, creating a very uncomfortable position for public administrators who must interpret and apply statutes. If they act beyond their statutory authority and cause harm, they may have to fight a damage suit. The famous state case of *Miller* v. *Horton,* 26 N.E. 100 (Mass., 1891), conveys the message that under common law doctrine even public officials are very vulnerable if they harm anyone through a mistaken application of the law, even if they acted in good faith. In this case, health officers killed a horse which they thought had glanders, a contagious disease the health officers were authorized to combat by destroying all animals infected with it. However, later it was discovered that the horse did not have glanders. The owner of the horse sued for damages, contending that the health officers were authorized to destroy only diseased animals. The court ruled that the officers were in fact personally liable for their actions because they had acted beyond their lawful jurisdiction. In sum, under common law, the government had sovereign immunity, but its officers were not protected from being sued for their tortious acts.

Toward Absolute Official Immunity

The realization by the courts that public officials were placed in a very precarious and probably unfair position under common law doctrine led judges gradually to abandon it so that they could provide governmental officers with reasonable immunity protections from liability suits. It also became clear to the courts that administrators could not perform their duties effectively if they had to worry constantly about the possibility of being sued for any injuries they might cause to persons while implementing the laws.

The *Spalding* Case Breaks Ground   To justify granting administrators immunities, the courts began to reason that just as judges need to be free from threatening liability suits to perform their jobs properly, so do administrators. In a precedential case, *Spalding* v. *Vilas,* 161 U.S. 483, 498 (1896), the Court held that "the same general considerations of public policy and convenience which demand for judges of courts of superior jurisdiction immunity from civil suits for damages arising from acts done by them in the course of the performance of their judicial functions, apply to a large extent to official communications made by heads of executive departments when engaged in the discharge of duties imposed upon them by law. The interests of the people require that due protection be accorded to them in respect of their official acts." More specifically, in regard to a postmaster general facing damage action, the Court commented: "In exercising the functions of his office, the head of an executive department, keeping within the limits of his authority, should not be under an apprehension that the motives that control his official conduct may at any time become the subject of inquiry in a civil suit for damages. It would seriously cripple the proper and effective administration of public affairs as entrusted to the executive branch of the government, if he were subjected to any such restraint" (at 498).

The *Spalding* case is significant for starting the trend toward granting official immunity to governmental officers. In particular, the Court in *Spalding* acknowledged that discretion does play a necessary role in policy implementation and that at least high-ranking administrators should not hesitate to use discretion because they fear that they may be sued for their discretionary decisions within their statutory jurisdiction. The *Spalding* case is also important for the Court's opinion that top administrators (for example, department heads) should be protected from tort suits against them, regardless of the *motives* that inspired their actions or whether their conduct was malicious: "The motive that impelled him to do that . . . is therefore wholly immaterial. If we were to hold that the demurrer admitted, for the purposes of the trial, that the defendant acted maliciously, that could not change the law" (at 499). In so ruling, the Court in effect sanctioned the immunization of public officials from damage suits, even if they decide to act maliciously and in bad faith toward individuals with the intention of harming them. The *Spalding* case raised an interesting question: Can intentional malicious treatment of persons by administrators in bad faith ever be considered action within their proper statutory authority?

David Rosenbloom contends that the Court's logic in *Spalding* became more open to question as the modern administrative state emerged. Rosenbloom considers that the decision in *Spalding* to allow top-level administrators to have virtually total immunity "underestimates the harm that might be done by administrative officials in a day and age when the penetration by government of the life of the society is so intense." He maintains that, surely, given the great powers of administrators today, "at the very least, the citizen needs some protection against a public official such as a department head who is acting in *bad* faith." But Rosenbloom also believes that the *Spalding* Court failed to understand where the power actually resides in public bureaucracy. That is, in *Spalding* the Court implied that real decision-making power lies at the top of the administrative hierarchy. To make decisions effectively, the Court reasoned, top-level administrators must be permitted to make executive decisions free from the worry that they could be held personally liable for damages caused by their decisions. However, Rosenbloom acknowledges that most scholars maintain the middle-range administrators make the most crucial decisions affecting persons: "Consequently, if one is concerned that civil suits 'would seriously cripple the proper and effective administration of public affairs as entrusted to the executive branch,' then some provisions for immunity for lower ranking administrators would be necessary."[18]

A Giant Step toward Granting Absolute Immunity to Public Officers: *Barr* v. *Matteo*   The courts after *Spalding* did in fact move toward making official immunity more comprehensive. In 1938, in *Cooper* v. *O'Connor, 99* F.2d 135 (D.C.Cir.), the court argued that all administrators performing quasi-judicial functions should be given the same immunity protections enjoyed by judges. This is necessary, the court reasoned, because such administrators are entrusted with settling disputes based upon questions pertaining to private rights and obligations.[19]

But it was in *Barr* v. *Matteo*, 360 U.S. 564 (1959), that the Supreme Court took a giant step in extending absolute immunity to virtually all administrative officials. The case stems from a libel suit filed against Barr, an acting director of the Federal Office of Rent Stabilization, for making public through a press release allegedly libelous remarks about two subordinates. Speaking for the divided Court, Justice John Harlan asserted that the Court had been called upon to consider two questions "of high importance which now and again come into sharp conflict—on the one hand, the protection of the individual citizen against pecuniary damage caused by oppressive or malicious action on the part of the officials of the Federal Government; and on the other, the protection of the public interest by shielding responsible governmental officers against the harassment and inevitable hazards of vindictive or ill-founded damage suits brought on account of action taken in the exercise of their official responsibilities" (at 565).

The *Barr* case is especially known for the Court's strong, and seemingly extreme, arguments in defense of a public administrator's right to absolute official immunity. The Court's basic argument throughout was rooted in the belief that absolute immunity protections for administrators are in the public interest. Specifically, Harlan acknowledged the validity of the old argument in support of official immunity that governmental administrators must be able to exercise their administrative duties free from the threat of damage suits. According to the Court, such suits "would consume time and energies which would otherwise be devoted to governmental service and the threat of which might appreciably inhibit the fearless, vigorous, and effective administration of policies of government" (at 571). Drawing from previous court decisions, especially *Gregoire* v. *Biddle,* 177 F.2d 579 (2d Cir., 1948), Harlan presented a utilitarian argument to substantiate the Court's conclusion that absolute immunity privileges should be extended to virtually all public officials during the performance of what can reasonably be considered their official duties: "To be sure, as with any rule of law which attempts to reconcile fundamentally antagonistic social policies, there may be occasional instances of actual injustice which will go unredressed, but we think that price a necessary one to pay for the greater good" (at 576).

It had been argued that the Court in *Barr* was insensitive to the argument that absolute official immunity protections could "open the door to wholesale oppression and abuses on the part of unscrupulous government officials" (at 576). Harlan asserted that this was a greatly exaggerated and unsubstantiated claim: "It is perhaps enough to say that fears of this sort have not been realized within the wide area of government where a judicially formulated absolute privilege of broad scope has long existed. It seems to us wholly chimerical to suggest that what hangs in the balance here is the maintenance of high standards of conduct among those in the public service" (at 576).

And finally, the *Barr* decision was instrumental in making it far easier for almost all public administrators to hide under the cloak of official immunity as long as their acts could be justified as barely within the scope of their official discretionary authority. Building upon *Spalding,* the Court reasoned: "The fact that the action here taken was within the outer perimeter of petitioner's line of duty is enough to render the privilege applicable, despite the allegations of malice" (at 575).

The *Barr* case was highlighted here because its reach was so extensive. In dissenting in *Barr,* Justice William J. Brennan argued that the Court had gone too far in extending absolute immunity privileges to virtually all officials in the federal administrative system. After the *Barr* ruling, federal courts did find it appropriate to apply *Barr* to even relatively low-ranking federal officers.

In *Carter* v. *Carlson,* 447 F.2d 358, 361 (D.C.Cir.; 1971), the court held that a public administrator "is protected by the doctrine of official immunity if the alleged tort was committed in the performance of a 'discretionary' rather than a 'ministerial' function." A *ministerial act* is a straight-line function in which no discretion is involved; rather, orders are only being carried out. However, this distinction has been criticized severely by judges and scholarly critics as too difficult to apply, since it is virtually impossible in practice to make a distinction between "discretionary" and "ministerial" functions. As noted in Chapter 7, Kenneth C. Davis argues that all governmental officials exercise discretion. Thus, by extending official immunity to all governmental officials who exercise discretion, the *Carter* holding, in the spirit of

Barr, in effect extends official immunity privileges to all governmental administrators. Can you think of any administrator who employs absolutely no administrative discretion in his or her work? If a public official were sued for damages, can you imagine a situation in which the defense attorney could not convince the court that his or her client, as a public official, exercises some administrative discretion? Clearly, any administrator could use discretionary powers to harm citizens.

In sum, the *Spalding-Barr* rationale served to immunize too many administrative actions, thus tipping the delicate balance between the needs of the administrative state and the needs of the citizenry too much in the favor of the former. Under the *Spalding-Barr* rule, David Rosenbloom noted, citizens had no opportunity to recover damages in court for harm done them by even the most malicious administrators. For all practical purposes, he maintained, the application of *Spalding-Barr* makes it impossible for citizens to hold administrators directly accountable for their actions. In short, under *Spalding-Barr,* "the needs of the administrative state for smooth operation are placed above protections for the citizenry."[20] Because abuses of administrative power were bound to increase under this immunity system, Rosenbloom concluded that "it was only a matter of time before the Supreme Court would have to readdress the concept of *absolute* immunity."[21]

Courts Reverse Direction and Adopt Qualified Immunity Standard: *Bivens* and After

Virtually every administrative law textbook author cites *Bivens* v. *Six Unknown Fed. Narcotics Agents,* 403 U.S. 388 (1971), as a case which played a major role in eroding the doctrine of absolute immunity and establishing the qualified immunity doctrine. This is because the Court in *Bivens* made it very clear that the judicial doors are always open to those who are victims of flagrant and unconstitutional abuses of administrative power. As Justice John Harlan stated in his strongly worded concurring opinion, judicial remedies should be made available when administrative actions are clearly unjustified and abusive: "Although litigants may not often choose to seek relief, it is important, in a civilized society, that the judicial branch of the Nation's government stand ready to afford a remedy in these circumstances" (at 411).

These particular circumstances involved a situation in which federal narcotics officers broke into the plaintiff's home at 6:30 A.M. without a search warrant and in the absence of probable cause. The narcotics agents handcuffed Bivens, searched his premises, employed excessive force, threatened to arrest his family, subjected him to a visual strip search in the federal courthouse, fingerprinted, photographed, interrogated, and booked him. When Bivens was brought before a United States Commissioner, however, charges against him were dismissed. Bivens filed against each of the narcotics officers for $15,000 in damages on the grounds that he had "suffered great humiliation, embarrassment, and mental suffering as a result of the agents' unlawful conduct" (at 389–90). The high Court had to decide whether violation of the Fourth Amendment "by a federal agent acting under color of his authority gives rise to a cause of action for damages consequent upon his constitutional conduct" (at 389).[22]

The Court majority reached a quick decision: "we hold that petitioner is entitled to recover money damages for any injuries he has suffered as a result of the agents' violation of the Amendment" (at 397).

The Court justified its decision in the logic espoused in the classic case, *Marbury* v. *Madison*, 1 Cranch 137, 163 (1803), where the Court explained: "The very essence of civil liberty certainly consists in the right of every individual to claim the protection of the laws, whenever he receives an injury." The Court also made clear that "federal courts may use any available remedy to make good the wrong done" (at 396). An important aspect of the *Bivens* case was the Court's rejection of the argument by the respondents that claim against the narcotics officers should be treated no differently than a civil action between two private parties in state court. But Justice William J. Brennan, speaking for the majority, contended that such a perspective underestimates the potentially destructive powers of modern administrators. Respondents "ignore the fact that power, once granted, does not disappear like a magic gift when it is wrongfully used. An agent acting—albeit unconstitutionally—in the name of the United States possesses a far greater capacity for harm than an individual trespasser exercising no authority other than his own" (at 392).

The Supreme Court in *Bivens* expressed only that the actions of the narcotics officers were appalling and that, under the circumstances, the damage suit was appropriate and the federal courts could provide relief by ordering money damages to be paid to Bivens to compensate for his injuries (the denial of Fourth Amendment protections by the narcotics agents). The Court did not decide whether the federal narcotics officers were immune from a liability suit because of their official government position. This question was remanded to the Second Circuit Court of Appeals.

On remand, the court found in *Bivens* v. *Six Unknown Named Agents*, 456 F.2d 1339 (1972), that these agents were not immune from tort action against them, rejecting the agents' argument that they were engaged in discretionary actions protected by official immunity. Specifically, the appeals court did maintain that governmental officials should be protected by the official immunity doctrine, as established in *Barr*, when they are engaged in discretionary actions "within the outer perimeter of [their] line of duty" (at 1345). However, in this case the court did not believe that the actions of the narcotics officers could even be considered within that outer perimeter, despite the fact that the court also found the discretionary test not very helpful in legitimately distinguishing discretionary from nondiscretionary acts in most cases. Thus, the court held that the narcotics agents were not entitled to absolute official immunity "because we do not agree that the Agents were alleged to be engaged in the performance of the sort of 'discretionary' acts that require the protection of immunity" (at 1343). Further, the court remarked: "It would be a sorry state of affairs if an officer had the 'discretion' to enter a dwelling at 6:30 a.m., without a warrant or probable cause, and make an arrest by employing unreasonable force" (at 1346). In other words, the court emphasized that federal officers are not entitled to immunity protections in all situations, especially when a damage suit is filed "based upon allegations of violations of constitutional rights" (at 1347). In so ruling, the appeals court established a qualified immunity standard based on circumstances. A dozen years later in *Davis* v. *Scherer,* 104 S.Ct. 3012 (1984), the Supreme Court interpreted certain "circumstances" to uphold qualified immunity protections for state officials.

The significance of the Court's action in *Bivens* should not be underestimated, because here the Court, playing a very activist role, radically changed the course of tort law involving public officials by holding that federal agents could be held liable for damages if their actions deprived persons of their constitutional rights even in the absence of federal statutes authorizing such remedies. Drawing from *Bivens* and other cases,[23] the Supreme Court in 1983 said emphatically: "the federal courts' power to grant relief not expressly authorized by Congress is firmly established" (*Bush* v. *Lucas,* 462 U.S. 367, 374).

Would future courts honor the *Bivens* ruling? They have done so. Actually, the qualified immunity doctrine since *Bivens* has been generally honored by the courts in an effort to provide persons with protections against flagrant abuses of administrative power by public officials insensitive to the constitutional rights of citizens. However, as we shall see, the courts have placed certain restrictions on the *Bivens* remedy, making it somewhat more difficult for plaintiffs to use the *Bivens* action successfully. In *Wood* v. *Strickland,* 420 U.S. 308 (1975), and *Harlow* v. *Fitzgerald,* 457 U.S. 800 (1982), the Supreme Court held that public officials were not immune to damage suits under *Bivens,* but plaintiffs had to prove to win a *Bivens* action that such officials "knew or reasonably should have known" that their actions violated established constitutional rights. *Davis* v. *Scherer,* 104 S.Ct. 3012 (1984), also granted only qualified immunity to public officials, but the Supreme Court made it even more difficult to win using the *Bivens* remedy by ruling that petitioners had to prove that at the time any governmental officer "violated" a person's constitutional rights that the right(s) had to have been "clearly established." The Supreme Court upheld *Scherer* in *Siegert* v. *Gilley,* 111 S.Ct. 1789 (1991), where Chief Justice Rehnquist, speaking for the majority, ruled that a former government employee could not pursue a *Bivens* claim against his former supervisor because he had failed to show that any "clearly established constitutional right" had been violated by his former supervisor, thus failing to satisfy the basic threshold test for a qualified immunity challenge. In *Schweiker* v. *Chilicky,* 487 U.S. 412 (1988), the high Court held that a *Bivens* suit cannot be brought when the government has provided adequate alternative remedies within the administration of the governmental program even if, as in this particular case, administrative wrongs led to the unconstitutional denial of benefits.

Applying Provision 1983   The concept of qualified immunity was upheld by the Supreme Court in *Scheuer* v. *Rhodes,* 416 U.S. 232 (1974). In one of the most publicized cases of the 1970s, the petitioners, who represented three students who had been killed by Ohio National Guard troops at Kent State University as they may have protested U.S. involvement in Vietnam, sued Governor James Rhodes of Ohio and others for money damages. The liability suit was predicated on 42 U.S. Code 1983, a provision incorporated into the Civil Rights Act of 1871. The provision states: "Every person who, under color of any statute, ordinance, regulation, custom, usage, or any State or Territory, subjects, or causes to be subjected, any citizen of the United States or other person within the jurisdiction thereof to the deprivation of any rights, privileges, or immunities secured by the Constitution and laws, shall be liable to the party injured in an action at law, suit in equity, or other proper proceeding for redress."[24]

Reversing two lower court rulings, Justice Warren Burger, writing the Court's opinion, argued that qualified immunity should be made available to governmental officials, but only in "varying scope." The variation, he continued, should be "dependent upon the scope of discretion and responsibilities of the office and all the circumstances as they reasonably appeared at the time of the action on which liability is sought to be based" (at 247). The Court concluded that granting qualified immunity to administrative officials depends on whether they can show that they acted *reasonably* under the circumstances and in *good faith* (at 248).

The Court in *Davis* v. *Scherer,* 105 S.Ct. 26 (1984), (noted before and discussed more fully in the next section), handed down a decision that would make it more difficult for plaintiffs to win Section 1983 litigations. To reiterate, in *Scherer* the Court ruled that to win a damage suit under Section 1983, the plaintiff would have to prove that the constitutional and/or statutory rights supposedly violated by public officials were *clearly established* at the time the violations took place. This "clearly established" threshold test or standard for pursuing a Section 1983 suit has proved to be a rather difficult legal obstacle for many petitioners to overcome (*Hunter* v. *Bryant,* 112 S.Ct. 534; 1991 and *Siegert* v. *Gilley,* op. cit.).

Section 1983 damage suits have been filed against public officials at such an accelerated pace since the early 1970s that strategies (some very questionable ethically) have been adopted by public officials to stop these suits. In an unusual Section 1983 case, *Town of Newton* v. *Rumery,* 107 S.Ct. 1187 (1987), the Supreme Court for the first time ruled on whether a prosecutor could enter into a "release-dismissal" agreement, in which the prosecutor would agree to drop charges against a person (even if the charges were very weak, as it appeared in this case) if the person would agree not to file a damage action suit against the city and its officials under Section 1983. (In this case, police misconduct was alleged; the prosecutor has absolute immunity.) A very divided Supreme Court upheld the "release-dismissal" agreement on the grounds that it was entered into voluntarily, deliberately, and in an informed manner. In addition, the plurality argued, the "enforcement of this agreement would not adversely affect the relevant public interest" (at 1195). However, the four dissenting justices (Stevens, Brennan, Marshall, and Blackmun) vehemently objected to the plurality's opinion. Speaking for the dissenters, Justice Stevens premised his argument on the contention that no completely innocent persons accused of a crime should "be required to choose between a threatened indictment and trial . . . and surrendering the right to a civil remedy against individuals who have violated his or her constitutional rights" (at 1198).

Recent Section 1983 Issues   Recently, the courts have been addressing other new issues in Section 1983 liability suits. One interesting Section 1983 question that has developed deals with whether qualified immunity claims under Section 1983 can be filed against private parties representing or acting in behalf of the government under statutory authorization. The trend toward "privatization" (i.e., the government's contracting out all kinds of services to private companies, e.g., a private management firm hired by Housing and Urban Development to manage a HUD housing project) since the beginning of President Reagan's administration has made the liability of such private parties a problematic legal question. Should these private parties, performing quasi-governmental functions, be entitled to qualified immunity protections, as government employees, in the face of Section 1983 damage actions against them?

The question has yet to be answered in any definitive way. In 1982 in *Lugar* v. *Edmondson Oil Company,* 457 U.S. 922, the Supreme Court held that private parties can be said to engage in "state action" through "attachment statutes" if their actions can be "fairly attributable to the state" (at 937), but the court failed to address the issue of whether private parties should enjoy qualified immunity in Section 1983 suits.

In 1992 in *Wyatt* v. *Cole,* 112 S.Ct. 1827, a divided Supreme Court addressed this private-party immunity issue, but not very well. In *Wyatt* the Court refused to extend qualified immunity protections to private parties in Section 1983 suits charged with violating a person's constitutional right(s) when engaged in state action or in the performance of quasi-governmental functions. The Court rooted its decision in revised common law reasoning that advanced the notion that immunity should be granted to public officials to protect them from lawsuits so they can vigorously administer public policies in the public interest without worrying about being sued for possible tortious actions. The Court argued that under common law the interest to protect public officials was not applicable to private parties.

Critics reacted immediately, charging that the *Wyatt* decision unfairly leaves private parties engaged in quasi-public activities sanctioned by statutes unprotected and very exposed to potentially devastating Section 1983 damage suits. As Scott C. Arakaki and Robert E. Badger, Jr. exclaim: "By refusing to extend qualified immunity to private defendants, Wyatt increases litigation costs for private parties who are unaware that the statutes upon which they rely will later be declared unconstitutional. The Supreme Court has long recognized that litigation costs present a significant public policy concern."[25] In sum, it is safe to say that the *Lugar* and *Wyatt* decisions have not successfully resolved the private-party liability question and have in fact caused confusion and division in the courts of appeals.[26]

In light of the relentless stream of Section 1983 suits, the courts have also been trying to answer some crucial questions pertaining to punitive damage awards. It is true that Section 1983 may provide parties with their only real chance for recovering punitive damages for having their constitutional rights violated by governmental officials or their "agents" (*Carlson* v. *Green,* 446 U.S. 14; 1980), yet key questions remain: What standards should be applied when awarding punitive damages? When are punitive damages excessive? What are the actual purposes of awarding punitive damages?[27]

In *Larez* v. *Los Angeles,* 946 F.2d 630 (9th Cir. 1991), an excessive police force case, the circuit court held that punitive damages may be awarded against the Police

Commissioners even in the absence of actual malice as long as evidence has shown reckless or callous indifference toward the plaintiff. In *TXO Production Corp.* v. *Alliance Resources Corp.,* 113 S.Ct. 2711 (1993), the Supreme Court argued that due process does impose caps on punitive damage awards, but the amount that can be awarded can be limited only by the arbitrary "reasonableness" standard. Frequently, courts have held that punitive damages should be linked to a defendant's net worth (which might be substantial if the public official is indemnified by, say, a municipality) and to the need to punish and deter such unconstitutional behavior. Normally, courts have argued that the chief purpose of Section 1983 punitive damage awards is to punish past unconstitutional behavior and to deter future unconstitutional conduct.

In the Rodney King case, *King* v. *Marci,* 993 F.2d 294 (2nd Cir. 1993), one of the most publicized cases in American legal history, the trial court, as well as the Second Circuit Court of Appeals, accepted King's attorney's summation argument before the jury when he was trying to convince the jury to award punitive damages. King's counsel argued that in light of the brutal beating of Rodney King, his false arrest, and malicious prosecution, punitive damages should be awarded so that the defendant and others in the future ". . . will no longer think they're above the law, so that they won't be arrogant and think they can do whatever they want, so that they won't think that because they have a badge and they have a uniform they can violate people's rights" and that such punitive damages would send ". . . that same message to others in a position to abuse their authority." (at 298).

The "Knew or Reasonably Should Have Known" Rule   The Supreme Court in *Wood* v. *Strickland,* 420 U.S. 308 (1975), added a new twist which served to make public officials even more vulnerable to tort actions against them. In this case local school board members were sued by high school students who argued that they had been deprived of constitutional due process rights when they were expelled from school for spiking a punch bowl at a school function. Specifically, the students claimed that they should not have been expelled without the benefit of a full hearing. Speaking for the majority, Justice Byron White ruled that the demonstration of good faith does not alone guarantee the extension of immunity to public officials if they were aware, or should have been aware, that their actions, even if within the "outer perimeter" of their duties, would violate the constitutional rights of those involved. Consequently, the Court held that a member of a school board cannot be found to be immune from damage suits "*if he knew or reasonably should have known* that the action he took within his sphere of official responsibility would violate the constitutional rights of the students affected, or if he took the action with the malicious intention to cause a deprivation of constitutional rights or other injury to the students" (my emphasis) (at 322).

In a 1980 article, David Rosenbloom applauded the *Wood* decision. He maintained that the "Wood standard goes a long way toward guaranteeing that public administrators will have a sufficient *personal* stake in their actions to force them to avoid engaging in arbitrary unconstitutional actions vis-a-vis members of the general public."[28] But he held that, on the other hand, the *Wood* standard is balanced in that it "is not so general or ill-defined as to invite a rash of unfounded law suits against public officials."[29] Reflecting upon the possible impact of *Bivens* and *Wood* soon after the *Wood* decision was handed down, Bernard Schwartz speculated that these cases may really open the door to liability suits against public administrators "since tortious official conduct can frequently be described in constitutional terms."[30] That is, administrative abuses of all kinds could be rationalized as violating due process guarantees. "If *Bivens* and *Wood* are pressed that far," Schwartz concluded, "it may make for a major extension of liability in cases involving constitutional deprivations by public officers, even those previously immunized under *Barr v. Matteo.*"[31] By the mid-1980s it had become clear that in fact the *Bivens, Scherer,* and *Wood* decisions, buttressed by several other Supreme Court rulings,[32] had led to a host of tort suits against public officials. Some interpreted this sudden onslaught of tort actions against public officials, especially on the municipal level, as a crisis constituting "the largest threat to municipalities in the 1980s—expanding tort liability and municipal insurance unavailability."[33]

According to the *Wood* principle, reiterated in *Harlow* v. *Fitzgerald,* 457 U.S. 800, 818 (1982), under the qualified immunity doctrine public officials (except for those few given absolute immunity—for example, judges, prosecutors, and the president) can be sued for damages if they "knew or reasonably should have known" that their actions violated established constitutional or statutory guarantees. But the *Wood* principle raises an obvious question. What if the statutory or constitutional rights were not clearly established when the alleged violations took place? This question was answered by the Supreme Court in 1984 in *Davis* v. *Scherer,* mentioned briefly in the last section because it involved a Section 1983 claim. In *Scherer,* Gregory Scherer, a radio teletype operator for the Florida Highway Patrol, sued his superiors for damages after he had been fired from his job. He charged that his constitutional due process rights under the Fourteenth Amendment had been violated because he was dismissed without the benefit of a pretermination or immediate posttermination hearing. The Supreme Court ruled against Scherer, arguing that his claim could not be upheld because at the time of the alleged constitutional violation it had not been *clearly established* that an employee had a right to a formal pretermination or post-termination hearing. Thus, to the Court, it would be unfair to allow the damage suit against Scherer's superiors since it cannot be shown that they "knew or reasonably should have known" that they were violating Scherer's constitutional rights when at the time of the alleged violation it was not *clearly established* that Scherer was entitled to such constitutional protections. Quoting from *Harlow,* the Court asserted that public officials " 'are shielded from liability for civil damages insofar as their conduct does not violate clearly established statutory or constitutional rights of which a reasonable person would have known.' Whether an official may prevail in his qualified immunity defense depends upon the 'objective reasonableness of [his] conduct as measured by reference to clearly established law.' No other 'circumstances' are relevant to the issue of qualified immunity" (at 3017). This new *Scherer* rule modifies the old *Wood* rule and serves to make it somewhat more difficult for plaintiffs to win tort liability claims against public officials, especially in situations in which there is some reasonable doubt about the status of statutory or constitutional rights.

In the early 1990s the Supreme Court in *Siegert* v. *Gilley,* 111 S.Ct. 1789 (1991), affirmed and expanded upon its decisions in *Harlow* and *Scherer.* The case involves a situation in which a former government employee, Siegert, filed a tort suit against his former supervisor, Gilley, charging that his former boss, in response to a request for information about his job performance, wrote a defamatory letter in bad faith, which Siegert felt would likely prevent him from obtaining a comparable job in the future. This, he claimed, violated his constitutional right to due process. But the Supreme Court, in rejecting *Siegert*'s claim, stressed that the plaintiff must establish that "clearly established" constitutional rights have been violated before discovery could be granted as a preparation for trial. The Court exclaimed: "One of the purposes of immunity, absolute or qualified, is to spare a defendant not only unwarranted liability, but unwarranted demands customarily imposed upon those defending a long drawn out lawsuit" (at 1793). The Court continued: "*Harlow* thus recognized an entitlement not to stand trial or face the other burdens of litigation, conditioned on the resolution of the essentially legal question whether the conduct of which the plaintiff complains violated clearly established law. The entitlement is an *immunity from suit* rather than a mere defense to liability; and like an absolute immunity, it is effectively lost if a case is erroneously permitted to go to trial" (at 1793–1794). In *Siegert* the Court concluded that it is not enough to argue simply that the constitutional right was deprived with malice, which if shown could make the defendant liable, because first "[T]he substantive defense of immunity controls" (at 1795). This ". . . heightened pleading standard is a necessary and appropriate accommodation between the state of mind component of malice and the objective test that prevails in qualified immunity analysis as a general matter" (at 1795).[34]

Qualified Immunity Should Be the General Rule When Federal Officials Violate Constitutional Rights: The Butz Ruling   Of all the official immunity cases handed down by the courts, none is more important, at least from the standpoint of its comprehensiveness, than *Butz* v. *Economou,* 434 U.S. 994 (1977). In *Butz,* the Supreme Court reviewed virtually all major official immunity cases decided previously in an effort to link these cases to the Court's present position on official immunity privileges for governmental administrators. The case stems from a situation in which Earl Butz, the secretary of agriculture, initiated action which led to the suspension of Economou's registration privilege, thus preventing him from being able to continue to work as a commodities futures trader. But upon review, the District of Columbia Appeals Court ruled that the action taken against Economou was improper because adequate warning was not accorded before the suspension. Economou then sued Butz and others for damages, specifically charging that press releases pertaining to the suspension hurt him as a businessman, and that the suspension itself was aimed at "chilling" his freedom of expression right under the First Amendment because he had been outspoken against DOA rule-makers. The Butz defense argued that Butz and his co-defendants were entitled to absolute immunity because their actions as top administrative officials were discretionary, not ministerial. Such, they claimed, was well-established federal law.

However, the high Court held that such executive officers as Butz are entitled to qualified immunity only when constitutional rights are involved; therefore, they can be held liable for damages. The *Butz* decision applied the qualified immunity doctrine *to federal* administrators (except law enforcement officers). Previously, the doctrine had been applied only to state and local governmental officers. The Court contended that "there is no basis for according to federal officials a higher degree of immunity from liability when sued for a constitutional infringement as authorized by *Bivens* than is accorded state officials when sued for the identical violation under Section 1983. . . . Surely, *federal* officials should enjoy no greater zone of protection when they violate *federal* constitutional rules than do state officers" (at 501).[35]

Arguing that public administrators should be protected against frivolous lawsuits, the Court, nevertheless, concluded "that, in a suit for damages arising from unconstitutional action, federal executive officials exercising discretion are entitled only to the qualified immunity specified in *Scheuer,* subject to those exceptional situations where it is demonstrated that absolute immunity is essential for the conduct of the public business" (at 507). However, although the Court in *Butz* did establish that public officials should in general enjoy only qualified immunity privileges from damage suits involving constitutional violations, it did insist that absolute immunity protections should be extended to public officers performing quasi-judicial functions (for example, agency attorneys functioning as prosecutors and administrative law judges performing adjudicative functions) to preserve the effectiveness of agency adjudications.

Despite the exclusion of a few types of federal officials from qualified immunity protections, it is clear that *Butz* significantly extended the *Bivens* rule of qualified immunity. The Court did so in an attempt to deter future federal administrators from violating the constitutional rights of citizens. In its decision, the Court noted that it might be a good idea for federal administrators, to avoid possible damage suits, to be trained more in constitutional law so that they are better equipped to recognize administrative actions which seem to violate constitutional due process dictates.[36] After nearly two decades the *Butz* ruling, despite some judicial modifications of *Butz,* still remains a guiding force for the courts (*Watts* v. *Burkhart,* 978 F2d 269 (6th Cir. 1992).

The Advantages of the *Bivens* Remedy   Supreme Court decisions in the 1980s have served to clarify the application of the official immunity decisions of the 1970s. In *Carlson* v. *Green,* 446 U.S. 14 (1980), the Court specifically upheld the qualified immunity doctrine as established in *Bivens,* concluding that "A federal official contemplating unconstitutional conduct similarly must be prepared to face the prospect of a *Bivens* action" (at 25). In this case Marie Green sued Carlson, director of the Federal Bureau of Prisons, and others for compensatory and punitive damages, charging that their negligent actions (denying proper medical attention to her son) caused his death. Specifically, Green claimed that these federal prison officials were liable for damage action under *Bivens* because they violated her son's "due process, equal protection, and Eighth Amendment rights" (at 16).

Carlson and his co-defendants argued that the suit against them is inappropriate because the Federal Tort Claims Act (FTCA) provides an avenue for relief. However, the Court replied tersely: "Petitioners do not enjoy such independent status in our constitutional scheme as to suggest that judicially created remedies against them might be inappropriate." Although the Court's upholding of the qualified immunity doctrine, as established in *Bivens, Scheuer,* and *Butz,* is noteworthy, the chief significance of *Carlson* is in the Court's argument on why those seeking damage settlements, when not prohibited by statutes, should be allowed to pursue a *Bivens* remedy, if they choose, instead of an FTCA remedy. Essentially, a *Bivens* action allows public officials to be held personally liable for their unconstitutional administrative actions, while under the FTCA, action is brought against the United States for torts committed by federal administrative officers.

Delivering the opinion of the Court's majority, Justice William J. Brennan maintained that a *Bivens* action should be made available to victims of tortious official behavior, if they so desire, since evidence suggests "that the *Bivens* remedy is more effective than the FTCA remedy" (at 20). The Court noted that the *Bivens* remedy is preferable to the FTCA remedy in at least four ways. First, since a *Bivens* action allows damage action against individual public officials instead of only the state, as in an FTCA action, it should have a deterrent effect on public officers who contemplate committing tortious acts against citizens: "Because the *Bivens* remedy is recoverable against individuals, it is a more effective deterrent than the FTCA remedy against the United States. It is almost axiomatic that the threat of damages has a deterrent effect" (at 21). Second, a *Bivens* suit permits punitive damages to be paid to victims, while FTCA action does not. And according to the Court, the payment of punitive damages is "especially appropriate to redress the violation by a government official of a citizen's constitutional rights" (at 22). Third, under a *Bivens* action a plaintiff is entitled to bring his or her case before a jury, while jury trials are prohibited under an FTCA suit. Although juries would not necessarily favor plaintiffs, Brennan asserted that there is no reason why plaintiffs should not be permitted to choose between a jury and a judge. And fourth, FTCA suits are permitted "only if the State in which the alleged misconduct occurred would permit a cause of action for that misconduct to go forward" (at 23). However, the Court argued that "it is obvious that the liability of federal officials for violation of citizens' constitutional rights should be governed by uniform rules" (at 23). *Bivens* allows for such uniformity since cause for legal action is not based on what state laws will allow. The Court reasoned that it made no sense that constitutional violations by public officials created cause for action in some states, but not in others. In sum, the Court held: "Plainly FTCA is not a sufficient protector of the citizens' constitutional rights, and without a clear congressional mandate we cannot hold that Congress relegated respondent exclusively to the FTCA remedy" (at 23).

It should be noted that the Supreme Court has never directly applied the *Bivens* remedy to tort claims against state officials, even though state officials may knowingly and maliciously violate U.S. constitutional rights when administering federal programs in their states. Of course the *Bivens* and *Carlson* cases involved tort suits against federal officers. So are state officials liable under *Bivens?* Davis and Pierce argue that "[L]ogic requires the answer that state officers are as much under the Constitution as federal officers, but the Supreme Court has never applied the *Bivens* doctrine to state officers."[37] However, they point out that in 1988 in *Schweiker* v. *Chilicky,* 487 U.S. 412, 418, the Supreme Court appeared to assume, without actually rendering a decision on the matter, that state officials who implement federal law are subject to *Bivens* suits. Lower courts have been split on the applicability of the *Bivens* remedy in tort suits against state officials.[38] Since state officers can be sued under Section 1983, which provides a remedy similar to *Bivens,* it is probably not that crucial that the Supreme Court rule soon on whether *Bivens* applies to state officers.

The Need to Establish a Direct Causal Connection between Official Action and Injury in Qualified Immunity Cases   In *Martinez* v. *California,* 444 U.S. 277, the Supreme Court ruled that, subject to qualified immunity, establishing that the state's action is related directly to the harm caused is necessary to justify a tort claim against a state or its public officials. In this case petitioners had sued California state parole board officials who had paroled a mentally disturbed sex offender who presented a "clear and present danger" to the public. Five months after being released, the parolee tortured and murdered a fifteen-year-old girl. The girl's survivors sued for damages, contending that the negligent and reckless decision by the parole board to parole this dangerous man led to the girl's death. Specifically, the petitioners claimed that the parole board's action deprived the girl of her life without due process of law and, thus, the board's members were liable to pay for the damages caused by the parolee. Also at issue, *inter alia,* was a California state statute which granted members of the parole board absolute immunity from tort claims.

The Court held that California statute did not violate due process property rights under the Fourteenth Amendment because in this case "the State's interest in fashioning its own rules of tort law is paramount to any discernible federal interest, except perhaps an interest in protecting the individual citizen from state action that is wholly arbitrary or irrational" (at 282). In *Martinez,* however, the Court believed that the parole board's actions were far from being "arbitrary and irrational"; thus it was reasonable for the state to protect such discretionary board decisions from tort suits. In fact, the Court argued that such board action was somewhat similar to judicial decision making and therefore should probably be protected from damage suits. The Court argued that some risk is always involved in paroling prisoners. To subject parole board members to liability claims, the Court maintained, would probably prevent the state from being able to implement any parole program designed to rehabilitate inmates. Besides, the Court held that the action taken by the parolee five months later "can not be fairly characterized as state action. . . . He was in no sense an agent of the parole board" (at 285). The Fourteenth Amendment, the Court argued, "protected her [the murdered child] only from deprivation by the 'State . . . of life . . .

without due process of law'" (at 284). In short, the Court believed that the relationship between the parolee's action and the parole board's decision was too indirectly related to justify a cause for tort action against the board's officials under the Fourteenth Amendment or any federal statutes (for example, the Federal Civil Rights Act, 42 U.S.C., Section 1983).

Liability Claims Not Honored When Congress Has Provided Alternative Remedies   In *Bush* v. *Lucas,* 462 U.S. 367 (1983), petitioner Bush, an aerospace engineer working at the Marshall Space Flight Center operated by the National Aeronautics and Space Administration, had often criticized the operations of the space center to the media. Subsequently, Lucas, director of the center, demoted Bush on the grounds that his statements to the media were false and misleading. Although the Federal Employee Appeals Authority upheld his demotion, on further appeal the Civil Service Commission's Appeals Review Board ruled that Bush's demotion had violated his First Amendment guarantees and, thus, recommended his reinstatement to his former position. Bush then filed a damage suit against Lucas, charging that Lucas had violated his First Amendment rights. The Supreme Court refused to grant the remedy sought by Bush. It maintained that Congress had evidently intended to not allow such remedial relief because it had provided appropriate and elaborate alternative remedies under the Civil Service Commission. Speaking for a unanimous Court, Justice Stevens said: "The question is not what remedy the court should provide for a wrong that would otherwise go unredressed. It is whether an elaborate remedial system that has been constructed step by step, with careful attention to conflicting policy considerations, should be augmented by the creation of a new judicial remedy for the constitutional violation at issue" (at 366). Arguing that Congress is in the best position to develop remedies that would balance the rights of employees with governmental efficiency, the Supreme Court declined to create any new judicial remedy (at 380-92). The Supreme Court affirmed this position in the late 1980s in *Schweiker* v. *Chilicky,* 487 U.S. 412 (1988), yet the high Court in 1992 in *McCarthy* v. *Madigan,* 112 S.Ct. 1081, confused its position in *Bush* and *Chilicky* by holding that a federal prisoner could in fact file a *Bivens* claim even though Congress had provided an alternative remedy under the Federal Tort Claims Act. Experts noted that this decision demonstrates the Court's reluctance to abandon the *Bivens* remedy, despite the burden this remedy places upon individual defendants, even when other remedies are available.

In sum, the Supreme Court, starting with *Bivens* in 1971 and continuing in such cases as *Scheuer, Wood, Butz,* and *Carlson,* did much to destroy the absolute immunity doctrine for public officials as established in *Barr,* while the high Court in more recent cases such as *Martinez, Bush, Scherer,* and *Chilicky* has conveyed the clear message that it is not willing to proceed recklessly in interpreting the qualified immunity doctrine to make public officials "too" susceptible to tort suits, especially under *Bivens* and Section 1983. *Madigan* reaffirms *Bivens* as a remedy, but it does not necessarily make it any easier for plaintiffs to win on the actual merits of the liability claim.

TOWARD INCREASED GOVERNMENTAL LIABILITY AND DECREASED OFFICIAL LIABILITY?

Today, the question of whether public officials or the government should be held liable for tortious acts committed against persons by governmental officers, and under what circumstances, still remains unresolved. Indeed, since the beginning of the Republic, our lawmakers and judges have oscillated on this liability question. To recapitulate, at first we drew upon common law to deprive individuals from suing the government for the tortious actions of its officers. But while common law gave the government sovereign immunity, it permitted liability suits to be filed against its officers.[39] However, the courts, with the tacit consent of Congress and state legislative bodies, eventually moved toward making federal and state officials increasingly immune from tort action suits.

The virtual immunity from liability suits of both the government and its officers created undue hardships for persons abused by public officials committing tortious acts.[40] In response to this unjust situation, legislators developed the doctrines of qualified and limited immunity (for example, the Federal Tort Claims Act), as did judges (for example, the *Bivens* remedy), thus again making public officials more vulnerable to tort actions against them, and the government, stripped of its almost untouchable sovereign immunity status, considerably more open to damage suits. Another trend, making public officials less liable and the government more liable to tort suits, has apparently been developing at the national and state levels. In moving gradually in this direction, the government has begun to turn itself into a mutual insurance agency, supported by tax dollars and dedicated to minimizing liability risks to public administrators, while compensating those who are injured by governmental actions.

This step toward a comprehensive liability insurance policy for governmental officers, paid for by tax dollars, represents an expected extension of the scope of responsibility assumed by the modern welfare state. But as with private insurance policies, the liability policy provides only limited liability coverage. The federal government, as well as state and local governments, are not interested in insuring all forms of tortious acts committed by their officers. The prevailing attitude seems to be that administrative errors committed in good faith in the line of duty, but which cause unintentional harm to persons, should be covered. However, the feeling is that fraudulent, corrupt, or malicious acts by governmental officials should not be given liability protection, especially if not committed in the line of duty. A California statute that substitutes governmental liability for officer liability typifies this new perspective on liability.[41] The statute obligates the State of California to assume most of the liability risks for its employees, but it still makes its employees liable for their fraudulent, malicious, or corrupt actions. This new concept in governmental liability is based upon the no-fault principle.[42] Thus, compensatory payments will be made to persons injured by governmental activities; but in order to save court costs, no judicial attempts will be made to prove fault. Overall, this trend away from officer liability to governmental liability represents a movement away from the doctrine of sovereign immunity.

Reasons for Moving toward Governmental Liability

Why are we apparently moving away from officer liability and toward governmental liability?[43] From the perspective of the governmental officials, it seems only fair that the government should extend a form of basic liability insurance to its employees. After all, it is argued, these officials are working for our benefit. That is, as a result of their efforts to implement needed governmental programs, society in general benefits. Should we, as a people, make them pay damages out of their own pockets for any innocent mistakes they make in the process of implementing public policies? As Davis and Pierce exclaimed in their 1994 *Administrative Law Treatise:* "Some of the most flagrant injustice in the legal system occurs when huge judgments are entered against conscientious public employees."[44] As mentioned previously, the use of administrative discretion in making policy implementation decisions almost guarantees that some parties will yell "Foul!" Besides, it is held, the government is in a much better position to absorb the costs of damage claims than its employees, who are struggling to balance their own family budgets. It is also noted that the vast majority of tortious acts are committed unintentionally, and errors which lead to injuries are bound to occur because the workloads of the typical administrator are so heavy and the laws guiding officials are often vague and difficult to understand. Under such conditions agency decision makers cannot possibly know for certain when they are violating the law. Yes, administrators may win such suits by successfully arguing that the law they violated was not "clearly established," but they still may have to fight the expensive and inconvenient tort suit.

From the perspective of the administrative system, as acknowledged before, the omnipresent danger of being sued for wrongdoing would tend to be disruptive to the administrative process because administrators would possibly hesitate to act unless they were certain that their actions were proper and that they would not have to worry about being sued for their acts. This might sound like a good thing, but in reality, in the world of public administration uncertainty exists behind virtually all administrative acts. Consequently, waiting to make no-risk decisions would probably tend only to promote needless indecision and costly inefficiency in the administrative process. Christopher H. Schroeder feels that this would harm American society greatly because public administrators must make hard decisions that involve inherently risky modern technologies if we are to advance as a society.[45] And the Supreme Court said in *Scheuer* that the danger of personal liability against public officials would deter their willingness to perform their duties with decisiveness, as is required to promote the public good (416 U.S. 232, 240; 1974). Thus, despite some of the disadvantages of substituting governmental liability for official liability, it is argued that, on the whole, the substitution is in the public interest because it serves to preserve the essential vitality of the public administration system.

Kenneth C. Davis argues that transferring tort liability from public officials to the government will have four positive effects. His first two reasons are reiterations of the typical arguments that the shift to governmental liability helps to promote the public interest by preserving the administrative process and that giving immunity to governmental officers is simply the just thing to do. His third and fourth points are more controversial. Davis claims that "the quality of justice to injured persons will be improved in that they will no longer lack a remedy if the officer happens to be judgment proof."[46] To him, *judgment proof* means that a public official is too poor to be able to afford to pay a judgment. Also helpful in making an officer judgment proof, according to Davis, is the sympathetic attitude that judges and juries hold toward public officials, making them extremely reluctant to conclude that public officials (with families and debts) should be made personally liable for their actions done in the line of public duty. Suits against governments make more sense to him, especially since governments do not elicit particular sympathy and they always have the resources to pay legitimate damage claims. These circumstances tend to make recovery for damages more realistic and fair from the point of view of the injured party."[47]

Davis' fourth reason for preferring governmental liability to officer liability is that tort suits filed against the government will deter officials from committing deliberate torts because the officer charged with committing the tortious act will be reprimanded by his or her superior for causing the governmental unit to fight and possibly pay a liability claim. To substantiate this contention, Davis notes that "all experience shows that subordinates respond more to discipline imposed by superiors than to the possibility that they will be held personally liable."[48] However, he fails to document this very questionable assertion. On the other hand, Justice Brennan argued in *Carlson* that public officials would be more likely to avoid tortious actions if they knew that they might have to suffer the financial consequence of their tortious acts themselves.

Davis and Pierce believe that it is so critical to shift liability for tortious actions from public employees to the government that they suggest specific ways for doing it. In particular, they urge Congress to pass a statute which would eliminate *Bivens* claims against federal employees, while also eliminating Section 1983 actions against state and local officials. In addition, they recommend that Congress amend the FTCA by dropping the exemptions for certain intentional torts. They also suggest that Congress should employ its power under the Fourteenth Amendment, Section 5, to make state and local governments liable under Section 1983 suits instead of their officials. Davis and Pierce acknowledge that Congress has already shifted liability in specific situations from federal officials to the federal government, but it seems reluctant to pass broad legislation which would shift liability to the federal government for federal employees. These scholars also note that the courts could do a lot to shift liability to the government at the federal, state, and local levels by, for example, specifically overruling *Bivens* and interpreting Section 1983 in such a way that state and local governments would be much more exposed to Section 1983 tort actions than their state and local officials.[49]

Suing the Government under the Federal Tort Claims Act   It was not until 1946, when the Federal Tort Claims Act (60 Stat. 842) was passed that Congress took a significant step toward stripping the federal government of its virtual sovereign immunity status, thus forcing the national government to start assuming some of the responsibility for the damages caused by the tortious actions of its agents. However, in

1946 Congress severely limited the sort of tort action suits that could be filed against the government. Although the FTCA allowed damage suits to be filed against the United States in U.S. district courts "for money only . . . on account of damage to or loss of property or on account of personal injury or death caused by the negligent or wrongful act or omission of any employee of the Government while acting within the scope of his office or employment, under circumstances where the United States, if a private person, would be liable for such damage," other key provisions in the act: (1) limited damage claims to only $10,000 or less (this amount has since been abandoned); (2) prohibited jury trials; (3) forbade claims for punitive damages; (4) exempted certain agencies, specific administrative operations, and claims originating in foreign nations; (5) failed to make the act applicable if the claim arises "out of assault, battery, false imprisonment, false arrest, malicious prosecution, abuse of process, libel, slander, misrepresentation, deceit, or interference with contract rights" (Section 421[h]); and (6) prohibited any tort suit "based upon an act or omission of an employee of the Government, *exercising due care, in the execution of a statute or regulation,* whether or not such statute or regulation be valid, or based upon the *exercise or performance or failure to exercise a discretionary function or duty* on the part of a Federal agency or an employee of the Government, whether or not the discretion involved be abused" (my emphasis) (Section 421[a]).[50]

In 1988 Congress passed the Federal Employees Liability Reform and Tort Compensation Act,[51] which amends the FTCA by: (1) broadening the scope of the FTCA to include legislative and judicial branch employees; and (2) transferring to the government liability for common law torts, not constitutional torts, committed by federal officers while acting within the scope of their official duties.[52] These two amendments, although not inconsequential, accomplish less than one may think. In the first place, legislative and judicial officials already enjoy absolute immunity from tort suits as long as they are performing legislative or judicial duties. Secondly, Congress did not immunize government officials from liability for constitutional torts committed while carrying out their duties. Since most common law torts can be argued from the standpoint of constitutional torts (i.e., most tortious acts that injure can be presented as a denial of constitutional due process, equal protection, etc.), chances are that federal employees won't gain much added protection from this amendment.

The loopholes in the FTCA are so numerous and broad that many have criticized its practical worth to those who have been victimized by the tortious acts of federal officials. After all, how many times would officers commit tortious acts while performing nonstatutory functions, and in how many cases would you say the exercise of discretion would not be a factor? Section 421(a) basically relieves the government of the burden of being responsible for abusive discretionary acts of its public officials (excluding law enforcement officers) while performing the tasks which they have been hired to carry out.

In fact, in 1963 in *Dalehite* v. *United States,* 346 U.S. 15 (1953), the Supreme Court applied essentially this interpretation. Filing for recovery of damages under the FTCA, petitioners argued that the negligent handling of ammonium nitrate fertilizer by the federal government caused an explosion which destroyed hundreds of millions of dollars in property, killed 560 people, and injured about 3,000 others. However, the Court had no difficulty in dismissing the hundreds of suits filed, arguing that the FTCA did not permit such suits since "immune discretion" was involved, even if it could be shown that negligence occurred or discretionary authority was abused.

The Supreme Court in 1957 in *Rayonier, Inc.* v. *United States,* 352 U.S. 315, found the U.S. Forest Service liable because it was negligent in providing fire protection services; and a year later, in *Indian Towing Co.* v. *United States,* 350 U.S. 61(1965), it held that the Coast Guard was liable because it failed to exercise "due care" in maintaining a lighthouse. It returned to the wisdom in *Dalehite* in 1972 in *Laird* v. *Nelms,* 406 U.S. 797. In *Laird* the Supreme Court ruled that the United States could not be held liable under the FTCA for damages caused by sonic booms resulting from military aircraft which flew over North Carolina at three times the speed of sound. Amazingly, the Court argued that no negligence could be shown in the planning of the flight or in the flight itself. As in *Dalehite,* the Court noted in essence that Congress, in drafting the FTCA, did not intend for a strict liability standard to be imposed upon the government. The Court's majority in *Laird* maintained that the important lesson conveyed "in *Dalehite* is that . . . the Federal Tort Claims Act itself precludes the imposition of liability if there has been no negligence or other form of 'misfeasance or nonfeasance'. . . on the part of the Government" (at 799).

Thus, as of 1972 the high Court had not ordinarily been very generous in permitting tort suits against the federal government. Actually, state court judges have, by and large, been more liberal in allowing tort suits in their respective states, reflecting to some extent the growing trend under state law "making state governments liable upon the same basis as private tortfeasors."[53] The *Laird* decision attracted heated protests from those who believed that the Supreme Court had gone far beyond the intent of the framers of the FTCA in disallowing tort actions against the government. For example, Bernard Schwartz concluded that the *Laird* ruling represented a step backward in tort law. He contended that the damage claim in *Laird* should have been allowed since clearly the FTCA "makes the United States liable for 'negligent or wrongful acts' where a private employer would be. Under applicable tort law, a private person who creates a sonic boom is absolutely liable for any injuries caused thereby. The creation of a sonic boom is thus a 'wrongful act' within the Tort Claims Act, regardless of whether negligence is shown."[54] But possibly the most vehement criticism of the Court's ruling in *Laird* comes from Justices William J. Brennan and Potter Stewart, who dissented in the case. They argued that the conclusion reached by the Court's majority lacks common sense and clearly contradicts the act's purpose: "Nothing in the language or the legislative history of the Act compels such a result, and we should not lightly conclude that Congress intended to create a situation so much at odds with common sense and the basic rationale of the Act" (at 809).

But in 1984 in *U.S.* v. *S.A. Empresa DeViacao Aerea Rio Grandense,* 467 U.S. 797, the Supreme Court again rooted its decision in the restricted line of reasoning developed over thirty years before in *Dalehite.* The legal issue in this case was whether the United States can be held liable under the Federal Tort Claims Act for the negligent certification by the Federal Aviation Administration of an aircraft. Because of an allegedly unsafe trash receptacle, the Boeing 707 caught fire in flight from Paris to Rio de Janeiro and crashed, killing most of the passengers. The airline sued for damages under the FTCA, charging that the Civil Aeronautics Board (the FAA's predecessor) negligently issued a type of certificate that in effect approved the lavatory trash receptacle used on the Boeing 707 that really failed to meet applicable air safety regulations.

Consistent with its decision in *Dalehite,* the Supreme Court ruled that the "discretionary function exception" to the FTCA precludes a damage suit against the FAA. Maintaining that the FTCA's discretionary function exception applies to federal agencies as well as to all federal employees exercising discretion, the Court argued that the courts should not intervene and provide relief because "it was precisely this sort of judicial intervention in policymaking that the discretionary function exception was designed to prevent" (at 820). In explanation, the Court elaborated: "Judicial intervention in such decisionmaking through private tort suits would require the courts to 'second-guess' the political, social, and economic judgments of an agency exercising its regulatory function. . . . FAA employees in executing the 'spot-check' program . . . are protected by the discretionary function. . . . The FAA employees who conducted compliance reviews of the aircraft involved in this case were specifically empowered to make policy judgments regarding the degree of confidence that might reasonably be placed in a given manufacturer, the need to maximize compliance with FAA regulations, and the efficient allocation of agency resources. In administering the 'spot-check' program, these FAA engineers and inspectors necessarily took certain calculated risks, but those risks were encountered for the advancement of a governmental purpose and pursuant to the specific grant of authority in the regulations and operating manuals. Under such circumstances, the FAA's alleged negligence in failing to check specific items in the course of certifying a particular aircraft falls squarely within the discretionary function exception of Section 2680(a)" (at 820). Given this reasoning, it is difficult to imagine how any plaintiff could win a damage suit under the FTCA. Could not the "discretionary function exception" be used to defeat any claim under the FTCA? If you were injured by a federal agency or its officials, in light of these Supreme Court rulings, what do you think the odds would be of winning a liability claim under the FTCA?

Recent court cases place these odds into perspective, suggesting that the odds of winning a damage award under the FTCA are not very good. The key to winning an FTCA suit seems to be in overcoming the "discretionary function exception." Stated simply, unless the plaintiff can show that a government official caused injury because the tortious action was outside his/her discretionary authority in the administration of some public policy, the plaintiff will not win. For example, in *United States* v. *Gaubert,* 111 S.Ct. 1267 (1991), the Supreme Court refused to allow tort action under the FTCA brought by a shareholder of an insolvent savings and loan association who charged essentially that negligent regulatory supervision on a day-to-day basis of directors and officers was responsible for the bankruptcy which caused damage to shareholders. Citing *Dalehite* and *Varig Airlines,* the Court held that the discretionary function exemption protects the government from liability as long as ". . . a regulation mandates particular conduct, and the employee obeys the direction. . . . If the employee violates the mandatory regulation, there will be no shelter from liability because there is no room for choice and the action will be contrary to policy. On the other hand, if a regulation allows the employee discretion, the very existence of the regulation creates a strong presumption that a discretionary act authorized by the regulation involves consideration of the same policies which led to the promulgation of the regulations" (at 1274). Consequently, the Court concluded: "Gaubert asserts that the discretionary function exception protects only those acts of negligence which occur in the course of establishing broad policies, rather than individual acts of negligence which occur in the course of day-to-day activities. . . . If the routine or frequent nature of a decision were sufficient to remove an otherwise discretionary act from the scope of the exception, then countless policy-based decisions by regulators exercising day-to-day supervisory authority would be actionable" (at 1279).

There are also jurisdictional limitations to the application of the FTCA. In *Smith* v. *United States,* 113 S.Ct. 1178 (1993), the Supreme Court denied a wrongful death claim brought by a spouse whose husband was killed in Antarctica while working for a construction company hired by the National Science Foundation. The Court dismissed the suit, arguing simply that the FTCA's waiver of sovereign immunity does not apply to tort claims occurring in foreign countries—and Antarctica should be regarded as a foreign country under the FTCA even though it has no recognized government.

Finally, under the FTCA the government is not liable to pay punitive damages. However, in *Molzof* v. *United States,* 112 S.Ct. 711 (1992), the Supreme Court awarded damages the government argued amounted to "punitive damages" (i.e., future supplemental medical expenses and loss of enjoyment of life). But the Court contended that FTCA ". . . bars the recovery only of what are *legally* considered 'punitive damages' under traditional common law principles" (at 718). The Court felt that the award of damages here did not comply with the common law understanding of *punitive* since the financial award was not awarded to punish the defendant officers for purposeful misconduct.

Suing Municipalities under Section 1983   We have already reviewed the liability of governmental officials under Section 1983. In this section the liability of municipalities under Section 1983 is discussed. In the early 1960s in *Monroe* v. *Pape,* 365 U.S. 167 (1961), the Supreme Court, holding to its pro sovereign immunity mood as developed in *Barr* just two years before, ruled that "Congress did not undertake to bring municipal corporations within the gambit of (Section 1983)" (at 187). However, Supreme Court decisions in the past decade have established that municipalities can be held liable under Section 1983 suits under certain conditions.

In *Monell* v. *Department of Social Services,* 436 U.S. 658 (1978), the Supreme Court, after reexamining the legislative history of the Civil Rights Act of 1871, Section 1983, concluded that the Court in *Monroe* had misread the legislative history and, thus, reached the wrong conclusion about the applicability of Section 1983 claims against municipalities. In *Monell,* the Court reversed *Monroe* in this regard, arguing that "our analysis of the legislative history of the Civil Rights Act of 1871 compels the conclusion that Congress *did* intend municipalities and other local government units to be included among those persons to whom Section 1983 applies" (at 690). Consequently, the Court held: "Local governing bodies . . . can be sued directly under Section 1983 for monetary, declaratory, or injunctive relief where, as here, the action that is alleged to be unconstitutional implements or executes a policy statement, ordinance, regulation, or decision officially adopted and promulgated by that body's officers" (at 690). In addition, the Court held that a municipality can be held liable under Section 1983, like any other "Section 1983 person," if the municipality's official policies can be shown to cause constitutional deprivations. On the other hand, the Court made clear that "Congress did not intend municipalities to be held liable unless action pursuant to official policy of some nature caused a constitution tort. In particular, we conclude that a municipality cannot be held liable *solely* because it employs a tortfeasor—or, in other words, a municipality cannot be held liable under Section 1983 on a *respondeat superior* theory" (at 691).

But could a municipality escape damage actions against it under Section 1983 for torts that deprive persons of their constitutional rights committed by its officers, even if it contends in defense that its officers acted in *good faith?* The Supreme Court said *no* to this question in *Owen* v. *City of Independence,* 445 U.S. 622 (1980). The Court's 5–4 majority argued that it would make no sense to allow municipalities a good faith defense since it would leave remediless victims of constitutional violations by municipalities. "Unless countervailing considerations counsel otherwise, the injustice of such a result should not be tolerated" (at 651). Further, the Court noted, "Section 1983 was intended not only to provide compensation to the victims of past abuses, but to serve as a deterrent against future constitutional deprivations, as well. . . . The knowledge that a municipality will be liable for all of its injurious conduct, whether committed in good faith or not, should create an incentive for officials who may harbor doubts about the lawfulness of their intended actions to err on the side of protecting citizens' constitutional rights. Furthermore, the threat that damages might be levied against the city may encourage those in a policymaking position to institute internal rules and programs designed to minimize the likelihood of unintentional infringements on constitutional rights" (at 651–652).

But maybe the most significant aspect of *Owen* is the Court's development of the concept of "equitable loss spreading," which seems to make the *Owen* decision appear very much ahead of its time. In its holding the Court acknowledged that it is crucial for tort law to evolve so that our notion of responsible government is preserved. To the *Owen* Court, "equitable loss spreading" is a fairer principle because it calls for distributing the costs of official misconduct, making no longer "individual 'blameworthiness' the acid test of liability" (at 657). Basically, the Supreme Court contended that the costs for damages caused by the tortious actions of governmental officials, especially under Section 1983, should be shared by the three principal parties: (1) the victim; (2) the officer(s) who committed the tort; and (3) the public (the governmental unit supported by the citizens' tax dollars, in this case the City of Independence, Missouri). Therefore, the Court concluded: "The innocent individual who is harmed by an abuse of governmental authority is assured that he will be compensated for his injury. The offending official, so long as he conducts himself in good faith, may go about his business secure in the knowledge that a qualified immunity will protect him from personal liability for damages that are more appropriately chargeable to the populace as a whole. And the public will be forced to bear only the costs of injury inflicted by the 'execution of a government's policy or custom, whether made by its lawmakers or by those whose edicts or acts may fairly be said to represent official policy'" (at 657).

The Supreme Court has attempted to clarify and apply the *Monell* rule that an official's tortious unconstitutional action must have been taken "pursuant to official municipal policy of some nature" before the municipality can be held liable under Section 1983. In *City of Oklahoma City* v. *Tuttle,* 105 S.Ct. 2427 (1985), the case focused on a *single incident* in which an Oklahoma City police officer shot and killed a man outside a bar where a robbery was reported to be in progress. The plaintiff, the man's wife, filed a Section 1983 suit against Oklahoma City, charging that the city's training and supervisory policies were inadequate and, as a result, had led to the unconstitutional action committed against her husband. The Court held: "Proof of a *single incident* of unconstitutional activity is not sufficient to impose liability under Monell, unless proof of the incident includes proof that it was caused by an existing, unconstitutional municipal policy, which can be attributed to a municipal policy-maker. Otherwise the existence of the unconstitutional policy, and its origin, must be separately proved. But where the policy relied upon is not itself unconstitutional, considerably more proof than the single incident will be necessary in every case to establish both the requisite fault on the part of the municipality, and the causal connection between the 'policy' and the constitutional deprivation" (my emphasis) (at 2436).

The key to understanding *Tuttle* is found in the emphasized phrases. A year later in *Pembaur* v. *Cincinnati,* 106 S.Ct. 1292 (1986), the Supreme Court, drawing on these emphasized phrases, reached a different conclusion in a case involving a single incident. This time the Court upheld the plaintiff's Section 1983 damage suit because it believed that it was clearly shown that the police officers who had violated the plaintiff's constitutional rights had in fact directly followed official county policy, specifically, the county prosecutor's "clear command." The single incident in this case involved a situation in which county deputy sheriffs used an axe to gain entry into a room barred by the plaintiff to arrest subpoenaed witnesses employed by the plaintiff at his clinic. However, the deputy sheriffs carried out such action only after they had called the county prosecutor's office and received the "clear command" from the county prosecutor to take such action. In light of these facts, the high Court ruled that Section 1983 liability may be imposed for a single incident on a governmental unit under such circumstances (at 1301).

A 1992 case also helps to clarify the scope of Section 1983 liability suits. In *Collins* v. *City of Harker Heights, Tex.,* 112 S.Ct. 1061, the widow of a sanitation worker employed by Harker Heights' sanitation department brought a Section 1983 suit against the city, claiming that her husband died of asphyxia after entering a manhole to repair a sewer line because the city had failed to train or warn its sanitation workers of known risks. She argued that such deprived her husband of "life" without "due process of law." The Supreme Court ruled, citing *Monell,* that "[T]he city is not liable under Section 1983 for the constitutional torts of its agents: It is only liable when it can be fairly said that the city itself is the wrongdoer" (at 1067). In *Monell,* ". . . we decided that a municipality can be found liable under Section 1983 only where the municipality *itself* causes the constitutional violation at issue. *Respondent superior* or vicarious liability will not attach under Section 1983" (at 1067). Elaborating, the Court explained that inadequate training of employees ". . . could be characterized as the cause of the constitutional tort—if and only if—the failure to train amounted to 'deliberate indifference' to the rights of persons . . ." (at 1068). Further, "[N]either the text nor the history of the Due Process Clause supports petitioner's claim that the governmental employer's duty to provide its employees with a safe working environment is a substantive component of the Due Process Clause" (at 1069). The intent of the Fourteenth Amendment's due process clause, the Court asserted, was ". . . to prevent government 'from abusing (its) power, or employing it as an instrument of oppression'" (at 1069). Showing some irritation with the claim in the suit, the Court exclaimed that the "[P]etitioner's submission that the city violated a federal constitutional obligation to provide its employees with certain minimal levels of safety and security is unprecedented. . . ." Due process does not ". . . guarantee municipal employees a workplace that is free of unreasonable risks of harm . . . (at 1071).

In concluding, it should be emphasized that Section 1983 suits, while often difficult to win, nonetheless in general have the effect of scaring state and local public officials and the governments that employ them to uphold the constitutional rights of their citizens because Section 1983 has emerged in modern tort law as a legal weapon with potentially fierce and broad teeth.[55] As Davis and Pierce note in summary, Section 1983 ". . . now authorizes damage actions against state and local government employees based on constitutional torts, damage actions against local governments based on constitutional torts committed while implementing law or official policy, and actions for declaratory and injunctive relief against state and local governments based on violations of either the U.S. Constitution or any federal law that is interpreted to create a judicially enforceable right in an individual. Moreover, because a Section 1983 plaintiff is not required to exhaust state or local judicial or administrative remedies and is often entitled to recover attorney fees under Section 1988, Section 1983 has become the preferred vehicle for obtaining relief based on alleged violations of federal law by state or local officials and institutions."[56] Optional state and local remedies are seldom used.

The Patchwork Quilt Today   In the mid-1970s Walter Gellhorn and Clark Byse, reflecting the sentiment of many administrative law scholars, concluded that "the system of governmental liability resembles a patchwork quilt, and a rather imperfectly constructed one, at that."[57] These scholars, and others, were reacting to a legal system that had failed to produce a clear picture on governmental and official immunity. However, by the 1990s the picture of public tort law is still very blurred, although Congress has made some amendments to public tort law, as noted in this chapter, in an attempt to resolve some issues. Even though some damage actions apply to the states in general (e.g., Section 1983), public tort law at the state level is even more confusing due to specific state enactments limiting sovereign immunity and qualifying official immunity. How federal and state tort laws apply to federal, state, and local officials, as well as to the governments that they serve, is very confusing. In fact, in their recent 1994 *Administrative Law Treatise,* Davis and Pierce concluded their chapter on public tort law with a section entitled "Inordinate Confusion and Complexity in Public Tort Law," which seems to encapsulate the problem very well.[58]

After reading this chapter you may feel that you still do not understand public tort law very well. You may feel that you still do not have a very good grasp of the applicability of various liability laws to state, local, and federal officials, as well as to their governments. Well, join the club! After carefully reviewing public tort law in their *Administrative Law Treatise,* Davis and Pierce concluded that "[T]he law in this area is so complex and uncertain that no judge or lawyer is likely to be able to address a single dispute in a manner that reflects all of the relevant statutory and decisional law."[59] These scholars, as well as other legal scholars, claim that despite the fact that courts hand down decisions every day pertaining to public liability questions, many, if not most, of the questions they "answer" are really "unanswerable" under our present system of "patchwork quilt" public tort law.[60]

In reading court decisions and the literature on public tort law, it becomes readily apparent that judges and scholars write in tentative, confusing, incomplete, and even contradictory terms. Judicial decisions may sound emphatic and clear in one context, but serious reflection almost always raises questions about how their interpretations would apply in even a slightly different situation or whether another court would give the same interpretation to the same questions of tort law and fact and reach the same decision. Public tort law scholars are afraid to draw emphatic conclusions about most issues in public liability law, making their writings confusing, because there are normally no definitive answers to most public tort questions.

Unquestionably, general principles have been developed in the field of public tort law, but applying these principles in specific cases becomes a very difficult and frustrating task because it is not easy to decide, for example, whether the government or its officials are liable, or both or neither, which liability laws apply, whether constitutional violations have occurred, whether the constitutional rights violated were "clearly established," whether alternative remedies should preclude the liability suit before the court, whether the discretionary exception should apply, etc. A strong consensus of scholars and practitioners contend that our lawmakers must draft statutes to help clear up the confusion in public tort law because it remains a "patchwork quilt."

THE QUESTION OF PRESIDENTIAL IMMUNITY

The attitude that certain governmental officials should be entitled to absolute immunity from judicial action against them while performing governmental functions had been well established by 1700 under British common law.[61] Drawing heavily upon the British legal system, our constitutional framers, legislators, and judges in American history at least eventually saw to it that most of our public officials were also extended immunity protections. Our legislators and judges have always enjoyed absolute immunity from judicial actions against them for acts committed in their line of duty.[62] In *Spalding,* in 1896, the Supreme Court gave absolute immunity protection to top executive officers (for example, a postmaster general in this case), while in 1959, in *Barr,* this immunity privilege was extended to cover almost all public administrators.

However, in recent years the courts have abandoned the absolute immunity principle of *Spalding-Barr* and, starting with *Bivens,* replaced it with only a qualified immunity status for public administrators. But given the unique constitutional and practical position of the president, should our chief executive also be accorded only a qualified immunity privilege? Should the president, like virtually all other public administrators, be made subject to lawsuits because of official presidential actions or even unofficial actions?[63] Would not the threat of lawsuits prevent the president from providing the nation with effective presidential leadership? Does the Constitution not recognize this and give the president absolute immunity protection?

Although *United States* v. *Nixon,* 418 U.S. 683 (1974), did not consider the presidential immunity question from the standpoint of whether the president can be brought before a federal court as a defendant in a tort suit, it was an important case for conveying to the public the Supreme Court's perspective on the presidential immunity issue in general. In *Nixon,* Special Watergate Prosecutor Archibald Cox petitioned U.S. District Judge John Sirica for an order that would entitle Cox to obtain from President Nixon certain Watergate tapes required by grand jury subpoena *duces tecum.* However, Nixon claimed executive privilege and filed a motion to have the subpoena dismissed. Judge Sirica denied this motion and then issued an order requesting that specific tapes be released for *in camera* inspection. Nixon appealed, arguing that the "intrabranch dispute" between Cox and himself was a nonjusticiable controversy which precluded court review. In so arguing, Nixon was in effect maintaining that he alone had the authority, under the doctrine of executive privilege, to determine what material should be kept privileged (in this case, away from the grand jury in a criminal prosecution).

The Court ruled essentially that, although it is "in the public interest to afford Presidential confidentiality the greatest protection," the president does not stand above the law (at 715). According to the Court, the presumption of executive "privilege must be considered in light of our historic commitment to the rule of law" (at 708). Quoting from *Marbury* v. *Madison,* 1 Cranch 137 (1803), the Court reasoned that, in order for our governmental system of separation of powers to work, it must be "emphatically the province and duty of the judicial department to say what the law is" (at 703). Flatly rejecting the argument by Nixon that he should be the only one to determine how the law applies to executive privilege, the Court exclaimed "that the Court has the authority to interpret claims with respect to powers alleged to derive from enumerated powers" (at 704).

The prevalent attitude in *Nixon* was that executive privilege should never be used without any regard to the impact its use may have on the due process rights of others. The Court argued that it had the responsibility to protect such due process rights. Thus, in the context of the case at hand, the Court asserted that it "must weigh the importance of the general privilege of confidentiality of Presidential communication in performance of the President's responsibilities against the inroads of such a privilege on the fair administration of criminal justice." All factors considered, the Court reasoned, the use of executive privilege "cannot prevail over the fundamental demands of due process of law. . . . The generalized assertion of privilege must yield to the demonstrated, specific need" (at 711–13).

This forceful decision against Nixon cannot be understood without an appreciation for the atmosphere in which it was made. Public opinion was strongly against Nixon, especially since many citizens believed that he opposed releasing the tapes not for any noble reason, but only to hide his criminal involvement in the Watergate affair. Consequently, some scholarly critics at the time felt that the Court might have gone too far in weakening executive privilege, especially since in the public's eye the Court's rhetoric boldly scolded Nixon for perceiving himself above the law.

In *Halperin* v. *Kissinger,* 606 F.2d 1192 (1979), the D.C. Circuit Court considered whether the president should be entitled to absolute immunity from damage suits filed against him.[64] The case stems from a suit filed by Halperin, ex-chief of the National Security Council Planning Group, for money damages. He argued that Nixon et al. had placed an illegal wiretap on his home telephone from 1969 to 1971, violating his Fourth Amendment right to privacy and Title III of the Omnibus Crime Control and Safe Streets Act of 1968.[65] Nixon argued, however, that the president is entitled to absolute immunity in such tort actions. Again, as in the case five years earlier, Nixon's arguments were rejected with judicial vigor.

First, because of the illegal wiretap, the D.C. Circuit Court overruled the nominal award of one dollar for damages awarded by the district court (424 F.Supp. 838; 1976). Arguing that such wiretaps require a warrant justifying their use, the Court noted that Halperin and his family were entitled to be paid more than nominal damages because their basic constitutional rights were violated by Nixon et al.: "This court has held that in cases involving constitutional rights, compensation 'should not be approached in a niggardly spirit . . .'" (at 1208).

Second, rooting its arguments in the reasoning espoused in *Butz,* the Court noted that to accept Nixon's contention that he should be absolutely immune in this suit, "we would have to hold that his status as President sets him apart from the other high Executive officials named as defendants to this action. Such a distinction would have to rest on a determination either that the Constitution impliedly exempts the President from all liability in cases like this or that the repercussions of finding liability would be drastically adverse. Because we are unable to make that distinction, we do not believe he is entitled to absolute immunity to a damage action by a citizen subjected to an unconstitutional or illegal wiretap" (at 1210). The Court acknowledged specifically that the Constitution does not grant the president any special immunities and this should not be interpreted as an oversight, especially since the founding fathers saw fit to grant legislators certain immunities (at 1211).

The appeals court also found that it made no sense to allow absolute presidential immunity on what is called "prudential grounds." That is, the Court did not feel that the threat of damage suits against a president would prove disruptive to presidential management. The Court also noted that legitimate suits against the president would be "quite rare" (at 1212). More specifically, the Court argued that the extra personal burden placed upon presidents by permitting tort suits to be filed against them is not heavy enough to justify extending to them absolute immunity privileges (at 1213).

The Court in *Halperin* v. *Kissinger* took a very clear stand on the issue of whether presidents should be accorded absolute immunity status. The Court answered with an emphatic "No!" In so ruling, the Court upheld the wisdom of *Butz* that only qualified immunity, not absolute immunity, should be extended to all governmental administrators, except, of course, to those involved in adjudications. Clearly, the Court here refused to place the president in a kingly position by placing him above the law.

However, in *Nixon* v. *Fitzgerald,* 457 U.S. 731(1982), the Supreme Court took a radically different stand by ruling that the rule of official liability established in *Scheuer* and *Butz* does not apply to the president because the president, due to his unique office, is entitled to absolute immunity from damage suits (at 749–758). Employing a balance test, the Court argued "that a court, before exercising jurisdiction, must balance the constitutional weight of the interest to be served against the dangers of intrusion on the authority and functions of the Executive Branch. . . . When judicial action is needed to serve broad public interest . . . the exercise of jurisdiction has been held warranted. In the case of this merely private suit for damages based on a President's official acts, we hold it does not" (at 754).

Anticipating that scholars would criticize the Court's decision for apparently placing the president above the law, since this decision now makes presidents absolutely immune from liability suits, the Court argued that alternative remedies and deterrents for presidential misconduct such as impeachment, scrutiny by the press, various formal and informal checks, the desire to earn reelection, the need to retain prestige, and the president's concern for a good name in history "establishes that absolute immunity will not place the President 'above the law.' For the President, as for judges and prosecutors, absolute immunity merely precludes a particular private remedy for alleged misconduct in order to advance compelling public ends" (at 758). However, Justice White in dissent, joined by Justices Brennan, Marshall, and Blackmun, emphatically disagreed with the majority's holding, arguing that now "a President, acting within the outer boundaries of what Presidents normally do, may, without liability, deliberately cause serious injury to any number of citizens even though he knows his conduct violates a statute or tramples on the constitutional rights of those who are injured. . . . He would be immune regardless of the damage he inflicts, regardless of how violative of the statute and of the Constitution he knew his conduct to be, and regardless of his purpose" (at 764–765).

It should be emphasized that in the companion case, *Harlow* v. *Fitzgerald*, 457 U.S. 800 (1982), the Supreme Court made very clear that, although the president is entitled to absolute immunity from tort liability, his aides are not. The Court concluded that presidential aides, like most other administrators, should be entitled to only qualified immunity. Applying only the "knew or reasonably should have known" rule, the Court held "that government officials performing discretionary functions generally are shielded from liability for civil damages insofar as their conduct does not violate clearly established statutory or constitutional rights of which a reasonable person would have known" (at 818). It is important to point out that in *Harlow* the Court dropped the good faith-malicious intent factor, arguing that experience has shown that trying to establish the subjective intent of public officials, whether their actions were committed in good faith or bad faith (maliciously), has led to too many long and costly litigations that ultimately fail to prove whether good or bad intentions motivated the alleged tortious actions (at 813–815). In sum, *Harlow* established, as confirmed two years later in *Scherer,* that the only question that matters in liability claims against public officials is whether the official "knew or reasonably should have known" that his or her actions were violating clearly established statutory or constitutional rights.[66]

After a very comprehensive review of the amenability of presidents to lawsuits, from President George Washington to President George Bush, Laura Ray concluded that the immunity status of presidents is unclear because the Supreme Court ". . . has failed to meet its institutional obligation to define for the lower courts and for the country the contours of the relationship of presidential power to the legal process."[67] In particular, she found disturbing polar opposite decisions handed down in the 1974 *Nixon* decision and the 1982 *Fitzgerald* holding. The *Nixon* ruling clearly grants only qualified immunity to presidents and places them under the law, while the latter emphatically places presidents above the law by granting presidents absolute immunity while in the performance of their official acts.[68] For Justice White, *Fitzgerald* represents an anomaly because the decision rejects the wisdom espoused in *Nixon,* which upholds precedent, history, and the intention of the founding fathers to make presidents democratically accountable.

In 1994 Paula Jones filed a civil suit against President Clinton, seeking $700,000 in damages for sexual harassment (making improper sexual advances) when she was an Arkansas state employee and he was governor. Whether such a damage claim can be filed against a president is very questionable since no court has addressed the question of whether a president can be sued for damages for unofficial actions before he became president. The *Fitzgerald* ruling suggests that a president is absolutely immune from all "merely private suits for damages," but in *Fitzgerald* the Supreme Court was concerned in particular with protecting presidents against liability suits while performing their official duties as president.

In 1995, a federal district court in Arkansas ruled that Jones's suit could not be heard until after President Clinton leaves office, although the discovery process could begin. However, in 1996 the Eighth Circuit Court reversed, holding that the case can proceed because a president can be sued for his unofficial acts even while in office.

Clinton has appealed to the Supreme Court, contending that the reasoning applied in *Fitzgerald* should make the president immune from *all* "merely private suits for damages."

SUMMARY

Should individuals be able to sue the government and its administrators for their tortious acts in the same manner liability claims can be filed against parties in the private sector? Under the common law doctrine that reflects our Anglo-Saxon heritage, the government was made totally immune from damage suits, while its administrative officers were made quite vulnerable to liability actions against them for tortious behavior. However, some courts did employ the sovereign immunity doctrine to protect the government, as well as its officials, reasoning that the actions of the two could not be separated in practice. Other courts insisted on adopting the old Anglo-Saxon common law argument that the government's administrators should not be exempted from liability suits because to do so would place them above the law, something which is not legitimate in a rule-of-law nation.

The sovereign immunity doctrine is rooted in the old British common law thinking that the king can do no wrong. Although this legal principle was never officially adopted by Congress, it was mysteriously recognized by American courts from the very beginning of the Republic. This was true in spite of the fact that the doctrine, especially when it was used to protect the government's officials, made sense for old monarchical Europe, but virtually no sense for America—a political system based on the rule of law. Regardless of the doctrine's apparent un-American character, it has been only very modestly modified.

Reformers had pushed for the abolition of the sovereign immunity doctrine since at least the 1930s because of its blatantly unfair character. The basic argument was that it was patently unfair to deprive persons of the right to sue the government for its tortious actions against them, especially since the powers of the government placed it in a strategic position to cause injury to parties. Nevertheless, the doctrine survived for so long because proponents of the doctrine, never defending it for being fair to individuals, contended that damage suits had the potential to destroy the government upon which society is dependent. Consequently, the doctrine was justified on the grounds that it is better to allow an individual or a few people to suffer than to permit liability suits to place society in jeopardy.

The development of qualified immunity status for government officials followed an uneven road, which can be divided into three basic stages. The first stage lasted until the late 1800s. During this stage the courts generally ruled that the government's administrators could be held liable for their tortious behavior toward citizens. But placing public administrators in such a position was considered unfair since they could ill afford to pay damage claims out of their own pockets. Besides, it was thought that making these devoted public servants vulnerable to tort liability claims tended to disrupt the administrative process.

In 1896 the Court which heard *Spalding* ruled that top-level administrators, who employ considerable discretion in making policy decisions, should not be placed in a position in which they would have to worry about whether they could be sued for their official discretionary decisions. But since virtually all administrators employ discretion in the line of duty, it was only a matter of time before the *Spalding* logic was employed by later courts to exempt practically all administrative officials from damage action suits. Indeed, the Supreme Court in *Barr* (1959) applied *Spalding* to cover virtually all governmental administrators. However, scholarly reaction to *Barr* was extremely negative and the courts soon shifted their position. After *Barr* the courts began to find governmental officials at all levels of government increasingly more vulnerable to liability actions against them, especially when it could be shown that they denied clearly established constitutional rights to persons when they knew, or should have known, better (*Scherer;* 1984).

Presently, the government has only limited immunity from liability claims, while its officers enjoy only qualified immunity. In many instances, this allows persons the opportunity to choose between suing the government or its officers, depending upon which course of action would be most beneficial. Although the courts have made suing the government and particularly its officials easier, these "generous" courts have created new financial burdens for government and its employees, even though the courts, applying various tests, have made winning tort suits quite difficult. Nonetheless, potentially tort suits can prove to be a financial disaster, especially if publicly insured public officials lose a *Bivens* or Section 1983 claim amounting to awards of millions of dollars in punitive damages. State and especially local governments have been particularly hard hit by the enormous increase in Section 1983 suits that have been filed against them, making it difficult for them to obtain and retain liability insurance at affordable rates. Consequently, state and local authorities have organized to meet what they perceive as the growing crisis in tort liability and insurance unavailability. They have turned to Congress for help, pleading with Congress to pass legislation that would reduce their liability under tort law (for example, doing away with punitive damage claims, placing ceilings on damage awards) and ease their tort liability insurance problems (for example, stabilize rates and prevent insurance companies from canceling liability insurance except for nonpayment or fraud). However, by the mid-1990s not much relief had been provided.

NOTES

1. For a good theoretical discussion of the costs and benefits of strict liability, see Richard A. Epstein, *A Theory of Strict Liability* (San Francisco: CATO Institute, 1980).
2. Harold J. Krent, "Reconceptualizing Sovereign Immunity," *Vanderbilt Law Review,* vol. 45 (November 1992), 1530.
3. However, the very fact that our lawmakers allowed the courts to employ the doctrine for so long implies that our legislators gave at least tacit approval to its use.
4. *Muskopf* v. *Corning Hospital District,* 359 P.2d 457, 458–459 (Cal., 1961).
5. John E. Sherry, "The Myth That the King Can Do No Wrong: A Comparative Study of the Sovereign Immunity Doctrine in the United States and the New York Court of Claims," *Administrative Law Review,* 22 (October 1969), 58, held that it is the citizen who needs protection, not the state: "Sovereign immunity is at best a judicial protective

device created to immunize a weak government against oppressive and insensitive citizen demands. . . . Today it is the citizen who is helpless in the face of growing governmental intrusion into his very life, often with unpredictable and tragic results. . . . Sovereign immunity is dangerous to our democratic institutions."

6. Bernard Schwartz, *Administrative Law,* 2nd ed. (Boston: Little, Brown and Company, 1984), 568.
7. Kenneth C. Davis, *Administrative Law Treatise.* vol. 4, 2nd ed. (San Diego: K.C. Davis Publishing Co., 1983), 191–192.
8. Kenneth C. Davis, *Administrative Law and Government* (St. Paul, Minn.: West Publishing Company, 1975), 111.
9. Davis makes this argument in several works, but his best argument against sovereign immunity is "Sovereign Immunity Must Go," *Administrative Law Review,* 22 (April 1970), 383–405. See also Davis, *Administrative Law Treatise,* 4: 191–198.
10. This should not imply, however, that the government should not do what it can to provide emergency relief and follow-up care to those harmed in such a tragedy, but the relief provided would be voluntary, not compelled by judicial orders as payment of damages.
11. Davis, *Administrative Law,* 220.
12. Bernard Schwartz, *Administrative Law,* 3rd ed. (Boston: Little, Brown and Company, 1991), 614.
13. Louis L. Jaffe, "Suits against Governments and Officers: Damage Actions," *Harvard Law Review,* 77 (December 1963), 213.
14. *United States* v. *Caltex (Philippines), Inc.,* 344 U.S. 149 (1952).
15. It should be recognized that the governmental and official immunity doctrine never existed in pure form. In other words, limited and qualified immunity always did exist since the courts have always honored some exceptions to the sovereign immunity doctrine. Even Congress early in our history recognized that the government should not be completely immune from suits. Congress did establish the United States Court of Claims in 1855, thereby eliminating the government's immunity status in the area of contracts. Thus, limited governmental immunity and qualified immunity imply a significant relaxation of immunity protection, which has occurred in recent years. It should be noted that some authors use the terms "limited" and "qualified" interchangeably to apply to governmental and official immunity. Of course, "limited" and "qualified" do convey the same meaning when applied to immunity. I make the distinction only for the sake of clarity.
16. Bernard Schwartz, *Administrative Law,* 3rd ed., 598.
17. A. V. Dicey, *Introduction to the Study of the Law of the Constitution,* 9th ed. (London: Macmillan, 1952), 193.
18. David H. Rosenbloom, "Public Administrators' Official Immunity and the Supreme Court: Developments during the 1970s," *Public Administration Review,* vol. 40 (March-April 1980), 168.
19. The Court in *Butz* v. *Economou,* 434 U.S. 994 (1978), upheld the validity of extending absolute immunity to governmental administrators who perform quasi-judicial functions, although in general the Court heartily endorsed the concept of qualified immunity for most public officials.
20. Rosenbloom, "Public Administrators' Official Immunity and the Supreme Court," 169.
21. Ibid.
22. The Fourth Amendment, of course, guarantees to citizens the right "to be secure in their persons, houses, papers, and effects, against unreasonable searches and seizures." The amend-

ment also states that "no warrants shall [be] issued but upon probable cause, supported by oath or affirmation, and particularly describing the place to be searched, and the persons or things to be seized." These protections, the amendment says, "shall not be violated."

23. *Davis* v. *Passman,* 442 U.S. 228 (1979); and *Carlson* v. *Green,* 446 U.S. 14 (1980).

24. Since *Bivens* this 1983 provision, as we shall see, has been employed as the basis of tort suits by many petitioners intending to win liability cases against governmental officials who have violated the constitutional rights of citizens.

25. Scott C. Arakaki and Robert E. Badger, Jr., "*Wyatt* v. *Cole* and Qualified Immunity for Private Parties in Section 1983 Suits," *Notre Dame Law Review,* vol. 69 (1995), 762.

26. Ibid., 737–739; 769–770.

27. Martin A. Schwartz and Eileen Kaufman, "Punitive Damages in Section 1983 Cases," *New York Law Journal,* November 16, 1993, 3–6.

28. Rosenbloom, "Public Administrators' Official Immunity and the Supreme Court," 170.

29. Ibid.

30. Bernard Schwartz, *Administrative Law* (Boston: Little, Brown, 1976), 560.

31. Ibid., 561.

32. *Butz* v. *Economou,* 434 U.S. 994 (1978); *Carlson* v. *Green,* 446 U.S. 14 (1980); and *Harlow* v. *Fitzgerald,* 457 U.S. 800 (1982).

33. National Institute of Municipal Law Officers Mid-Year Seminar, "The Tort Liability and Municipal Insurance Crises," Executive Committee Report (Washington, D.C., 1986), 1. Also see Eric Wiesenthal, "Public Liability Crisis Sparks Reform," *Public Administration Times, 9* (March 1, 1986), 1 and 3. Wiesenthal reports that Section 1983 lawsuits against states and localities have increased from 260 in 1960 to more than 38,000 in 1981, causing a crisis for states and localities. To alleviate the crisis, state and local officials have asked Congress to place new regulations on insurance companies to stabilize insurance coverage and rates and to reduce the liability of states and cities and their officials (for example, eliminating or lowering punitive damage awards, shortening time limit to file damage claims, and setting liability ceilings).

34. See Kenneth C. Davis and Richard J. Pierce, Jr., *Administrative Law Treatise,* 3rd ed., vol. III, 223–226 for a discussion of applying the "clearly established" test in cases.

35. It should be noted that Sec. 1983 does not, according to Judge Levanthal in *Expeditions Unlimited, Inc.* v. *Smithsonian Institution,* 566 F.2d 289 (D.C.Cir., 1977), necessarily overrule *Barr's* application of absolute immunity in cases not involving constitutional violations of citizens' rights by federal officers. However, the impact of *Barr* has been softened by the weight of many "anti-Barr" decisions throughout the 1970s and into the 1990s.

36. For a review of the significance of the *Butz* decision, especially as it applies to Section 1983 liability suits at all governmental levels, see Robert H. Freilich and Richard G. Carlisle, *Section 1983: A Sword and Shield* (Chicago: American Bar Association, 1983), 60, 301, and 336.

37. Kenneth C. Davis and Richard J. Pierce, Jr., *Administrative Law Treatise,* 3rd ed., vol. III, 277.

38. Ibid.

39. See Philip L. Gregory, Jr., "Executive Immunity: For Constitutional Torts after *Butz* v. *Economou,*" *Santa Clara Law Review,* 20 (Spring 1980), 467–72; Schuck, *Suing Government: Citizen Remedies for Official Wrongs* (New Haven, Conn.: Yale University Press, 1983); and Paul T. Hardy and J. Devereaux Weeks, *Personal Liability of Public*

Officials under Federal Law (Athens, Ga.: Carl Vinson Institute of Government, The University of Georgia, 1985).

40. It could be argued that under social contract theory, as developed through the ages by Thomas Hobbes, Jean Jacques Rousseau, and especially John Locke, citizens should have a right to redress governmental officials' violations of the agreed-upon contract (for example, the Constitution). Under contract theory, the sovereign's power is limited by the contract to certain actions. For example, the sovereign, the U.S. government, cannot, under the Constitution, take away private property without due process of law. Thus, freedom would be severely jeopardized if citizens could not sue the government or its officials for tortious actions against them, since these citizens would be left without remedies short of rebellion (justified, incidentally, by Locke under these conditions) to redress violations of the contract. In short, the undue hardships mentioned above are created, in reality, by unconstitutional actions.

41. Cal. Gov't Code, Secs. 825.4, 825.6.

42. For a fascinating discussion of the pros and cons of the application of this principle, see Epstein, *Theory of Strict Liability,* esp. chaps. 1–3, 8, and 10.

43. I say "apparently" because at this point it is uncertain in which direction we are headed in the area of liability, especially since court decisions in recent years have caused dramatic changes in public tort laws. Davis and Pierce in their recent *Administrative Law Treatise,* 3rd ed., vol. III, state that the entire area of tort law is very complex and very confused (p. 276).

44. Kenneth C. Davis and Richard J. Pierce, Jr., *Administrative Law Treatise,* 3rd ed., vol. III, 204.

45. Christopher H. Schroeder, "Rights Against Risks," *Columbia Law Review,* 86 (April 1986), 496–562. Peter Huber makes an even stronger case for this position in "Safety and the Second Best: The Hazards of Public Risk Management in the Courts," *Columbia Law Review,* 85 (March 1985), 277–337.

46. Kenneth C. Davis, *Administrative Law,* 218.

47. Kenneth C. Davis and Richard J. Pierce, Jr., *Administrative Law Treatise,* 3rd ed., vol. III, 206.

48. Kenneth C. Davis, *Administrative Law,* 218.

49. Kenneth C. Davis and Richard J. Pierce, *Administrative Law Treatise,* 3rd ed., vol. III, 206–207.

50. Section 421(h) was amended in 1974 (88 Stat. 50) in light of the *Bivens* decision to make law enforcement officers essentially liable for committing the tortious acts specified in Sec. 421(h). That is, the United States is presently liable for assault, battery, false imprisonment, false arrest, abuse of process, or malicious prosecution committed by its law enforcement officers.

51. 102 Stat. 4564.

52. In *United States* v. *Smith,* 111 S.Ct. 1180 (1991), the Court ruled that the plaintiff has no remedy if an FTCA exclusion makes the government not liable.

53. Bernard Schwartz, *Administrative Law,* 3rd ed., 613.

54. Ibid., 612.

55. The original purpose of Section 1983 of the Civil Rights Act of 1871 was to enforce the Fourteenth Amendment on the states, making state and local governments and their officers liable if they violated the constitutional rights of their citizens. After the Civil War and the passage of the Fourteenth Amendment in 1868, many states and their local gov-

ernments, as well as their officials, refused to honor the due process and equal protection clauses of the Fourteenth Amendment. In fact, many state and local officials were members of the Ku Klux Klan or at least were KKK sympathizers. Because the Civil Rights Act of 1871 targeted such KKK supporters, the Act was popularly known as the KKK Act. Its purpose then, as it is still today, was in part to scare officials into compliance, threatening them and their governments with tort suits if they don't.

56. Kenneth C. Davis and Richard J. Pierce, Jr., *Administrative Law Treatise,* 3rd ed., vol. III, 261–262.
57. Walter Gellhorn and Clark Byse, *Administrative Law,* 377.
58. Kenneth C. Davis and Richard J. Pierce, Jr., *Administrative Law Treatise,* 3rd ed., vol. III, 276.
59. Ibid.
60. Ibid., 276–281.
61. See Margaret J. Copernoll, *"Halperin* v. *Kissinger:* The D.C. Circuit Rejects Presidential Immunity from Damage Action," *Loyola Law Review,* 26 (Fall 1980), 147. Also see Peter M. Shane, "Legal Disagreement and Negotiation in a Government of Laws: The Case of Executive Privilege Claims against Congress," *Minnesota Law Review,* 71 (February 1987), 481–84.
62. The courts have generally interpreted "official duty" very liberally, thus assuring legislators and judges of very comfortable immunity protections so that they could perform their official duties without fear that they might have to defend their actions in court. However, in *United States* v. *Brewster,* 408 U.S. 501 (1972), the Supreme Court argued that legislators should not be immune from being prosecuted for criminal conduct (for example, accepting bribes) under the Speech or Debate Clause.
63. It is important to remember that the Court, in *Butz* v. *Economou,* 434 U.S. 994 (1978), recognized that prosecutors, administrative law judges, and other administrators connected directly with adjudicative processes needed immunity protection to perform their jobs properly. Thus, some administrators today do enjoy absolute immunity privileges.
64. In this case Richard M. Nixon was named as a defendant, along with former National Security Advisor Henry Kissinger, former United States Attorney General John Mitchell, and seven others.
65. 18 U.S.C., Secs. 2510–20 (1976).
66. For a comprehensive analysis of the immunity of presidential aides in light of the *Harlow* decision, see Kathryn Dix Dowle, "The Derivative and Discretionary-Function Immunities of Presidential and Congressional Aides in Constitutional Torts," *Ohio State Law Journal,* 44 (1983), 944–85.
67. Laura Krugman Ray, "From Prerogative To Accountability: The Amenability of the President to Suit", *Kentucky Law Journal,* vol. 80 (1991/1992), 813.
68. Ibid.

CHAPTER 10

AN ADMINISTRATIVE LAW CHALLENGE: BALANCING SOCIETAL AND INDIVIDUAL RIGHTS

BALANCING: A TOUGH CHALLENGE FOR ADMINISTRATORS

When public administrators take steps to implement public policies, they must cope with the extremely frustrating and challenging question: due process or fair treatment for whom—the individual at issue in any particular case or society? Administrators face a difficult choice because, obviously, what may seem fair for an individual may be unjust for society, and vice versa. In short, administrators must make difficult daily choices between the interests of society and those of the individual. And despite how critical these decisions may be to the individual or our society, a viable common value framework has not been developed to guide these choices. Thus, this decision-making process, which affects our fundamental liberties, is imperfect at best.

The purpose of this chapter is to highlight some of the issues and difficulties of trying to balance the rights of society with the rights of the individual. This is a vital administrative law topic which should not be understated. Unquestionably, the administrator's task of balancing societal and individual rights when implementing public policies has presented and will continue to present the toughest general administrative challenge.[1] To convey how involved the balancing issue is, I have relied heavily upon relevant and informative court opinions.

PRESERVING INDIVIDUAL LIBERTIES IN THE FACE OF MASS CONTROL EFFORTS: AN INTRODUCTORY COMMENT

The social contract theorists (Thomas Hobbes, John Locke, and Jean-Jacques Rousseau) once argued that individuals would be willing to surrender some of their personal freedoms to a governmental authority in exchange for peace, security, and order. Essentially, these theorists imagined that society without government was chaotic and full of dangers and human suffering. To escape such a wretched life, reasonable persons would realize that more pleasant living could be attained if governmental institutions were created to order, regulate, and elevate society. Consequently, the prospects of a better life led people to form a "contract" with the government, eagerly consenting to the right of government to make the rules necessary to preserve harmony in the social system (to promote "ordered liberty").

For all practical purposes, this conceptualization of the status of individuals in society before government is still accurate today and helps us to comprehend a problem which plagues all modern societies. Fundamentally, as suggested, administrative law implicitly aims at striking an equitable and practical balance between the rights of individual citizens and the rights of the collective citizenry (society). But the intensifying problem in modern American society, according to some critics, is that more and more institutional decisions appear to be made to protect group or societal interests at the expense of the individual. It appears that the costs to individuals for the administration of "ordered liberty" in the United States are soaring upward, despite attempts by the American Civil Liberties Union and other such organizations to reverse this trend by fighting to protect the constitutional rights of individual citizens.

We have noted thus far in this text that many relatively recent laws and court rulings have helped to preserve the rights of citizens. But given the rapid expansion of administrative government, some have argued that the preservation and extension of individual rights have not kept pace with the liberties the new administrative state has taken away. Indeed, Herbert Kaufman asserts that all of the new regulations that have been adopted for the sake of society may have taken too much freedom away from individuals.[2]

It just might be that to uphold its contractual obligation to preserve ordered liberty in our society, the government has been justified in taking the regulatory steps it has. Increases in crime, consumer rip-offs, and the poisoning of our drinking water by the illicit dumping of toxic wastes provide just a few reasons that increased governmental regulations may have been justified. Nevertheless, the individual freedom we enjoy in America may be in jeopardy; certainly it is already much different from the freedoms of our ancestors. One major problem for administrative law is this: How can individual liberties still be protected in an atmosphere in which governmental officials are struggling to keep order and continued socioeconomic prosperity in a society increasing in numbers and complexity and in which urban decay, crime, environmental pollution, and so on threaten to disrupt and destroy the nation's health?

Every time an administrative agency or a court makes a decision which benefits a larger group at the expense of the individual, another liberty is lost and our way of life changes. For example, because hijacking airplanes was a real threat to air passengers during the 1970s, governmental officials decided in good faith that the public could best be protected if they required each person boarding planes to be searched. The thorough search may involve opening up purses, attache cases, and even holiday gifts. Likewise, the increase in drug traffic has caused authorities to carry out humiliating searches at border stations, the persons seemingly selected almost at the whim of border officials who try to judge possible smugglers. These searches occasionally involve embarrassing naked body searches. Under normal circumstances judges have demanded probable cause before they would issue search warrants permitting particular individuals to be searched. When a search warrant is issued, the signed and dated warrant specifies the place, the person or persons to be searched, and the things to be seized. In the 1990s new satellite remote sensing technology poses a new threat to privacy rights because now the government can conduct broad, invasive "open field" searches using powerful cameras such as the KFA-1000 to view tiny details in objects or on persons from great distances.

In short, searches administered to protect society against hijackings, drug abuse, etc. have a noble purpose, but nevertheless, such searches are not specifically aimed at individuals where probable cause can be established, but against anyone who boards an airplane or passes through a border station. In many respects, such governmental actions against individuals not only take away previously enjoyed freedoms; such administrative procedures tend to be insulting and dehumanizing as well. Elaborating, Herbert Kaufman comments that it is not surprising that the vast majority of decent citizens become resentful of all the abusive rigmarole (red tape) that they must endure so that a tiny fraction may be caught and punished. From this perspective, Kaufman concludes, such governmental rules and regulations, which tend to restrict individual freedom, "are neither justified nor justifiable."[3]

The true constitutional legitimacy of such bothersome administrative searches is highly questionable, since the Fourth Amendment clearly prohibits "unreasonable" searches and seizures, and Amendments Five and Fourteen in general call for citizens to be accorded due process. However, despite such infringements upon the constitutional rights of citizens, such administrative practices will probably continue to be allowed so that society can be protected. Whether this will prove beneficial or harmful in the long run, when all costs and benefits are considered, is difficult to judge.[4] But administrative policymakers and reviewing courts, as well as our legislators, must acknowledge the fact that groups are mere *abstractions* and only individuals are *real*. When administrative decisions are made to benefit a large group or society in general, in reality only individuals are affected. This is so because groups, in the final analysis, are made up of nothing more than individuals. Consequently, the critical question for our political system has become: Should we permit public administrators, supposedly for the sake of the public welfare, to execute administrative measures which help to bury our constitutional liberties?

To the late Justice William O. Douglas, by the early 1970s the central question in America had become "whether the government by force of its largesse has the power to 'buy up' rights guaranteed by the Constitution."[5] This had become the crucial question for Douglas because he perceived modern bureaucracy as "not only slow, lumbering, and oppressive; it is omnipresent. It touches everyone's life at numerous points. It pries more and more into private affairs, breaking down the barriers that individuals erect to give them some insulation from the intrigues and harassments of modern life."[6] Thus, one task of administrative law in the 1990s is to seek solutions to societal problems which do not crush individual liberty for the sake of promoting some abstract noble social goal. History should have taught us by now that totalitarian societies tend to emerge when leaders insist that individuals surrender their liberties for the sake of a greater common good. This is not to assert that no sense of a common good or public interest exists. In a free society no state efforts to promote the general welfare should be achieved by robbing citizens of their inalienable rights.

ADMINISTRATIVE PRACTICES AND THE BILL OF RIGHTS

What is the Bill of Rights, and what precise relevance does it have to administrative law? The first ten amendments to the United States Constitution constitute the Bill of Rights. State constitutions also have bills of rights. Applicable provisions in the Bill of Rights have been applied to the states by various court decisions over the years. The Bill of Rights places restrictions upon what the government can do while exercising its powers; thus it is quite consistent with the democratic principle of limited government. Actually, the Bill of Rights was added to the Constitution to satisfy those who insisted at the time of its ratification that they would oppose ratification of the Constitution unless a clear statement of rights was attached to specify the personal freedoms individuals would retain under the new government. The Bill of Rights, which guarantees the retention of basic liberties for individuals, has always been considered by constitutional scholars as absolutely essential to the maintenance of a free society.[7]

Specific provisions in the Bill of Rights guarantee American citizens various protections against arbitrary governmental intrusions into their personal life. For example, it protects persons against arbitrary invasions of their privacy by public officials; preserves the right of citizens to state what they think publicly; prohibits the government from stopping citizens from organizing to, say, protest governmental policies; guarantees persons accused of crimes certain due process rights so that they can have an opportunity to prove their innocence; and forbids the taking of life, liberty, and private property without due process under law. In sum, the Bill of Rights places restrictions upon the government by underwriting the principle that individuals should be left alone unless the government can show good legal cause that they should not be.

It should be emphasized that the courts have not interpreted these rights to be absolute. Common sense should dictate that certain circumstances would not justify the absolute extension of these rights, especially if they are used to commit illegal acts which threaten the rights and safety of other citizens. In some situations, Justice

Oliver Wendell Holmes argued, the misuse of such rights creates "a clear and present danger" for others or for society. In regard to the acceptable limits of the right of free speech, Justice Holmes remarked: "The question in every case is whether the words used are in such circumstances and are of such a nature as to create a clear and present danger that they will bring about the substantive evils that Congress has a right to prevent. It is a question of proximity and degree." In the same famous decision, he noted, for example, that no one should have the right to yell "Fire!" in a crowded theater and then claim a constitutional right to do so.[8]

The courts have traditionally employed a balancing doctrine to determine whether individuals have abused their constitutional rights, causing an undue threat to the public interest. When the courts employ the balancing doctrine, they are faced with the difficult task of choosing between the rights of the individual and the rights of society. That is, the courts must protect the interests of society while simultaneously preserving the constitutional rights of citizens. This task is becoming more difficult as societal problems become more acute, requiring more intense governmental involvement.

But when making legislation and administering public policies, legislators and administrators must also be guided by the balancing principle. Administrators especially are faced with the daily chore of balancing Bill of Rights guarantees with the apparent needs of society. Although many administrative activities do not involve the application of the Bill of Rights, many do. Administrators are particularly restricted in their regulatory functions by the provisions of the Fourth Amendment, although they must frequently be cognizant of the restrictions placed upon them by the Fifth and First Amendments and, to a much lesser extent, some of the other constitutional amendments.

The remainder of the chapter is an analysis of how well administrative agencies have been doing in preserving Bill of Rights liberties for individuals while implementing public programs aimed at protecting and promoting our nation's general welfare. Only topics not discussed in previous chapters are considered here. The analysis begins with the Fourth Amendment, since it has the greatest relevance to administrative law.

ADMINISTRATIVE ACTIONS UNDER THE FOURTH AMENDMENT

What does the Fourth Amendment guarantee, and how has it been applied to restrict the behavior of administrative officials? The Fourth Amendment is clearly one of the most important constitutional amendments because it protects individuals "in their persons, houses, papers, and effects, against unreasonable searches and seizures." The amendment specifically prohibits search warrants from being issued except "upon probable cause, supported by oath or affirmation, and particularly describing the place to be searched, and the persons or things to be seized."

Despite its critical relevance to the preservation of individual liberties, this amendment has always been difficult to interpret and apply in practice. What constitutes an unreasonable search and seizure has not always been easy to determine. Generally, the courts have ruled that the particular circumstances surrounding the search and seizure determine the reasonableness of the search and seizure. For example, warrantless searches and seizures have been allowed by the courts when it could be demonstrated that circumstances made it unfeasible to obtain a warrant. Consequently, the constitutionality of certain search and seizure tactics has often been decided on a case-to-case basis, creating great uncertainty in search and seizure law. But one thing is certain: evidence obtained through illegal searches and seizures cannot normally be used in federal or state courts, although such evidence may be used for questioning witnesses before grand juries.[9] For our purposes, the major question is whether Fourth Amendment protections should be applied to administrative law cases which involve noncriminal, or civil, proceedings.

Historically, the prevalent attitude has been that certain Bill of Rights guarantees, such as Fourth Amendment rights, should apply only to criminal procedures, not to civil procedures. For example, Fourth Amendment safeguards have not been applied customarily to deportation proceedings involving the Immigration and Naturalization Service, because such proceedings are considered civil and not criminal proceedings protected by the Bill of Rights. It was apparently not considered necessary to apply Fourth Amendment protections, as well as other Bill of Rights safeguards, to civil cases, because the penalties for civil offenses were not perceived as severe enough to warrant elaborate Bill of Rights protections for individuals. Besides, it was maintained that the state could not afford to absorb the extra administrative costs for such protections and that the extension of such safeguards would make efficient and effective administration impossible.

But it would be patently naive to hold that administrative actions cannot result in the severe deprivation of a person's personal liberties since Congress, as well as state legislatures, has delegated to administrators the power to inflict grave punishments upon individuals or corporate persons without providing them with the benefit of independent judicial judgment.[10] Consequently, concerned observers have begun to question very seriously how fair it is to deny persons constitutional due process protections in certain situations just because the proceedings are labeled "civil" instead of "criminal."[11]

The Administrative Power to Arrest and Imprison

Is it possible in this civilized and free democratic country to be arrested and imprisoned for relatively long periods of time, sometimes for many months, without ever stepping into a courtroom? Shocking as it is, the answer is yes. In *Wong Wing* v. *United States,* 163 U.S. 228 (1896), the Court held that persons cannot be imprisoned *as a punishment* unless they are first given a criminal trial, according to constitutional requirements, and sentenced by a judicial tribunal. Such a due process safeguard has always been considered essential to any society which cherishes liberty. According to Bernard Schwartz, "the absence of nonjudicial powers of imprisonment sharply distinguishes our legal system from those we disparagingly describe as totalitarian."[12]

However, it is crucial for our purposes to point out that the court in *Wong Wing* ruled explicitly that in America persons can be apprehended and sent to jail as long as the incarceration is not done with the intent to punish. In this immigration case, the Court reasoned that immigration administrators can legitimately detain or confine persons temporarily in order to carry out effectively their congressionally mandated legislative functions (at 235).

Thus, Congress has delegated to administrators the power to arrest and imprison temporarily persons who have not been accused of or convicted of any criminal wrongdoings. But why should Congress want to give administrators the discretionary authority to arrest and imprison noncriminals? In some cases the administrative power to seize and confine persons appears quite reasonable and necessary to protect the larger interests of society; but in other situations the power seems to permit administrators to exploit and punish innocent persons in a patently unreasonable way. On the reasonable side, it seems sensible that public health administrators, to protect the public health, should have the authority to apprehend and confine those who pose a dangerous health threat to a community.[13] In *Ex parte Hardcastle,* 208 S.W. 531 (Tex., 1919), the court asserted that it makes good sense to uphold laws which call for the confinement of those who have been exposed to or are carriers of infectious diseases, even if the laws call for the confinement of such persons without the benefit of a judicial proceeding. Obviously, to protect the general welfare by preventing the spread of a contagious disease, public officials would have to possess powers to enable them to act quickly to stop such individuals from walking freely in the community. For example, the recent AIDS crisis has caused some to recommend the radical step of rounding up and confining those with AIDS to stop the spread of the deadly disease. This suggestion has created much controversy. In fact, early in President Clinton's administration numerous Haitian refugees were detained at Guantanamo Bay Naval Base against their will for long periods of time with U.S. authorities refusing to grant them parole because they had tested HIV-positive. Was this action fair to the refugees? A U.S. district court thought not, ruling that Attorney General Reno and other federal officials had abused their discretion by refusing to grant these Haitian refugees parole simply because they had tested HIV-positive [*Haitian Centers Council, Inc.* v. *Sale,* 823 F.Supp. 1028 (E.D. N.Y. 1993)]. But were Attorney General Reno and the other federal authorities just trying to promote America's public health and safety?

The vital questions seem to be: When do seizures and confinements become unreasonable and unjustified, even in light of administrative efforts to promote the public interest? How much should the individual be expected to suffer for the good of the public welfare? The public has an interest in a public prosecutor's being able to prosecute a murder case successfully. Therefore, it may be in the interest of the prosecutor to hold a key material witness to a murder in jail until the trial. But how long should the prosecutor be allowed to detain the witness—days, weeks, many months? Continued postponements of trial dates have been known to push trial dates back for months, possibly delaying the trial's outcome for more than a year. Can any society in good conscience hold a material witness, guilty of no crime, in jail for such a long period of time?[14] Should an INS administrator be permitted to seize and incarcerate for months, without benefit of bail, an illegal alien, whose deportability is being determined by the INS? Are not such administrative arrests and detentions flatly contrary to the spirit of the Fourth Amendment, however technically legal they may be in the eyes of the courts?[15] Is not a legal system rather strange if it provides more due process protections from arrests and imprisonment to those accused of violent crimes than to those accused of no criminal conduct at all?

Abel v. *United States,* 362 U.S. 217 (1960), is an excellent case for conveying the potential dangers behind the use of administrative arrests and detentions. Specifically, the case serves to demonstrate how an administrative official, with powers granted by Congress, can work with law enforcement officers to undermine Fourth Amendment safeguards. Abel was a Soviet spy who the FBI believed was engaged in espionage activities against the United States. Upon learning about his whereabouts, the FBI wanted to arrest him at his hotel, but FBI officers lacked enough evidence against him to satisfy the probable cause requirement needed before a judge would be willing to sign an arrest warrant. To circumvent the constitutional red tape, those FBI agents sought the assistance of INS officials. Having been told by the FBI that Abel was an illegal alien, the district director of the INS made out an arrest warrant. Both FBI and INS officers then went to Abel's hotel with the administrative arrest warrant to make the arrest. This FBI-INS cooperative effort allowed the FBI to obtain an arrest which the FBI alone would not have been able to make if it had to uphold Fourth Amendment due process restrictions. After the arrest, Abel was placed in solitary confinement for five weeks at a detention camp. It was not until criminal charges were finally filed against him that the judicial branch was brought into his case.

The Court in *Abel* had to decide whether the administrative procedures leading to the arrest and imprisonment of Abel were lawful under the Fourth Amendment. Specifically, Abel had charged that the arrest was unconstitutional because the arrest warrant did not satisfy the Fourth Amendment's warrant requirements. However, the court upheld the constitutionality of such "standard" INS arrest procedures (at 233).

From the very beginning this decision attracted heated protests from liberal critics who believed that the ruling sanctioned actions against individuals which the constitutional framers, in writing the Fourth Amendment, definitely wanted to prevent. In a dissent to *Abel,* Justice William J. Brennan argued that the Fourth Amendment was written to prevent such violations of a person's basic rights. Brennan made the point that under this administrative arrest, where no judicial voice was heard, the INS never had to justify any of its actions to an independent judge. Clearly, he maintained, some judicial control over such administrative actions is needed to preserve constitutional due process requirements (at 248–56).

However, not all lower courts have always followed the controversial *Abel* holding. For example, in 1994 in *Alexander* v. *City and County of San Francisco,* 29 F.3d 1355, the Ninth Circuit Court ruled that an administrative search warrant obtained by health inspectors to check for health code violations did not authorize police officers to enter a home to arrest the occupant, which actually led to police killing the occupant. The court stressed that prior cases, including, ironically, *Abel,*

". . . make it very clear that an administrative search may not be converted into an instrument which serves the very different needs of law enforcement officials. If it could, then all of the protections traditionally afforded against intrusions by the police would evaporate, to be replaced by the much weaker barriers erected between citizens and other governmental agencies. It is because the mission of those agencies is less potently hostile to a citizen's interests than are the missions of the police that the barriers may be weak as they are and still not jeopardize Fourth Amendment guarantees" (at 1361).

Three years after *Abel,* in *United States* v. *Alvarado,* 321 F.2d 336 (2d Cir., 1963), the court upheld the constitutionality of an administrative arrest during which immigration authorities took even greater liberties with the Fourth Amendment. This time, acting according to statute, they arrested an alien without first obtaining an administrative warrant.[16] In *Abel,* at least an administrative warrant was obtained before the arrest was made. Admittedly, the administrative warrant, as contrasted to a regular judicial warrant, does not go very far in protecting an individual under the Fourth Amendment. Nevertheless, some reasons must be given to show cause for deportability before the administrative warrant can be signed by an administrative officer.

What, then, is the real significance of *Abel* and *Alvarado* in light of the Fourth Amendment? The Fourth Amendment, to reiterate, guarantees essentially that persons cannot be subjected to "unreasonable searches and seizures." If searches and seizures were to be carried out, the constitutional framers required probable cause to be established before search and seizure warrants could be issued, presumably by an independent judicial officer. These quite simple constitutional procedures seemed to provide the necessary safeguards to ensure that if searches and seizures were executed, they would be kept within reasonable bounds, consistent with the concept of limited government. The Fourth Amendment emphasizes that its provisions "shall not be violated," and nothing in the amendment suggests that its provisions cannot be violated by law enforcement officers but can be violated by other governmental administrators—regardless of how the courts have interpreted the applicability of the Fourth Amendment.

Circumstances dictate that some reasonable exceptions occasionally should be tolerated in any laws, but it does appear that the courts went unwisely and too far in *Abel* and *Alvarado.* The courts in *Abel* and *Alvarado* permitted law enforcement officers (FBI and U.S. customs officials, respectively) to achieve their search, seizure, and confinement objectives by calling upon INS agents to do the job that they were not able to do legally under the constitutional restrictions of the Fourth Amendment. With the information obtained from the administrative searches, the FBI and customs officials were then able to build criminal cases against Abel and Alvarado. Justice Douglas believed that such underhanded and tricky governmental actions defeat the noble purpose of the Fourth Amendment, and that the facts of the *Abel* case suggest clearly "that the FBI agents wore the mask of INS to do what otherwise they could not have done. They did what they could do only if they had gone to a judicial officer pursuant to the requirements of the Fourth Amendment."[17]

The *Abel* and *Alvarado* holdings conflict with the separation-of-powers doctrine in that the courts in both cases allowed administrators to act as arresting officers, prosecutors, and judges. Specifically, the courts accepted as constitutional a situation in which officials from the same agency were allowed to: (1) decide whether sufficient probable cause existed to justify the issuance of an arrest warrant; (2) issue the arrest warrant itself; (3) carry out the arrest; (4) conduct a general search of the premises to obtain damaging evidence to be used in a criminal trial; and (5) determine whether the arrested person should be confined. Adding further to the consolidation of administrative power under these circumstances, a prior case had upheld a statute giving such administrative officials the power to determine whether bail should be given and, if so, at what amount over five hundred dollars.[18] Ironically, the courts have allowed such a concentration of power in the hands of administrators because the Fourth and Eighth Amendments were not perceived to be applicable to such administrative actions but were held to be applicable to police actions against suspected criminals. But regardless of the labels given to these state actions taken against persons, Bernard Schwartz concluded that they "can scarcely conceal the reality of individuals being deprived of liberty without the essential safeguards contemplated by the Bill of Rights."[19]

Today, many legal scholars believe that the United States has gone too far in employing various rationales to deprive persons of their fundamental constitutional due process rights. In a criminal case that has considerable relevance to administrative law, a divided Supreme Court, in 1987, in *United States* v. *Salerno*, 107 S.Ct. 2095, upheld the constitutionality of the Bail Reform Act of 1984, 18 U.S.C., Section 3142(e), which permits courts to order pre-trial detention of persons charged with serious crimes if it is felt, after a pre-trial hearing, that they would impose a threat to the community. The *Salerno* holding immediately drew harsh criticism from liberal groups as well as the three dissenting justices in the case (Justices Marshall, Brennan, and Stevens). Justice Marshall started his dissent by addressing the potentially tyrannical character of the Bail Reform Act: "This case brings before the Court for the first time a statute in which Congress declares that a person innocent of any crime may be jailed indefinitely . . . if the Government shows to the satisfaction of a judge that the accused is likely to commit crimes, unrelated to the pending charges, at any time in the future. Such statutes, consistent with the usages of tyranny and the excesses of what bitter experience teaches us to call the police state, have long been thought incompatible with the fundamental human rights protected by our Constitution" (at 2105–2106).

Justice Marshall objected vigorously to what he felt was the Court's absurd and destructive distinction between *regulatory* and *punitive* legislation, even though a similar distinction and application of the distinction had been made long ago in *Wong Wing*. To Marshall, the distinction made by the majority could allow constitutional guarantees to be taken away by the state, under the administrative or regulatory rationale, any time the state felt that certain persons may in the future commit acts that would pose a danger to society. Marshall concluded: "The majority's technique for infringing this right (due process) is simple: merely redefine any measure which is claimed to be punishment as 'regulation,' and, magically, the Constitution no longer prohibits its imposition" (at 2108). The blatant point that Marshall is making, and it has clear implications for administrative law, is that it is dangerous to uphold laws or regulations, especially when basic constitutional rights are at stake, on the premise that they serve a legitimate regulatory goal of making the community safer. Such could lead to the destruction of our cherished constitutional liberties since virtually all statutes and rules could be justified on such "regulatory interest" grounds.

However, possibly responding to the harsh criticisms it received for its *Salerno* decision, the Supreme Court in *Foucha* v. *Louisiana,* 112 S.Ct. 1780 (1992), softened the clout of *Salerno* by stating: "It was emphasized in *Salerno* that the detention we found constitutionally permissible was strictly limited in duration. . . . Here, in contrast, the state asserts that because Foucha once committed a criminal act and now has an antisocial personality that sometimes leads to aggressive conduct, a disorder for which there is no effective treatment, he may be held indefinitely. This rationale would permit the state to hold indefinitely any other insanity acquittee not mentally ill who could be shown to have a personality disorder that may lead to criminal conduct. . . . Freedom from physical restraint being a fundamental right, the state must have a particularly convincing reason, which it has not put forward, for such discrimination against insanity acquittees who are no longer mentally ill" (at 1787–1788).

The Administrative Power to Search and Inspect

From the perspective of administrative law, probably the most serious threat to the guarantees of individual liberty under the Fourth Amendment is posed by the power of administrative officials to employ their discretionary authority to have arrested and imprisoned, in the absence of judicial intervention, persons not charged with any criminal misconduct. Fortunately, however, administrative arrests (seizures) and detentions are relatively uncommon. But administrative searches are very common. For example, at the peak of its regulatory prowess, in fiscal 1976, the Occupational Safety and Health Administration conducted 90,369 workplace inspections.[20] Typically, administrative searches are used to inspect premises (for example, a person's house or a company's plant), documents (for example, a person's tax receipts or a corporation's records), and regulated operations (for example, how a chemical manufacturer complies with federal standards in disposing of its toxic wastes). Such administrative inspections may also present challenges to the right to privacy under the Fourth Amendment.

Why have Congress and state legislatures given administrators the authority to carry out administrative inspections? The reasons should appear quite obvious. As Max Weber acknowledged in his scholarly writing on public bureaucracy, the real strength of bureaucratic organizations resides in the information they collect, store, and use. To function properly, administrative agencies must be able to obtain vital information which can help them perform their assigned regulatory activities. Bernard Schwartz points out that "information is the fuel without which the administrative engine could not operate; the old saw that knowledge is power has the widest application in administrative law."[21] Actually, agencies can obtain most of the information they seek without much difficulty. In fact, much of the data they need can be found by simply referring to their own records, files elsewhere in the governmental bureaucracy, governmental publications, and other readily accessible data sources. Agency staffs can also obtain information through normal research processes which do not involve any direct investigations into the private affairs of individuals and businesses. And even if agency administrators feel that they must obtain certain information from persons and businesses, most times such private parties cooperate rather cheerfully, freely disclosing to these governmental officials what they want to know. There are occasions, however, when individuals and businesses believe that requests for information, frequently in the form of physical administrative inspections, encroach too far upon their right to privacy as protected by the Fourth Amendment. When such resistance occurs, administrators can compel private parties to disclose to them the information they want, sometimes by forcing them to submit to administrative inspections, as long as statutes permit such investigations. Almost all agencies do possess such statutory power. Actually, to protect the administrative investigatory function from possible impotence, virtually all agencies have been given the weapon of the administrative subpoena. It was established in *Cudahy Packing Co.* v. *Holland,* 315 U.S. 357, 363 (1942), that the administrative subpoena can be employed coercively to subpoena records and witnesses.

A Note on the Record-Keeping Requirement   Since the beginning of our Republic, it has always been recognized that it is necessary for effective governmental administration to require private parties to keep essential records and present reports to which the government, for the sake of the general welfare, has a legitimate regulatory interest. Consequently, legislated statutes have routinely included record-keeping and reporting provisions.

Obviously, regulatory agencies could not be expected to regulate if the regulated did not have to keep records of its activities. That is, to see whether an industry has been complying with required statutes and rules, the regulatory agency would have to review the industry's records and its reports. For example, how could the FCC decide on whether to renew the license of a television station if the station were not required to keep records and submit reports which help to provide the FCC with valuable information on how well the particular station has complied with approved standards of television broadcasting in the past? To anyone who understands the nature of the governmental regulatory process, it is quite clear that regulatory activities are interrelated and that specific regulatory functions relate to and are dependent upon one another. For instance, record keeping, inspections, and licensing are mutually dependent upon one another. That is, standard and sensible licensing practices require that information pertinent to licensing requirements must be inspected and evaluated periodically so that intelligent decisions can be reached regarding whether licenses should be granted, denied, renewed, or suspended.

The record-keeping and reporting requirements have never faced serious legal challenges.[22] The courts have held in general that the record-keeping requirement does not violate the Constitution as long as "there is a sufficient relation between the activity sought to be regulated and the public concern so that the government can constitutionally regulate or forbid the basic activity concerned, and can constitutionally require the keeping of particular records, subject to inspection by the administration" (*Shapiro* v. *United States,* 335 U.S. 1, 32; 1948). Earlier, the Supreme Court held in *United States* v. *Darby,* 312 U.S. 100, 125 (1941): "The requirement for records . . . is an appropriate means to a legitimate end." According to the high Court in *United States* v. *Morton Salt Co.,* 338 U.S. 632, 652 (1950), even legitimate "official curiosity" can justify agencies to compel parties to keep records because such agencies as the FTC "have legitimate right to satisfy themselves that corporate behavior is consistent with the law and the public interest." Naturally, however, limits must be placed upon an agency's appetite to satisfy its "official curiosity." Once again, the primary task in a democratic system is to try to balance the government's need to obtain information in the public interest with the Fourth Amendment's privacy rights for persons. Regarding record keeping, the only constitutional limitation under the Fourth Amendment seems to be, as expressed in *Shapiro* and many other cases, that record-keeping and reporting requirements be confined to regulatory activities sanctioned by statute. Such records can be required because they are considered in reality *public* records. To satisfy an agency's curiosity, officials cannot require that private parties keep records and submit reports which have no legitimate regulatory value. Such agency requirements would constitute an unfounded invasion of a person's purely *private* affairs.[23]

Fourth Amendment Limitations on Administrative Inspections In a genuinely free society (of course, within the limits of what is necessary to maintain socioeconomic and political stability), persons should be protected from unreasonable encroachments upon their personal privacy, whether the intention of the state's search is to uncover criminal evidence or to discover code violations in a person's home or business. Although heated arguments still persist over whether administrative inspections should be restricted by Fourth Amendment provisions, it is clear that personal liberties cannot survive in a nation if governmental officials show wanton disrespect for a person's right to privacy. It is therefore obvious that if personal privacy rights are to be protected, no governmental officials can be allowed to intrude at their discretion into a person's private life, whether the public officials be FBI agents or OSHA inspectors. The Court in *United States* v. *Martinez-Fuerte,* 428 U.S. 543, 569 (1976), made the point that limits must restrict official intrusions into the private affairs of others or administrative tyranny will surely result. As the Court emphasized in *Wolf* v. *Colorado,* 338 U.S. 25, 27 (1949), protection against arbitrary invasions of a person's privacy is fundamental to the preservation of a free society; it is at the core of the Fourth Amendment. To permit any public administrator to exercise unconfined, unstructured, and unchecked discretion in the area the Fourth Amendment was written to guard is to place the liberty of everyone and every business at the absolute discretion of any administrator who has an interest in anyone's personal or business affairs. Such a situation would surely spell the end of freedom. The freedom fighter Justice William O. Douglas conveyed this point succinctly in his dissent in *New York*

v. *United States,* 342 U.S. 882, 884 (1951): "Absolute discretion, like corruption, marks the beginning of the end of liberty." And in *California* v. *Hodari D.,* 111 S.Ct. 1547, 1561 (1991), dissenting Justices Stevens and Marshall, criticizing the Court's majority's lack of respect for the Fourth Amendment's protective rights, warned, quoting Justice Brandeis, that our constitutional framers conferred upon us "'. . . the right to be let alone—the most comprehensive of rights and the right most valued by civilized men. To protect that right, every unjustifiable intrusion by the Government upon the privacy of the individual, whatever the means employed, must be deemed a violation of the Fourth Amendment.'"

It should not be overlooked that totalitarian governments retain their position of dominance over their citizenry by allowing their state officers to exercise shockingly broad discretionary powers to spy on persons and business operations, as well as to search and seize individuals and their property. Because personal freedom poses a threat to the survival of totalitarian regimes, governmental laws are typically aimed at destroying individual liberties (for example, freedom of speech, freedom of the press, and the right to be free from unreasonable searches and seizures). In police states, very few, if any, searches and seizures are perceived by governmental authorities as unreasonable. The right to privacy carries little meaning in such regimes, where state rights are considered far superior to individual rights. In reflecting upon the character of totalitarian states, Ronald Bacigal concluded: "Unchecked power to search and seize is crucial to the maintenance of a totalitarian state."[24]

The causes of tyranny were well known and publicized by the founders of our nation. A reading of *The Federalist* would convince anyone of this. The colonists, under British rule, had become quite sensitive to the abuses and excesses of governmental power. As a matter of historical fact, it was largely the reactions by the colonists to oppressive British rule that caused the American Revolution. It is in this context that Justice Felix Frankfurter exclaimed in his dissent to *United States* v. *Rabinowitz,* 339 U.S. 56, 69 (1950), that the drafting of the Fourth Amendment's "unreasonable searches and seizures" provision must be understood. The precise intent of the constitutional framers in including the Fourth Amendment in the Constitution cannot be known for sure as no records were kept, but the Supreme Court, in *Chimel* v. *California,* 395 U.S. 752–763 (1969), contended that credible historians have acknowledged that the Bill of Right's authors, who had suffered at the hands of oppressive British governors, wanted future generations of Americans protected against arbitrary intrusions into their private affairs by any governmental officials.

But how have the courts applied the Fourth Amendment to administrative searches, which mostly involve inspections aimed at discovering whether persons and businesses are complying with various agency regulations in the areas of health (including perceived moral health), safety, and welfare? Once again, because the regulatory activities of the emerging administrative state are relatively new to the American scene, well-established law on how the Fourth Amendment should be applied to administrative intrusions into the private practices of individuals and businesses has not yet developed. Opinions on how the Fourth Amendment should apply to administrative searches have varied greatly from court to court and even within the same courts. In 1971 in *Wyman* v. *James,* 400 U.S. 309, for example, the Supreme Court said essentially that administrative inspections were not searches restricted by the Fourth Amendment since they are not intended to produce evidence which could be used in criminal prosecutions. However, two decades earlier, in *Rabinowitz,* the high Court recognized that search and seizure standards must be applied to administrative officials to prevent capricious and malicious administrative behavior.

To help clarify the Supreme Court's position on the applicability of the Fourth Amendment to administrative inspections, Kevin MacKenzie, several years ago, classified Supreme Court decisions in this area into three general categories. His categories still remain very helpful. In the first category, he includes the cases of *Camara* v. *Municipal Court,* 387 U.S. 523 (1967), *See* v. *City of Seattle,* 387 U.S. 541 (1957), and *Marshall* v. *Barlow's, Inc.,* 436 U.S. 307 (1978). In each of these cases, the Court held that governmental officials must, as a general rule, obtain a search warrant before they can force an individual or company to undergo an inspection. MacKenzie's second category includes the cases of *Colonnade Catering Corp.* v. *United States,* 397 U.S. 72 (1970), and *United States* v. *Biswell,* 406 U.S. 311 (1972). In these two cases, because the businesses were already closely supervised by regulatory agencies, the Court felt it was reasonable to except such businesses from the normal warrant requirement. MacKenzie includes in the third grouping *United States* v. *Martinez-Fuerte,* 428 U.S. 543 (1976), and *South Dakota* v. *Opperman,* 428 U.S. 364 (1976). In these two cases, the Supreme Court also believed an exception to the warrant requirement was justified, but here because adequate administrative safeguards already existed to protect privacy interests in much the same way a search warrant would. A review of what the cases in these three categories seem to establish helps one better understand the present judicial position on the Fourth Amendment's applicability to administrative inspections. The cases MacKenzie places into his three categories are reviewed, along with more recent cases bringing us into the 1990s.[25]

Cases Promoting the Administrative Search Requirement: *Camara, See, Barlow's, Inc., Dow Chemical,* and *Riley*   In both *Frank* v. *Maryland,* 359 U.S. 360 (1959), and in *Ohio ex rel. Eaton* v. *Price,* 364 U.S. 263 (1960), the Supreme Court took the position that administrative officials could conduct reasonable inspections without first having to obtain an administrative search warrant. However, in *Camara* and *See,* both decisions handed down on the same day, the Supreme Court reversed its attitude toward warrantless administrative inspections and argued that warrantless administrative inspections are unconstitutional because they violate the Fourth Amendment's provision which prohibits the government from carrying out unreasonable searches against persons. The high Court held in *Camara:* "except in certain carefully defined classes of cases, a search of private property without proper consent is 'unreasonable' unless it has been authorized by a valid search warrant" (at 528–529).

Prior to *Camara* and *See,* it was uncertain whether the warrant requirement of the Fourth Amendment, if applied to administrative searches, should apply to business establishments, as well as to individuals. But in *Camara* and *See* the Court made it very clear that both individuals and businesses have a constitutional right to be protected against warrantless searches by administrators. In *See*, the high Court reiterated what it had just finished saying in *Camara*: "As we explained in Camara, a search of private houses is presumptively unreasonable if conducted without a warrant. The businessman, like the occupant of a residence, has a constitutional right to go about his business free from unreasonable official entries upon his private commercial property. The businessman, too, has that right placed in jeopardy if the decision to enter and inspect for violations of regulatory laws can be made and enforced by the inspector in the field without official authority evidenced by a warrant" (at 543).

The *Camara* and *See* rulings also answered another vital administrative question which had been left unresolved. By 1967, when the *Camara* and *See* opinions were reached, it had been well established that the Fourth Amendment's guarantee against warrantless searches did apply to criminal investigations; but it was widely questioned whether the amendment's warrantless search clause should be made applicable to civil or administrative searches. However, the *Camara* Court presented a well-developed, forceful argument that the Fourth Amendment protects persons and businesses against warrantless invasions of their privacy, whether the investigations are civil or criminal in nature.

Rejecting the reasoning in *Frank*, which had upheld the constitutionality of a warrantless administrative inspection of private premises, the Court in *Camara* reasoned that in a free society the Fourth Amendment should be applied broadly so that privacy rights are properly respected. The Court further rejected the majority's contention in *Frank* that administrative inspections such as health and safety inspections are covered only "peripherally" by the Fourth Amendment: "But we cannot agree that the Fourth Amendment interests at stake in these inspection cases are merely 'peripheral.' It is surely anomalous to say that the individual and his private property are fully protected by the Fourth Amendment only when the individual is suspected of criminal behavior" (at 530). The Supreme Court in *Camara* emphasized that Fourth Amendment privacy rights should be respected in administrative searches because in practice discovered violations may lead to criminal charges, prosecution, fines, and even jail sentences for the offenders. In some cases, the Court noted, refusal to comply with an administrative compliance order is in itself a criminal offense (at 531). To the Court, warrantless searches, as upheld in *Frank*, "unduly discount the purposes behind the warrant machinery contemplated by the Fourth Amendment" (at 532). "The basic purpose of the Fourth Amendment," according to the *Camara* Court, "is to safeguard the privacy and security of individuals against arbitrary invasions by governmental officials" (at 528). Without the warrant requirement in administrative searches, the Court reasoned, privacy rights are threatened unnecessarily by administrative inspectors because "when the inspector demands entry, the occupant has no way of knowing whether enforcement of the municipal code involved requires inspection of his premises, no way of knowing the lawful limits of the inspector's power to search, and no way of knowing whether the inspector himself is acting under proper authorization. These are questions which may be reviewed by a neutral magistrate without any reassessment of the basic agency decision to canvass an area" (at 532).

In 1978 the Supreme Court, in *Barlow's, Inc.,* affirmed and expanded upon its holdings in *Camara* and *See.* This time the Court ruled that Section 8(a) of the Occupational Safety and Health Act of 1970 (29 USCS Sec. 657[a]), which authorizes warrantless searches by OSHA inspectors, violates the search warrant provisions of the Fourth Amendment. Specifically, the Court rejected the argument by the secretary of labor, in whose department OSHA is housed, that warrantless inspections of business premises are constitutional, although such searches of private dwellings may not be. In an attempt to put to rest the skepticism over whether the constitutional framers intended the Fourth Amendment's provisions to apply to business establishments, the Court built a fairly convincing case to support its contention that the founding fathers definitely intended to protect business proprietors against unreasonable invasions of their privacy. Drawing from historians, the *Barlow's, Inc.* Court noted that general administrative search warrants were included in the Virginia Bill of Rights, which the Court noted has been recognized as the basic model for the Bill of Rights. The Court argued that it was common historical knowledge that such legislation as the 1765 Stamp Act, the 1767 Townshend Revenue Act, and the 1773 tea tax were found to be particularly offensive to colonial businessmen and merchants because these acts gave British colonial administrators virtually unlimited discretion to inspect the premises, products, and records of American businessmen and merchants. The Court had noted only a year before, in *United States* v. *Chadwick,* that "the Fourth Amendment's commands grew in large measure out of the colonists' experience with the writs of assistance . . . (that) granted sweeping power to customs officials and other agents of the King to search at large for smuggled goods" (at 311). "Against this background," the Court concluded, "it is untenable that the ban on warrantless searches was not intended to shield places of business as well as of residence" (at 312).

In *Barlow's, Inc.,* the Court was very careful to point out that in obtaining an administrative search warrant, governmental officials do not have to demonstrate probable cause in the same strict manner as is required of law enforcement officers seeking warrants for criminal investigations. To protect the privacy interests of private businesses, the Court held that administrative officials need show only that the searches or inspections are: (1) authorized by statute; (2) consistent with legislative goals and standards; (3) based in a "general administrative plan" necessary to enforce the legislation; and (4) going to be carried out against a Specific business cited on the warrant (at 309, 320).

The Court in *Barlow's, Inc.,* did a fairly commendable job in placing into a balanced perspective business privacy interests with the legitimate interests of agency administrators trying to perform their mandated regulatory functions. The Court made its position clear: It would not tolerate warrantless searches of the premises of businesses simply because the intrusions into private areas were being conducted for administrative regulatory purposes and not for the collection of criminal evidence. Reiterating much of what was said previously in *Camara* and *See,* the Court stressed the dangers of the warrantless searches and emphasized the value of the Fourth Amendment's warrant requirement. In particular, it noted that the warrantless search allows administrators to enjoy almost unbridled discretionary power as to when, what, and whose premises ought to be searched: "A warrant, by contrast, would provide assurances for a neutral officer that the inspection is reasonable under the Constitution, is authorized by statute, and is pursuant to an administrative plan containing specific neutral criteria. Also, a warrant would then and there advise the owner of the scope and objects of the search, beyond which limits the inspector is not expected to proceed" (at 323).

The Court did not adopt the general warrant requirement rule for administrative inspections without first considering the possible burden the warrant requirement might have on administrators. It rejected the argument that the warrant requirement would place a heavy strain on the administrative regulatory system and the courts, making administrative regulation in particular less effective. For one thing, the Court noted, most businesses would consent to the inspections without demanding that the administrators obtain a warrant first.[26] In rebuttal to the specific argument that "surprise searches" are necessary to promote "inspection efficiency," the Court pointed out that after inspectors are refused entry, they can then obtain an *ex parte* warrant and reappear at the business site at any reasonable "surprise time" they desire, since inspectors need not provide any further notice (at 317–20).[27] *Barlow's, Inc.* is an important case because it established a strong precedent that under normal conditions (i.e., when special circumstances do not permit a warrantless search) administrative search warrants must be obtained before a search can be conducted [*Tri-State Steel* v. *OSHA*, 26 F.3d 173 (D.C. Cir. 1994)].

In 1986 in *Dow Chemical Co.* v. *United States,* 106 S.Ct. 1819, the Supreme Court handed down a decision rooted in what many may perceive as enigmatic judicial logic. Refusing to overrule the warrant requirement for the administrative searches of business premises as established in *Camara, See,* and *Barlow's, Inc.,* yet upholding a warrantless search of the grounds of Dow Chemical Company by the Environmental Protection Agency, the Court ruled that the EPA's warrantless search was lawful because the "search" really didn't constitute a search under the Fourth Amendment. The facts are these: The EPA wanted to conduct an on-site inspection of Dow Chemical's 2,000-acre chemical plant that is under tight security and hidden from ground level public view. However, Dow refused to allow the inspection. Instead of obtaining an administrative search warrant (this is perplexing because such warrants are normally very easy to obtain), the EPA hired an aerial photographer, using a standard aerial mapping camera, to take photographs of Dow's facilities. All photographs were taken at legal altitudes. Learning of the aerial photographic search of its plant, Dow filed suit, charging that the EPA's warrantless investigative actions constituted an illegal search extending beyond the EPA's statutory investigative authority, which violated Dow's right to privacy under the Fourth Amendment.

Unsympathetic to Dow's allegations, the Supreme Court argued that the EPA's aerial search was within the EPA's statutory authority, not only because Congress did not prohibit such searches specifically, but also because the EPA must be able to conduct investigations or searches to carry out its mandated regulatory mission (in this case, enforcing the provisions of Section 114(a) of the Clean Air Act). The Court also maintained that the aerial search did not constitute a search under Fourth Amendment protection because the "search" was conducted in lawful navigable air space open to the public and was done with standard aerial photography equipment that only enhanced human vision and was commonly used by aerial mappers. Although the Court found no constitutional problems in the use of this equipment to conduct searches, it implied that more sophisticated aerial spy equipment may pose constitutional problems under the Fourth Amendment (at 1823-24).

It must be stressed that the Supreme Court rested its precedential decision in search law mostly on the contention that the EPA's "search" was not a search subject to Fourth Amendment due process privacy protections because the area "searched" was similar to a public or "open field" where no legitimate demand for privacy can be demanded (at 1821). Regarding such aerial searches of companies, the Court explained "that the open areas of an industrial plant complex with numerous plant structures spread over an area of 2,000 acres are not analogous to the 'curtilage' of a dwelling for purposes of aerial surveillance; such an industrial complex is more comparable to an open field and as such is open to the view and observation of persons in aircraft lawfully in the public airspace immediately above or sufficiently near the area for the reach of cameras." Therefore, the Court held "that the taking of aerial photographs of an industrial plant complex from navigable airspace is not a search prohibited by the Fourth Amendment" (at 1827). A divided Supreme Court in *Florida* v. *Riley,* 109 S.Ct. 693, 705 (1989), also upheld the constitutionality of warrantless aerial searches, even though dissenting Justices Brennan, Marshall, and Stevens (Justice Blackmun wrote a separate dissenting opinion) thought such searches could sanction George Orwell's dreaded vision of Big Brother watching us.[28] Although this involved a helicopter police search, *Riley* has implications for warrantless administrative searches because the courts apply less strict Fourth Amendment restrictions when administrative searches are involved.

In sum, the significance of *Dow Chemical* is that it upholds the warrant requirement for legitimate Fourth Amendment searches that normally involve intimate inspections, as established in *Camara, See,* and *Barlow's, Inc.,* because businesses have a reasonable expectation of privacy; but regulatory agencies do not require warrants for certain kinds of searches that can be classified as nonintimate and nondetailed inspections that could be conducted by anyone in the general public.

However, Lisa Steele is very concerned that new technologies will allow invasive, "intimate" warrantless searches, given general judicial sympathy for such searches, and such will bring ". . . Orwell's vision closer to reality."[29] Since *Dow Chemical,* federal, state, and local governments have been experimenting with various new technologies that have allowed "Big Brother" to get a better peek at what businesses and citizens are doing. For example, sophisticated radar equipment can produce high-resolution radar images (reflections) by sending a high energy pulse at objects in homes and businesses or within the "curtilage" of these homes and businesses. Infrared sensors have been used to detect infrared light and heat through the walls of homes and businesses, while aerial searches of "open fields" within the "curtilage" of private homes and businesses can be conducted from space by high-tech satellite equipment.

Unfortunately, in recent years courts have used all sorts of rationales, some patently absurd, to justify high-tech governmental searches. Often courts have argued that such searches are reasonable and the person or place being searched had no reasonable expectation of privacy because the high-tech equipment "only assisted" or "materially enhanced" the natural senses or that the equipment used is "widely available commercially" or that the searched party did not do enough to guarantee privacy, such as stopping detectable heat losses from a structure, or that the person did too much to guarantee privacy, thus creating reasonable suspicion to justify a search warrant, or that the searched party "knew or should have known that he was observable" even if the observation was made from a distance high in the sky.[30] Steele concludes that the courts should carefully examine the implications of such high-tech searches on our Fourth Amendment privacy rights.[31]

Cases Upholding Exceptions to Warrant Requirement When Activities Are Already Tightly Regulated: *Donovan, Pullin, Shoemaker,* and *Krull*   To understand the Court's decision in *Barlow's, Inc.,* clearly, it is crucial to acknowledge that the Court, while upholding *Camara* and *See,* took a rather flexible position over the warrant requirement and did not rigidly hold that it was necessary to obtain an administrative warrant under all inspection or search circumstances. Actually, the Court in *Barlow's, Inc.* acknowledged (at 313) that administrative search warrants are not necessary if the businesses subject to searches are already "pervasively regulated" (*Biswell,* at 316) and "closely regulated" industries which have been under tight governmental control for a long time (*Colonnade Catering Corp.,* at 7–1). However, the Court stressed that the *Biswell* and *Colonnade Catering Corp.* decisions represent reactions to "relatively unique circumstances." Therefore, these holdings cannot be applied generally to the more normal situations, as existed in *Barlow's, Inc.,* where it is necessary to protect the privacy interests of businesses by requiring administrative search warrants if consent to search premises, papers, and so on, is refused to inspectors (at 313–16).

What were the unique circumstances that existed in both *Colonnade Catering Corp.* and *Biswell* which convinced the Supreme Court that agency officials should be permitted to carry out warrantless searches? How did these circumstances differ from the situation that existed in *Barlow's, Inc.?* In *Colonnade Catering Corp.,* federal inspectors, under federal legislation regulating licensed dealers in alcoholic beverages, forcibly entered a locked liquor storeroom and illegally seized stored liquor. The federal inspectors did this without a search warrant. The Court held that, although the statutes did not provide for forcible entry, inspectors could execute warrantless searches, as authorized by federal statutes, because the liquor business had historically been a heavily regulated industry in order "to meet the evils at hand" (at 76).

A similar situation existed in *Biswell,* only this time a federal treasury agent searched an unlocked storeroom and seized illegally kept sawed-off rifles. Biswell, a pawnshop operator licensed to deal in sporting weapons, but not sawed-off rifles, at first refused to allow the search but then permitted it after the inspector cited the Gun Control Act of 1968 (18 USCA, Sec. 923), which allows such warrantless searches. The chief issue in *Biswell* was whether the statute which authorized warrantless searches was constitutional. The *Biswell* Court believed that the circumstances in *Colonnade Catering Corp.* and *Biswell* were very similar because both cases involved statutes authorizing warrantless searches of federally licensed dealers trading in goods (liquor and firearms) which the federal government historically had a very serious interest in regulating: "Federal regulation of the interstate traffic in firearms is not as deeply rooted in history as is governmental control of the liquor industry, but close scrutiny of this traffic is undeniably of central importance in federal efforts to prevent violent crime and to assist the States in regulating the firearms traffic within their borders. . . . Large interests are at stake, and inspection is a crucial part of the regulatory scheme, . . ." (at 315).

The *Biswell* Court perceived a significant difference between the inspection in *See* and the inspection here. Justice Byron White, speaking for the majority in *Biswell,* pointed out that in *See* a warrantless search was found to be unreasonable and, therefore, unconstitutional under the Fourth Amendment because inspectors sought only to discover whether building codes and the like had been violated, conditions fairly difficult to rectify in a hurry. Thus, the *See* Court concluded rightly that warrantless searches constituted unnecessary intrusions of privacy under the circumstances. But in *Biswell,* the regulation of dangerous firearms is involved. The Court claimed: "Here, if inspection is to be effective and serve as a credible deterrent, unannounced, even frequent, inspections are essential. In this context, the prerequisite of a warrant could easily frustrate inspection; and if the necessary flexibility as to time, scope and frequency is to be preserved, the protections afforded by a warrant would be negligible" (at 316).

To justify its ruling in *Biswell* that warrantless searches are constitutional in this special area of "urgent federal interest," the Court reasoned: "When a dealer chooses to engage in this pervasively regulated business and to accept a federal license, he does so with the knowledge that his business records, firearms and ammunition will be subject to effective inspection" (at 316). This reasoning has been severely criticized by many administrative law scholars who hold that it is absurd to maintain that any businessperson knowingly and willfully surrenders Fourth Amendment rights when entering even closely regulated licensed businesses.[32] For example, Kevin MacKenzie argues that it is unsound to base a decision not upon the genuine reasonableness of the actual inspection, but upon the fictional grounds that those "pervasively regulated" have given their "implied consent" to be, in effect, unreasonably searched. He acknowledges that lower federal courts have already started the dangerous practice of employing the unacceptable "implied consent" rule to settle cases quickly without probing the real constitutional issues.[33]

Several more recent decisions uphold the constitutionality of warrantless administrative searches under the "pervasively regulated" rationale, as established in *Colonnade Catering Corp.* and *Biswell.* In *Donovan v. Dewey,* 452 U.S. 594 (1981), relying heavily on its argument for "pervasively regulated" businesses as developed in *Biswell,* the Supreme Court ruled that the warrantless search of stone quarries, as required by Section 103(a) of the Federal Mine Safety and Health Act of 1977, does not violate the Fourth Amendment. The Court asserted that "it is undisputed that there is a substantial federal interest in improving the health and safety conditions in the Nation's underground and surface mines. In enacting the statute, Congress was plainly aware that the mining industry is among the most hazardous in the country and that the poor health and safety record of this industry has significant deleterious effects on interstate commerce. Nor is it seriously contested that Congress in this case would reasonably determine, as it did with respect to the Gun Control Act in *Biswell,* that a system of warrantless inspections was necessary 'if the law is to be properly enforced and inspection made effective. . . .' In designing an inspection program, Congress expressly recognized that a warrant requirement could significantly frustrate effective enforcement of the Act. Thus, it provided in Section 103(a) of the Act 'no advance notice of inspection shall be provided to any person.'" In addition, the Court noted that "the Act is specifically tailored to address those concerns, and the regulation of mines it imposes is sufficiently pervasive and defined that the owner of such a facility cannot help but be aware that he 'will be subject to effective inspections'" (at 602-3). Recently, the argument presented in *Donovan* that "exigent circumstances" permit exceptions to the warrant requirement was upheld in *O'Brien* v. *City of Grand Rapids,* 23 F.3d 990, 997 (6th Cir. 1994).

In *Pullin* v. *Louisiana State Racing Com'n,* 477 So.2d 683 (1985), the Supreme Court of Louisiana upheld a warrantless search of a race track barn that led to the discovery of drugs prohibited in the horse barns. The seized drugs were then used as evidence in an administrative hearing conducted by the Louisiana Racing Commission that resulted in the suspension of Vernon Pullin, a licensed horse owner and trainer who owned the seized drugs. Pullin sought judicial review of the commission's decision, arguing that evidence seized in the warrantless search of the barn violated his Fourth Amendment rights. Drawing on *Biswell* and *Donovan,* the court held that the warrantless search did not violate Pullin's Fourth Amendment privacy rights because he was in "a closely regulated and licensed business" and, therefore, "consents to certain restrictions on his expectation of privacy" (at 686). Elaborating further, the court emphasized that "because horse racing is a strictly regulated activity, licenses to participate in the sport are only issued under certain terms and conditions. . . . Among other things, a licensee must agree to being searched within the grounds of a racing association. This type of consent is valid, *despite the element of coercion*" (my emphasis) (at 686–87).

The Third Circuit Court of Appeals reached a similar conclusion a year later in *Shoemaker* v. *Handel,* 795 F.2d 1136 (1986), a well-publicized case because several famous horse racing jockeys, including William Shoemaker and Angel Cordero, brought suit against the New Jersey Racing Commission, charging that warrantless random breath and urine testing of jockeys violated their Fourth Amendment privacy protections. The court disagreed, contending that the administrative search exception (reduced privacy expectation) applies in this case because employees in such a heavily regulated business as horse racing have necessarily limited privacy expectations,

'We've Pretty Much Taken Out The Fourth Amendment — Which One Should We Start On Next?'

Source: Reprinted with permission of Tom Engelhardt and the *St. Louis Post-Dispatch,* June 2, 1991.

especially considering the state's strong interest in assuring the public of the integrity of those engaged in the business (at 1142).

In *Illinois* v. *Krull,* 107 S.Ct. 1160 (1987), the Supreme Court extended the *pervasively regulated rule,* established in *Colonnade-Biswell-Donovan* (allowing warrantless searches of liquor dealers, gun dealers, and mine operators, respectively), to cover auto parts dealers (in this case, a wrecking yard dealer selling used auto parts). Under question in this case was the constitutionality of an Illinois statute that required licensed motor vehicle and vehicle parts dealers to permit state officials to carry out inspections at the time of the search. Rooting its argument in *Donovan* in particular, the Supreme Court upheld the statute and the challenged inspection, asserting that the Illinois statute was "directed at one specific and heavily regulated industry, the authorized warrantless searches were necessary to the effectiveness of the inspection system, and licensees were put on notice that their businesses would be subject to inspections pursuant to the state administrative scheme" (at 1172). The administrative scheme, the Court pointed out, promoted the strong public interest of controlling the theft of automobiles and automobile parts (at 1172).

Administrative search law has remained virtually the same in recent years since the Supreme Court has not handed down a decision in this area since 1987. Critics such as Susan McDonough hold that this is unfortunate because they believe that the "pervasively regulated standard" is applied too broadly and is unfair since ". . . administrations have been empowered to determine when an industry is pervasively regulated, thus jeopardizing the protection of a warrant."[34] McDonough claims that the courts need to provide a better balance test to balance more fairly the means used to conduct an administrative search with the rights of parties to be protected against unreasonable searches and seizures.[35]

Martinez-Fuerte and *Opperman* Permit an Exception to Warrant Requirement When Other Acceptable Administrative Safeguards Exist

In *Barlow's, Inc.*, the Court, in requiring administrative search warrants as a general rule, did not in fact overrule the holdings in *Martinez-Fuerte* and *Opperman* that warrantless searches may be acceptable as long as it can be demonstrated that alternative administrative safeguards exist to prevent inspection searches which are flagrantly offensive to Fourth Amendment privacy rights. The *Barlow's, Inc.*, Court flatly rejected the secretary of labor's argument that if OSHA's warrantless inspections violate the Fourth Amendment, all regulatory actions involving warrantless searches are unconstitutional. The Court maintained: "The reasonableness of a warrantless search, however, will depend upon the specific enforcement needs and privacy guarantees of each statute. . . . In short, we base today's opinion on the facts and law concerned with OSHA" (at 321–22).

Warrantless searches were upheld by the Supreme Court in *Martinez-Fuerte* because the Court believed that the administrative circumstances under which the warrantless searches were carried out provided sufficient alternative safeguards to preclude the need for administrative search warrants. Specifically, the Court held that routine searches of vehicles by the border patrol officers did not require administrative search warrants because, *inter alia:* (1) the searches conducted were reasonably limited in scope; (2) inspection officers had limited discretionary powers; (3) checkpoint authorities were quite stationary and visible; (4) inspection checkpoint stops were placed at fixed and known border locations; and (5) checkpoint sites were selected not by field inspectors, but by those officials responsible for making general policy pertaining to the enforcement of immigration statutes (at 545–66).

However, in *U.S. v. Santa Maria*, 15 F.3d 879 (9th Cir. 1994), the court refused to extend *Martinez-Fuerte* to allow the Border Patrol to conduct a warrantless search for drugs when the statute permitted Border Patrol agents to enter private land within 25 miles of the border only to find illegal aliens. The Ninth Circuit Court concluded ". . . that Section 1357(a)(3) does not authorize the Border Patrol to search only for drugs. The Border Patrol is empowered . . . to conduct administrative searches for aliens. To expand this power to include searches for narcotics is impermissible. Absent probable cause or consent, this search was both unauthorized and a violation of the Fourth Amendment" (at 883).

During the same year, the high Court, in *Opperman,* held that warrantless administrative searches can be constitutional in some situations if administrative procedural checks exist which guard against the possibility that the searches may be administered arbitrarily. This time the Court ruled that warrantless "inventory" searches of automobiles held in police custody are reasonable under the Fourth Amendment because standard procedures for such routine searches are set by high-ranking policy-makers in the police department. The Court asserted that such standard operating procedures can easily be assessed by the courts as to their reasonableness under the Fourth Amendment. The Court also noted that it is not necessary for probable cause to be established in such routine caretaker searches: "The probable-cause approach is unhelpful when analysis centers upon the reasonableness of routine administrative caretaking functions" (at 370 n. 5).

In 1990 the Supreme Court in *Florida* v. *Wells,* 110 S.Ct. 1632, relying upon *Opperman,* declared unconstitutional an inventory search that led officers to open a closed container in Wells' car absent any policy established by the Florida Highway patrol with respect to searching closed containers. The high Court noted that ". . . the Florida Highway Patrol had no policy whatever with respect to the opening of closed containers encountered during an inventory search" (at 1635). Consequently, the court held: "We hold that absent such a policy, the instant search was not sufficiently regulated to satisfy the Fourth Amendment . . ." (at 1635). The court emphasized that establishing a policy to regulate ". . . inventory searches is based on the principle that an inventory search must not be a ruse for a general rummaging in order to discover incriminating evidence" (at 1635). And in 1994 in *U.S.* v. *Andrews,* 22 F.3d 1328, the Fifth Circuit Court of Appeals upheld an inventory search because the court held that established policy regulated sufficiently the discretion that could be employed by the city's police officers in conducting the search. However, the court upheld *Wells* by acknowledging that "[T]he requirement to be distilled from the line of cases culminating in *Wells* is that inventory policies must be adopted which sufficiently limit the discretion of law enforcement officers to prevent inventory searches from becoming evidentiary searches" (at 1336). Parenthetically, it should be noted that even though these searches are conducted by police officers, they are technically administrative searches to produce an inventory of items "'. . . to protect the property of the owner and to reduce the potential liability of the police department'" (at 1336).

A Postscript to *Barlow's, Inc.*   In 1973 Roger B. Dworkin remarked in disgust: "The Fourth Amendment cases are a mess!"[36] He essentially meant by this that judicial applications of the Fourth Amendment's warrant requirements to administrative searches and inspections have been too inconsistent to protect either the government's interest or privacy rights. However, the Supreme Court, in *Barlow's, Inc.,* did a great deal to resolve some of the problems that had contributed to the mess. Shortly after the *Barlow's, Inc.,* decision was handed down, Bernard Schwartz predicted that the case promised to become the leading case on administrative inspection power because it went far toward resolving most issues on the subject which the Court had left unanswered in its prior decisions. More directly, he believed that the *Barlow's, Inc.*, Court answered in relatively clear terms the following vital questions pertaining to the basic reasoning for and the scope of the warrantless search/inspection exception: "Did it apply to all regulated businesses or only to those subject to pervasive regulation by an ICC-type regulatory agency? Did it turn upon the fact that the business operated under a license, so that implied consent could be assumed? Or could the legislature authorize warrantless inspections in every case where there was a direct public interest in effective enforcement of the agency's regulatory scheme?"[37]

Professor Schwartz's prediction seems to have come true. Cases handed down since the 1978 *Barlow's, Inc.* ruling have pretty much followed the Court's thinking on administrative searches of businesses as developed in *Barlow's, Inc.* Fourth Amendment administrative search cases since *Barlow's, Inc.* have refined *Barlow's, Inc.* somewhat, but these cases have mainly affirmed the wisdom on administrative case law established in *Barlow's, Inc.* Today, compared to other areas of administrative law, administrative search case law in this specific area is quite well developed, consistent, and clear—so clear that legal scholars should be able to predict with fair accuracy the outcomes of administrative search cases before the courts. Such is the real test for the clarity of any area of law.[38]

Inspections Involving Welfare Recipients

The Supreme Court, in *Barlow's, Inc.*, concluded that administrative search warrants should generally be obtained if business operators refuse entry to inspectors. But what has the Supreme Court said if the premises or papers to be searched do not involve private businesses receiving no direct financial aid from government, but instead those who are receiving public welfare payments? Do welfare recipients have the same privacy rights under the Fourth Amendment as businesses or individuals not receiving welfare benefits?

The answer appears to be a shaky yes, but at a very high price to those on welfare. That is, in *Wyman v. James*, 400 U.S. 309 (1971), the Supreme Court held, in a precedential case which still stands, that warrantless administrative searches cannot be carried out against the wishes of the welfare recipients under the Aid to Families of Dependent Children program; but if entry is refused, welfare benefits may be cut off, as is authorized by statute. In this case, the Court specifically upheld the constitutionality of a New York statute which did require the consent of the welfare recipient before inspectors (caseworkers) could lawfully conduct searches of their homes. However, the statute also authorized public assistance benefits to be discontinued at the agency's discretion if home visitation inspections were refused.

The Court was not sympathetic to the argument by the plaintiff, a mother receiving welfare under the AFDC program, that she had a constitutional right not to consent to the home visitation inspections without having to forfeit her public assistance. She based her argument on the premise that such inspections constituted unconsented-to warrantless searches, in violation of her Fourth and Fourteenth Amendment rights. But the Court disagreed, resting its decision on two major arguments: First, Justice Harry Blackmun, speaking for the 6–3 majority, maintained that home visitation inspections of this nature do not constitute searches within the proper meaning of the Fourth Amendment, since these searches are performed primarily for rehabilitative reasons and not so much for investigatory purposes. Second, even if the home visitation search could be placed under the protection of the Fourth Amendment, Blackmun contended this type of inspection "visit does not fall within the Fourth Amendment's proscription. This is because it does not descend to the level of unreasonableness" (at 317). To the Court's majority, the home visitation inspection appeared reasonable mainly because: (1) the needs of the dependent children are of paramount importance; (2) the state has a legitimate interest in monitoring how its tax dollars are spent; (3) continuations of benefits should reasonably depend on how public monies are now being spent; (4) visitation inspections are an essential aspect of proper welfare administration; (5) forced entry, entry under false pretenses, entry during unreasonable hours (for example, midnight searches), and snooping are all prohibited by statute; (6) trained caseworkers making the inspections are friends to those in need, their central objective being to protect the interests of the welfare recipient; (7) the inspection is performed for purely administrative purposes; (8) a warrant under such circumstances would be inappropriate; and (9) refusal to grant entry does not lead to criminal charges, but only possibly to the denial of future public assistance (at 318–24).

The three dissenting judges strongly objected to the majority's holding. Justice William O. Douglas asserted that the government should not be permitted to "buy up" constitutional rights in such situations. In so saying, Douglas meant that a citizen should not have to agree to forfeit one right (for example, Fourth Amendment protection) to receive another (the right to receive public assistance, if eligible) (at 328). Justices Thurgood Marshall and William J. Brennan also remarked in dissent: "We are told that the visit is designed to rehabilitate, to provide aid. This is strange doctrine indeed. A paternalistic notion that a complaining citizen's constitutional rights can be violated so long as the State is somehow helping is alien to our Nation's philosophy" (at 343). Quoting Justice Louis Brandeis in his dissent in *Olmstead* v. *United States,* 277 U.S. 438, 479 (1928), these dissenters noted that more than forty years before, Brandeis cautioned that "experience should teach us to be most on our guard to protect liberty when the government's purposes are beneficent" (at 343).

Marshall and Brennan were particularly disturbed over the distinction the majority made between *See* and this case. The majority contended that a *genuine* search was involved in *See,* but not in *Wyman.* The majority also noted that in *See* it was a criminal offense to refuse entry, while such was not the case in *Wyman.* However, the dissenters argued that "apart from the issue of consent, there is neither logic in, nor precedent for, the view that the ambit of the Fourth Amendment depends not on the character of the governmental intrusion but on the size of the club that the State wields against a resisting citizen. . . . For protecting the privacy of her home, Mrs. James lost the sole means of support for herself and her infant son. For protecting the privacy of his commercial warehouse, Mr. See received a $100 suspended fine" (at 340). This implies the major reason for their dissent; it also reflects the chief criticism others have voiced against the *Wyman* decision. That is, the majority's holding in *Wyman,* for all practical purposes, seems to discriminate against the poor in its application of the Fourth Amendment. It is debatable whether this is the case, but Marshall, Brennan, and legal scholars think so. Marshall, in writing the dissent in which Brennan joined, concluded: "Perhaps the majority has explained why a commercial warehouse deserves more protection than does this poor woman's home. I am not convinced; and, therefore, I must respectfully dissent" (at 347).

Kenneth C. Davis agrees with Justices Marshall and Brennan that the *Wyman* majority seemed to discriminate against poor parents. However, Davis attacks more the apparent illogic of the decision. He claims that the Court is either discriminating against poor parents, as well as nonpoor children, or—if it does not mean to discriminate—the Court is saying in effect that governmental inspectors have a right to enter and inspect *all* homes as to various kinds of health, safety, and welfare administrative inspections, since the *Wyman* Court argued that entry was essential to see to it that the needs of the children, which it viewed as of "paramount importance," were being handled adequately. Davis suggests that the *Wyman* Court "may mean that *all* children could be protected by home visits, on the theory that the children give implied consent to visits that are for their own benefit. . . . If that is so, all homes . . . may be entered without warrants."[39] Thus, *Wyman's* illogic, Davis asserts, could cause one to infer that refusal to allow a social security caseworker to inspect Mr. X's home, to provide another example, might not result in any criminal charges against him, but Mr. X might forfeit his social security checks because he insisted on his Fourth Amendment rights.

Because of the illogic of *Wyman,* Davis contends that the probability that the Supreme Court will continue to follow it in the future appears very unlikely.[40] However, Davis may be right regarding a few specific contentions in *Wyman,* but wrong about the general strength of the decision. Although some of the arguments in *Wyman* are admittedly weak, the tone of the ruling in general can be justified in the context of efficient public administration and tight fiscal control over the public treasury. But the *Wyman* Court did leave unanswered one vital question which Davis and others have addressed: Can any private party who receives some form of public assistance (for example, grants, subsidies, unemployment compensation) be placed in the precarious position of having to choose between what it needs from government and its Fourth Amendment rights? In this case, did the Court do a good job in applying the Fourth Amendment to balance the individual's interest with the public interest? Given constant and vehement charges that the government throws our money away, that public bureaucracy is wasteful and inefficient, that too many are on welfare, that too many collect public assistance fraudulently, and that too many children are neglected, would you have ruled differently? Examine carefully the two basic sides to the argument in *Wyman* in the context of the criticisms above and other such criticisms of government. The majority argued that home visitation inspections are necessary for the children's sake and administrative efficiency and effectiveness, while the dissenters argued that such inspections violate the Fourth Amendment. Running a government is often a tough, frustrating, and thankless job.

Although the *Wyman* decision still stands, the case is rarely cited by the courts and, thus, has had little impact on the development of case law in the area of warrantless searches. Some scholars speculate that *Wyman* is seldom cited because the Supreme Court in *Wyman* was bitterly divided over the decision, the ruling itself constituted bad law that was poorly received by legal scholars, and the decision was forcefully attacked by those who felt that the holding established a double standard that blatantly discriminated against the poor.

THE DECLINE OF THE INDIVIDUAL'S RIGHT AGAINST SELF-INCRIMINATION DURING THE RISE OF THE ADMINISTRATIVE STATE

One clear trait of the modern administrative state is that it has an insatiable appetite for information. Indeed, the state's bureaucratic apparatus needs vast information about people and things to function properly. Nevertheless, free societies have placed limits on how the government can obtain information about its citizens, what information it can legally seize, and how it can use the information it does collect. While the previously discussed Fourth Amendment is aimed largely at prohibiting unreasonable invasions of personal privacy in the face of official efforts to gather information, the Fifth Amendment's self-incrimination clause essentially prohibits the government from forcing persons to implicate themselves in criminal misconduct. Specifically, the Fifth Amendment provides that "no person . . . shall be compelled in any criminal case to be a witness against himself."

Initially the self-incrimination privilege was used only to protect those in court charged with criminal offenses. However, the Supreme Court has extended the privilege to apply to virtually any official proceeding. For example, in *Murphy* v. *Waterfront Commission of New York Harbor,* 378 U.S. 52 (1964), the Court held that individuals have the constitutional right to avoid being compelled to provide incriminating evidence against themselves in any federal, state, or local proceeding, civil or criminal, administrative or judicial, adjudicative or investigative.[41] But because the guarantee against self-incrimination has been applied quite narrowly in these proceedings, especially since the 1930s, the protection in actuality is not as great as it may seem. In fact, virtually every legal scholar in recent decades has talked about how meaningless the privilege against self-incrimination has become. For instance, in a *Harvard Law Review* article, Justice William J. Brennan once argued that recent court decisions have greatly damaged the protective shield once offered by the Fifth's self-incrimination privilege, as interpreted by the Court in *Boyd* v. *United States,* 116 U.S. 616 (1886).[42] A lengthy *Harvard Law Review* "Note" takes the position that "values of privacy" have been seriously eroded in modern law by "legal realism." Legal realism, as opposed to the nineteenth-century adherence to absolute legal ideals, is characterized by a pragmatic and relativist approach to the application of our legal principles—for example, the privilege against self-incrimination. This modern approach, it is held, has allowed the practical informational needs of the state to be honored increasingly at the expense of the constitutional privilege against self-incrimination.[43] Kenneth C. Davis asserts that the Supreme Court, especially during the 1940s and 1970s, did much to drastically reduce the privacy protections once provided by both the Fourth and Fifth Amendments, the protection against self-incrimination being no exception. He also believes that Fourth and Fifth Amendment privacy protections have been severely compromised to satisfy the practical informational demands of the modern administrative state.[44] And recently Joel Cohen concluded, given the present trend of at least the Second Circuit Court, that under the new "act of production" doctrine ". . . there will be precious little Fifth Amendment protection covering private documents prepared by individuals. . . ."[45]

Before commencing the analysis of the rise and fall of the Fifth's self-incrimination privilege, a few comments on the logic of the presentation are necessary. In the first place, it is very difficult to discuss the privilege against self-incrimination outside the context of the Fourth Amendment. This is because the gathering of information, protected under the Fourth, and the use of the gathered information, protected under the Fifth but also under both, depending upon one's perspective, cannot be neatly separated—even for analytical purposes. In many instances, search and seizure and self-incrimination questions seem to be very intertwined legally. For example, Justice William R. Day, in *Weeks* v. *United States,* 232 U.S. 383, 392–394, 398 (1914), argued that the seizing and later use of evidence at a trial involves a single evidentiary transaction by the government. Therefore, the defendant has the constitutional right under the Fifth to demand the exclusion of the use of incriminating evidence obtained under the jurisdiction of the Fourth. Justice Joseph P. Bradley had recognized this close relationship between the Fourth and Fifth Amendments' privacy protections years before. In *Boyd,* he declared that "the Fourth and Fifth Amendments run almost into each other" (at 630). Elaborating, Bradley reasoned that the Fourth and Fifth Amendments "throw great light on each other. For the 'unreasonable searches and seizures' condemned in the Fourth Amendment are almost always made for the purpose of compelling a man to give evidence against himself, which in criminal cases is condemned in the Fifth Amendment; and compelling a man 'in a criminal case to be a witness against himself,' which is condemned in the Fifth Amendment, throws light on the question as to what is an 'unreasonable search and seizure' within the meaning of the Fourth Amendment. And we have been unable to perceive that the seizure of a man's private books and papers to be used in evidence against him is substantially different from compelling him to be a witness against himself" (at 633).

Although this assertion was made about a century ago, it has survived the test of time. Most legal scholars and justices today appear to recognize the "convergence theory" or "doctrine of mutuality" as established in *Boyd.* Even as late as 1976, in *Andresen* v. *Maryland,* 427 U.S. 463 (1976), the Supreme Court acknowledged that the Fourth and Fifth Amendments seem to provide more privacy protection when viewed together rather than separately (at 492). Thus, in the following discussion it is sometimes necessary to consider search and seizure points in order to develop an examination of the Fifth's guarantee against self-incrimination.

It is also necessary to include criminal law cases, as contrasted to purely administrative law cases, since the former help to explain the development of the courts' general attitude toward the applicability of the self-incrimination protection. Besides, as the Court noted in *Boyd*, it is not always fair or practical to draw a sharp distinction between civil and criminal law cases for purposes of applying Fourth and Fifth Amendment protections. In response to the question of whether a governmental prosecutor can deprive citizens of their Fourth and Fifth Amendment rights by seeking desired information under a civil heading rather than under a criminal heading, the Court said not when criminal charges and penalties could result: "The information, though technically a civil proceeding, is in substance and effect a criminal one" (at 634). Recently, the Third Circuit Court diminished the worth of the exclusionary rule, a rule that may exclude illegally seized evidence, by holding that the fact that ". . . an unlawful search and seizure has occurred does not diminish the probative value of the illegally seized evidence in any way. . . . Evidence seized illegally by state officials" (in a criminal matter) "may be used in a federal civil proceeding" [*U.S.* v. *Torres*, 926 F.2d 321, 323 (3rd. Cir. 1991)].

The Fifth Amendment's Protection against Self-Incrimination under the Philosophy of Legal Formalism

Nineteenth-century legal formalism was a legal philosophy dedicated to the preservation of democratic ideals. And certainly, in the Bill of Rights, which was written near the end of the eighteenth century, many democratic ideals were espoused that needed judicial protection. In the ideal, the Fifth's privilege against self-incrimination meant that individuals should not be compelled to reveal incriminating evidence which can be used by the government against them in criminal cases. This liberty is regarded as necessary in a free society because it places the burden of proof on the state's prosecutor, not on the individual possibly facing criminal charges. But the freedom runs deeper than this in practice. Prohibiting the state from using self-incriminating evidence serves to deter the government from trying to seize incriminating evidence through the use of ruthless inquisitional practices (for example, interrogations continuing for literally days), torture (for example, beating confessions out of individuals), and unreasonable searches (for example, unconscionable warrantless, early-morning bedroom searches). While the legal formalists refused to significantly weaken the coverage of the Fifth's protection against self-incrimination during the 1800s and early 1900s, the emergence of the legal realists brought a rather abrupt end to the thinking that the privacy protections of the Fourth and Fifth Amendments should be applied in any absolute or extreme manner.

Boyd Epitomizes the Legal Formalism Perspective   Kenneth C. Davis remarked some years ago that "the clear fact is that the law of 1978 is in sharp contrast with the law of *Boyd* (1886) and *American Tobacco* (1924)."[46] To understand why recent judicial applications of Fourth and Fifth Amendment rights differ so dramatically from the application of these rights in *Boyd* v. *United States,* 116 U.S. 616, or *American Tobacco,* 264 U.S. 298, it is imperative that the different legal philosophies which guided and presently guide judicial determinations be examined and compared. It is worth reviewing the *Boyd* case in relative detail because in its decision, the Court captured the legal formalism perspective which dominated the thinking of so many justices during the nineteenth and early twentieth centuries. One who comprehends the justifications behind the Court's arguments in *Boyd* will become better equipped to appreciate why the demands of contemporary American society pressured the justices of modern America to abandon the rigidity of legal formalism for the flexibility of legal realism.

The unanimous Supreme Court ruled in *Boyd* that all governmental efforts to obtain an individual's personal papers violate the Fourth Amendment's prohibition against unreasonable searches and seizures and the Fifth Amendment's protection against self-incrimination (at 636–38). In reaching this decision, the Court based its argument in the rationale that the privacy rights of the Fourth and Fifth Amendments are in effect "sacred" and "indefeasible" rights "of personal security, personal liberty and private property" (at 630). Employing the uncompromising attitude characteristic of legal formalism, the Court maintained that there are certain rights which must be carefully preserved if liberty is to have any concrete meaning. Compromising the privacy protections of the Fourth and Fifth Amendments, Justice Bradley declared in *Boyd,* may serve the ends of despots, but certainly not the ends of those who cherish liberty. He stressed that "any compulsory discovery by extorting the party's oath, or compelling the production of his private books and papers, to convict him of crime, or to forfeit his property, is contrary to the principles of a free government. It is abhorrent to the instincts of an Englishman; it is abhorrent to the instincts of an American. It may suit the purposes of despotic power; but it cannot abide the pure atmosphere of political liberty and personal freedom" (at 632).

This attitude can be seen somewhat in the Court's decision in *American Tobacco,* although by 1924 the influence of legal formalism was rapidly fading. In *American Tobacco* the Court strongly objected to public agencies' (in this case, the FTC) using general subpoena power to permit them to carry out "fishing expeditions" while conducting administrative investigations. The Court exclaimed: "Anyone who respects the spirit as well as the letter of the Fourth Amendment would be loath to believe that Congress intended one of its subordinate agencies to sweep all our traditions into the fire," yet "to allow a search through all of [the American Tobacco Company's] records, relevant or irrelevant, in the hope that something will turn up" would accomplish this (at 306).

What makes the *Boyd* ruling so characteristic of the legal formalism approach, as contrasted to today's legal realism approach, is the espoused absolutism of the constitutional privacy values set forth in the Fourth and Fifth Amendments. To the *Boyd* Court, protections against unreasonable searches and seizures and against self-incrimination seemed to constitute absolute moral values which should not be questioned as to their rightness in all situations. Rejecting the possible relative nature of these privacy values, depending upon various circumstances, the Court argued that these "sacred" and "indefeasible" rights should not be allowed to be undermined by the government, even for the sake of promoting the general welfare. The question in *Boyd* was essentially the constitutionality of Section A of the 1874 customs law, which authorized a United States court, upon request by government attorney, to compel persons suspected of avoiding customs duties in revenue cases to produce in court relevant personal documents (such as private papers, books, invoices, and the like) or, by not presenting such materials, be faced with, in effect, admitting to being guilty of the charges.

E. A. Boyd and Sons, an importer of glass, was charged by customs officials with not paying customs duties under the 1874 act on thirty-five cases of imported plate glass. Although the proceeding was on its face a civil or administrative law proceeding, under Section 12 of the act, severe penalties could be imposed on those found to be in violation of the customs laws. Penalties for each offense could include fines of not less than fifty dollars or more than five thousand dollars, or imprisonment not to exceed two years, or both. Additionally, the merchandise would be forfeited.

The Court addressed a few basic Fourth and Fifth Amendment questions. One, is an act constitutional which compels a person to produce in court for inspection evidence which can later be used against him in the prosecution of his case? Two, does not the compulsion of such private and incriminating evidence, for all practical purpose, compel a person to present testimony against himself or herself? And three, does not the forced production of such evidence in effect constitute an unreasonable search and seizure of private property (at 621-25)?

To answer these questions, the *Boyd* Court relied heavily upon the arguments presented by Lord Camden in a famous 1765 English case, *Entick* v. *Carrington and Three Other King's Messengers,* 19 Howell's State Trials, 1029, as well as on the American experience which led to the development of the privacy clauses in the Fourth and Fifth Amendments. The contentions of Lord Camden, which embrace the spirit of legal formalism adopted by Justice Bradley in *Boyd,* are worth emphasis. The action under dispute in *Entick* involved a situation in which the plaintiff's house was entered by the king's agents, his desks, boxes, and so on, were broken into, and his personal papers were searched and examined with the intention of securing evidence which could be used against him to convict him of a crime (in this case, of seditious libel).

Lord Camden condemned such governmental action as being essentially a violation of the basic social contract, as conceptualized by John Locke and other contract theorists. According to natural law philosophy, quite adequately expressed in the writings of John Locke, individuals possessed certain inalienable rights which the state had no business taking away, even under the social contract. To Locke, to formalist legal scholars such as Lord Camden, and later to Justice Bradley and American capitalist thinkers, the most important of the inalienable rights was the private property right. In fact, Locke asserted that the chief purpose of entering into the social contract was the protection of private property: "The great and *chief end,* therefore, of men's uniting into Commonwealths, and putting themselves under Government, is the *Preservation of their Property.*"[47]

When Locke spoke of private property, he was not referring to merely land or goods; he had a broader meaning in mind. Under the heading of property, Locke included "Lives, Liberties, and Estates."[48] Thus, when Lord Camden defended the property rights of individuals, he applied Locke's conceptualization of private property as extending to personal privacy kinds of property rights.

Echoing Locke's fundamental thinking on property rights, Lord Camden claimed that "the great end for which men entered into society was to secure their property. That right is preserved sacred and incommunicable. . . . By laws of England, every invasion of private property, be it ever so minute, is a trespass" (at 627). Camden challenged the Crown to show any written laws which allow the government to trespass on private property rights as did the government in *Entick*. Answering his own question, he responded: "I can safely answer, there is none; and therefore, it is too much for us, without such authority, to pronounce a practice legal which would be subversive of all the comforts of society" (at 628). More specifically, Lord Camden pointed out that no English law permits searches of personal property which would serve to help a person convict himself in either civil or criminal cases (at 629).

Why did the *Boyd* Court devote several pages of its opinion exclusively to Lord Camden's judgment in *Entick?* A reading of *Boyd* makes it readily apparent that Justice Bradley used Camden's argument to substantiate the point that the constitutional framers intended the Fourth and Fifth Amendments to have the same absolute meaning that Camden had earlier given to such private property freedoms. The Court made evident in *Boyd* that all American political leaders were aware of Lord Camden's monumental defense of such liberties at the time the Constitution was drafted: "As every American statesman, during our revolutionary and formative period as a nation, was undoubtedly familiar with this monument of English freedom and considered it as the true and ultimate expression of constitutional law, it may be confidently asserted that its propositions were in the minds of those who framed the Fourth Amendment to the Constitution, and were considered as sufficiently explanatory of what was meant by unreasonable searches and seizures" (at 626–27). One must remember that Justice Bradley considered the privacy clauses in the Fourth and Fifth Amendments to be inseparable. Thus, it must be assumed that Camden's wisdom also stands behind the Fifth Amendment's provision against self-incrimination.

To the *Boyd* Court, it is incredible that the constitutional framers, in light of Camden's condemnation of governmental invasions of sacred private property entitlements under natural law, would have ever signed into law the 1874 customs revenue laws. The Court stressed that for decades the colonists fought the British because they had imposed similar arbitrary and exploitive revenue laws (for example, writs of assistance), which empowered British revenue officers to carry out blatantly unreasonable searches and seizures of private property for the purpose of securing incriminating evidence against colonists. Undoubtedly, the Court contended, the implementation of "writs of assistance in Boston, were fresh in the memories of those who achieved our independence and established our form of government" (at 625). Consequently, Justice Bradley concluded in *Boyd* that our founders would have flatly rejected, as offensive to the ideals standing behind our Republic, the use of the customs laws in question in this case (at 630).

In summation, the *Boyd* Court, rooting its judgment in the canons of legal for-malism, attacked administrative governmental actions which threatened to erode the privacy protections set forth by the constitutional framers in the Fourth and Fifth Amendments. During this period in American judicial history, the courts adhered to the belief that they had the vital duty of preserving the constitutional rights of indi-vidual citizens. Legal arguments, presented mostly by the government, which held that the Bill of Rights should be compromised somewhat so that society in general may benefit were not accepted by formalist justices. Prevailing judicial opinion of the 1800s and early 1900s was that slight encroachments upon the absolute libertarian standards incorporated in the Bill of Rights served only to start the beginning of the end for limited and popular government in America. According to the logic of *Boyd,* "illegitimate and unconstitutional practices get their first footings . . . by silent ap-proaches and slight deviations from legal modes of procedure (at 635). Accordingly, the Court in *Boyd* felt that it had to set aside the constitutionality of the 1874 customs revenue laws, which sanctioned unreasonable searches and seizures of private prop-erty, as well as permitted the government in effect to compel persons to provide tes-timonial evidence against themselves.

The *Boyd* decision is particularly noteworthy for its strong endorsement of the use of the *exclusionary rule* as a protective constitutional remedy for citizens. The exclusionary rule allows individuals to have excluded in trials and possibly adminis-trative hearings all incriminating evidence which was obtained improperly (in viola-tion of constitutional or statutory dictates). The logic behind the exclusionary rule, as developed in *Boyd,* is simply that the government has no right to use evidence which was obtained illegally. Wiretaps of home telephones, forced confessions, and admin-istrative or judicial subpoenas which require persons to produce self-incriminating evidence are examples of what courts have considered illegally obtained and, there-fore, inadmissible evidence. However, since *Boyd,* the courts have in general permit-ted the submission of an increasing quantity of evidence which the *Boyd* Court would have considered inadmissible. Today in the 1990s, whether in criminal or civil pro-ceedings, the exclusionary rule plays only a minor role in helping to uphold the Fifth Amendment's protections against self-incrimination because the courts have allowed so many exceptions to the exclusionary rule to permit the submission of various kinds of illegally seized evidence.[49] [*United States* v. *Payner,* 447 U.S. 727; 1980; *INS* v. *Lopez-Mendoza,* 468 U.S. 1032; 1984; *Pullin* v. *Louisiana State Racing Com'n,* 477 So.2d 683; La. 1985; *Illinois* v. *Krull,* 107 S.Ct. 1160; 1987; and *Trinity Industries, Inc.* v. *OSHRC,* 16 F.3d 1455 (6th Cir. 1994)].

The Erosion of the Fifth Amendment's Protection against Self-Incrimination under the Legal Realism Philosophy

After *Boyd* the Supreme Court began to view the Constitution in general less from the perspective of strict constructionalism. Even though the Court since *Boyd* has oc-casionally interpreted Fourth and Fifth Amendment rights in a rather inflexible and literal manner, the clear trend has been for the Court to reject the rigid or strict constructionalist viewpoint expressed by the *Boyd* Court.[50] A few decades ago, the liberal individual rights philosophy of legal formalism could be seen in the dissenting opinions of Justices William O. Douglas and William J. Brennan.[51] But radically liberal applications of the privacy clauses of the Fourth and Fifth Amendments have accomplished little else except to remind us of how the Supreme Court perceived privacy rights in America's distant past. For all practical purposes, the moral absolutism and democratic idealism which formed the basis of the legal formalist philosophy which guided the unanimous Court in *Boyd* have been almost totally rejected by twentieth-century courts. For example, in *Fisher v. United States,* 425 U.S. 391 (1976), the Court spent considerable time repudiating the underlying philosophy expressed in *Boyd,* concluding that "the foundations for the *(Boyd)* rule (against self-incrimination) have been washed away" (at 109).

For at least the past half century the vast majority of court justices in America have adopted the philosophy of legal realism as the guiding light for their decisions. For many reasons, legal formalism, whether fortunately or unfortunately, was destined to be replaced by the more flexible legal realist philosophy as American society became more complex and the citizenry requested the government to become more deeply involved in the craft of social engineering.

Legal formalism appears, in the context of democratic government, theoretically more sound than legal realism because the principles of legal formalism embrace the principles of democratic theory much more consistently and comfortably. In fact, legal realism calls for the compromising or rationalizing away of democratic values (allowing certain "inalienable" property rights to be sacrificed for the good of the whole community). Lord Camden's masterful defense of privacy liberties, in contrast, expressed the legal formalist attitude that democratic values cannot be compromised if limited popular government is to survive. Yet the inflexible principles of legal formalism seemed better suited for the much simpler American society of the 1700s and 1800s. By the twentieth century it became evident to most legal and political thinkers that a less formal and more flexible and realistic legal philosophy had to be applied to constitutional issues if the Constitution was to survive. Kenneth C. Davis has noted that modern justices began to recognize that constitutional guarantees could not always be feasibly applied as absolute rights for individuals but had to be balanced so that the interests of both individuals and society could be extended adequate constitutional protections. Davis thinks today's justices are "wise enough to know that such balancing is absolutely essential to keeping the Constitution alive and responsive to the needs of a rapidly changing society and an ever-growing degree of governmental intervention in affairs that were once regarded as private."[52] Once more, he asserts that since government has decided to pick up the regulatory ball, "for better or for worse . . . then what it does must be guided by information and cannot be based on ignorance of the relevant facts."[53]

Therefore, the legal realist school emerged early in the 1900s to replace impractical and outmoded legal formalism and serve modern American government. But the death of legal formalism raised some serious questions about the viability of democracy which should not be overlooked by any student of American government. If the legal formalist philosophy is more sound than legal realism from the standpoint of democratic theory, does the death of legal formalism mean in reality that "genuine" democratic government is a luxury modern America cannot afford because of the pressures modern American society has placed upon its government? Have not fundamental democratic principles, once held to be the vanguard of democratic constitutionalism, been cast aside by the legal realist justices? Does not the legal realist philosophy simply make it too easy for the courts today to rationalize away guarantees promised to individuals in the Bill of Rights? Since legal realism (relativism) has been guiding court decisions, have not the constitutional rights of individuals been severely compromised?[54] In the late 1970s a writer in the *Harvard Law Review* reached this conclusion: "While it is true that balancing need not invariably lead to results undercutting personal privacy, the history of fourth and fifth amendment protections since the shift to legal relativism demonstrates that there is no reason to assume balancing will reinforce privacy values."[55] Regarding the privacy protections offered by the Fourth and Fifth Amendments in particular, most legal scholars have concluded that these constitutional guarantees have been drastically reduced, especially in the past half century.[56]

Legal Realism in a Nutshell   By now the general picture of legal realism should be clear. As contrasted to legal formalism, legal realism is a much more flexible and relativistic philosophy. But what is the specific nature of legal realism, and how has this philosophical perspective contributed to the quashing of privacy rights for individuals and businesses? Under legal formalism, the argument was posited that privacy protections were absolute rights guaranteed by the Constitution. In regard to the Fifth Amendment's privilege against self-incrimination, this meant that in practice governmental officials could not encroach upon these absolute rights. For all practical purposes, the personal papers, books, and the like, of individuals and private business were strictly off limits for governmental officials. But the legal realists rejected the legal formalist contention that any constitutional rights should be perceived as absolute. The legal realists, or relativists, argued that rights vary from one situation to the next. Thus, they advanced the argument that no absolute rights exist. In so arguing, they repudiated the platonic contention, basic to legal formalism, that absolute rights or standards could be discovered and employed to guide governmental actions. In the *Republic* Plato maintained that true justice, if it was discovered, would be applicable to all state regulatory situations, since what is just in one situation could not be found to be unjust in another. To Plato, justice was an absolute which could not be compromised and still be preserved. Likewise, for the legal formalists of the 1800s, constitutional privacy rights were also considered absolute values which could not be regarded as right in one situation but wrong in another. The legal formalists believed compromising privacy rights would serve only to destroy them as well as democratic government.

Rooting their thinking in a pragmatic consciousness, the legal realists adopted essentially the Aristotelian notion of moral relativism. That is, they espouse the position that what may be right, proper, moral, or just, given one set of circumstances, may be found to be quite wrong, improper, immoral, or unjust under other conditions.[57] To philosopher William James, the pragmatic consciousness of the legal realists meant that single perceptions of moral right could not endure from one place at one time to another at a different time: "The true . . . is only the expedient in our way of thinking, just as the right is only the expedient in our way of behaving."[58]

This pragmatic thinking led directly to the idea that, in making judicial decisions, justices had the task of balancing individual with societal rights so that a fair compromise could be reached. Thus, the new legal realist judges became social engineers, entrusted with the difficult task of interpreting the Constitution in such a way that both individual and societal rights were given protection. Whether playing this twofold role is possible remains an unresolved question. In any event, "balancing and accommodating competing societal interests in the pursuit of compromise and expediency emerged as the keynote of the realist approach."[59] This new role for the courts was applauded by some because it prevented justices from forcing their own moral values upon society under the veil of moral absolutism.[60]

The development of legal realism largely paralleled the growth of what Max Weber perceived as scientism and the new rationality in Western society.[61] Weber believed that this new scientism and rationality not only cultivated the growth of modern bureaucracy, but they also tended to destroy absolute traditional and religious values which were based upon faith rather than upon empirical observation. In particular, the school of scientism espoused the belief that principles must be verified through empirical scientific testing before they can be accepted as true. But since social principles cannot be easily proved true or false through scientific tests, if at all, it was easy for the legal realists to attack the weak premises on which the principles of the Bill of Rights stood, and then to make the claim that the constitutional ideals should be regarded as guiding standards, not as absolute rights. As Justice Oliver Wendell Holmes, one of the most celebrated legal realists, once remarked, "Such words as 'right' are a constant solicitation to fallacy" (*Jackman* v. *Rosenbaum,* 260 U.S. 22, 31; 1922).

To function as viable social engineers, the legal realists had to cast aside the unverifiable assumptions and moral principles underlying the natural law base of legal formalism for a pragmatic consciousness.[62] Adopting the methodology of the "exact" sciences, these legal realist social engineers demanded that democratic principles survive the test of practical social experience, or in the words of Benjamin Cardozo, years before he took his place on the Supreme Court, survive the experiences of "life itself."[63] To pass the practical test of life itself, the application of constitutional principles would have to generate a net benefit for society. Thus, judicial social engineering would involve weighing the costs and benefits to individuals and society according to the facts on a case-by-case basis. For instance, in deciding whether an individual's claim against self-incrimination should be honored under the Fifth Amendment, the court would have to weigh the costs of not granting the individual this privilege against the costs to society if it did. This is exactly what the Court did in reaching its decision in *INS* v. *Lopez-Mendoza, 468* U.S. 1032 (1984). In ruling the exclusionary rule inapplicable in deportation hearings, Justice O'Connor, writing the majority opinion, concluded that although it is important to safeguard privacy protections, applying cost-benefit analysis, the social costs of allowing the exclusionary rule to apply in deportation proceedings would be too high. In her words: "In these circumstances we are persuaded that the *Janis* balance between costs and benefits comes out against applying the exclusionary rule in civil deportation hearings held by the INS" (at 1050).

However, a review of decisions handed down by the legal realist courts conveys the clear message that legal realist justices have a pro-social welfare bias. In general, when individual rights have clashed with the public interest, the courts have normally opted to reduce the scope of individual rights. For example, in administrative law cases, the courts have become increasingly more supportive of regulatory agency efforts to search for, seize, and use personal materials once considered so private that they were placed beyond the reach of administrative officials. But the courts have held that encroachments upon personal privacy are necessary if governmental regulatory activities are to be efficiently handled. In sum, to the legal realist courts of the twentieth century, the costs to society are weighed much more heavily on the scale of justice than are the costs to individuals.

Toward the Virtual Elimination of the Fifth's Privilege against Self-Incrimination for Business

In 1973, in *Couch* v. *United States,* 409 U.S. 322, Justice William O. Douglas, dissenting, acknowledged the relentless historical trend toward the elimination of Fifth Amendment privacy protections in the realm of business. He voiced serious concern over the expanded investigatory authority of governmental agencies which had allowed public administrators to pry into the private affairs of businesses, once thought to be sacred and inviolable. Objecting to what the courts had already done to diminish Fourth and Fifth Amendment privacy privileges for businesses, Douglas feared that the courts might go still further in future decisions, causing those in business not to trust even their closest business associates with their business papers. Douglas considered that this would have a crippling impact on democratic society since it would tend to discourage those in the business world from exchanging their *recorded* ideas because of the prevailing risk that such records might at some time be seized by governmental officials and possibly be used to implicate them in some illegal activities. Justice Douglas wrote: "Are we now to encourage meddling by the Government and even more ingenious methods of obtaining access to sought-after materials? The premium now will be on subterfuge, on bypassing the master of domain by spiriting the materials away or compelling disclosure by a trusted employee or confidant" (at 341–42). Such, he maintained, "would lead those of us who cherish our privacy to refrain from recording our thoughts or trusting anyone with even temporary custody of documents we want to protect from public disclosure. In short, it will stultify the exchange of ideas that we have considered crucial to our democracy" (at 342).

How prophetic these words of warning now seem! In light of more recent judicial opinions, especially *Fisher* v. *United States,* 425 U.S. 391 (1976); *Andresen* v. *Maryland,* 427 U.S. 463 (1976); *Matter of Grand Jury Empanelled,* 597 F.2d 851 (3rd Cir., 1979); *United States* v. *Doe,* 465 U.S. 605 (1984); and *In Re Grand Jury Subpoena,* 21 F.3d 226 (8th Cir. 1994), it now appears that businesspersons have lost virtually all Fifth Amendment protections against self-incrimination in regard to compelled production of private and possibly incriminating business records. That is, it seems that governmental administrators can now compel persons in business to release personal, incriminating business documents unless these things are always kept in their possession and locked safely away.[64]

Earlier Decisions Setting the Stage for *Fisher* and After   Although the *Boyd* Court held that the government was prohibited by the self-incrimination clause of the Fifth Amendment to compel businesses to produce private and incriminating business documents, not too long after *Boyd* the courts began to restrict its scope. In 1906, in *Hale* v. *Henkel,* 201 U.S. 43, the Court ruled essentially that the Fifth Amendment's protection against self-incrimination does protect individuals themselves, but not corporations set up by individuals as third parties. The Court reasoned: "The Amendment is limited to a person who shall be compelled in any criminal case to be a witness against himself, and if he cannot set up the privilege of a third person, he certainly cannot set up the privilege of a corporation" (at 70).

Five years later, in *Wilson* v. *United States,* 221 U.S. 361, 382 (1911), the Court affirmed the *Hale* opinion, asserting that corporations cannot resist attempts by governmental officials to force the production of corporate documents on the basis of the self-incrimination protection. The chief point made by the Court in *Wilson* was that corporate officers do not have the constitutional right to refuse to surrender corporate records to governmental officials even though the records could incriminate them personally. The Court held that "the books and papers are held subject to examination by the demanding authority, the custodian has no privilege to refuse production although their contents tend to incriminate him. In assuming their custody he has accepted the incident obligation to permit inspection" (at 381–82). Some legal experts argue that the reasoning of the Supreme Court in *Hale* and *Wilson* is illogical because, despite the fact that the Fifth Amendment prohibits the government from compelling self-incriminating testimony from individuals, the logic of *Hale* and *Wilson* allows the government to use corporations to make individuals in corporations produce incriminating evidence against themselves.[65] Thus, the question raised by *Hale* and *Wilson* is this: Does the spirit of the Fifth Amendment really permit the government to compel individuals to produce self-incriminating records simply because these records also happen to be corporate records?

Whether within the spirit of the Fifth or not, the Supreme Court's answer was yes and has been ever since *Hale.* Actually, the high Court since *Hale* and *Wilson* has reached out to prohibit the use of the self-incrimination privilege in other types of organizations. In *United States* v. *White,* 322 U.S. 694 (1944), during the 1940s when the federal courts struck many severe blows against the privacy protections under both the Fourth and Fifth Amendments, the Supreme Court specifically held that neither an unincorporated labor union nor its officers are entitled to Fifth Amendment self-incrimination privileges in regard to union documents. However, the case is significant because the Court argued that self-incrimination protections should not apply to any associations (incorporated or unincorporated) or their officers in the face of governmental investigations into association records. The Court reasoned that governmental regulatory actions for the sake of the public interest necessitate probings into the books and records of associations. Particularly noteworthy in *White* was the Court's contention that the Fifth Amendment's protection against self-incrimination be restricted to cover only *natural* individuals or persons, as contrasted to *artificial* individuals such as corporations. Although previous courts may have disagreed, the *White* Court asserted that protecting natural persons has been the historic role of the Fifth Amendment's self-incrimination clause: "Basically, the power to compel the production of any organization, whether it be incorporated or not, arises out of the inherent and necessary power of the federal and state governments to enforce their laws, with the privilege against self-incrimination being limited to its historic function of protecting only the *natural individual* from compulsory incrimination, through his own testimonial or *personal records*"(italics mine) (at 700–01).

The significance of the Court's phrase, "personal records," should not be underplayed, because this dictum set the stage for later courts to really close the door on persons claiming that the self-incrimination clause prohibits the government from using their business records to provide testimonial evidence against them. Davis and Pierce claim that "the language opened the way for a holding that all business records, whether of an individual or an organization, are unprotected by the privilege."[66] *White,* then, established the notable position that the records of corporations, associations, or even the records of individual entrepreneurs, should properly be regarded as business records, not personal records, and therefore not protected by the Fifth Amendment's privilege against self-incrimination.

Some questioned whether the *White* Court had meant to include quite small organizations, since very small associations tend to assume a more personal character. Could such small and personal organizations as partnerships including only a few persons or sole proprietorships to some extent escape the regulatory eyes of government by hiding under the Fifth Amendment protection against self-incrimination? In *Bellis* v. *United States,* 417 U.S. 85 (1974), the Supreme Court answered this question in part by saying *no* to partnerships. Quoting the language of the lower court, the high Court maintained that a partnership consists of more than just an association of a few individuals but has "a recognizable juridical existence apart from its members" (at 87). The specific question in *Bellis* was whether one of the partners in a law partnership, holding the partnership's records in a representative capacity, could guard the partnership's records against compelled disclosure by asserting his rights against self-incrimination under the Fifth Amendment. According to the Court, the partnership had "an established institutional identity independent of its individual partners" because the partnership constituted a formal institutional structure formed to conduct legal practices, it had a separate bank account in the name of the partnership, stationery was used in the partnership's name, "and, in general, [the firm] held itself out to third parties as an entity with an independent institutional identity" (at 101). With this being the case, the *Bellis* Court concluded that partnership records were impersonal enough to be easily classified "partnership property," not personal property. Since only personal records are entitled to protection against self-incrimination, such business records had to be excepted from this constitutional protection. The Court left unanswered the question of whether the business records of sole proprietors, which cannot be so easily separated from what might be considered personal records, should also be excepted from the Fifth Amendment's protection against self-incrimination.

Fisher* and *Andresen   By the time the *Bellis* decision was made, the stage had already been set for the virtual elimination of the Fifth Amendment privilege against self-incrimination when business and personal records are intermixed. Court rulings during the 1970s, 1980s, and into the 1990s have almost totally upheld the idea that governmental administrators could compel the release of any business records, as long as they were not of a purely personal nature (for example, one's personal diary). What constitutes records of a purely personal nature has not been resolved as yet, but with each passing year it seems that the courts have made more and more records public which previous courts had regarded as strictly personal records protected by the Fifth's provision against self-incrimination.[67]

Justice Douglas's fears about how "ingenious methods" for obtaining personal information might evolve in the near future seemed justified in light of *Fisher* v. *United States.* In *Fisher,* the Internal Revenue Service was investigating taxpayers (husband and wife) for possible civil or criminal violations of federal income tax statutes. Shortly after IRS agents had interviewed the taxpayers, they secured from their accountants work papers relating to the preparation of their tax returns. Shortly thereafter, they turned their accountants' workpapers over to their attorneys. Upon learning that their accountants' workpapers were in the hands of their attorneys, the IRS subpoenaed the workpapers from their attorneys. But their attorneys refused to produce the documents which the IRS sought. This action caused the IRS to initiate enforcement action. One attorney contended that forced release of the workpapers would violate "the taxpayer's accountant-client privilege, his attorney-client privilege, and his Fourth and Fifth Amendment rights," while the other taxpayer's attorney "claimed that enforcement would involve compulsory self-incrimination of the taxpayers in violation of their Fifth Amendment privilege, would involve a seizure of the papers without necessary compliance with the Fourth Amendment, and would violate the taxpayers' right to communicate in confidence with their attorney" (at 395).

However, the Supreme Court rejected these arguments. The Court reasoned that although the evidence sought was incriminating in nature, the taxpayers were not being compelled to produce the incriminating evidence themselves. The incriminating papers, the Court argued, were being provided by a third party, and the Fifth Amendment's privilege against self-incrimination was meant only to prevent the government from compelling individuals to provide testimonial communications against themselves. Quoting from *Couch,* the Court stressed: "It is extortion of information from the accused himself that offends our sense of justice" (at 398). The Court continued: "Agent or no, the lawyer is not the taxpayer. The taxpayer is the 'accused,' and nothing is being extorted from him" (ibid.).

Not only did the Court contend that the taxpayer was not entitled to Fifth Amendment protections against self-incrimination because he was *not compelled to do anything,* but the Court also pointed out that the papers were not even the property of the taxpayer and thus, "the Fifth Amendment would not be violated by the fact alone that the papers on their face might incriminate the taxpayer, for the privilege protects a person only against being incriminated by his own compelled testimonial communications. . . . The accountant's workpapers are not the taxpayer's. They were not prepared by the taxpayer, and they contain no testimonial declarations by him" (at 409). Thus, the Court concluded that attorney-client privilege could not be honored in this instance because the workpapers would not be protected under the self-incrimination clause even if they were in the hands of the taxpayer, since they belonged to the accountant (at 402–03).

One final point is worth mentioning in regard to the *Fisher* case. The argument was made in *Fisher* that even though the taxpayers transferred the workpapers over to their attorneys, irrespective of whether these papers could be lawfully subpoenaed on other grounds, the taxpayers actually retained "constructive possession" of them.[68] But the Court rejected this argument, too, maintaining that the transfer of the workpapers was not "so temporary and insignificant as to leave the personal compulsion upon the taxpayer substantially intact." In so holding, the Court was suggesting that the "constructive possession" argument would be upheld only as long as the records sought were only very temporarily out of the direct possession of the owner.

During the same term, the Supreme Court, in *Andresen* v. *Maryland,* immediately affirmed its contention in *Fisher* that the Fifth Amendment's privilege against self-incrimination is not applicable when the individual is *not compelled to do anything* in the production of the incriminating evidence. But this time the Court took the "not compelled to do anything" doctrine one step further. The central question in *Andresen* was "whether the seizure of . . . [personal] business records, and their admission into evidence at his trial, compelled petitioner to testify against himself in violation of the Fifth Amendment" (at 471). The petitioner had claimed that the "prohibition against compulsory self-incrimination applies as well to personal business papers seized from his offices as it does to the same papers being required to be produced under a subpoena" (ibid.). The petitioner rested his argument on the following contention of the *Boyd* Court: "We have been unable to perceive that the seizure of a man's private books and papers to be used in evidence against him is substantially different from compelling him to be a witness against himself" (ibid.).

However, the *Andresen* Court was unsympathetic to the petitioner's contentions. Citing *Fisher,* Justice Harry A. Blackmun, writing the opinion for the majority, maintained simply that the Fifth's self-incrimination privilege does not apply because, as in *Fisher,* the "petitioner was not asked to say or do anything. The records seized contained statements that petitioner had voluntarily committed to writing. The search for and seizure of these records were conducted by law enforcement personnel. Finally, when these records were introduced at trial, they were authenticated by a handwriting expert, not by petitioner. Any compulsion of petitioner to speak; other than the inherent psychological pressure to respond at trial to unfavorable evidence, was not present" (at 473). Blackmun also noted that such governmental action was consistent with the principle espoused by Justice Oliver Wendell Holmes in *Johnson v. United States,* 228 U.S. 457, 458 (1913): "A party is privileged from producing the evidence but not from its production." Finally, citing *Couch,* Blackmun explained that the Holmes principle "recognizes that the protection afforded by the Self-Incrimination Clause of the Fifth Amendment 'adheres basically to the person, not to information that may incriminate him.'"

Criticism of *Fisher* and *Andresen*   Critics have harshly attacked the Supreme Court's rulings in *Fisher* and *Andresen* because they claim that these holdings have virtually destroyed individuals' Fifth Amendment protections against being compelled by governmental officials to, in effect, provide the government with self-incriminating personal business records—testimonial materials which, according to William J. Brennan in his dissent in *Andresen,* fall clearly within the "zone of privacy" protected by the Fifth's self-incrimination clause.[69] Justice Brennan asserted that it was unquestionable that the incriminating papers seized from the petitioner's own offices and used as evidence against him were self-incriminating materials protected by the Fifth Amendment. Quoting from *Bellis,* Brennan argued that the Court had only two years before acknowledged that the privilege against self-incrimination "applies to the business records of the sole proprietor or sole practitioner as well as to personal documents containing more intimate information about the individual's private life" (at 435–36). Such records, he continued, "are at least an extension of an aspect of a person's activities, though concededly not the more intimate aspects of one's life. Where the privilege would have protected one's mental notes of his business affairs in a less complicated day and age, it would seem that the protection should not fall away because the complexities of another time compel one to keep business records" (at 436).

According to Brennan, the assault on the self-incrimination protection in *Andresen* is not confined only to narrowing the scope of this privacy protection, because the Court seeks also to circumvent the purpose of this constitutional protection by making "an unjustified distinction between production compelled by subpoena and production secured against the will of the petitioner through warrant" (at 436). To him, the Fifth Amendment's protection against being compelled to provide the government with self-incriminating material means nothing if all the government has to do to get it is to secure a search warrant and then seize the incriminating evidence. Brennan considers that such incriminating material is compelled in the sense that individuals are not free to stop governmental investigators from searching for and seizing incriminating evidence from their files, as was the case in *Andresen.* Worse yet, as contrasted to the situation in *Fisher,* the individual in *Andresen* had possession of his personal records when they were seized. Brennan noted that the *Couch* Court had recognized rightly that "actual possession of documents bears the most significant relationship to Fifth Amendment protections against governmental compulsions upon the individual accused of crime" (ibid.).

The majority in *Andresen* held that the seizure of the incriminating evidence did not violate the privacy protections under the Fifth Amendment because not only did the petitioner not have "to do anything" to produce the incriminating evidence, but a legal search warrant was used to secure the records, thus making the search and seizure reasonable. However, Brennan contended that despite what the majority had said, it has never been established that an illegal search and seizure must be executed before the Fifth Amendment's protection against self-incrimination can apply. He pointed out that the Court, in *Gouled* v. *United States,* 255 U.S. 298 (1921), made "it clear that the illegality of the search and seizure is not a prerequisite for a Fifth Amendment violation. Under *Gouled,* a Fifth Amendment violation exists because the '[accused] is the unwilling source of the evidence,' a matter which does not depend on the illegality *vel non* of the search and seizure" (at 439).

But in the final analysis, Brennan rested the basis for his dissenting argument in the *Boyd* Court's claim that it could not "perceive that the seizure of a man's private books and papers to be used in evidence against him is substantially different from compelling him to be a witness against himself" (489). Brennan also asserted that he could "perceive no distinction of meaningful substance between compelling the production of such records through subpoena and seizing such records against the will of the petitioner" (at 435). Emerging from Brennan's argument is the clear viewpoint that men and women and their personal records, business or purely personal, cannot be easily separated for the convenient application of the Fifth Amendment's protection against self-incrimination. Obviously, Brennan maintains by implication that personal records represent an extension of the self. That is, what we say, what we write, and what we do reflect what we are. From this line of reasoning, it is quite clear that the Holmes principle does little to strengthen the majority's argument in *Andresen,* since written communications cannot be separated from the person who drafted them. Thus, when a person's personal records are seized by governmental officials and used in court, they can be as self-incriminating as if the person provided direct testimony in court against himself or herself by confessing about what was in the personal records. From this standpoint, echoing the attitude of the Court in *Boyd* and Justice Brennan in *Andresen,* for the government to compel a person to turn over personal records is to compel individuals, in effect, to testify against themselves contrary to the Fifth Amendment's guarantee against self-incrimination. To hold, as the majority did in *Andresen,* that the individual was not compelled "to do anything" to produce the self-incriminating evidence seems absurd.

According to a *Harvard Law Review* critique of *Fisher* and *Andresen,* the holdings appear quite shocking from a historical perspective because these rulings have suddenly, but not without warning, dampened the constitutional privilege against self-incrimination in areas previously enjoyed by individuals under the Fifth: "Historically, the fifth amendment was read to allow an individual a privacy interest in his personal business papers. Now the Court has interpreted the fifth amendment to allow the government to obtain indirectly the information that it cannot obtain directly from the individual, if the information leaves the individual's possession or is seized pursuant to a search warrant."[70] The *Fisher* and *Andresen* decisions have apparently made virtually all "private" business records the public's business.

In another *Harvard Law Review* analysis of these cases, it was maintained that the Constitution has been recast by *Fisher* and *Andresen* so that the Constitution now provides "no protection to privacy other than the procedural standards of the warrant clause."[71] Kenneth C. Davis is in comfortable agreement with this insight. He concludes likewise that the judicial propositions developed in *Fisher* and *Andresen* have together reduced "the Fifth Amendment's protection of records to almost nothing."[72] Davis speculates, nevertheless, that future court decisions will likely further erode what few privacy protections remain under the Fifth Amendment in the name of the public interest.

Recent Court Decisions Regarding the Fifth

Less than a year after Davis made the speculative remark just quoted, the Third Circuit Court of Appeals handed down a decision which conveyed that his speculation was on target. In *Matter of Grand Jury Empanelled,* 597 F.2d 851 1979, this circuit court ruled that a subpoena to produce personal records of a sole proprietor could be served on the proprietor's "trusted employees," to employ Justice Douglas's phrase, without violating the Fifth Amendment's protection against self-incrimination. In previous cases the Supreme Court had left open the question of whether the government could compel the release of business records of sole proprietors because such records, it was commonly believed, were much more personal than other business records, especially those of larger and more impersonal organizations. To recall, in 1911 the Supreme Court in *Wilson* excepted corporate records from Fifth Amendment privacy guarantees. In 1944, in *White,* the business records of associations were excepted by the high Court. And in 1974 the Supreme Court excepted partnerships' business records.

The *Grand Jury Empanelled* decision goes far in actualizing some of the fears expressed by William O. Douglas's previously mentioned dissenting opinion in *Couch.* In *Grand Jury Empanelled,* Dominick Colucci, a sole proprietor of a trucking and excavating business which had grown fairly large in its twenty-year history, employed an office manager, Marion DeMato, who kept the business records, specifically, job folders and billing records. The government served *subpoenas duces tecum* on both Colucci and DeMato for the production of Colucci's personal business records. Colucci contended that compelled disclosure of his private business records violated his Fifth Amendment right against compelled self-incrimination.

Finally saying that "a sole proprietor has no legal existence apart from its owner," as contrasted to corporations, associations, or partnerships, the court concluded that Colucci's personal business records are protected by the Fifth Amendment's protection against self-incrimination as long as they are in *his* possession (at 859). However, the court defeated Colucci's purpose of blocking the compelled release of his business records by ruling that anyone who holds business records in a representative capacity, such as Colucci's office manager, cannot assert the Fifth

Amendment privilege. Citing *Fisher*, the circuit court contended that "the Fifth Amendment is a personal right which may be exercised only by the person against whom governmental compulsion is directed. . . . Therefore, Colucci's right under the Fifth Amendment was not infringed by the order and *subpoena* served on DeMato" (at 860). Thus, employers today lose their Fifth Amendment protection against self-incrimination regarding their personal business papers if they place them in the "hands" of their "trusted employees," even their "personal" secretaries.

Not only was the court's unsympathetic rejection of Colucci's argument that he had "constructive possession" of his business papers of import in this case, but also of significance was the general negative tone toward the possible use of constructive possession, as developed in *Couch*. The *Grand Jury Empanelled* court claimed that "possession" for the purpose of the Fifth Amendment "is determined as of the time that governmental compulsion is exerted to produce the documents" (at 865). At the time the *subpoena* was issued, the business records were in DeMato's possession; thus she was under a legal obligation to produce the papers for the government. On the other hand, "once that official compulsion had been placed on DeMato, Colucci could not rightfully take possession of the records for the purpose of preventing the performance of DeMato's duty called for by the *subpoena*" (at 865).

The fact that the Third Circuit Court rejected the constructive possession argument in this case is very significant because the Supreme Court in *Couch* suggested that the constructive possession doctrine would probably apply in the sort of situation which existed in *Grand Jury Empanelled*. In *Couch* the Court rejected the taxpayer's contention of her tax records because they were in the possession of her accountant, and "the accountant himself worked neither in petitioner's office nor as her employee." But in *Grand Jury Empanelled* the situation exists where Colucci's business records were kept by his office manager in his office. Despite this, however, the Third Circuit Court decided to dismiss *Couch's* suggestive comment regarding the limits of constructive possession as mere dictum (at 862). Overall, *Grand Jury Empanelled* represents a ruling of major consequence to the status of Fifth Amendment privacy protections for those in business because "the decision limits the operation of the right against self-incrimination to circumstances where the sole proprietor himself prepares and maintains the records, a circumstance unlikely to be found in any but the smallest business."[73]

In 1984 the Supreme Court in *United States* v. *Doe* reached a decision that limits the protective shield of the Fifth Amendment for businesspersons even more. In *Doe* the Court resolved the question over constructive possession raised in *Grand Jury Empanelled* by simply asserting that the possession question is irrelevant since the only relevant question is whether the self-incriminating records are compelled. Because it is important to capture the precise reasoning of the Court in this complex legal area, it is best to defer to the Court's exact holding: "As we noted in *Fisher*, the Fifth Amendment protects the person asserting the privilege only from *compelled* self-incrimination. . . . Where the preparation of business records is voluntary, no compulsion is present. A subpoena that demands production of documents 'does not compel oral testimony; nor would it ordinarily compel the taxpayer to restate, repeat, or affirm the truth of the contents of the documents sought.'. . . This reasoning applies with equal force here. Respondent does not contend that he prepared the documents involuntarily or that the subpoena would force him to restate, repeat, or affirm the truth of their contents. *The fact that the records are in respondent's possession is irrelevant to the determination of whether the creation of the records was compelled.* We therefore hold that the contents of those records are not privileged" (emphasis mine) (at 610–12).

A few key decisions decided in the 1990s reaffirm, clarify, and expand prior case law, especially *Fisher,* establishing current law regarding the Fifth Amendment's privilege against self-incrimination. In 1990 in *Baltimore City Dept. of Social Services* v. *Bouknight,* 110 S.Ct. 900 (1990), the Supreme Court held that a mother (Bouknight) could be ordered to produce her abused child, who was in her custody and was receiving public assistance, even though production of the child would amount to testimonial, self-incriminating action normally protected by the Fifth Amendment. The Court made clear that the Supreme Court ". . . has on several occasions recognized that the Fifth Amendment privilege may not be invoked to resist compliance with a regulatory regime constructed to effect the state's public purposes . . ." (at 905). The court, quoting from *Fisher,* argued that "[W]hen the government demands that an item be produced, the only thing compelled is the act of producing the (item)" (at 905). To the high Court, the child represented a "required record" that the Department of Social Services had a regulatory right to see or have produced by the mother. The Court noted that "[W]hen a person assumes control over items that are the legitimate object of the government's noncriminal regulatory powers, the ability to invoke the privilege is reduced" (at 906).

The Court in *Bouknight* reaffirmed the "production doctrine," as established in *Fisher,* and developed the "required records exception doctrine" under the Fifth Amendment, first established in *Shapiro* v. *United States,* 335 U.S. 1 (1948), and elaborated on in *Grosso* v. *United States,* 390 U.S. 62 (1968). The Eighth Circuit Court in 1994 placed these doctrines into clear perspective *In Re Grand Jury Subpoena,* 21 F.3d 226. The only question before the court *In Re Grand Jury Subpoena* was ". . . whether the required records exception applies to an incriminating act of production by a sole proprietor" (at 228). In this case Spano, a car dealer being investigated for odometer tampering, moved to quash a grand jury subpoena requesting that he produce required business records under federal and state law, including federally required odometer readings. Spano, a sole proprietor, argued that to produce the documents would violate his privilege against self-incrimination under the Fifth Amendment.

However, the court ruled that although the act of production could cause testimonial self-incrimination, in this case the required records exception doctrine applies. In its holding, the Eighth Circuit Court did an excellent job of summarizing the reasoning behind how the act of production doctrine and the required records exception doctrine apply to privilege against self-incrimination. "We hold that the required records exception applies to Spano . . . , despite the self-incriminating and testimonial aspects of the production for the following reasons: (1) the public interest in obtaining the information necessary to the regulatory scheme outweighs the private interest in disclosure, and if a private individual were able to invoke the privilege the regulatory purpose of the scheme would be frustrated; (2) the individual, by engaging in the regulated activity, is deemed to have waived his privilege as to the production of those records which are required to be kept; and (3) the individual admits little of significance by the act of production because of the public aspects of the documents. We hold that the required records exception to the Fifth Amendment privilege will apply to the act of production by a sole proprietor even where the act of production could involve compelled testimonial self-incrimination" (at 230).

A 1994 Sixth Circuit Court case, *United States* v. *Ritchie*, 15 F.3d 592, followed almost exactly the decision the Supreme Court rendered in *Fisher*, making it very clear law that the attorney-client privilege does ". . . not prohibit the enforcement of a summons issued by the IRS to the taxpayer's attorney for accounting documents related to the representation . . ." (at 602). (Presumably, this would apply to any similar summons or subpoena issued by an administrative agency or court). In this case, Ritchie, a prominent criminal defense attorney, tried to quash IRS summonses that requested Ritchie's law firm to submit records on three of his clients who had paid services by cash amounting to over ten thousand dollars each. The summonses demanded that Ritchie's firm supply names, addresses, and taxpayer identification of these clients, as well as the nature of the services provided to them.

Ritchie contended that forcing him to provide such information would deprive his clients of their Fifth Amendment protection against self-incrimination. Relying mostly upon *Fisher*, the court flatly rejected Richie's position, arguing that "[T]he privilege against self-incrimination is a personal privilege . . . and here the client is not the one being compelled. And the attorney may not object that the client may be incriminated by the attorney's testimony; . . . the attorney may, of course, assert the attorney-client privilege if the requested information is actually privileged. Furthermore, the information required must be incriminating or integrally linked with the behavior deemed offensive in order for the Fifth Amendment to be implicated, . . . paying one's attorney in cash does not fall within this category" (at 602).

Further Erosion of the Fifth's Protection against Self-Incrimination through the Judiciary's Virtual Rejection of the Exclusionary Rule   Courts since *Fisher* and *Andresen* have drawn upon these cases to justify their rulings, which have generally had the impact of further limiting the privacy rights of businesspersons and private persons under the closely related Fourth and Fifth Amendments. During the last two decades especially, the courts have consistently rejected the use of the exclusionary rule, thus allowing certain self-incriminating evidence to be used against business and private persons in administrative proceedings and trials even though the evidence was illegally obtained. As noted, critics believe that the almost total abandonment of the use of the exclusionary rule has seriously jeopardized the functional value of the Fifth Amendment's protection against self-incrimination. The first case reviewed below is *United States* v. *Payner*, 447 U.S. 727 (1980). The Court's rejection of the exclusionary rule under the outrageous circumstances in this case is shocking.

In *Payner* the high Court ruled that the federal courts' supervisory power does not permit a court to exclude otherwise admissible incriminating evidence, even though the evidence was obtained illegally from a third party not standing before the court (at 737) (upheld in *U.S. Dept. of Labor* v. *Triplett,* 110 S.Ct. 1428; 1990). In this case the Internal Revenue Service had paid a person, Casper, eight thousand dollars in cash to steal a briefcase (the Supreme Court called the case the "briefcase caper" case) containing incriminating evidence to be later used at trial to help convict another party. Justices Marshall, Brennan, and Blackmun joined in drafting one of the most vehement dissenting opinions ever written by Supreme Court justices.

The dissenting justices concluded that the evidence was illegally obtained by the IRS and, therefore, should not be used to help the government obtain a conviction. But their strong dissent stems from the fact that they perceived the IRS's lawlessness as blatantly evil, conducted in bad faith, and patently offensive to the operations and standards of any righteous democratic government (at 738–51). Specifically, the dissenters held that the actions of the paid IRS agent in "stealing the briefcase, opening it, and photographing all the documents inside" were patently violative of constitutional due process standards in regard to the collection and the use of evidence for government prosecutions (at 746). The three dissenters exclaimed: "If the IRS is permitted to obtain a conviction in federal court based almost entirely on the illegally obtained evidence from its fruits, then the judiciary has given full effect to the deliberate wrongdoings of government. The federal court does indeed become the accomplice of the government lawbreaker, an accessory after the fact, for without judicial use of the evidence the 'caper' would have been for naught. Such a pollution of the federal courts should not be permitted" (at 747–48). The dissenters stressed that the IRS had absolutely no case unless it illegally chose "to sacrifice the constitutional rights of one person in order to prosecute another" (at 748).

In *INS* v. *Lopez-Mendoza,* 468 U.S. 1032 (1984), the Supreme Court ruled that the exclusionary rule does not apply in a deportation hearing. This means that any evidence seized from an illegal arrest or in any other unlawful manner can be submitted as evidence in a deportation hearing. The Court rejected the application of the exclusionary rule on the grounds that the exclusionary rule is used to protect persons in criminal trials, while a deportation hearing is a "purely civil" proceeding "intended to provide a streamlined determination of eligibility to remain in this country, nothing more. The purpose of deportation is not to punish past transgressions but rather to put an end to a continuing violation of the immigration laws" (at 1039). Although the Court tried to minimize the significance of a deportation hearing, some scholars feel that the stakes for individuals in a deportation case are so high that in reality an adverse decision in a deportation case may result in a more severe deprivation than an adverse decision in a criminal case. This reality motivated Justice Brandeis to conclude many years ago that deportation decisions may be more harmful to persons in deportation hearings than verdicts in criminal trials because adverse deportation rulings may "result . . . in loss of both property and life; or of all that makes life worth living" (*Ng Fung Ho* v. *White,* 259 U.S. 276, 284; 1922).[74]

In reviewing the *Lopez-Mendoza* ruling, Bernard Schwartz expressed concern that the *Lopez-Mendoza* decision may signal the end to the use of the exclusionary rule in all administrative proceedings because the Court's rationale to exclude the exclusionary rule in this case could be employed in all other administrative law or civil cases. He argues that "an agency hearing is not just another civil trial, particularly where, as is most often the case, the agency is one of the parties. In addition, in the agency case, the tainted evidence is the fruit of a governmental, not private, crime. The law should not allow a public agency to be the known beneficiary of stolen goods. It is anomalous to enforce opposite rules in administrative and criminal proceedings concerning evidence blighted by the same pollution; an unlawful search violates the identical privacy, whether its fruits are used to convict in a criminal case or to forfeit a personal right in an agency proceeding. An administrative agency, just as any other public organ, is obligated to conduct its activities in conformity with the demands of the Constitution. When its agents exceed those limits, it should not be permitted to avail itself of the fruits of such unlawful activity."[75]

Consistent with the argument made in *Lopez-Mendoza,* the Louisiana Supreme Court in *Pullin* v. *Louisiana State Racing Com'n.* (1985), op. cit., ruled that even if the evidence were obtained illegally, the evidence should not be excluded from the administrative hearing before the Louisiana State Racing Commission under the exclusionary rule, because the hearing was only a civil proceeding, not a criminal trial. In the court's tongue: "Even if the evidence were illegally seized, no purpose is served by excluding it in a civil administrative proceeding" (at 690).

Finally, in 1994 in *Trinity Industries* v. *OSHRC,* op. cit., the Sixth Circuit Court seemed to employ an illogical agreement to allow illegally seized evidence to be used in an Occupational Safety and Health Review Commission proceeding. The court noted that a "full-scope" physical OSHA inspection which produced incriminating evidence was conducted without probable cause and in clear violation of the requirements for administrative inspections as set forth in *Barlow*'s and, thus, should normally cause the evidence to be excluded. The court also rejected OSHA's argument, based upon *Lopez-Mendoza,* that the exclusionary rule should not apply because the benefits of including the illegally seized evidence outweigh the costs to Trinity Industries. Further, the court asserted that the exclusionary rule does not apply to agency enforcement actions for the purpose of correcting violations, but does apply when the objective of the administrative inspection is to gather evidence for the purpose of assessing penalties for violations, which was OSHA's objective in this case. Nonetheless, despite noting such objections to the illegally seized evidence, the court held that the evidence should not be suppressed under the exclusionary rule because the inspectors acted in "good faith" under a restrictive search warrant and, therefore, the "good faith exception" to the exclusionary rule should apply. Given all of these "exceptions" to the application of the exclusionary rule, it is really difficult to imagine when the exclusionary rule would apply, especially in administrative proceedings.

It should be emphasized that the chief reason for the exclusionary rule is to deter the government from using its law enforcement and administrative officials to gather and use incriminating evidence against businesses and individuals in an unconstitutional manner. Supposedly, such governmental officers would find it cost-ineffective to illegally gather information if the illegally seized evidence could not be used. Unfortunately, the courts, employing the legal realist philosophy to an extreme,

'Live It Up, Guys!'

Source: Reprinted with permission of Tom Engelhardt and the *St. Louis Post-Dispatch,* June 27, 1980.

have very often handed down decisions that tend to encourage the illegal gathering and use of information, much to the dismay of civil libertarians who believe that the Fourth and Fifth Amendment privacy rights are worth saving. The practical question remains: how far should we drift from upholding "pure" constitutional principles to catch and punish those who violate our laws and rules?

SUMMARY

Systems theory has made it quite clear that public administrators are constantly faced with the frustrating problem of satisfactorily balancing the conflicting demands of their environments. Without much doubt, probably the most difficult task for our administrators, especially for those who make significant public policy choices, is balancing fairly the rights of individual parties with the rights and apparent needs of society. To perform their functions properly, they must carry out certain administrative actions which necessarily invade the privacy interests of individual parties. Such administrative behavior makes administrators vulnerable to criticisms from opposite sides. If administrators become overzealous in gathering essential regulatory information, individuals may bitterly attack them, possibly in court, for illegally encroaching upon constitutionally protected privacy rights, as protected by the Fourth and Fifth Amendments. On the other hand, if regulatory officials fail to obtain information which is considered crucial for proper regulatory operations, legislators, the media, citizen action groups, and the general public may charge that an agency has favored special parties and, in so doing, failed to act responsibly in promoting the public interest.

In this chapter, special attention was devoted to assessing how well administrative officials have been doing in upholding Fourth and Fifth Amendment privacy guarantees, while serving as regulators. The Fourth Amendment provides individuals with protection against unreasonable searches and seizures. Convincing historical evidence suggests that the constitutional framers incorporated these privacy protections into the Bill of Rights in reaction to the unreasonable searches and seizures that they had to endure while under British colonial rule. The Fifth Amendment protects individuals from being compelled to witness against themselves. Ideally, this constitutional guarantee was supposed to prevent governmental officials from forcing individuals to produce testimonial evidence, either oral or written, which would be self-incriminating. At first it was questioned whether the Fourth and Fifth Amendment privacy rights should be made applicable to only criminal cases, but the courts soon extended these constitutional privacy protections to apply to civil matters (for example, administrative inspections).

During the 1800s administrative power was severely restricted and administrators seldom violated Fourth and Fifth Amendment privacy rights. When administrators did appear to transgress upon these privacy protections, the courts were usually quick to overturn such administrative intrusions into the private affairs of individuals and private businesses. In a famous nineteenth-century case, *Boyd* v. *United States,* 116 U.S. 616 (1886), the Supreme Court, guided by the prevailing philosophy of legal formalism, argued essentially that constitutional privacy rights were absolute and should not be compromised by administrators. Legal formalism, which espoused the basic belief that Bill of Rights guarantees should be strictly upheld if democratic liberties were to be preserved, reigned as the major philosophical force guiding judicial decision making until the early 1900s.

As society became more complex and the need for more comprehensive and rigorous governmental regulation increased during the twentieth century, the courts began to turn to the philosophy of legal realism to guide their judgments. Legal realism seemed better suited to the demands of the emerging administrative state. Basically, it is a pragmatic legal philosophy which has had the effect of permitting administrative agencies to gather and use information which appears necessary if they are to competently perform essential regulatory functions for the good of society. In practice, this has allowed the courts to uphold administrative searches and seizures, as well as to permit agencies to use self-incriminating evidence, especially as applied to the use of personal business papers.

In response to the growing complexities of modern technological society, the administrative agencies have felt compelled to gather and use more and more information so that they can function as effective regulators. Adequate information on what is being regulated, administrative officials argue, provides the key to regulatory success. The courts, sympathetic to the regulators' plight, have been charged in recent decades with employing the balance doctrine to favor agency regulatory interests, while freely permitting the dangerous erosion of constitutionally protected privacy guarantees. Critics admit that the regulatory problems which confront our administrators are massive and real, but they maintain that the judiciary has gone too far in sanctioning agency actions which have clearly violated Fourth and Fifth Amendment privacy rights.

In recent cases the Supreme Court has upheld unscrupulous, invasive, and illegal methods for obtaining material to be used as incriminating evidence against individuals. These rulings indicate that the high Court at least has little respect for the exclusionary rule and, as a result, is unwilling to make decisions that would discourage administrative agencies from adopting investigative and prosecutorial procedures that blatantly undermine the intent of the Fourth and Fifth Amendment privacy protections. Recently, federal, state and local officials have pushed intimate, mandatory urine and blood testing of governmental employees, targeting those thought to occupy jobs key to the promotion of public health and safety (for example, air traffic controllers, military personnel, and police and firefighters). Thus far, the courts have ruled against such mandatory testing unless probable cause can be established in specific circumstances to justify such an intrusive search, or the government after applying a balance test, can show that such an invasion of personal privacy can be justified on a group level by demonstrating its clear and weighty benefits to society. The contagious and deadly disease AIDS presents a serious threat to the public health of this nation and indeed to world civilization. In dealing with this terrible and complex problem, governmental officials will have to be careful to balance the rights of individuals with the rights of society.

Democracy is a fragile governing mechanism which can only be preserved if governmental officials, while carrying out the tasks of government, respect and uphold fundamental constitutional liberties reserved for private parties. Probably the chief difference between democratic and totalitarian governing structures is in how each regards and treats individuals, especially in regard to personal privacy rights. Judging from recent trends in regulatory behavior in America, we must act together as a society to make regulatory procedures more administratively effective and at the same time more sensitive to personal privacy rights. Since the survival of genuine democratic governmental practices in America depends upon our commitment to this task, we cannot afford not to accept this challenge.

NOTES

1. Of course, in drafting public policies and resolving disputes in court, legislators and judges must also choose between societal and individual rights. Consequently, one could validly say that seeking an equitable balance to these frequently competing rights is government's single biggest task.

2. Herbert Kaufman, *Red Tape* (Washington, D.C.: Brookings Institution, 1977), 19.

3. Ibid.

4. For a thorough analysis of the costs and benefits of preserving protected interests, see Kenneth C. Davis and Richard J. Pierce, Jr., *Administrative Law Treatise,* 3rd ed. (Boston: Little, Brown and Company, 1994), vol. 1, chap. 4, and vol. II, chap. 1.

5. Dissenting in *Wyman* v. *James,* 400 U.S. 309, 328 (1971).

6. Ibid., at 335.

7. Michael J. Perry, *The Constitution, the Courts, and Human Rights: An Inquiry into the Legitimacy of Constitutional Policymaking by the Judiciary* (New Haven, Conn.: Yale University Press, 1982), especially chaps. 3 and 4; Ronald C. Kahn, *The Supreme Court and Constitutional Democracy* (Ithaca, N.Y.: Cornell University Press, 1984); and Bruce A. Ackerman, "The Storrs Lecture: Discovering the Constitution," *The Yale Law Journal,* 93 (May 1984), 1013–1072.

8. *Schenck* v. *United States,* 249 U.S. 47 (1919).

9. *Weeks* v. *United States,* 232 U.S. 383 (1914); *Mapp* v. *Ohio,* 367 U.S. 643 (1961). Recently, however, courts have been ruling that illegally seized evidence can be used in a variety of imaginative ways. For example, evidence illegally seized by state authorities may be used not in state proceedings, but in federal civil proceedings (*United States* v. *Torres,* 926 F.2d 321, 1991).

10. Bernard Schwartz, *Administrative Law,* 3rd ed. (Boston: Little, Brown, 1991), 94–107.

11. Ronald F. Wright, "The Civil and Criminal Methodologies of the Fourth Amendment," *The Yale Law Review,* 93 (May 1984), 1127–46. Also see dissenting opinions in *United States* v. *Salerno,* 107 S.Ct. 2095 (1987).

12. Bernard Schwartz, *Administrative Law,* 3rd ed., 98–99.

13. See Walter Gellhorn, Clark Byse, Peter L. Strauss, Todd Rakoff, and Roy A. Schotland, *Administrative Law: Cases and Comments,* 8th ed. (Mineola, N.Y.: The Foundation Press, 1987), 673–701.

14. Several years ago, there was a good deal of publicity about the case of a Spanish-speaking immigrant who had witnessed a murder in Boston shortly after he had moved to the United States. Because he was regarded as an unreliable witness (one who might vanish before being called to testify), the prosecutor's office ordered that he be detained in the Suffolk County Jail, a jail known for its deplorable conditions, until he could testify at the trial. His story received media attention when it was learned that he had been kept in the jail for six months and that, because the defense had just been granted another postponement of the trial date, it appeared that the unfortunate witness, guilty of no crime, would likely have to spend at least another half year in jail. Public comment centered on the quality of welcome to the country that this man had received.

15. Incidentally, a writ of *habeas corpus* would not be used to obtain the release of individuals lawfully held by administrators. A writ of *habeas corpus* can be employed only to obtain the release of persons *illegally* held by administrators.

16. An immigration statute, 8 U.S.C., Sec. 1357(a)(2), permits immigration officials to make an arrest without an administrative warrant if it is thought that the alien would likely "escape before a warrant can be obtained for his arrest."

17. Justice William O. Douglas, dissenting in *Abel,* at 245.

18. *Carlson* v. *Landon,* 342 U.S. 524 (1952). This decision may be questioned under the Eighth Amendment's provision guaranteeing persons the right to be released after posting reasonable bail. For current conservative and liberal thinking on the use of bail, see *United States* v. *Salerno,* 107 S.Ct. 2095 (1987).

19. Bernard Schwartz, *Administrative Law,* 3rd ed., 107.

20. *U.S. Department of Labor Annual Report,* 37 (Washington, D.C.: Government Printing Office, 1976). This figure dropped to 59,932 in fiscal 1977 because of public reaction to the quantity of OSHA inspections. To systems theorists, the reduction in inspections from 1976 to 1977 points out perfectly how agencies adjust to the feedback demands from their environments. OSHA has had to make appropriate adjustments in order to survive (*U.S. Department of Labor Annual Report,* 48 [Washington, D.C.: Government Printing Office, 1977]). As reported earlier, OSHA inspections dropped off dramatically during the Reagan administration.

21. Bernard Schwartz, *Administrative Law,* 3rd ed., 110.

22. Ibid.

23. For a commentary on the "required records" doctrine, see Unauthored Note, "Organizational Papers and the Privilege against Self-Incrimination," *Harvard Law Review,* 99 (January 1986), 652–654.

24. Ronald J. Bacigal, "Some Observations and Proposals on the Nature of the Fourth Amendment," *George Washington Law Review,* 46 (May 1978), 559.

25. Kevin I. MacKenzie, "Administrative Searches and the Fourth Amendment: An Alternative to the Warrant Requirement," *Cornell Law Review,* 64 (1979), 864–871.

26. The Court acknowledged that its decision in this case would cause more businesses to demand in the future that inspectors go back and obtain a search warrant before they allowed the inspection. However, since the warrants can be obtained very easily, I doubt whether many astute businesspeople, who have some understanding of human psychology, would want to irritate administrative inspectors, who can exercise vast discretion in spotting violations, by inconveniencing them and forcing them to get warrants. For a zoologist's fascinating view of how we make certain responses that tend to elicit hostile attitudes in others, see Desmond Morris, *The Naked Ape* (London: Corgi Books, 1967), chap. 5. To avoid being cited for so-called extra violations, Morris' advice to business managers would be to take on a noncombative, submissive role in an effort to avoid putting the inspectors in positions where they feel compelled to demonstrate their power and dominance. Morris says that once animals (including humans) establish dominance, they no longer feel compelled to act aggressively, since the challenge has been met.

27. It should be noted that surprise inspections probably have little value in the administrative regulatory process, as compared to the criminal law area, because, minor violations aside, serious violations cannot normally be kept hidden from inspectors (for example, cracks in the walls of nuclear power plant chambers or unhealthy and unsafe working conditions).

28. These four dissenting justices have all left the Supreme Court, thus leading to the speculation that now the more conservative court would most likely find most aerial searches constitutional under the Fourth Amendment. See Susan M. McDonough, "The Fourth Power? Administrative Searches vs. the Fourth Amendment," *New England Journal on Criminal and Civil Confinement,* vol. 20 (Winter 1993), 195–237.

29. Lisa J. Steele, "The View From On High: Satellite Remote Sensing Technology and the Fourth Amendment," *High Tech Law Journal,* vol. 6 (Fall, 1991).

30. Ibid., 302–333.
31. Ibid., 333–334. Also, see Lisa J. Steele, "Waste Heat and Garbage: The Legalization of Warrantless Infrared Searches," *Criminal Law Bulletin,* vol. 29 (January–February, 1993), 19–39.
32. Justice Potter Stewart presents an argument against the use of implied consent to take away a person's Fourth Amendment rights in his dissenting opinion in *Donovan* v. *Dewey,* 101 S.Ct. 2534 (1981).
33. MacKenzie, "Administrative Searches and the Fourth Amendment," 867.
34. Susan M. McDonough, "The Fourth Power? Administrative Searches vs. The Fourth Amendment," 236.
35. Ibid., 237.
36. Roger B. Dworkin, "Fact Style Adjudication and the Fourth Amendment: The Limits of Lawyering," *Indiana Law Journal,* 48 (Spring 1973), 329.
37. Bernard Schwartz, "Administrative Law Cases During 1978," *Administrative Law Review,* 31 (Spring 1979), 146.
38. For some articles on administrative searches, see Steven T. Wax, "The Fourth Amendment, Administrative Searches and the Loss of Liberty," Environmental Law, vol. 18 (Summer 1988); John C. Sheldon, "Sobriety Checkpoints, The Rational-Basis Test, and the Law Court," *Maine Bar Journal,* vol. 8 (March 1993); and Evelyn M. Oswad et al., "Criminal Law Project: Administrative Searcher," *Georgetown Law Review,* vol. 82 (March–April 1994), 688–697.
39. Kenneth C. Davis, *Administrative Law Treatise,* 2nd ed. vol. 1 (San Diego: K.C. Davis Publishing, 1979), 261.
40. Ibid., 262.
41. Actually, as far back as *Boyd* v. *United States,* 116 U.S. 616 (1886), the Court recognized that Fourth Amendment protections should sometimes be extended to cover civil proceedings since civil proceedings frequently assume a quasi-criminal nature, especially when refusal to comply with requests under civil laws can lead to criminal charges and eventual fines or imprisonment (at 634–35).
42. William J. Brennan, Jr., "State Constitutions and the Protection of Individual Rights," *Harvard Law Review, 90* (January 1977), 495.
43. "Formalism, Legal Realism, and Constitutionally Protected Privacy under the Fourth and Fifth Amendments," *Harvard Law Review, 90* (March 1977), 945–991.
44. Kenneth C. Davis, *Administrative Law Treatise,* 2nd ed., vol. 1, 299.
45. Joel Cohen, "Are John Doe's Personal Papers Protected by the Fifth Amendment Any More?," *New York Law Journal,* vol. 210 (September 21, 1993), 1 and 4.
46. Kenneth C. Davis, *Administrative Law Treatise,* 2nd ed., vol. 1, 299.
47. John Locke, *Two Treatises of Government,* introduction by Peter Laslett (Cambridge: Cambridge University Press, 1960), 368.
48. Ibid.
49. Deborah Connor, "Criminal Procedure Project: The Exclusionary Rule," *Georgetown Law Review,* vol. 82 (March-April 1994), 755–769.
50. Several Supreme Court decisions have supported the *Boyd* ruling at least in principle (specifically, the holding that a person should not be compelled to produce self-incriminating evidence), although in practice the decisions served to undermine the application of the *Boyd* principle. See *Wilson* v. *United States,* 221 U.S. 361 (1911); *Wheeler* v. *United States,* 226 U.S. 478 (1913); *United States* v. *White,* 332 U.S. 694 (1944); *Couch* v. *United States,* 409 U.S. 322 (1973); and *Bellis* v. *United States,* 417 U.S. 85 (1974).

51. See Douglas' dissenting opinions in *Abel* v. *United States*, 362 U.S. 217 (1960); *Warden* v. *Hayden*, 387 U.S. 294 (1967); *Wyman* v. *James*, 400 U.S. 309 (1971); and *Couch* v. *United States*, 409 U.S. 322 (1973).

   In *Fisher* v. *United States*, 425 U.S. 391, 414 (1976), Justice Brennan, concurring, voiced strong objections to the Court's majority opinion regarding compelled production of one's private papers. He maintained that it struck another crippling blow to the privilege against self-incrimination. In his own words, "it is but another step in the denigration of privacy principles settled nearly 100 years ago in *Boyd* v. *United States*, 116 U.S. 616 (1886)."

52. Kenneth C. Davis, *Administrative Law Treatise*, 2nd ed., vol. 1, 299–300.

53. Ibid.

54. See "Formalism, Legal Realism, and Constitutionally Protected Privacy under the Fourth and Fifth Amendments," 979–91; Steven T. Wax, "The Fourth Amendment, Administrative Searches and the Loss of Liberty," *Environmental Law*, vol. 4 (Summer 1988); and Thomas M. Blumenthal, "Judicial Activism—The Politicization of the Right of Privacy," *Saint Louis University Public Law Review*, vol. 11 (Fall 1992).

55. "Formalism, Legal Realism, and Constitutionally Protected Privacy under the Fourth and Fifth Amendments," 932.

56. For an excellent analysis of how the employment of "balancing" has compromised Fourth and Fifth Amendment private protections, see Ronald F. Wright, "The Civil and Criminal Methodologies of the Fourth Amendment," *The Yale Law Journal*, 93 (May 1984), 1127–16. Basically, Wright contends that when the balance test (i.e., balancing between the privacy rights of an individual and the public interest) is applied by the courts, it is easier to rule in favor of the public interest, while if a more "concrete" standard is used (for example, showing probable cause), it is more difficult to side with the public interest. Like most legal scholars addressing this issue, he believes that the increased use of balancing in recent years has unfortunately resulted in individuals' being denied their Fourth and Fifth Amendment privacy rights too often.

57. For discussions of this theoretical background, see Morton Gabriel White, *Social Thought in America* (Mineola, N.Y.: Foundation Press, 1957), 7; and Edwin Wilhite Patterson, *Jurisprudence* (New York: Foundation Press, 1957), 472.

58. William James, *Pragmatism: A New Name for Old Ways of Thinking* (New York: Green and Company, 1947), 222.

59. "Formalism, Legal Realism, and Constitutionally Protected Privacy under the Fourth and Fifth Amendments," 966.

60. Ibid.

61. Reinhard Bendix, *Max Weber: An Intellectual Portrait* (New York: Doubleday, 1962), chaps. 3, 12–15.

62. Roscoe Pound, "The Scope and Purpose of Sociological Jurisprudence," *Harvard Law Review*, 25 (April 1912), 514.

63. Benjamin N. Cardozo, *The Nature of the Judicial Process* (New Haven, Conn.: Yale University Press, 1921), 113.

64. For a review of some key decisions since *Boyd*, see Cohen, "Are John Doe's Personal Papers Protected by the Fifth Amendment Any More?"

65. Davis and Pierce, Jr., *Administrative Law Treatise*, 3rd ed., vol. 1, 167–171.

66. Ibid.

67. In *United States* v. *Osborn*, 561 F.2d 1334, 1338 (9th Cir., 1977), the court noted that records kept by persons who are connected with an industry regulated by the govern-

ment (for example, bank accounts, utility bills, sales transactions of personal property, or tax statements) are not personal records. Since government regulation is so pervasive today, it appears that only a few of our records could be classified as purely personal.

68. In this case, "constructive possession" means that the taxpayer actually retained legal possession of the workpapers, even though he had temporarily transferred them from his hands to his attorney's.

69. Justice Thurgood Marshall also wrote a separate dissenting opinion in which he supported Brennan's basic position that the seized personal business records should have been suppressed at the petitioner's trial.

70. "Fifth Amendment: Compulsory Production of Incriminating Business Records," 52.

71. "Formalism, Legal Realism, and Constitutionally Protected Privacy under the Fourth and Fifth Amendments," 978.

72. Davis, *Administrative Law Treatise,* 2nd ed., vol. 1, 284.

73. "Fifth Amendment: Compulsory Production of Incriminating Business Records," 53.

74. This is not an exaggerated statement. During the Iranian hostage crisis that plagued the last year of the Carter administration, Carter ordered many Iranians in the United States, many of them students, sent back to Iran. However, many of these Iranians feared that their lives would be in danger if they were sent back to Iran because many of them and their families in Iran (some of their family members had already been killed) were bitter and vocal enemies of Iran's new leader, Ayatollah Khomeini, and friends and even aides of the deposed Shah. Consequently, several Iranians in the United States vigorously fought their deportation in INS hearings. Haitians, seeking political asylum in the United States during the Clinton administration, had similar fears regarding being returned to Haiti.

75. Bernard Schwartz, "Administrative Law Cases during 1984," *Administrative Law Review,* 37 (Spring 1985), 141.

APPENDIX

Federal Administrative Procedure Act

TITLE 5, U.S. CODE

Chapter 5—Administrative Procedure

---

[1]So in original. Does not conform to section catchline.

§551. Definitions

For the purpose of this subchapter—

(1) "agency" means each authority of the Government of the United States, whether or not it is within or subject to review by another agency, but does not include—

(A) the Congress;

(B) the courts of the United States;

(C) the governments of the territories or possessions of the United States;

(D) the government of the District of Columbia; or except as to the requirements of section 552 of this title;

(E) agencies composed of representatives of the parties or of representatives of organizations of the parties to the disputes determined by them;

(F) courts martial and military commissions;

(G) military authority exercised in the field in time of war or in occupied territory; or

(H) functions conferred by sections 1738, 1739, 1743, and 1744 of title 12; chapter 2 of title 41; or sections 1622,1884,1891-1902, and former section 1641(b)(2), of title 50, appendix;

(2) "person" includes an individual, partnership, corporation, association, or public or private organization other than an agency;

(3) "party" includes a person or agency named or admitted as a party, or properly seeking and entitled as of right to be admitted as a party, in an agency proceeding, and a person or agency admitted by an agency as a party for limited purposes;

(4) "rule" means the whole or a part of an agency statement of general or particular applicability and future effect designed to implement, interpret, or prescribe law or policy or describing the organization, procedure, or practice requirements of an agency and includes the approval or prescription for the future of rates, wages, corporate or financial structures or reorganizations thereof, prices, facilities, appliances, services or allowances therefor or of valuations, costs, or accounting, or practices bearing on any of the foregoing;

(5) "rule making" means agency process for formulating, amending, or repealing a rule;

(6) "order" means the whole or a part of a final disposition, whether affirmative, negative, injunctive, or declaratory in form, of an agency in a matter other than rule making but including licensing;

(7) "adjudication" means agency process for the formulation of an order;

(8) "license" includes the whole or a part of an agency permit, certificate, approval, registration, charter, membership, statutory exemption or other form of permission;

(9) "licensing" includes agency process respecting the grant, renewal, denial, revocation, suspension, annulment, withdrawal, limitation, amendment, modification, or conditioning of a license;

(10) "sanction" includes the whole or a part of an agency—

(A) prohibition, requirement, limitation, or other condition affecting the freedom of a person;

(B) withholding of relief;

(C) imposition of penalty or fine;

(D) destruction, taking, seizure, or withholding of property;

(E) assessment of damages, reimbursement, restitution, compensation, costs, charges, or fees;

(F) requirement, revocation, or suspension of a license; or

(G) taking other compulsory or restrictive action;

(11) "relief" includes the whole or a part of an agency—

(A) grant of money, assistance, license, authority, exemption, exception, privilege, or remedy;

(B) recognition of a claim, right, immunity, privilege, exemption, or exception; or

(C) taking of other action on the application or petition of, and beneficial to, a person;

(12) "agency proceeding" means an agency process as defined by paragraphs (5), (7), and (9) of this section;

(13) "agency action" includes the whole or a part of an agency rule, order, license, sanction, relief, or the equivalent or denial thereof, or failure to act; and

(14) "ex parte communication" means an oral or written communication not on the public record with respect to which reasonable prior notice to all parties is not given, but it shall not include requests for status reports on any matter or proceeding covered by this subchapter.

(Pub. L. No. 89-554, Sept. 6, 1966, 80 Stat. 381; Pub. L. No. 94-409, §4(b), Sept. 13, 1976, 90 Stat. 1247.) . . .

§553. Rulemaking

(a) This section applies, according to the provisions thereof, except to the extent that there is involved—

(1) a military or foreign affairs function of the United States; or

(2) a matter relating to agency management or personnel or to public property, loans, grants, benefits, or contracts.

(b) General notice of proposed rule making shall be published in the Federal Register, unless persons subject thereto are named and either personally served or otherwise have actual notice thereof in accordance with law. The notice shall include—

(1) a statement of the time, place, and nature of public rule making proceedings;

(2) reference to the legal authority under which the rule is proposed; and

(3) either the terms or substance of the proposed rule or a description of the subjects and issues involved.

Except when notice or hearing is required by statute, this subsection does not apply

(A) to interpretative rules, general statements of policy, or rules of agency organization, procedure, or practice; or

(B) when the agency for good cause finds (and incorporates the finding and a brief statement of reasons therefor in the rules issued) that notice and public procedure thereon are impracticable, unnecessary, or contrary to the public interest.

(c) After notice required by this section, the agency shall give interested persons an opportunity to participate in the rule making through submission of written data, views, or arguments with or without opportunity for oral presentation. After consideration of the relevant matter presented, the agency shall incorporate in the rules adopted a concise general statement of their basis and purpose. When rules are required by statute to be made on the record after opportunity for an agency hearing, sections 556 and 557 of this title apply instead of this subsection.

(d) The required publication or service of a substantive rule shall be made not less than 30 days before its effective date, except—

(1) a substantive rule which grants or recognizes an exemption or relieves a restriction;

(2) interpretative rules and statements of policy; or

(3) as otherwise provided by the agency for good cause found and published with the rule.

(e) Each agency shall give an interested person the right to petition for the issuance, amendment, or repeal of a rule.

(Pub. L. No. 89-554, Sept. 6, 1966, 80 Stat. 383.)

§554. Adjudications

(a) This section applies, according to the provisions thereof, in every case of adjudication required by statute to be determined on the record after opportunity for an agency hearing, except to the extent that there is involved—

(1) a matter subject to a subsequent trial of the law and the facts de novo in a *court;*

(2) the selection or tenure of an employee, except a[2] administrative law judge appointed under section 3105 of this title;

(3) proceedings in which decisions rest solely on inspections, tests, or elections;

(4) the conduct of military or foreign affairs functions;

(5) cases in which an agency is acting as an agent for a court; or

(6) the certification of worker representatives.

(b) Persons entitled to notice of an agency hearing shall be timely informed of—

(1) the time, place, and nature of the hearing;

(2) the legal authority and jurisdiction under which the hearing is to be held; and

---

[2]So in original.

(3) the matters of fact and law asserted.

When private persons are the moving parties, other parties to the proceeding shall give prompt notice of issues controverted in fact or law; and in other instances agencies may by rule require responsive pleading. In fixing the time and place for hearings, due regard shall be had for the convenience and necessity of the parties or their representatives.

(c) The agency shall give all interested parties opportunity for-

(1) the submission and consideration of facts, arguments, offers of settlement, or proposals of adjustment when time, the nature of the proceeding, and the public interest permit; and

(2) to the extent that the parties are unable so to determine a controversy by consent, hearing and decision on notice and in accordance with sections 556 and 557 of this title.

(d) The employee who presides at the reception of evidence pursuant to section 556 of this title shall make the recommended decision or initial decision required by section 557 of this title, unless he becomes unavailable to the agency. Except to the extent required for the disposition of ex parte matters as authorized by law, such an employee may not—

(1) consult a person or party on a fact in issue, unless on notice and opportunity for all parties to participate; or

(2) be responsible to or subject to the supervision or direction of an employee or agent engaged in the performance of investigative or prosecuting functions for an agency.

An employee or agent engaged in the performance of investigative or prosecuting functions for an agency in a case may not, in that or a factually related case, participate or advise in the decision, recommended decision, or agency review pursuant to section 557 of this title, except as witness or counsel in public proceedings. This subsection does not apply—

(A) in determining applications for initial licenses;

(B) to proceedings involving the validity or application of rates, facilities, or practices of public utilities or carriers; or

(C) to the agency or a member or members of the body comprising the agency.

(e) The agency, with like effect as in the case of other orders, and in its sound discretion, may issue a declaratory order to terminate a controversy or remove uncertainty.

(Pub. L. No. 89-554, Sept. 6, 1966, 80 Stat. 384; Pub. L. No. 95-251, §2(a)(1), Mar. 27, 1978, 92 Stat. 183.)

§555. Ancillary matters

(a) This section applies, according to the provisions thereof, except as otherwise provided by this subchapter.

(b) A person compelled to appear in person before an agency or representative thereof is entitled to be accompanied, represented, and advised by counsel or, if permitted by the agency, by other qualified representative. A party is entitled to appear in person or by or with counsel or other duly qualified representative in an agency proceeding. So far as the orderly conduct of public business permits, an interested person may appear before an agency or its responsible employees for the presentation, adjustment, or determination of an issue, request, or controversy in a proceeding, whether interlocutory, summary, or otherwise, or in connection with an agency function. With due regard for the convenience and necessity of the parties of their representatives and within a reasonable time, each agency shall proceed to conclude a matter presented to it. This subsection does not grant or deny a person who is not a lawyer the right to appear for or represent others before an agency or in an agency proceeding.

(c) Process, requirement of a report, inspection, or other investigative act or demand may not be issued, made, or enforced except as authorized by law. A person compelled to submit data or evidence is entitled to retain or, on payment of lawfully prescribed costs, procure a copy or transcript thereof, except that in a nonpublic investigatory proceeding the witness may for good cause be limited to inspection of the official transcript of his testimony.

(d) Agency subpenas authorized by law shall be issued to a party on request and, when required by rules of procedure, on a statement or showing of general relevance and reasonable scope of the evidence sought. On contest, the court shall sustain the subpena or similar process or demand to the extent that it is found to be in accordance with law. In a proceeding for enforcement, the court shall issue an order requiring the appearance of the witness or the production of the evidence or data within a reasonable time under penalty of punishment for contempt in case of contumacious failure to comply.

(e) Prompt notice shall be given of the denial in whole or in part of a written application, petition, or other request of an interested person made in connection with any agency proceeding. Except in affirming a prior denial or when the denial is self-explanatory, the notice shall be accompanied by a brief statement of the grounds for denial.

(Pub. L. No. 89-554, Sept. 6, 1966, 80 Stat. 385.)

§556. Hearings; presiding employees; powers and duties; burden of proof; evidence; record as basis of decision

(a) This section applies, according to the provisions thereof, to hearings required by section 553 of 554 of this title to be conducted in accordance with this section.

(b) There shall preside at the taking of evidence—

(1) the agency;

(2) one or more members of the body which comprises the agency; or

(3) one or more administrative law judges appointed under section 3105 of this title.

This subchapter does not supersede the conduct of specified classes of proceedings, in whole or in part, by or before boards or other employees specially provided for by or designated under statute. The functions of presiding employees and of employees participating in decisions in accordance with section 557 of this title shall be conducted in an impartial manner. A presiding or participating employee may at any time disqualify himself. On the filing in good faith of a timely and sufficient affidavit of personal bias or other disqualification of a presiding or participating employee, the agency shall determine the matter as a part of the record and decision in the case.

(c) Subject to published rules of the agency and within its powers, employees presiding at hearings may—

(1) administer oaths and affirmations;

(2) issue subpenas authorized by law;

(3) rule on offers of proof and receive relevant evidence;

(4) take depositions or have depositions taken when the ends of justice would be served;

(5) regulate the course of the hearing;

(6) hold conferences for the settlement or simplification of the issues by consent of the parties or by the use of alternative means of dispute resolution as provided in subchapter IV of this chapter;

(7) inform the parties as to the availability of one or more alternative means of dispute resolution, and encourage use of such methods;

(8) require the attendance at any conference held pursuant to paragraph (6) of at least one representative of each party who has authority to negotiate concerning resolution of issues in controversy;

(9) dispose of procedural requests or similar matters;

(10) make or recommend decisions in accordance with section 557 of this title; and

(11) take other action authorized by agency rule consistent with this subchapter.

(d) Except as otherwise provided by statute, the proponent of a rule or order has the burden of proof. Any oral or documentary evidence may be received, but the agency as a matter of policy shall provide for the exclusion of irrelevant, immaterial, or unduly repetitious evidence. A sanction may not be imposed or rule or order issued except on consideration of the whole record or those parts thereof cited by a party and supported by and in accordance with the reliable, probative, and substantial evidence. The agency may, to the extent consistent with the interests of justice and the policy of the underlying statutes administered by the agency, consider a violation of section 557(d) of this title sufficient grounds for a decision adverse to a party who has knowingly committed such violation or knowingly caused such violation to occur. A party is entitled to present his case or defense by oral or documentary evidence, to submit rebuttal evidence, and to conduct such cross-examination as may be required for a full and true disclosure of the facts. In rule making or determining claims for money or benefits or applications for initial licenses an agency may, when a party will not be prejudiced thereby, adopt procedures for the submission of all or part of the evidence in written form.

(e) The transcript of testimony and exhibits, together with all papers and requests filed in the proceeding, constitutes the exclusive record for decision in accordance with section 557 of this title and, on payment of lawfully prescribed costs, shall be made available to the parties. When an agency decision rests on official notice of a material fact not appearing in the evidence in the record, a party is entitled, on timely request, to an opportunity to show the contrary.

(Pub. L. No. 89-554, Sept. 6, 1966, 80 Stat. 386; Pub. L. No. 94-409, §4(c), Sept. 13, 1976, 90 Stat. 1247; Pub. L. No. 95-251, §2(a)(1), Mar. 27, 1978, 92 Stat. 183; Pub. L. No. 101-552, §4(a), Nov. 15, 1990, 104 Stat. 2737.)

§557. Initial decisions; conclusiveness; review by agency; submissions by parties; contents of decisions; record

(a) This section applies, according to the provisions thereof, when a hearing is required to be conducted in accordance with section 556 of this title.

(b) When the agency did not preside at the reception of the evidence, the presiding employee or, in cases not subject to section 554(d) of this title, an employee qualified to preside at hearings pursuant to section 556 of this title, shall initially decide the case unless the agency requires, either in specific cases or by general rule, the entire record to be certified to it for decision. When the presiding employee makes an initial decision, that decision then becomes the decision of the agency without further proceedings unless there is an appeal to, or review on motion of, the agency within time provided by rule. On appeal from or review of the initial decision, the agency has all the powers which it would have in making the initial decision except as it may limit the issues on notice or by rule. When the agency makes the decision without having presided at the reception of the evidence, the presiding employee or an employee qualified to preside at hearings pursuant to section 556 of this title shall first recommend a decision, except that in rule making or determining applications for initial licenses—

(1) instead thereof the agency may issue a tentative decision or one of its responsible employees may recommend a decision; or

(2) this procedure may be omitted in a case in which the agency finds on the record that due and timely execution of its functions imperatively and unavoidably so requires.

(c) Before a recommended, initial, or tentative decision, or a decision on agency review of the decision of subordinate employees, the parties are entitled to a reasonable opportunity to submit for the consideration of the employees participating in the decisions—

(1) proposed findings and conclusions; or

(2) exceptions to the decisions or recommended decisions of subordinate employees or to tentative agency decisions; and

(3) supporting reasons for the exceptions or proposed findings or conclusions. The record shall show the ruling on each finding, conclusion, or exception

presented. All decisions, including initial, recommended, and tentative decisions, are a part of the record and shall include a statement of—

    (A) findings and conclusions, and the reasons or basis therefor, on all the material issues of fact, law, or discretion presented on the record; and

    (B) the appropriate rule, order, sanction, relief, or denial thereof.

(d)(1) In any agency proceeding which is subject to subsection (a) of this section, except to the extent required for the disposition of ex parte matters as authorized by law—

    (A) no interested person outside the agency shall make or knowingly cause to be made to any member of the body comprising the agency, administrative law judge, or other employee who is or may reasonably be expected to be involved in the decisional process of the proceeding, an ex parte communication relevant to the merits of the proceeding;

    (B) no member of the body comprising the agency, administrative law judge, or other employee who is or may reasonably be expected to be involved in the decisional process of the proceeding, shall make or knowingly cause to be made to any interested person outside the agency an ex parte communication relevant to the merits of the proceeding;

    (C) a member of the body comprising the agency, administrative law judge, or other employee who is or may reasonably be expected to be involved in the decisional process of such proceeding who receives, or who makes or knowingly causes to be made, a communication prohibited by this subsection shall place on the public record of the proceeding:

    (i) all such written communications;

    (ii) memoranda stating the substance of all such oral communications; and

    (iii) all written responses, and memoranda stating the substance of all oral responses, to the materials described in clauses (i) and (ii) of this subparagraph;

    (D) upon receipt of a communication knowingly made or knowingly caused to be made by a party in violation of this subsection, the agency, administrative law judge, or other employee presiding at the hearing may, to the extent consistent with the interests of justice and the policy of the underlying statutes, require the party to show cause why his claim or interest in the proceeding should not be dismissed, denied, disregarded, or otherwise adversely affected on account of such violation; and

    (E) the prohibitions of this subsection shall apply beginning at such time as the agency may designate, but in no case shall they begin to apply later than the time at which a proceeding is noticed for hearing unless the person responsible for the communication has knowledge that it will be noticed, in which case the prohibitions shall apply beginning at the time of his acquisition of such knowledge.

(2) This subsection does not constitute authority to withhold information from Congress.

(Pub. L. No. 89-554, Sept. 6, 1966, 80 Stat. 387; Pub. L. No. 94-409, §4(a), Sept. 13, 1976, 90 Stat. 1246.)

§558. Imposition of sanctions; determination of applications for licenses; suspension, revocation, and expiration of licenses

(a) This section applies, according to the provisions thereof, to the exercise of a power or authority.

(b) A sanction may not be imposed or a substantive rule or order issued except within jurisdiction delegated to the agency and as authorized by law.

(c) When application is made for a license required by law, the agency, with due regard for the rights and privileges of all the interested parties or adversely affected persons and within a reasonable time, shall set and complete proceedings required to be conducted in accordance with sections 556 and 557 of this title or other proceedings required by law and shall make its decision. Except in cases of willfulness or those in which public health, interest, or safety requires otherwise, the withdrawal, suspension, revocation, or annulment of a license is lawful only if, before the institution of agency proceedings therefor, the licensee has been given—

(1) notice by the agency in writing of the facts or conduct which may warrant the action; and

(2) opportunity to demonstrate or achieve compliance with all lawful requirements.

When the licensee has made timely and sufficient application for a renewal or a new license in accordance with agency rules, a license with reference to an activity of a continuing nature does not expire until the application has been finally determined by the agency.

(Pub. L. No. 89-554, Sept. 6, 1966, 80 Stat. 388.)

§559. Effect on other laws; effect of subsequent statute

This subchapter, chapter 7, and sections 1305, 3105, 3344, 4301(2)(E), 5372, and 7521 of this title, and the provisions of section 5335(a)(B) of this title that relate to administrative law judges, do not limit or repeal additional requirements imposed by statute or otherwise recognized by law. Except as otherwise required by law, requirements or privileges relating to evidence or procedure apply equally to agencies and persons. Each agency is granted the authority necessary to comply with the requirements of this subchapter through the issuance of rules or otherwise. Subsequent statute may not be held to supersede or modify this subchapter, chapter 7, sections 1305, 3105, 3344, 4301(2)(E), 5372, or 7521 of this title, or the provisions of section 5335(a)(B) of this title that relate to administrative law judges, except to the extent that it does so expressly.

(Pub. L. No. 89-554, Sept. 6, 1966, 80 Stat. 388; Pub. L. No. 90-623, §1(1), Oct. 22, 1968, 82 Stat. 1312; Pub. L. No. 95-251, §2(a)(1), Mar. 27, 1978, 92 Stat. 183; Pub. L. No. 95-454, title VIII, §801(a)(3)(B)(iii), Oct. 13, 1978, 92 Stat. 1221.)

Chapter 7—Judicial Review

§701. Application; definitions.
§702. Right of review.
§703. Form and venue of proceeding.
§704. Actions reviewable.
§705. Relief pending review.
§706. Scope of review.

§701. Application; definitions

(a) This chapter applies, according to the provisions thereof, except to the extent that—
 (1) statutes preclude judicial review; or
 (2) agency action is committed to agency discretion by law.
(b) For the purpose of this chapter—
 (1) "agency" means each authority of the Government of the United States whether or not it is within or subject to review by another agency, but does not include—
  (A) the Congress;
  (B) the courts of the United States;
  (C) the governments of the territories or possessions of the United States;
  (D) the government of the District of Columbia;
  (E) agencies composed of representatives of the parties or of representatives of organizations of the parties to the disputes determined by them;
  (F) courts martial and military commissions;
  (G) military authority exercised in the field in time of war or in occupied territory; or
  (H) functions conferred by sections 1738, 1739, 1743, and 1744 of title 12; chapter 2 of title 41; or sections 1622, 1884, 1891-1902, and former section 1641(b)(2), of title 50, appendix; and
 (2) "person", "rule", "order", "license", "sanction", "relief", and "agency action" have the meanings given them by section 551 of this title.
(Pub. L. No. 89-554, Sept. 6, 1966, 80 Stat. 392.)

§702. Right of review

A person suffering legal wrong because of agency action, or adversely affected or aggrieved by agency action within the meaning of a relevant statute, is entitled to judicial review thereof. An action in a court of the United States seeking relief other than money damages and stating a claim that an agency or an officer or employee thereof acted or failed to act in an official capacity or under color of legal authority shall not be dismissed nor relief therein be denied on the ground that it is against the United States or that the United States is an indispensable party. The United States may be named as a defendant in any such action, and a judgment or decree may be entered against the United States:

Provided, That any mandatory or injunctive decree shall specify the Federal officer or officers (by name or by title), and their successors in office, personally responsible for compliance. Nothing herein (1) affects other limitations on judicial review or the power or duty of the court to dismiss any action or deny relief on any other appropriate legal or equitable ground; or (2) confers authority to grant relief if any other statute that grants consent to suit expressly or impliedly forbids the relief which is sought. (Pub. L. No. 89-554, Sept. 6, 1966, 80 Stat. 392; Pub. L. No. 94-574, §1, Oct. 21, 1976, 90 Stat. 2721.)

§703. Form and venue of proceeding

The form of proceeding for judicial review is the special statutory review proceeding relevant to the subject matter in a court specified by statute or, in the absence or inadequacy thereof, any applicable form of legal action, including actions for declaratory judgments or writs of prohibitory or mandatory injunction or habeas corpus, in a court of competent jurisdiction. If no special statutory review proceeding is applicable, the action for judicial review may be brought against the United States, the agency by its official title, or the appropriate officer. Except to the extent that prior, adequate, and exclusive opportunity for judicial review is provided by law, agency action is subject to judicial review in civil or criminal proceedings for judicial enforcement.
(Pub. L. No. 89-554, Sept. 6, 1966, 80 Stat. 392; Pub. L. No. 94-574, §1, Oct. 21, 1976, 90 Stat. 2721.)

§704. Actions reviewable

Agency action made reviewable by statute and final agency action for which there is no other adequate remedy in a court are subject to judicial review. A preliminary, procedural, or intermediate agency action or ruling not directly reviewable is subject to review on the review of the final agency action. Except as otherwise expressly required by statute, agency action otherwise final is final for the purposes of this sec-

tion whether or not there has been presented or determined an application for a declaratory order, for any form of reconsiderations, or, unless the agency otherwise requires by rule and provides that the action meanwhile is inoperative, for an appeal to superior agency authority.
(Pub. L. No. 89-554, Sept. 6, 1966, 80 Stat. 392.)

§705. Relief pending review

When an agency finds that justice so requires, it may postpone the effective date of action taken by it, pending judicial review. On such conditions as may be required and to the extent necessary to prevent irreparable injury, the reviewing court, including the court to which a case may be taken on appeal from or on application for certiorari or other writ to a reviewing court, may issue all necessary and appropriate process to postpone the effective date of an agency action or to preserve status or rights pending conclusion of the review proceedings.
(Pub. L. No. 89-554, Sept. 6, 1966, 80 Stat. 393.)

§706. Scope of review

To the extent necessary to decision and when presented, the reviewing court shall decide all relevant questions of law, interpret constitutional and statutory provisions, and determine the meaning or applicability of the terms of an agency action. The reviewing court shall—

(1) compel agency action unlawfully withheld or unreasonably delayed; and

(2) hold unlawful and set aside agency action, findings, and conclusions found to be—

(A) arbitrary, capricious, an abuse of discretion, or otherwise not in accordance with law;

(B) contrary to constitutional right, power, privilege, or immunity;

(C) in excess of statutory jurisdiction, authority, or limitations, or short of statutory right;

(D) without observance of procedure required by law;

(E) unsupported by substantial evidence in a case subject to sections 556 and 557 of this title or otherwise reviewed on the record of an agency hearing provided by statute; or

(F) unwarranted by the facts to the extent that the facts are subject to trial de novo by the reviewing court.

In making the foregoing determinations, the court shall review the whole record or those parts of it cited by a party, and due account shall be taken of the rule of prejudicial error.
(Pub. L. No. 89-554, Sept. 6, 1966, 80 Stat. 393.)

§1305. Administrative law judges

For the purpose of section[3] 3105, 3344, 4301(2)(D), and 5372 of this title and the provisions of section 5335(a)(B) of this title that relate to administrative law judges, the Office of Personnel Management may, and for the purpose of section 7521 of this title, the Merit Systems Protection Board may investigate, require reports by agencies, issue reports, including an annual report to Congress, prescribe regulations, appoint advisory committees as necessary, recommend legislation, subpoena witnesses and records, and pay witness fees as established for the courts of the United States. (Pub. L. No. 89-554, Sept. 6, 1966, 80 Stat. 402; Pub. L. No. 90-83, §1(3), Sept. 11, 1967, 81 Stat. 196; Pub. L. No. 95-251, §2(a)(1), (b)(1), Mar. 27, 1978, 92 Stat. 183; Pub. L. No. 95-454, title VIII, §801(a)(3)(B)(iii), title IX, §906(a)(12), Oct. 13 1978, 92 Stat. 1221, 1225.)

§3105. Appointment of administrative law judges

Each agency shall appoint as many administrative law judges as are necessary for proceedings required to be conducted in accordance with sections 556 and 557 of this title. Administrative law judges shall be assigned to cases in rotation so far as practicable, and may not perform duties inconsistent with their duties and responsibilities as administrative law judges.
(Pub. L. No. 89-554, Sept. 6, 1966, 80 Stat. 415; Pub. L. No. 95-251, §2(a)(1), (b)(2), (d)(1), Mar. 27, 1978, 92 Stat. 183, 184.)

§3344. Details; administrative law judges

An agency as defined by section 551 of this title which occasionally or temporarily is insufficiently staffed with administrative law judges appointed under section 3105 of this title may use administrative law judges selected by the Office of Personnel Management from and with the consent of other agencies. (Pub. L. No. 89-554, Sept. 6, 1966, 80 Stat. 425; Pub. L. No. 95-251, §2(a)(1) (b)(2), Mar. 27, 1978, 92 Stat. 183; Pub. L. No. 95-454, title IX, §906(a)(2), Oct. 13, 1978, 92 Stat. 1224.)

§5372. Administrative law judges

(a) For the purposes of this section, the term "administrative law judge" means an administrative law judge appointed under section 3105.

(b)(1) There shall be 3 levels of basic pay for administrative law judges (designated as AL-1, 2, and 3, respectively), and each such judge shall be paid at 1 of those

---

[3]So in original. Probably should be "sections".

levels, in accordance with the provisions of this section. The rates of basic pay for those levels shall be as follows:

AL-3, rate A 65 percent of the rate of basic pay for level IV of the Executive Schedule.

AL-3, rate B 70 percent of the rate of basic pay for level IV of the Executive Schedule.

AL-3, rate C 75 percent of the rate of basic pay for level IV of the Executive Schedule.

AL-3, rate D 80 percent of the rate of basic pay for level IV of the Executive Schedule.

AL-3, rate E 85 percent of the rate of basic pay for level IV of the Executive Schedule.

AL-3, rate F 90 percent of the rate of basic pay for level IV of the Executive Schedule.

AL-2 95 percent of the rate of basic pay for level IV of the Executive Schedule.

AL-1 The rate of basic pay for level IV of the Executive Schedule.

(2) The Office of Personnel Management shall determine, in accordance with procedures which the Office shall by regulation prescribe, the level in which each administrative-law-judge position shall be placed and the qualifications to be required for appointment to each level.

(3)(A) Upon appointment to a position in AL-3, an administrative law judge shall be paid at rate A of AL-3, and shall be advanced successively to rates B, C, and D of that level upon completion of 52 weeks of service in the next lower rate, and to rates E and F of that level upon completion of 104 weeks of service in the next lower rate.

(B) The Office of Personnel Management may provide for appointment of an administrative law judge in AL-3 at an advanced rate under such circumstances as the Office may determine appropriate.

(c) The Office of Personnel Management shall, prescribe regulations necessary to administer this section.

(Pub. L. No. 89-554, Sept. 6, 1966, 80 Stat. 473, §5362; Pub. L. No. 95-251, §2(a)(1), (b)(1), Mar. 27, 1978, 92 Stat. 183; renumbered §5372 and amended Pub. L. No. 95-454, title VIII, §801(a)(3)(A)(ii), title IX, §906(a)(2), Oct. 13, 1978, 92 Stat. 1221, 1224; Pub. L. No. 101-509, title V, §529 [title I, §104(a)(1)], Nov. 5, 1990, 104 Stat. 1427, 1445.)

AMENDMENTS

1990 Pub. L. No. 101-509 amended section generally. Prior to amendment, section read as follows: "Administrative law judges appointed under section 3105 of this title are entitled to pay prescribed by the Office of Personnel Management independently of agency recommendations or ratings and in accordance with subchapter III of this chapter and chapter 51 of this title."

§7521. Actions against administrative law judges

(a) An action may be taken against an administrative law judge appointed under section 3105 of this title by the agency in which the administrative law judge is employed only for good cause established and determined by the Merit System Protection Board on the record after opportunity for hearing before the Board.

(b) The actions covered by this section are—

    (1) a removal;

    (2) a suspension;

    (3) a reduction in grade;

    (4) a reduction in pay; and

    (5) a furlough of 30 days or less; but do not include—

        (A) a suspension or removal under section 7532 of this title;

        (B) a reduction-in-force action under section 3502 of this title; or

        (C) any action initiated under section 1215 of this title.

(Added Pub. L. No. 95-454, title II, §204(a), Oct. 13, 1978, 92 Stat. 1137 amended Pub. L. No. 101-12, §9(a)(2), Apr. 10, 1989, 103 Stat. 35.)

Name Index

SUBJECT INDEX

Absolute discretion, 289–90
Absolute immunity, 368, 372–75
Absolutism, 72
Abstention doctrine, 347
Accountability. *See* Administrative accountability
Actual bias, 241
Ad hoc decisions, 292, 301
Adjudication
  defined, 468
  of public and private rights, 58
  section in APA, 470–71
  See also Order-making
Adjudicative facts, 239
Administrative accountability, 102–48
Administrative actions
  Bill of Rights and, 411–12
  Fourth Amendment on, 412–13
  judicial review of, 332–48
  proper scope of review over, 350–58
  reviewable, 333–35
  unreviewable, 335–37
Administrative agencies
  cabinet departments as, 17
  caseloads of, 295–97
  decision-making by, 218
  delegation of power to, 50–59
  discretion of, 24–25, 276–324
  first- and second-class, 185
  growth of, 39–50
  lead roles of, 12–22
  order-making by, 218–75
  policy-making powers of, 62
  policy statements issued by, 198–99
  power of, 62–68

  proliferation of, 39–40
  public administrators in, 14–19
  resistance to FOIA by, 132
  rule-making by, 182–217
Administrative behavior
  Administrative Procedures Act on, 129–39
  conflict-of-interest laws and, 151
  democratically responsible, 104–5
  guidance legislation for, 115–28
  judicial review of, 325–64
  undermining of, 149
Administrative centralization, 206
Administrative courts, 309–11. *See also*
    Administrative hearings
Administrative decisions, 10, 65–67. *See also*
    Decision making; Decisions
Administrative discretion, 276–324
  cases overruling, 299–303
  cases upholding, 303–9
  courts' control of, 297–99
  Davis on, 283–97
  defined, 278–81
  formal versus informal, 276–78
  Gifford's model of, 294–97
  history of, 281–83
  See also Administrative power; Discretion
Administrative growth, 68–80
Administrative hearings
  concluding business of, 269–70
  court trials vs., 232–37
  in district courts, 330
  exclusionary rule in, 255
  fair, 231
  formality of, 233